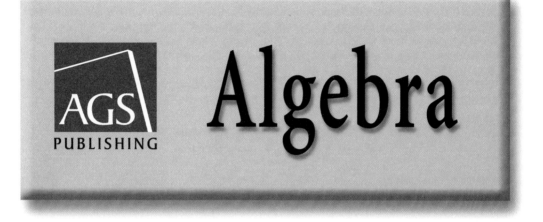

Algebra

by
Siegfried Haenisch

AGS Publishing
Circle Pines, Minnesota 55014-1796
800-328-2560

About the Author

Siegfried Haenisch, Ed.D. has taught mathematics at every level, from elementary to graduate school, most recently as Professor in the Department of Mathematics and Statistics at the College of New Jersey. The Mathematical Association of America granted him the 1995 Award for Distinguished Teaching of Mathematics. Dr. Haenisch was the site director for the training of teachers in the New Jersey Algebra Project. He was a member of the National Science Foundation Institutes in Mathematics at Rutgers University, Oberlin College, and Princeton University. At Yale University, he was a member of the Seminar in the History of Mathematics, sponsored by the National Endowment in the Humanities. Dr. Haenisch currently serves as a mathematics curriculum consultant to school districts.

Photo credits for this textbook can be found on page 526.

The publisher wishes to thank the following educators for their helpful comments during the review process for *Algebra*. Their assistance has been invaluable.

Maria Antonopoulou, Algebra Teacher, Hastings Education Centre, Vancouver, B.C., Canada; **David Arnold,** SLD Teacher, Winter Park Ninth Grade Center, Winter Park, Florida; **Tamara Bell,** Special Education Teacher, Muncie Community Schools, Southside High School, Muncie, Indiana; **Jacqueline DeWitt,** Cooperative Consultant, Umatilla High School, Sorrento, Florida; **Tina Dobson,** Special Education Math Resource Specialist, Sandridge Junior High School; Roy, Utah; **Connie Eichhorn,** Career Center and Adult Education Program, Omaha Public Schools, Omaha, Nebraska; **Dr. Rita Giles,** Program Director, Fairfax County Public Schools, Alexandria, Virginia; **Anne Hobbs,** Special Education Secondary Coordinator, Hobbs Municipal Schools, Hobbs, New Mexico; **Deborah Horn,** Wayne City High School, Wayne City, Illinois; **Rosanne Hudok,** Learning Support Teacher, Keystone Oaks High School, Pittsburgh, Pennsylvania; **Robert Jones,** Mathematics Supervisor, Cleveland Public Schools, Cleveland, Ohio; **Lee Kucera,** Math Teacher, Capistrano Valley High School, Mission Viejo, California; **Anne Lally,** Algebra Teacher, Eli Whitney School, Chicago, Illinois; **Christine Lansford,** Coordinator of Special Education, Melville Comprehensive School, Melville, Saskatchewan, Canada; **Robert Maydak,** Math Specialist, Pittsburgh Mt. Oliver Intermediate Unit, Pittsburgh, Pennsylvania; **Kathe Neighbor,** Math Chair, Crawford High School, San Diego, California; **Rachelle Powell,** Department Chair, Dr. Ralph H. Poteet High School, Mesquite, Texas; **Jacqueline Smith,** Resource Department Chair, Sterling High School, Baytown, Texas; **Carol Warren,** Math Teacher, Crockett County High School, Alamo, Tennessee; **William Wible,** Math Resource Teacher, San Diego Unified, San Diego, California

Publisher's Project Staff

Vice President of Product Development, Kathleen T. Williams, Ph. D. NCSP; Associate Director, Product Development, Teri Mathews; Managing Editor: Partick Keithahn; Editor: Jody Peterson; Development Assistant: Bev Johnson; Graphic Designer: Katie Sonmor; Creative Services Manager: Nancy Condon; Desktop Publishing Specialist: Linda Peterson; Purchasing Agent: Mary Kaye Kuzma; Senior Marketing Manager/Secondary Curriculum: Brian Holl

4201 Woodland Road
Circle Pines, MN 55014-1796
800-328-2560 • www.agsnet.com

Printed in the United States of America

ISBN 0-7854-3567-0

Product Number 93820

A 0 9 8 7 6 5 4 3 2

Contents

Chapter 7 Data, Statistics, and Probability . . . 182

Chapter 8 Fractions and Algebra . . . 218

Chapter 9

Chapter 10

How to Use This Book: A Study Guide

Welcome to *Algebra.* In this book, you will learn about the concepts of algebra. You will learn to use mathematical skills and algebra skills. Why do you need these skills? Many jobs use mathematics and algebra. People who work in banking, food service, printing, electronics, construction, surveying, insurance, and retail all use these skills on the job. Algebra skills are also useful in your everyday life, at home and in school.

As you read this book, notice how each lesson is organized. Information will appear at the beginning of each lesson. Read this information carefully. A sample problem with step-by-step instructions will follow. Use the instructions to learn how to solve a certain kind of problem. Once you know how to solve this kind of problem, you will have the chance to solve similar problems on your own. If you have trouble with a lesson, try reading it again.

Before you start to read this book, it is important that you understand how to use it. It is also important to know how to be successful in this course. This first section of the book is here to help you achieve these things.

How to Study

These tips can help you study more effectively:

- Plan a regular time to study.
- Choose a quiet desk or table where you will not be distracted. Find a spot that has good lighting.
- Gather all the books, pencils, paper, and other equipment you will need to complete your assignments.
- Decide on a goal. For example: "I will finish reading and taking notes on Chapter 1, Lesson 1, by 8:00."
- Take a five- to ten-minute break every hour to keep alert.
- If you start to feel sleepy, take a break and get some fresh air.

Chapter

1 Algebra: Arithmetic with Letters

Do you know what causes lightning? It is actually electricity. Lightning happens when positive and negative electrons in the clouds crash into each other. During a storm, a cloud separates into two parts called electrical fields. The top part stores positive electrons. The bottom part is filled with negative electrons. The two parts build energy until they crash into each other. When they do, we get a thunder and lightning show! In algebra, we work with positive numbers and their opposites, negative numbers. Together, these are called integers. In a flash, you'll be solving algebra problems using positive and negative numbers.

In Chapter 1, you will learn the basics of algebra.

Goals for Learning
- To recognize numerical and algebraic expressions
- To understand the use of variables in algebraic expressions
- To understand positive and negative integers, opposites, and absolute value
- To discover and use rules related to adding, subtracting, multiplying, and dividing integers
- To simplify expressions with one or more variables
- To read and write exponents
- To use formulas with variables

1

Before Beginning Each Chapter

- Read the chapter title and study the photograph. What does the photo tell you about the chapter title?
- Read the opening paragraphs.
- Study the Goals for Learning. The Chapter Review and tests will ask questions related to these goals.
- Look at the Chapter Review. The questions cover the most important information in the chapter.

Note the Chapter Features

Application

A look at how a topic in the chapter relates to real life

Application

Notes

Hints or reminders that point out important information

Look for this box for helpful tips!

Technology Connection
Use technology to apply math skills

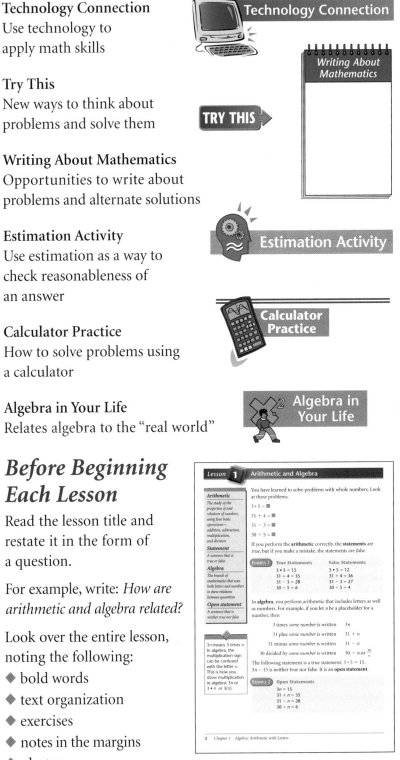

Try This
New ways to think about problems and solve them

Writing About Mathematics
Opportunities to write about problems and alternate solutions

Estimation Activity
Use estimation as a way to check reasonableness of an answer

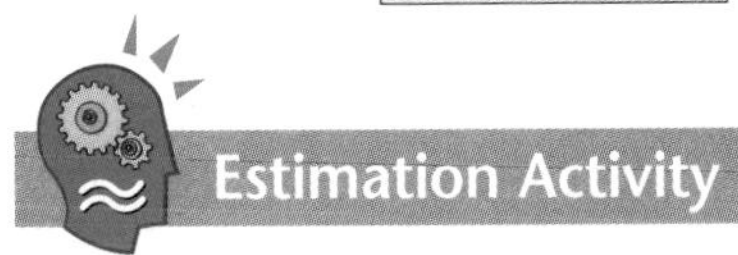

Calculator Practice
How to solve problems using a calculator

Algebra in Your Life
Relates algebra to the "real world"

Before Beginning Each Lesson

Read the lesson title and restate it in the form of a question.

For example, write: *How are arithmetic and algebra related?*

Look over the entire lesson, noting the following:

- bold words
- text organization
- exercises
- notes in the margins
- photos

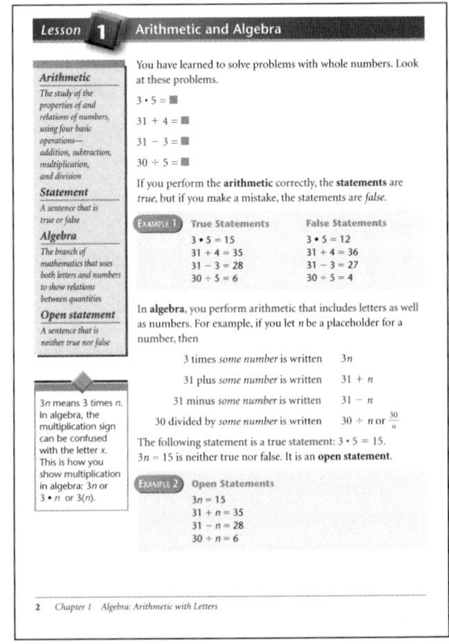

Lesson 1 Arithmetic and Algebra

Arithmetic
The study of the properties of and relations of numbers, using four basic operations—addition, subtraction, multiplication, and division

Statement
A sentence that is true or false

Algebra
The branch of mathematics that uses both letters and numbers to show relations between quantities

Open statement
A sentence that is neither true nor false

You have learned to solve problems with whole numbers. Look at these problems.

$3 \cdot 5 = ■$

$31 + 4 = ■$

$31 - 3 = ■$

$30 \div 5 = ■$

If you perform the **arithmetic** correctly, the **statements** are *true*, but if you make a mistake, the statements are *false*.

EXAMPLE 1

True Statements	False Statements
$3 \cdot 5 = 15$	$3 \cdot 5 = 12$
$31 + 4 = 35$	$31 + 4 = 36$
$31 - 3 = 28$	$31 - 3 = 27$
$30 \div 5 = 6$	$30 \div 5 = 4$

In **algebra**, you perform arithmetic that includes letters as well as numbers. For example, if you let n be a placeholder for a number, then

3 times *some number* is written $3n$

31 plus *some number* is written $31 + n$

31 minus *some number* is written $31 - n$

30 divided by *some number* is written $30 \div n$ or $\frac{30}{n}$

The following statement is a true statement: $3 \cdot 5 = 15$. $3n = 15$ is neither true nor false. It is an **open statement**.

$3n$ means 3 times n. In algebra, the multiplication sign can be confused with the letter x. This is how you show multiplication in algebra: $3n$ or $3 \cdot n$ or $3(n)$.

EXAMPLE 2 **Open Statements**

$3n = 15$
$31 + n = 35$
$31 - n = 28$
$30 \div n = 6$

2 *Chapter 1 Algebra: Arithmetic with Letters*

As You Read the Lesson

- Read the major headings.
- Read the subheads and paragraphs that follow.
- Read the content in the example boxes.
- Before moving on to the next lesson, see if you understand the concepts you read. If you do not, reread the lesson. If you are still unsure, ask for help.
- Practice what you have learned by doing the exercises in each lesson.

Using the Bold Words

Bold type

Words seen for the first time will appear in bold type

Glossary

Words listed in this column are also found in the glossary

Knowing the meaning of all the boxed words in the left column will help you understand what you read.

These words appear in **bold type** the first time they appear in the text and are often defined in the paragraph.

A **statement** is a sentence that is true or false.

All of the words in the left column are also defined in the **glossary**.

Statement (stāt′ mənt) a sentence that is true or false (p. 2)

What to Do with a Word You Do Not Know

When you come to a word you do not know, ask yourself:

- **Is the word a compound word?**
  Can you find two words within the word? This could help you understand the meaning. For example: *rainfall.*
- **Does the word have a prefix at the beginning?**
  For example: *improper.* The prefix *im-* means "not," so this word refers to something that is not proper.
- **Does the word have a suffix at the end?**
  For example: *variable, -able.* This means "able to vary."
- **Can you identify the root word? Can you sound it out in parts?** For example: *un known.*
- **Are there any clues in the sentence that will help you understand the word?**

Look for the word in the margin box, glossary, or dictionary. If you are still having trouble with a word, ask for help.

Using the Chapter Reviews

- For each Chapter Review, answer the multiple choice questions first.
- Answer the questions under the other parts of the Chapter Review.
- To help you take tests, read the Test-Taking Tips at the end of each Chapter Review.

When learning math vocabulary, make flash cards with words and abbreviations on one side and definitions on the other side. Draw pictures next to the words, if possible. Then use the flash cards in a game to test your vocabulary skills.

Preparing for Tests

- Complete the exercises in each lesson. Make up similar problems to practice what you have learned. You may want to do this with a classmate and share your questions.
- Review your answers to lesson exercises and Chapter Reviews.
- Test yourself on vocabulary words and key ideas.
- Practice problem-solving strategies.

Using the Answer Key

Pages 432–464 of this book show answers and solutions to selected problems. The problems with black numbers show answers. The problems with red numbers also show step-by-step solutions. Use the answers and solutions to check your work.

Using a Calculator

An electronic calculator can help you with many algebra problems. There are many different kinds of calculators available. Some calculators have a few keys and perform only a few simple operations. Other calculators have many keys and do many advanced calculations. It is important to know what your calculator can do and how to use it. Here are some tips for using the keys on most calculators. To learn more about your own calculator, read the instructions that come with it.

The diagram shows an example of a scientific calculator. It describes the keys that you will most likely use in algebra.

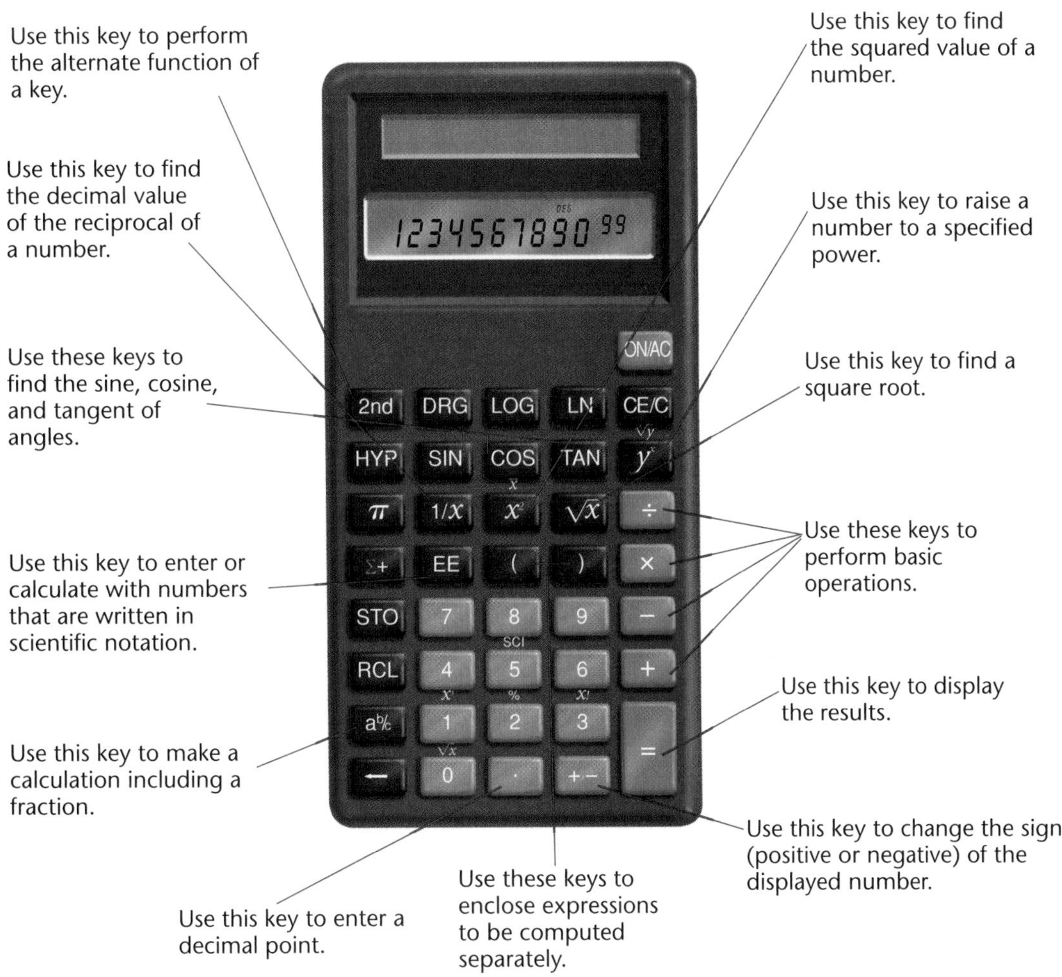
Use this key to perform the alternate function of a key.
Use this key to find the decimal value of the reciprocal of a number.
Use these keys to find the sine, cosine, and tangent of angles.
Use this key to enter or calculate with numbers that are written in scientific notation.
Use this key to make a calculation including a fraction.
Use this key to enter a decimal point.
Use these keys to enclose expressions to be computed separately.
Use this key to change the sign (positive or negative) of the displayed number.
Use this key to display the results.
Use these keys to perform basic operations.
Use this key to find a square root.
Use this key to raise a number to a specified power.
Use this key to find the squared value of a number.
1234567890 99
ON/AC
2nd
DRG
LOG
LN
CE/C
HYP
SIN
COS
TAN
π
1/x
EE
(
)
STO
7
8
9
RCL
4
5
6
+
1
2
3
0
.
=
×
÷
−

Problem-Solving Strategies

The main reason for learning math skills is to help us use math to solve everyday problems. You will notice sets of problem-solving exercises throughout your text. When you learn a new math skill, you will have a chance to apply this skill to a real-life problem.

Following these steps will help you to solve the problems.

1 Read

Read the problem to discover what information you are to gather. Study the problem to decide if you have all the information you need or if you need more data. Also study the problem to decide if it includes information you do not need to solve the problem. Begin thinking about the steps needed to solve the problem.

Ask yourself:

- Am I looking for a part of a number?
- Am I looking for a larger number?
- Am I looking for more than one number?
- Will solving the problem require multiple steps?

For example, read this problem:

Keesha's brother, Jackson, is one year older than she is. Their ages added together equal 25. Keesha's mother is 38 years old and her father is 40. How old is Keesha? How old is Jackson?

This problem asks you to find out Keesha's and her brother's ages. It gives information about the difference in their ages and the sum of their ages. It also gives unnecessary information about their parents' ages.

In order to answer the questions, you see that you are looking for the part of 25 that is Keesha's age and the part that is Jackson's age. You will solve for two numbers.

2 Plan

Think about the steps you will need to do to solve the problem. Decide if you are going to calculate this mentally, on paper, or with a calculator. Will you need to add, subtract, multiply, or divide? Will you need to do more than one step? If possible, estimate your answer.

These strategies may help you to find a solution:

- ✔ Simplify or reword the problem
- ✔ Draw a picture
- ✔ Make a chart or graph to illustrate the problem
- ✔ Divide the problem into smaller parts
- ✔ Look for a pattern
- ✔ Use a formula or write an equation

In the example problem, you will need to subtract and divide. You can write an equation to solve the problem.

- ✔ Let x stand for Keesha's age.
- ✔ Let $x + 1$ stand for Jackson's age.
- ✔ Together their ages equal 25, so your equation is $x + (x + 1) = 25$ or $2x + 1 = 25$.

3 Solve

Follow your plan and do the calculations. Check your work. Make sure to label your answer correctly.

$2x + 1 = 25$

$2x + 1 - 1 = 25 - 1$

$2x = 24$

$2x \div 2 = 24 \div 2$

$x = 12$

x stands for Keesha's age, so Keesha is 12 years old.

$x + 1$ stands for her brother's age, so Jackson is $12 + 1$ for 13 years old.

4 Reflect

Reread the problem and ask yourself if your answer makes sense. Did you answer the question? You can also check your work to see if your answer is correct.

Keesha and Jackson are one year apart. If Keesha is 12, then it makes sense to say that her older brother is 13. Their ages add up to 25. $12 + 13 = 25$, so the answer is correct.

Chapter

Algebra: Arithmetic with Letters

Do you know what causes lightning? It is actually electricity. Lightning happens when positive and negative electrons in the clouds crash into each other. During a storm, a cloud separates into two parts called electrical fields. The top part stores positive electrons. The bottom part is filled with negative electrons. The two parts build energy until they crash into each other. When they do, we get a thunder and lightning show! In algebra, we work with positive numbers and their opposites, negative numbers. Together, these are called integers. In a flash, you'll be solving algebra problems using positive and negative numbers.

In Chapter 1, you will learn the basics of algebra.

Goals for Learning

- To recognize numerical and algebraic expressions
- To understand the use of variables in algebraic expressions
- To understand positive and negative integers, opposites, and absolute value
- To discover and use rules related to adding, subtracting, multiplying, and dividing integers
- To simplify expressions with one or more variables
- To read and write exponents
- To use formulas with variables

Lesson 1 Arithmetic and Algebra

Arithmetic
The study of the properties of and relations of numbers, using four basic operations—addition, subtraction, multiplication, and division

Statement
A sentence that is true or false

Algebra
The branch of mathematics that uses both letters and numbers to show relations between quantities

Open statement
A sentence that is neither true nor false

You have learned to solve problems with whole numbers. Look at these problems.

$3 \cdot 5 = ■$

$31 + 4 = ■$

$31 - 3 = ■$

$30 \div 5 = ■$

If you perform the **arithmetic** correctly, the **statements** are *true*, but if you make a mistake, the statements are *false*.

EXAMPLE 1

True Statements	False Statements
$3 \cdot 5 = 15$	$3 \cdot 5 = 12$
$31 + 4 = 35$	$31 + 4 = 36$
$31 - 3 = 28$	$31 - 3 = 27$
$30 \div 5 = 6$	$30 \div 5 = 4$

In **algebra**, you perform arithmetic that includes letters as well as numbers. For example, if you let n be a placeholder for a number, then

3 times *some number* is written	$3n$
31 plus *some number* is written	$31 + n$
31 minus *some number* is written	$31 - n$
30 divided by *some number* is written	$30 \div n$ or $\frac{30}{n}$

The following statement is a true statement: $3 \cdot 5 = 15$. $3n = 15$ is neither true nor false. It is an **open statement**.

$3n$ means 3 times n. In algebra, the multiplication sign can be confused with the letter x. This is how you show multiplication in algebra: $3n$ or $3 \cdot n$ or $3(n)$.

EXAMPLE 2

Open Statements

$3n = 15$
$31 + n = 35$
$31 - n = 28$
$30 \div n = 6$

Open statements become true or false statements when you substitute numbers for letters.

EXAMPLE 3 Is $3n = 15$ true or false when $n = 1, 2, 3, 4$, or 5?

When $n = 1$, $3n = 15$ becomes $3 \cdot 1 = 15$ or $3 = 15$ False.
When $n = 2$, $3n = 15$ becomes $3 \cdot 2 = 15$ or $6 = 15$ False.
When $n = 3$, $3n = 15$ becomes $3 \cdot 3 = 15$ or $9 = 15$ False.
When $n = 4$, $3n = 15$ becomes $3 \cdot 4 = 15$ or $12 = 15$ False.
When $n = 5$, $3n = 15$ becomes $3 \cdot 5 = 15$ or $15 = 15$ True.

Exercise A Write true or false for each statement.

1. $3 \cdot 4 = 12$

2. $6 + 12 = 15$

3. $19 - 7 = 12$

4. $14 \div 7 = 2$

5. $\frac{42}{6} = 8$

6. $42 + 8 = 50$

7. $6 + 18 = 22$

8. $41 - 5 = 45$

9. $4 \cdot 9 = 36$

10. $84 - 44 = 50$

Exercise B Write true, false, or open for each statement.

11. $4 + 6 = 10$

12. $4n = 16$

13. $20 \div 5 = 5$

14. $60 - n = 50$

15. $60 - 10 = 50$

16. $60 + 17 = 67$

17. $\frac{3}{n} = 1$

18. $51 + n = 70$

19. $46 - 16 = 30$

20. $4 \cdot 6 = 24$

Exercise C Write true or false for each example.

Is $6 + n = 10$ true or false when

21. $n = 1$ **22.** $n = 3$ **23.** $n = 4$

Is $50 - n = 40$ true or false when

24. $n = 10$ **25.** $n = 5$ **26.** $n = 15$

Is $24 \div n = 4$ true or false when

27. $n = 12$ **28.** $n = 4$ **29.** $n = 6$

30. $n = 2$

Lesson 2 Representing Numbers Using Letters

Numerical expression
A mathematical sentence that includes operations and numbers

Operation
The mathematical processes of addition, subtraction, multiplication, and division

Algebraic expression
A mathematical sentence that includes at least one operation and a variable

Variable
A letter or symbol that stands for an unknown number

Coefficient
The number that multiplies the variable

A **numerical expression** includes only numbers and at least one **operation**.

$9 + 2$ $\quad$ $15 - 11$

$7 \cdot 2$ $\quad$ $64 \div 8$

An **algebraic expression** includes a **variable** with its **coefficient**, if it has one, and at least one operation.

$3y + 4$ $\quad$ $m - 17$

$3 + 2q$ $\quad$ $x \div 6$

EXAMPLE 1 Study the table.

$5 + 11$ is a numerical expression. Addition is the operation.

$6x + 1$ is an algebraic expression and x is the variable. The coefficient of x is 6. There are two operations in this expression—multiplication and addition.

	Numerical	Algebraic	Operation	Variable
$5 + 11$	Yes	No	Addition	None
$6x + 1$	No	Yes	Multiplication Addition	x
$c \div 4$	No	Yes	Division	c
$2 \cdot 8$	Yes	No	Multiplication	None

Exercise A Write numerical or algebraic for each expression. Identify the operations.

1. $m \div 8$

2. $9 \cdot 4.5$

3. $x + 10$

4. $6 + 9$

5. $14 - 3$

6. $1.5 - 1.2$

7. $4 + 6n$

8. $13 \cdot 2$

9. $2 \cdot 3n$

10. $\frac{n}{4}$

Exercise B Name the variable in each expression.

11. $6d + 8$

12. $5 + m$

13. $18 - e$

14. $4h$

15. $k - 7$

16. $5 + y$

17. $5y + 5$

18. $\frac{7}{x}$

19. $n \div 22$

20. $5c + 2$

Exercise C Identify the operation or operations in each expression.

21. $2x$

22. $n \div 4$

23. $3d - 2$

24. $9 + s$

25. $7v \div 3$

26. $7 - 2p$

27. $6(n)$

28. $\frac{r}{7}$

29. $4y$

30. $6m + 1$

Exercise D Classify each expression, name the operation or operations, and identify any variables.

31. $3 + 6$

32. $8 - 4$

33. $3x$

34. $m \div 6$

35. $2y + 7$

36. $9 - n$

37. $11 \cdot 4$

38. $9 + 3$

39. $8m + 2$

40. $9 \div 2$

PROBLEM SOLVING

Exercise E Solve each problem.

41. Write a numerical expression for the number of days in three weeks.

42. There are twenty years in a score. Write a numerical expression to represent the number of years in four scores.

43. Juan was born three years before his brother, who is now 18 years old. Write a numerical expression that represents Juan's age.

44. Write an algebraic expression to represent how far a car travels at 50 mph in *d* hours.

45. Write an algebraic expression for the following pattern. Use *n* as the variable.

$3 \cdot 1, 3 \cdot 2, 3 \cdot 3, 3 \cdot 4, 3 \cdot 5, 3 \cdot 6, \ldots$

Lesson 3 Integers on the Number Line

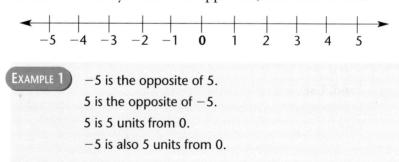

Real number

A number on the number line

Integer

A whole number or its opposite (…–2, –1, 0, 1, 2,…)

Negative integer

A whole number less than zero

Positive integer

A whole number greater than zero

Opposites

Numbers the same distance from zero but on different sides of zero on the number line

Numbers on the number line are examples of **real numbers**. Every point on the number line corresponds to a specific real number. The arrows at the end of the number line show that the pattern of numbers continues.

Positive and negative whole numbers and zero are called **integers**. Numbers to the left of zero are **negative integers** and are read as negative 1, negative 2, and so on.

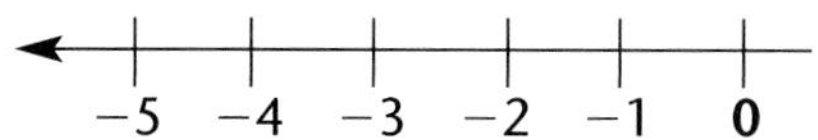

Numbers to the right of zero are **positive integers** and are read as positive 1 or 1, positive 2 or 2, and so on. Zero is neither negative or positive.

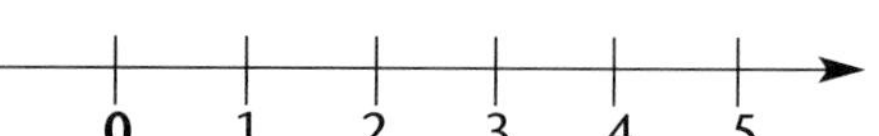

For every number other than **0**, there is an **opposite** number on the other side of zero. Opposites are the same distance from zero. When you add two opposites, their sum is zero.

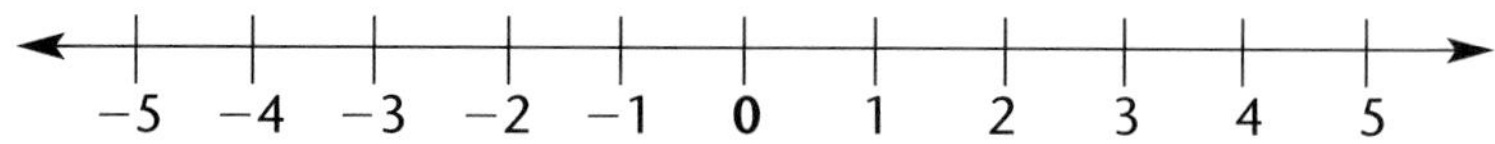

EXAMPLE 1

−5 is the opposite of 5.
5 is the opposite of −5.
5 is 5 units from 0.
−5 is also 5 units from 0.

Absolute value

The distance a number on the number line is from zero

The distance an integer is from zero on the number line is called its **absolute value**.

EXAMPLE 2 In algebra,

$|-5|$ is read "the absolute value of negative 5."

$|-5| = 5$, 5 units from 0.

$|5| = 5$, 5 units from 0.

Exercise A Find the opposite of each integer.

1. 4
2. -1
3. 6
4. -8
5. $+11$
6. -17
7. -24
8. $+14$
9. 9
10. -3

Exercise B Find each absolute value.

11. $|-2|$
12. $|13|$
13. $|+4|$
14. $|5|$
15. $|-6|$
16. $|10|$
17. $|-3|$
18. $|-11|$
19. $|-8|$
20. $|0|$

PROBLEM SOLVING

Exercise C Solve each problem.

21. A football team gained 15 yards on the first play and lost 8 yards on the second. Use + and − numbers to show the team's progress.

22. How does a temperature of 4°F compare to −7°F?

23. How does a temperature of −2°F compare to −6°F?

24. Two different integers are the same distance apart on a number line. What word could you use to describe those integers?

25. Explain how you could use a number line to represent the time when an event happened in the past.

TRY THIS A bell will sound in exactly two minutes to signal the end of your class. Would you use −2 or +2 to describe the number of minutes until the bell rings? Explain.

Lesson 4 Adding Integers

Addition

The arithmetic operation of combining numbers to find their sum or total

Addend

A number that is added to one or more numbers

Sum

The answer to an addition problem

Addition is combining numbers to form a total. Each number being added is an **addend**. The answer is the **sum**.

Adding a positive to a positive makes the result more positive.

EXAMPLE 1 $3 + 4 = \blacksquare$

Start at 3, move 4 units to the right. Since you stopped at 7, $3 + 4 = 7$.

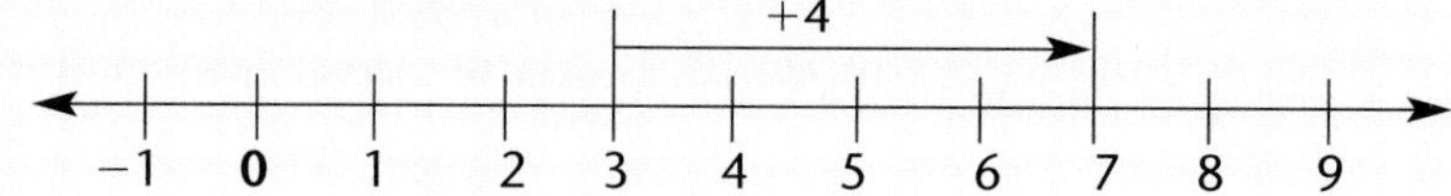

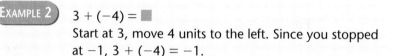

Adding a negative to a positive makes the result more negative.

EXAMPLE 2 $3 + (-4) = \blacksquare$

Start at 3, move 4 units to the left. Since you stopped at −1, $3 + (-4) = -1$.

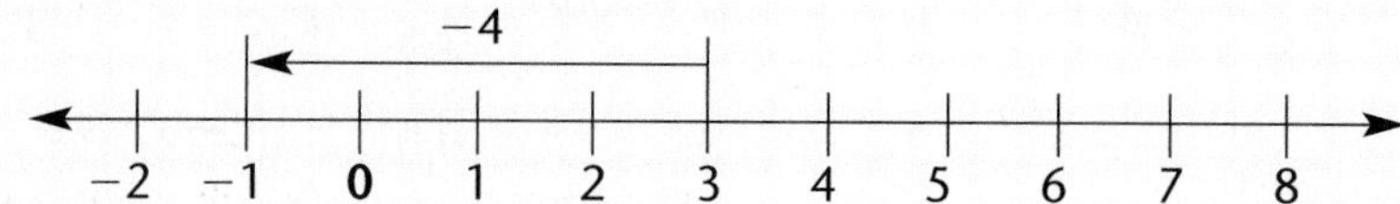

Adding a positive to a negative makes the result more positive.

EXAMPLE 3 $-3 + 4 = \blacksquare$

Start at −3, move 4 units to the right. Since you stopped at 1, $-3 + 4 = 1$.

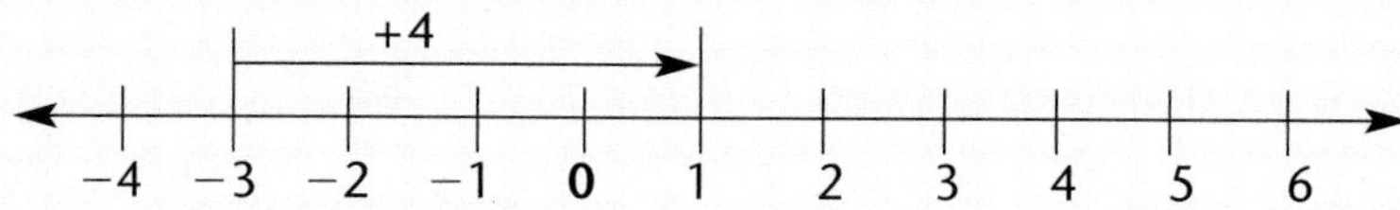

Adding a negative to a negative makes the result more negative.

EXAMPLE 4 $-3 + (-4) = \blacksquare$

Start at −3, move 4 units to the left. Since you stopped at −7, $-3 + (-4) = -7$.

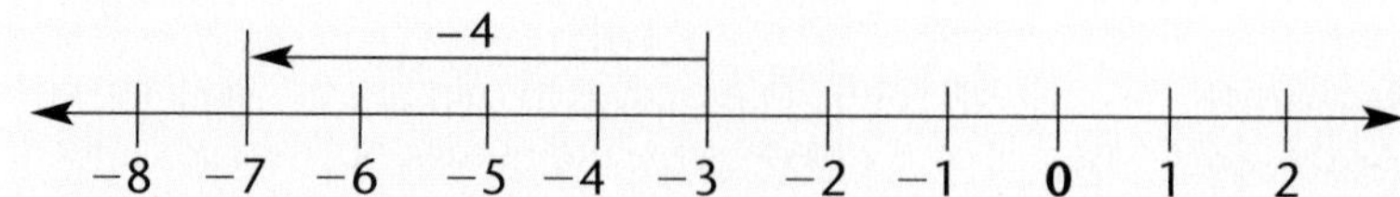

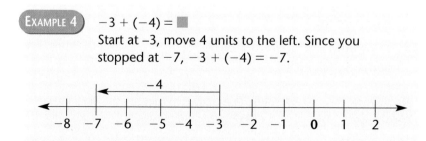

Exercise A Find each sum.

1. $5 + 8$
2. $-9 + (-3)$
3. $-4 + 8$
4. $2 + 7$
5. $-10 + 2$
6. $-8 + (-6)$
7. $-5 + 3$
8. $6 + 9$
9. $-2 + (-2)$
10. $6 + (-10)$
11. $-4 + (-2)$
12. $3 + 2$
13. $5 + (-9)$
14. $-7 + (-4)$
15. $3 + (-3)$

Exercise B Find each temperature.

16. $-5°F + 4°F$
17. $-8°F + 6°F$
18. $13°F + 7°F$
19. $4°F + (-4)°F$
20. $-15°F + (-9)°F$
21. $-3°F + 11°F$
22. $6°F + (-15)°F$
23. $-5°F + 15°F$
24. $2°F + (-10)°F$

Exercise C Find each temperature.

25. $-5°C + (-5)°C$
26. $9°C + 7°C$
27. $-4°C + 10°C$
28. $3°C + (-3)°C$
29. $7°C + -18°C$
30. $-2°C + (-9)°C$

Calculator Practice

The [+/−] key on your calculator changes the sign of the number entered. You can use the [+/−] key to add integers.

EXAMPLE 5

$5 + -1$

Press 5 [+] 1 [+/−] [=] 4

$-4 + 8$

Press 4 [+/−] [+] 8 [=] 4

Exercise D Find each sum using a calculator.

31. $651 + -821$
32. $-725 + -265$
33. $658 + -427$
34. $326 + 989$
35. $-951 + 458$

Lesson 5 Subtracting Integers

Subtraction

The arithmetic operation of taking one number away from another to find the difference

Difference

The answer to a subtraction problem

Subtracting a positive from a positive makes the result less positive or more negative, so you move to the left.

EXAMPLE 1 $3 - (+4) = ■$ Start at 3, move 4 units to the left. Since you stopped at -1, $3 - (+4) = -1$.
Note: $3 - (+4) = -1$ gives the same result as $3 + (-4) = -1$ because 4 and -4 are opposites.

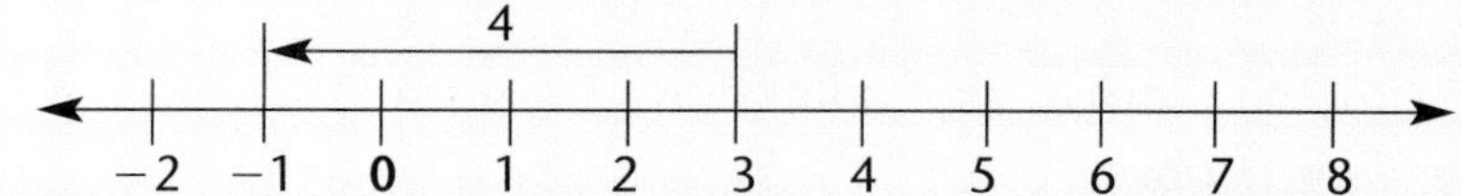

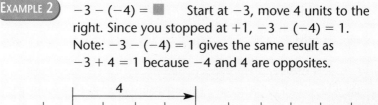

Subtracting a negative from a negative makes the result less negative or more positive, so you move to the right.

Subtraction and addition are opposite arithmetic operations. In addition, two (or more) numbers are combined. In subtraction, one number is taken away from another number. The answer is the **difference**.

EXAMPLE 2 $-3 - (-4) = ■$ Start at -3, move 4 units to the right. Since you stopped at $+1$, $-3 - (-4) = 1$.
Note: $-3 - (-4) = 1$ gives the same result as $-3 + 4 = 1$ because -4 and 4 are opposites.

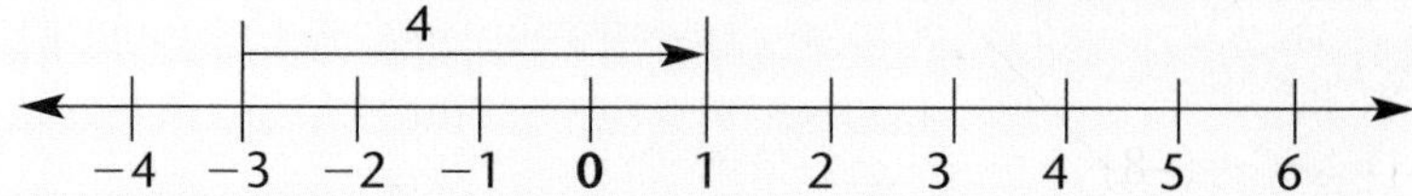

Subtracting a negative from a positive makes it less negative or more positive, so you move to the right.

EXAMPLE 3 $3 - (-4) = ■$ Start at 3, move 4 units to the right. Since you stopped at $+7$, $3 - (-4) = 7$.

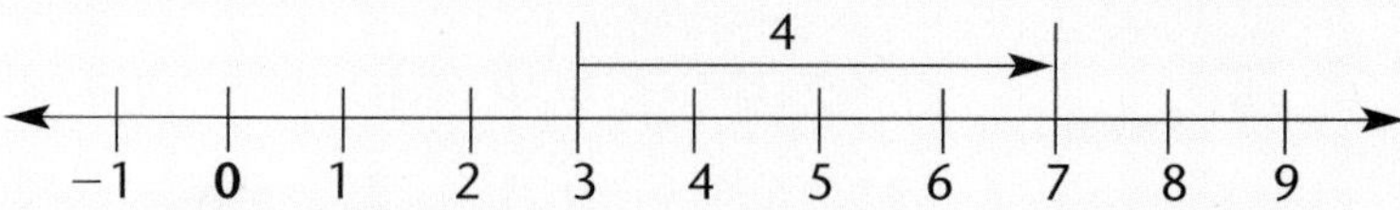

Subtracting a positive from a negative makes it less positive or more negative, so you move to the left.

EXAMPLE 4 $-3 - (+4) = ■$ Start at -3, move 4 units to the left. Since you stopped at -7, $-3 - 4 = -7$.

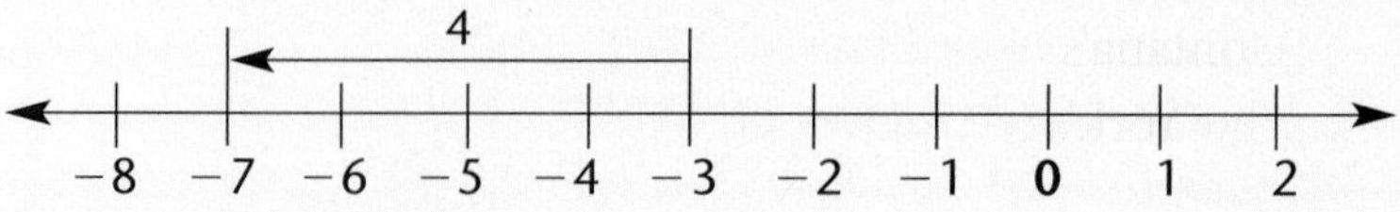

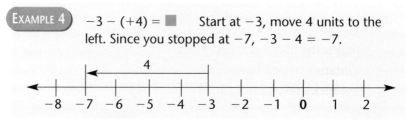

IN SUMMARY:

$3 - (+4) = -1$	is the same as	$3 + (-4) = -1$
$-3 - (-4) = 1$	is the same as	$-3 + 4 = 1$
$3 - (-4) = 7$	is the same as	$3 + 4 = 7$
$-3 - (+4) = -7$	is the same as	$-3 + (-4) = -7$

Rule To subtract in algebra, add the opposite.
$3 - (+4) = 3 + (-4)$
$a - (b) = a + (-b)$

Exercise A Rewrite each subtraction expression as an addition expression. Solve the new expression.

1. $5 - (+4)$

2. $8 - 2$

3. $-5 - (-6)$

4. $-9 - (-8)$

5. $-7 - (+5)$

6. $-3 + 5$

7. $-3 - (-10)$

8. $11 - (+6)$

9. $8 - (-1)$

10. $4 - 3$

11. $-6 - (+2)$

12. $7 - 3$

Exercise B Find each difference.

13. $9 - 6$

14. $-5 - (-8)$

15. $8 - (-8)$

16. $-5 - (+10)$

17. $12 - (-3)$

18. $-7 - (-3)$

19. $7 - (+9)$

20. $-6 - 6$

21. $3 - 6$

22. $-3 - (+5)$

23. $5 - 8$

24. $-7 - (+6)$

25. $6 - (-9)$

26. $-10 - (-7)$

27. $8 - 2$

PROBLEM SOLVING

Exercise C Solve each problem.

28. The record high temperature for Pennsylvania is 111°F. The record low is –42°F. What is the difference between the high and low?

29. What is the difference between Montana's record low of −70°F and New York's record low of −52°F?

30. Lake Eyre, Australia, has an elevation of −52 feet, while Lake Torrens, Australia, has an elevation of 92 feet. What is the difference between the elevations?

Lesson 6 Multiplying Integers

Multiplication
The arithmetic operation of adding a number to itself many times

Factor
A number that is multiplied in a multiplication problem

Product
The answer to a multiplication problem

In **multiplication**, you simply add a number many times. The order in which you multiply two **factors** does not change the **product**.

In algebra, "3 times 3" is written as (3)(3) and "3 times n" is written as $3n$. You know that $(3)(3) = 9$. You can think of this as three groups of 3.

EXAMPLE 1 $(3)(3) = 9$

Start at zero and count by 3's on the number line.

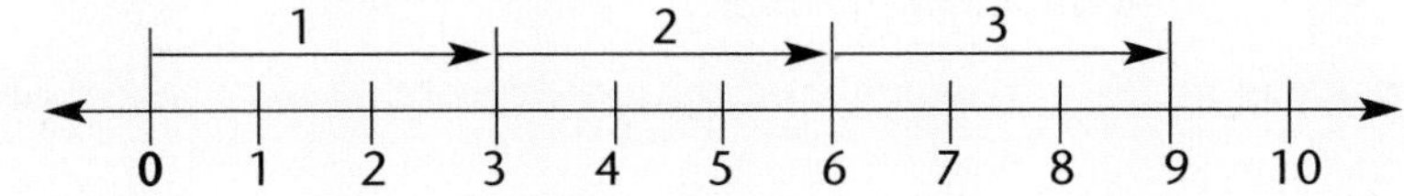

Rule (Positive) • (Positive) = (Positive)

EXAMPLE 2 $(3)(-3) = \blacksquare$

Start at zero and count by -3 on the number line.
$(3)(-3)$ means three groups of -3.
$(-3) + (-3) + (-3)$. Therefore, $(3)(-3) = -9$.

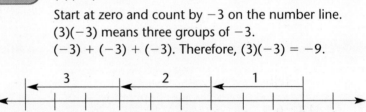

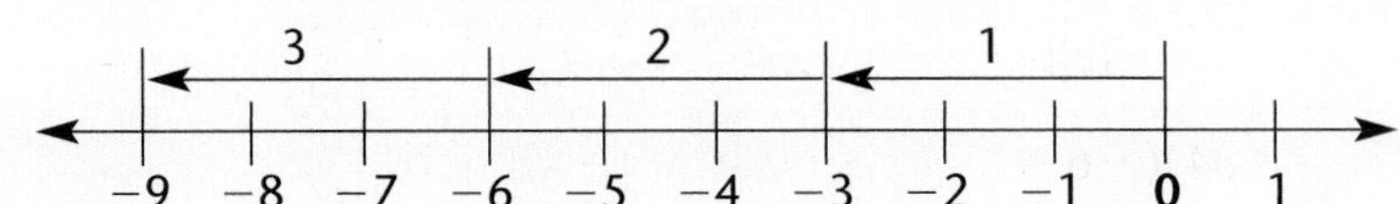

Rule (Positive) • (Negative) = (Negative)

EXAMPLE 3 $(-3)(3) = \blacksquare$

Treat this the same as $(3)(-3)$.
$(-3)(3)$ means three groups of (-3) or
$(-3) + (-3) + (-3)$. Therefore, $(-3)(3) = -9$.

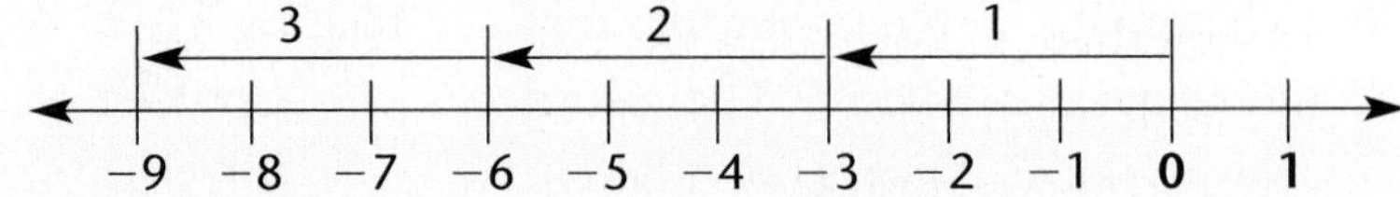

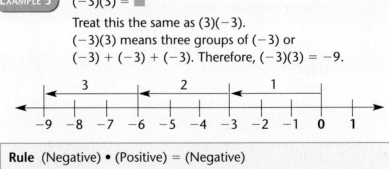

Rule (Negative) • (Positive) = (Negative)

EXAMPLE 4 This leaves only one other case, namely (−3)(−3) or a (Negative) (Negative).
This case cannot be shown on the number line.
The product is 9. You need to solve exercises such as these using the following rule:

> **Rule** (Negative) • (Negative) = (Positive)

So, $(-3)(-3) = 9$

Exercise A Find each product.

1. $(7)(8)$	**8.** $(-4)(13)$	**15.** $(-6)(-5)$
2. $(-4)(-3)$	**9.** $(6)(-10)$	**16.** $(-8)(-2)$
3. $(-5)(6)$	**10.** $(3)(9)$	**17.** $(5)(-10)$
4. $(9)(-8)$	**11.** $(-7)(-9)$	**18.** $(15)(4)$
5. $(9)(9)$	**12.** $(-7)(3)$	**19.** $(-4)(5)$
6. $(-5)(-9)$	**13.** $(8)(3)$	**20.** $(-11)(-8)$
7. $(5)(12)$	**14.** $(-9)(2)$	

Exercise B Tell whether each product is positive, negative, or zero.

21. $(-34)(-63)$	**24.** $(-400)(205)$	**27.** $(-771)(-522)$
22. $(67)(-326)$	**25.** $(0)(-345)$	**28.** $(389)(399)$
23. $(-487)(-351)$	**26.** $(800)(-72)$	

PROBLEM SOLVING

Exercise C Solve these problems.

29. One side of a ship has marks spaced three feet apart. Four marks are underwater. How many feet of the ship are underwater?

30. Is $(-3)(0)$ equal to -3 or 0? Why?

Lesson 7 Dividing Positive and Negative Integers

Division

The arithmetic operation that finds how many times a number is contained in another number

Quotient

The answer to a division problem

Dividend

A number that is divided

Divisor

The number by which you are dividing

Division is the arithmetic operation that finds how many times a number is contained in another number. The answer is the **quotient**.

EXAMPLE 1 $30 \div 6 = 5$

$$6\overline{)30}\ \text{with quotient } 5$$

Division and multiplication are opposite operations. Multiplying 3 by 4, then dividing the product by 4 gets you back to 3: $(3)(4) = 12$ and $12 \div 4 = 3$. You can use this information to discover the rules for division with negatives.

EXAMPLE 2

	Multiplication		Division
	$(3)(4) = 12$	and	$12 \div 4 = 3$
Rule	$(+)(+) = (+)$		$(+) \div (+) = (+)$

EXAMPLE 3

	$(3)(-4) = -12$	and	$(-12) \div (-4) = 3$
Rule	$(+)(-) = (-)$		$(-) \div (-) = (+)$

EXAMPLE 4

	$(-3)(4) = -12$	and	$(-12) \div (4) = (-3)$
Rule	$(-)(+) = (-)$		$(-) \div (+) = (-)$

EXAMPLE 5

	$(-3)(-4) = 12$	and	$(12) \div (-4) = (-3)$
Rule	$(-)(-) = (+)$		$(+) \div (-) = (-)$

Rules Like signs create positive products and quotients.
Unlike signs create negative products and quotients.

Division is the opposite of multiplication. A **dividend** is divided by a **divisor** to find a quotient.

Writing About Mathematics

Explain how to check division problems using multiplication. Then write about ways you can use division and multiplication in daily activities.

Exercise A Find each quotient.

1. $42 \div 6$

2. $-12 \div 4$

3. $16 \div (-4)$

4. $-25 \div (-5)$

5. $81 \div 9$

6. $-36 \div (-6)$

7. $-54 \div (-9)$

8. $48 \div 8$

8. $-56 \div 7$

10. $-8 \div (-4)$

11. $0 \div (-1)$

12. $40 \div (-5)$

13. $50 \div 5$

14. $-40 \div (-40)$

15. $21 \div 3$

16. $32 \div (-8)$

17. $64 \div 8$

18. $21 \div (-3)$

19. $-18 \div (-6)$

20. $-72 \div 9$

Exercise B Tell whether each quotient is positive, negative, or zero.

21. $2226 \div (-42)$

22. $-3458 \div 19$

23. $676 \div (-26)$

24. $5402 \div (73)$

25. $-8514 \div (-33)$

26. $121 \div (-11)$

27. $-3563 \div 7$

28. $0 \div (-21)$

Exercise C Write + or − in each ■ to make each statement true.

29. ■ $21 \div 3 = 7$

30. ■ $30 \div 3 = -10$

Algebra in Your Life

Creating Color

Want to paint your room? You can choose from thousands of shades of color. To create each shade, a specified number of drops of one or more base colors is added to white paint. Want to work with color on your computer? Open a computer's drawing or paint program. Go to the "custom color" option where you'll see several cells with numbers. Experiment. If you add or subtract from the numbers in one or more of the cells, you'll see the new color you've created.

Lesson 8 Simplifying Expressions—One Variable

Term
Part of an expression separated by an addition or subtraction sign

Like terms
Terms that have the same variable

Simplify
Combine like terms

In algebra, you need to add, subtract, multiply, and divide using variables to stand for numbers.

In algebra $3n$ means $n + n + n$.
$2n$ means $n + n$.
n means $1n$ (the 1 is not written).

$3n$ and $2n$ and n are all called **terms**. $3n + 2n$ is an example of an algebraic expression that includes **like terms.**

To **simplify** an algebraic expression, combine the like terms.

EXAMPLE 1 $3n + 2n$

Combine the like terms, $3n$ and $2n$.

$3n + 2n$ means the same as

$$\underbrace{n + n + n}_{3n} + \underbrace{n + n}_{2n} = 5n$$

EXAMPLE 2 $3x - 15 - 10x$

Combine the like terms by subtracting the x's:

$3x - 10x$ (Think $3 - 10 = -7$)

$3x - 10x = -7x$

Since you cannot combine -15 with $-7x$, you are finished.

The simplified answer: $3x - 15 - 10x = -7x - 15$

Exercise A Simplify each expression.

1. $m + m$

2. $s + s + s + s$

3. $v + v + v$

4. $b + b + b$

5. $c + c + c + c$

Exercise B Simplify each expression.

6. $2m + m$
7. $6h + 4h$
8. $3t + 6t$
9. $k + 7k$
10. $j + 3j + 6j$
11. $5p + 6 + 8p$
12. $7 + 2i + 4i$
13. $7y + 3y - 4$
14. $6z + 4z - 11$
15. $9 + 6c - 2c$
16. $8x + 4 - 3x$
17. $6q - 3 - 2q$
18. $10p + 12 - 8p$
19. $20v + 9 + 9v$
20. $17w - 5 - 12w$
21. $-6g + g$
22. $k + (-12k)$
23. $6m + (-18m)$
24. $-5t + t + (-12t)$
25. $14x - (-14x)$
26. $6 + j + (-15j)$
27. $2r + 18 - 18r$
28. $5f + (-3f) + 14$
29. $15u - 18 - 17u$
30. $7 + 23m - (-14m)$

Exercise C Find the missing term to make each statement true.

31. $c + ■ = 10c$
32. $6j - ■ = 3j$
33. $18e + ■ = 12e$
34. $■ - (-21x) = 21x$
35. $90z + ■ = 80z$

Exercise D Write an expression for each statement.

36. The sum of four x and twenty.
37. The difference between $2n$ and thirty.
38. The sum of $5d$ and seventeen.
39. Three subtracted from $4p$.
40. Twenty-five added to $17q$.

Estimation Activity

Estimate: Will the result of a multiplication or division problem be positive or negative?

$(37)(-0.12) = ?$
$(37)(-0.12) \div 1.5 = ?$
$(37)(-0.12) \div (-1.5) = ?$
$(x)(-x^2)(-x) \div (x^3)(-x) = ?$

Solution: For multiplication and division, an odd number of negative factors or divisors will give a negative result. An even number of negative factors or divisors will give a positive result.

Lesson 9 Simplifying Expressions—Several Variables

Unlike terms

Terms that have different variables

You may have more than one variable in an expression.

EXAMPLE 1 $3a + b$

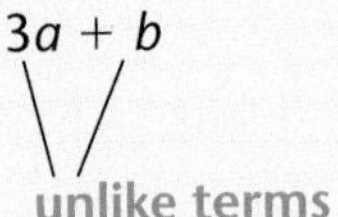

unlike terms

You cannot combine terms because a and b are unlike terms.

$3a + a$

like terms

$3a + a$ are like terms and can be combined to create $4a$.

To simplify expressions, combine all like terms.

EXAMPLE 2 $3x + 15 + 6x - 7 + y$

Combine x terms: $3x + 6x = 9x$

Combine integers: $15 - 7 = +8$

Note: You cannot combine unlike terms $9x$, y, and 8, so you are finished.

Rewrite $3x + 15 + 6x - 7 + y$ as $9x + y + 8$.

Exercise A Combine like terms. Simplify each expression.

1. $5x + 3x + 4 + 7b$

2. $14m + 7c + 4c + 4m$

3. $16 + 4a - 2a + 7u + 2u$

4. $5h - 3h + 14 + 15n$

5. $7y + 10p + 18 + 10p + 17y$

6. $13r + 25 - 8r + 14g + 5g$

7. $m + 10 + 2m + 7t$

8. $20p - 4 - 12p + 5q + 2q$

9. $8w - 13 - 4w + y$

10. $32j + 14 - 30j + 3h + 2h$

11. $8u + 7b + 17 + 2b - 4u$

12. $25 + 16a - 22 + 7d - 15a + 7d$

13. $9g + 2 + 16r - 7g + 15 - 13r$

14. $8 + j - 3 + 4j + 17m$

15. $3m + 7y + 5 - m - 6y$

Exercise B Combine like terms. Simplify each expression.

16. $7t - 14 - 16t + 9c + (-14c)$

17. $8 - 8c - 8c - 4b - 12b$

18. $10n - 15 - 5n + 6 + 2c$

19. $3x + (-17) + 21f + 3x - (-21f)$

20. $-19m + 5 - (-m) + c - 7c$

21. $y - 14 + 30c - 2y + 16c$

22. $10 + (-4g) + 10 - 13x - 2g + 5x$

23. $20j + 20j - 16m - 16m + 16$

24. $-25d + 2s - 7 + 15s - 20d$

25. $9m - 14 - 6m + 4r + 12r$

Exercise C Tell whether each statement is true or false.

26. $m + 15c + (-3m) - 4$ simplifies to $8mc$

27. $30x + 9 + 9m + 14x - 3m$ simplifies to $34x + 9 + 6m$

28. $6 + 4m - 17g + 6m + 3g$ simplifies to $6 + 10m - 14g$

29. $17 + 6y - 10 + m + 7m$ simplifies to $27 + 6y + 8m$

30. $-j + 10s - j + 12 - 8s$ simplifies to $-2j + 2s + 12$

Technology Connection

Software Programs Use Formulas

Balancing your checkbook is easy when you use a software program. Just enter the dollar amounts of your checks and deposits in the right place. The software calculates your balance for you. In the same way, other software programs help businesses to do payroll. They also help insurance companies to figure out premiums, and scientists to calculate the growth of bacteria and viruses. These software programs have one thing in common—they all use formulas with variables!

Lesson 10 Positive Exponents

Exponent
Number that tells the times another number is a factor

Base
The number being multiplied; a factor

Power
The product of multiplying any number by itself once or many times

2^3 is an example of a way to show a number (2) multiplied by itself three times.

2^3 The 3 is called the **exponent**.
The 2 is called the **base**.

$a \cdot a \cdot a$ can be written as a^3 — Exponent, Base

$y \cdot y \cdot y \cdot y$ can be written as y^4 — Exponent, Base

You can multiply and divide by adding or subtracting exponents with the same base.

EXAMPLE 1 $y^2 \bullet y^3 = y \bullet y \bullet y \bullet y \bullet y = y^5$
or $y^2 \bullet y^3 = y^{2+3} = y^5$

Rule To multiply, add exponents with the same base.

EXAMPLE 2 $y^3 \div y^2 = \frac{y^3}{y^2} = \frac{y \bullet \not{y} \bullet \not{y}}{\not{y} \bullet \not{y}} = y$
or $y^3 \div y^2 = y^{3-2} = y^1 = y$

Rule To divide, subtract exponents with the same base.

Terms such as x^2 or x^3 have no numerical value until you substitute numbers for x.

EXAMPLE 3 If $x = 3$, $x^2 = 3 \bullet 3$ or 9 and $x^3 = 3 \bullet 3 \bullet 3$ or 27.
3 to the second **power** is 9.
3 to the third power is 27.

Exercise A Tell whether each statement is true or false. If the statement is false, write the correct solution.

1. $2^3 = 8$
2. $x \cdot x \cdot x = x^3$
3. $m^2 \cdot m^5 = m^{10}$
4. $3^2 = 6$
5. $c^5 \cdot c^4 \cdot c^2 = c^{11}$
6. $y^3 \cdot y^3 = 6^y$
7. $n^{10} \div n^2 = n^8$
8. $\frac{b^{16}}{b^4} = b^{12}$
9. $a^{25} \div a^5 = a^5$
10. $\frac{t^8}{t^5} = t^3$

Exercise B Simplify each expression.

11. $w^8 \cdot w^7$
12. $p^4 \div p^3$
13. $b^2 \cdot b$
14. $c^{10} \div c^2$
15. $v^7 \cdot v^7$
16. $x^{11} \div x^5$
17. $d^4 \cdot d^3 \cdot d$
18. $j^{18} \div j^6$
19. $t \cdot t^8 \cdot t^{10}$
20. $m^{20} \div m^{18}$
21. $x^3 \cdot x \cdot x^5 \cdot x^4$
22. $\frac{y^{16}}{y^{16}}$
23. $\frac{g^{14}}{g^3}$
24. $r^4 \div r$
25. $v^2 \cdot v^2 \cdot v^8 \cdot v^7$

Exercise C Find the value of n to make each statement true.

26. $y^3 \cdot b^4 \cdot y^6 = y^9 b^n$
27. $a^3 \cdot c^4 \cdot c^3 \cdot a^7 = a^{10} c^n$
28. $\frac{e^{14}}{e^n} = e^{10}$
29. $t \cdot v^6 \cdot t^2 = t^n v^6$
30. $i^n \div i^{10} = i^{35}$
31. $\frac{w^{12}}{w^6} = w^n$
32. $x^4 \cdot y^3 \cdot x^5 \cdot y^2 = x^n y^5$
33. $p^3 \cdot q^4 \cdot q^7 = p^n q^{11}$
34. $z^n \div z^8 = z^6$
35. $\frac{s^{20}}{s^n} = s^5$

Calculator Practice

Use the y^x or x^y key on your calculator to compute with exponents.

EXAMPLE 4 Find 5^4.

Press 5 y^x 4 = .

The display will show 625.

Exercise D Use a calculator to find the value of each expression.

36. 25^4
37. $(4.1)^2$
38. $(\frac{1}{2})^3$
39. $(0.01)^2$
40. 3^{10}

Lesson 11 Formulas with Variables

Perimeter

The distance around the outside of a shape

Equilateral triangle

A triangle with three equal sides

In the formula for finding the **perimeter**, or distance around, any **equilateral triangle**, s stands for the length of a side of the triangle. The letter s represents an unknown quantity or variable. To find perimeter, add the length of each side of a figure.

EXAMPLE 1 **Perimeter** $= s + s + s = 3s$

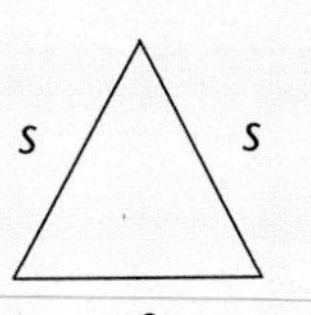

If $s = 2$, then $3s = (3)(2) = 6$

If $s = 15$, then $3s = (3)(15) = 45$

Square

s

s s

s

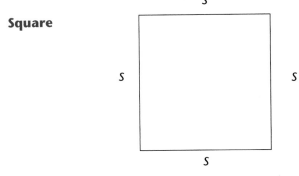

Exercise A Use the square for Problems 1–4.

1. What is the formula for finding the perimeter of this square?
2. Find the perimeter of a square, when $s = 4$ cm.
3. Find the perimeter of a square, when $s = 10$ m.
4. What is the length of each side of a square when the perimeter is 36 meters?

Triangle

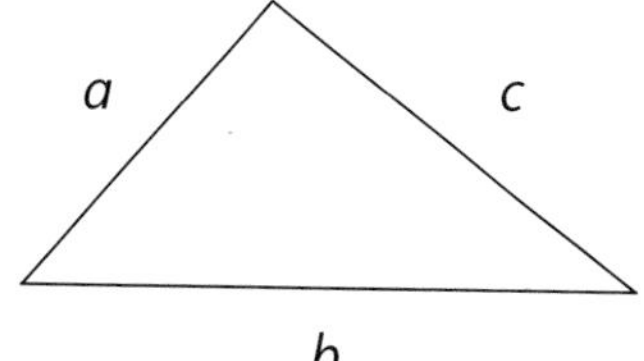

Exercise B Use the triangle for Problems 5–8.

5. What is the formula for finding the perimeter of this triangle?

6. Find the perimeter, when $a = 13$ cm, $b = 10$ cm, and $c = 20$ cm.

7. Find the perimeter, when $a = 20$ cm, $b = 30$ cm, and $c = 40$ cm.

8. What is the length of side c when the perimeter is 100 m, $b = 35$ m, and $a = 40$ m?

Rectangle

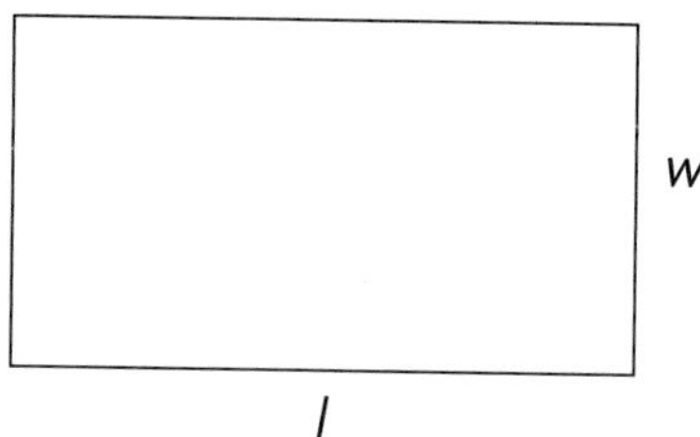

Exercise C Use the rectangle for Problems 9–12.

9. What is the formula for finding the perimeter of this rectangle?

10. Find the perimeter, when $l = 15$ mm and $w = 8$ mm.

11. Find the perimeter, when $l = 10$ cm and $w = 9$ cm.

12. What is the width of a rectangle when the perimeter is 14 m and the length is 4 m?

Pentagon

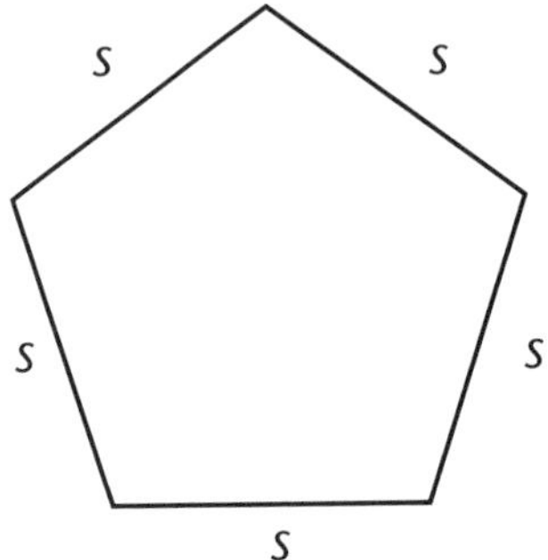

Exercise D Use the pentagon for Problems 13–16.

13. What is the formula for finding the perimeter of this regular pentagon?

14. Find the perimeter, when $s = 6$ m.

15. Find the perimeter, when $s = 8$ cm.

16. What is the length of each side of a regular pentagon when the perimeter is 100 km?

The Pentagon in Arlington, Virginia, has five wedge-shaped sections.

Rhombus

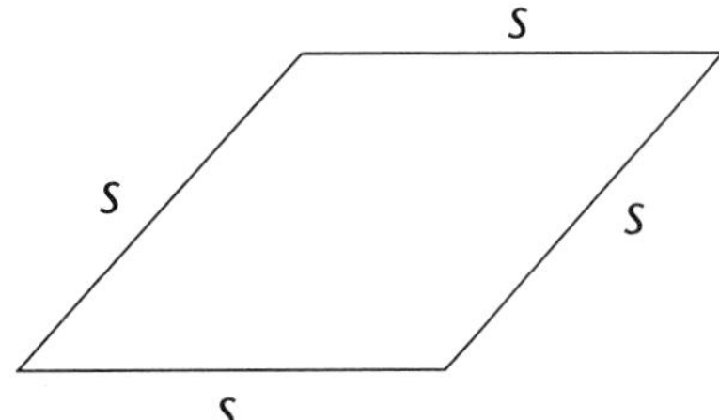

Exercise E Use the rhombus for Problems 17–21.

17. What is the formula for finding the perimeter of this rhombus?

18. Find the perimeter, when $s = 15$ km.

19. Find the perimeter, when $s = 8$ km.

20. What is the length of each side of a rhombus when the perimeter is 28 km?

21. A rhombus has the same perimeter formula as what other polygon?

Hexagon

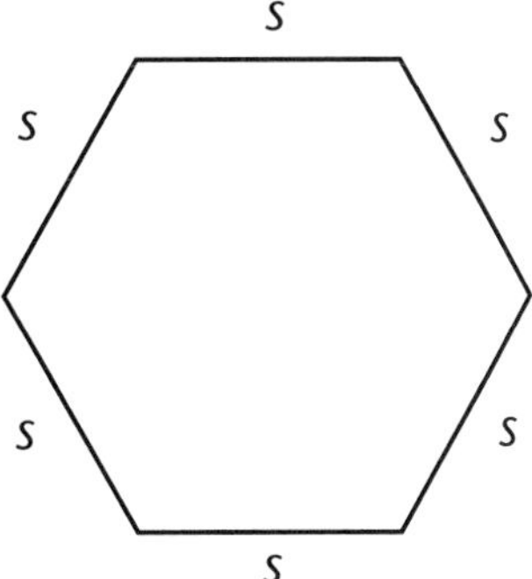

Exercise F Use the hexagon for Problems 22–25.

22. What is the formula for finding the perimeter of this hexagon?

23. Find the perimeter, when $s = 10$ mm.

24. Find the perimeter, when $s = 8$ km.

25. What is the length of each side of a regular hexagon when the perimeter is 72 m?

Application $\pi^2 \sum + \Omega \sqrt{x^2} \% \neq y \geq n = \nabla 30^\circ \pi$

Using a Formula

The speed that an airplane travels is calculated by the formula $g = a - h$. Ground speed (g) equals air speed (a) minus head wind speed (h).

	Ground speed (g)	=	Air speed (a)	−	Head wind speed (h)
EXAMPLE 1	g	=	200 mph	−	67 mph

$g = 200 - 67 = 133$ The ground speed (g) equals 133 mph.

EXAMPLE 2	133 mph	=	a	−	67 mph

$133 = a - 67$

$a = 133 + 67 = 200$ The air speed (a) equals 200 mph.

EXAMPLE 3	133 mph	=	200 mph	−	h

$133 = 200 - h$

$h = 200 - 133 = 67$ The head wind speed (h) equals 67 mph.

Exercise Copy the table. Find each missing value.

	Ground speed (g)	air speed (a)	head wind speed (h)
1.	g	175 mph	53 mph
2.	273 mph	293 mph	h
3.	155 mph	a	15 mph
4.	g	112 mph	27 mph
5.	g	305 mph	41 mph

You can find an airplane's speed by using an algebraic formula.

Chapter 1 REVIEW

Write the letter of the correct answer.

1. Find the sum of $15 + (-13)$.

A 28
B 2
C -2
D -28

2. Find the difference of $-6 - (-7)$.

A 1
B -1
C 14
D -14

3. Find the quotient of $-25 \div (-5)$.

A 5
B -20
C -5
D -30

4. Simplify the equation $8x + 14 + 14x$.

A $28x + 8$
B $22 + 14x$
C $22x + 14$
D $28x + 8x$

5. Simplify the equation $a^3 \cdot b^4 \cdot a^6 \cdot b^2$.

A a^{15}
B b^{15}
C $a^{36} \cdot b^8$
D a^9b^6

6. The perimeter of a regular hexagon is $6s$. Find the perimeter when $s = 9$ m.

A 54 m
B 36 m
C 45 m
D 27 m

Identify each expression as either a numerical or an algebraic expression.

Example: $s + 14$ Solution: algebraic expression

7. $5x - 3$ **8.** $9 + 6$ **9.** $4y$ **10.** $p \div 7$ **11.** $16 \div 4$

Find the absolute value, or distance from zero.

Example: $|-7|$ Solution: $|-7| = 7$

12. $|2|$ **13.** $|-3|$ **14.** $|6|$ **15.** $|14|$ **16.** $|-25|$

Find each opposite.

Example: -8 Solution: $+8$ or 8

17. $+4$ **18.** -6 **19.** -1.5 **20.** 0 **21.** $(\frac{3}{4})$

Find each sum.

Example: $-8 + -8$ Solution: $-8 + -8 = -16$

22. $-8 + (-10)$ **23.** $14 + 14$ **24.** $7 + (-7)$ **25.** $-12 + 20$

Find each difference.

Example: $-4 - 2$ Solution: $-4 - 2 = -6$

26. $3 - 7$ **27.** $-3 - (-2)$ **28.** $10 - 4$ **29.** $0 - 5$

Find each product.

Example: $(-4)(4)$ Solution: $(-4)(4) = -16$

30. $(-5)(-8)$ **31.** $(6)(-10)$ **32.** $(-9)(6)$ **33.** $(10)(0)$

Find each quotient.

Example: $8 \div -2$ Solution: $8 \div -2 = -4$

34. $16 \div (-4)$ **35.** $-100 \div 10$ **36.** $27 \div 9$ **37.** $0 \div (-8)$

Simplify each expression.

Example: $-12a + 5a$ Solution: $-12a + 5a = -7a$

38. $-3m + 16 - (-13m)$

39. $15y - 20y + 15$

40. $-7n + 11 - 3x + 9x + 8n$

41. $1.2k - 3.4k$

42. $9 + 4g - 5$

43. $128v + 11r - 150v - 3r$

44. $x^4 \cdot x^3 \cdot x$

45. $n^{10} \div n^2$

46. $v^{14} \div v^5$

47. $(e^2)(g)(g^4)(e^3)$

48. $(d)(d^2)(d^3)$

49. $n^{10} \div n^4$

50. $(e)(e^7)(e)$

51. $j^7 \div j$

Use a formula to solve the problems.

Example: The width of a rectangle is x. Its length is twice the measure of its width. Write an expression in simplest form to represent the perimeter of the rectangle.

Solution: Let x = length
Let $2x$ = width
$p = x + x + 2x + 2x$
$p = 6x$

52. The perimeter of a square is $4s$. Find the perimeter when $s = 12$ mm.

53. The perimeter of an equilateral triangle is $3s$. Find the perimeter, when $s = 15$ km.

54. If the perimeter of a square is 152 cm, what is the length of each side?

55. If the perimeter of a regular hexagon is 96 m, what is the length of each side?

Test-Taking Tip

When studying for a test, write your own test problems with a partner. Then complete each other's test. Double-check your answers.

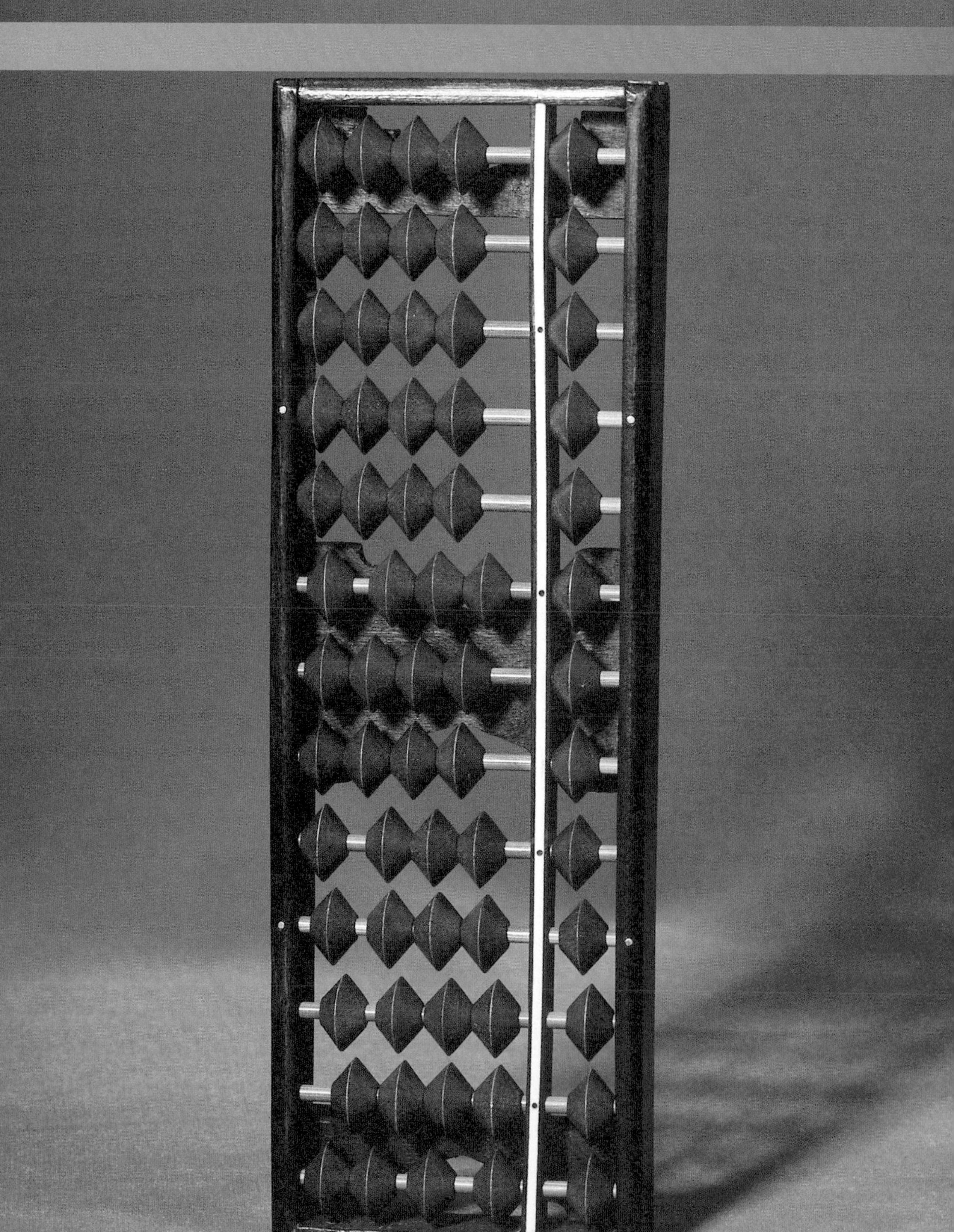

Chapter

The Rules of Arithmetic

Have you ever tried using an abacus? If so, you know that an abacus is a simple kind of calculator. Ancient cultures in China, Japan, and Russia used abacuses to count money. People also used them to keep track of how much things weighed. The ancient Chinese based their arithmetic on the numbers 2 and 16. Our numbering system is based on the number 10. To use an abacus, you slide the beads up and down or left and right to add, subtract, multiply and divide. As you learn algebra, you will use your arithmetic skills to add, subtract, multiply, and divide in order to solve equations.

In Chapter 2, you will be introduced to basic rules of arithmetic as they apply to algebra.

Goals for Learning

- To recognize the commutative property of addition and multiplication
- To understand the associative property of addition and multiplication
- To understand the distributive property and factoring
- To recognize the properties of the numbers 0 and 1
- To identify and use powers and roots of numbers
- To discover and use the order of operations in making calculations

Lesson 1 Commutative Property of Addition

Expanded notation

An algebraic expression written to show its smallest terms

Commutative property of addition

The order in which two numbers are added does not change their sum

Commutative is related to the word **commute**. Remember commute means to go from point A to point B and back from B to A. The distance between the two points is the same whether you go from A to B or B to A.

A number line can be used to show that the sum of 3 + 4 is equal to the sum of 4 + 3.

EXAMPLE 1 $3 + 4 = \blacksquare$

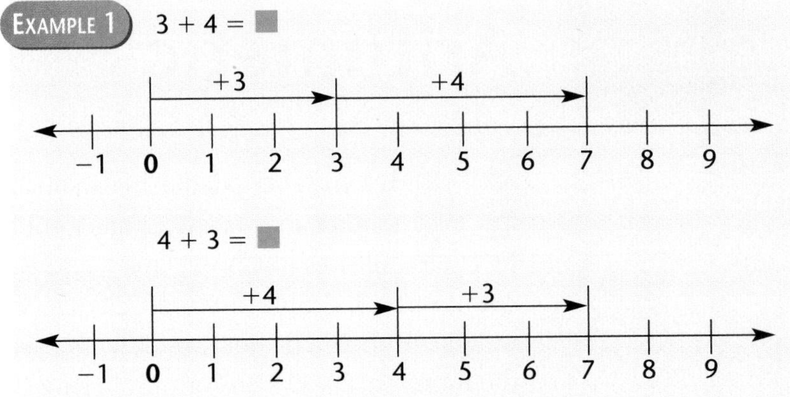

In algebra, you can use **expanded notation** to show that $3a + 4a$ and $4a + 3a$ both add to $7a$. Expanded notation means that the expression is written to show its smallest terms.

EXAMPLE 2 Write each equation in expanded notation.

$3a + 4a = \blacksquare$

$$a + a + a + a + a + a + a = a + a + a + a + a + a + a$$

$$3a \quad + \quad 4a \quad = \quad 7a$$

EXAMPLE 3 $4a + 3a = \blacksquare$

$$a + a + a + a + a + a + a = a + a + a + a + a + a + a$$

$$4a \quad + \quad 3a \quad = \quad 7a$$

The **commutative property of addition** states that you can rewrite any sum to change the order of the terms.

EXAMPLE 4 $6 + 4 = 4 + 6$

$m + n = n + m$

$10w + 12y = 12y + 10w$

Commutative Property of Addition

Two numbers may be added in either order without changing the sum. In general, for all terms or numbers a and b, $a + b = b + a$.

Exercise A Draw a number line to show that the sums are equal.

1. $1 + 3 = 3 + 1$

2. $2 + 3 = 3 + 2$

3. $1 + 2 = 2 + 1$

4. $5 + 2 = 2 + 5$

5. $3 + 4 = 4 + 3$

6. $3 + 6 = 6 + 3$

7. $4 + 5 = 5 + 4$

8. $1 + 6 = 6 + 1$

9. $3 + 5 = 5 + 3$

10. $7 + 2 = 2 + 7$

Exercise B Find each sum using expanded notation.

11. $2x + 4x$

12. $3c + c$

13. $4t + 2t$

14. $5j + 2j$

15. $6m + m$

16. $6v + 2v$

17. $y + 2y$

18. $3s + 5s$

Exercise C Rewrite each sum showing the commutative property of addition.

19. $a + 3$

20. $a + b$

21. $x + y$

22. $2x + 6$

23. $5g + 8g$

24. $b + 9b$

25. $4r + 7r$

26. $2p + 6p$

27. $2x + y$

28. $9k + 2k$

29. $6p + 7p$

30. $11 + 6$

31. $16q + 2q$

32. $8i + i$

33. $x + 10$

34. $2l + 3l$

35. $5y + y$

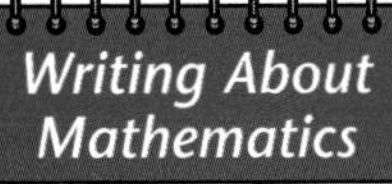

Write about things you do in your day that are commutative. For example, does it matter whether you brush your teeth, then comb your hair, or if you reverse the order?

Lesson 2 Commutative Property of Multiplication

> ***Geometry***
> *The study of points, lines, angles, surfaces, and solids*
>
> ***Commutative property of multiplication***
> *The order in which two numbers are multiplied does not change their product*

A number line can be used to show that the product of 3 • 4 is equal to the product of 4 • 3.

EXAMPLE 1 $(3)(4) = 12$

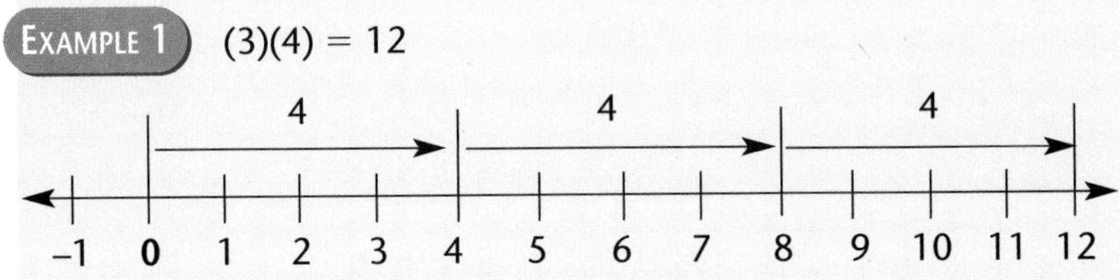

3 groups of 4 is the same as 12.

$(4)(3) = 12$

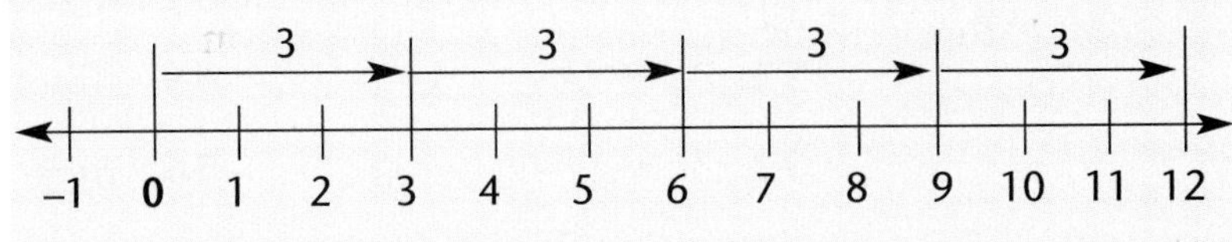

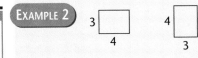

4 groups of 3 is the same as 12.

In **geometry**, you can find the area of a rectangle by multiplying its length (l) by its width (w).

> Even though $3n$ is equal to $n3$, the number is usually written before the variable. Therefore, $3n$ is the preferred form.

EXAMPLE 2

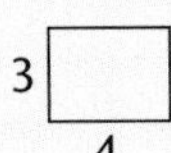

4 3

Because $(4)(3) = (3)(4)$, the area of each figure is 12 square units.

The **commutative property of multiplication** states that you can rewrite any product to change the order of the factors.

EXAMPLE 3 $xy = yx$

$(5a)(2b) = (2b)(5a)$

$15 \bullet 4 = 4 \bullet 15$

> **Commutative Property of Multiplication**
> Two numbers may be multiplied in either order without changing their product. In general, for all terms or numbers a and b, $ab = ba$.

Exercise A Draw a number line to show that each pair of products are equal.

1. $(2)(3) = (3)(2)$
2. $(4)(2) = (2)(4)$
3. $(5)(3) = (3)(5)$
4. $(2)(5) = (5)(2)$
5. $(4)(1) = (1)(4)$
6. $(1)(3) = (3)(1)$

Exercise B Write the factors and the product for the area of each rectangle.

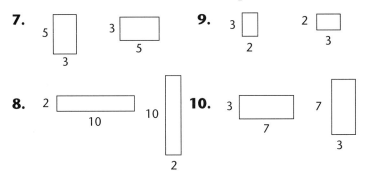

7. 5, 3; 3, 5

8. 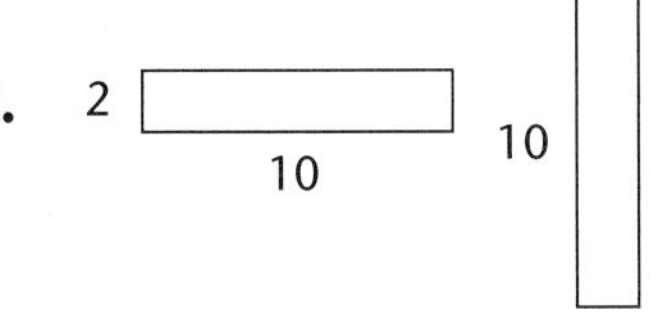

9. 3, 2; 2, 3

10. 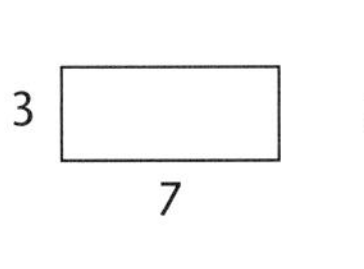

Exercise C Rewrite each expression showing the commutative property of multiplication.

11. ab
12. xy
13. zw
14. $z(2w)$
15. $(3z)(2)$
16. $5m(6b)$
17. $h(9w)$
18. $(14k)(12y)$

PROBLEM SOLVING

Exercise D Read each statement. If the commutative property can be used in the situation, write *yes.* If it cannot, write *no.*

19. Matt and Jenny order cheese, sausage, and onions on their pizza.
20. Juanita and Jose run inside the house, grab their game, and run back outside to play the game.
21. To get ready, Yung washes his face and hands and combs his hair.
22. Violet first finishes her math homework; then she finishes her history reading.
23. Mike reads his literature assignment and answers the review questions.
24. Rosalia cuts the lawn, pulls weeds out of the garden, and waters the plants.
25. Quentin reads the lesson on integers and then takes the mastery test.

Lesson 3 Associative Property of Addition

Associative property of addition

The same terms added in different groupings result in the same answer

Add: $98 + 9 + 1$

You can add several numbers in the order in which they appear.

$$\begin{array}{r} 98 \\ +\ 9 \\ \hline 107 \end{array} \qquad \begin{array}{r} 107 \\ +\ 1 \\ \hline 108 \end{array}$$

Another way is to change the order of the numbers.

$$\begin{array}{r} 9 \\ +\ 1 \\ \hline 10 \end{array} \qquad \begin{array}{r} 10 \\ +\ 98 \\ \hline 108 \end{array}$$

You can use parentheses to show the order in which the numbers should be added.

$(98 + 9) + 1 = 108 \qquad 98 + (9 + 1) = 108$

$(98 + 9) + 1 = 108$ is the same as $98 + (9 + 1) = 108$.

The **associative property of addition** allows you to add terms in any order.

EXAMPLE 1 $7r + (2r + 3r) = (7r + 2r) + 3r$

EXAMPLE 2 $5x + (4x + 6x) = (5x + 4x) + 6x$

Associative Property of Addition

Numbers may be added with different groupings. The final answer does not change. In general, for all terms or numbers a, b, and c, $(a + b) + c = a + (b + c)$.

Exercise A Find the sum for each pair of expressions. Add the terms in parentheses first.

1. $(4 + 6) + 15$

$4 + (6 + 15)$

2. $9 + (8 + 1)$

$(9 + 8) + 1$

3. $(15 + 5) + 7$

$15 + (5 + 7)$

4. $(12 + 8) + 5$

$12 + (8 + 5)$

5. $14 + (16 + 7)$

$(14 + 16) + 7$

6. $(4 + 6) + 14$

$4 + (6 + 14)$

7. $25 + (25 + 13)$

$(25 + 25) + 13$

8. $18 + (12 + 14)$

$(18 + 12) + 14$

9. $(33 + 17) + 22$

$33 + (17 + 22)$

10. $18 + (12 + 11)$

$(18 + 12) + 11$

Exercise B Use the associative property of addition to show each expression in two equal ways.

11. $x + y + z$

12. $m + n + o$

13. $g + h + j$

14. $3t + f + h$

15. $w + 4c + p$

16. $5r + x + 7t$

17. $4f + 9y + 2x$

18. $13a + 8e + 9f$

19. $21k + 13u + 16s$

20. $33x + 41h + 18k$

Exercise C Rewrite each expression showing the associative property of addition.

21. $3 + (6 + z)$

22. $(y + 13) + b$

23. $2b + (3c + 8)$

24. $16 + (2x + 9)$

25. $(5s + 3d) + 28$

TRY THIS Could there be an associative property of subtraction? Why or why not?

Lesson 4 Associative Property of Multiplication

Associative property of multiplication

The same terms multiplied in different groupings result in the same answer

The product of 3 • 4 • 10 can be found in two different ways. One way is to perform the operations from left to right in the order they appear.

3 times 4 is 12.

12 times 10 is 120.

This is written as $(3 \cdot 4)10 = 12 \cdot 10 = 120$.

The second way is to change the order and multiply 4 by 10 to get 40, then multiply 3 times 40 to get 120.

This is written as $3(4 \cdot 10) = 3 \cdot 40 = 120$.

Both ways give the same product.

$(3 \cdot 4)10 = 3(4 \cdot 10)$

$12 \cdot 10 = 3 \cdot 40$

$120 = 120$

In geometry, you find the volume of a rectangular solid (such as a box) by multiplying its length (l) times its width (w) times its height (h), or volume = lwh.

Brackets are used as a second set of parentheses. For example, instead of writing 6((3 + 2) − 4), we can write 6[(3 + 2) − 4]. This way it is easier to see what operation must be done first. In this case, add 3 and 2, subtract 4, and then multiply by 6.

$h = 2 \quad w = 5 \quad l = 10$

The base of this solid figure measures 10 by 5.

Volume = $(10 \bullet 5) \bullet 2 = 50 \bullet 2 = 100$ cubic units

$\quad\quad l \quad w \quad h$

$l = 5 \quad w = 2 \quad h = 10$

The base of this solid figure measures 5 by 2.

Volume = $(5 \bullet 2)10 = 10 \bullet 10 = 100$ cubic units

$\quad\quad l \quad w\ h$

The volumes are equal because it is the same box.

The **associative property of multiplication** states that you can place parentheses in any product of three factors, and the products will remain equal.

Associative Property of Multiplication

All terms or numbers may be multiplied with different groupings. The final answer does not change. In general, for all terms or numbers a, b, and c, $(ab)c = a(bc)$.

EXAMPLE 2 Use the associative property of multiplication to place parentheses in two ways for the product xyz.

$(xy)z = x(yz)$

Exercise A Copy the problems. Find the products by multiplying the factors in parentheses first.

1. $(3 \cdot 5)20 = 3(5 \cdot 20)$

2. $4(6 \cdot 10) = (4 \cdot 6)10$

3. $[5(4 \cdot 13)] = [(5 \cdot 4)13]$

4. $8(2 \cdot 5) = (8 \cdot 2)5$

5. $[(15 \cdot 3)3] = [15(3 \cdot 3)]$

6. $(25 \cdot 4)9 = 25(4 \cdot 9)$

7. $17(5 \cdot 2) = (17 \cdot 5)2$

8. $[(14 \cdot 10)2] = [14(10 \cdot 2)]$

9. $[20(5 \cdot 4)] = [(20 \cdot 5)4]$

10. $8(15 \cdot 2) = (8 \cdot 15)2$

Technology Connection

Binary System

Computers process all information using a binary system. A binary system uses only two digits—0 and 1. A binary digit, called a "bit," is the smallest unit of information in the computer world. The 0 stands for "off," "no," or "false." The 1 stands for "on," "yes," or "true." Bits combine into large units called "bytes." A byte is 8 digits. In binary code, the byte for number 237 is 11101101. But computers aren't smarter than humans. After all, when we program them, we tell the computers what to do!

Exercise B Find the volume of each figure in two different ways.

11.

12.

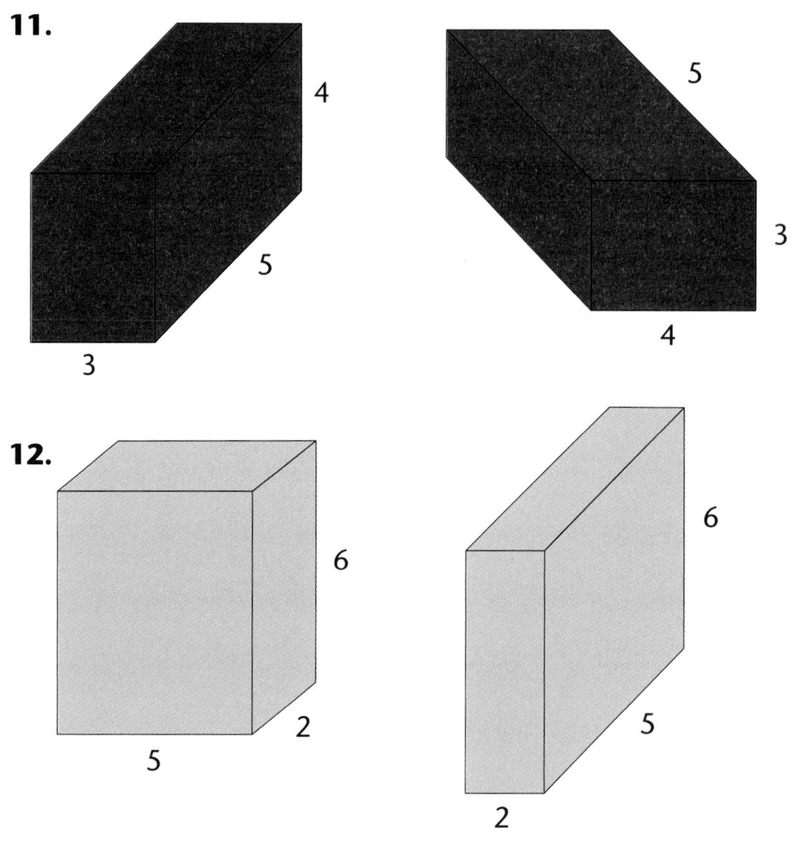

You can find the volume of rectangular solids by using the associative property of multiplication.

13.

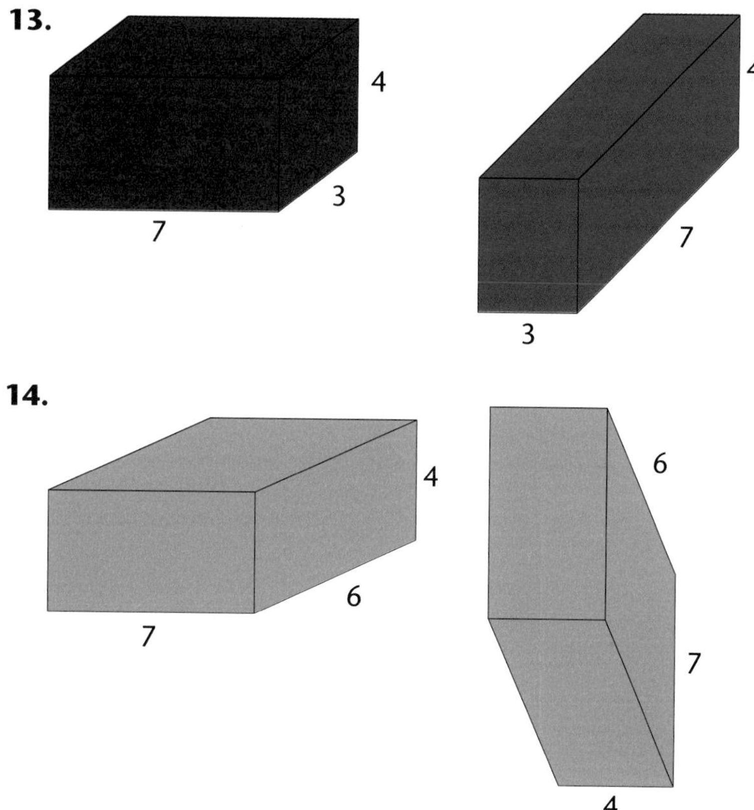

14.

Exercise C Use the associative property of multiplication to place parentheses in two different ways.

15. *lwh*

16. *xyz*

17. *fpn*

18. *cdj*

19. *mks*

20. *ghy*

Algebra in Your Life

Stepping through a Process

There are times when you need to do things in a certain order, and there are times when you don't. You follow step-by-step directions to build models from kits, bake cakes, or mix chemical formulas. Doing steps in the given order helps you get the results you want. The same is true of the order of operations in algebra. If you follow the steps in the right order, you end up with the correct answer.

Lesson 5 The Distributive Property—Multiplication

Distributive property

Numbers within parentheses can be multiplied by the same factor

Three times the sum of $10 + 5$ is written as $3(10 + 5)$.
You can find the result in two ways.
One way is to perform the operation inside parentheses first.

$3(10 + 5)$

$3(15)$

45

Another way is to use the **distributive property**.

$3(10 + 5) = 3(10 + 5)$

$3 \cdot 10 + 3 \cdot 5$

$30 + 15$

45

EXAMPLE 1 Simplify $3(a + b)$.

Since you cannot perform the operation inside parentheses first (because you do not know the values of a and b), use the distributive property.

$3(a + b) = a + b \ + \ a + b \ + \ a + b$

$= 3a + 3b$ or

$3(a + b)$

$(3 \bullet a) + (3 \bullet b)$

$3a + 3b$

$3 \bullet a$

$3\,(a + b) = 3a + 3b$

$3 \bullet b$

Use the distributive property to simplify these expressions.

EXAMPLE 2 $3(2x + 4y)$

$3(2x + 4y) = 2x + 4y \ + \ 2x + 4y \ + \ 2x + 4y$

$= 6x + 12y$ or

$3(2x + 4y) = (3)(2x) + (3)(4y) = 6x + 12y$

EXAMPLE 3 Let 10 be the height of two rectangles whose bases are 3 and 5. The areas of these rectangles represent the two products of the distributive property.

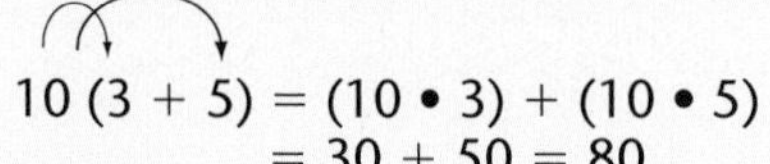

$10\,(3 + 5) = (10 \bullet 3) + (10 \bullet 5)$

$= 30 + 50 = 80$

10 | 30 | 50

3 5

Distributive Property of Multiplication

In a problem that mixes multiplication with addition or subtraction, you can multiply each term in parentheses by a single factor. In general, for all terms or numbers a, b, and c, $a(b + c) = ab + ac$.

Exercise A Copy and complete using the distributive property.

1. $4(10 + 5) = 4 \cdot ■ + 4 \cdot ■$
2. $18(9 + 8) = 18 \cdot ■ + 18 \cdot ■$
3. $4(b + 14) = 4 \cdot ■ + 4 \cdot ■$
4. $8(m + b) = 8 \cdot ■ + 8 \cdot ■$
5. $-2(6 + 7) = -2 \cdot ■ + -2 \cdot ■$
6. $7(22 + -6) = 7 \cdot ■ + 7 \cdot ■$
7. $-3(-9 + n) = -3 \cdot ■ + -3 \cdot ■$
8. $-9(31 + 16) = -9 \cdot ■ + -9 \cdot ■$

Exercise B Use the distributive property to simplify each expression.

9. $4(a + b)$
10. $6(8 + c)$
11. $-2(d + k)$
12. $3(-x + y)$
13. $-4(a + b)$
14. $7[-c + (-x)]$
15. $-9(-v + 9)$
16. $-5(-z + 10)$
17. $8(z + 4)$
18. $2(-b + m)$
19. $3[-x + (-4)]$

Exercise C Use the distributive property to find the area of each figure.

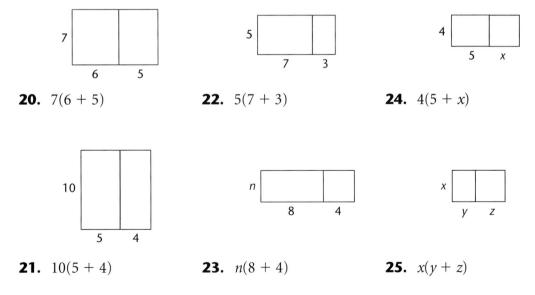

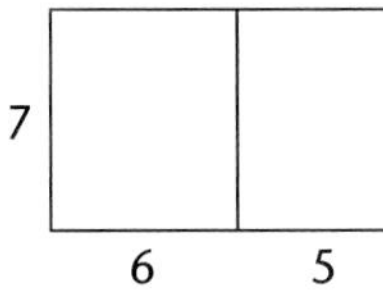

20. $7(6 + 5)$

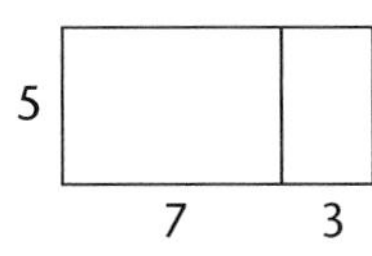

22. $5(7 + 3)$

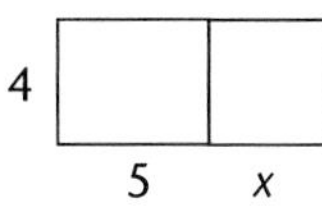

24. $4(5 + x)$

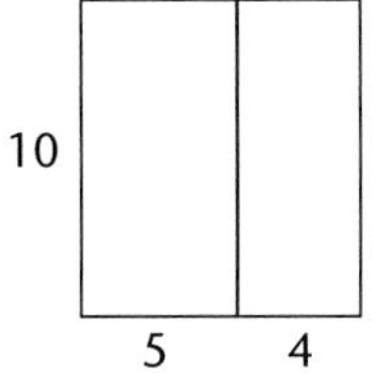

21. $10(5 + 4)$

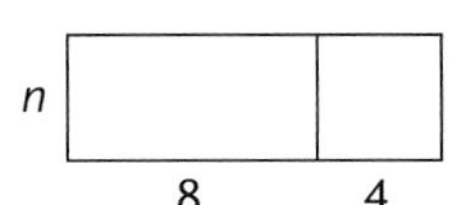

23. $n(8 + 4)$

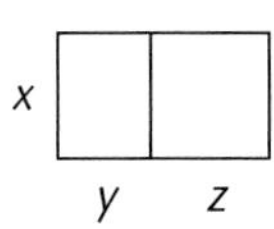

25. $x(y + z)$

Lesson 6 The Distributive Property—Factoring

Common factor

A multiplier shared by the terms in an expression

Factoring

Using the distributive property to separate the common factor from the terms in the expression

Recall that like terms in an expression can be combined.

$$2a + 3a = (a + a) + (a + a + a) = 5a$$

In the expression $2a + 3a$, a is common to both terms, so a is a **common factor** of $2a + 3a$. Therefore, $2a + 3a = a(2 + 3) = 5a$.

Common factors and the distributive property can be used to factor, or rewrite, expressions.

EXAMPLE 1 Factor the expression $ab + ax$.

Since a is common to both terms, a is a common factor, and using the distributive property, you can rewrite $ab + ax$ as $a(b + x)$. So the expression $ab + ax$ factored is $a(b + x)$.

Since $a(b + x)$ is the product of two factors, this use of the distributive property is called **factoring**.

EXAMPLE 2 $-3x - 3y = -3(x + y)$

(-3) is the common factor.

You can always check by multiplying:

Since $-3(x + y) = -3x + (-3y) = -3x - 3y$, the factoring is correct.

Remember: subtracting means adding the opposite.

$6 - (-2) =$

$6 + 2 = 8$

$-4 - 2 =$

$-4 + (-2) = -6$

EXAMPLE 3 $ax^2 - ay^2 = a(x^2 - y^2)$

a is the common factor.

Check: $a(x^2 - y^2) = a[x^2 + (-y^2)] = ax^2 + a(-y^2)$

$= ax^2 - ay^2$

Exercise A Identify the common factor in each expression.

1. $2a + 3a$
2. $5w + 7w$
3. $4x + 5x$
4. $-8e + 9e$
5. $6b - 2b$
6. $-10e - 4e$
7. $-3z - 2z$
8. $7w - 2w$
9. $3a - 2a$
10. $-2x + 3x$

Exercise B Use the distributive property to factor each expression.

11. $4x + 4y$
12. $5y + 5w$
13. $3j - 3p$
14. $-8k - 8g$
15. $6y + 6z$
16. $15s - 15t$
17. $-4m - 4y$
18. $fp + fg$
19. $ax - ay$
20. $mi - mb$
21. $-as + aj$
22. $ky - kx$
23. $-uv - um$
24. $tj - tr$
25. $bx^2 + by^2$
26. $cw^3 - cx^2$
27. $wx^4 + wm^2$
28. $-ha - hx^2$

PROBLEM SOLVING

Exercise C Solve each problem.

29. Sylvia is in grade 9 homeroom b, and her friend Mai is in grade 9 homeroom c. What do they have in common? Use the distributive property to write an expression that shows the common factor.

30. Mai's class schedule has her taking 4 classes before lunch and 3 classes after lunch. Allow c to represent classes. Use the distributive property to write an expression that shows the number of classes Mai takes.

Lesson 7 Properties of Zero

Addition property of zero

A number does not change if 0 is added or subtracted

Additive inverses

Numbers that equal 0 when added together; also called opposites

If you add zero to any number, that number does not change. If you subtract zero from any number, that number does not change.

EXAMPLE 1 $3 + 0 = 3$ and $0 + 3 = 3$

$-1 + 0 = -1$ and $-1 - 0 = -1$

Addition Property of Zero

Adding zero to a number does not change the number.

$4 + 0 = 4$ $0 + 4 = 4$ $a + 0 = a$ $0 + a = a$

Any two numbers whose sum is 0 are opposites of each other.

EXAMPLE 2 $3 + (-3) = 0$

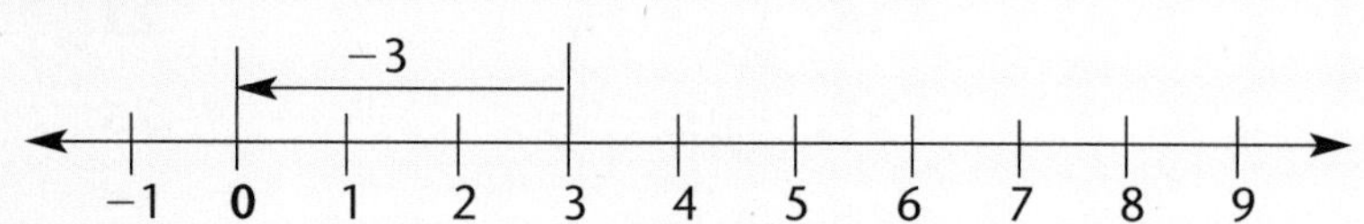

EXAMPLE 3 $a + (-a) = 0$

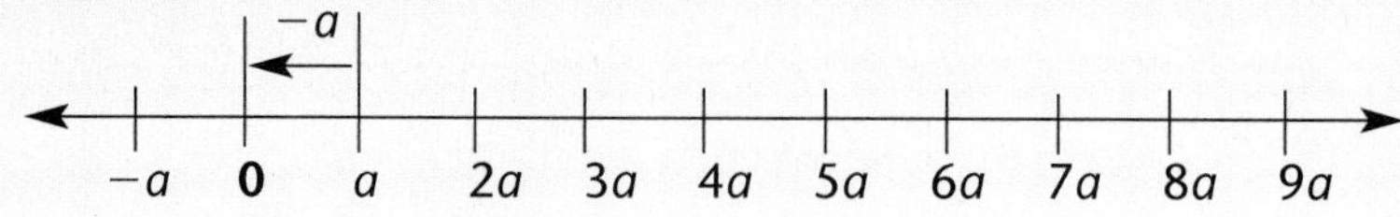

Additive Inverse Property

Any two numbers whose sum is 0 are **additive inverses**, or *opposites*, of each other.

Because there is only one point for 0 on the number line, zero is its own opposite.

EXAMPLE 4 $5 + ■ = 0$

Since the opposite of 5 is -5, $5 + (-5) = 0$.

$-x + ■ = 0$

Since the opposite of $-x$ is x, $-x + x = 0$.

Multiplication property of zero

Zero times any number is zero

Writing About Mathematics

Explain what the opposite of a positive integer is and what the opposite of a negative integer is.

If you add or subtract zero with any number, that number does not change.

EXAMPLE 5 Counting by 2's

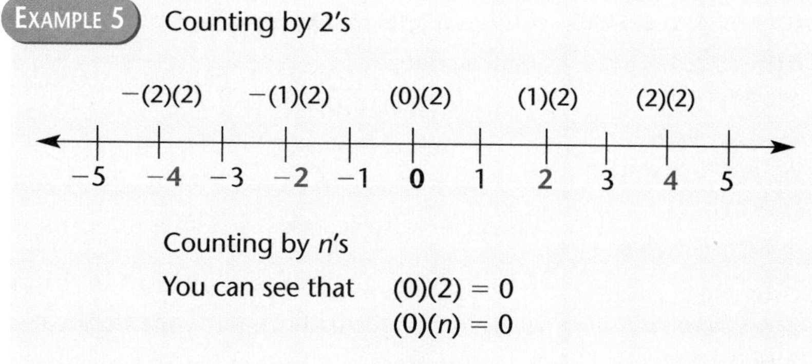

Counting by n's

You can see that $(0)(2) = 0$
$(0)(n) = 0$

(0)(n)

−5n −4n −3n −2n −n 0 1n 2n 3n 4n 5n

Multiplication Property of Zero

Zero times any number is zero.

$(0)(n) = 0$ where n is any number.

$0(a + b) = 0$ because $0(a + b) = (0)(a) + 0(b) = 0 + 0$.

Exercise A Write each sum.

1. $3 + 0$ **2.** $0 - 7$ **3.** $x^2 + 0$ **4.** $0 - y^3$

Exercise B Copy and fill in the missing number or letter.

5. $-5 + n = 0$ **6.** $4 - n = 0$ **7.** $a + n = 0$ **8.** $-x^2 + n = 0$

Exercise C Write each product.

9. $0(5)$ **10.** $(0)(y)$ **11.** $(-8)(0)$ **12.** $(ax)(0)$ **13.** $(a + b)(0)$

Exercise D Write your answer to each question.

14. How are 23 meters below sea level and 23 meters above sea level related to each other?

15. Explain why 5° Fahrenheit is 10 degrees warmer than −5° Fahrenheit.

Lesson 8 Properties of 1

Multiplication property of 1

A number or term does not change when multiplied by 1

Multiplicative inverses

Any two numbers or terms whose product equals 1

Reciprocals

Multiplicative inverses

One is a special number. It is a factor of any number or variable.

3 means one 3 or $(1)(3)$.

x means one x or $(1)(x)$.

$(a + b)$ means one $(a + b)$ or $(1)(a + b)$.

In each of these cases, 1 is a factor, even when it is not written.

Multiplying any number or term by 1 does not change the number or term. This is the **multiplication property of 1.**

$(1)(n) = n = (n)(1)$ for any number n.

Multiplication Property of 1

A number or term does not change when multiplied by 1.

Knowing that multiplying by 1 does not change the value of a term is very helpful in arithmetic and algebra.

EXAMPLE 1 Arithmetic:

$\frac{1}{2} \bullet 1 = \frac{1}{2}$; $1 = \frac{3}{3}$, so $\frac{1}{2} \bullet \frac{3}{3} = \frac{3}{6} = \frac{1}{2}$

Algebra:

$(a)(1) = a$; $1 = \frac{b}{b}$ so $(a)(\frac{b}{b}) = \frac{ab}{b} = a$

$\frac{b}{b}$ is the same as $b \div b = 1$; any number divided by itself equals 1. You also know that $(\frac{1}{2})(2) = 1$ and $a(\frac{1}{a}) = \frac{a}{a} = 1$.

Important note: 0 does not have an inverse, or reciprocal. $\frac{1}{0}$ is not a number or symbol for a number.

When two numbers or terms are multiplied and their product is 1, they are called **multiplicative inverses**, or **reciprocals**, of each other.

$\frac{1}{2}$ and $\frac{2}{1}$ or 2 are reciprocals of each other.

a and $\frac{1}{a}$ are reciprocals of each other.

Multiplicative Inverses (Reciprocals)

Any two numbers or terms whose product equals 1 are multiplicative inverses, or reciprocals, of each other.

EXAMPLE 2 What is the reciprocal of 3?

$\frac{1}{3}$ because $(3)(\frac{1}{3}) = 1$

EXAMPLE 3 What is the reciprocal of x?

$\frac{1}{x}$ because $(x)(\frac{1}{x}) = \frac{x}{x} = 1$

EXAMPLE 4 What is the reciprocal of $\frac{1}{y}$?

y because $(y)(\frac{1}{y}) = \frac{y}{y} = 1$

Exercise A Copy and write the missing factor.

1. $\frac{1}{2} \blacksquare = \frac{5}{10}$
2. $\frac{3}{4} \blacksquare = \frac{18}{24}$
3. $\frac{7}{8} \blacksquare = \frac{14}{16}$
4. $\frac{1}{3} \blacksquare = \frac{7}{21}$
5. $\frac{3}{8} \blacksquare = \frac{12}{32}$
6. $a \blacksquare = \frac{ab}{b}$
7. $m \blacksquare = \frac{mk}{k}$
8. $w \blacksquare = \frac{wp}{p}$
9. $x \blacksquare = \frac{3x}{3}$
10. $t \blacksquare = \frac{6t}{6}$

Exercise B What is the reciprocal of each term? Check by multiplying.

11. $\frac{1}{3}$
12. 7
13. c
14. $\frac{1}{x^3}$
15. n^2
16. 12
17. $\frac{1}{d}$
18. $\frac{1}{y}$

PROBLEM SOLVING

Exercise C Solve each problem.

19. An apple is cut into 4 equal slices. How many fourths are in the apple?
20. If today's temperature of 1° F is the multiplicative inverse of yesterday's temperature, what was yesterday's temperature?

Lesson 9 Powers and Roots

Root

An equal factor of a number

Recall what you have learned about powers and positive exponents such as 2^3, 4^2, a^3, and x^5. The opposite of taking a power of a number is called taking a **root** of a number.

EXAMPLE 1

Area = s^2

$5^2 = (5)(5) = 25$

5 squared equals 25.

Area of square = 25

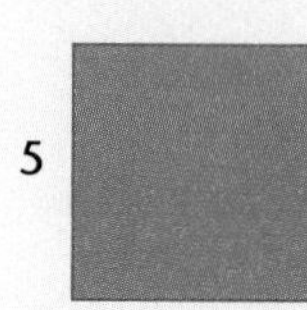

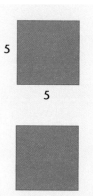

$s = \sqrt{\text{Area}}$

$\sqrt{25} =$

The square root of 25 equals 5.

Side of square = $\sqrt{25} = 5$

$A = 25$

EXAMPLE 2

Volume = s^3

$5^3 = (5)(5)(5) = 125$

5 cubed equals 125.

Volume of cube = 125

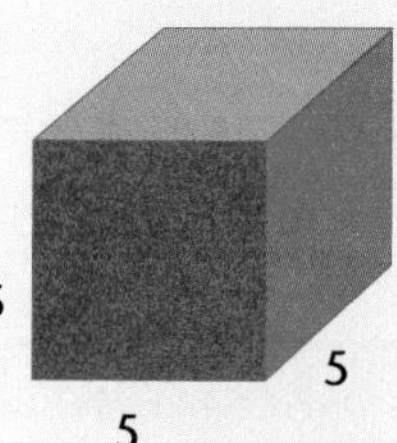

$s = \sqrt[3]{\text{Volume}}$

$\sqrt[3]{125} = 5$

The cube or third root of 125 equals 5.

Side of cube = $\sqrt[3]{125} = 5$

$V = 125$

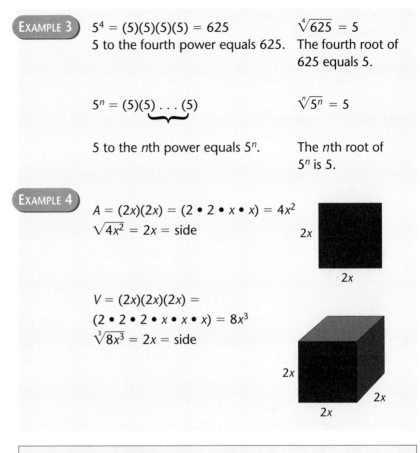

EXAMPLE 3

$5^4 = (5)(5)(5)(5) = 625$ | $\sqrt[4]{625} = 5$
5 to the fourth power equals 625. | The fourth root of 625 equals 5.

$5^n = \underbrace{(5)(5)\ldots(5)}$ | $\sqrt[n]{5^n} = 5$

5 to the *n*th power equals 5^n. | The *n*th root of 5^n is 5.

EXAMPLE 4

$A = (2x)(2x) = (2 \bullet 2 \bullet x \bullet x) = 4x^2$

$\sqrt{4x^2} = 2x = \text{side}$

$V = (2x)(2x)(2x) =$

$(2 \bullet 2 \bullet 2 \bullet x \bullet x \bullet x) = 8x^3$

$\sqrt[3]{8x^3} = 2x = \text{side}$

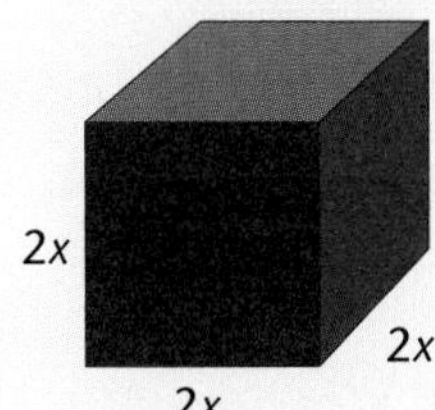

Rule For any number *x*,
$\sqrt[n]{x} = a$ if and only if $a^n = x$.
The *n*th root of *x* is a number *a* if and only if an gives you *x*.

By the examples you just did,

$\sqrt{25} = 5$ because $5^2 = 25$

$\sqrt[3]{125} = 5$ because $5^3 = 125$

$\sqrt[4]{625} = 5$ because $5^4 = 625$

To find roots that are not whole numbers, you can estimate the whole number that is less than the root and the whole number that is greater than the root.

Remember what the signs mean:
$<$ is read as "is less than."
$>$ is read as "is greater than."

EXAMPLE 5 $\sqrt{14}$ is between which two integers?

Study the list of square roots:

$$\underset{}{\overset{1}{\sqrt{1}}} < \sqrt{2} < \sqrt{3} < \overset{2}{\sqrt{4}} < \sqrt{5} < \sqrt{6} < \sqrt{7} < \sqrt{8} < \overset{3}{\sqrt{9}} <$$

$$\sqrt{10} < \sqrt{11} < \sqrt{12} < \sqrt{13} < \sqrt{14} < \sqrt{15} < \overset{4}{\sqrt{16}}$$

So $\sqrt{14}$ is between 3 and 4.

You can write this in algebra as $3 < \sqrt{14} < 4$.

Exercise A Find the length of a side of each figure.

1.

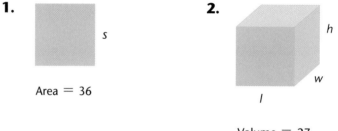

Area = 36

2.

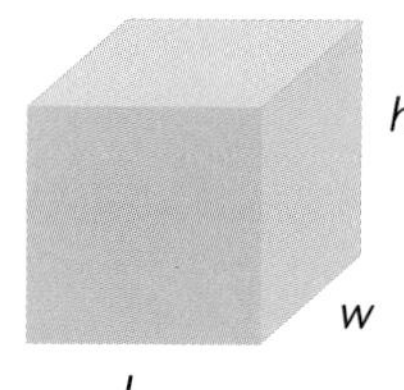

Volume = 27

Estimation Activity

Estimate: Find the square root of a number that is not a perfect square.

What is $\sqrt{45}$?

Solution: To estimate a square root, put the square root between the closest perfect square integers above and below the given number.

$6^2 = 36$ and $7^2 = 49$
$\sqrt{36} < \sqrt{45} < \sqrt{49}$ or $6 < \sqrt{45} < 7$
The square root of 49 is closer to 6 than 7.

Exercise B Estimate the value of each square root by finding a whole number greater than and a whole number less than the square root.

3. $\sqrt{15}$

4. $\sqrt{24}$

5. $\sqrt{7}$

6. $\sqrt{48}$

7. $\sqrt{83}$

8. $\sqrt{105}$

To find a value of a root more precisely and quickly, use a calculator.

EXAMPLE 6 Find $\sqrt{14}$.

Enter 14

Press $\boxed{\sqrt{\ }}$

Read 3.74166

$\sqrt{14} = 3.74166$

Use the calculator to find 3.74166^2. Because $3.74166^2 = 14.00002$, you know that 3.74166 is a very precise approximation of the square root of 14.

Exercise C Use your calculator to find the square root of each term.

9. $\sqrt{655.36}$

10. $\sqrt{103426.56}$

11. $\sqrt{3.0625}$

12. $\sqrt{6593.44}$

Lesson 10 More on Powers and Roots

When you use letters as variables, you cannot find roots and powers. You can only write their symbols. Only after you substitute numbers for variables can you evaluate the terms and expressions.

EXAMPLE 1 y to the fourth power y^4
the fourth root of y $\sqrt[4]{y}$

EXAMPLE 2 x to the tenth x^{10}
the fifth root of x $\sqrt[5]{x}$

What is the value of y^4 when $y = 2$?
$y^4 = 2^4 = (2)(2)(2)(2) = 16$
What is the value of $\sqrt[4]{y}$ when $y = 16$?
$\sqrt[4]{y} = \sqrt[4]{16} = 2$

Square roots can be negative as well as positive.

$(5)(5) = 25$ $(-5)(-5) = 25$
$\sqrt{25} = 5$ $\sqrt{25} = -5$

Note: $\sqrt{-25}$ is not an integer, because
$5^2 = 25$ and $(-5)^2 = 25$,
so neither 5 nor -5 is a root of $\sqrt{-25}$.

The square root of a negative number is not a real number.

EXAMPLE 3 $\sqrt{36} = 6$ or -6 because $6^2 = 36$ and $(-6)^2 = 36$

EXAMPLE 4 $\sqrt{a^2} = a$ or $-a$ because $(a)(a) = a^2$ and $(-a)(-a) = a^2$
Because $(-2)(-2)(-2) = -8$, $\sqrt[3]{-8} = -2$.
It is possible to find cube roots of negative numbers.

Powers	Roots
$(-2a)^2 = (-2a)(-2a) = 4a^2$	$\sqrt[3]{-27} = -3$ because $(-3)(-3)(-3) = -27$
$(-2a)^3 = (-2a)(-2a)(-2a) = -8a^3$	$\sqrt[3]{-x^3} = -x$ because $(-x)(-x)(-x) = -x^3$
$(-5x)^3 = (-5x)(-5x)(-5x) = -125x^3$	$\sqrt[3]{-x^6} = -x^2$ because $(-x^2)(-x^2)(-x^2) = -x^6$

Exercise A Find each value.

1. $\sqrt{49}$
2. $\sqrt{a^4}$
3. $\sqrt{b^6}$
4. $\sqrt{81}$
5. $\sqrt[3]{-8}$
6. $\sqrt[3]{64}$
7. $\sqrt[3]{-x^6}$
8. $\sqrt[3]{-y^9}$

Exercise B Find the value of each expression when $a = 8$, $b = 16$, and $c = 64$.

9. $\sqrt{c}$
10. $\sqrt[3]{a}$
11. $\sqrt[4]{b}$
12. $\sqrt[3]{c}$
13. $\sqrt{b}$
14. $\sqrt[5]{c}$

Calculator Practice

Use your calculator to simplify $(-3m)^4$.
First, think of this problem in terms of expanded notation:

$$(-3m)^4 = (-3m)(-3m)(-3m)(-3m)$$

Notice we're multiplying -3 four times. Then use your calculator.

EXAMPLE 5 Simplify $(-3m)^4$.

Enter 3 [+/−] [×] 3 [+/−] [×] 3 [+/−] [×] 3 [+/−]

Press [=]

The display reads *81*.

You know that $(m)(m)(m)(m) = m^4$

Therefore, $(-3m)^4 = 81m^4$

Exercise C Use your calculator to simplify each term.

15. $(-5x)^3$
16. $(2y)^5$
17. $(-4m)^4$
18. $(-8g)^3$
19. $(16w)^2$
20. $(5z)^4$
21. $(-3n)^5$
22. $(4t)^2$
23. $(-3v)^6$
24. $(-2x)^3$
25. $(-6a)^4$

Lesson 11 Order of Operations

If you have an expression with a number of different operations, there are rules to help you decide the order in which the operations must be performed.

EXAMPLE 1 $3 + (4)(5) = ■$

Should you add or multiply first?

If you add first:	If you multiply first:
$3 + (4)(5)$	$3 + (4)(5)$
$7 \quad (5)$	$3 + 20$
35	23

The correct answer is 23. The only way to get 23 from $3 + (4)(5)$ is to multiply first, and then add 3; $3 + 20 = 23$.

Order of Operations

1. If grouping symbols such as parentheses are used, perform the operations inside the grouping symbols first.
2. Evaluate powers.
3. Multiply and divide in order from left to right.
4. Add and subtract in order from left to right.

EXAMPLE 2 $3^2 \bullet 2$

Step 1 Square 3.
$3^2 = (3)(3) = 9$

Step 2 Multiply by 2.
$9 \bullet 2 = 18$
$3^2 \bullet 2 = 18$

EXAMPLE 3 $(2^2 \div 2) \bullet x$

Step 1 Square 2.
$2^2 = (2)(2) = 4$

Step 2 Divide by 2.
$4 \div 2 = 2$

Step 3 Multiply by x.
$2 \bullet x = 2x$
$(2^2 \div 2) \bullet x = 2x$

Exercise A Find the value using the order of operations.

1. $3 - (2)(5)$
2. $(3 + 4) \cdot 5$
3. $5 + 16 \div 4$
4. $(4 + 12) \div 2^2$
5. $10 \div (5)(2)$
6. $8^2 - 3 \cdot 5$
7. $4^3 - 8^2 + (-3)$
8. $6(2 + 4)$
9. $10 - (15)(2)$
10. $6 + (-8^2) - 3$
11. $8 + 6 \div 2$
12. $5^2 + (6)(2)$

Exercise B Use the order of operations to simplify.

13. $10c - 3c(2)$
14. $(5x + 4x) \div 3$
15. $8k + 6(k + 2k)$
16. $8n - 6n + (2n - n)$
17. $25y + (-15y - 3y)$
18. $(6)(2t) - 4t$
19. $4b^2 + (3b)(b)$
20. $5s^3 + 3s^3 + 2s^3$
21. $3z^2 + 2z^2 - z^2$
22. $7d^2 - (d^2 + 2d^2)$

PROBLEM SOLVING

Exercise C Solve each problem.

23. Corinne pays $5.00 for materials to make pillows. She makes 3 pillows and sells 2 for $10.00 each and 1 for $5.00. What is Corinne's profit?

24. Martha buys three sets of earrings for $2.99 each, four bracelets for $5.99 each, and a bottle of nail polish for $2.79. How much does she spend?

25. John buys a poster for $5.00. He also buys 3 CDs for $8.00 each. How much does he spend?

Application $\pi^2 \sum + \Omega \sqrt{x^2} \% \neq y \geq n = \nabla 30^\circ \pi$

Using Square Root

A square root is a tool that can be used when exploring the area of a square.

EXAMPLE 1 Suppose the damage caused by an earthquake is enclosed by an imaginary square that has an area of 10,000 square blocks. In blocks, what is the measure of one side of the square?

Step 1 Write the formula for finding the area of a square. $A = s^2$

Step 2 Substitute 10,000 into the formula. $10{,}000 = s^2$

Step 3 Find the square root to find the length of one side of the square. $\sqrt{10{,}000} = \sqrt{s^2}$

$100 = s$ One side of the square measured 100 blocks.

Exercise Use the information about the damage caused by different earthquakes to answer the following questions.

Earthquake	Area
Earthquake A	100 square blocks
Earthquake B	625 square blocks
Earthquake C	324 square blocks
Earthquake D	1,369 square blocks
Earthquake E	1,024 square blocks

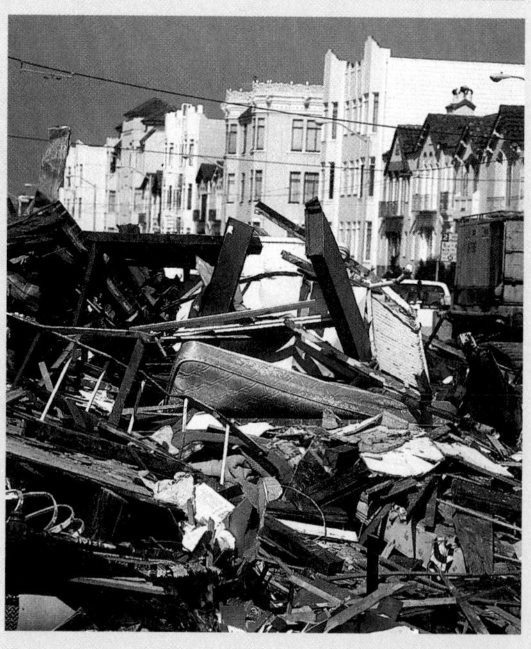

1. If the damage caused by Earthquake A is measured in the shape of a square, what is the measure in blocks of one side of the damaged area?

2. If the damage caused by Earthquake B is measured in the shape of a square, what is the measure in blocks of one side of the damaged area?

3. If the damage caused by Earthquake C is measured in the shape of a square, what is the measure in blocks of one side of the damaged area?

4. If the damage caused by Earthquake D is measured in the shape of a square, what is the measure in blocks of one side of the damaged area?

5. If the damage caused by Earthquake E is measured in the shape of a square, what is the measure in blocks of one side of the damaged area?

Chapter 2 REVIEW

Write the letter of the correct answer.

1. How would the product of $(5n)(3y)$ be rewritten using the commutative property of multiplication?

A $(3y)(5n)$
B $8yn$
C $(8y)(8n)$
D $3yn$

2. Using the associative property of addition, what would be two equal ways to write the expression $3x + 4w + z$ with parentheses?

A $z(3x + 4w) = 3x + (4w + z)$
B $3x + 4(w + z) = (3x + 4)(w + z)$
C $3(x + 4)w + 4z = 7x + (7w + 7z)$
D $(3x + 4w) + z = 3x + (4w + z)$

3. Find the product of $7(4 \cdot 5) = (7 \cdot 4)5$. Remember to multiply the factors in the parentheses first.

A $120 = 120$
B $140 = 120$
C $140 = 140$
D $160 = 140$

4. Find the value of $\sqrt[3]{-27}$.

A 3
B 9
C -3
D 18

5. Find the value of 7^2.

A 2^7
B 49
C -49
D 14

6. Simplify the expression $6 + (-5)^2 - 4$.

A -8
B 12
C 27
D -27

7. Simplify the expression $3(9n + 3n) + n$ using the order of operations.

A $37n$
B $27n$
C $13n$
D $16n$

Rewrite each sum using the commutative property of addition.

Example: $s + 14$ Solution: $14 + s$

8. $m + 8$

9. $3x + b$

10. $2p + 11$

11. $14g + 8a$

Write each expression with parentheses in two equal ways, using the associative property of addition.

Example: $a + b + c$ Solution: $(a + b) + c = a + (b + c)$

12. $x + y + z$

13. $h + t + s$

14. $7r + f + 3c$

15. $2m + 6n + s$

16. $d + 6c + p$

17. $4b + x + 2$

Copy the problems. Find each product. Remember to multiply the factors in the parentheses first.

Example: $4(3 \bullet 2) = (4 \bullet 3)2$ Solution: $4(6) = 12(2)$
$24 = 24$

18. $4(6 \cdot 5) = (4 \cdot 6)5$

19. $25(2 \cdot 2) = (25 \cdot 2)2$

20. $(10 \cdot 4)25 = 10(4 \cdot 25)$

Use the distributive property to multiply.

Example: $3(a + b)$ Solution: $3a + 3b$

21. $6(m + n)$

22. $-5(d + e)$

23. $2(-x + z)$

24. $-4(r + b)$

25. $7[-h + (-p)]$

26. $4[-p + (-r)]$

Use the distributive property to factor each expression.

Example: $3x + 3y$ Solution: $3(x + y)$

27. $5n + 5s$

28. $4x - 4v$

29. $2b + 3b$

30. $xg^3 - xr^2$

Copy and fill in the missing number or letter.

Example: $6 + \blacksquare = 0$ Solution: $6 + (-6) = 0$

31. $8 + \blacksquare = 0$

32. $6 - \blacksquare = 0$

33. $w + \blacksquare = 0$

34. $-y^3 + \blacksquare = 0$

35. $-5 + \blacksquare = 0$

36. $n^2 + \blacksquare = 0$

What is the reciprocal of each term?

Example: 4 Solution: $\frac{1}{4}$

37. $\frac{1}{8}$

38. x^3

39. $\frac{1}{c}$

40. a^2

Find each value.

Example: 5^2 Solution: $(5)(5) = 25$

41. $\sqrt{64}$

42. $\sqrt[3]{x^3}$

43. 6^3

44. 10^3

Simplify each term.

Example: $(-4x)^2$ Solution: $(-4x)(-4x) = 16x^2$

45. $(-3y)^3$

46. $(2c)^5$

47. $(-2m)^4$

48. $(4g)^3$

49. $(7j)^2$

50. $(-5z)^5$

Test-Taking Tip

When you review your notes to prepare for an exam, use a marker to highlight key words and example problems.

43148

Chapter

Linear Equations with One Variable

Before the telegraph was invented, train brakemen sometimes walked the tracks to a point ahead of waiting trains. Why? They were looking for trains coming from the other direction that were behind schedule. When the brakeman spotted a late train coming his way, he waved a red flag. The train would then stop and wait at the nearest town until the other train could pass. This prevented speeding trains from crashing into each other. Using algebra, you can calculate the answer to problems involving distance, speed, and time using the formula *distance* = *rate* × *time.* If you know any two of the variables, you can easily solve for the third.

In Chapter 3, you will explore how to write and solve linear equations.

Goals for Learning

- To write and solve equations
- To use formulas for perimeter and area to solve problems
- To use the Pythagorean theorem to solve problems
- To graph inequalities on the number line
- To solve inequalities

Lesson 1 Writing Equations

Equation

A mathematical sentence stating that two quantities are equal and written as two expressions separated by an equal sign
$(4n + 4n = 8n)$

An algebraic **equation** such as $3n = 15$ is read "3 times some number equals 15." The equation $3n = 15$ is neither true nor false—it is an open statement because the value of the variable n is unknown.

$3n = 15$ is a true statement when $n = 5$;
5 is called the root of the equation.

$3n = 15$ is a false statement when $n \neq 5$,
which is read "n is not equal to 5."

Statements of equality can be written as equations.

EXAMPLE 1 6 times some number equals 18.
Let x be that number.
Solution: $6x = 18$

The root of an equation can be found by substituting different numbers for the variable. If the number is the root, the statement is true. If the number is not the root, the statement is false.

When working with algebraic equations, remember that any letter of the alphabet can be used to represent a variable

EXAMPLE 2 $4x = 20$ $\quad x = 1, 4, 5$

$(4)(1) = 20$ False
$(4)(4) = 20$ False
$(4)(5) = 20$ True

Exercise A Write an equation for each statement. Let x be the variable in the equation.

1. 9 times some number equals 36.

2. Sixteen times some number plus 3 equals 51.

3. Nine times some number minus 18 equals zero.

Remember that *equals, is,* and *is equal to* are all terms used for the equal sign.

4. 8 times some number equals 40.

5. 5 times some number plus three equals 28.

6. 2 times some number minus 3 equals 3.

7. 3 multiplied by some number is equal to 27.

8. 7 times some number equals 49.

9. Ten times some number minus 13 equals 47.

10. 8 times some number plus 7 equals 71.

11. 6 subtracted from some number is 25.

12. 14 times some number minus 28 equals 14.

13. 4 subtracted from some number is 10.

14. Four multiplied by some number plus six equals 46.

Writing About Mathematics

Write a comparison of a sentence and an equation explaining the parts of each and how they are similar. Then create several sentence problems with their related equations.

Exercise B Find the root of each equation by writing T (true) or F (false) for each value.

15. $2s = 14$ $s = 5, 6, 7, 8$

16. $3p = 15$ $p = 2, 3, 4, 5$

17. $9m = 63$ $m = 1, 3, 6, 7$

18. $8w = 72$ $w = 9, 10, 11, 12$

19. $6n = 18$ $n = 1, 2, 3, 4$

20. $2s = 30$ $s = 10, 15, 20, 25$

21. $5a = 10$ $a = 2, 4, 6, 8$

22. $7e = 21$ $e = 1, 3, 5, 7$

23. $4y = 16$ $y = 4, 5, 6, 7$

24. $3j = 9$ $j = 2, 3, 6, 9$

25. $8g = 32$ $g = 2, 3, 4, 5$

TRY THIS Use mental math to find a solution to the equation $19 = y - 20$.

Lesson 2 Solving Equations: $x - b = c$

Whenever you find the root of an equation, you are solving the equation. Some equations can be solved mentally. For example, to solve $n - 1 = 4$, think "If you subtract 1 from a number, you get 4. What is the number?" Since $5 - 1 = 4$, $n = 5$.

When equations cannot be solved mentally, you can add equal amounts to both sides of an equation to find the root, or value, of the variable.

EXAMPLE 1 Solve $n - 17 = 81$ for n.

Step 1 Write the equation. $n - 17 = 81$

Step 2 Add 17 to both sides of the equation.

$$\begin{aligned} n - 17 &= 81 \\ +17 &= +17 \end{aligned}$$

Step 3 Simplify.

$$\begin{aligned} n - 17 &= 81 \\ +17 &= +17 \\ n &= 98 \end{aligned}$$

Step 4 Check. $98 - 17 = 81$

EXAMPLE 2 Solve $x - 29 = 43$ for x.

Step 1 Write the equation. $x - 29 = 43$

Step 2 Add 29 to both sides of the equation.

$$\begin{aligned} x - 29 &= 43 \\ +29 &= +29 \end{aligned}$$

Step 3 Simplify.

$$\begin{aligned} x - 29 &= 43 \\ +29 &= +29 \\ x &= 72 \end{aligned}$$

Step 4 Check. $72 - 29 = 43$

EXAMPLE 3 Solve $g -(-2) = 7$ for x.

Step 1 Rewrite the equation. $g + 2 = 7$

Step 2 Add (-2) to both sides of the equation.

$$\begin{aligned} g + 2 &= 7 \\ +(-2) &= +(-2) \end{aligned}$$

Step 3 Simplify.

$$\begin{aligned} g + 2 &= 7 \\ +(-2) &= +(-2) \\ g &= 5 \end{aligned}$$

Step 4 Check. $5 - (-2) = 7$

> Subtracting a negative is the same as adding the opposite.

Remember b and $-b$ are opposites because they add to zero.

In these examples, each equation was solved by adding the opposite. Whenever you add an opposite, remember to add the opposite to both sides of the equation.

Rule To solve equations of the form $x - b = c$, add b to both sides of the equation.

Exercise A Find the solution for each equation. Check your answer.

1. $x - 7 = 9$

2. $m - 6 = 1$

3. $e - 5 = 6$

4. $y - 2 = 3$

5. $j - 8 = 15$

6. $u - 3 = 0$

7. $p - 12 = 25$

8. $w - 20 = 29$

9. $t - 32 = 15$

10. $a - 14 = 9$

11. $h - 20 = 35$

12. $n - 17 = 19$

13. $d - 22 = 70$

14. $z - 11 = 2$

Exercise B Find the solution for each equation by rewriting the subtraction as addition. Check your answer.

15. $m-(-2)=9$

16. $x-(-3)=2$

17. $m-(-4)=4$

18. $f-(-6)=9$

19. $z-(-8)=2$

20. $j-(-2)=3$

PROBLEM SOLVING

Exercise C Write an equation for each problem. Solve the equation.

21. The price of a CD is reduced by \$4.50. If Juanita pays \$5.00 for the CD, what was its original price?

22. Phil pays \$16.97 for a computer game. The price was reduced by \$4.99. What was the original price?

23. The price of a shirt is reduced by \$11.50. If Jenny pays \$9.83 for the shirt, what was its original price?

24. Melvin pays \$2.97 for a paperback book. The price was reduced by \$1.50. What was the original price?

25. Adam wants to know the original price of a bag of popcorn. He could only remember he paid \$3.73, which was \$2.51 less than the original price. What was the original price?

Lesson 3 Solving Equations: $x + b = c$

Recall that you used the idea of opposites to solve equations of the form $x - b = c$. The same idea of opposites can be used to solve equations of the form $x + b = c$.

EXAMPLE 1 Solve $a + 24 = 51$ for a.

Step 1 Write the equation. $a + 24 = 51$

Step 2 Subtract 24 from both sides of the equation. This is the same as adding −24 to both sides.

$$\begin{aligned} a + 24 &= 51 \\ -24 &= -24 \end{aligned}$$

Step 3 Simplify.

$$\begin{aligned} a + 24 &= 51 \\ -24 &= -24 \\ a &= 27 \end{aligned}$$

Step 4 Check. $27 + 24 = 51$

EXAMPLE 2 Solve $r + 1.4 = 3.7$ for r.

Step 1 Write the equation. $r + 1.4 = 3.7$

Step 2 Subtract 1.4 from both sides of the equation.

$$\begin{aligned} r + 1.4 &= 3.7 \\ -1.4 &= -1.4 \end{aligned}$$

Step 3 Simplify.

$$\begin{aligned} r + 1.4 &= 3.7 \\ -1.4 &= -1.4 \\ r &= 2.3 \end{aligned}$$

Step 4 Check. $2.3 + 1.4 = 3.7$

Remember that subtraction is the same as adding the opposite.

EXAMPLE 3 Solve $k + (-2) = 7$ for k.

Step 1 Rewrite the equation. $k - 2 = 7$

Step 2 Add 2 to both sides of the equation.

$$\begin{aligned} k - 2 &= 7 \\ +2 &= +2 \end{aligned}$$

Step 3 Simplify.

$$\begin{aligned} k - 2 &= 7 \\ +2 &= +2 \\ k &= 9 \end{aligned}$$

Step 4 Check. $9 + (-2) = 7$

Again, each equation was solved by adding the opposite. Whenever you add an opposite, remember to add the opposite to both sides of the equation.

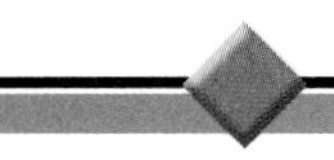

Remember b and $-b$ are opposites because they add to zero.

Rule To solve equations of the form $x + b = c$, add $-b$ to both sides of the equation.

Exercise A Find the solution for each equation. Check your answer.

1. $x + 4 = 10$

2. $y + 3 = 7$

3. $g + 6 = 9$

4. $j + 2 = 3$

5. $k + 1 = 6$

6. $c + 10 = 15$

7. $e + 12 = 25$

8. $i + 23 = 27$

9. $m + 16 = 30$

10. $v + 32 = 50$

11. $t + 80 = 89$

12. $w + 51 = 67$

13. $b + 17 = 17$

14. $f + 10 = 58$

15. $h + 30 = 37$

16. $s + 3.5 = 3.7$

17. $y + 1.6 = 4$

18. $t + 9.2 = 15.6$

19. $r + 6.9 = 11.3$

20. $a + 31.5 = 40$

Exercise B Find the solution for each equation. Check your answer.

21. $c + (-3) = 9$

22. $d + (-4) = 2$

23. $a + (-7) = 7$

24. $t + (-5) = 15$

25. $y + (-16) = 29$

26. $p + (-11) = 13$

PROBLEM SOLVING

Exercise C Write an equation for each problem. Solve the equation.

27. Marsha notices the original price of a calculator is $13.99. The discount is $5.22. How much does she pay?

28. Amphone wants to buy a pair of jeans, which were originally $29.99. The discount is $4.75. How much do the jeans cost?

29. Gary buys a CD player that was originally $99.99. The discount is $27.99. What is the sale price?

30. Karim notices the original price of a computer is $1,300.00. The discount is $275.00. How much does he pay?

Lesson 4 Solving Multiplication Equations

Some equations that include multiplication can be solved mentally. For example, to solve $9q = 36$, think "Nine times what number is 36?" Since $9 \cdot 4 = 36$, $q = 4$.

When equations that include multiplication cannot be solved mentally, you can find the value of the variable by multiplying both sides of the equation by the reciprocal of the coefficient.

EXAMPLE 1 Solve $3w = 57$ for w.

Step 1 Write the equation. $3w = 57$

Step 2 Multiply both sides of the equation by $\frac{1}{3}$, the reciprocal of 3. $(\frac{1}{3})3w = 57(\frac{1}{3})$

Step 3 Simplify.

$$(\tfrac{1}{3})\tfrac{3}{1}w = \tfrac{57}{1}(\tfrac{1}{3})$$

$$\tfrac{3}{3}w = \tfrac{57}{3}$$

$$w = 19$$

Step 4 Check. $3 \bullet 19 = 57$

Multiplying by $\frac{1}{3}$ is the same as dividing by 3. In general, dividing by a number n is the same as multiplying by $\frac{1}{n}$. This fact gives you a choice—you can solve equations that include multiplication by dividing or by multiplying by the reciprocal of the coefficient.

EXAMPLE 2 Find the value of the variable in the expression $5c = 125$.

Divide each side by 5.

$$5c = 125$$

$$\tfrac{5}{5}c = \tfrac{125}{5}$$

$$c = 25$$

Check. $5 \bullet 25 = 125$

Multiply each side by $\frac{1}{5}$.

$$5c = 125$$

$$(\tfrac{1}{5})5c = 125(\tfrac{1}{5})$$

$$\tfrac{5}{5}c = \tfrac{125}{5}$$

$$c = 25$$

Check. $5 \bullet 25 = 125$

Exercise A Find the solution for each equation.

1. $5x = 25$
2. $2z = 8$
3. $8m = 32$
4. $6b = 54$
5. $4x = 40$
6. $3v = 24$
7. $7a = 63$
8. $4c = 12$
9. $7n = 14$
10. $5y = 35$
11. $6.2x = 12.4$
12. $3.7h = 11.1$
13. $4.5d = 18$
14. $8.8f = 17.6$
15. $7.5p = 45$
16. $1.9t = -19$
17. $-0.5z = 25$
18. $-2.3u = -18.4$
19. $5.3a = 31.8$
20. $11.1w = -44.4$
21. $25.2e = -50.4$
22. $-35.5x = 248.5$
23. $0.9c = 8.1$
24. $-22.7b = -204.3$
25. $-4.4t = 48.4$
26. $8.6i = -137.6$

Exercise B Write an equation for each statement. Solve the equation.

27. A number x multiplied by 13 is 52. What is the value of x?
28. A number f multiplied by 32 is 192. What is the value of f?
29. A number g multiplied by -6 is 66. What is the value of g?
30. A number n multiplied by 5.5 is -33. What is the value of n?

Technology Connection

Let the Spreadsheet Do the Work

Software spreadsheet programs allow you to calculate totals in columns and rows. You simply type in the equation you need. Suppose you want the total of the numbers in column A, rows 1 through 10. Just write the correct equation in column A, row 11 to show the total. Every time you change a number in any one of the rows, the total will change in row 11. Imagine what it was like when people had to do all that with just a pencil and paper!

Lesson 5 Solving Equations with Fractions

Some algebra equations involve multiplication with fractions. To solve these equations, multiply both sides of the equation by the reciprocal of the fraction.

Always check your work. Replace the variable with your answer and solve the problem.

EXAMPLE 1 Solve $\frac{1}{4}h = 6$ for h.

Step 1 Write the equation. $\frac{1}{4}h = 6$

Step 2 Multiply both sides of the equation by $\frac{4}{1}$, the reciprocal of $\frac{1}{4}$. $\left(\frac{4}{1}\right)\frac{1}{4}h = 6\left(\frac{4}{1}\right)$

Step 3 Simplify.

$$\left(\frac{4}{1}\right)\frac{1}{4}h = \frac{6}{1}\left(\frac{4}{1}\right)$$

$$\left(\frac{4}{1}\right)\frac{1}{4}h = \frac{6}{1}\left(\frac{4}{1}\right)$$

$$\frac{4}{4}h = \frac{24}{1}$$

$$h = 24$$

Step 4 Check. $\frac{1}{4}(24) = 6$

EXAMPLE 2 Solve $-\frac{2}{3}m = 12$ for m.

Step 1 Write the equation. $-\frac{2}{3}m = 12$

Step 2 Multiply both sides of the equation by $-\frac{3}{2}$, the reciprocal of $-\frac{2}{3}$.

$$(-\tfrac{3}{2}) -\tfrac{2}{3}m = 12(-\tfrac{3}{2})$$

Step 3 Simplify.

$$(-\tfrac{3}{2}) -\tfrac{2}{3}m = 12(-\tfrac{3}{2})$$

$$(-\tfrac{3}{2}) -\tfrac{2}{3}m = \tfrac{12}{1}(-\tfrac{3}{2})$$

$$\frac{6}{6}m = -\frac{36}{2}$$

$$m = -18$$

Step 4 Check.

$$(-\tfrac{2}{3})(-18) = 12$$

$$\frac{36}{3} = 12$$

Rule To solve an equation that involves multiplication with fractions, multiply both sides of the equation by the reciprocal of the fraction.

Exercise A Find the solution for each equation.

1. $\frac{1}{2}x = 3$

2. $\frac{1}{3}y = 4$

3. $\frac{1}{5}c = 7$

4. $\frac{1}{8}d = 2$

5. $\frac{1}{4}a = 5$

6. $\frac{2}{3}f = 6$

7. $\frac{3}{5}g = 9$

8. $\frac{7}{8}h = 14$

9. $\frac{5}{7}m = 5$

10. $\frac{8}{9}p = 16$

11. $\frac{5}{8}y = 20$

12. $\frac{3}{4}x = 12$

13. $\frac{1}{2}w = 8$

14. $\frac{6}{10}e = 18$

15. $\frac{5}{8}r = 25$

16. $\frac{8}{16}s = -8$

17. $-\frac{3}{5}d = 24$

18. $-\frac{9}{10}g = 18$

19. $-\frac{2}{5}x = -20$

20. $\frac{15}{16}c = 30$

21. $\frac{9}{10}v = -18$

22. $-\frac{6}{7}b = 12$

23. $\frac{10}{15}n = 40$

24. $-\frac{1}{8}j = -8$

25. $\frac{3}{4}i = 27$

26. $\frac{1}{2}u = -10$

PROBLEM SOLVING

Exercise B Write an equation for each problem. Solve the equation.

27. Two-thirds of Mrs. Minsinski's class are football fans. How many students are in the class if there are 16 football fans altogether?

28. A box contains eight calculators. It is one-sixth full. If the box were full, how many calculators would be in the box?

29. Jon answers nine questions on a test. He is only finished with one-half of the test. How many questions are on the test?

30. Maggie ordered three-fifths of a truckload of mulch for her garden. She receives eight cubic yards of mulch. How much mulch is in a full truckload?

Lesson 6 Solving Equations—More Than One Step

Some equations have more than one operation. You may need to combine two or more solutions to find the value of the variable.

EXAMPLE 1 $3x - 7 = 5$

To solve for x, you can proceed in two ways.

Method 1

Step 1 Multiply each side by $\frac{1}{3}$.

$$\frac{1}{3}(3x - 7) = \frac{1}{3}(5)$$

$$\frac{3}{3}x - \frac{7}{3} = \frac{5}{3}$$

Step 2 Add $\frac{7}{3}$ to each side.

$$x - \frac{7}{3} + \frac{7}{3} = \frac{5}{3} + \frac{7}{3}$$

$$x = \frac{12}{3} = 4$$

$$x = 4$$

Method 2

Step 1 Add 7 to each side.

$$\begin{aligned} 3x - 7 &= 5 \\ +7 &= +7 \\ 3x &= 12 \end{aligned}$$

Step 2 Divide each side by 3. $\frac{3}{3}x = \frac{12}{3}$

$$x = 4$$

Step 3 Check. $3(4) - 7 = 5$

You might try performing some steps mentally.

$2c = 18$ Think: 2 times what number is 18? $c = 9$

$4e + 1 = 21$ Think: Subtract 1 from each side.
4 times what number is 20? $e = 5$

To solve equations with more than one operation, you should always complete one operation before beginning the other.

EXAMPLE 2 $-3k - 6 = -27$

Step 1 Add 6 to each side.

$$\begin{aligned} -3k - 6 &= -27 \\ +6 &= +6 \\ -3k &= -21 \end{aligned}$$

Step 2 Divide each side by -3.

$$\frac{-3k}{-3} = \frac{-21}{-3}$$

$$k = 7$$

Step 3 Check. $-3(7) - 6 = -27$

EXAMPLE 3 $\frac{3}{4}p + 12 = 0$

Step 1 Subtract 12 from each side.

$$\begin{aligned} \tfrac{3}{4}p + 12 &= 0 \\ -12 &= -12 \\ \tfrac{3}{4}p &= -12 \end{aligned}$$

Step 2 Multiply each side by $\frac{4}{3}$, the reciprocal of $\frac{3}{4}$.

$$\left(\frac{4}{3}\right)\frac{3}{4}p = -\frac{12}{1}\left(\frac{4}{3}\right)$$

$$p = -\frac{48}{3} \text{ or } -16$$

Step 3 Check.

$$\frac{3}{4}(-16) + 12 = 0$$

Exercise A Solve each equation.

1. $3x - 6 = 6$
2. $3y + 1 = 7$
3. $2m - 3 = 7$
4. $5b - 2 = 13$
5. $2g + 4 = 16$
6. $7a + 2 = 16$
7. $4e - 3 = 1$
8. $2k + 3 = 17$
9. $2w - 8 = 8$
10. $9d - 25 = 2$
11. $4t + 5 = 25$
12. $6s - 10 = 10$
13. $3p + 20 = 50$
14. $3i - 4 = 23$
15. $5p + 0 = 0$
16. $2t - 4 = 8$

Exercise B Solve each equation.

17. $-6b + 20 = -16$
18. $-4m + 2 = 14$
19. $-9c - 4 = -4$
20. $2y - (-10) = 18$
21. $-\frac{1}{2}g + 2 = 6$
22. $3r - 25 = 5$
23. $\frac{2}{3}s - (-4) = 8$
24. $\frac{4}{5}a + (-5) = 0$
25. $-\frac{2}{7}w - 6 = -4$

PROBLEM SOLVING

Exercise C Solve each problem by using an equation.

26. To find the number of square miles in Adair County, Kentucky, solve $s = 57 + (77)(5)$.
27. By solving $s + 27 = (20)(30)$, you will find the number of square miles in Clay County, Iowa.
28. To calculate the number of square miles in Dane County, Wisconsin, solve $s = 35^2 - 28$.
29. Solve the equation $s - 26 = (9)(5)$ to find the number of square miles in Kings County, New York.
30. You will find the number of square miles in Los Angeles County, California, by solving $s = (4 \cdot 10^3) + 71$.

Lesson 7 Equations Without Numbers

Literal equation

An equation that has only letters

Constant

Specific real number

In algebra, it is possible to have no numbers at all in an equation, only letters. These are called **literal equations.** Here is an example:

$ax + b = c$

In the equation, *a, b,* and *c* represent real numbers, and *x* represents the variable. The letters *x, y,* and *z* usually represent variables, while *a, b,* and *c* usually represent **constants,** or specific real numbers.

You can solve literal equations using the same methods you have learned for numbers.

EXAMPLE 1 Solve the equation for *x*.

Step 1 Write the equation. $3x + 4 = 13$

Step 2 Subtract 4 from both sides.

$$\begin{aligned} 3x + 4 &= 13 \\ -4 &= -4 \\ 3x &= 9 \end{aligned}$$

Step 3 Divide each side by 3.

$$\begin{aligned} \frac{3x}{3} &= \frac{9}{3} \\ x &= 3 \end{aligned}$$

Step 4 Check.

$$\begin{aligned} (3)(3) + 4 &= 13 \\ 13 &= 13 \end{aligned}$$

True

EXAMPLE 2 Solve for *x*.

Step 1 Write the equation. $ax + b = c$

Step 2 Subtract *b* from both sides.

$$\begin{aligned} ax + b &= c \\ -b &= -b \\ ax &= (c - b) \end{aligned}$$

Step 3 Divide each side by *a*.

$$\begin{aligned} \frac{ax}{a} &= \frac{(c - b)}{a} \\ x &= \frac{c - b}{a} \end{aligned}$$

Step 4 Check.

$$\begin{aligned} a\frac{(c - b)}{a} + b &= c \\ (c - b) + b &= c \\ c &= c \end{aligned}$$

True

EXAMPLE 3 Solve for x.

$$3x = 12$$
$$\frac{3x}{3} = \frac{12}{3}$$
$$x = 4$$

Check.

$$3(4) = 12$$

True

EXAMPLE 4 Solve for x.

$$ax = b$$
$$\frac{ax}{a} = \frac{b}{a}$$
$$x = \frac{b}{a}$$

Check.

$$a(\tfrac{b}{a}) = b$$
$$b = b$$

True

These examples show that literal equations can be solved in the same way as equations with numbers.

Exercise A Solve for x.

1. $-ax = b$
2. $cx + ax = b$
3. $-b = -ax$
4. $cx - bx = a$
5. $-a = bx$
6. $ax + bx = c$
7. $-c = bx + ax$
8. $ax - bx = c$
9. $cx = -b$
10. $cx + bx = a$
11. $bx - ax = c$
12. $-bx = c$
13. $cx - bx = a$
14. $ax + bx = -c$
15. $-a = cx + bx$
16. $cx - bx = -a$
17. $bx + ax = c$
18. $-c = ax - bx$
19. $cx + ax = -b$
20. $cx + ax = b$

Algebra in Your Life

Packaging a Product

When you're at the store, do you ever think about why a package or can is the size it is? Package designers use volume formulas to determine how much of a product will fit into a container. Designers know that two differently shaped containers with the same volume may not hold the same amount. However, the package that holds the most isn't always the best design. Designers must also think about how the product will look to customers and how it will fit on a shelf.

Lesson 8 Formulas

Formulas are examples of literal equations. Most formulas you have learned are found in geometry. Sometimes you will need to rearrange a formula to solve a problem.

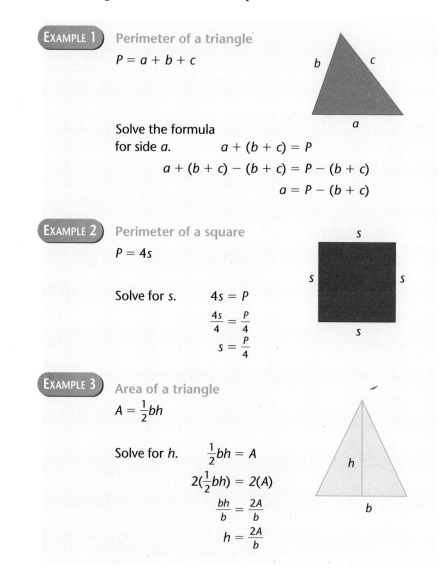

EXAMPLE 1 Perimeter of a triangle

$P = a + b + c$

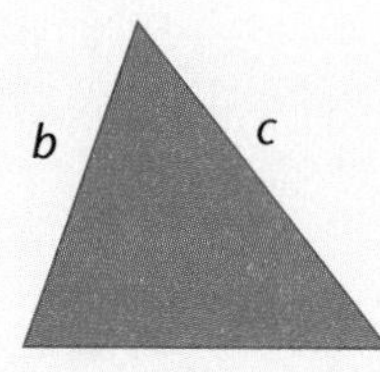

Solve the formula for side a.

$$a + (b + c) = P$$
$$a + (b + c) - (b + c) = P - (b + c)$$
$$a = P - (b + c)$$

EXAMPLE 2 Perimeter of a square

$P = 4s$

Solve for s.

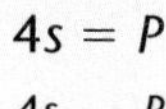

$$4s = P$$
$$\frac{4s}{4} = \frac{P}{4}$$
$$s = \frac{P}{4}$$

EXAMPLE 3 Area of a triangle

$A = \frac{1}{2}bh$

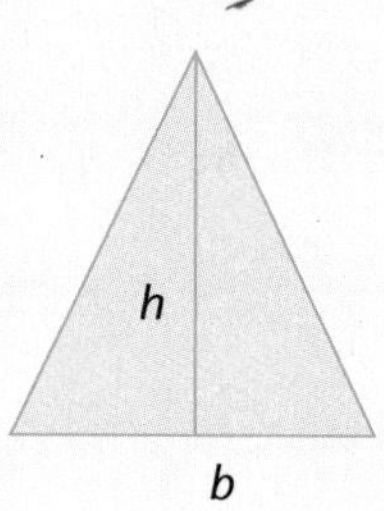

Solve for h.

$$\frac{1}{2}bh = A$$
$$2(\frac{1}{2}bh) = 2(A)$$
$$\frac{bh}{b} = \frac{2A}{b}$$
$$h = \frac{2A}{b}$$

EXAMPLE 4 Area of a rectangle

$A = bh$

Solve for b. $bh = A$

$$\frac{bh}{h} = \frac{A}{h}$$

$$b = \frac{A}{h}$$

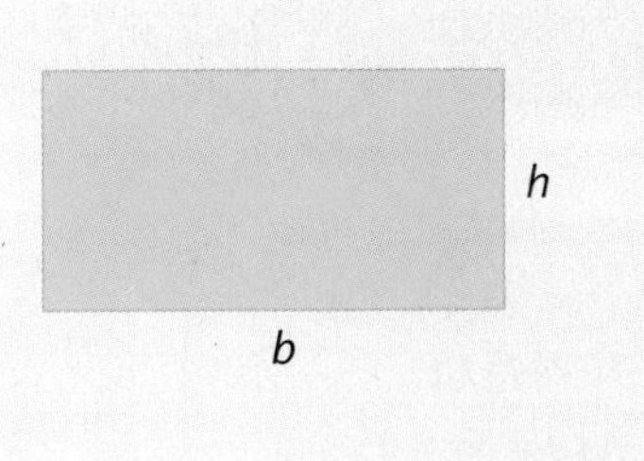

Exercise A Solve each equation.

1. $A = bh$ for h.
2. $A = lw$ for w.
3. $P = 3s$ for s.
4. $A = \frac{1}{2}bh$ for h.
5. $W = fd$ for d.
6. $A = \frac{1}{2}bh$ for b.
7. $A = bh$ for b.
8. $d = rt$ for t.
9. $P = 5s$ for s.
10. $P = a + b + c$ for a.
11. $d = rt$ for r.
12. $P = a + b + c$ for b.
13. $W = fd$ for f.
14. $P = 2\pi r$ for r.
15. $A = \frac{1}{2}(b_1 + b_2)h$ for h.
16. $A = sd$ for d.
17. $P = a + c$ for a.
18. $A = yz$ for z.
19. $A = \frac{d}{n}$ for d.
20. $P = c - d$ for c.
21. $A = \frac{1}{2s}$ for s.
22. $V = hm$ for h.
23. $\frac{a}{P} = s$ for a.
24. $P = c + d - e$ for c.
25. $\frac{c}{d} = A + b$ for A.

Lesson 9 The Pythagorean Theorem

Pythagorean theorem
A formula that states that in a right triangle, the length of the hypotenuse squared is equal to the length of side b squared and the length of side a squared

Right triangle
A three-sided figure, or triangle, with one right, or 90°, angle

Hypotenuse
The longest side in a right triangle

The Pythagorean Theorem

The **Pythagorean theorem** is an important formula. It states that in any **right triangle,** c is the longest side known as the **hypotenuse,** and a and b are the other sides: $c^2 = a^2 + b^2$.

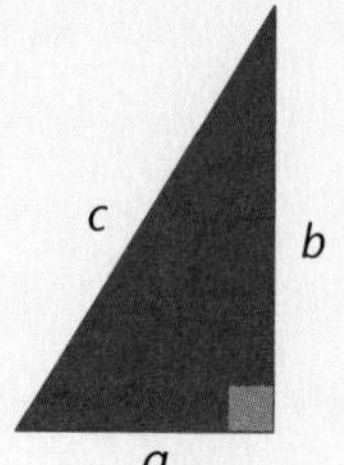

A proof of this can be shown algebraically.

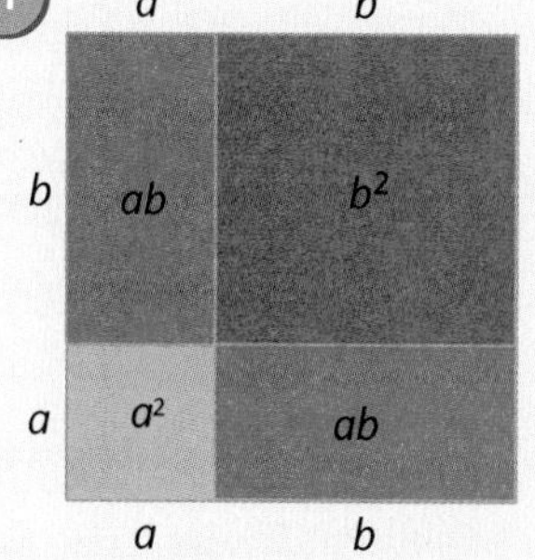

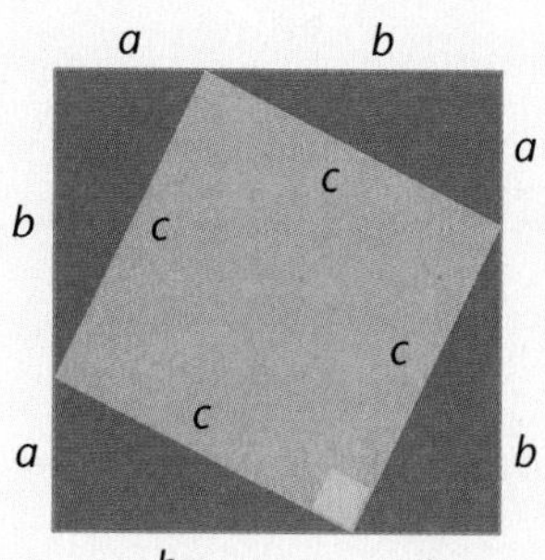

Add the areas in each of the equal squares.

$a^2 + 2ab + b^2 = c^2 + 4\left(\frac{1}{2}ab\right)$

$a^2 + 2ab + b^2 = c^2 + 2ab$ Subtract $2ab$ from both sides.

$a^2 + b^2 = c^2$

The Pythagorean theorem was named for Pythagoras, a Greek who lived in the sixth century B.C.

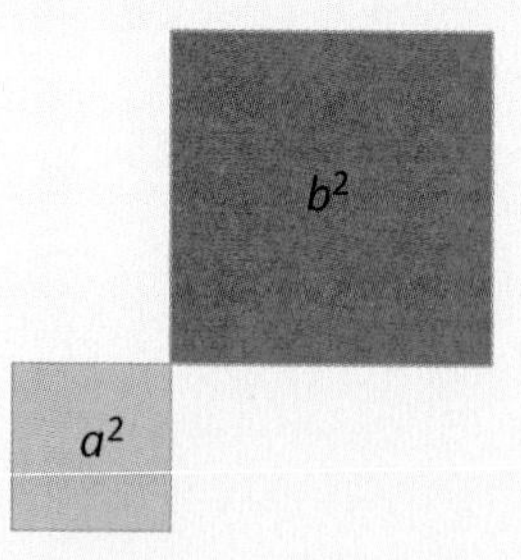

The area $a^2 + b^2$ is equal to the area c^2.

EXAMPLE 2 Using the Pythagorean theorem: $c^2 = a^2 + b^2$

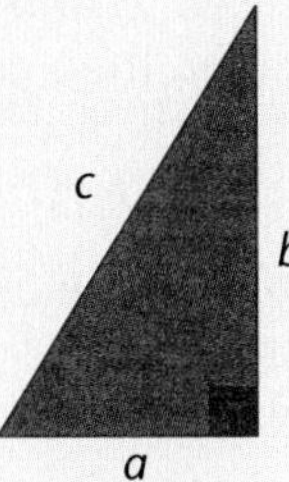

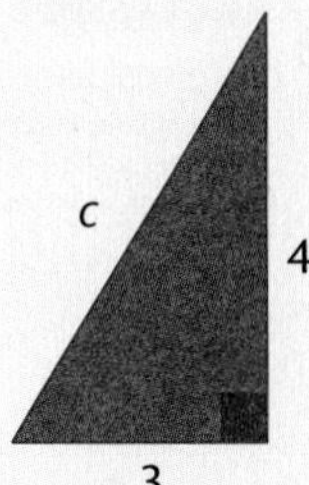

Suppose you know $a = 3$, $b = 4$, and c is unknown. Solve for c.

$c^2 = a^2 + b^2$

$c^2 = 3^2 + 4^2$

$c^2 = 9 + 16$

$c^2 = 25$ Find the square root of 25.

$c = 5$

Check. $5^2 = 3^2 + 4^2$

$25 = 25$ True

Solve for a. $c^2 = a^2 + b^2$

$c^2 - b^2 = a^2$

$\sqrt{c^2 - b^2} = a$ Find the square root of both sides of the equation.

Exercise A Use the Pythagorean theorem to find the missing value.

1. $a^2 = ■$ $b^2 = 50$ $c^2 = 100$

2. $a^2 = 36$ $b^2 = 75$ $c^2 = ■$

3. $a^2 = 64$ $b^2 = ■$ $c^2 = 90$

4. $a^2 = 10$ $b^2 = ■$ $c^2 = 55$

5. $a^2 = ■$ $b^2 = 27$ $c^2 = 78$

The *square key* x^2 and the *square root key* $\sqrt{\ }$ on your calculator can be used to find the missing side of a right triangle, using the Pythagorean theorem.

$a = 32$ $b = ■$ $c = 40$

Step 1 Set up the problem using the Pythagorean theorem.
$c^2 = a^2 + b^2$
$40^2 = 32^2 + b^2$

Step 2 Use the calculator square key x^2 to simplify.

Press 40 x^2 =. The display reads 1600.

Press 32 x^2 =. The display reads 1024.

Now $40^2 = 32^2 + b^2$

becomes $1600 = 1024 + b^2$.

Step 3 Solve for b^2.
$1600 - 1024 = 1024 + b^2 - 1024$
$576 = b^2$

Step 4 Solve by finding the square root of each side of the equation. Use the *square root key* $\sqrt{\ }$ to find the value of *b*.

$\sqrt{576} = b^2$

Press 576 $\sqrt{\ }$ =. The display reads 24.

$\sqrt{576} = 24$

Therefore, $b = 24$.

Exercise B Use a calculator to find the missing side of each right triangle. Round your answer to the nearest tenth.

6. $a = 9$ $b = 40$ $c = ■$

7. $a = ■$ $b = 6$ $c = 10$

8. $a = 18$ $b = ■$ $c = 30$

9. $a = 39$ $b = 36$ $c = ■$

10. $a = 12$ $b = ■$ $c = 20$

11. $a = 25$ $b = 9$ $c = ■$

PROBLEM SOLVING

Exercise C Use the Pythagorean theorem to solve each problem.

12. Martin leaves school and walks four blocks north and then three blocks east. How far is Martin from school?

13. A 10-foot ladder is leaning against a pole. The base of the ladder is six feet away from the pole. How high up the pole does the ladder reach?

14. To get to the grocery store from her house, Francine walks 12 blocks east and then 5 blocks south. Using a straight line, how far is the grocery store from Francine's house?

15. A 10-foot telephone pole has a support wire attached to the top of the pole and the ground. It is attached 24 feet away from the bottom of the pole. How long is the support wire?

Estimation Activity

Estimate: The area of a triangle when you only know the length of one side.

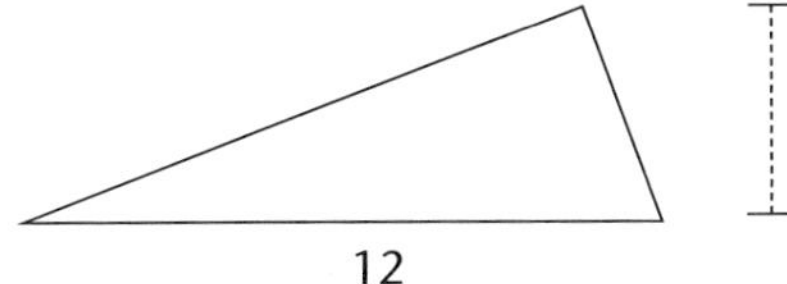

Solution: Estimate the height based on the length of the known side. Then calculate the area.

Height = about $\frac{1}{3}$ of the base.

Area $\approx \frac{1}{2}(12)(\frac{12}{3})$ or $(6)(4) = 24$ units^2

Lesson 10 Inequalities on the Number Line

Graphing
Showing on a number line the relationship of a set of numbers

Equality
The state of being equal; shown by the equal sign

Inequality
The state of being unequal; shown by the less than, greater than, and unequal to signs

Disjunction
A compound statement that uses the word or to connect two simple statements

Recall that a number line can be used to display positive and negative integers. A number line can also help give you a *picture* of number sets. This *picturing* is called **graphing.**

The statement $x = 3$ is an **equality.**

When $x \neq 3$ (read as "x is not equal to 3"), the statement is an **inequality.**

EXAMPLE 1 Graph $x = 3$. The closed dot means 3 is a solution.

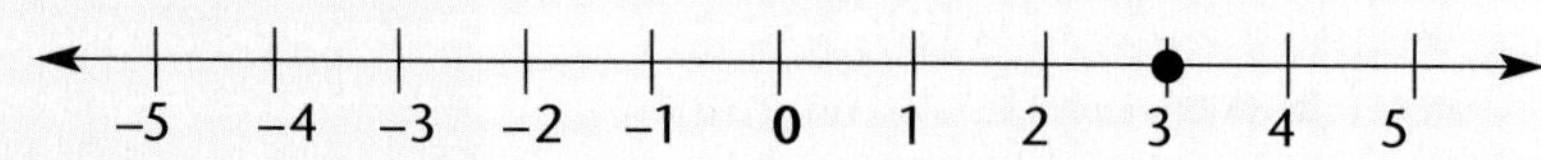

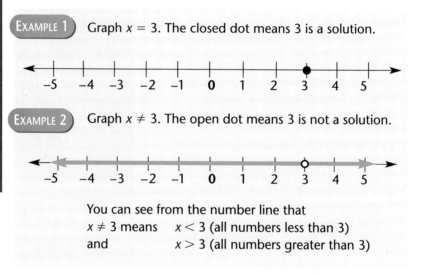

EXAMPLE 2 Graph $x \neq 3$. The open dot means 3 is not a solution.

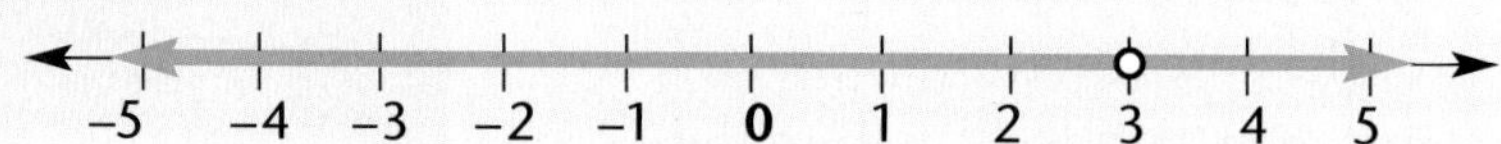

You can see from the number line that
$x \neq 3$ means $x < 3$ (all numbers less than 3)
and $x > 3$ (all numbers greater than 3)

The inequality $3 \leq 5$ is read "$3 < 5$ or $3 = 5$." This is an example of an *or* statement called a **disjunction.**

A disjunction is a compound statement using the word *or* to connect two simple statements. There is a rule that tells you when a disjunction is True (T) or False (F).

> **Rule for Disjunctions**
> A disjunction is always true except when both parts of the disjunction are false.

So "$3 < 5$ or $3 = 5$" is a true disjunction
(T) or F

and $3 \leq 5$ is a True statement.

Truth table

A table of true and false values

If p is any statement, p can be T or F (2 possibilities).
If q is any statement, q can be T or F (2 possibilities).
p and q together have $2 \cdot 2 = 4$ possible combinations.

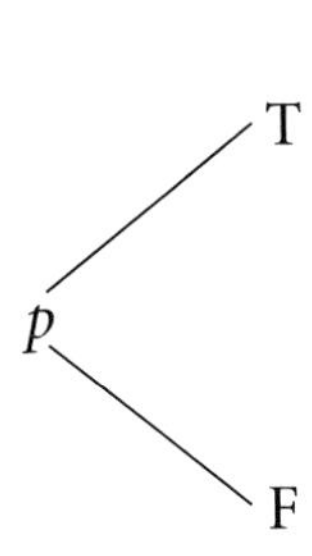

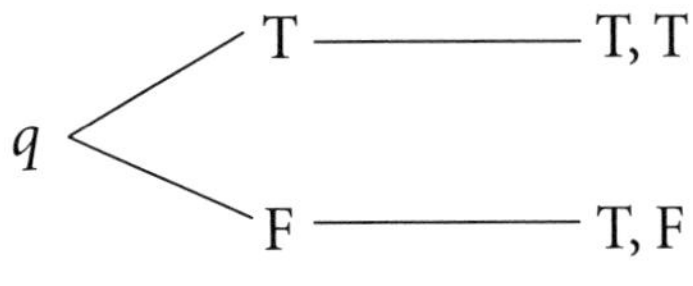

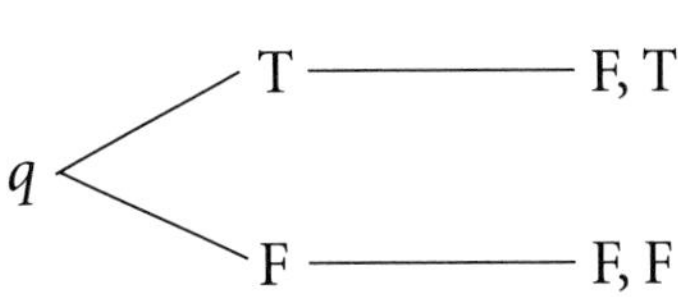

The rule for disjunctions can be summarized by a **truth table,** a table of T and F values like this:

p	q	Disjunction p or q
T	T	T
T	F	T
F	T	T
F	F	F

EXAMPLE 3 Use the rule for disjunctions to give the truth-value of each inequality.

$4 \leq 10$

$4 \leq 10$ means $4 < 10$ or $4 = 10$
$\quad$ T $\quad$ F $\qquad$ T or F means the statement is T.

Conclusion: $4 \leq 10$ is T.

EXAMPLE 4

$-2 \geq 2$

$-2 \geq 2$ means $-2 > 2$ or $-2 = 2$.
$\quad$ F $\quad$ F $\qquad$ F or F means the statement is F.

Conclusion: $-2 \geq 2$ is F.

To graph the inequality $x \leq 3$, you want to graph all points for which $x \leq 3$ is true.

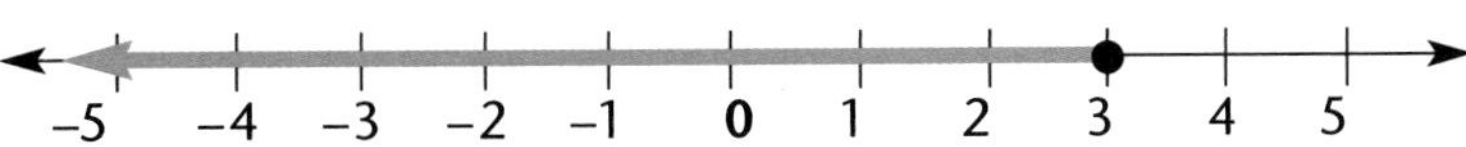

$x \leq 3$ means $x < 3$ or $x = 3$
$\quad$ T $\quad$ T

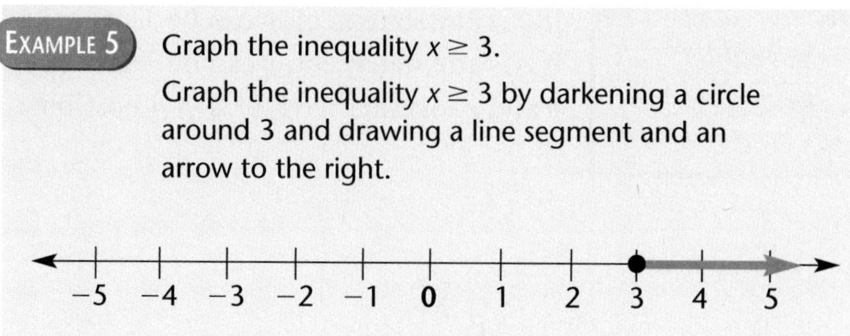

EXAMPLE 5
Graph the inequality $x \geq 3$.
Graph the inequality $x \geq 3$ by darkening a circle around 3 and drawing a line segment and an arrow to the right.
−5 −4 −3 −2 −1 0 1 2 3 4 5

This graph shows all numbers between −1 and 1.

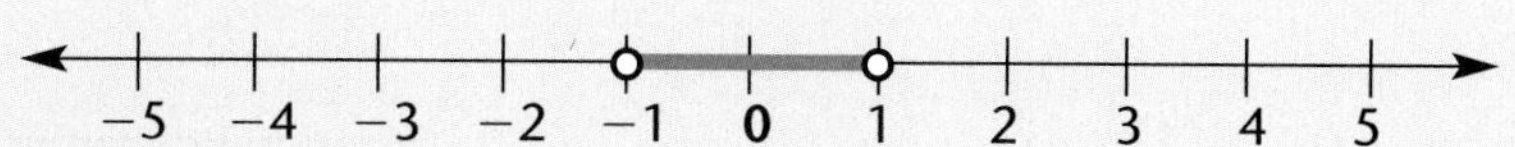

In algebra, the data displayed by the graph are $-1 < x < 1$ or -1 is less than x, which is less than 1.
(This also can be read as x is between −1 and 1.)

This graph shows all numbers between −1 and 1 *including* the points −1 and 1.

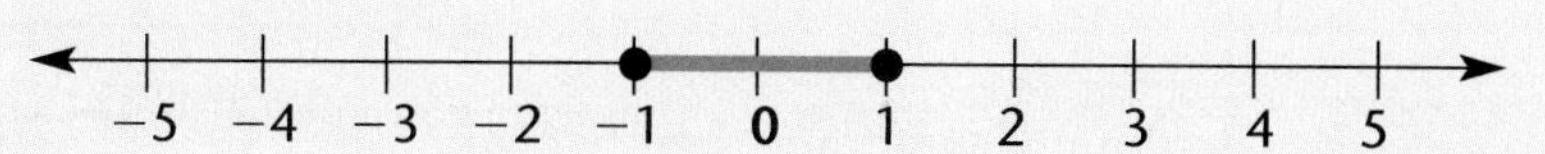

The data displayed by the graph can be written as $-1 \leq x \leq 1$.

Exercise A Write a statement of equality or inequality for each graph on the number line. Use x as the variable.

1.

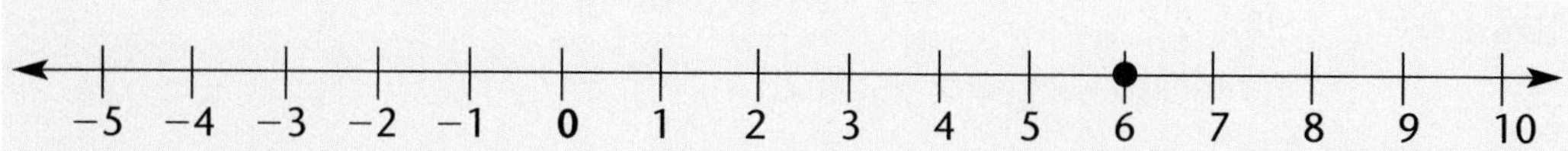

2.

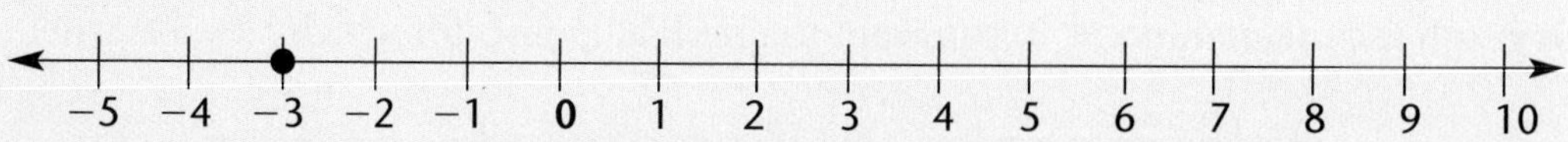

3.

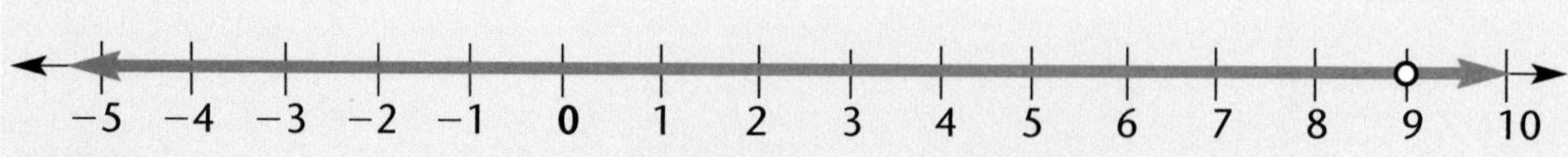

4.

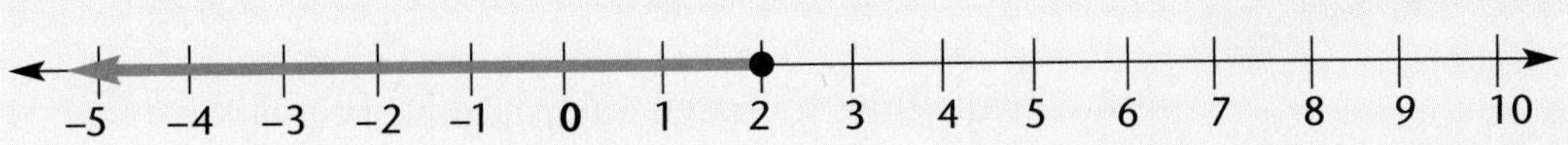

5.

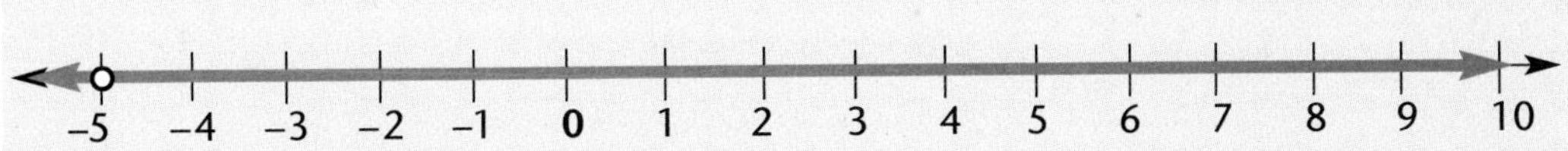

6.

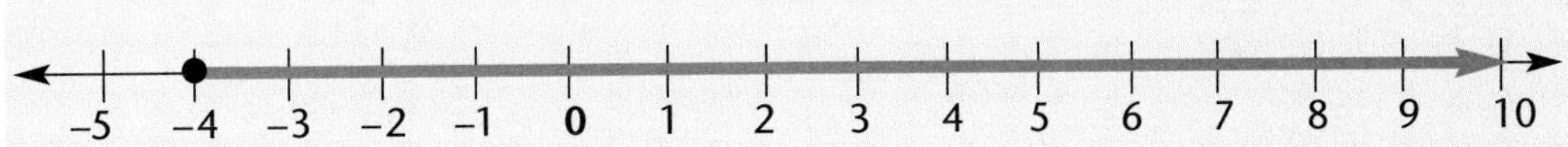

7.

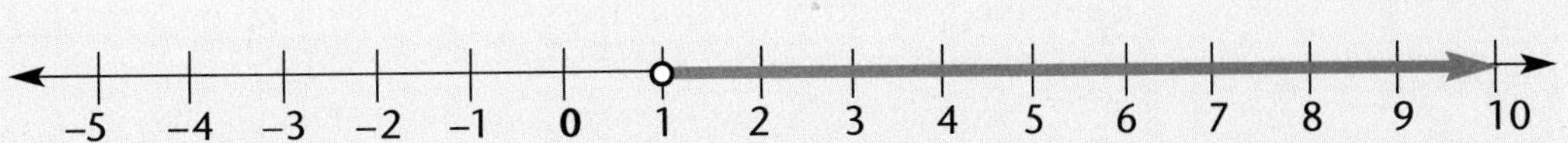

Exercise B Graph each of the equalities or inequalities on a number line.

8. $x < 2$

9. $x = 2$

10. $x \geq -5$

11. $x \leq -3$

12. $x = -10$

13. $x > -4$

14. $x \neq 6$

15. $1 < x < 4$

16. $-2 < x < 0$

17. $-8 \leq x \leq 8$

18. $7 \leq x \leq 10$

19. $x \neq 3$

Exercise C Write T if the disjunction is True or F if the disjunction is False.

20. $1 \leq 10$

21. $10 \leq 10$

22. $-2 \geq 1$

23. $-2 \geq -2$

24. $7 \leq 10$

25. $x \leq -1$ when $x = 0$

Lesson 11 Solving Inequalities with One Variable

Solve inequalities the same way you solved equalities.

EXAMPLE 1

Inequality		Equality
$x - 3 < 10$		$x - 3 = 10$
$+3 \quad +3$	Add 3 to both sides.	$+3 = +3$
$x < 13$		$x = 13$
$x + 3 > 10$		$x + 3 = 10$
$-3 \quad -3$	Subtract 3 from both sides.	$-3 = -3$
$x > 7$		$x = 7$
$3x \leq 15$		$3x = 15$
$\frac{1}{3}(3x) \leq \frac{1}{3}(15)$	Divide by 3 or multiply by $\frac{1}{3}$.	$\frac{1}{3}(3x) = \frac{1}{3}(15)$
$x \leq 5$		$x = 5$

Rule You can add or subtract the same number from both sides of an inequality, and you can multiply or divide both sides of an inequality by a *positive* number without changing the value of the inequality.

The reason you *cannot* divide or multiply by a negative number without changing the direction of the inequality sign is as follows:

EXAMPLE 2 $3 < 10$ True

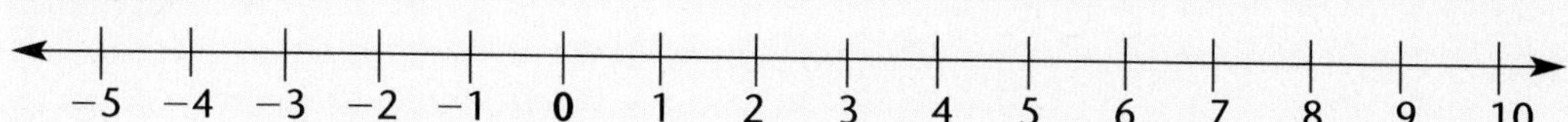

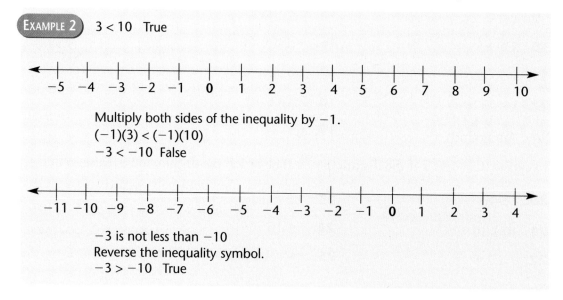

Multiply both sides of the inequality by -1.
$(-1)(3) < (-1)(10)$
$-3 < -10$ False

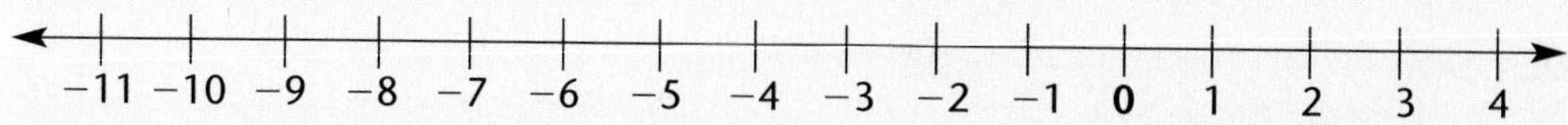

-3 is not less than -10
Reverse the inequality symbol.
$-3 > -10$ True

EXAMPLE 3 Divide both sides of $6 > 4$ by -2.

Divide both sides by -2.	$\frac{6}{-2} > \frac{4}{-2}$	
	$-3 > -2$	False
Reverse the inequality sign.	$-3 < -2$	True

Rule When you multiply or divide an inequality by a negative number, you must reverse the direction of the inequality sign to keep the statement true.

Exercise A Solve each inequality.

1. $x + 4 > 10$

2. $\frac{7}{8}b < -21$

3. $w + 8 > 15$

4. $6s \leq 42$

5. $g + (-5) \leq 15$

6. $4f < 44$

7. $\frac{1}{2}m < -7$

8. $p - 4 \leq 5$

Exercise B Solve each inequality. Remember to use the rule for multiplying or dividing an inequality by a negative number.

9. $-5c < 20$

10. $-\frac{1}{3}y \geq 3$

11. $-2t \geq -20$

12. $-\frac{1}{6}k \leq -3$

13. $-4x > 16$

14. $-\frac{3}{8}c > -9$

15. $-11m \leq 33$

16. $-\frac{2}{3}n > -14$

PROBLEM SOLVING

Exercise C Write an inequality to solve each problem.

17. Juan finds the growth rate of snow peas is always less than 95 mm per day. Describe the growth rate of peas using an inequality and the letter *p*.

18. At the county agricultural center, Young finds that the germination temperature for Kentucky bluegrass has to be greater than 58°F. Write an inequality that uses the letter *g* to describe the temperature.

19. Kim learns the number of grubs in a city lawn is always less than 2,500. Show the number of grubs as an inequality that includes the letter *i*.

20. During a pumpkin-growing contest, John finds the number of Connecticut field pumpkins entered is never more than $\frac{1}{3}$ the number of people attending the contest. One hundred fifty people are registered. Use the letter *c* and an inequality to show the number of Connecticut field pumpkins entered in the contest.

Application $\pi^2 \sum + \Omega \sqrt{x^2} \% \neq y \geq n = \nabla 30° \pi$

Using Equations Set up equations to solve problems. First identify the unknown. Assign a letter to represent the unknown. Create an equation that relates the unknown to the known. Then solve the equation.

EXAMPLE 1 The Osborn Building in St. Paul has two-thirds as many stories as the Xerox Tower in Rochester, Minnesota. The Osborn Building has 20 stories. How many stories does the Xerox Tower have?

Step 1 Read the problem carefully to set up the equation.

j = number of stories in the Xerox Tower

$\frac{2}{3}j = 20$

Step 2 Solve the equation.

$$\frac{2}{3}j = 20$$

$$\frac{2}{3}j \bullet \frac{3}{2} = 20 \bullet \frac{3}{2}$$

$$j = 30$$

(multiply each side by $\frac{3}{2}$, the reciprocal of $\frac{2}{3}$)

Step 3 Write your answer in sentence form. The Xerox Tower has 30 stories.

Exercise Use equations to solve the following problems about buildings around the country.

1. One Liberty Place is the tallest building in Philadelphia, measuring 945 feet, which is 397 feet taller than Philadelphia's City Hall Tower. How tall is the City Hall Tower?

2. One Liberty Place is 585 feet taller than Philadelphia's City Hall Tower, not including the statue of William Penn. How tall is the statue of William Penn on top of City Hall Tower?

3. The 333 Market Building in San Francisco is only half the size of Society Center in Cleveland. The 333 Market Building is 474 feet tall. How tall is Society Center?

4. The John Hancock Tower in Boston has triple the number of stories as the Southern National Finance Center building in Winston-Salem. The John Hancock Tower has 60 stories. How many stories does the Southern National Finance Center building have?

5. Chicago's Amoco Building is 1,136 feet tall, which is 688 feet taller than Denver's Amoco Building. How tall is Denver's Amoco Building?

Chapter 3 REVIEW

Find the solution for the equation.
Write the letter of the correct answer.

1. $m - 3 = 4$

A $m = 1$
B $m = -7$
C $m = 7$
D $m = -1$

2. $j + 2 = -8$

A $j = -10$
B $j = 6$
C $j = -6$
D $j = -8$

3. $\frac{1}{4}x = 8$

A $x = 2$
B $x = 12$
C $x = 32$
D $x = 16$

4. $-6x = 24$

A 4
B -4
C 18
D -30

5. $3.2h = -6.4$

A $h = 2$
B $h = -3.2$
C $h = 9.6$
D $h = -2$

Solve for x. Write the letter of the correct answer.

6. $-a = bx$

A $b = \frac{-a}{x}$
B $x = \frac{-a}{b}$
C $x = \frac{-b}{a}$
D $x = \frac{a}{b}$

7. $cx + ax = b$

A $x = \frac{b}{(c + a)}$
B $x = \frac{(c + a)}{b}$
C $x = b(a + c)$
D $x = \frac{b}{2ac}$

Write an equation for each statement. Let x be the variable in each equation.

Example: 4 times some number equals 32. Solution: $4x = 32$

8. 3 times some number equals 36.

9. 14 times some number plus 5 equals 33.

10. 6 times some number minus 18 equals 24.

11. 8 times some number equals 24.

Solve each problem using a formula for perimeter or area.

Example: $P = 3s$ Solve for s. Solution: $P = 3s$ (divide each side by 3)

$$\frac{P}{3} = \frac{3s}{3}$$

$$\frac{P}{3} = s$$

12. $P = 5s$ Solve for s.

13. $\frac{A}{h} = w$ Solve for A.

14. $P - c = a + b$ Solve for P.

15. $2A = bh$ Solve for A.

16. $P = a + b + c$ Solve for a.

Use the Pythagorean theorem and a calculator to find the missing side of each right triangle.

Example:
Solution:

b 5
4

Step 1: Set up the problem using the Pythagorean theorem.
$5^2 = 4^2 + b^2$

Step 2: Simplify. $25 = 16 + b^2$

Step 3: Solve for b. $25 - 16 = 16 + b^2 - 16$

$9 = b^2$

$3 = b$

Find the length of the missing side of each triangle.

17.

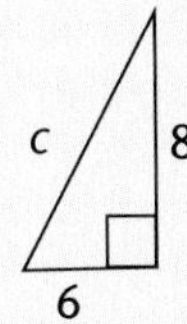

18.

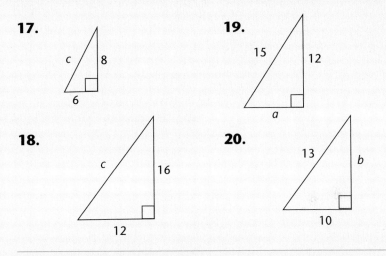

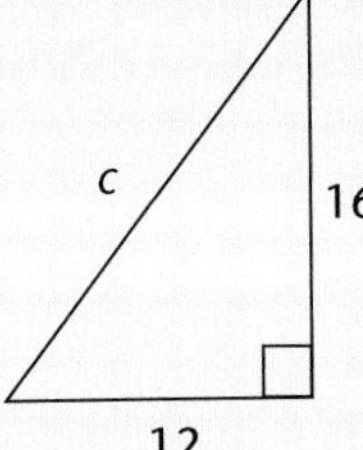

19.

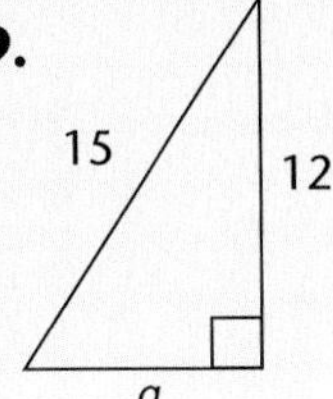

20.

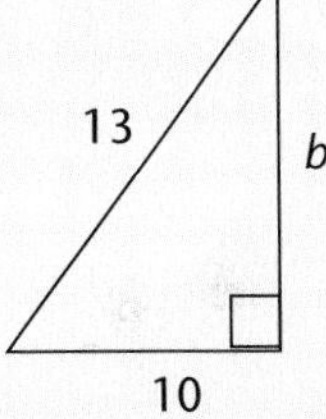

Graph each equality or inequality using a number line.

Example: $x \leq 3$ Solution:

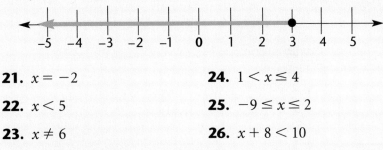

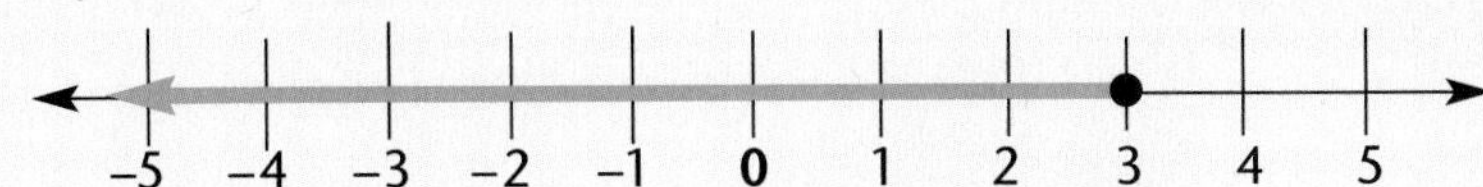

21. $x = -2$

22. $x < 5$

23. $x \neq 6$

24. $1 < x \leq 4$

25. $-9 \leq x \leq 2$

26. $x + 8 < 10$

Solve each inequality.

Example: $3s < 27$

Solution: $3s < 27$

(divide each side by 3)

$\frac{3s}{3} < \frac{27}{3}$

$s < 9$

27. $b + (-5) \geq 13$

28. $-6d \leq 48$

29. $v - 4 \leq 5$

30. $3x > -21$

Test-Taking Tip

When taking a mathematics test, complete the answers that you know before tackling more difficult problems.

Chapter

Applications of Algebra

Scientists create and test formulas to search for cures to diseases or to prove new theories. Equations and formulas have many common uses in daily life. For example, recipes are formulas. Leave out an ingredient and you get a flat cake! There are formulas for every kind of mixture problem. The correct antifreeze-to-water ratio is important for a car radiator. Even artists use formulas to mix just the right color or to cast a metal sculpture. If you think about it, you probably use formulas almost every day of the week.

In Chapter 4, you will write and apply algebraic equations and formulas.

Goals for Learning

- To write an algebraic equation for a number sentence
- To identify formulas to use in specific types of problems
- To write problems using algebraic formulas
- To solve problems by applying algebraic equations

Lesson 1 Writing Equations—Odd and Even Integers

Consecutive

Following one after the other in order

A number sentence gives information about an unknown number or numbers. A number sentence can be written as an algebraic equation. Then the equation can be solved to identify the number.

EXAMPLE 1 Six times a number added to 15 is 27. What is the number?

Step 1 First, make a "model" of the problem.
Choose a letter to represent the number.
Decide if the letter has a coefficient.
Let $n =$ the number.
Let $6n$ represent six times the number.

Step 2 Write and solve the algebraic equation.

$$15 + 6n = 27$$
$$15 - 15 + 6n = 27 - 15$$
$$6n = 12$$
$$n = 2$$

Step 3 Check. $15 + (6)(2) = 27$ $15 + 12 = 27$ True
The number is 2.

A number sentence may describe **consecutive** integers. Algebraic equations can be used to find the consecutive numbers.

EXAMPLE 2 The sum of two consecutive integers is 31. What are the integers?
Think of the integers on the number line.

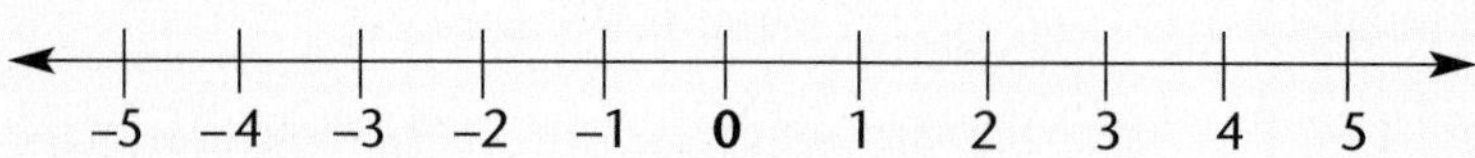

The common difference between consecutive integers is 1.

Step 1 Let $n =$ one of the integers.
Let $n + 1 =$ the consecutive integer.

Step 2 Write and solve the equation.

$$n + (n + 1) = 31$$
$$2n + 1 = 31$$
$$2n = 30$$
$$n = 15 \text{ and } n + 1 = 16$$

Step 3 Check. $15 + 16 = 31$ True
The two consecutive integers are 15 and 16.

EXAMPLE 3 The sum of three consecutive *odd* integers is 33. What are the integers?
Think of the set of odd integers on the number line.

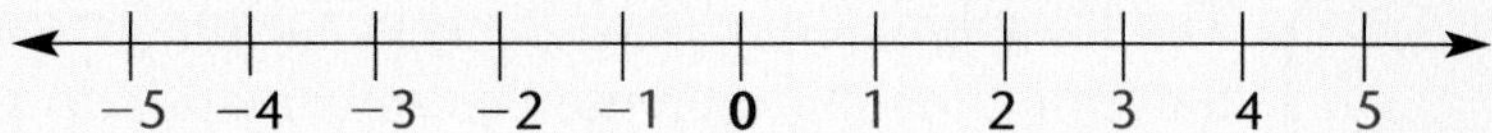

The common difference between consecutive odd numbers is 2.

Step 1 Let $n =$ the smallest odd integer.
Let $n + 2 =$ the next odd integer.
Let $n + 4 =$ the greatest odd integer.

$$\underbrace{n \quad n+2}_{2}\ \underbrace{\quad n+4}_{2}$$

Step 2 Write the equation. $n + (n + 2) + (n + 4) = 33$

$$3n + 6 = 33$$
$$3n = 27$$
$$n = 9 \quad n + 2 = 11 \quad n + 4 = 13$$

Step 3 Check. $9 + 11 + 13 = 33$ True

The three consecutive odd integers are 9, 11, and 13.

Exercise A Let *n* represent an even integer. Write an expression for each of the following.

1. the next consecutive integer

2. the next even integer

3. the previous even integer

Exercise B Write the equation and solve to answer each question.

4. Seven times a number decreased by 2 is 19. What is the number?

5. An integer added to 24 equals 16. What is the integer?

6. The sum of two consecutive odd integers is -8. What are the integers?

7. The sum of three consecutive even integers is 36. What are the integers?

8. The sum of two consecutive integers is -13. What are the integers?

Exercise C Show that the following equations are true. Express your answers in terms of variables.

9. even integer + even integer = even integer

10. odd integer + odd integer = even integer

Lesson 2 Using the 1% Solution to Solve Problems

Percent
Part per one hundred

The 1% solution method is a way of solving percent problems. Solve first for 1%, then use that information to answer the question.

Recall that **percent** means "part per one hundred."

For example, $20\% = \frac{20}{100} = 0.20 = \frac{1}{5}$, and $100\% = \frac{100}{100} = 1$.

The 1% solution method can be used to find the total number from a percentage.

EXAMPLE 1 There are 120 seniors at Belmont High. If 20% of the students in the school are seniors, how many students attend Belmont High?

20% of population = 120	Given.
20% ÷ 20 = 120 ÷ 20	Divide both sides by 20 to solve for 1%.
1% of population = 6	
100% of population = 600	Multiply both sides by 100 to find the total population.

600 students attend Belmont High.

The 1% solution method can be used to find a portion of the total number from a percentage.

EXAMPLE 2 A city has a population of 100,000. If 23% of the population are 18 years old or younger, how many people are 18 or younger?

100% of population = 100,000	Given.
1% of population = 1,000	Divide both sides by 100 to solve for 1%.
23% of population = (1,000)(23) = 23,000	Multiply both sides by 23 to find the total youth population that is 18 years old or younger.

23,000 people are 18 years old or younger.

The 1% solution method can be used to find what percentage a portion is of the total number.

EXAMPLE 3 You want to raise $1,000 for charity. You have raised $550. What percent of the total did you raise?

100% of the total = $1,000	Given.
1% = $10	Divide both sides by 100.
55% = $550	Multiply both sides by 55 to find the percent of the total raised.

55% of the total was raised.

PROBLEM SOLVING

Exercise A Use the 1% solution to solve each problem.

1. Jay earns $2,500 a month. He pays $850 a month to rent an apartment. What percent of Jay's income does he pay for rent?

2. A tennis resort has 1,200 guests. If 65% of the guests play doubles and singles, how many guests will play both games?

3. 24,600 people attend a baseball game. If 75% of the seats are filled, how many seats are in the ball park?

4. Jeremy wants to buy a computer that costs $1,600. He has already saved $1,280. What percent of the total has he saved?

5. Suppose 40 people come to your party. If 15% of your guests arrive early, how many people arrive early?

6. Maria has an annual income of $32,000. If she saves 8% of her income, how much money does she save?

7. There are 30 mystery books in Chin's book collection. If 6% of his books are mysteries, how many books does Chin have in his collection?

8. There are 10,000 people at a concert. Of those people, 6,250 are adults. What percent of the people at the concert are adults?

9. A cable television provider offers six different news stations. If 25% of the stations offered are news, how many stations are offered by the provider?

10. In an apartment building, 45% of the families have pets. If 27 families have pets, how many families live in the building?

Lesson  3

Using the Percent Equation

Remember that percent means part of 100. For example, 20% is equal to $\frac{20}{100}$.

Another way to solve a percent problem is to find a fraction of a number. First, you change the percent into a fraction. Use the percent equation.

Percent Equation

Fraction • Number = Result

$(\frac{p}{100}) \bullet (n) = r$

where

p = the number that is the percent

n = the total number

r = result

In percent problems, you will be given two variables. You can solve for a third one using algebra.

You can use the percent equation to find out what the percent number is when the percent and the total are known.

EXAMPLE 1 25% of the 20 students in the class have seen the latest hit movie. How many of the students have seen the movie?

Substitute the values into the percent equation. Then solve for r.

25% of 20 is what number?

Step 1 Write the percent equation. $(\frac{p}{100})(n) = r$

Step 2 Change the percent into a fraction.

$p = 25$ $(\frac{25}{100})(n) = r$

Step 3 Write the total number.

$n = 20$ $(\frac{25}{100})(20) = r$

Step 4 Simplify the fraction. $(\frac{1}{4})(20) = r$

Step 5 Solve the equation. $(\frac{1}{4})(20) = 5$

25% of 20 is 5. Five students have seen the movie.

Circle graph

A graphic way to present information using the parts of a circle

You can use the percent equation to find percent when the percent number and the total are known.

EXAMPLE 2 4 of the 5 students who saw the movie would like to see it again. What percent of students would like to see the movie again?

4 is what percent of 5?

Substitute the values into the percent equation. Then solve for p.

$$(\frac{p}{100})(n) = r$$

$n = 5 \quad r = 4 \qquad (\frac{p}{100})(5) = 4$

$$5p = 400$$

$$p = 80$$

4 is 80% of 5.

You can use the equation to find the total when the percent and the percent number are known.

EXAMPLE 3 15 is 25% of what number?

Substitute the values into the percent equation. Then solve for n.

$$(\frac{p}{100})(n) = r$$

$p = 25 \qquad r = 15 \quad (\frac{25}{100})(n) = 15$

$$25n = 1500 \qquad n = 60$$

15 is 25% of 60.

The percent equation can also be used to solve percent problems that are displayed by a circle graph. A **circle graph** shows the different parts into which a whole is divided. For example, the circle graph below shows that 60% of 30 students attended a school sports event last week, while 40% of 30 students did not.

Did You Attend a School Sports Event Last Week?

(30 students surveyed)

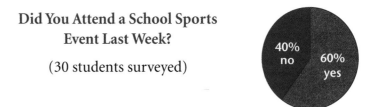

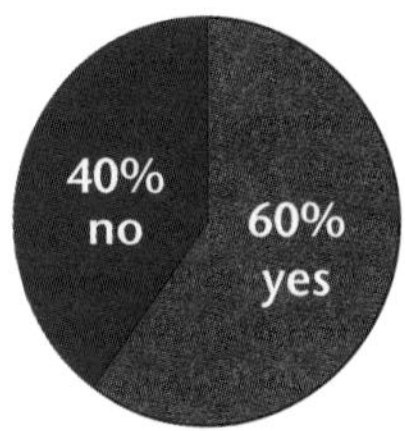

You can also use percents to make a circle graph.

EXAMPLE 4 A professional sports team earns \$40 million of revenue annually. Of that amount, 30% is from ticket sales and 70% is from other sources. Represent the information in a circle graph.

Step 1 Write a title for the circle graph and draw a circle to represent the whole.

Annual Team Revenue

Step 2 The circle graph will be made up of two parts (70% of the whole and 30% of the whole). Since a circle measures 360°, divide the circle into two parts by finding 70% of 360° and 30% of 360°.

Annual Team Revenue

70% of 360° = 252°

30% of 360° = 108°

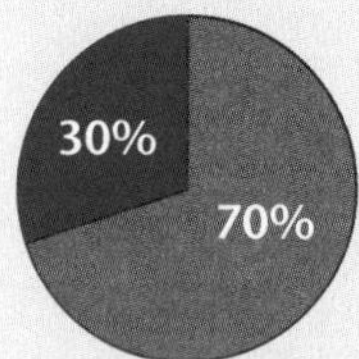

Step 3 Determine the information that the circle graph is supposed to display by finding 70% of \$40 million and 30% of 40 million. Then write the answers on the graph. Add labels identifying each part.

Annual Team Revenue

70% of \$40 million = \$28 million

30% of \$40 million = \$12 million

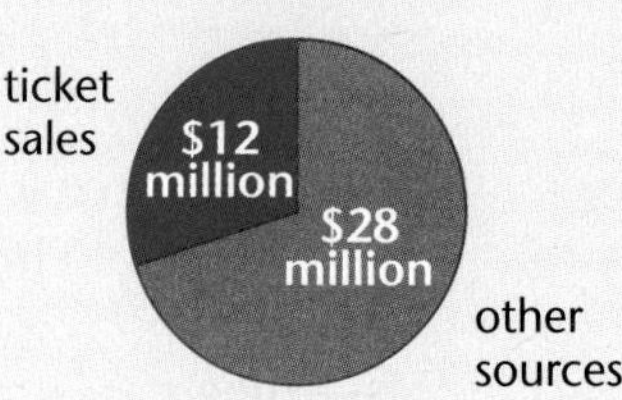

Exercise A Find the percent of each number.

1. 25% of 40

2. 42% of 720

3. 50% of 82

4. 80% of 200

5. 65% of 510

6. 70% of 90

7. 30% of 450

8. 92% of 800

9. 18% of 75

10. 45% of 60

PROBLEM SOLVING

Exercise B Solve each problem using the percent equation.

11. All of the students in Ms. Elgin's science class are going on the class field trip to the planetarium. There are 20 students in the class. What percentage of students in Ms. Elgin's class are going on the field trip?

12. Of the 450 students in the school, 75 students take biology classes. What percentage of students in the school are taking biology classes?

13. Every day, school bus 101 carries 40 students to and from school. Fifteen of the students live more than 10 miles from school. What percent of the students live more than 10 miles from school?

14. Of the 16 students in the school orchestra, 12.5% play the violin. How many students play the violin?

15. This room is the homeroom for 25 freshmen. That is 25% of all the freshmen in the school. How many freshmen does the school have?

Exercise C Use the information on calculating with percents to explore information about sports teams earnings. Compute the dollar values for each percent and make a circle graph to show the information.

16. Major League Baseball Teams—Average Earnings: $66 million

Ticket Sales	40%
Television and Radio	35%
Stadium Revenue	18%
Licensing and Other Sources	7%

17. National Basketball Association Teams—Average Earnings: $50 million

Ticket Sales	41%
Television and Radio	40%
Arena Revenue	12%
Licensing and Other Sources	7%

18. National Football League Teams—Average Earnings: $64 million

Ticket Sales	24%
Television and Radio	63%
Arena Revenue	9%
Licensing and Other Sources	4%

19. National Hockey League Teams—Average Earnings: $35 million

Ticket Sales	63%
Television and Radio	17%
Arena Revenue	16%
Licensing and Other Sources	4%

20. Identify the sport that makes the most money from
a. Ticket Sales
b. Television and Radio

Lesson 4 Solving Distance, Rate, and Time Problems

Writing About Mathematics

What property of equality was used to transform $d = rt$ into $r = \frac{d}{t}$? Explain.

The total distance traveled is equal to the average rate of speed multiplied by the total time.

Formulas for Distance, Rate, and Time

Total distance = Average rate of speed • Total time $d = rt$

Average rate of speed = $\frac{\text{total distance}}{\text{total time}}$ $r = \frac{d}{t}$

Total time = $\frac{\text{total distance}}{\text{average rate of speed}}$ $t = \frac{d}{r}$

Average rate of speed is expressed as miles per (one) hour or kilometers per (one) hour.

EXAMPLE 1 Suppose you drive for $3\frac{1}{2}$ hours at 50 miles per hour (mph).

How many miles have you driven?

50 mph means 50 miles in one hour.

50 miles	50 miles	50 miles	25 miles
1 hour	2 hours	3 hours	$3\frac{1}{2}$ hours

= 175 miles

This diagram shows that you drove 50 miles in 1 hour, 100 miles in 2 hours, 150 miles in 3 hours, and 175 miles in $3\frac{1}{2}$ hours.

Or, you can use the formula $d = rt$ to find out how many miles, or the distance, you drove.

$d = rt$

$d = (50)(3\frac{1}{2}) = 175$ miles

EXAMPLE 2 Suppose you travel 378 miles in 7 hours.

What is your average rate of speed?

(Hint: How many miles did you travel in one hour?)

1 hour	2 hours	3 hours	4 hours	5 hours	6 hours	7 hours	378 miles

Divide the total number of miles driven (378 miles) by the number of hours (7 hours) to find average speed.

$\frac{378}{7} = 54$ miles per (one) hour.

The formula $r = \frac{d}{t}$ uses the same steps to find average rate of speed.

$r = \frac{d}{t} \quad r = \frac{378}{7} = 54$ miles per hour

PROBLEM SOLVING

Exercise A Solve each problem using miles.

1. Fernando drives 165 miles at a constant speed of 55 miles per hour. How many hours does he drive?

2. Maria and Julia live 690 miles apart. They decide to meet. Maria drives toward Julia at 60 miles per hour and Julia drives toward Maria at 55 miles per hour. How long will it take for them to meet?

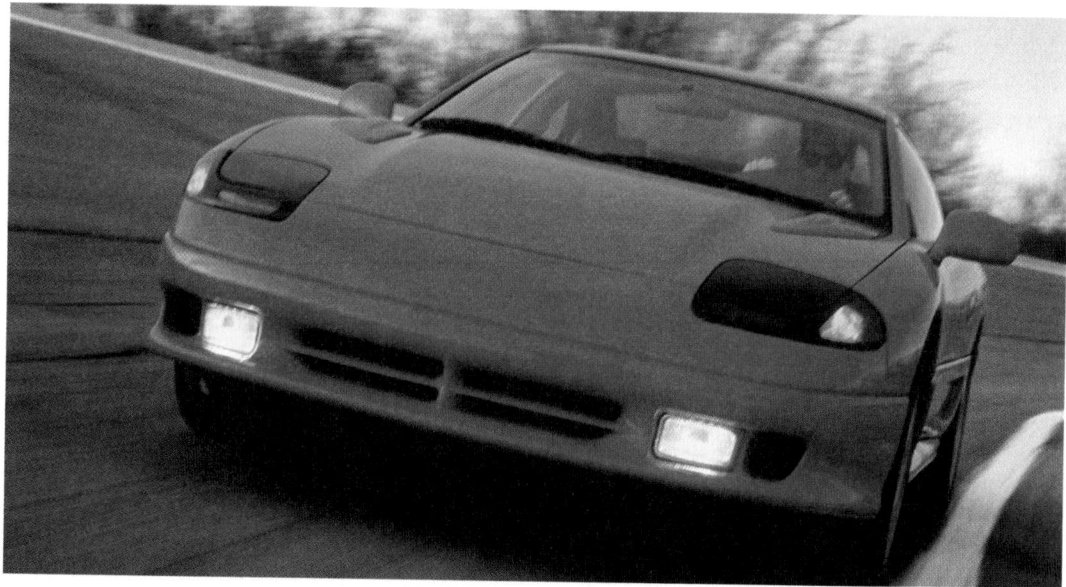

EXAMPLE 3 Suppose you drive 80 kilometers per hour for $1\frac{1}{2}$ hours and 90 kilometers per hour for $\frac{1}{2}$ hour. What is your average rate of speed?

80 km/h means 80 kilometers in one hour, or 120 kilometers in $1\frac{1}{2}$ hours.

90 km/h means 90 kilometers in one hour, or 45 kilometers in $\frac{1}{2}$ hour.

$$\begin{array}{l} \quad 120 \text{ kilometers in } 1\frac{1}{2} \text{ hours} \\ + \ 45 \text{ kilometers in } \frac{1}{2} \text{ hour} \\ \hline \quad 165 \text{ kilometers in 2 hours, or } 165 \div 2 = 82.5 \end{array}$$

kilometers in 1 hour

Use the formula Average rate $= \frac{\text{Total distance}}{\text{Total time}}$ and solve for r.

$$r = \frac{d}{t}$$

$$= \frac{(80)(1\frac{1}{2}) \ + \ 90(\frac{1}{2})}{1\frac{1}{2} \ + \ \frac{1}{2}}$$

$$= \frac{120 + 45}{2}$$

$$= \frac{165}{2}$$

$$= 82.5 \text{ km/h}$$

Estimation Activity

Estimate: Sammi buys a sweater that costs $29.67. If the sales tax is 6%, how much sales tax will Sammi pay?

Solution:
Round $29.67 to $30.00.
Figure 1% of $30.00 = $0.30 or 30%
Multiply $0.30 by 6 $0.30 x 6 = $1.80

Sammi will pay $1.80 in sales tax.

PROBLEM SOLVING

Exercise B Solve each problem using kilometers.

3. Jessica rides her bicycle for $2\frac{3}{4}$ hours at an average rate of speed of $14\frac{1}{2}$ kilometers per hour. How many kilometers does she ride?

4. On Saturday, Erica and Bianca travel 324 kilometers. They reach their destination in 4 hours. What is their average speed?

5. Jake and Lisa walk at a rate of 9 kilometers per hour for $1\frac{1}{4}$ hours and 6 kilometers per hour for 15 minutes. What is their average speed?

Algebra in Your Life

Building, Baking, Candlestick Making . . . Everything we build, cook, and mix uses ratio and proportion. We build houses from plans drawn to scale. We bake cookies by mixing specific proportions of ingredients. A one-to-one ratio of blue and yellow paint makes green. Changing the ratio produces different shades of blue-greens and yellow-greens. A two-to-one ratio of hydrogen and oxygen atoms produces water. Let's face it—we just can't get away from ratios and proportions!

Lesson 5 Using a Common Unit—Cents

American money is made up of coins and bills. Each coin and bill is a specific amount of money.

1 penny = 1 cent
1 nickel = 5 cents
1 dime = 10 cents
1 quarter = 25 cents
1 half-dollar = 50 cents
1 dollar = 100 cents

To solve problems dealing with money, you can write and solve algebraic equations.

EXAMPLE 1 John has \$5.00 in nickels and dimes. If he has twice as many dimes as nickels, how many of each coin does he have?

Let x = number of nickels. Let $2x$ = number of dimes since there are twice as many dimes as nickels.

Write an equation. To eliminate the decimal point, multiply dollar amounts by 100. \$5.00 is the same as 500 cents.

nickels + dimes = total amount

$x(5¢) + 2x(10¢) = 500$

$25x = 500$

$x = 20$ and $2x = 40$

John has 20 nickels and 40 dimes.

Check. $20(5¢) + 40(10¢) = 100¢ + 400¢ = 500¢$

Divide cents by 100 to get dollars.
$500¢ \div 100 = \$5.00$

EXAMPLE 2 Andrea has six times as many dimes as quarters. If her dimes and quarters total \$12.75, how many of each coin does she have?

Let x = number of quarters.

Let $6x$ = number of dimes since there are six times as many dimes as quarters.

$$6x(10) + (25)x = 1{,}275$$
$$60x + 25x = 1{,}275$$
$$85x = 1{,}275$$
$$x = 15 \text{ and } 6x = 90$$

Andrea has 15 quarters and 90 dimes.

Check. $15(25¢) + 90(10¢) = 375¢ + 900¢ =$ $1{,}275¢$, or \$12.75

PROBLEM SOLVING

Exercise A Solve the problems by answering the questions.

1. Tricia has the same number of nickels and dimes in her pocket. The coins total \$3.60.

a. How many of each coin does she have?

b. How many coins are in Tricia's pocket?

2. Gilberto has three times as many quarters as half-dollars. The coins total \$13.75.

a. How many of each coin does he have?

b. How many coins does Gilberto have?

3. Kristi has \$13.20 in dimes and half-dollars. She has one-half as many dimes as half-dollars.

a. How many of each coin does she have?

b. How many coins does Kristi have?

4. Latisha noticed that she has the same number of nickels, dimes, quarters, and half-dollars in her drawer. The coins total \$12.60.

a. How many of each coin does she have?

b. The nickels and dimes total what amount?

c. The quarters and half-dollars total what amount?

You can use a calculator to solve problems involving money.

EXAMPLE 3 $3.50, three times more dimes than nickels

Set up your equation: $3x(10¢) + x(5¢) = 350¢$

Press: 3 [×] 10 [+] 5 [=]. Your calculator will read 35.

Clear, and then press: 350 [÷] 35 [=] 10, the number of nickels.

Press: [×] 3 [=] 30, the number of dimes.

Exercise B Use a calculator to tell how many nickels and how many dimes in each problem.

5. $2.40, two times more nickels than dimes

6. $3.00, the same number of nickels as dimes

7. 900¢, 4 times more dimes than nickels

8. 350¢, 5 times more nickels than dimes

9. $1.70, 8 times more dimes than nickels

10. 520¢, 6 times more nickels than dimes

Technology Connection

Internet Calculators

There's a calculator on the Internet for just about any type of number you want to know. There are calculators that compute interest for a loan. There are calculators to figure the distance from one place to another and how much gas you'll use. Other calculators figure the cost of living in different cities. You can also find what your car is worth, or how long it will take to build a house. And that's just for starters. Type "online calculator" into a search engine, and see what you can find!

Lesson 6 Calculating Simple Interest

Interest

The amount of money paid or received for the use of borrowed money

Principal

The amount of money deposited, borrowed, or loaned

When you deposit money in a bank, your money earns **interest** because the bank is using (borrowing) your money to make investments. The rate of interest is applied to your money for 1 year at a time. The money you earn is simple annual interest.

Simple Interest Formula

$I = p \bullet r \bullet t$ or $I = prt$

where I is the interest in dollars, p is the **principal** in dollars, r is the rate in percent, and t is the time in years.

EXAMPLE 1 If you deposit \$500 at a rate of 6% for 2 years, how much interest will you earn?

Substitute the values into the formula $I = prt$ to solve.

$p = \$500$ $\qquad I = prt$

$r = 6\% = 0.06$ $\qquad = (\$500)(6\%)(2 \text{ years})$

$t = 2$ years $\qquad = (500)(0.06)(2)$

$I =$ interest $\qquad I = 60$

The interest earned is \$60.

EXAMPLE 2 Find the principal in an account that has a rate of 7.5% for 1 year and earns \$900 in interest.

Use the formula $I = prt$ to solve for p.

$I = prt \quad \frac{I}{rt} = \frac{prt}{rt} \quad \frac{I}{rt} = p$

Substitute the values into the formula to solve.

$p = \frac{I}{rt}$

$r = 7.5\% = 0.075$ $\quad p = \frac{\$900}{(0.075)}$

$t = 1$ year

$I = \$900$

$p =$ principal $\qquad p = \$12{,}000$

The principal is \$12,000.

EXAMPLE 3 Keesha borrows $3,000 for 1 year. At the end of the year, she has paid $210 in interest. Find the rate of interest.

Use the formula $I = prt$ to solve for r.

$r = \frac{I}{pt}$

Substitute the values into the formula to solve.

$p = \$3{,}000$ $\qquad r = \frac{\$210}{\$3{,}000}$

$t = 1$ year

$I = \$210$

$r =$ rate of interest $\quad r = 0.07 = 7\%$

The rate of interest is 7%.

Exercise A Find the interest.

1. Principal: $3,000

Rate: 5.5%

Time: 1 year

2. Principal: $8,000

Rate: 8%

Time: 2 years

3. Principal: $5,000

Rate: 11.5%

Time: 4 years

Exercise B Find the principal or rate of interest.

4. Interest: $640

Rate: 4%

Time: 1 year

5. Interest: $2,016

Rate: 12%

Time: 3 years

6. Principal: $4,000

Interest: $720

Time: 2 years

PROBLEM SOLVING

Exercise C Solve each problem.

7. Find the interest earned on $4,200 at a 6.25% annual interest rate for 5 years.

8. Terence opens a savings account with a deposit of $1,000. After 1 year, he receives $50 in interest. What is the annual interest rate?

9. Suppose you lend a friend $400 for 2 years. You loan the money at a rate of 6%. How much should your friend pay you in interest at the end of 2 years?

10. Credit cards usually have high interest rates. Jennifer has a credit card bill of $1,350. The interest rate is 18% per year. How much interest will Jennifer pay at the end of 1 month? (Hint: 1 month $= \frac{1}{12}$ of a year)

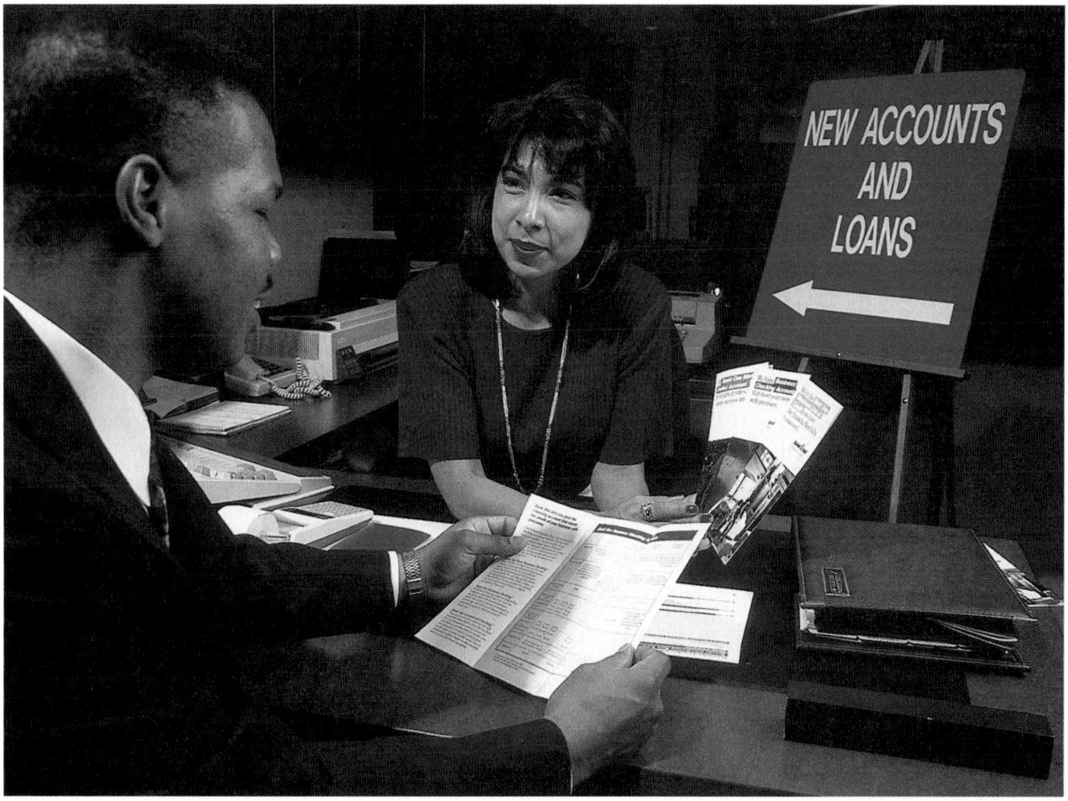

Lesson 7 Deriving a Formula for Mixture Problems

Mixture problems can be solved in different ways.

EXAMPLE 1 Peanuts cost \$3.00 per pound and walnuts cost \$5.00 per pound. If you mix three pounds of peanuts with two pounds of walnuts, what is the cost for one pound of the mixture?

Peanuts cost	\$3.00 for 1 pound
	\$9.00 for 3 pounds
Walnuts cost	\$5.00 for 1 pound
	\$10.00 for 2 pounds

Add the amounts to get the total price and the total weight.

Peanuts	\$ 9.00 for 3 pounds
Walnuts	\$10.00 for 2 pounds
Mixture:	\$19.00 for 5 pounds

One pound of the mixture costs \$19.00 ÷ 5 or \$3.80.

In algebra, the following formula copies the steps used above.

$$\text{Price per pound} = \frac{\text{cost of total mixture}}{\text{number of pounds}}$$

$$\text{Price per pound} = \frac{(3)(\$3) + (2)(\$5)}{3+2}$$

$$= \frac{\$19}{5} = \$3.80$$

EXAMPLE 2 A grocer wants to mix peanuts and walnuts. Peanuts cost \$3.00 per pound and walnuts cost \$5 per pound. If she wants 100 pounds of a mixture to sell for \$3.50 a pound, how much of each kind of nut should she use?

Let x represent the number of pounds of peanuts and $100 - x$ represent the number of pounds of walnuts.

You know that 100 pounds at \$3.50 per pound is \$350.00 for the total mixture.

Cost of peanuts + cost of walnuts = \$350

$$\$3x + \$5(100 - x) = \$350$$

Write the equation and solve for x.

$$3x + 5(100 - x) = 350$$
$$3x + 500 - 5x = 350$$
$$500 - 2x = 350$$
$$-2x = -150$$
$$2x = 150$$
$$x = 75 \text{ and } 100 - x = 25$$

The grocer should use 75 pounds of peanuts and 25 pounds of walnuts.

Check. $(\$3)(75) + (\$5)(25) = \$225 + \$125 = \$350$

PROBLEM SOLVING

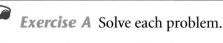

Exercise A Solve each problem.

1. Cashews cost $4 per pound and peanuts cost $2.50 per pound. If you mix 4 pounds of cashews and 4 pounds of peanuts, what is the cost of one pound of the mixture?

2. The price for one pound of a mixture of cashews and walnuts is $6.25. The total cost of the mixture is $27. What is the total number of pounds in the mixture?

3. Peanuts cost $4 per pound and walnuts cost $5.50 per pound. A 40-pound mixture sells for $184. How many pounds of each kind of nut are in the mixture?

4. Suppose you want to make a mixture of peanuts and walnuts that costs $2.70 per pound. How many pounds of peanuts at $1.50 per pound should be mixed with 24 pounds of walnuts at $3.50 per pound?

5. A grocer purchased a 100-pound mixture of nuts for $150. The mixture contains 40 pounds of walnuts that cost $2.25 per pound. What is the average cost per pound of the other nuts in the mixture?

TRY THIS Create a formula for solving mixture problems. Use *C* for total cost, *V* for value (price per pound), and *A* for amount (number of pounds).

Lesson 8 Ratio and Proportion

Ratio

A comparison of two quantities using division

Proportion

An equation made up of two equal ratios

Cross products

The result of multiplying the denominator of one fraction with the numerator of another

A **ratio** is a comparison between two like quantities or numbers. Examples of ratios include

$\frac{3}{5}$ $\frac{3\text{ ft}}{5\text{ ft}}$ $\frac{3\text{ min}}{5\text{ min}}$

In algebra, the ratio of a to b is written as $a{:}b$, or $\frac{a}{b}$.

EXAMPLE 1 An algebra class has 32 students. What is the ratio of males to females if there are 15 boys and 17 girls in the class?

The ratio of males to females is $\frac{15}{17}$.

You can also write 15:17 or 15 to 17.

Note that $15 + 17 = 32$, the total number of students.

What is the ratio of girls to boys?

$\frac{17}{15}$, 17:15, or 17 to 15.

Both ratios contain the same information, but have different values since $\frac{15}{17} \neq \frac{17}{15}$.

Two equal ratios make up a **proportion**.

For example, $\frac{2}{4} = \frac{1}{2}$ are equal ratios that form a proportion.

In any true proportion, the **cross products** of the proportion are equal to one another.

EXAMPLE 2 Is $\frac{1}{3} = \frac{3}{9}$ a proportion?

Step 1 Find the cross products of the proportion.

$\frac{1}{3} \times \frac{3}{9}$

The cross products are $1 \bullet 9 = 9$ and $3 \bullet 3 = 9$.

Step 2 Compare the cross products.

Since $1 \bullet 9 = 9$ and $3 \bullet 3 = 9$, the cross products are equal and

$\frac{1}{3} = \frac{3}{9}$ is a proportion.

To find the missing term in any proportion, set the cross products equal to each other. Then solve for the variable.

EXAMPLE 3 Find the missing term in the proportion $\frac{3}{4} = \frac{9}{x}$.

Step 1 Set the cross products equal to each other.

$$\frac{3}{4} \times \frac{9}{x} \qquad (3)(x) = (9)(4)$$

$$3x = 36$$

Step 2 Solve for x.

$$3x = 36$$

$$\frac{3x}{3} = \frac{36}{3}$$

$$x = 12$$

Step 3 $\frac{3}{4} = \frac{9}{12}$

$$3 \bullet 12 = 4 \bullet 9$$

$$36 = 36$$

PROBLEM SOLVING

Exercise A Solve each problem. Your answer will be a ratio. Write the ratio as a fraction in lowest terms.

1. In a small business, 64 of the employees are women and 40 of the employees are men. What is the ratio of
- **a.** women to men?
- **b.** men to women?
- **c.** men to the total number of employees?
- **d.** women to the total number of employees?

2. An algebra test of 50 questions included 15 questions on Chapter 4. What is the ratio of questions from Chapter 4 to the other questions on the test?

3. A rectangular garden measures 12 feet (length) by 8 feet (width). What is the ratio of
- **a.** length to width?
- **b.** width to length?
- **c.** length to area?
- **d.** width to area?

Exercise B Find the missing term in each proportion.

4. $\frac{2}{3} = \frac{n}{9}$

5. $\frac{6}{8} = \frac{y}{4}$

6. $\frac{4}{11} = \frac{20}{x}$

7. $\frac{2}{4} = \frac{n}{18}$

8. $\frac{x}{15} = \frac{3}{5}$

9. $\frac{6}{x} = \frac{48}{40}$

10. $\frac{8}{n} = \frac{5}{10}$

11. $\frac{9}{27} = \frac{y}{9}$

12. $\frac{1}{4} = \frac{x}{32}$

13. $\frac{3}{5} = \frac{24}{n}$

14. $\frac{12}{15} = \frac{x}{50}$

15. $\frac{18}{24} = \frac{30}{x}$

Application

Using Proportions

Many answers can be found by writing and solving proportions.

EXAMPLE 1 If the large gear turns 5 times, how many times will the small gear turn?

Step 1 Find how many times the small gear turns for one turn of the large gear.

$\frac{\text{Large gear}}{\text{Small gear}} = \frac{20}{12} = \frac{5}{3} = 1\frac{2}{3}$

For one turn of the large gear, the small one turns $\frac{5}{3}$ or $1\frac{2}{3}$ times.

Step 2 Write the proportion. $\frac{\text{1 turn of large gear}}{\text{5 turns of large gear}} = \frac{\frac{5}{3}\text{turns of small gear}}{x}$

Step 3 Rewrite the proportion algebraically. Then solve for x.

$\frac{1}{5} = \frac{5}{3} \div x \quad x = (5)(\frac{5}{3}) \quad x = \frac{25}{3} = 8\frac{1}{3}$

For five turns of the large gear, the small one turns $8\frac{1}{3}$ times.

Exercise Solve each problem.

1. Jody can swim 18 laps in 25 minutes. At that rate, how many laps can she swim in 125 minutes?
2. Darrell drives 147 miles in 3 hours. If he drives at the same speed, how many miles can he drive in 7 hours?
3. If 5 gallons of gasoline cost $6.60, how much do 9 gallons of gasoline cost?

The scale on a map reads 2 inches = 60 miles.

4. If two cities measure $5\frac{1}{2}$ inches apart, how far apart are they in actual miles?
5. If the actual distance between two cities is 280 miles, what is the distance on the map?

Chapter 4 REVIEW

Write the letter of the correct answer.

1. What is 30% of 150?

A 40

B 90

C 120

D 45

2. 63 is what percent of 90?

A 70%

B 63%

C 30%

D 143%

3. 135 is 30% of what number?

A 105

B 450

C 165

D 45

4. Louis drives for $5\frac{1}{2}$ hours at an average rate of 65 miles per hour. How many miles does he drive?

A $357\frac{1}{2}$ mi

B 325 mi

C 455 mi

D 330 mi

5. Peanuts cost \$2.50 per pound and walnuts cost \$5.00 per pound. If you mix 4 pounds of peanuts with 4 pounds of walnuts, what is the cost of one pound of the mixture?

A \$7.50

B \$30.00

C \$3.75

D \$15.00

6. Peanuts cost \$2 per pound and cashews cost \$4 per pound. A 50-pound mixture cost \$164. How many pounds of each kind of nut are in the mixture?

A 12 pounds of peanuts, 24 pounds of cashews

B 18 pounds of peanuts, 32 pounds of cashews

C 32 pounds of peanuts, 18 pounds of cashews

D 38 pounds of peanuts, 12 pounds of cashews

Solve each problem.

Example: The sum of two consecutive numbers is 13. What are the numbers? Solution: $n + (n + 1) = 13$ $2n = 12$ $n = 6, n + 1 = 7$

7. The sum of three consecutive integers is 114. What are the integers?

8. The sum of two consecutive odd integers is 36. What are the integers?

Solve each problem using the 1% solution method.

Example: Shari has 6 cousins who are boys. If 60 percent of her cousins are boys, how many cousins does Shari have?
Solution: 60% of cousins = 6

$$60\% \div 60 = 6 \div 60$$
$$1\% = \frac{1}{10}$$
$$1\% \bullet 100 = \frac{1}{10} \bullet 100$$
$$100\% = 10 \text{ cousins}$$

9. There are 40 oak trees in the park. If 10% of the trees in the park are oak trees, how many trees are in the park?

10. Jason wants to buy a mountain bike that costs $350. He has already saved $105. What percent of the total cost has he saved?

11. A town has a population of 4,800 people. If 25% of the population are senior citizens, how many people are senior citizens?

Solve each problem.

Example: Marisa rides her bicycle for two hours at an average rate of speed of 15 km/h. How far does she ride? Solution: $d = 15(2)$ $d = 30$

12. Bette drives at 60 miles per hour for $2\frac{1}{2}$ hours and at 75 miles per hour for $1\frac{1}{2}$ hours. What is her average rate of speed?

13. Kim has $4.75 in nickels and dimes. If she has twice as many dimes as nickels, how many of each coin does she have?

14. Find the interest earned on a deposit of \$800 at 5.5% annual interest rate for 3 years. (Hint: Use the formula $I = prt$.)

15. Chen has \$2.10 in nickels, dimes, and quarters. He has three times as many quarters as dimes and four times as many nickels as dimes. How many of each coin does Chen have?

16. Miwa borrows \$1,250 for 1 year. At the end of the year, she pays \$112.50 in interest. Find the rate of interest she was charged. (Hint: Use the formula $I = prt$.)

Find the missing term in each proportion.

Example: $\frac{1}{2} = \frac{4}{x}$ Solution: $1x = 2(4)$ $x = 8$

17. $\frac{x}{21} = \frac{5}{35}$

18. $\frac{12}{15} = \frac{x}{20}$

Solve using a proportion.

Example: If 2 gallons of milk cost \$3.50, how much would 3 gallons cost?
Solution: $\frac{3.50}{2} = \frac{x}{3}$ $3.50(3) = 2x$ $10.50 = 2x$ $\$5.25 = x$

19. A bicyclist completes a 120-mile race in 4 hours 30 minutes. What is the average speed, in miles per hour, of the bicyclist?

20. If 8 feet of fencing costs \$12.40, how much does 36 feet of fencing cost?

Test-Taking Tip

Read a problem thoroughly before you begin to solve it. After you have completed your answer, read the problem again to be sure your answer makes sense.

SOLD
FOR SALE
985-4575

Chapter

Exponents and Polynomials

Most people don't have thousands of dollars to buy expensive things like houses or cars. To buy a house, you go to a bank and apply for a loan called a mortgage. You need to borrow enough money to pay for the cost of the house. That is called the "principal." Along with the principal, you pay the bank extra money, or interest. Bankers use an algebraic formula to divide the total mortgage into monthly payments. Each month, the interest you owe decreases and the principal you're paying off increases. This kind of calculation is a polynomial. Polynomials involve doing several arithmetic functions using exponents.

In Chapter 5, you will examine exponents and polynomials.

Goals for Learning

- ◆ To recognize and use exponents in computations
- ◆ To identify the benefit of using scientific notation in some calculations
- ◆ To define, name, and solve polynomials

Lesson 1 Exponents

In Chapter 1, you learned how to multiply $(x^3)(x^4)$:

$(x^3)(x^4) = (x \cdot x \cdot x)\,(x \cdot x \cdot x \cdot x) = x^7$.

In other words, $(x^3)(x^4) = x^{3+4} = x^7$.

> **Rule** The general rule is $(x^n)(x^m) = x^{n+m}$. To multiply terms with exponents, add the exponents.

You can use what you know about exponents to find the value of $(x^2)^4$:

$(x^2)^4$ can be written as $\overbrace{(x^2)(x^2)(x^2)(x^2)}^{\text{4 times}} = x^8$.

In other words, $(x^2)^4 = x^{2 \cdot 4} = x^8$.

> **Rule** The general rule is $(x^n)^m = x^{n \cdot m}$.
> To raise a power to a power, multiply the exponents.

Suppose you need to simplify $x^7 \div x^3$.
You can rewrite the problem as

$$\frac{x^7}{x^3} = \frac{\cancel{x} \cdot \cancel{x} \cdot \cancel{x} \cdot x \cdot x \cdot x \cdot x}{\cancel{x} \cdot \cancel{x} \cdot \cancel{x}} = \frac{x \cdot x \cdot x \cdot x}{1} = x^4.$$

In other words, $\frac{x^7}{x^3} = x^{7-3} = x^4$.

> **Rule** The general rule is $x^n \div x^m = x^{n-m}$.
> To divide terms with exponents, subtract the exponents.
>
> **Important note** This is only true when $x \neq 0$. $\frac{0}{0}$ is undefined.

EXAMPLE 1 $x^5 \div x^2 = \frac{x^5}{x^2} = \frac{\cancel{x} \bullet \cancel{x} \bullet x \bullet x \bullet x}{\cancel{x} \bullet \cancel{x}} = \frac{x \bullet x \bullet x}{1} = x^3,\ x \neq 0$

EXAMPLE 2 $\frac{m^7}{m^2} = m^{7-2} = m^5,\ m \neq 0$

EXAMPLE 3 $(y^3)^2 = (y^3)(y^3) = y^{2 \bullet 3} = y^6$

Writing About Mathematics

Any number (except zero) raised to the power of zero is 1. For example, $3^0 = 1$. Tell why.

Raising a number to the zero power is a special case.

EXAMPLE 4 $\frac{32}{32} = \frac{2^5}{2^5} = 2^{5-5} = 2^0 = 1$

or $\frac{2^5}{2^5} = \frac{2 \cdot 2 \cdot 2 \cdot 2 \cdot 2}{2 \cdot 2 \cdot 2 \cdot 2 \cdot 2} = 1$

What is the value of x^0, when $x \neq 0$?

You already know that $1 = \frac{x^2}{x^2}$

and that $\frac{x^2}{x^2} = x^{2-2} = x^0$.

You can put these two statements together:

$1 = \frac{x^2}{x^2} = x^{2-2} = x^0$, so $1 = x^0$.

Rule $x^0 = 1$ when $x \neq 0$.

You can use what you know about multiplying and dividing exponents to find solutions to problems.

$(2^2)^2 = 2^{2 \cdot 2} = 2^4 = 2 \cdot 2 \cdot 2 \cdot 2 = 16$

Exercise A Show why these statements are true.

1. $(3^2)^3 = 729$

2. $(2^2)^5 = 1{,}024$

3. $(x^3)^4 = x^{12}$

4. $(y^5)^3 = y^{15}$

5. $(m^4)^4 = m^{16}$

6. $[(x + y)^2]^3 = (x + y)^6$

7. $[(2x + 3y)^4]^2 = (2x + 3y)^8$

Exercise B Simplify each expression.

8. $(3^5) \div (3^3)$

9. $\frac{4^4}{4^3}$

10. $\frac{x^5}{x^4}, x \neq 0$

11. $y^5 \div y^3, y \neq 0$

12. $\frac{m^7}{m^3}, m \neq 0$

13. $(x + y)^5 \div (x + y)^2, (x + y) \neq 0$

14. $\frac{(2p + 3q)^6}{(2p + 3q)^2}, (2p + 3q) \neq 0$

Exercise C Show two ways to simplify each expression.

15. $(3^5) \div (3^5)$

16. $\frac{2^{10}}{2^{10}}$

17. $\frac{x^7}{x^7}, x \neq 0$

18. $(4x + 2y)5 \div (4x + 2y)^5, (4x + 2y) \neq 0$

19. $\frac{(p + q)^3}{(p + q)^3}, (p + q) \neq 0$

20. $\frac{p^4}{p^4}, p \neq 0$

Lesson 2 Negative Exponents

Negative exponent

For any nonzero integers a and n,

$a^{-n} = \frac{1}{a^n}$

The number patterns below show how to use **negative exponents** to show numbers less than 1.

$10^3 = 1{,}000$ ÷ 10 gives
$10^2 = 100$ ÷ 10 gives
$10^1 = 10$ ÷ 10 gives
$10^0 = 1$ ÷ 10 gives
$10^{-1} = \frac{1}{10} = \frac{1}{10^1}$ ÷ 10 gives
$10^{-2} = \frac{1}{100} = \frac{1}{10^2}$ ÷ 10 gives
$10^{-3} = \frac{1}{1{,}000} = \frac{1}{10^3}$

and so on

$2^3 = 8$ ÷ 2 gives
$2^2 = 4$ ÷ 2 gives
$2^1 = 2$ ÷ 2 gives
$2^0 = 1$ ÷ 2 gives
$2^{-1} = \frac{1}{2} = \frac{1}{2^1}$ ÷ 2 gives
$2^{-2} = \frac{1}{4} = \frac{1}{2^2}$ ÷ 2 gives
$2^{-3} = \frac{1}{8} = \frac{1}{2^3}$

and so on

Rewrite $\frac{1}{10^4}$ with a negative exponent: $\frac{1}{10^4} = 10^{-4}$

Rewrite $\frac{1}{(x+y)^5}$ with a negative exponent, $(x + y) \neq 0$:

$$\frac{1}{(x+y)^5} = (x+y)^{-5}$$

You can also use the rule for exponents in division to find negative exponents. Remember $3^0 = 1$.

$$\frac{1}{3^2} = \frac{3^0}{3^2} = 3^{0-2} = 3^{-2}$$

$$\frac{1}{x^3} = \frac{x^0}{x^3} = x^{0-3} = x^{-3}$$

Writing About Mathematics

Explain why $\frac{1}{3^2}$ can be rewritten as 3^{-2}.

EXAMPLE 1

$$\frac{x^5}{x^7} = \frac{\cancel{x} \cdot \cancel{x} \cdot \cancel{x} \cdot \cancel{x} \cdot \cancel{x}}{\cancel{x} \cdot \cancel{x} \cdot \cancel{x} \cdot \cancel{x} \cdot \cancel{x} \cdot x \cdot x} = \frac{1}{x^2} = x^{-2}$$

or

$$\frac{x^5}{x^7} = x^{5-7} = x^{-2}$$

EXAMPLE 2

$$\frac{(2x + 3y)^8}{(2x + 3y)^{11}} = (2x + 3y)^{8-11} = (2x + 3y)^{-3}$$

EXAMPLE 3 Write $(2x + 3y)^{-3}$ with a positive exponent:

$$(2x + 3y)^{-3} = (2x + 3y)^{-3} \bullet 1 = (2x + 3y)^{-3} \bullet \frac{(2x + 3y)^3}{(2x + 3y)^3}$$

$$= \frac{(2x + 3y)^{-3} \bullet (2x + 3y)^3}{(2x + 3y)^3} = \frac{(2x + 3y)^{-3+3}}{(2x + 3y)^3}$$

$$= \frac{(2x + 3y)^0}{(2x + 3y)^3} = \frac{1}{(2x + 3y)^3}$$

Exercise A Rewrite using a negative exponent.

1. $\frac{4^5}{4^9}$

2. $\frac{1}{5^3}$

3. $\frac{1}{10^5}$

4. $2^5 \div 2^{10}$

5. $10^{10} \div 10^{20}$

6. $\frac{1}{10^{23}}$

7. $\frac{1}{15^2}$

8. $14^3 \div 14^5$

9. $\frac{203^3}{203^7}$

10. $5{,}280^2 \div 5{,}280^3$

Exercise B Rewrite using a negative exponent.

11. $\frac{x^5}{x^7}, x \neq 0$

12. $\frac{1}{m^3}, m \neq 0$

13. $\frac{1}{(x+2y)^4}, (x + 2y) \neq 0$

14. $(x+3y)^3 \div (x+3y)^5,$
$(x + 3y) \neq 0$

15. $\frac{(x+y)^3}{(x+y)^6}, (x + y) \neq 0$

16. $(2x + 3y)^2 \div (2x + 3y)^8,$
$(2x + 3y) \neq 0$

17. $(-3m-9)^3 \div (-3m - 9)^6,$
$(-3m-9) \neq 0$

18. $\frac{x^3}{x^7}, x \neq 0$

Exercise C Rewrite using a positive exponent.

19. 3^{-2}

20. 10^{-2}

21. 10^{-23}

22. x^{-4}

23. $2y^{-6}$

24. $(4p + 3q)^{-3}$

25. 4^{-2}

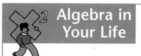

Algebra in Your Life

On Opposite Ends of the Ruler
Particle physicists are scientists who study things smaller than atoms—particles measuring as small as 10^{-16} meters! They have found quarks and leptons, and they suspect even smaller particles exist. Astrophysicists study things in the largest scale you can imagine—the universe. They have found that less than 10 percent of the mass of the universe consists of the kind of matter we can see. The last century revealed much about our universe. Just imagine what this one will bring!

Lesson 3 Exponents and Scientific Notation

Scientific notation

A number written as the product of a number between 1 and 10 and a power of ten.

Any number in scientific notation $= (1 \leq x < 10)(10^n)$

Scientists and researchers often need to record and work with very large or very small numbers. To make writing these numbers easier, they have developed a way of writing these numbers called **scientific notation.**

EXAMPLE 1 Write 394.74 in scientific notation.

$394.74 = 3.9474(10^2)$

Step 1 Move the decimal point so the number is between 1 and 10.

394.74

Step 2 Write the new number and then count the number of places the decimal point moved. In this example, the decimal point moved *2* places to the *left.*

3.9474

Step 3 Multiply the number from Step 2 times 10 raised to the number of places the decimal point moved.

$3.9474(10^2)$

Use a positive exponent if the decimal point moved to the left.

Use a negative exponent if the decimal point moved to the right.

EXAMPLE 2 Write 0.0003947 in scientific notation.

Step 1 Move the decimal point so the number is between 1 and 10.

0.0003947

Step 2 Write the new number, and then count the number of places the decimal point moved. In this example, the decimal point moved *4* places to the *right.*

3.947

Step 3 Multiply the number from Step 2 times 10 raised to the number of places the decimal point moved.

$3.947 \bullet 10^{-4}$

Writing About Mathematics

Find a use of scientific notation in a science book or an encyclopedia. Write a sentence about what you found and share your findings with other students.

Exercise A Write each number in scientific notation.

1. 186,000

2. 0.00563

3. 276,000,000,000

4. 0.0156

5. 1,342.54

6. 0.002010

7. 0.0000000001

8. 1,000,000,000

9. 935,420,000

10. 0.00000305

Exercise B Rewrite these numbers so they are no longer in scientific notation.

11. $3.28 \cdot 10^{-3}$

12. $5.42 \cdot 10^{6}$

13. $1.86(10^{2})$

14. $2.71(10^{-8})$

15. $5.280(10^{3})$

16. $5.42 \cdot 10^{-6}$

17. $1.6 \cdot 10^{-27}$

18. $1.1122(10^{-4})$

19. $1.1122(10^{4})$

20. $3.1 \cdot 10^{-4}$

Calculator Practice

You can use a calculator to translate numbers into scientific notation. Some calculators have a *function* or *mode* that will translate the number immediately.

EXAMPLE 3 Translate 250 into scientific notation.

Select scientific mode

Enter number 250

Press [×] Enter 1

Press [=]

Read 2.5000 02

Read the display as $2.5(10^{2})$

Some calculators translate numbers using these steps:

Enter 250

Press [×] 1 [EE] [=]

Read 2.5000 02

Exercise C Use a calculator to check your answers in Exercise A.

Lesson 4 Computing in Scientific Notation

Scientific notation is useful for multiplying or dividing very large or very small numbers.

EXAMPLE 1 Find $(13{,}000{,}000)^2$.

Step 1 Write the number in scientific notation.

$13{,}000{,}000 = 1.3 \bullet 10^7$

$(13{,}000{,}000)^2 = (1.3 \bullet 10^7)^2$

Step 2 Change the order of the factors to make the multiplication easier.

$(1.3 \bullet 10^7)^2 = (1.3 \bullet 10^7)(1.3 \bullet 10^7)$

$= 1.3 \bullet 1.3 \bullet 10^7 \bullet 10^7$

$= (1.3)^2(10^7)^2$

Step 3 Complete the multiplication, using the rule for raising exponents to a power.

$(1.69)(10^{7 \bullet 2}) = (1.69)(10^{14})$

Step 4 Check that the product is written in scientific notation.

The answer is $1.69(10^{14})$.

EXAMPLE 2 Find the product of $0.0000006 \bullet 32{,}000{,}000 \bullet 0.0043$.

Step 1 Write each number in scientific notation.

$(6.0 \bullet 10^{-7})(3.2 \bullet 10^7)(4.3 \bullet 10^{-3})$

Step 2 Use the commutative property to change the order of the factors.

$(6.0 \bullet 3.2 \bullet 4.3)(10^{-7} \bullet 10^7 \bullet 10^{-3})$

Step 3 Complete the multiplication, using the rule for multiplying with exponents.

$(82.56)(10^{-7+7-3}) = (82.56)(10^{-3})$

Step 4 Write the product in scientific notation.

$(8.256)(10)(10^{-3}) = 8.256(10^{-2})$

EXAMPLE 3 Find the quotient of 9,250,000 ÷ 25,000.

Step 1 Write each number in scientific notation.

$9.25 \bullet 10^6 \div 2.5 \bullet 10^4$

Step 2 Rewrite the division as a fraction.

$\frac{9.25 \bullet 10^6}{2.5 \bullet 10^4} = \frac{9.25}{2.5} \bullet \frac{10^6}{10^4} = (9.25 \div 2.5)(10^6 \div 10^4)$

Step 3 Complete the division, using the rule for dividing with exponents.

$(3.7)(10^{6-4}) = (3.7)(10^2)$

Step 4 Check that the product is written in scientific notation.

The answer is $3.7(10^2)$.

Exercise A Find the products. Write your answer in scientific notation.

1. $1.4(10^3) \bullet 6.3(10^{-4})$
2. $8.1(10^{14}) \bullet 9.0(10^{-6})$
3. $(4.01 \bullet 10^2)^3$
4. $(3.4 \bullet 10^2)(1.3 \bullet 10^5)(2.54 \bullet 10^{-6})$
5. $52{,}000{,}000 \bullet 706{,}000$
6. $(11{,}000{,}000)^2$
7. $(0.00008) \bullet (640{,}000{,}000)$
8. $(350{,}000) \bullet (1{,}200) \bullet (16{,}000{,}000)$
9. $(0.00645) \bullet (0.00004302 \bullet (0.000000035)$
10. $[(2000)^3 \bullet (50{,}000)^2]^2$

Exercise B Find each quotient. Write your answer in scientific notation.

11. $(6.8 \cdot 10^2) \div (3.4 \cdot 10^6)$

12. $(7.62 \cdot 10^{-2}) \div (2.54 \cdot 10^6)$

13. $1.6(10^6) \div 4.0(10^{-2})$

14. $4.1(10^9) \div 8.2(10^{-2})$

15. $545{,}000{,}000 \div 100{,}000$

16. $350{,}000 \div 1{,}400{,}000$

17. $\frac{0.00008}{640{,}000{,}000}$

18. $\frac{1{,}200}{240{,}000{,}000}$

19. $\frac{0.000645}{0.005}$

20. $\frac{50{,}000^2}{0.00001}$

Exercise C Use a calculator with a scientific mode to check your answers to Exercises A and B.

Technology Connection

Smashing Atoms

Scientists use accelerators—atom smashers—to release the parts of atoms called quarks and leptons. One accelerator in the United States uses 1,000 superconducting magnets. Each magnet weighs about 20 tons. The magnets steer bunches of protons—parts of atoms—around the accelerator, or ring, as the scientists call it. Each bunch contains more than one trillion protons. No wonder scientific notation was invented! How else could scientists work with such huge numbers?

Lesson 5 Defining and Naming Polynomials

Polynomial

An algebraic expression made up of one term or the sum or difference of two or more terms in the same variable

Monomial

A term that is a number, a variable, or the product of a number and one or more variables

Degree of a polynomial

Greatest power of the variable

You have already worked with algebraic expressions such as $3a - b + 5 - 2a$. In this lesson, you will be introduced to algebraic expressions known as **polynomials.**

EXAMPLE 1 These expressions are polynomials in one variable.

Polynomial	Number of Terms	Name of Polynomial
$3x^2$	one term	***mono**mial*
$3x^2 + x$	two terms	*bi*nomial
$3x^2 + x + 1$	three terms	*tri*nomial
$x^3 + 2x^2 - x + 5$	many terms	*poly*nomial

Some algebraic expressions are *not* polynomials.

$x^{-4} + x^2 + 3$	has a negative exponent
$\frac{1}{x^2 + 3}$	is not a sum or difference
$\frac{5}{x^{-3}}$	is not a sum, has a negative exponent
$2y^3 + x^2 + x + 1$	has more than one variable
$\frac{3}{x^2}$	has a variable in the denominator

Polynomials can be named by their terms.

EXAMPLE 2
binomial (or polynomial) in x $\quad x^2 + 1$
trinomial (or polynomial) in x $\quad x^2 + x + 1$
trinomial (or polynomial) in y $\quad y^2 + y + 1$
polynomial in z $\quad 2z^3 + z^2 + z + 1$

The greatest power of the variable is called the **degree of a polynomial.**

EXAMPLE 3
6 degree 0 (The degree of a constant is 0.)
$x - 3$ degree 1
$x^2 + x + 1$ degree 2
$x^3 + 4x^2 + 1$ degree 3

Standard form

Arrangement of variables from left to right, from greatest to least degree of power

The terms in a polynomial can be arranged in any order. However, in **standard form,** they are arranged left to right, from greatest to least degree of power. Always place the terms in standard form before using a polynomial in a computation.

EXAMPLE 4 $x^5 - x^3 + 7x$

Exercise A Name each expression by the number of its terms. Use monomial, binomial, trinomial, and polynomial.

1. $y^2 + 1$

2. $n^2 + n + 1$

3. $5x^2 + 2x - 4$

4. $5z^4 + z^3 + z + 1$

5. $2p^3 + p^2 + p - \frac{1}{3}$

6. $2x^5 + x^3 + x + 23$

7. $7y^4 + 4y + 8$

8. $7a^3 + a^2$

9. $b^7 + b^6 + b^5 + b^4 + b^3 + b^2 + b$

10. b^{10}

Exercise B Give the degree of each polynomial.

11. $3n^2 + 2n + 1$

12. $3w^2 + 2w + w - 31$

13. $5x^4 + 2x^3 + 54$

14. $5a^5 + a^3 + a + 1$

15. $2s^3 + s^2 + s - \frac{1}{2}$

16. $2x^5 + x^4 + x^3 + x + 23$

17. $z^7 + 5z^4 + z^3 + z + 432$

18. $7b^4 + 7b^3 + 4b^2 + 8$

19. $a^3 + a^2 + a$

20. $b^7 + 2b^6 + 3b^5 + 4b^4 + 5b^3 + 6b^2 + 7b$

Exercise C Write one polynomial for each description.

21. a trinomial in *x*, degree 3

22. a polynomial in *y*, degree 4

23. a binomial in *b*, degree 5

24. a polynomial in *z*, degree 3

25. a monomial in *r*, degree *n*

Exercise D Tell why these expressions are not polynomials.

26. $3n^{-2} + 2n + 23$

27. $3w^2 \div 2w$

28. $5x^4 + \frac{1}{3x^3}$

29. $\frac{5}{x^n}$

30. $x^3 + 5y^2 + x - 5$

Lesson 6 Adding and Subtracting Polynomials

You can find the sum of two or more polynomials by adding like terms.

EXAMPLE 1 Add $(5x^4 + x^3 - 2x^2 + 7x - 5)$ and $(-2x^3 + x^2 - 5x + 3)$.

Step 1 Rewrite the expression and line up like terms.

$$\begin{array}{rrrrrrrrr} & 5x^4 & + & x^3 & - & 2x^2 & + & 7x & - & 5 \\ + & & - & 2x^3 & + & x^2 & - & 5x & + & 3 \\ \hline \end{array}$$

Step 2 Add like terms.

$$\begin{array}{rrrrrrrrrr} & 5x^4 & + & x^3 & - & 2x^2 & + & 7x & - & 5 \\ + & & - & 2x^3 & + & x^2 & - & 5x & + & 3 \\ \hline & 5x^4 & - & x^3 & - & x^2 & + & 2x & - & 2 \end{array}$$

You can find the difference of two or more polynomials by subtracting like terms.

EXAMPLE 2 Subtract $(-2x^3 + x^2 - 5x + 3)$ from $(5x^4 + x^3 - 2x^2 + 7x - 5)$.

Step 1 Remember that to subtract, you add the opposite.

$-(-2x^3 + x^2 - 5x + 3)$ is equal to

$(-1)(-2x^3 + x^2 - 5x + 3) = 2x^3 - x^2 + 5x - 3$

Step 2 Rewrite the expression and line up like terms.

$$\begin{array}{rrrrrrrrrr} & 5x^4 & + & x^3 & - & 2x^2 & + & 7x & - & 5 \\ + & & & 2x^3 & - & x^2 & + & 5x & - & 3 \\ \hline \end{array}$$

Step 3 Add like terms.

$$\begin{array}{rrrrrrrrrr} & 5x^4 & + & x^3 & - & 2x^2 & + & 7x & - & 5 \\ + & & & 2x^3 & - & x^2 & + & 5x & - & 3 \\ \hline & 5x^4 & + & 3x^3 & - & 3x^2 & + & 12x & - & 8 \end{array}$$

Exercise A Find each sum.

1. $(2y^5 + y^3 + 7y + 33)$ and $(4y^6 + y^3 - 4y^2 - 7y - 5)$
2. $(2x^4 - 4x^3 - 15x^2 + 21x + 4)$ and $(4x^4 + 2x^3 + 17)$
3. $(b^4 + b^3 - 2b^2 + 7b - 5)$ and $(-3b^4 - b^3 - 2b^2 - 2b)$
4. $(m^4 + m^2 - 5)$ and $(m^3 + m + 5)$
5. $(4x^4 + 7x^3 + 15x^2 + 4)$ and $(4x^3 + 2x^2 + 17x)$
6. $(2b^5 + 3b^4 - 4b^3 + 7b^2)$ and $(-2b - 12)$
7. $(-4x^7 - 6x^5 - 7x^3 - 9x - 2) + (-x^7 + 6x^6 + 2x^2 + 8)$
8. $(5m^4 + 2m^2 - 5m)$ and $(5m^3 + 2m + 10)$
9. $(x^7 + x^5 - 3x^3) + (x^7 - 6x^6 + 8x - 2) + (-2x^2 + 8x - 14)$
10. $(7y^5 + 8y^2 + 3) + (7y^5 + y^3) + (-4y^2 - y - 3)$

Exercise B Find each difference. Remember to add the opposite.

11. $(2y^5 + y^3 + 7y + 33) - (4y^6 + y^3 - 4y^2 - 7y - 5)$
12. $(2x^4 - 4x^3 - 15x^2 + 21x + 4) - (4x^4 + 2x^3 + 17)$
13. $(b^4 + b^3 - 2b^2 + 7b - 5) - (-3b^4 - b^3 - 2b^2 - 2b)$
14. $(m^4 + m^2 - 5) - (m^3 + m - 5)$
15. $(x^7 + x^5 - 3x^3 + 8x - 2) - (x^7 - 6x^6 - 3x^3 + 8x - 14)$
16. Subtract $(7y^5 + y^3 - 4y^2 - y - 3)$ from $(7y^5 + 8y^2 + 3)$
17. Subtract $(4x^3 + 2x^2 + 17x)$ from $(4x^4 + 7x^3 + 15x^2 + 4)$
18. Subtract $(-2b - 12)$ from $(2b^5 + 3b^4 - 4b^3 + 7b^2)$

PROBLEM SOLVING

Exercise C Follow the directions.

19. Franco is remodeling his kitchen. He is going to put baseboards around the perimeter of the room. Write an expression that shows the perimeter of Franco's kitchen.

20. For an art project, Clarissa is decorating the lid of a box shaped like a triangle. She is gluing lace to the perimeter of the triangle-shaped lid. She wants to know what the perimeter of the lid is so that she can cut the right amount of lace. Write an expression to help her find the perimeter of the lid.

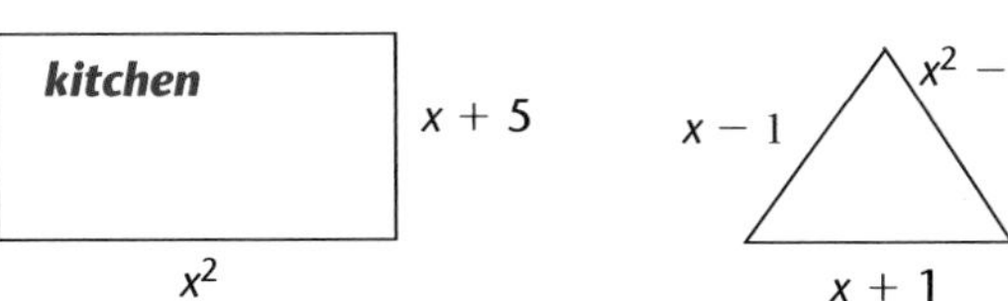

Lesson 7 Multiplying Polynomials

You can use the distributive property to multiply monomials and polynomials.

EXAMPLE 1

$x^2(2x^2 + 1) = (x^2 \bullet 2x^2) + x^2 = 2x^4 + x^2$

EXAMPLE 2

$x^2(3x^3 + x + 1) = (x^2 \bullet 3x^3) + (x^2 \bullet x) + x^2 = 3x^5 + x^3 + x^2$

EXAMPLE 3

$x^2(4x^5 + x^3 - 2x^2 + x - 5) =$

$(x^2 \bullet 4x^5) + (x^2 \bullet x^3) - (x^2 \bullet 2x^2) + (x^2 \bullet x) - 5x^2 =$

$4x^7 + x^5 - 2x^4 + x^3 - 5x^2$

Suppose you must simplify the following expression: $3(a + b) + 2(a + b)$. You can use the distributive property and simplify this sum in two ways. **Hint:** Think of $(a + b)$ as a single variable as in $3x + 2x = 5x$.

$3(a + b) + 2(a + b)$	$=$	$(3 + 2)(a + b)$
$3a + 3b + 2a + 2b$		$5(a + b)$
$5a + 5b$		$5a + 5b$

You can use the distributive property to multiply two binomials.

EXAMPLE 4 Find the product of $(x + 1)(x - 4)$.

$$(x + 1)(x - 4) = x(x - 4) + (1)(x - 4)$$
$$= (x^2 - 4x) + (x - 4)$$
$$= x^2 - 3x - 4$$

EXAMPLE 5 Find the product of $(x - 1)(x - 4)$.

$$(x - 1)(x - 4) = x(x - 4) - (1)(x - 4)$$
$$= (x^2 - 4x) - (x + 4)$$
$$= x^2 - 5x + 4$$

TRY THIS

Explain in words or draw a diagram showing how you would multiply $(a+b+c)(x+y+z)$.

You can use the distributive property to find the product of a binomial and a trinomial.

EXAMPLE 6 Find the product of $(x + 4)(x^2 + 3x + 1)$.

$$\begin{aligned}(x + 4)(x^2 + 3x + 1) &= x(x^2 + 3x + 1) + (4)(x^2 + 3x + 1)\\ &= (x^3 + 3x^2 + x) + (4x^2 + 12x + 4)\\ &= x^3 + 7x^2 + 13x + 4\end{aligned}$$

Exercise A Find each product.

1. $(x + 2)(8x - 2)$
2. $(-8y^2 + 3)(-4y - 3)$
3. $(b^4 + b^3)^2$
4. $(m^4 + 5)(m^3 + m^2 + 1)$
5. $(15x^2 + 4)(4x^3 - 17x)$
6. $(2y + 3)(4y^3 - 7y - 2)$
7. $(2x^4 - x)(x^2 + 2x + 1)$
8. $(-9x - 2)(-x^6 + 2x^2 + 8)$
9. $(5m^4 + 2m^2 - 5m)(2m + 10)$
10. $(-2b - 12)(2b^5 + 3b^4 - 4b^3 + 7b^2)$

PROBLEM SOLVING

Exercise B Write a polynomial for each problem.

11. Ellie and Terrell are carpeting their square living room. They need to know the area of the room to buy the carpeting. What is the area of the room with each side measuring $a + 2b$?

$a + 2b$

12. Before the carpeting is put down in the living room, Ellie is going to paint the baseboards. She needs to know the perimeter of the room to help her estimate how much paint she will need. What is the perimeter of the room?

13. Ellie and Terrell are also putting new carpeting in their family room, which is a rectangle having length $= x + 3$ and width $= x + 1$. What is the area of the family room?

$x + 3$

$x + 1$

14. If their family room had a length twice that of its actual length, what would the area of the room be?

15. The kitchen has a width that is three times the width of the family room but the same length. What is the area of the kitchen?

Lesson 8 Special Polynomial Products

The products of some polynomials form a pattern.

EXAMPLE 1 Find $(a + b)^2$.

$$(a + b)^2 = (a + b)(a + b) = a(a + b) + b(a + b)$$
$$a^2 + ab + ba + b^2$$
$$a^2 + ab + ab + b^2$$
$$(a + b)^2 = a^2 + 2ab + b^2$$

EXAMPLE 2 Find $(a - b)^2$.

$$(a - b)^2 = (a - b)(a - b) = a(a - b) - b(a - b)$$
$$a^2 - ab - ba + b^2$$
$$a^2 - ab - ab + b^2$$
$$(a - b)^2 = a^2 - 2ab + b^2$$

EXAMPLE 3 Find $(a + b)(a - b)$.

$$(a + b)(a - b) = a(a - b) + b(a - b)$$
$$a^2 - ab + ba - b^2$$
$$a^2 - ab + ab - b^2$$
$$(a + b)(a - b) = a^2 - b^2$$

EXAMPLE 4 Find $(a + b)^3$.

$$(a + b)^3 = (a + b)(a + b)(a + b)$$
$$(a + b)[(a + b)(a + b)]$$
$$(a + b)(a^2 + 2ab + b^2)$$
$$a^3 + 2a^2b + ab^2 + a^2b + 2ab^2 + b^3$$
$$(a + b)^3 = a^3 + 3a^2b + 3ab^2 + b^3$$

What polynomial represents $(a + b)^4$?

Exercise A Find each product. Compare your solutions with the patterns on page 138.

1. $(x + y)^2$
2. $(p - q)^2$
3. $(m - n)(m + n)$
4. $(x + y)^3$
5. $(x + 2)^2$
6. $(y + 3)^3$
7. $(z - 3)(z + 3)$
8. $(m - 4)^2$
9. $(x + 5)(x - 5)$
10. $(n + 2)^3$
11. $(x + 3)^2$

PROBLEM SOLVING

Exercise B Find the product for each problem.

12. Tanyika is going to buy potting soil for a flowerpot shaped like a cube. Knowing the volume of the flowerpot will help Tanyika choose the size of package of dirt to buy. The flowerpot has a side length of $z + 4$. What is its volume?

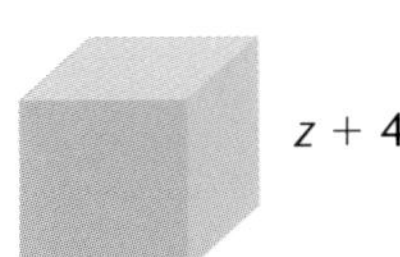

13. Maura's flower box has a length of $x + 3$, a width of $x + 1$, and a height of $x + 2$. What is its volume?

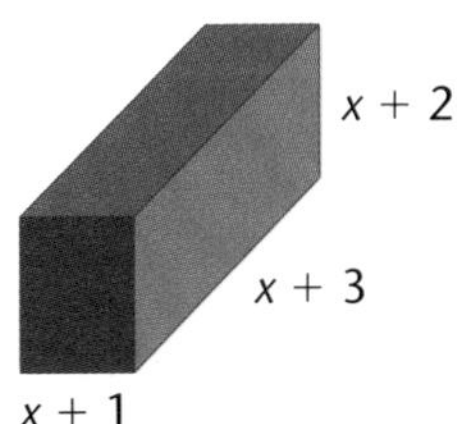

14. Maura also wants to line the bottom of her flower box with plastic sheeting. She needs to determine the area of the box bottom to know how much sheeting she will need. What is the area?

15. Aaron is packing groceries in a rectangular grocery bag. He wants to know the volume of the bag. The bag's dimensions are $m - n$, $m - n$, and $m + n$. What is its volume?

Lesson 9 Dividing a Polynomial by a Monomial

The distributive property can be used to divide a polynomial by a monomial.

EXAMPLE 1 Find the quotient of $(12x^4 - 8x^3 + 4x^2) \div 4$.

Step 1 Rewrite the problem.

$$\frac{12x^4 - 8x^3 + 4x^2}{4} \qquad \frac{\text{(dividend)}}{\text{(divisor)}}$$

Step 2 Divide each term of the numerator by the term in the denominator.

$$\frac{12x^4}{4} - \frac{8x^3}{4} + \frac{4x^2}{4} = \frac{12}{4}x^4 - \frac{8}{4}x^3 + \frac{4}{4}x^2 = 3x^4 - 2x^3 + x^2$$

Step 3 Check the answer. In this example, because there is no remainder (or a remainder of 0), you can check the answer by multiplying:

$$\text{(quotient)} \bullet \text{(divisor)} = \text{(dividend)}$$

$$(3x^4 - 2x^3 + x^2) \bullet (4) = 12x^4 - 8x^3 + 4x^2$$

EXAMPLE 2 Find the quotient of $(3x^3 - 5x^2 + 4x) \div x$.

Step 1 Rewrite the problem.

$$\frac{3x^3 - 5x^2 + 4x}{x} \qquad \frac{\text{(dividend)}}{\text{(divisor)}}$$

Step 2 Divide each term of the numerator by the term in the denominator.

$$\frac{3x^3}{x} - \frac{5x^2}{x} + \frac{4x}{x} = 3x^{3-1} - 5x^{2-1} + 4x^{1-1}$$

$$= 3x^2 - 5x + 4$$

Step 3 Check the answer by multiplying.

$$\text{(quotient)} \bullet \text{(divisor)} = \text{(dividend)}$$

$$(3x^2 - 5x + 4) \bullet (x) = 3x^3 - 5x^2 + 4x$$

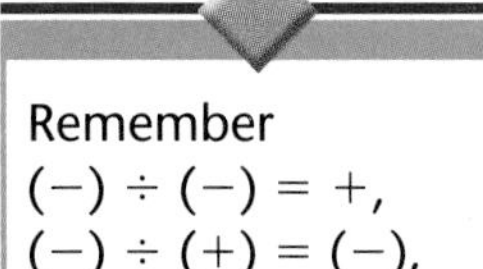

Remember
$(-) \div (-) = +$,
$(-) \div (+) = (-)$,
and $(+) \div (-) = (-)$.

Be sure to watch for + and – signs when dividing polynomials.

EXAMPLE 3 $\frac{-3y^4}{-y^2} = 3y^2$; check: $(3y^2)(-y^2) = -3y^4$

while $\frac{-3y^4}{y^2} = -3y^2$; check: $(-3y^2)(y^2) = -3y^4$

and $\frac{3y^4}{-y^2} = -3y^2$; check: $(-3y^2)(-y^2) = 3y^4$

Exercise A Find each quotient. Check your work using multiplication.

1. $\frac{(16x^2 + 4)}{4}$

2. $\frac{(9y^3 + 6y - 3)}{3}$

3. $\frac{(-32x^3 + 24x^2 - 16x + 8)}{8}$

4. $\frac{(-32a^3 + 24a^2 - 16a + 8)}{-4}$

5. $(7m^2 - 7m + 7) \div 7$

6. $(-18p^3 + 36p^2 + 9p) \div 9$

Exercise B Find each quotient. Check your work using multiplication.

7. $\frac{(26x^3 + 4x^2)}{x}$

8. $\frac{(-21y^9 - 6y^4 - 21y}{y}$

9. $\frac{(23x^6 - 41m^4 + 31x^2)}{x^2}$

10. $(-5m^7 - 7m^2 + 7m) \div m$

11. $(-25x^6 + 14x^2 + 9x) \div -x$

12. $\frac{(-32a^3 + 24a^2 - 16a)}{-4a}$

Exercise C Find each quotient. Check your work using multiplication.

13. $\frac{(15y^5 + y^4 + 5y^3 - 17y^2 + y)}{y}$

14. $\frac{(x^6 + 6x^5 - 15x^4 + 20x^3 - 15x^2)}{x^2}$

15. $\frac{(a^7 - 12a^6 - 18a^5 - 20a^3)}{-a^3}$

Lesson 10 Dividing a Polynomial by a Binomial

Dividing a polynomial by a binomial is similar to the long division you learned in arithmetic. As in arithmetic, division can result in a quotient and no remainder or a quotient and a remainder that is not zero.

Case I   Remainder = 0

Example 1 Find the quotient of 345 ÷ 15.

Step 1 Divide 15 into 34.

$$15\overline{)345}\text{ quotient } 2 \qquad 15\overline{)34}\text{ quotient } 2$$

Step 2 Multiply and subtract product.

$$\begin{array}{r} 2 \\ 15\overline{)345} \\ -\underline{30} \\ 4 \end{array} \qquad (2)(15) = 30 \qquad 34 - 30 = 4$$

Step 3 Bring down 5 and divide 15 into 45.

$$\begin{array}{r} 23 \\ 15\overline{)345} \\ -\underline{30} \\ 45 \end{array} \qquad 15\overline{)45}\text{ quotient } 3$$

Step 4 Multiply and subtract product.

$$\begin{array}{r} 23 \\ 15\overline{)345} \\ -\underline{30} \\ 45 \\ -\underline{45} \\ 0 \end{array} \qquad (3)(15) = 45 \qquad 45 - 45 = 0$$

Step 5 Check by multiplication.

(23)(15) = 345

Example 2 Find the quotient of $(x^2 - x - 6) \div (x + 2)$.

Step 1 Divide x into x^2.

$$x + 2\overline{)x^2 - x - 6}\text{ quotient } x \qquad x\overline{)x^2}\text{ quotient } x$$

Step 2 Multiply and subtract product.

$$\begin{array}{r} x \\ x + 2\overline{)x^2 - x - 6} \\ \underline{-(x^2 + 2x)} \\ -3x \end{array} \qquad (x)(x + 2) = x^2 + 2x \qquad \begin{array}{r} x^2 - x \\ \underline{-x^2 - 2x} \\ 0 - 3x \end{array}$$

Step 3 Bring down − 6 and divide x into − 3x.

$$\begin{array}{r} x - 3 \\ x + 2\overline{)x^2 - x - 6} \\ \underline{-(x^2 + 2x)} \\ -3x - 6 \end{array} \qquad x\overline{)-3x}\text{ quotient } -3$$

Step 4 Multiply and subtract product.

$$\begin{array}{r} x - 3 \\ x + 2\overline{)x^2 - x - 6} \\ \underline{-(x^2 + 2x)} \\ -3x - 6 \\ \underline{-(-3x - 6)} \\ 0 \end{array} \qquad (-3)(x+2) = -3x-6$$

Step 5 Check by multiplication.

$(x - 3)(x + 2) = x^2 - x - 6$

Case II Remainder $\neq 0$

EXAMPLE 3 Find the quotient of $346 \div 15$.

Step 1 Divide 15 into 34.

$$15\overline{)346} \quad 2 \qquad 15\overline{)34} \quad 2$$

Step 2 Multiply and subtract product.

$$\begin{array}{r} 2 \\ 15\overline{)346} \\ -\underline{30} \\ 4 \end{array} \qquad \begin{array}{l} (2)(15) = 30 \\ 34 - 30 = 4 \end{array}$$

Step 3 Bring down 6 and divide 15 into 46.

$$\begin{array}{r} 23 \\ 15\overline{)346} \\ -\underline{30} \\ 46 \end{array} \qquad \begin{array}{r} 3 \\ 15\overline{)46} \end{array}$$

Step 4 Multiply and subtract product.

$$\begin{array}{r} 23 \\ 15\overline{)346} \\ -\underline{30} \\ 46 \\ -\underline{45} \\ 1 \text{ remainder} \end{array} \qquad \begin{array}{l} (3)(15) = 45 \\ 46 - 45 = 1 \end{array}$$

Step 5 Check by multiplication.

$(23)(15) + 1 = 346$

EXAMPLE 4 Find the quotient of $(x^2 - x - 7) \div (x + 2)$.

Step 1 Divide x into x^2.

$$(x + 2)\overline{)x^2 - x - 7} \quad x \qquad x\overline{)x^2} \quad x$$

Step 2 Multiply and subtract product.

$$\begin{array}{r} x \\ x + 2\overline{)x^2 - x - 7} \\ \underline{-(x^2 + 2x)} \\ -3x \end{array} \qquad \begin{array}{r} (x)(x + 2) = x^2 + 2x \\ x^2 - x \\ \underline{-x^2 - 2x} \\ 0 - 3x \end{array}$$

Step 3 Bring down -7 and divide x into $-3x$.

$$\begin{array}{r} x - 3 \\ x + 2\overline{)x^2 - x - 7} \\ \underline{-(x^2 + 2x)} \\ -3x - 7 \end{array} \qquad \begin{array}{r} -3 \\ x\overline{)-3x} \end{array}$$

Step 4 Multiply and subtract product.

$$\begin{array}{r} x - 3 \\ x + 2\overline{)x^2 - x - 7} \\ \underline{-(x^2 + 2x)} \\ -3x - 7 \\ \underline{-(-3x - 6)} \\ 0 - 1 \text{ remainder} \end{array} \qquad (-3)(x+2) = -3x-6$$

Step 5 Check by multiplication.

$$\begin{aligned}(x + 2)(x - 3) - 1 &= x^2 - x - 6 - 1 \\ &= x^2 - x - 7\end{aligned}$$

Check to be sure the powers are in descending order before dividing a polynomial.

If the coefficient of one power of the variable is zero, then mark its place with a zero. Be sure to keep terms with the same power aligned in the same column.

EXAMPLE 5 Find the quotient of $\frac{(8p^3 - 125)}{2p - 5}$.

$$
\begin{array}{r}
4p^2 + 10p + 25 \\
2p - 5 \,\overline{)\, 8p^3 + 0 + 0 - 125} \\
\underline{-(8p^3 - 20p^2)} \\
+ 20p^2 + 0 \\
\underline{-(20p^2 - 50p)} \\
+ 50p - 125 \\
\underline{-(50p - 125)} \\
0 \quad 0
\end{array}
$$

Check. $(4p^2 + 10p + 25)(2p - 5)$

$$
\begin{array}{r}
8p^3 + 20p^2 + 50p \\
- 20p^2 - 50p - 125 \\
8p^3 - 125 \quad \text{True}
\end{array}
$$

Exercise A Find each quotient.

1. $\frac{x^2 - 2x - 8}{(x + 2)}$
2. $\frac{x^2 + 8x + 15}{(x + 5)}$
3. $\frac{x^2 - 5x + 6}{(x - 3)}$
4. $\frac{x^2 - 3x + 2}{(x - 1)}$
5. $\frac{x^2 + 5x - 50}{(x - 5)}$
6. $\frac{x^2 - 11x + 28}{(x - 4)}$
7. $\frac{x^2 + 10x + 24}{(x + 6)}$
8. $\frac{x^2 - 36}{(x - 6)}$
9. $\frac{x^2 - 4}{(x + 2)}$
10. $\frac{x^2 - 100}{(x - 10)}$

Exercise B Find each quotient. Identify any remainder.

11. $\frac{x^2 - 7x + 11}{(x - 2)}$

12. $\frac{x^2 + x - 15}{(x + 4)}$

13. $\frac{x^2 + 9x + 9}{(x + 7)}$

14. $\frac{x^2 - 8x + 15}{(x - 4)}$

15. $\frac{x^2 - 2x - 22}{(x + 4)}$

Exercise C Find each quotient.

16. $\frac{15m^3 - 5m^2 - 6m + 2}{(3m - 1)}$

17. $\frac{-8m^2 - 14m - 16}{(2m + 5)}$

18. $\frac{a^2 - 16}{(a - 4)}$

19. $\frac{12y^3 - 3y^2 - 20y + 5}{(4y - 1)}$

20. $\frac{3x^3 + 7x^2 - 7x - 9}{(3x + 1)}$

21. $\frac{x^3 + x^2 - 22x + 8}{(x - 4)}$

22. $\frac{27p^3 - 8}{(3p - 2)}$

23. $\frac{2y^3 - 5y^2 + 39}{(2y + 3)}$

24. $\frac{8p^3 - 125}{(2p - 5)}$

25. $\frac{15z^4 - 15z + 1}{(3z^3 - 3)}$

Exercise D Check your answers to Exercises A, B, and C by multiplying (quotient • divisor) and adding any remainder.

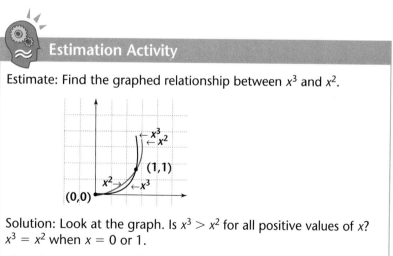

Estimation Activity

Estimate: Find the graphed relationship between x^3 and x^2.

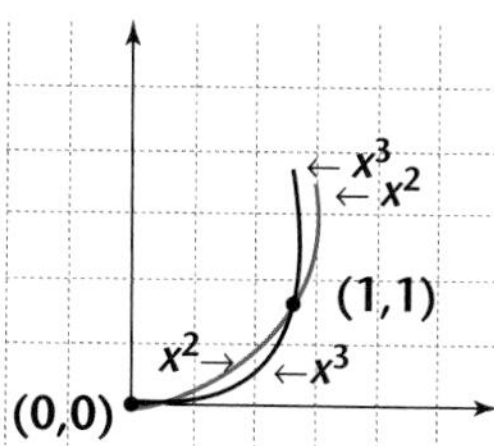

Solution: Look at the graph. Is $x^3 > x^2$ for all positive values of x? $x^3 = x^2$ when $x = 0$ or 1.

$x^3 < x^2$ when $0 < x < x^3 > x^2$ when $x > 1$ x^3 is $\leq x^2$ for all positive values of x.

Lesson 11 Polynomials in Two or More Variables

The expression $(x + y)^2 = x^2 + 2xy + y^2$ is an example of a polynomial in two variables. The variables are x and y. The notation for "P of x and y equals $x^2 + 2xy + y^2$" is

$$P(x, y) = x^2 + 2xy + y^2.$$

The variables x and y are placeholders for numbers and are called independent variables. By replacing x and y with numbers, you evaluate the polynomial.

EXAMPLE 1 Given: $P(x, y) = x^2 + 2xy + y^2$

Evaluate $P(x, y)$ for $x = 2$ and $y = -1$.

$$P(x, y) = P(2, -1) = (2)^2 + 2(2)(-1) + (-1)^2$$
$$= 4 - 4 + 1 = 1$$
$$P(2, -1) = 1$$

EXAMPLE 2 Given: $P(x, y) = x^3 + 2x^2y + xy^2 + y^3$

Evaluate $P(x, y)$ for $x = 1$ and $y = -2$.

$$P(x, y) = P(1, -2) = 1^3 + 2(1)^2(-2) + (1)(-2)^2 + (-2)^3$$
$$= 1 - 4 + 4 - 8 = -7$$
$$P(1, -2) = -7$$

EXAMPLE 3 Given: $P(x, y, z) = x^2y + xy^2z + y^2z^2$

Evaluate $P(x, y, z)$ for $x = -1$, $y = 2$, $z = 3$.

$$P(x, y, z) = P(-1, 2, 3) = (-1)^2(2) + (-1)(2^2)(3) + (2^2)(3^2)$$
$$= 2 - 12 + 36 = 26$$
$$P(-1, 2, 3) = 26$$

Exercise A Evaluate $P(x, y) = x^2 + xy + y^2$ for

1. $x = 0, y = -1$

2. $x = -2, y = 5$

3. $x = \frac{1}{2}, y = -4$

4. $x = -3, y = 5$

5. $x = \frac{1}{3}, y = 9$

Exercise B Evaluate $P(x, y) = x^3y^2 + x^2y + xy^3$ at

6. $P(2, 1)$

7. $P(-1, -1)$

8. $P(5, 0)$

9. $P(9, 1)$

10. $P(-2, -3)$

Exercise C Evaluate $P(x, y, z) = x^3yz^2 + x^2y^2z^2 + xy^3 + yz$ for

11. $x = 1, y = 1, z = 1$

12. $x = -1, y = 0, z = 5$

13. $x = 2, y = -1, z = 2$

14. $x = 0, y = 5, z = -2$

15. $x = 1, y = -2, z = -3$

Polynomial Interest

One type of savings account is a simple savings account. If you invest an amount, P, called the principal, at an annual interest rate of r, you will have $P + (P \cdot r)$ dollars at the end of one year. If you let S stand for savings, you can write this as

$$S = P + (P \cdot r) \text{ or } S = P(1 + r).$$

How much savings will you have if you place $100 for one year in an account that pays 5 percent interest?

$$S = P(1 + r)$$
$$S = \$100(1 + .05) = \$105$$

If you leave your savings in the account for a second year, the new principal is $105. The amount of savings becomes

$$S = [P(1 + r)](1 + r) \text{ or } S = P(1 + r)^2$$

If a principal, P, is invested at an interest rate, r, and interest is compounded annually for t years, the total savings will be $S = P(1 + r)^t$.

In some savings accounts, interest is computed (or compounded) more frequently than once a year. Some accounts compound interest quarterly (four times a year); some compound interest daily!

EXAMPLE 1 You place $100 in a savings account. The annual interest rate is 5 percent and is compounded quarterly. What is your total savings after one year? In this example, $P = \$100$; $r = 5$ percent; $n = 4$, the number of times the interest is compounded in a year; and $t = 1$, the number of years.

$$S = P(1 + \tfrac{r}{n})^{nt} \qquad S = 100(1 + 0.0125)^4$$
$$S = 100(1 + \tfrac{.05}{4})^{4 \cdot 1} \qquad S = 100(1.0509453) = \$105.09$$

Exercise Find the amount of savings in each instance.

1. $1,000 deposited for one year at 5 percent annual interest, compounded every six months.

2. $1,000 deposited for one year at 5 percent annual interest, compounded quarterly.

3. $1,000 deposited for two years at 5 percent annual interest, compounded quarterly.

4. $1,000 deposited for three years at 8 percent annual interest, compounded annually.

5. $1,000 deposited for three years at 8 percent annual interest, compounded quarterly.

Chapter 5 REVIEW

Write the letter of the correct answer.

1. Simplify $(x^6)^3$.

A x^9

B x^3

C x^{18}

D x^2

2. Simplify $[(a + b)^3]^2$.

A $(a + b)^{\frac{3}{2}}$

B $(a + b)^5$

C $(a + b)^1$

D $(a + b)^6$

3. Find the quotient of $\frac{4^5}{4^4}$.

A 4

B $1\frac{1}{4}$

C 1

D 64

4. Find the quotient of $(4x + 2y)^5 \div (4x + 2y)^7, 4x + 2y \neq 0$.

A $(4x + 2y)^2$

B $(4x + 2y)^{12}$

C $(4x + 2y)^{-2}$

D $(4x + 2y)^{\frac{5}{7}}$

5. What is 4,000,000,000 in scientific notation?

A $4.0 \cdot 10^8$

B $4.0 \cdot 10^9$

C 40^9

D $4.0 \cdot 10^{10}$

6. What is $3.14(10^{-4})$ in standard notation?

A 31,400

B 0.000314

C 0.00314

D 3.000014

Find the sum, difference, product, or quotient.
Write your answer in scientific notation.

Example: $2(10^3) + 2(10^3)$ Solution: $2(10^3) + 2(10^3) = 4(10^3)$

7. $3.1(10^{-4}) + 4.2(10^{-4})$

8. $4.7(10^{-2}) - 3.6(10^{-2})$

9. $1.3(10^{-6}) \cdot 4.2(10^{-4}) \cdot 1.9(10^{2})$

10. $8.58(10^{-4}) \div 4.29(10^{-4})$

11. $0.2825(10^{-6}) \div 1.13(10^{2})$

Find the sum and the difference for each pair of polynomials.

Example: $x^2 + 2y + 2$, $x^2 - y + 1$ Solution: Add

$$\begin{array}{r} x^2 + 2y + 2 \\ + \; x^2 - y + 1 \\ \hline 2x^2 + y + 3 \end{array}$$

Subtract

$$\begin{array}{r} x^2 + 2y + 2 \\ - \; (x^2 - y + 1) \\ \hline \end{array} = \begin{array}{r} x^2 + 2y + 2 \\ (-1)(x^2 - y + 1) \\ \hline \end{array} = \begin{array}{r} x^2 + 2y + 2 \\ - \; x^2 + y - 1 \\ \hline 3y + 1 \end{array}$$

12. $3y^5 + 2y^3 + 1y + 3$

$4y^5 + 5y^3 - 7y - 8$

13. $2x^4 - 4x^3 - 6x^2 + 8x + 10$

$3x^4 + 5x^3 + 7$

14. $b^4 + 4b^3 - 6b^2 + 4b - 1$

$-3b^4 - 3b^3 - 5b^2 - 4b$

15. $m^5 + m^3 - 5$

$m^4 + m^2 + 5$

16. $4x^4 + 8x^3 + 16x^2 + 4$

$4x^3 + 2x^2 + 16x$

Find the product.

Example: $(x + 2)(x + 2)$ Solution: $(x + 2)(x + 2) = x(x + 2) + 2(x + 2)$
$= x^2 + 4x + 4$

17. $2x^2(9x^2 + x - 7)$

18. $(x + 3)(9x^4)$

19. $(4y^2 + 4)(-3y - 3)$

20. $(x + 5)(x + 4)$

21. $(4x + 3)(x - 2)$

22. $(m^3 + m^2)^2$

23. $(m^4 + 5)(2m^3 + 3m^2 + 2)$

Find the quotients. Identify any remainder. Use multiplication to check your answer.

Example: $\frac{10x^2 + 20x + 5}{5}$ Solution: $\frac{10x^2 + 20x + 5}{5} = 2x^2 + 4x + 1$

24. $\frac{(12y^3 - 18y - 36)}{6}$

25. $\frac{(-30x^3 + 25x^2 - 20x + 10)}{-5}$

26. $\frac{(p^2 - 2p)^2}{(p^2 - 2p)}$

27. $\frac{(3x^2 - 6x)}{x(x - 2)}$

28. $(33x^3 + 24x^2 + 18x - 12) \div 3x$

29. $(x^3 - 49x) \div (x + 7)$

30. $(5x - 1)\overline{)\,15x^3 - 13x^2 - 18x + 4}$

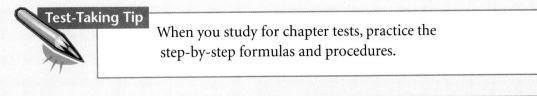

Test-Taking Tip

When you study for chapter tests, practice the step-by-step formulas and procedures.

Chapter

6 Factoring

If there are eight cars parked in a row and there are four rows, how many cars are in the parking lot? The quickest way to the answer is by multiplying eight by four to get 32. You can also do it the other way around. Suppose you know that the parking lot has 32 spaces and you know there are four rows. How many cars are in each row? You divide 32 by four and get eight. To simplify algebraic expressions, you must divide, or factor. Knowing the multiplication tables makes factoring easy.

In Chapter 6, you will factor integers and algebraic expressions.

Goals for Learning

- ◆ To completely factor integers
- ◆ To find the greatest common factor of polynomials
- ◆ To factor trinomials
- ◆ To factor algebraic expressions
- ◆ To identify zero as a factor
- ◆ To use factoring as a means of solving equations

Lesson 1 Greatest Common Factor

Prime number

An integer that can be divided only by itself and 1

Composite number

An integer that is not a prime number

Factoring completely

Expressing an integer as a product of only prime numbers

An integer that can be divided only by itself and 1 is a **prime number.** Integers that are not prime numbers are called **composite numbers.** Composite numbers can be written as a product of two or more prime numbers.

EXAMPLE 1

$17 = 17 \bullet 1$ — 17 is a prime number.

$18 = 2 \bullet 3 \bullet 3$ — 2 and 3 are prime factors of 18.

18 is a composite number.

Expressing an integer as a product of only prime numbers is called **factoring completely.**

Study the chart showing the prime factorization for the integers 1 to 50. Note that 1 is not a prime number.

Remember factors are numbers that are multiplied in a multiplication problem.

Prime Factorization for Integers 1–50		
1	**18** $2 \cdot 3^2$	**35** $5 \cdot 7$
2 prime	**19** prime	**36** $2^2 \cdot 3^2$
3 prime	**20** $2^2 \cdot 5$	**37** prime
4 2^2	**21** $3 \cdot 7$	**38** $2 \cdot 19$
5 prime	**22** $2 \cdot 11$	**39** $3 \cdot 13$
6 $2 \cdot 3$	**23** prime	**40** $2^3 \cdot 5$
7 prime	**24** $2^3 \cdot 3$	**41** prime
8 2^3	**25** 5^2	**42** $2 \cdot 3 \cdot 7$
9 3^2	**26** $2 \cdot 13$	**43** prime
10 $2 \cdot 5$	**27** 3^3	**44** $2^2 \cdot 11$
11 prime	**28** $2^2 \cdot 7$	**45** $3^2 \cdot 5$
12 $2^2 \cdot 3$	**29** prime	**46** $2 \cdot 23$
13 prime	**30** $2 \cdot 3 \cdot 5$	**47** prime
14 $2 \cdot 7$	**31** prime	**48** $2^4 \cdot 3$
15 $3 \cdot 5$	**32** 2^5	**49** 7
16 2^4	**33** $3 \cdot 11$	**50** $2 \cdot 5^2$
17 prime	**34** $2 \cdot 17$	

EXAMPLE 2 Factor 120 completely.

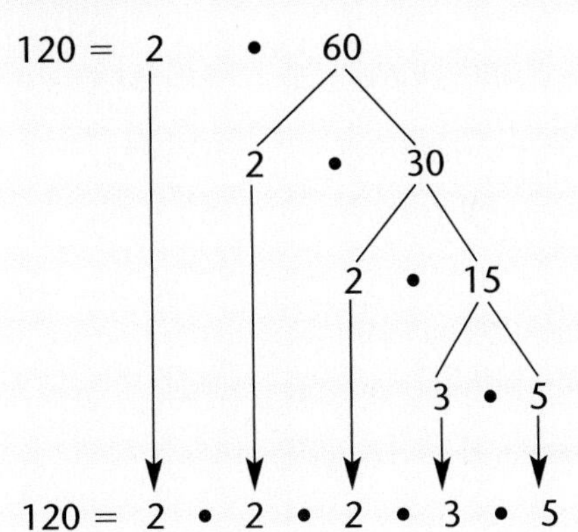

$120 = 12 \cdot 10$

$12 = 4 \cdot 3$, $10 = 5 \cdot 2$

$4 = 2 \cdot 2$

$120 = 2 \cdot 2 \cdot 3 \cdot 5 \cdot 2$

$120 = 2 \cdot 2 \cdot 2 \cdot 3 \cdot 5$

Greatest common factor (GCF)

The largest factor of two or more numbers or terms

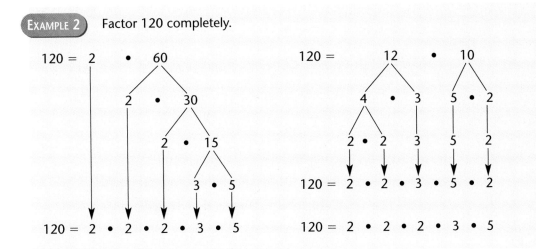

The **greatest common factor** is the greatest factor that divides into each term or number. The greatest common factor is often abbreviated as GCF.

EXAMPLE 3 Find the GCF of 120 and 28.

Step 1 Write the complete factorization of each number.

$120 = \boxed{2 \cdot 2} \cdot 2 \cdot 3 \cdot 5$

$28 = \boxed{2 \cdot 2} \cdot 7$

Step 2 Identify the common prime factors.

$2 \cdot 2$ is common to both numbers.

Step 3 The GCF is the product of all the common prime factors.

2^2 is the GCF of 120 and 28.

Algebra in Your Life

Turning a Big Decision into Smaller Ones

You have probably needed to make a big decision in your life. Maybe you will soon need to decide what you are going to do after graduation. You can make this big decision easier by breaking it into several smaller decisions. In other words, you use factoring. Some of the factors you might list are your interests, education, living situation, and job. List all the factors you can, and your decision gets easier—just as factoring an equation can make finding its solution easier.

You can find the GCF of algebraic expressions using these same steps.

EXAMPLE 4 Find the GCF of $21a^3$ and $18a^5$.

Step 1 Write the complete factorization of each number.

$21a^3 = 3 \bullet 7 \bullet a \bullet a \bullet a$

$18a^5 = 2 \bullet 3 \bullet 3 \bullet a \bullet a \bullet a \bullet a \bullet a$

Step 2 Identify the common prime factors.

$3 \bullet a \bullet a \bullet a$ are common to both numbers.

Step 3 The GCF is the product of all the common prime factors.

$3a^3$ is the GCF of $21a^3$ and $18a^5$.

EXAMPLE 5 Find the GCF of $24a^3b^3$ and $28a^5b$.

Step 1 Write the complete factorization of each number.

$24a^3b^3 = 2 \bullet 2 \bullet 2 \bullet 3 \bullet a \bullet a \bullet a \bullet b \bullet b \bullet b$

$28a^5b = 2 \bullet 2 \bullet 7 \bullet a \bullet a \bullet a \bullet a \bullet a \bullet b$

Step 2 Identify the common prime factors.

$2 \bullet 2 \bullet a \bullet a \bullet a \bullet b$ are common to both numbers.

Step 3 The GCF is the product of all the common prime factors.

2^2a^3b is the GCF of $24a^3b^3$ and $28a^5b$.

Exercise A Find the GCF for these groups of integers.

1. 72, 36

2. 24, 48

3. 27, 24

4. 72, 24

5. 72, 36, 24

6. 78, 26

7. 66, 99

8. 39, 169

9. 25, 225

10. 132, 512

Exercise B Find the GCF for these groups of expressions.

11. $3x^2, 3x$

12. $18y^2, 3y^2$

13. $m^2n^2, 3m^2$

14. $27p^3, 9p$

15. $12x^2, 8x$

16. $33a^3b^5, 66a^2b^3$

17. $21x^3y^2, 7x^2y, 42xy$

18. $3a^6, 4a^5, a^4$

19. $24x^2y, 36x^2y^2, 20xy^2$

20. $42ab^2, 42$

Exercise C Answer these questions using the table of prime numbers 1–50 on page 156.

21. What is the largest prime integer less than 50?

22. Why is 2 the only even prime number?

23. How many composite integers are less than 50?

24. How many prime numbers are less than 50?

25. How can you use the table to factor 180 completely?

Calculator Practice

Use the exponent key on a scientific calculator to check the prime factorization of any number. This key raises a number to a power. On some calculators, it is y^x and on others it is ^ .

EXAMPLE 6 Does $2^4 \bullet 7^2 = 784$?

Clear your calculator display, then enter:

2 y^x 4 × 7 y^x 2 =

2 ^ 4 × 7 ^ 2 =

Your display will show 784.

Exercise D Use a scientific calculator to find the number represented by these prime factorizations.

26. $2^3 \cdot 3^2$

27. $3^2 \cdot 5^3$

28. $2^5 \cdot 5^2 \cdot 7^3$

29. $5^4 \cdot 7^2 \cdot 11^2$

30. $2^6 \cdot 3^3 \cdot 5^2 \cdot 7^2$

Lesson 2 Factoring Polynomials

You can use what you know about finding a GCF to factor an algebraic sum or difference.

EXAMPLE 1 Factor $a^3b^2 + a^2b$.

Step 1 Find the GCF.

$a^3b^2 = a \bullet a \bullet a \bullet b \bullet b$

$a^2b = a \bullet a \bullet b$

The GCF is $a \bullet a \bullet b = a^2b$.

Step 2 Write the expression using the GCF.

$a^3b^2 + a^2b = a^2b(ab) + a^2b(1)$

$= a^2b(ab + 1)$

(using the distributive property)

Step 3 Check. $a^2b(ab + 1) = a^3b^2 + a^2b$

EXAMPLE 2 Factor $5x^4 + 10x^2$.

Step 1 Find the GCF.

$5x^4 = 5 \bullet x \bullet x \bullet x \bullet x$

$10x^2 = 2 \bullet 5 \bullet x \bullet x$

The GCF is $5 \bullet x \bullet x = 5x^2$.

Step 2 Write the expression using the GCF.

$5x^4 + 10x^2 = 5x^2(x^2) + 5x^2(2)$

$= 5x^2(x^2 + 2)$

(using the distributive property)

Step 3 Check. $5x^2(x^2 + 2) = 5x^4 + 10x^2$

Writing About Mathematics

How is a common factor different from the greatest common factor? Give an example.

When you factor algebraic expressions, there may be more than two terms to factor, and the factors may be numbers as well as variables.

EXAMPLE 3 Factor $6t^3 - 3t^2 + 9$.

Because 9 is a constant and not a coefficient of t, you know that t cannot be a factor of each term in the expression. Therefore, you need only find the GCF for the coefficients of 9, 6, and -3. The GCF of these numbers is 3.

$6t^3 - 3t^2 + 9 = 3(2t^3 - t^2 + 3)$

Exercise A Find the GCF, then factor these expressions.

1. $3x^2 + 3$

2. $18y^2 - 6$

3. $m^2n^2 + 3m^2$

4. $6x^3 + 18$

5. $6x^3 + 18x^2 + 24$

6. $5a^3 + 25a^2 - 35a + 20$

7. $16m^3 + 24m^2 + 16$

8. $25x^2y + 15xy^2 + 30$

9. $32x^5 + 64x^4 + 16x$

10. $21x^3y^2 - 7x^2y + 42xy$

11. $-3a^6 - 4a^5 - a^4$

12. $4x^2y - 16x^2y^2 + 20xy^2$

13. $-24x^2y + 6x^2y^2 + 30y^2$

14. $18a^2 - 36a^2b^2 + 44b^2$

15. $-15x^3y^2 - 45x^2y^2 - 33xy^2$

16. $4a^2b^7 - 32a^2b^6 + 8ab^2$

17. $17x^2y - 34xy$

18. $3m^2n - 39m^2n^2 - 13n$

19. $-40t^2 + 5t^2s + 20ts^2$

20. $6p^4q + pqr - 3pr$

Lesson 3 Factoring Trinomials: $x^2 + bx + c$

A trinomial is a polynomial that is made up of three terms. There are several different forms of trinomials. This lesson explores trinomials of the form $x^2 + bx + c$. Examples of these trinomials include $x^2 + 8x + 12$ and $x^2 - 3x - 10$.

A trinomial is the product of two factors. For example, if the factors of a trinomial were $(x + 2)$ and $(x - 1)$, the trinomial would be

$$\begin{aligned}(x + 2)(x - 1) &= x(x - 1) + 2(x - 1)\\ &= x^2 - x + 2x - 2\\ &= x^2 + x - 2\end{aligned}$$

This shows that $x^2 + x - 2 = (x + 2)(x - 1)$

a trinomial = product of 2 factors

If you start with the trinomial and try to find the factors, you might think of the model in this way:

$x^2 + x - 2 = (\blacksquare + \blacksquare)(\blacksquare - \blacksquare)$ You know each factor contains an x because the product contains x^2.

$x^2 + x - 2 = (x + \blacksquare)(x - \blacksquare)$ The factors of -2 must be either $(2)(-1)$ or $(-2)(1)$.

The middle term tells you that the sum of the factors of -2 must be 1 (because $1x = x$).

Possible factors include $(2) + (-1) = 1$ and $(-2) + (1) = -1$. The factors must then be $(2) + (-1)$. $x^2 + x - 2 = (x + 2)(x - 1)$

EXAMPLE 1 Factor $x^2 + 5x - 14$.

Step 1 $x^2 + 5x - 14 = (\blacksquare + \blacksquare)(\blacksquare - \blacksquare)$

Step 2 $x^2 + 5x - 14 = (x + \blacksquare)(x - \blacksquare)$ to give x^2

Step 3 $x^2 + 5x - 14 = (x + \blacksquare)(x - \blacksquare)$

Find factors of -14 whose sum is 5.
$(-2)(7) = -14$, and $(-2) + (7) = 5$
$x^2 + 5x - 14 = (x + 7)(x - 2)$.

Step 4 Check by multiplying.

$$\begin{aligned}(x + 7)(x - 2) &= x(x - 2) + 7(x - 2)\\ &= x^2 - 2x + 7x - 14\\ &= x^2 + 5x - 14\end{aligned}$$

Not every trinomial can be factored in this way. For example, in $x^2 + x - 3$, the factors of -3 are $(-3)(1)$ or $(3)(-1)$.

The coefficient of the middle term is (1), so you know the sum of the factors of -3 must be 1. But $(-3) + (1) = -2$, and $(3) + (-1) = 2$. Neither combination of factors gives the correct middle term.

Some trinomials may have a common factor. In these cases, you will need to find the GCF first.

EXAMPLE 2 Factor $2x^4 + 10x^3 - 28x^2$.

Step 1 Find the common factors.
$2x^4 + 10x^3 - 28x^2 = 2x^2(x^2 + 5x - 14)$

Step 2 Factor the polynomial.
$2x^2(x^2 + 5x - 14) = 2x^2(x + 7)(x - 2)$
from previous example
so $2x^4 + 10x^3 - 28x^2 = 2x^2(x + 7)(x - 2)$.

Exercise A Factor the following expressions. Check by multiplying.

1. $x^2 + 5x + 6$

2. $m^2 - 4m - 12$

3. $a^2 - 6a + 8$

4. $x^2 + 5x - 24$

5. $y^2 + 3y - 18$

6. $m^2 - 8m - 20$

7. $t^2 - t - 20$

8. $y^2 - 4y - 5$

9. $x^2 + 16x - 17$

Exercise B Factor these expressions. Be sure to find any common factors.

10. $x^4 + 7x^3 + 12x^2$

11. $2b^3 + 10b^2 + 8b$

12. $3p^4 - 24p^3 + 45p^2$

13. $a^4 + 7a^2 + 12$

PROBLEM SOLVING

Exercise C Solve these problems.

14. Suppose the trinomial $x^2 - x - 2$ represents the area of a rectangle. What factors represent the length and width of that rectangle?

15. Suppose the trinomial $x^2 + 4x + 3$ represents the area of a rectangle. What is the perimeter of that rectangle?

Lesson 4 Factoring Trinomials: $ax^2 + bx + c$

Another form of a trinomial is $ax^2 + bx + c$. Examples of these trinomials include $4x^2 + 8x + 3$ and $20x^2 - 29x + 6$. In these trinomials, the coefficient of the x^2 term is some number other than 1.

$4x^2 + 8x + 3$	$20x^2 - 29x + 6$
The coefficient of x^2 is 4.	The coefficient of x^2 is 20.

When the coefficient of the x^2 term is some number other than 1, you must find the factors of this coefficient in order to factor the trinomial.

EXAMPLE 1 Factor $6x^2 + 13x + 5$.

Step 1 $6x^2 + 13x + 5 = (\blacksquare x + \blacksquare)(\blacksquare x + \blacksquare)$

to give x^2

Step 2 Find factors of 6 and 5 whose sum is 13.

Factors of 6 = (6)(1) or (2)(3)
Factors of 5 = (5)(1)
Try different combinations using trial and error.

There are four possible combinations:

$$(1x + 1)(6x + 5) = 1x(6x + 5) + 1(6x + 5) = 6x^2 + 5x + 6x + 5 = 6x^2 + 11x + 5$$

$$(1x + 5)(6x + 1) = 1x(6x + 1) + 5(6x + 1) = 6x^2 + x + 30x + 5 = 6x^2 + 31x + 5$$

$$(2x + 5)(3x + 1) = 2x(3x + 1) + 5(3x + 1) = 6x^2 + 2x + 15x + 5 = 6x^2 + 17x + 5$$

$$(2x + 1)(3x + 5) = 2x(3x + 5) + 1(3x + 5) = 6x^2 + 10x + 3x + 5 = 6x^2 + 13x + 5$$

The last combination gives us the desired product.

The factors of $6x^2 + 13x + 5$ are $(2x + 1)(3x + 5)$.

EXAMPLE 2 Factor $3x^2 + 14x - 5$.

Note that in this expression the constant is a negative. In this case, you will need to test for proper signs as well as correct factors.

Step 1 $3x^2 + 14x - 5 = (\blacksquare x + \blacksquare)(\blacksquare x - \blacksquare)$
to give x^2

Step 2 Find factors of 3 and -5 whose sum is $+14$.

Factors of $-5 = (5)(-1)$ or $(-5)(1)$
Factors of $3 = (3)(1)$

Try different combinations using trial and error.
There are four possible combinations:

$$(1x + 1)(3x - 5) = x(3x - 5) + 1(3x - 5) = 3x^2 - 5x + 3x - 5$$
$$= 3x^2 - 2x - 5$$
$$(3x + 1)(1x - 5) = 3x(x - 5) + 1(x - 5) = 3x^2 - 15x + x - 5$$
$$= 3x^2 - 14x + 5$$
$$(1x - 1)(3x + 5) = x(3x + 5) - 1(3x + 5) = 3x^2 + 5x - 3x - 5$$
$$= 3x^2 + 2x - 5$$
$$(3x - 1)(1x + 5) = 3x(x + 5) - 1(x + 5) = 3x^2 + 15x - x - 5$$
$$= 3x^2 + 14x - 5$$

The last combination gives us the desired product.
The factors of $3x^2 + 14x - 5$ are $(3x - 1)(1x + 5)$.

Exercise A Factor these expressions.

1. $3y^2 + 14y + 8$
2. $12b^2 + 17b + 6$
3. $6c^2 + 19c + 15$
4. $20r^2 + 104r + 20$
5. $20m^2 + 50m + 20$
6. $20x^2 + 40x + 20$
7. $20y^2 + 401y + 20$
8. $42x^2 + 84x + 42$

Exercise B Factor these expressions. Don't forget about positive and negative signs.

9. $7x^2 + 4x - 3$
10. $8a^2 - 26a + 15$
11. $49x^2 + 7x - 6$
12. $7a^2 + 19a - 6$
13. $6y^2 - 10y - 24$
14. $11x^2 - 41x - 12$
15. $6x^2 - 26x + 28$
16. $2x^2 - 14x + 12$
17. $3x^2 - 2x - 16$

Exercise C Factor these expressions. First find the GCF.

18. $4x^3 + 20x^2 + 16x$
19. $12x^4 + 26x^3 - 16x^2$
20. $10x^2 + 48x - 10$

Lesson 5 Factoring Expressions: $a^2 - b^2$

> ***Perfect square***
> *The square of an integer*

The squares of integers are called **perfect squares**. Examples of perfect squares include a^2 (because $a \cdot a = a^2$) and b^2 (because $b \cdot b = b^2$). Since a^2 is a perfect square and b^2 is a perfect square, $a^2 - b^2$ represents the difference of two perfect squares.

You can check this fact using multiplication:

$$(a + b)(a - b) = a(a - b) + b(a - b)$$
$$= a^2 - ab + ba - b^2$$

Using the commutative property of multiplication:

$$= a^2 - ab + ab - b^2$$
$$= a^2 - b^2$$

You can use geometry to visualize this process.

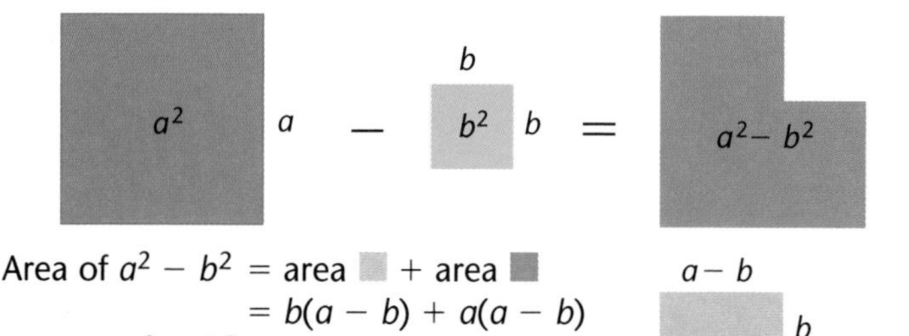

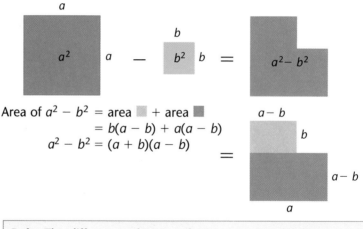

Area of $a^2 - b^2$ = area ▢ + area ■
$= b(a - b) + a(a - b)$
$a^2 - b^2 = (a + b)(a - b)$

> **Rule** The difference of two perfect squares can be factored using the model: $a^2 - b^2 = (a + b)(a - b)$, where $a = \sqrt{a^2}$ and $b = \sqrt{b^2}$.

EXAMPLE 1 You know that $25 = 5^2$, $9 = 3^2$, $25 - 9 = 16$.
You can use these facts to test the model:
Let $a = 5$ and $b = 3$. Then $a^2 - b^2 = 25 - 9 = 16$ True
and $(5 - 3)(5 + 3) = (2)(8) = 16$ True
Use the model to find the factors of $x^2 - 9$.

Step 1 Find the square roots of a and b:
$\sqrt{x^2} = x$ and $\sqrt{9} = 3$

Step 2 Place the values in the model.
$x^2 - 9 = (x + 3)(x - 3)$

Writing About Mathematics

Can you use the model to factor $8y^3 - 8$? Explain why or why not.

EXAMPLE 2 Find the factors of $9y^4 - 1$.

Step 1 Find the square roots of a and b:

$\sqrt{9y^4} = 3y^2$ and $\sqrt{1} = 1$

Step 2 Place the values in the model.

$9y^4 - 1 = (3y^2 + 1)(3y^2 - 1)$

Find the factors of $25x^6 - 4y^2$.

$\sqrt{25x^6} = 5x^3$ and $\sqrt{4y^2} = 2y$

$25x^6 - 4y^2 = (5x^3 + 2y)(5x^3 - 2y)$

Exercise A Use the model to factor these differences. Check your answers using arithmetic.

1. 144 − 100

2. 81 − 49

3. 36 − 25

4. 25 − 16

5. 121 − 81

6. 100 − 49

Exercise B Use the model to factor these expressions. Check your answers using multiplication.

7. $y^2 - 49$

8. $m^2 - 81$

9. $p^2 - 121$

10. $q^2 - 169$

11. $z^2 - 225$

12. $t^6 - 36$

Exercise C Factor these expressions. Check your answers.

13. $49x^2 - 1$

14. $25m^2 - 25$

15. $36t^4 - 121$

16. $64x^6 - 49$

17. $25r^8 - 1$

18. $100x^{10} - 100$

Exercise D Write these expressions as a product.

19. $49x^4 - 25y^2$

20. $121y^4 - 144z^6$

21. $36a^2b^2 - 1$

22. $225k^8 - 169h^4$

23. $81m^2 - 64n^{10}$

24. $625h^6 - 324h^8$

PROBLEM SOLVING

Exercise E Solve the problem.

25. A square fountain is planned for a city plaza. The plan calls for the plaza to be paved in decorative tiles. What area will the tiles need to cover?

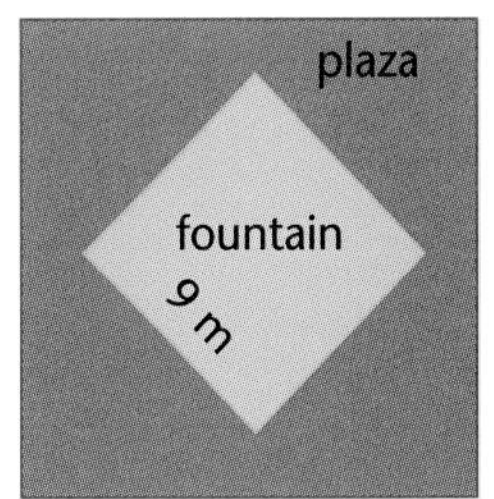

Lesson 6 Factoring Expressions: $a^2 + 2ab + b^2$

Perfect square trinomial

The result of multiplying a binomial by itself or squaring a binomial

You can use what you know about multiplying binomials to find the factors of some trinomials.

EXAMPLE 1 $(a + b)(a + b) = (a + b)^2 = a(a + b) + b(a + b)$

$= a^2 + ab + ba + b^2$

Using the commutative property of multiplication:

$= a^2 + 2ab + b^2$

$a^2 + 2ab + b^2$ is a **perfect square trinomial.**

You can use geometry to visualize this process.

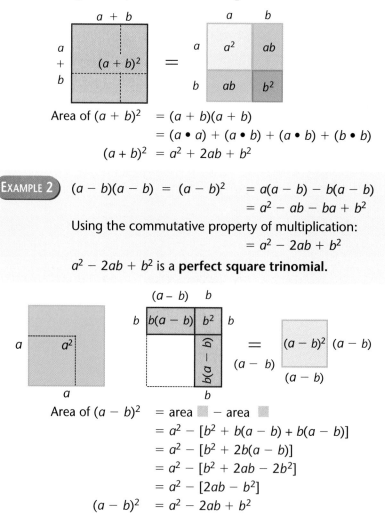

Area of $(a + b)^2 = (a + b)(a + b)$

$= (a \cdot a) + (a \cdot b) + (a \cdot b) + (b \cdot b)$

$(a + b)^2 = a^2 + 2ab + b^2$

EXAMPLE 2 $(a - b)(a - b) = (a - b)^2 = a(a - b) - b(a - b)$

$= a^2 - ab - ba + b^2$

Using the commutative property of multiplication:

$= a^2 - 2ab + b^2$

$a^2 - 2ab + b^2$ is a **perfect square trinomial.**

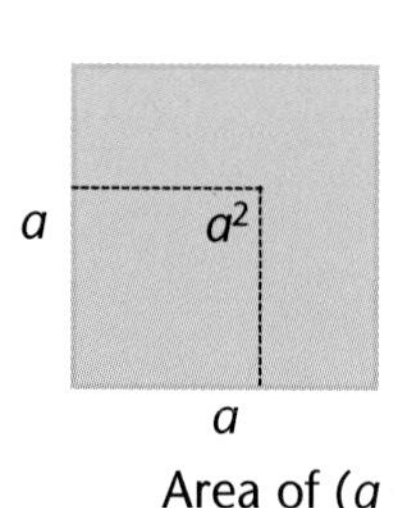

Area of $(a - b)^2$ = area ▭ − area ▭

$= a^2 - [b^2 + b(a - b) + b(a - b)]$

$= a^2 - [b^2 + 2b(a - b)]$

$= a^2 - [b^2 + 2ab - 2b^2]$

$= a^2 - [2ab - b^2]$

$(a - b)^2 = a^2 - 2ab + b^2$

Rule The perfect square trinomial can be factored using the model: $a^2 + 2ab + b^2 = (a + b)^2$.

EXAMPLE 3 Use the model to find the factors of $x^2 + 4x + 4$.

Step 1 Assign values to $x^2 + 4x + 4$ from the model:

$a^2 = x^2$ or $a = x$

$b^2 = 4$ or $b = 2$, this means that

$2ab = 2(2x) = 4x$

Step 2 Place the values in the model.

$x^2 + 4x + 4 = (x + 2)(x + 2) = (x + 2)^2$

EXAMPLE 4 Find the factors of $x^2 + 6x + 9$.

Step 1 Assign values from the model:

$a^2 = x^2$ or $a = x$

$b^2 = 9$ or $b = 3$, this means that

$2ab = 2(3x) = 6x$

Step 2 Place the values in the model.

$x^2 + 6x + 9 = (x + 3)(x + 3) = (x + 3)^2$

Exercise A Give the area of each region of the square as well as the total area of the large square.

1.

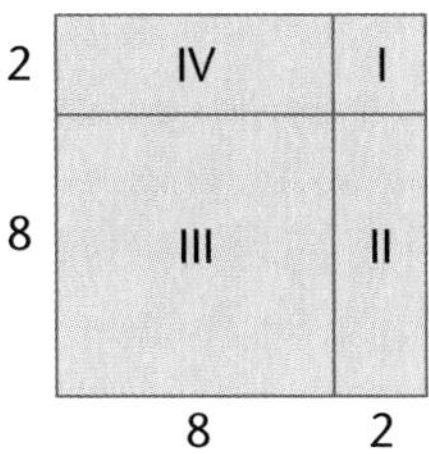

2.

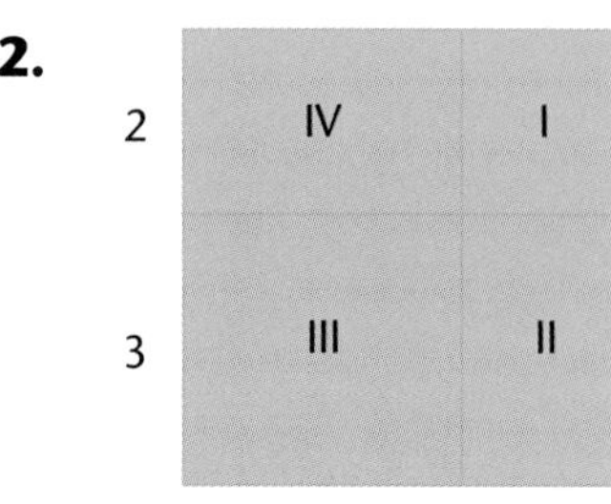

3.

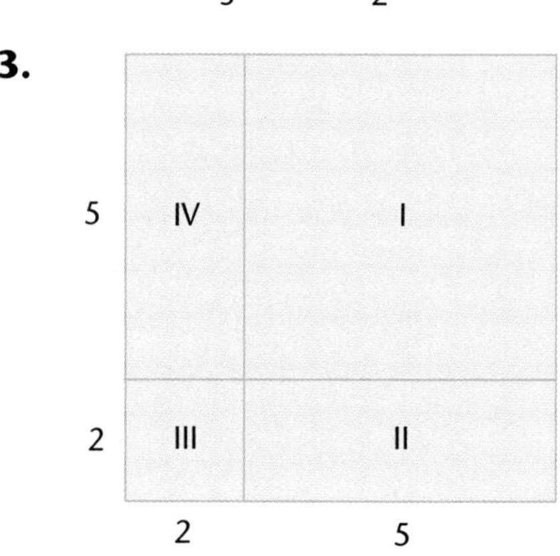

Exercise B Use the model to find the factors of these perfect square trinomials.

4. $m^2 - 24m + 144$

5. $x^2 + 24x + 144$

6. $p^2 - 18p + 81$

7. $t^2 + 18t + 81$

8. $z^2 + 30z + 225$

9. $x^2 + 26x + 169$

Exercise C Find the factors of these trinomials.

10. $4m^2 + 48m + 144$

11. $4r^2 - 48r + 144$

Writing About Mathematics

Is $64m^5 + 128m^3 + 64m^2$ a perfect square trinomial? Tell why or why not. Find all the factors of the trinomial.

12. $16x^4 - 16x^2 + 4$

13. $81p^6 + 90p^3 + 25$

14. $4x^2 - 60x + 225$

15. $25x^4 + 50x^2 + 25$

16. $36y^2 - 156y + 169$

17. $144b^4 - 24b^2 + 1$

18. $49q^8 + 28q^4 + 4$

PROBLEM SOLVING

Exercise D Solve each problem.

19. An architect drew this sketch to show how she would enlarge an existing room. The area of the existing room is 49 square units. The area of the new room will be 100 square units. What is the length and width of each region?

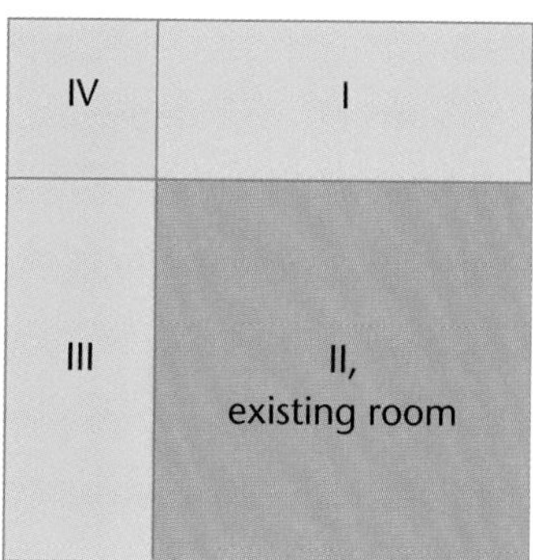

20. Use the diagram below to show that the area of the large square is $16y^2 - 8y + 1$.

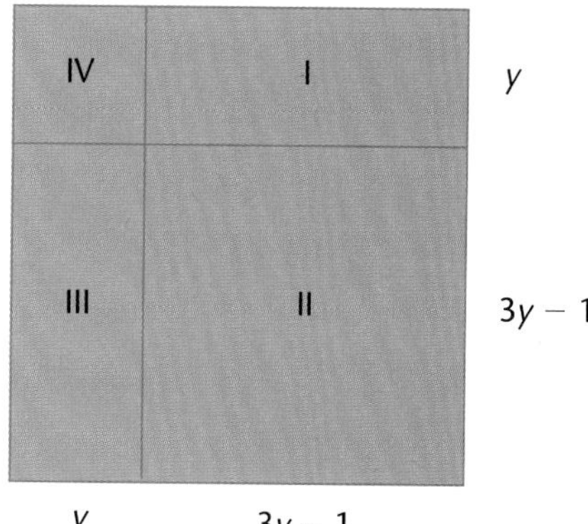

Lesson 7 Zero as a Factor

You already know that 0 times any number equals zero. So if $3x = 0$, you know that x must equal 0.

Suppose you know that the product of two unknown numbers is 0. What are the numbers?

Let a, b be the two numbers, then

$ab = 0$

Either a or b or both must be zero because

if	$a = 0$,	then $(0)(b) = 0$	True
if	$b = 0$,	then $(a)(0) = 0$	True
if	$a = 0$ and $b = 0$,	then $(0)(0) = 0$	True

Conclusion: $ab = 0$ whenever $a = 0$ or $b = 0$, or $a = b = 0$

EXAMPLE 1 Find the value of the variable.

$5y$	=	0	Since $5 \neq 0$, y must be 0.
y	=	0	because $(5)(0) = 0$

EXAMPLE 2

$3x^2$	=	0	Since $3 \neq 0$, x^2 must be 0.
x^2	=	0	because $(3)(0) = 0$, $x = 0$
x	=	0	

EXAMPLE 3

$5(x + 1)$	=	0	Since $5 \neq 0$, $x + 1$ must be 0.
$(x + 1)$	=	0	because $(5)(0) = 0$
so $(x + 1)$	=	0	and $x = -1$

Check. $5(x - 1) = 5(-1 + 1) = 5(0) = 0$

EXAMPLE 4

$(x + 1)(x - 2)$	=	0	implies
$(x + 1)$	=	0	because $(0)(x - 2) = 0$
or $(x - 2)$	=	0	because $(x + 1)(0) = 0$
if $(x + 1)$	=	0	then $x = -1$

Check. $(-1 + 1)(-1 - 2) = 0(-3) = 0$

if $(x - 2) = 0$ then $x = 2$

Check. $(2 + 1)(2 - 2) = 3(0) = 0$

so $x = -1$ or $x = 2$

Exercise A Find the value of the variable in each expression. Check your work.

1. $4m = 0$

2. $34k = 0$

3. $16y = 0$

4. $23x = 0$

5. $12x^2 = 0$

6. $14y^3 = 0$

7. $21b^4 = 0$

8. $44m^2 = 0$

9. $9x^3 = 0$

10. $33d^2 = 0$

Exercise B Solve these equations for the variable. Check your solutions.

11. $17(x - 5) = 0$

12. $21(y + 1) = 0$

13. $12(m + 21) = 0$

14. $12(m + 4) = 0$

15. $(n - 12)(n + 4) = 0$

16. $(x - 6)(x + 5) = 0$

17. $14(m - 4) = 0$

18. $(3x - 9)(x + 1) = 0$

19. $(4x - 6)(x + 6) = 0$

20. $(x - 6)^2(x + 5) = 0$

21. $(9z - 18)(12z + 6) = 0$

22. $(4t - 12)(5t - 25) = 0$

23. $(3x + 6)(2x - 10) = 0$

24. $(5x - 5)(14x + 28) = 0$

25. $(4p - 4)(13p + 27) = 0$

TRY THIS $(2x^2 - 32)(x - 9) = 0$

Lesson 8 Solving Quadratic Equations—Factoring

Quadratic equation

An equation in the form of $ax^2 + bx + c = 0$

Solution

The value of a variable that makes an open statement true

Recall that if

$$\begin{aligned} (x+1)(x-2) &= 0 \quad \text{then either} \\ (x+1) &= 0 \quad \text{and } x = -1 \text{ or} \\ (x-2) &= 0 \quad \text{and } x = +2 \end{aligned}$$

Also recall you can rewrite $(x + 1)(x - 2)$ as a trinomial:

$$\begin{aligned} (x+1)(x-2) &= x(x-2) + 1(x-2) \\ &= x^2 - 2x + x - 2 \\ &= x^2 - x - 2 \end{aligned}$$

So, $(x + 1)(x - 2) = 0$ is the same as $x^2 - x - 2 = 0$

$x^2 - x - 2 = 0$ is an example of a **quadratic equation.** *Quadratic* means square and in a quadratic equation the highest power of the variable is 2. The expression is an equation because it is equal to zero.

> **Rule** The general form of a quadratic equation is $ax^2 + bx + c = 0$.

$x = -1$ and $x = +2$ are called **solutions** to the quadratic equation $x^2 - x - 2 = 0$. When these values are substituted for x in the equation, the resulting statements are true.

Let $x = -1$, then $x^2 - x - 2 =$

$(-1)^2 - (-1) - 2 = 1 + 1 - 2 = 0$ True

Let $x = 2$, then $x^2 - x - 2 =$

$(2)^2 - 2 - 2 = 4 - 4 = 0$ True

Therefore, -1 and 2 represent the solutions for $x^2 - x - 2 = 0$. To solve a quadratic equation, you must find the solutions for the equation.

EXAMPLE 1 Solve $x^2 + 3x + 2 = 0$.

Step 1 Factor the equation. $x^2 + 3x + 2 = (x + 2)(x + 1) = 0$

Step 2 Set each factor equal to 0. $x + 2 = 0$ or $x + 1 = 0$

Step 3 Solve each factor for x. $x + 2 = 0, x = -2$ or $x + 1 = 0, x = -1$

Step 4 Check. Let $x = -2$, $x^2 + 3x + 2 = (-2)^2 + 3(-2) + 2 = 4 - 6 + 2 = 0$ True

Let $x = -1$, $x^2 + 3x + 2 = (-1)^2 + 3(-1) + 2 = 1 - 3 + 2 = 0$ True

The solutions are -2 and -1.

EXAMPLE 2 Solve $2m^2 - m - 3 = 0$.

Step 1 Factor the equation. The factors of 2 are 1 and 2, and the factors of 3 are 1 and 3. Arrange these factors as many ways as possible.

$(2m - 1)(m + 3)$

$(2m + 1)(m - 3)$

$(m - 1)(2m + 3)$

$(m + 1)(2m - 3)$

Step 2 Decide which arrangement is equal to $2m^2 - m - 3$, the given equation.

$(2m - 1)(m + 3) = 2m^2 + 5m - 3$

$(2m + 1)(m - 3) = 2m^2 - 5m - 3$

$(m - 1)(2m + 3) = 2m^2 + m - 3$

$(m + 1)(2m - 3) = 2m^2 - m - 3$

Step 3 Since $(m + 1)(2m - 3) = 2m^2 - m - 3$, the given equation, set $(m + 1)$ and $(2m - 3)$ equal to zero. Then solve.

$m + 1 = 0 \qquad 2m - 3 = 0$

$m = -1 \qquad 2m = 3$

$m = \frac{3}{2}$

Step 4 Check.

Let $m = -1$, then $2m^2 - m - 3 = 2(-1)^2 - (-1) - 3$

$= 2(1) + 1 - 3$

$= 2 + 1 - 3$

$= 3 - 3$

$= 0$ True

Let $m = \frac{3}{2}$, then $2m^2 - m - 3 = 2(\frac{3}{2})^2 - (\frac{3}{2}) - 3$

$= 2(\frac{9}{4}) - \frac{3}{2} - 3$

$= \frac{18}{4} - \frac{3}{2} - 3$

$= \frac{18}{4} - \frac{6}{4} - 3$

$= \frac{12}{4} - 3$

$= 3 - 3$

$= 0$ True

Exercise A Solve each of these quadratic equations. Be sure to check your work.

1. $x^2 + 5x + 6 = 0$
2. $m^2 - 4m - 12 = 0$
3. $a^2 - 6a + 8 = 0$
4. $x^2 + 5x - 24 = 0$
5. $y^2 + 3y - 18 = 0$
6. $m^2 - 8m - 20 = 0$
7. $t^2 - t - 20 = 0$
8. $y^2 - 4y - 5 = 0$
9. $x^2 + 16x - 17 = 0$
10. $q^2 - q - 30 = 0$
11. $x^2 + 7x + 12 = 0$
12. $y^2 - 9y + 14 = 0$
13. $2t^2 - 12t - 32 = 0$
14. $2d^2 - 18d - 20 = 0$
15. $2x^2 + 13x + 15 = 0$

Exercise B Find the solutions. Check your work.

16. $8n^2 - 40n - 48 = 0$
17. $2x^2 + 4x - 30 = 0$
18. $3x^2 - 6x - 9 = 0$
19. $4x^2 + 18x - 36 = 0$
20. $6x^2 - 18x - 60 = 0$

Estimation Activity

Estimate: Find the product.

13×17		8×14

Solution:
Use the distributive property to help figure out products.

Think:	$(10 + 3)17$	$8(10 + 7)$
Do:	$10 \times 17 = 170$ $3 \times 17 = 51$	$8 \times 10 = 80$ $8 \times 4 = 32$
Total:	$170 + 51 = 221$	$80 + 32 = 112$

Exercise C Find the solutions. Be sure to factor completely.

21. $3b^2 + 15b + 12 = 0$

22. $2p^2 - 16p + 30 = 0$

23. $12x^2 + 18x + 6 = 0$

24. $3y^2 + 12y - 36 = 0$

25. $12c^2 + 60c + 72 = 0$

PROBLEM SOLVING

Exercise D Solve the problems.

These possibilities exist for some quadratic equations.

A The equation has no solution.

B The equation has one solution.

C The equation has two solutions.

Study the following equations. For each equation, choose A, B, or C.

26. $x^2 = 9$

27. $x^2 + 9 = 25$

28. $x^2 + 1 = 0$

29. $2x^2 - 10 = -10$

30. $25x^2 = 49$

Technology Connection

Measuring Mattes

When you frame a picture, you can use the quadratic equation to find the dimensions of the matte that goes around the picture. The equation calculates the exact, or geometric, center of the matte. But there is a piece of technology that solves the same problem—a print positioner. It positions a print in the optical center of a matte. Optical center means exactly centered between left and right, but slightly above center between top and bottom. What will they think of next?

Application

Frame Factor Factoring equations is useful for computing the area of a shape without knowing the exact dimensions.

EXAMPLE 1 The overall dimensions of this picture frame are 20 in. by 14 in. The picture inside the frame has an area of 160 in^2. How wide should the matte surrounding the picture be?

Step 1 Area = length • width

$160 = (20 - 2x)(14 - 2x)$

$= 20 \cdot 14 - 20 \cdot 2x - 28x + 4x^2$

$280 - 68x + 4x^2 = 160$ or $4x^2 - 68x + 280 = 160$

Step 2 Set equation equal to zero.

$4x^2 - 68x + 280 - 160 = 160 - 160$

$4x^2 - 68x + 120 = 0$

Factor 4 from each term. $4(x^2 - 17x + 30) = 0(4)$

$x^2 - 17x + 30 = 0$ $(x - 15)(x - 2) = 0$ So either $x = 15$ or $x = 2$.

Check. $160 = (20 - 2x)(14 - 2x)$ for $x = 15$. Substituting 15 in the equation leads to a negative length, which is impossible, so 15 is not a solution.

Check. $160 = (20 - 2x)(14 - 2x)$ for $x = 2$ $160 = (20 - 2 \cdot 2)(14 - 2 \cdot 2)$

$160 = (16)(10)$ True. The matte should be 2 inches wide.

Exercise Factor to solve each problem.

1. The outside edges of a rectangular frame are 3 ft by 4 ft. The matte covers $\frac{1}{2}$ the area inside the frame. How wide is the matte?

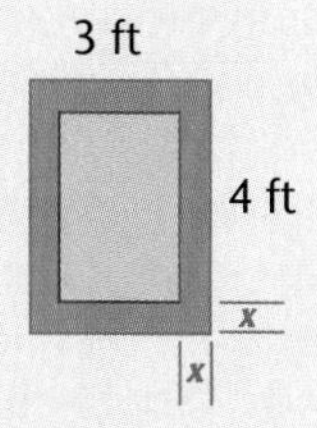

2. The area of a walkway around a rectangular garden is equal to the area of the garden alone. The garden measures 6 m by 9 m. What is the width of the walkway?

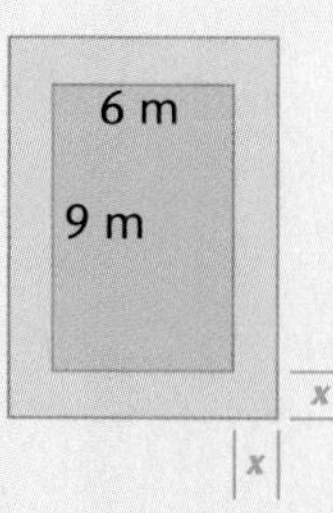

3. If the sides of a square are lengthened by 3 ft, the area of the square becomes 81 ft^2. What is the length of the side of the original square?

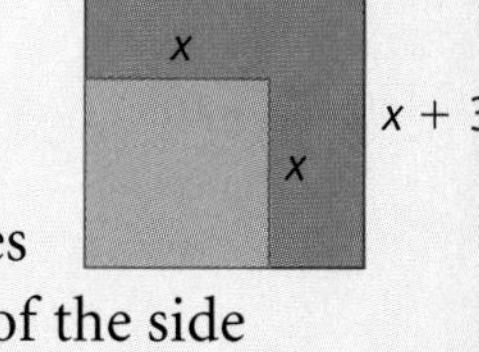

Chapter 6 REVIEW

Write the letter of the correct answer.

1. What is the greatest common factor of 24 and 36?

A 12

B 8

C 4

D 16

2. What is the greatest common factor for $54pq$, $108p$, and $27p$?

A 9

B $27p$

C $3p$

D 27

Factor the expression. Write the letter of the correct answer.

3. $24m^2 - 8$

A $m - 1$

B $8(3m^2 - 1)$

C $3(8m^2 - 2)$

D $24m^2 - (2 \cdot 4)$

4. $4x^4 - 32x^3 + 28x^2$

A $4x^2$

B $x^2 - 8x + 7$

C $4x(x - 8)$

D $4x^2(x - 7)(x - 1)$

5. $p^2 - 81$

A $p - 9$

B $p + 9$

C $(p + 9)(p - 9)$

D $(p - 9)^2$

6. $15x^2 - 35x + 10$

A $(5x - 10)(3x - 1)$

B $(3x + 5)(5x + 5)$

C $(3x + 1)(5x + 10)$

D $(3x - 5)(5x - 5)$

7. Solve for m. $13(m + 6) = 0$

A $m = 6$

B $m = -7$

C $m = -6$

D $m = 19$

Find the solutions for these equations.

Example: $x^2 + 5x + 6 = 0$ Solution: $x^2 + 5x + 6 = 0$
$(x + 3)(x + 2) = 0$
$(x + 3) = 0; x = -3$
$(x + 2) = 0; x = -2$

8. $a^2 - 2a - 8 = 0$

9. $2x^2 + 9x + 4 = 0$

10. $6x^2 - 8x = 8$

11. $9x^2 = -18x$

12. $3x^2 + 15x = -18$

13. $4y^2 - 10y + 6 = 0$

14. $5b^2 - 16b = -3$

15. $4z^2 = 9$

16. $x^2 + 45 = -18x$

17. $y^2 - 121 = 0$

18. $b^3 - 16b = 0$

19. $5c^2 + 45c = 0$

20. $x^2 + 6x = -5$

Find the solution to each problem.

Example: What is the area of the rectangle?
Solution: $A = (10)(x + 1)$
$A = 10x + 10$

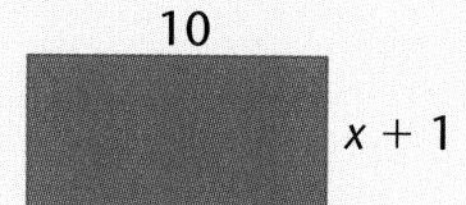

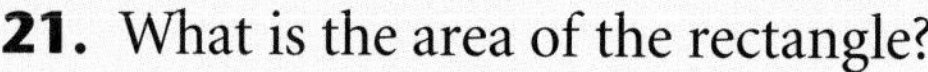

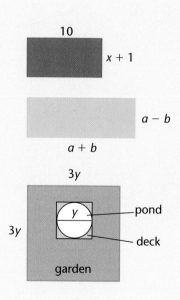

21. What is the area of the rectangle?

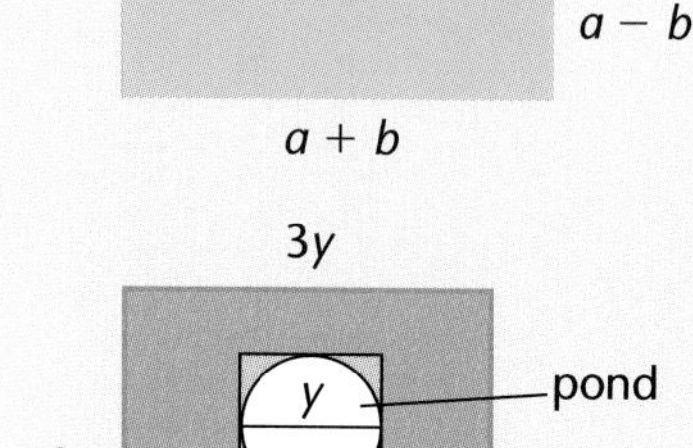

22. A pond and its square deck are part of a garden. What area of the garden is not occupied by the pond and its deck? If the diameter of the pond is 10 ft, what is the area of the garden not occupied by the pond and its deck?

23. This sketch shows how a contractor plans to enlarge an existing family room. The area of the existing room is 64 square units. The area of the new room will be 144 square units. What is the length and width of each region?

IV | I, existing room | III | II

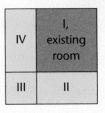

24. Describe two ways to find the area of the addition in problem 23.

25. What is the area of the large square?

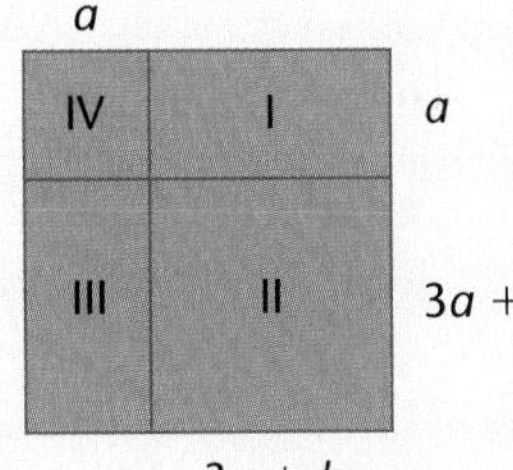

26. A rectangle has a length 3 cm greater than its width. The area of the rectangle is 28 cm^2. What is the length and width of the rectangle?

27. The length of a rectangle is two more than twice its width. The area of the rectangle is 60 units. What is the length and width of the rectangle?

28. A rectangle has an area of 108 m^2. Its width is 3 m less than its length. What are the dimensions of the rectangle?

29. The sides of a square are increased by 4 cm. The area of the newly created square is 121 cm^2. What was the original length of one side of the square?

30. Each side of a square is lengthened by 6 ft. This makes the area of the square 64 ft^2. What was the original length of a side of the square?

When studying for a test, review any tests or quizzes you took earlier that cover the same information.

Chapter

Data, Statistics, and Probability

Suppose the weather forecast calls for a 60 percent chance of rain. This prediction is based on similar past conditions and corresponding times of past years. In 60 percent of past cases, it rained. In 40 percent, it didn't rain. People who predict the weather collect, record, and study statistics on weather. They use this data to make predictions. You can use data and probability to predict many things besides weather. What are the chances you'll get heads in a coin toss or draw the winning card? Figure it out!

In Chapter 7, you will read and interpret data.

Goals for Learning

- To organize data into graphs
- To read and interpret graphic representations
- To determine range and measures of central tendency
- To compute probabilities and complementary events involving statistics

Lesson 1 Organizing Data

Frequency table

A way of showing the count of items or number of times in different groups or categories

Data

Information given in numbers

Stem-and-Leaf Plot

A way of showing place value by separating the data by powers of ten

Information can be organized and shown in many different ways. A **frequency table** is a method of summarizing data. The following data table shows how old some adults were when they bought their first home.

How old were you when you bought your first home? (in years)		
63	24	35
31	44	61
41	36	23
48	54	49
27	60	37
42	24	50
29	43	29
30	56	41

The frequency table was made using the **data** from the table. The frequency table is much easier to read and interpret than the data table.

Frequency Table		
Interval	Tally	Frequency
0–9		0
10–19		0
20–29	𝍸 I	6
30–39	𝍸	5
40–49	𝍸 II	7
50–59	III	3
60–69	III	3
70–79		0

A stem-and-leaf plot is another way to show how frequently data occur. **A stem-and-leaf plot** organizes and displays data using stems and leafs. In the following stem-and-leaf plot, the first data value is made up of a stem of 1 and a leaf of 0. The stem (1) represents the place value of the tens place (1 ten) and the leaf (0) represents the place value of the ones place (0 ones). So stem (1) and leaf (0) represents 1 ten—(10) + 0—ones (0), or $10 + 0 = 10$.

Bar Graph

A way of showing how information can be compared using rectangular bars

Time Spent Studying (in minutes)	
1	0 0 5 5 5
2	0 5 5
3	0 0 0 5
4	5

1 | 0 = 10

This stem-and-leaf plot shows:

- there are 13 data values
- the data values 15 and 30 occur most often
- the greatest data value is 45
- the least data value is 10

A **bar graph** uses rectangular bars to show data. The bar graph below shows the number of minutes five students spent getting ready for school.

Minutes Spent Getting Ready for School

number of minutes

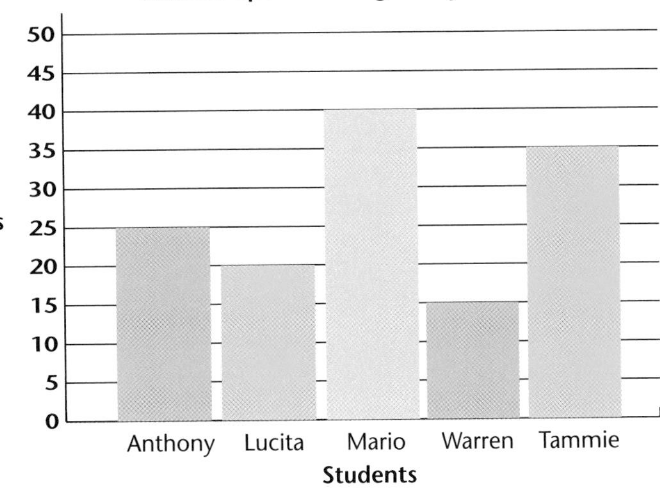

This bar graph contains

- a title
- horizontal and vertical axes with labels
- individual data values

To compare data shown by a bar graph, compare the heights of the bars. The tallest bars represent the greatest data values.

Histogram

A way of showing the frequency of data using rectangular bars and the area they contain

A **histogram** uses rectangular bars and area to represent the frequency of data. The histogram below shows how a class scored on a recent quiz.

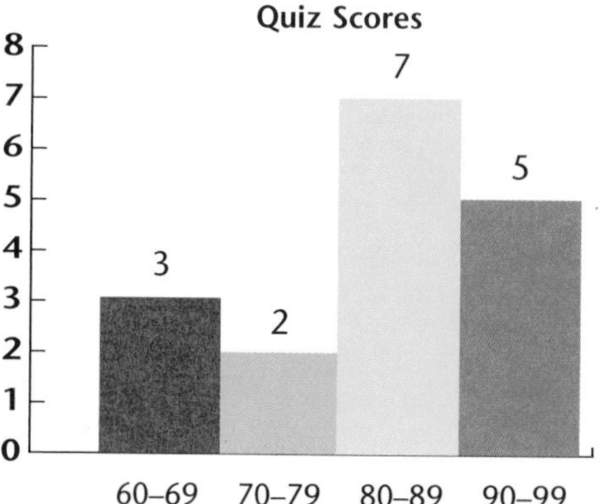

This histogram contains

- a title
- horizontal and vertical axes with regular intervals and labels
- data

Exercise A Consider the data in the chart.

1. Display the data in a stem-and-leaf plot.
2. Display the data in a frequency table.
3. Display the data in a bar graph.
4. Display the data in a histogram.

Age in Years		
21	2	13
10	11	7
20	19	26
27	14	6
3	30	25
4	20	11
16	22	4
12	5	24

Exercise B Use the graphs you made in Exercise A to answer these questions.

5. How are the graphs alike?

6. How are the graphs different?

7. Which data value occurs most often? Which occurs least often?

8. In which graph can you most easily find the data value or values that occur most often?

9. In which graph can you most easily find the data value or values that occur least often?

10. In which graph is the greatest data value easiest to find? In which graph is the least data value easiest to find? Explain.

Algebra in Your Life

Making a Budget

How much money do you spend? Here's a way to find out. Get a small notebook. Divide each page into columns and title each column. You might use these titles: recreation, clothes, gifts, food, gasoline, and savings. Carry your notebook with you everywhere. For three months, record everything you spend. After three months, divide the total amount you've spent in each category by three. This will give you the average of what you spend each month. From that information, you can develop a budget you can work with.

Lesson 2 Range, Mean, Median, and Mode

Range

The difference between the greatest and least values in a set of data

Mean

The sum of the values in a set of data divided by the number of pieces of data in the set

The stem-and-leaf plot you learned about in Lesson 1 uses numerals to display data. Range, median, mean, and mode are numerical ways to describe data.

Study this set of data: {\$6.50, \$7.31, \$10.00, \$25.95, \$10.00, \$4.50, \$2.13, \$6.50, \$10.00}

The **range** of the set of data is the difference between the greatest and least values. To compute the range, subtract the least value from the greatest value.

\$25.95	greatest value
−\$2.13	least value
\$23.82	

The range is \$23.82.

The arithmetic **mean** of a set of data is the sum of the values in the set divided by the number of values in the set.

EXAMPLE 1 Find the arithmetic mean of the set of data {\$6.50, \$7.31, \$10.00, \$25.95, \$10.00, \$4.50, \$2.13, \$6.50, \$10.00}.

Step 1 Find the sum of the data values in the set.

```
 $ 6.50
   7.31
  10.00
  25.95
  10.00
   4.50
   2.13
   6.50
+ 10.00
 $82.89
```

Step 2 Count the number of data values in the set. Divide the sum by the number of data values in the set.

\$82.89 ÷ 9 = \$9.21

The mean is \$9.21.

Median

The middle value in an ordered set of data

The **median** of a set of data is the middle value when the set is ordered from greatest to least or least to greatest.

EXAMPLE 2 Find the median of the set of data {$10.00, $25.95, $2.13, $10.00, $7.31, $6.50, $10.00, $6.50, $4.50}.

Step 1 Order the data values from greatest to least or from least to greatest.

$25.95 $10.00 $10.00 $10.00 $7.31 $6.50 $6.50 $4.50 $2.13

Step 2 Cross off the greatest and least values in the set. Continue crossing off greatest and least pairs until one value remains in the middle of the set.

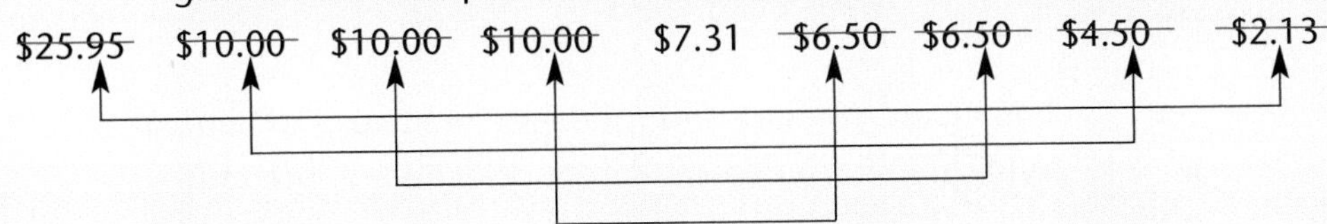

The data value remaining in the middle of the set is the median. The median of the set of data is $7.31.

The data set above has an odd number of values. Any set of data that has an odd number of values will always have a middle value. However, some sets of data have an even number of values. To find the median of such a set, arrange the values in order from greatest to least or least to greatest, and cross off greatest and least pairs until two values remain in the middle of the set. The median is the mean, or average, of these values.

EXAMPLE 3 Find the median of the set of data {9, 4, 2, 10}.

Step 1 Arrange the values from greatest to least or least to greatest.

2 4 9 10

Step 2 Cross off greatest and least pairs until two values remain in the middle of the set.

~~2~~ 4 9 ~~10~~

Step 3 Find the mean of the two values in the middle of the set. Add the values, then divide by 2 because there are 2 values in the set.

$$\begin{array}{r} 4 \\ +\,9 \\ \hline 13 \end{array} \qquad 13 \div 2 = 6.5 \text{ or } 6\tfrac{1}{2}$$

The median of the set of data is 6.5 or $6\frac{1}{2}$.

Mode

The value or values that occur most often in a set of data

Measures of central tendency

The mean, median, and mode of a set of data

The **mode** of a set of data is the value or values that occur most often. To compute the mode of a set of data, count the number of times each value appears. The value or values that appear most often is the mode.

EXAMPLE 4 Find the mode of the set of data

{1, 8, 6, 8, 2, 4, 9, 6}.

↑ ↑ ↑ ↑

The values 8 and 6 appear twice. All of the other values appear only once. Therefore, the modes are 8 and 6.

The mean, median, and mode are **measures of central tendency.** Each describes a set of data in a different way.

Exercise A Use this data set for the following exercise.

{8.2, 3.005, 2.03, 14, 7.75, 3, 1.01, 3.005}

1. Compute the range.

2. Compute the mean.

3. Compute the median.

4. Compute the mode.

Exercise B

5. Create a set of data that contains at least six values. Compute the range, mean, median, and mode of the set.

Exercise C

6. Create a data set that contains five values and has a range of 10.

7. Create a data set that contains four values and has a mean of 24.

8. Create a data set that contains seven values and has a median of 2.75.

9. Create a data set that contains three values and has a mode of $\frac{1}{3}$.

10. Which measure—range, mean, median, or mode—best describes the ages of your classmates? Explain.

A calculator can be used to compute the arithmetic mean, or average, of a set of data.

EXAMPLE 5 Find the average of the set of data {4.1, 2.5, 13.8}.

Step 1 Use a calculator to find the sum of the data values in the set.

Enter 4.1 [+] 2.5 [+] 13.8 [=]

Step 2 The calculator will display 20.4.

Divide by 3—the number of data values in the set.

Press [÷] 3 [=] The display reads 6.8.

The average of {4.1, 2.5, 13.8} is 6.8.

If your calculator has a sum [Σ+] key and a mean [$\bar{x}$] key, enter 4.1 [Σ+] 2.5 [Σ+] 13.8 [Σ+]. Then press [$\bar{x}$].
(On most calculators, you will need to press [SHIFT] [$\bar{x}$] or [2nd] [$\bar{x}$].) The display reads 6.8.

Exercise D Use a calculator to find the average of each set of data.

11. {12, 21, 34, 7}

12. {3.2, 16.5, 9.1}

13. {110, 158, 86}

14. {73.02, 11.145, 11.955}

15. {10, 550, 212, 623, 1914.06}

Lesson 3 Box-and-Whiskers Plots

Box-and-whiskers plot
A way to describe the concentration and the spread of data in a set

Lower quartile
The median of the scores below the median

Upper quartile
The median of the scores above the median

The bar graph and histogram you learned about in Lesson 1 are visual ways to represent data. A **box-and-whiskers plot** is another visual way to describe the concentration and the spread of data in a set. A box-and-whiskers plot with its box and two whiskers looks like this:

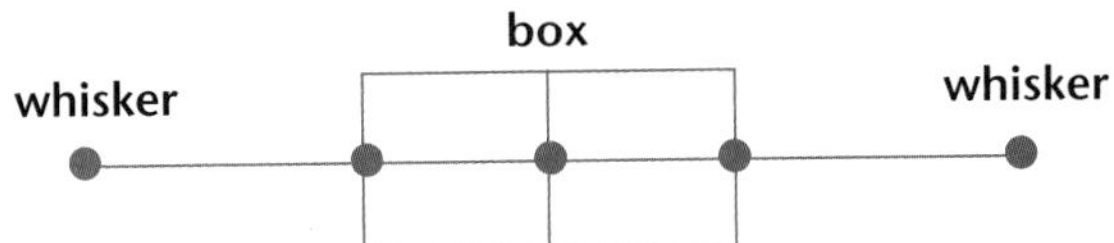

EXAMPLE 1 Construct a box-and-whiskers plot for the data set. The data represents the number of points seven players on a basketball team scored during a game.

{8, 3, 13, 10, 17, 12, 5}

Step 1 Arrange the data in order from greatest to least or least to greatest.

3 5 8 10 12 13 17

Step 2 Identify the greatest and least values of the data. These values are called the upper and lower extremes.

3 5 8 10 12 13 17
↑ (3) lower extreme ↑ (17) upper extreme

Step 3 Find the median of the data.

3 5 8 10 12 13 17
↑ (10) median

Step 4 Find the median of all of the scores below the median. This median is called the **lower quartile.** Then find the median of all of the scores above the median. This median is called the **upper quartile.**

3 5 8 10 12 13 17
↑ (5) lower quartile ↑ (13) upper quartile

Step 5 Draw a number line that can display all of the data in the set.

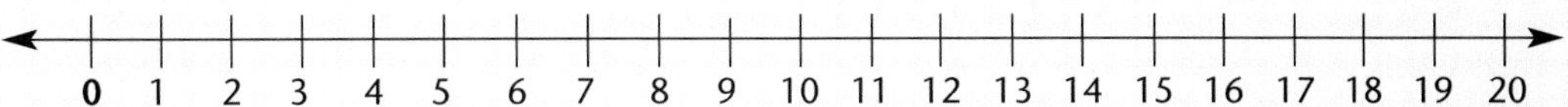

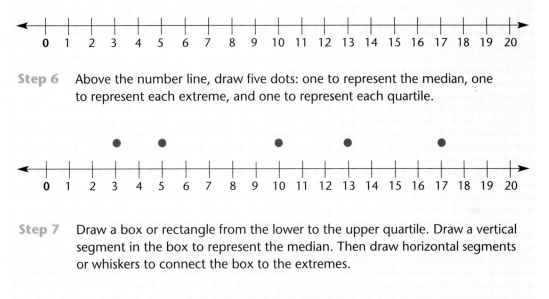

Step 6 Above the number line, draw five dots: one to represent the median, one to represent each extreme, and one to represent each quartile.

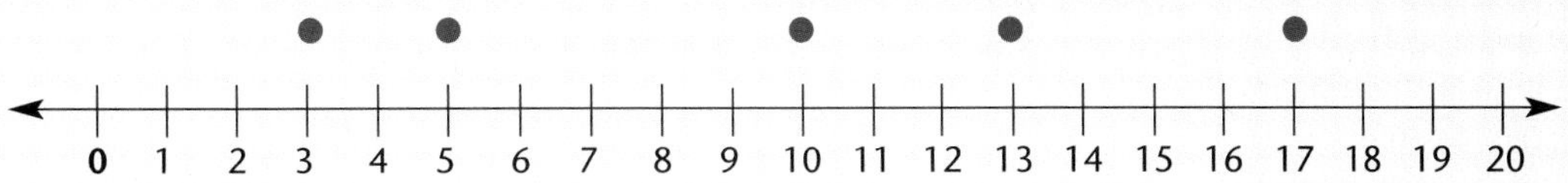

Step 7 Draw a box or rectangle from the lower to the upper quartile. Draw a vertical segment in the box to represent the median. Then draw horizontal segments or whiskers to connect the box to the extremes.

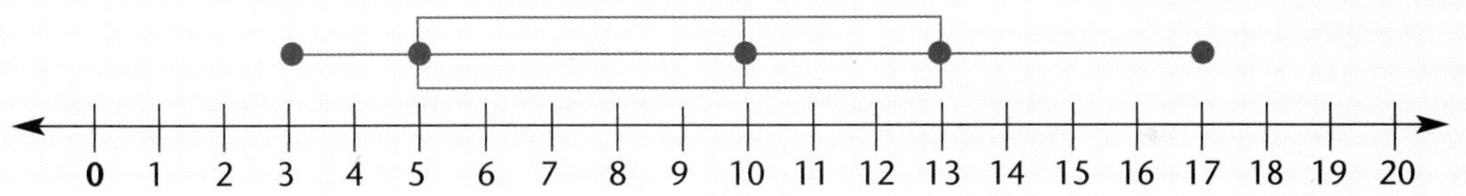

The box in a box-and-whiskers plot contains approximately 50% of the data. The box-and-whiskers plot above tells you that the middle 50% of the data range, or cluster, is from 5 to 13. Box-and-whiskers plots are especially useful when comparing large sets of data.

Writing About Mathematics

Survey your classmates. Ask them to estimate the average number of minutes they study each week. Record the data you collect and construct a box-and-whiskers plot from it.

Exercise A Use the following data set {42, 48, 44, 45, 41, 39, 45, 49, 47, 44, 40, 51, 49} to make a box-and-whiskers plot.

1. Arrange the data in order from greatest to least or least to greatest. Identify the greatest value of the data and label it upper extreme.
2. Identify the least value of the data and label it lower extreme.
3. Find the median of the data and label it median.
4. Find the median of all of the data above the median and label it upper quartile. Find the median of all of the data below the median and label it lower quartile.
5. Draw a number line that can display all of the data in the set. Draw dots for the median, both extremes, and both quartiles. Draw a box or rectangle from the lower to the upper quartile. Draw a vertical segment in the box to represent the median. Then draw horizontal segments or whiskers to connect the box to the extremes.

TRY THIS If a box-and-whiskers plot would also include the mean of the data, would the mean be in the box or on a whisker? Explain.

Estimation Activity

Estimate: Find the average (mean) of a set of numbers.

Find the average of 39, 42, 44, 45, 47, 48, 51

Solution: Take the highest and lowest numbers and add them.
$51 + 39 = 90$
Divide by 2 $90 \div 2 = 45$

The estimated average is 45.

Exercise B Use the following data set {18, 16, 12, 22, 21, 16, 20, 21, 14, 17, 15} to make a box-and-whiskers plot.

6. Arrange the data in order from greatest to least or least to greatest. Identify the greatest value of the data and label it upper extreme.

7. Identify the least value of the data and label it lower extreme.

8. Find the median of the data and label it median.

9. Find the median of all of the data above the median and label it upper quartile. Find the median of all of the data below the median and label it lower quartile.

10. Draw a number line that can display all of the data in the set. Draw dots for the median, both extremes, and both quartiles. Draw a box or rectangle from the lower to the upper quartile. Draw a vertical segment in the box to represent the median. Then draw horizontal segments or whiskers to connect the box to the extremes.

Lesson 4 The Probability Fraction

Statistics

Numerical facts about people, places, or things

Probability

The chance or likelihood of an event occurring

In Lesson 2, you explored the mean, median, and mode of a set of data. Mean, median, and mode are examples of **statistics.** Statistics also include **probability**—the chance or likelihood that an outcome will occur.

Probability experiments always include an event and one or more outcomes. To find the probability (P) that an outcome will occur, use the fraction

$$P = \frac{\text{number of favorable outcomes}}{\text{number of possible outcomes}}$$

EXAMPLE 1 Suppose a coin is tossed once. What is the probability P that the coin will land heads up?

Step 1 Use the probability fraction.

$$P = \frac{\text{number of favorable outcomes}}{\text{number of possible outcomes}}$$

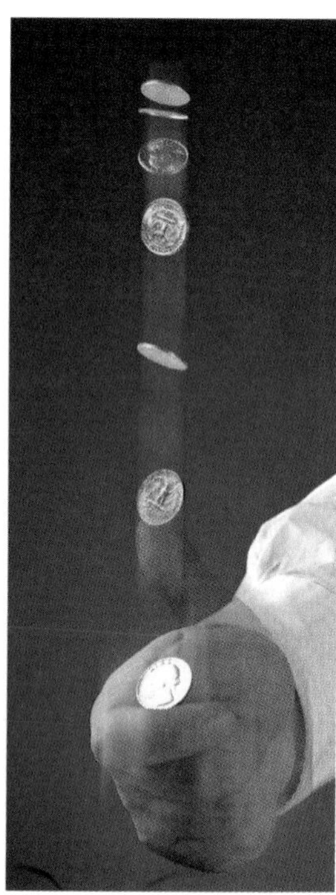

Step 2 Find the denominator. Since there are two possible outcomes when the coin is tossed—the coin will land either heads up or tails up—the denominator is two.

$$P = \frac{\text{number of favorable outcomes}}{2}$$

Step 3 Find the numerator. Since one outcome is favorable—the coin landing heads up—the numerator is one.

$$P = \frac{1}{2}$$

The probability of tossing a coin and having it land heads up is $\frac{1}{2}$.

Since you know how to change a fraction to a percent, you can also say that the probability of flipping a coin and having it land heads up is 50%. This is because $\frac{1}{2} = 50\%$.

Theoretical probability

The predicted likelihood of what should happen in an experiment

EXAMPLE 2 Suppose the 1–6 number cube at the right is rolled once. What is the probability of rolling an even number?

Step 1 Use the probability fraction.

$$P = \frac{\text{number of favorable outcomes}}{\text{number of possible outcomes}}$$

Step 2 Find the denominator. Since there are six possible outcomes when the cube is rolled—1, 2, 3, 4, 5, or 6—the denominator is six.

$$P = \frac{\text{number of favorable outcomes}}{6}$$

Step 3 Find the numerator. Since three outcomes are favorable—2, 4, or 6—the numerator is three.

$$P = \frac{3}{6}$$

Step 4 Simplify if possible.

$$P = \frac{3}{6} = \frac{1}{2}$$

The probability of rolling a 1–6 number cube and rolling an even number is $\frac{1}{2}$ or 50%.

In each of these examples, the probability you found is the **theoretical probability** of each event. Theoretical probability describes what will happen if the experiment is performed many times. In other words, if you toss a coin many times, the probability that the coin lands heads up (or tails up) approaches $\frac{1}{2}$ or 50%, and if you roll a 1–6 number cube many times, the probability of an even (or odd) outcome approaches $\frac{1}{2}$ or 50%.

The theoretical probability of any event will always be 0, 1, or a fraction between 0 and 1.

EXAMPLE 3 The probability of rolling a 1–6 number cube and rolling a 7 is zero because the outcome 7 is not possible. $P = \frac{0}{6} = 0$

EXAMPLE 4 The probability of tossing a coin and having it land heads up or tails up is one because either outcome is favorable. $P = \frac{2}{2} = 1$

Exercise A In a probability experiment, a 1–6 number cube is rolled once. Find the theoretical probability (P) of each event. Express your answer as a fraction in simplest form.

1. P (2)

2. P (3 or 5)

3. P (odd number)

4. P (2, 3, or 4)

5. P (prime number)

6. P (composite number)

Exercise B In a probability experiment, a painted cube is rolled once. One side of the cube is painted red, two sides are painted yellow, and three sides are painted green. Find the theoretical probability (P) of each event.

7. P (yellow)

8. P (green)

9. P (red)

10. P (yellow or green)

11. P (blue)

12. P (red or yellow or green)

Exercise C Suppose you write each letter of your first name on a slip of paper. All the slips of paper are the same size. The slips are placed in a bag and you take out one slip, without looking.

13. Find (P) of getting a vowel.

14. Find (P) of getting a consonant.

15. Find (P) of getting the first letter of your name.

16. Find (P) of getting the last letter of your name.

Exercise D

17. Describe an experiment that has a probability of 1.

18. Describe an experiment that has a probability of 0.

19. Describe an experiment that has a probability that is greater than 0 but less than 1.

20. Why can't the probability of any event ever exceed 1?

Technology Connection

Cell Phones + Pagers = More Phone Numbers

The number of ways we can "reach out and touch" one another continues to multiply. Less than a decade ago, there was usually one telephone number per household. Now a household may have a phone line for the computer, two or three cell phones, and a pager. All of these lines need a number different from the regular phone line. Phone companies began running out of numbers. The solution was to add more area codes. Adding just three digits has increased the combinations of phone numbers by the millions!

Lesson 5 Probability and Complementary Events

Remember that the probability of any outcome occurring is 0, 1, or a fraction between 0 and 1. The word *impossible* is sometimes used to describe a probability of 0, and the word *certain* is sometimes used to describe a probability of 1.

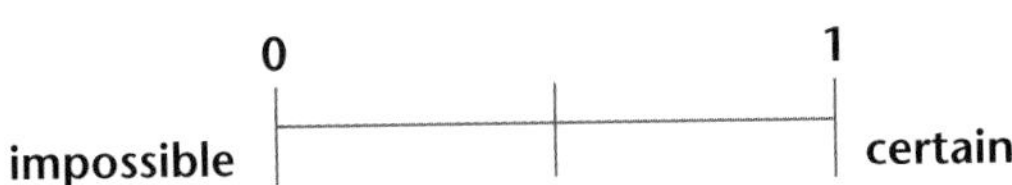

Phrases are sometimes used to describe a probability between 0 and 1. These phrases include *not likely* and *very likely*.

EXAMPLE 1 Suppose you roll a 1–6 number cube once and are looking for an outcome of 1, 2, 3, 4, or 5. You are *very likely* to be successful because there are five favorable outcomes (1, 2, 3, 4, 5) in the event and only one unfavorable outcome (6).

Suppose you roll a 1–6 number cube once and are looking for an outcome of 6. You are *not likely* to be successful because there is only one favorable outcome (6) in the event and five unfavorable outcomes (1, 2, 3, 4, 5).

Phrases such as *more likely* and *less likely* are sometimes used when probabilities are compared.

EXAMPLE 2 Suppose each letter of the alphabet is written on a slip of paper. All the slips of paper are the same size and are folded in the same way. If you choose one slip without looking, you will be *more likely* to choose a consonant than a vowel because there are 21 consonants and only 5 vowels in the alphabet. Also, you will be *less likely* to choose a vowel than a consonant for the same reason.

These words and phrases are used in a general way to describe probability. Probability can also be described in a specific or exact way. Recall that you explored how to find the probability of an outcome occurring. You can also find the probability of an outcome *not* occurring.

Complement of a probabilty event

The set of outcomes that are not in the event

Example 3 What is the probability of tossing a coin and not getting an outcome that is heads?

Step 1 Use the probability fraction.

$$P = \frac{\text{number of favorable outcomes}}{\text{number of possible outcomes}}$$

Step 2 Find the denominator. Since there are two possible outcomes when the coin is tossed—the coin will land either heads up or tails up—the denominator is two.

$$P = \frac{\text{number of favorable outcomes}}{2}$$

Step 3 Find the numerator. Since you are looking for an outcome that is not heads, the outcome that is favorable is tails. There is one favorable outcome.

$$P = \frac{1}{2}$$

The probability of tossing a coin and not getting an outcome that is heads is $\frac{1}{2}$. It is also an example of the complement of a probability event. The **complement of a probability event** is the set of outcomes that are not in the event.

Example 4 Find (P) not blue.

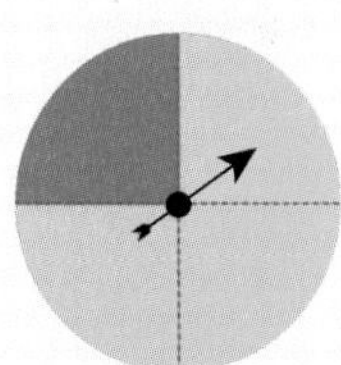

Since the probability of the spinner pointing to blue is $\frac{1}{4}$, the probability of the spinner not pointing to blue is $\frac{3}{4}$, because $\frac{1}{4} + \frac{3}{4} = \frac{4}{4} = 1$.

(P) not blue $= \frac{3}{4}$

Exercise A Write each sentence on a sheet of paper. Use one of these words or phrases to complete each sentence: *certain, impossible, very likely, not likely, more likely, less likely.*

1. The probability of tossing a coin and getting an outcome of heads or tails is ______.
2. An outcome of 2 or 4 on a 1–6 number cube is ______ than an outcome of any odd number.
3. An outcome of tossing a coin and getting an outcome of tails is ______ than rolling a 1–6 number cube and getting an outcome of 3.
4. The probability of tossing a coin and getting an outcome of heads and tails is ______.
5. An outcome of an odd number on a 1–6 number cube is ______ than an outcome of 3 or 5.
6. The probability of tossing a coin and getting an outcome of heads and tails is ______ than the probability of flipping a coin and getting an outcome of heads or tails.
7. It is ______ that a person was born during the month of February.
8. It is ______ that a person's age is a one-digit or a two-digit number.

Exercise B Refer to the spinner at the right. Express the probability of each event below as a fraction in simplest form.

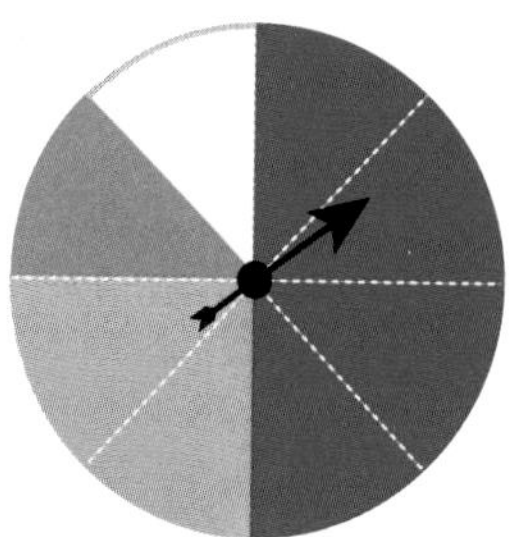

9. P (blue)
10. P (orange)
11. P (green)
12. P (not white)
13. P (not orange)
14. P (not white and not blue)
15. P (white or green)
16. P (green or not blue)
17. P (blue or white)
18. P (not green and not white)

PROBLEM SOLVING

Exercise C Determine the probability in each of the following problems.

19. Suppose your teacher randomly selects a student from your class. What is the probability that the student selected is you?

20. Suppose your teacher randomly selects a student from your class. What is the probability that the student selected is not male?

Lesson 6 Tree Diagrams and Sample Spaces

Sample space
The set of all possible outcomes of an experiment

In probability, a **sample space** is the set of all possible outcomes of an experiment. A tree diagram can be used to generate a sample space.

EXAMPLE 1 There are two children in a family. What is the probability that the first child is a girl and the second child is a boy? Use a tree diagram to solve.

Step 1 Show the possible outcomes for the first child. The first child could be a girl or a boy.

first child → girl boy

Step 2 Show the possible outcomes for the second child. If the first child was a girl, the second child could be a girl or a boy. If the first child was a boy, the second child could be a girl or a boy.

first child → girl boy
second child → girl boy girl boy

Step 3 Draw branches for your tree diagram. Each complete branch represents one possible outcome.

first child → girl boy
second child → girl boy girl boy

The sample space shows there are four possible combinations of children: (girl, girl), (girl, boy), (boy, girl), and (boy, boy). The probability that the first child was a girl and the second child was a boy is one of those combinations, or $\frac{1}{4}$.

EXAMPLE 2 A coin is tossed and the spinner at the right is spun once. What is the probability that the coin will land tails up and the spinner will point to 3?

Step 1 Show the possible outcomes for the coin.

coin → heads tails

Step 2 Show the possible outcomes for the spinner.

coin → heads tails

spinner → 1 2 3 1 2 3

If the outcome of the coin is heads, the outcome of the spinner can be 1, 2, or 3.

If the outcome of the coin is tails, the outcome of the spinner can be 1, 2, or 3.

Step 3 Draw branches for your tree diagram.

coin → heads tails

spinner → 1 2 3 1 2 3

The sample space shows there are six possible combinations: (heads and 1), (heads and 2), (heads and 3), (tails and 1), (tails and 2), (tails and 3). The probability that the coin was tails and the spinner pointed to 3 is one of those combinations, or $\frac{1}{6}$.

Exercise A Suppose you spin the spinner at the right and toss a coin. Use a tree diagram to determine the probability of each outcome below.

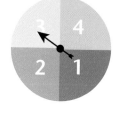

1. Find P (heads and 1)

2. Find P (tails and an odd number)

3. Find P (tails and a multiple of 3)

4. Find P (heads and a prime number)

5. Find P (not heads and not 4)

6. Find P (not tails and not a whole number)

7. Find P (heads or tails and a whole number)

How many different outcomes are possible if two 1–6 number cubes are rolled? What is the probability of rolling a 6 with each cube?

Exercise B Suppose you spin the spinner at the right and roll a 1–6 number cube.

8. Find P (B and 6)

9. Find P (R and an even number)

10. Find P (M or V and 4)

11. Find P (a consonant and a composite number)

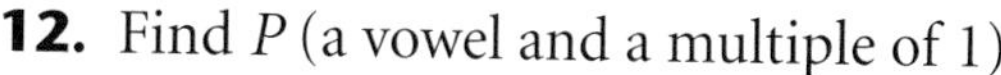

12. Find P (a vowel and a multiple of 1)

13. Find P (not M and not an odd number)

14. Find P (not B or not E and not a multiple of 2)

15. Find P (not B and 6)

Lesson 7 Dependent and Independent Events

Probability consists of events, trials, and outcomes. A coin toss, for example, is an event, tossing the coin is a trial, and (heads) and (tails) are the outcomes that could occur. Events in a probability experiment can be dependent or independent

EXAMPLE 1 Suppose a bag contains four marbles, all the same size. Two marbles are red and two marbles are yellow. You reach into the bag, choose a marble, record its color, and put the marble in your pocket. Then you take another marble from the bag. What is the probability that you will take out two yellow marbles? The experiment contains two events. Find the probability of each event.

Step 1 Find the probability of the first event—taking a yellow marble from the bag.
Use the probability fraction.

$$P = \frac{\text{number of favorable outcomes}}{\text{number of possible outcomes}}$$

In this event, there are four possible outcomes because there are four marbles in the bag. The denominator of the fraction is four. Since choosing either yellow marble that is in the bag is a favorable outcome, the numerator of the fraction is 2. The probability of this event is $\frac{2}{4}$.

Step 2 Find the probability of the second event—taking a yellow marble from the bag. Remember, you put the first marble that was taken from the bag in your pocket.

$$P = \frac{\text{number of favorable outcomes}}{\text{number of possible outcomes}}$$

In this event, there are three possible outcomes because there are three marbles in the bag. The denominator of the fraction is three. In the first trial, assume you chose a yellow marble. Since choosing the yellow marble that is still in the bag is a favorable outcome, the numerator of the fraction is 1. The probability of this event is $\frac{1}{3}$.

Step 3 To find the probability of taking out two yellow marbles, multiply the probability of the first event by the probability of the second event.

$$P = \frac{2}{4} \bullet \frac{1}{3} = \frac{2}{12} = \frac{1}{6}$$

Dependent event

In a probability experiment, the outcome of one event is affected by the outcome of any other event

The probability of the outcome is $\frac{1}{6}$. The events in this experiment were dependent. In **dependent events,** the outcome of the first event affects the outcome of all other events in the experiment.

EXAMPLE 2 Suppose a bag contains four marbles, all the same size. Two marbles are black and two marbles are white. You reach into the bag, choose a marble, and record its color. Then you replace the marble in the bag and take out a marble again. What is the probability that you will take out two white marbles? The experiment contains two events. Find the probability of each event.

Step 1 Find the probability of the first event—taking a white marble from the bag.
Use the probability fraction.

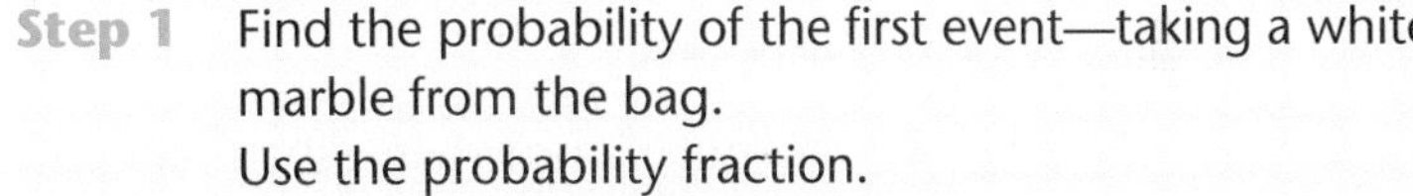

$$P = \frac{\text{number of favorable outcomes}}{\text{number of possible outcomes}}$$

In this event, there are four possible outcomes because there are four marbles in the bag. The denominator of the fraction is four. Since choosing either white marble that is in the bag is a favorable outcome, the numerator of the fraction is 2. The probability of this event is $\frac{2}{4}$.

Step 2 Find the probability of the second event—taking a white marble from the bag. Remember, you put the first marble that was taken from the bag back into the bag.

$$P = \frac{\text{number of favorable outcomes}}{\text{number of possible outcomes}}$$

In this event, there again are four possible outcomes because there are four marbles in the bag. The denominator of the fraction is four. Since choosing either white marble that is in the bag is a favorable outcome, the numerator of the fraction is 2. The probability of this event is $\frac{2}{4}$.

Step 3 To find the probability of taking out two white marbles, multiply the probability of the first event by the probability of the second event.

$$P = \frac{2}{4} \bullet \frac{2}{4} = \frac{4}{16} = \frac{1}{4}$$

Independent event

In a probability experiment, the outcome of any event does not affect the outcome of any other event

The probability of the outcome is $\frac{1}{4}$. The events in this experiment were independent. In **independent events,** the outcome of an event does not affect the outcome of any other event in the experiment.

Exercise A

1. To find the probability of tossing five tails in a row, you toss the same coin five times. Are the events in the experiment dependent or independent? Explain.
2. Suppose a consonant of the alphabet is chosen at random and removed. Then a different consonant is chosen. Are the events in the experiment dependent or independent? Explain.
3. Suppose a number cube is rolled and the outcome is 6. The cube is rolled a second time and again the outcome is 6. If the cube is rolled again, what will the outcome be? Explain.

Exercise B

Suppose a bag contains 6 marbles. All the marbles are the same size. One marble is green, two marbles are orange, and three marbles are purple. A marble will be taken from the bag two times. Each time a marble is taken out, it is replaced.

4. Find P (orange and green).
5. Find P (green and purple).
6. Find P (not purple and not orange).

Exercise C

Suppose a bag contains 8 marbles. All the marbles are the same size. One marble is red, two marbles are white, and five marbles are blue. A marble will be taken from the bag two times. Each time a marble is taken, it is *not* replaced.

7. Find P (white and red).

8. Find P (blue and white).

9. Find P (red and not white).

10. Find P (blue).

TRY THIS Look again at Exercise C. Suppose you take out a marble three times. What is the probability of (red and white and blue)? Express your answer as a percent rounded to the nearest whole number.

Writing About Mathematics

You might expect to get 5 heads and 5 tails in 10 coin tosses. Toss a coin 10 times. Tally the results. Compare your results to your prediction.

Lesson 8 The Fundamental Principle of Counting

Fundamental principle of counting

A general rule that states that if one task can be completed p *different ways, and a second task can be completed* q *different ways, the first task followed by the second task can be completed* p • q, *or* pq, *different ways*

Recall that a tree diagram can be used to generate a sample space.

EXAMPLE 1 Suppose you plan to travel from Detroit, Michigan, to Cheyenne, Wyoming, and pass through Lincoln, Nebraska, on the way. If there are three different roads you can travel from Detroit to Lincoln and two different roads you can travel from Lincoln to Cheyenne, how many different ways can you travel from Detroit to Cheyenne? Make a tree diagram.

Step 1 Show the different roads you can travel from Detroit to Lincoln. There are three different roads you can travel from Detroit to Lincoln.

Detroit

Lincoln

Step 2 Show the different roads you can travel from Lincoln to Cheyenne. There are two different roads you can travel from Lincoln to Cheyenne.

Detroit

Lincoln

Cheyenne

Step 3 Since there are 3 different roads you can travel from Detroit to Lincoln, and 2 different roads you can travel from Lincoln to Cheyenne, there are 3 • 2 or 6 different ways you can travel from Detroit to Cheyenne and pass through Lincoln.

A tree diagram helps you find all of the different ways without forgetting any.

Another method you could use to find the answer is the fundamental principle of counting. The **fundamental principle of counting** is a general rule that states that you can multiply the number of choices for each task to find the total number of choices.

Permutation

An arrangement of some or all of a set of numbers in a specific order

Factorial notation

The product of all positive integers from a given integer to 1 represented by the symbol (!)

EXAMPLE 2 How many different ways can Geri rearrange the letters of her name? Use the fundamental principle of counting to find out.

Step 1 Find the number of letters Geri could use for the first letter of her name.

4			

Any of four letters—G, E, R, or I—could be used for the first letter of her name.

Step 2 Find the number of letters Geri could use for the second letter of her name.

4 •	3 •		

A letter must have been used for the first letter of her name. So there are three letters remaining to choose from.

Step 3 Find the number of letters Geri could use for the third letter of her name.

4 •	3 •	2 •	

Two letters—one for the first letter in her name and one for the second—have been used. So there are two letters remaining to choose from.

The ways in which the members of a set can be arranged in an ordered fashion are called **permutations.** You can use the fundamental principle of counting to determine the number of permutations in a set.

Step 4 Find the number of letters Geri could use for the last letter of her name.

4 •	3 •	2 •	1

Three letters have been used, and only one letter remains.

Geri can arrange the letters of her name $4 \cdot 3 \cdot 2 \cdot 1$ or 24 different ways.

The computation $4 \cdot 3 \cdot 2 \cdot 1 = 24$ is an example of a factorial. The factorial is the product of all positive integers from a given integer to 1 and is represented by the symbol (!). In **factorial notation,** $4! = 4 \cdot 3 \cdot 2 \cdot 1 = 24$.

Example 3 Find 4!.

Find the product 4 • 3 • 2 • 1.

4! = 24

Find 6!.

Find the product 6 • 5 • 4 • 3 • 2 • 1.

6! = 720

When finding factorials, you may find it helpful to use a calculator. If you use a scientific calculator, look for the [!] key.

PROBLEM SOLVING

Exercise A Identify the number of arrangements possible for each of the following situations.

1. Choose any two letters of the alphabet. How many different ways can those letters be arranged?
2. Suppose that you want to read three books, and you can read them in any order. In how many different ways can you read the books?
3. Five students are waiting in a line. As they wait, how many different ways can they arrange themselves in that line?
4. How many different ways can Tamika, Miguel, Blevian, Trina, and Mark be seated in five chairs if Miguel must always sit in the first chair?
5. Jason has four winter hats, three scarves, and three pairs of mittens. How many different combinations of one hat, one scarf, and one pair of mittens can Jason wear?

PROBLEM SOLVING

Exercise B Use a calculator for these exercises.

6. A computer password is made up of four characters. Two characters must be letters of the alphabet and two characters must be digits (numbers). If no characters can be repeated, how many different passwords are possible?

7. A student is taking a true/false quiz. The quiz has ten questions. If the student guesses every answer, how many different arrangements of answers are possible?

8. Some of the license plates on automobiles display six characters—the first three characters are letters of the alphabet and the last three characters are digits (numbers). Characters may be repeated any number of times. How many different license plates of this style can be made?

9. Consider the phone number 924-xxxx. How many different phone numbers are possible with a 924 prefix?

10. How many different orders of finish can there be if there are eight people in a race and each person finishes the race?

Application

Multistage Experiments

To find the probability that any outcome in an experiment will occur, use the fraction

$$P = \frac{\text{number of favorable outcomes}}{\text{number of possible outcomes}}$$

Some probability experiments are multistage experiments. To find the probability of a multistage experiment, first determine the probability of each stage. Then find the product of the probabilities.

EXAMPLE 1 The following box contains the letters that spell the word mathematics.

m a t h e m a t i c s

Suppose you were to draw a letter from the box without looking and not replace it. Then you repeat the procedure three more times. What is the probability that you will first draw *c*, then *a*, then *t*, and then *s* to spell the word *cats*?

Step 1 Find the probability of each stage. Remember that you do not replace the letter after each draw.

Stage 1: Drawing the letter *c*. $P = \frac{1}{11}$

Stage 2: Drawing the letter *a*. $P = \frac{2}{10}$

Stage 3: Drawing the letter *t*. $P = \frac{2}{9}$

Stage 4: Drawing the letter *s*. $P = \frac{1}{8}$

Step 2 Find the product of the probability for each stage.

$$\frac{1}{11} \bullet \frac{2}{10} \bullet \frac{2}{9} \bullet \frac{1}{8} = \frac{4}{7{,}920} \text{ or } \frac{1}{1{,}980}$$

Exercise Suppose a launched rocket must burn three separate stages of fuel to reach orbit. The probability of failure for the first stage is $\frac{1}{10}$, for the second stage is $\frac{1}{10}$, and for the third stage is $\frac{1}{100}$.

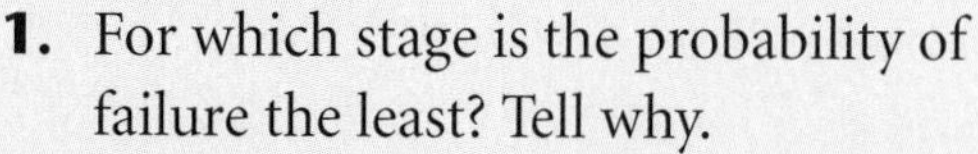

1. For which stage is the probability of failure the least? Tell why.

2. For which stage is the probability of success the greatest? Tell why.

3. Determine the probability of an overall failure. (Stages 1, 2, and 3 all fail.)

4. How many times less likely is the third stage to fail than the first or second stage? Explain.

5. In one million launches of this rocket, how many launches would you expect to fail?

Chapter 7 REVIEW

Use the data in the table to answer questions 1 through 4. Write the letter of the correct answer.

Age in Years		
37	30	84
42	4	49
14	11	13
21	28	51
54	61	26

1. What is the mean of the data in the table?

A 30 **C** 35

B 51 **D** 37

2. What is the median of the data in the table?

A 35 **C** 11

B 30 **D** 80

3. What is the range of the data in the table?

A 80 **C** 35

B 30 **D** 88

4. What is the mode of the data in the table?

A 11 **C** 30

B no mode **D** 35

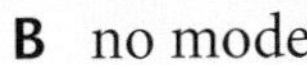

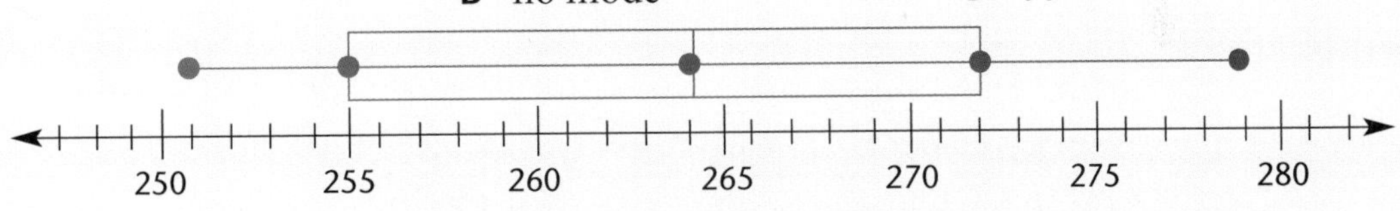

Use the box-and-whiskers plot above to answer questions 5 through 7. Write the letter of the correct answer.

5. Which values represent the quartiles?

A 251 and 272 **C** 251 and 279

B 255 and 272 **D** 264 and 279

6. Which value represents the median?

A 250 **C** 255

B 132 **D** 264

7. Which values represent the extremes?

A 255 and 272 **C** 251 and 279

B 251 and 255 **D** 272 and 279

Decide if the probability of each of the following events is 0, 1, close to 0, or close to 1.

Example: A day of the week is chosen at random.
The name of the weekday begins with a B.
Solution: Since no day of the week has a name that begins with B, the outcome is impossible, and the event has a probability of zero.

8. A person is chosen at random. The second digit of the person's age is 7.

9. A month of the year has only 27 days.

10. A person is born in winter, spring, or summer.

11. A day of the week chosen at random ends with the letter *y*.

In a probability experiment, two 1–6 number cubes are rolled once. Find the theoretical probability (P) of each event. Express your answer as a fraction in simplest form.

Example: $P(1, 2)$
Solution: Find the probability of each outcome and then find the product of the probabilities. $\frac{1}{6} \bullet \frac{1}{6} = \frac{1}{36}$

12. $P(1, 1)$

13. $P(0, 4)$

14. $P(3, 3 \text{ or } 6, 6)$

15. P(a multiple of 2 and a multiple of 3)

16. P(1 and 1 or 2 and 2 or 5 and 5 or 6 and 6)

17. P(a prime number and not a prime number)

Solve the following probabilities involving marbles.

Example: A bag contains 3 marbles—one red, one blue, and one white. Each time a marble is taken out, it is not replaced. Find the probability (P) of choosing a blue marble and then a red one.
Solution: $P(\text{blue}) = \frac{1}{3}$ $P(\text{red}) = \frac{1}{2}$ $P(\text{blue and red})$ $\frac{1}{3} \bullet \frac{1}{2} = \frac{1}{6}$

Suppose a bag contains 5 marbles. One is white, two are red, and two are yellow. Each time a marble is taken out, it is replaced.

18. Find P(red and yellow).

19. Find P(yellow and white).

Use the spinner at the right.

Example: Describe an event that could not happen.
Solution: The pointer cannot point to yellow because yellow is not on the spinner.

20. Describe an event that is certain.

21. Describe an event that is impossible.

Answer the following questions.

Example: Three chairs are arranged in a row. How many different ways can three students sit in those chairs?
Solution: Any of the three students can sit in the first chair. Once a person is in that chair, any of the two other students can sit in the middle chair. The remaining student sits in the last chair. The students can sit in $3 \bullet 2 \bullet 1 = 6$ different ways.

22. Four friends are waiting in a line. How many different ways can they arrange themselves in that line?

23. If six horses start and finish a race, how many different orders of finish are possible?

24. Jan has five books. How many different ways can she arrange the books on her shelf?

25. Miguel and his three friends say their names aloud one at a time. In how many different ways can they recite their names?

Test-Taking Tip

It is a good idea to double-check the location of numbers or other data that you identify in a table or chart.

60DH
CURRY
40DH
PIMENT

Chapter

Fractions and Algebra

We live in a three-dimensional world. Objects have height, width, and depth, or thickness. The amount of space any object takes up is its volume. Whether it is one of the great pyramids of Egypt or a grain of curry powder, every object has volume. You have been learning to apply your algebra skills to formulas. You can apply these skills to the formula for finding volume. To calculate the volume of a pyramid, for example, you will need to know how to multiply fractions. When you multiply one-third ($\frac{1}{3}$) of the pyramid's height by the area of its base, you find exactly how much space the entire pyramid occupies. With a little practice, working with fractions in algebra can be easy.

In Chapter 8, you will study and use fractions in algebraic equations.

Goals for Learning

- ◆ To write fractions in their simplest form
- ◆ To find the greatest common factor of two or more fractions
- ◆ To multiply and divide algebraic fractions
- ◆ To simplify complex fractions
- ◆ To find the least common multiple and prime factors of algebraic fractions
- ◆ To add and subtract algebraic fractions
- ◆ To solve problems involving proportions and fractions
- ◆ To solve equations with algebraic fractions

Lesson 1 Fractions as Rational Numbers

Rational number

Any number that is expressed as an integer or as a ratio between two integers when 0 does not serve as the denominator

Simplest form

A fraction in which the only common factor of the numerator and denominator is 1

A fraction is one or more parts of a whole. Examples of fractions include $\frac{1}{3}$, $\frac{-3}{4}$, and $\frac{0}{10}$. Fractions such as $\frac{1}{3}$ are positive. Fractions such as $\frac{3}{-4}$ or $\frac{-3}{4}$ or $-\frac{3}{4}$ are negative. When simplified, fractions such as $\frac{0}{10}$ are neither positive nor negative because $\frac{0}{10} = 0$.

Fractions are examples of **rational numbers.**

These numbers are rational numbers:

$\frac{1}{3}$, $\frac{-1}{3}$, $\frac{1}{-3}$, $\frac{5}{-7}$, $\frac{0}{5}$, and $\frac{-7}{5}$

These numbers are not rational numbers:

$\frac{0}{0}$, $\frac{1}{0}$, or $\frac{n}{0}$ where $n =$ any number.

Each of these fractions is equivalent to $\frac{1}{2}$.

$$\frac{1}{2} = \frac{2}{4} = \frac{3}{6} = \frac{4}{8} = \frac{5}{10} = \frac{6}{12} = \frac{7}{14} = \ldots \frac{1(n)}{2(n)} \text{ for all } n \neq 0.$$

The fraction $\frac{1}{2}$ is in **simplest form** because the greatest common factor of the numerator (1) and the denominator (2) is 1.

Remember that a proportion is an equation made up of two equal ratios. For example, $\frac{6}{12} = \frac{1}{2}$ is a proportion. To check, use cross products $6 \bullet 2 = 12$ and $12 \bullet 1 = 12$. Since the cross products are equal, $\frac{6}{12} = \frac{1}{2}$ is a true proportion.

Rule To write a fraction in simplest form, divide the numerator and denominator by the greatest common factor (GCF).

EXAMPLE 1 Write $\frac{6}{12}$ in simplest form.

Step 1 Write the prime factorization of 6 and 12.

$\frac{6}{12} = \frac{2 \bullet 3}{2 \bullet 2 \bullet 3}$

Step 2 Identify the common prime factors. The product of the common prime factors is the GCF.

$\frac{2 \bullet 3}{2 \bullet 2 \bullet 3}$ $\quad 2 \bullet 3 = 6$

Step 3 Divide the numerator and denominator of the fraction you want to simplify by 6.

$\frac{6}{12} \div \frac{6}{6} = \frac{1}{2}$

Step 4 Check your work. Use the idea that if two rational numbers are equivalent, they form a true proportion. In a true proportion, the cross products are equal.

EXAMPLE 2 Write $-\frac{1}{2}$ in two other forms.

$$-\frac{1}{2} = (-1)\frac{1}{2} = \left[\frac{-1}{1}\right] \bullet \frac{1}{2} = \frac{-1 \bullet 1}{2} = \frac{-1}{2} \text{ or}$$

$$-\frac{1}{2} = (-1)\frac{1}{2} = \left[\frac{1}{-1}\right] \bullet \frac{1}{2} = \frac{1}{-1 \bullet 2} = \frac{1}{-2}$$

Exercise A Find the GCF, then use it to write each fraction in simplest form. Check your work.

1. $\frac{9}{63}$

2. $\frac{21}{63}$

3. $\frac{-16}{64}$

4. $\frac{15}{75}$

5. $\frac{18}{72}$

6. $\frac{36}{-81}$

7. $\frac{12}{144}$

8. $-(\frac{25}{225})$

9. $\frac{18}{81}$

10. $\frac{-19}{38}$

11. $\frac{42}{64}$

12. $\frac{24}{192}$

13. $\frac{27}{72}$

14. $\frac{14}{-28}$

Exercise B Write each fraction in simplest form. Check your work.

15. $\frac{121}{891}$

16. $\frac{43}{172}$

17. $\frac{43}{-215}$

18. $\frac{95}{-135}$

19. $\frac{90}{135}$

20. $\frac{16}{128}$

21. $\frac{270}{720}$

22. $\frac{-42}{441}$

23. $\frac{125}{-525}$

24. $-(\frac{81}{405})$

25. $\frac{81}{405}$

Writing About Mathematics

Explain why $\frac{-a}{b} = \frac{a}{-b} = -[\frac{a}{b}]$ are equivalent expressions in which a and b are integers and $b \neq 0$. You may use numbers to illustrate your answer.

Lesson 2 Algebraic Fractions—Rational Expressions

Algebraic fraction

A single algebraic term divided by a single algebraic term

Rational expression

An algebraic expression divided by another algebraic expression

The expressions $\frac{x^2}{x^3}$ and $\frac{15x^2}{45x^3}$ are examples of **algebraic fractions.** Like all fractions, algebraic fractions can be simplified, or written in simplest form.

EXAMPLE 1 Simplify $\frac{x^2}{x^3}$.

Step 1 Find the GCF of the numerator and the denominator.

$\frac{x^2}{x^3} = \frac{x \bullet x}{x \bullet x \bullet x}$ The GCF is $x \bullet x$ or x^2.

Step 2 Divide both the numerator and the denominator by the GCF.

$\frac{x^2}{x^3} \div \frac{x^2}{x^2} = \frac{1}{x}$

Step 3 Does $\frac{x^2}{x^3} = \frac{1}{x}$? Check by comparing the cross products.

$x^2 \bullet x = x^3 \bullet 1$

$x^3 = x^3$ True

EXAMPLE 2 Simplify $\frac{15x^2}{45x^3}$.

Step 1 Find the GCF of the numerator and the denominator.

$\frac{15x^2}{45x^3} = \frac{3 \bullet 5 \bullet x \bullet x}{3 \bullet 3 \bullet 5 \bullet x \bullet x \bullet x}$ The GCF is $15x^2$.

Step 2 Divide both the numerator and the denominator by the GCF.

$\frac{15x^2}{45x^3} = \frac{15x^2}{45x^3} \div \frac{15x^2}{15x^2} = \frac{1}{3x}$

Step 3 Check. Does $\frac{15x^2}{45x^3} = \frac{1}{3x}$?

$15x^2 \bullet 3x = 45x^3 \bullet 1$

$45x^3 = 45x^3$ True

A **rational expression** is a fraction that compares two algebraic expressions. Many rational expressions can be written in simplest form.

Example 3 Simplify $\frac{(x + 2)}{(x + 2)^3}$.

Step 1 If possible, factor the numerator and denominator.

$$\frac{(x + 2)}{(x + 2)^3} = \frac{(x + 2)}{(x + 2)(x + 2)(x + 2)}$$

Step 2 Simplify. $\frac{\cancel{(x + 2)}}{\cancel{(x + 2)}(x + 2)(x + 2)} = \frac{1}{(x + 2)(x + 2)}$ or $\frac{1}{(x + 2)^2}$

Step 3 Check. Does $\frac{(x + 2)}{(x + 2)^3} = \frac{1}{(x + 2)^2}$?

$$\frac{(x + 2)}{(x + 2)^3} = \frac{1}{(x + 2)^2} \rightarrow (x + 2)(x + 2)^2 = (x + 2)^3 \bullet 1$$

$(x + 2)^3 = (x + 2)^3$ True

Example 4 Simplify $\frac{(x - 4)}{(x^2 - 8x + 16)}$.

Step 1 If possible, factor the numerator and denominator.

$$\frac{(x - 4)}{(x^2 - 8x + 16)} = \frac{x - 4}{(x - 4)(x - 4)}$$

Step 2 Simplify. $\frac{\cancel{x - 4}}{\cancel{(x - 4)}(x - 4)} = \frac{1}{(x - 4)}$

Step 3 Check. Does $\frac{(x - 4)}{(x^2 - 8x + 16)} = \frac{1}{(x - 4)}$?

$$\frac{(x - 4)}{(x^2 - 8x + 16)} = \frac{1}{(x - 4)} \text{ or } (x - 4)(x - 4) = x^2 - 8x + 16$$

> **Writing About Mathematics**
>
> What happens when you simplify $\frac{(16x^3y^2)}{(56x5y^3)}$ using $2xy$ instead of the GCF? Can you still factor completely? Explain.

Exercise A Use the GCF to simplify these expressions. Check your work.

1. $\frac{m^5}{m^6}$
2. $\frac{r^5}{r^3}$
3. $\frac{5x^3}{25x^2}$
4. $\frac{-45x^2}{90x^3}$
5. $\frac{125x^7}{25x^5}$
6. $\frac{13m^2n^2}{-39mn^2}$
7. $\frac{42xy}{63x^2y^3}$
8. $\frac{56r^2s^2}{28r^3s^3}$
9. $\frac{72x^3y^3z^3}{-144x^2y^2z}$
10. $\frac{(x - 3)}{(x - 3)^3}$
11. $\frac{(-a^2 - 4)}{(a^2 + 4)^2}$
12. $\frac{(m - 6)}{m^2 - 36}$
13. $\frac{(x^2 - 25)}{(x + 5)}$
14. $\frac{(d - 7)}{(d^2 - 49)}$

Exercise B Simplify. Check your work.

15. $\frac{(-x^2 + 25)}{(x + 5)}$
16. $\frac{-(r - 12)}{(r^2 - 24r + 144)}$
17. $\frac{(w^2 + 14w + 49)}{(w + 7)}$
18. $\frac{(-n^2 + 36)}{(n - 6)(n^2 + 12n + 36)}$
19. $\frac{(a - 4)}{(a^2 - 6a + 8)}$
20. $\frac{(-m - 8)}{(m^2 + 5m - 24)}$

Lesson 3 Multiplying and Dividing Algebraic Fractions

Follow the same method you learned to check basic division facts. To check $6 \div 3 = 2$, multiply the quotient (2) by the divisor (3). The product of the quotient and the divisor should equal the dividend: $(2)(3) = 6$.

Recall that the reciprocal of any non-zero number x is $\frac{1}{x}$. Dividing by a number is the same as multiplying by its reciprocal. For example, $12 \div 3 = 4$ is the same as $(12)(\frac{1}{3})$. Both equal 4.

In algebra, you divide fractions by multiplying by the reciprocal of the divisor.

$\frac{a}{b} \div \frac{c}{d} = \frac{a}{b} \bullet \frac{d}{c}$ $\frac{c}{d}$ and $\frac{d}{c}$ are reciprocals.

EXAMPLE 1 Find the quotient of $\frac{3}{4} \div \frac{2}{3}$.

Step 1 Write the equation.

Step 2 Divide by multiplying by the reciprocal.

$\frac{3}{2}$ is the reciprocal of $\frac{2}{3}$.

$\frac{3}{4} \div \frac{2}{3} = \frac{3}{4} \bullet \frac{3}{2}$

$\frac{3}{4} \div \frac{2}{3} = \frac{3}{4} \bullet \frac{3}{2} = \frac{9}{8}$

Step 3 Simplify if possible.

$\frac{9}{8} = 1\frac{1}{8}$.

Step 4 Check. Does $\frac{3}{4} \div \frac{2}{3} = 1\frac{1}{8}$?

$\frac{3}{4}$	$\div$	$\frac{2}{3}$	$=$	$1\frac{1}{8}$
dividend		divisor		quotient

Quotient • divisor = dividend

$\frac{9}{8} \bullet \frac{2}{3} = \frac{9 \bullet 2}{8 \bullet 3} = \frac{18}{24} = \frac{3}{4}$ True

EXAMPLE 2 Find the quotient of $1\frac{1}{2}x \div \frac{3x^2}{4}$.

Step 1 Rewrite $1\frac{1}{2}$ as an improper fraction.

$$1\frac{1}{2}x \div \frac{3x^2}{4} = \frac{3x}{2} \div \frac{3x^2}{4}$$

Step 2 Divide by multiplying by the reciprocal.

In this example, $\frac{3x^2}{4}$ and $\frac{4}{3x^2}$ are reciprocals.

$$\frac{3x}{2} \div \frac{3x^2}{4} = \frac{3x}{2} \bullet \frac{4}{3x^2} = \frac{12x}{6x^2}$$

Step 3 Simplify if possible.

$$\frac{12x}{6x^2} = \frac{2 \bullet \cancel{2} \bullet \cancel{3} \bullet \cancel{x}}{\cancel{2} \bullet \cancel{3} \bullet \cancel{x} \bullet x} = \frac{2}{x}$$

Step 4 Check. Does $1\frac{1}{2}x \div \frac{3x^2}{4} = \frac{2}{x}$?

$1\frac{1}{2}x$	$\div$	$\frac{3x^2}{4}$	$=$	$\frac{2}{x}$
dividend		divisor		quotient

Quotient • divisor = dividend

$$\frac{2}{x} \bullet \frac{3x^2}{4} = \frac{6x^2}{4x} = \frac{\cancel{2} \bullet 3 \bullet x \bullet \cancel{x}}{\cancel{2} \bullet 2 \bullet \cancel{x}} = \frac{3x}{2} \text{ or } 1\frac{1}{2}x \qquad \text{True}$$

> **Writing About Mathematics**
>
> Show why a number times its reciprocal is equal to 1. Explain your work.

Exercise A Find each product. Simplify your answers whenever possible.

1. $\frac{3}{4} \bullet \frac{5}{6}$
2. $\frac{7}{8} \bullet \frac{2}{3}$
3. $(3\frac{1}{3}) \bullet \frac{4}{5}$
4. $(2\frac{7}{8})(1\frac{5}{6})$
5. $(\frac{x}{a^2})(\frac{a^3}{x^2})$
6. $(\frac{d}{t^2}) \bullet \frac{d^2}{t}$
7. $\frac{1}{(a^2 - 25)} \bullet \frac{(a + 5)}{(a - 5)}$
8. $\frac{(x + 1)}{(b^2x^2 + b^2)} \bullet \frac{(b^2)}{(x + 1)}$
9. $\frac{(1 - x^2)}{(b^2x^2 - 1)} \bullet \frac{(bx + 1)}{(x + 1)}$
10. $\frac{(a^2 + 10a + 25)}{(b - 5)} \bullet \frac{(b^2 - 10b + 25)}{(a + 5)}$

Exercise B Find and check each quotient. Simplify your answers whenever possible

11. $\frac{3}{4} \div \frac{5}{6}$
12. $\frac{7}{8} \div \frac{2}{3}$
13. $(3\frac{1}{3}) \div \frac{4}{5}$
14. $(2\frac{7}{8}) \div (1\frac{5}{6})$
15. $(\frac{x}{a^2}) \div (\frac{a^3}{x^2})$
16. $(\frac{-d}{t^2}) \div \frac{d^2}{t}$
17. $\frac{1}{(a^2 - 25)} \div \frac{(a + 5)}{(a - 5)}$
18. $\frac{(x + 1)}{(b^2x^2 + b^2)} \div \frac{(b^2)}{(x + 1)}$
19. $\frac{(x^2 - 1)}{(b^2x^2 - 1)} \div \frac{(bx + 1)}{(x + 1)}$
20. $\frac{(a^2 + 10a + 25)}{(b - 5)} \div \frac{(b^2 - 10b + 25)}{(a + 5)}$

Lesson 4 Complex Fractions and the LCM

Complex fraction

A fraction in which the numerator, the denominator, or both the numerator and the denominator are fractions

Least common multiple (LCM)

The smallest number that two or more numbers can divide into without leaving a remainder

Recall there are two ways to represent a whole number division computation.

$12 \div 4 = 3$ and $\frac{12}{4} = 3$

There are also two ways to represent division of fractions.

$\frac{3}{2} \div \frac{3}{4} = 2$ can also be written as $\frac{\frac{3}{2}}{\frac{3}{4}} = 2$.

$\frac{\frac{3}{2}}{\frac{3}{4}}$ is an example of a **complex fraction.**

Other examples of complex fractions include

$$\frac{3}{\frac{5}{7}} \qquad \frac{\frac{1}{3}}{5} \qquad \frac{x}{\frac{a}{b}} \qquad \frac{\frac{a}{b}}{\frac{c}{d}}$$

You can simplify a complex fraction by removing the denominator in each fractional part.

EXAMPLE 1 Simplify $\frac{\frac{1}{3}}{5}$.

Step 1 One way to simplify complex fractions is to think of the fraction bar as a division symbol.

$\frac{\frac{1}{3}}{5} = \frac{1}{3} \div 5$

Step 2 Find $\frac{1}{3} \div 5$.

Write the whole number 5 as the improper fraction $\frac{5}{1}$.

$\frac{1}{3} \div 5 = \frac{1}{3} \div \frac{5}{1} = \frac{1}{3} \bullet \frac{1}{5} = \frac{1}{15}$

To find a quotient of two fractions, multiply the dividend by the reciprocal of the divisor.

Another way to simplify complex fractions is to find and multiply the numerator and denominator by the **least common multiple,** or **LCM,** of the two denominators.

EXAMPLE 2

Simplify $\dfrac{\frac{2}{15}}{\frac{3}{10}}$.

Step 1 Find the LCM of each denominator.

Multiples of 15: 15, **30**, 45, 60, 75, ...

Multiples of 10: 10, 20, **30**, 40, 50, ...

The LCM is 30.

Step 2 Multiply the numerator and denominator of the complex fraction by 30.

$$\frac{\frac{2}{15}}{\frac{3}{10}} \bullet \frac{30}{30}$$

Multiplying by $\frac{30}{30}$ is the same as multiplying by $\frac{1}{1}$ or 1—multiplying by 1 does not change the value of the fraction.

Step 3 Simplify.

$$\frac{\frac{2}{15}}{\frac{3}{10}} \bullet \frac{30}{30} = \frac{\frac{2}{15}}{\frac{3}{10}} \bullet \frac{\frac{30}{1}}{\frac{30}{1}} = \frac{\frac{60}{15}}{\frac{90}{10}} = \frac{4}{9}$$

EXAMPLE 3

Simplify $\dfrac{\frac{5}{7x}}{\frac{2}{3x}}$.

Step 1 Find the LCM of each denominator.

Multiples of $7x$: $7x$, $14x$, $\mathbf{21x}$, $28x$, $35x$, $42x$, ...

Multiples of $3x$: $3x$, $6x$, $9x$, $12x$, $15x$, $18x$, $\mathbf{21x}$, $24x$, $27x$, ...

The LCM is $21x$.

Step 2 Multiply the numerator and denominator of the complex fraction by $21x$.

$$\frac{\frac{5}{7x}}{\frac{2}{3x}} \bullet \frac{21x}{21x}$$

Step 3 Simplify.

$$\frac{\frac{5}{7x}}{\frac{2}{3x}} \bullet \frac{21x}{21x} = \frac{\frac{5}{7x}}{\frac{2}{3x}} \bullet \frac{\frac{21x}{1}}{\frac{21x}{1}} = \frac{\frac{105x}{7x}}{\frac{42x}{3x}} = \frac{15}{14} = 1\frac{1}{14}$$

EXAMPLE 4 $\frac{a}{b} \div \frac{c}{d}$ can be written as $\dfrac{\frac{a}{b}}{\frac{c}{d}}$

and $\dfrac{\frac{a}{b}}{\frac{c}{d}} \bullet \dfrac{(\frac{d}{c})}{(\frac{d}{c})} = \dfrac{\frac{ad}{bc}}{\frac{\cancel{cd}}{\cancel{dc}}} = \dfrac{ad}{bc}$.

Therefore, the rule for division of fractions is

$\frac{a}{b} \div \frac{c}{d} = \frac{a}{b} \bullet \frac{d}{c}$.

Exercise A Find the least common multiple for each pair.

1. 3, 4

2. 5, 2

3. 7, 8

4. 6, 7

5. 4, 9

6. 8, 3

7. 7, 21

8. 10, 12

9. 18, 6

10. $4a, 7a$

11. $8n, 2n$

12. $9x, 7x$

13. $4r, 5r$

14. $4m, 25m$

15. $9b, 11b$

Exercise B Simplify.

16. $\dfrac{1}{\frac{3}{5}}$

17. $\dfrac{4}{\frac{1}{2}}$

18. $\dfrac{\frac{2}{3}}{7}$

19. $\dfrac{\frac{5}{6}}{3}$

20. $\dfrac{\frac{3}{4}}{2}$

21. $\dfrac{4}{\frac{11}{12}}$

22. $\dfrac{6}{\frac{7}{8}}$

23. $\dfrac{\frac{3}{8}}{5}$

24. $\dfrac{10}{\frac{1}{5}}$

25. $\dfrac{\frac{3}{8}}{\frac{2}{3}}$

Writing About Mathematics

Take any two prime numbers, such as 3 and 5. Can you figure out an easy way to find their LCM? Test your theory by trying it out on another pair of prime numbers.

26. $\dfrac{\frac{2}{5}}{\frac{5}{6}}$

27. $\dfrac{\frac{2}{3}}{\frac{3}{4}}$

28. $\dfrac{\frac{2}{9}}{\frac{3}{7}}$

29. $\dfrac{\frac{1}{2n}}{\frac{9}{10n}}$

30. $\dfrac{\frac{4}{7x}}{\frac{2}{9x}}$

31. $\dfrac{\frac{6}{25n}}{\frac{3}{4n}}$

32. $\dfrac{\frac{2x}{3}}{5x}$

33. $\dfrac{\frac{1}{2a}}{\frac{5}{6a}}$

34. $\dfrac{\frac{3x}{16}}{\frac{1}{4}}$

35. $\dfrac{\frac{1}{8h}}{\frac{2}{9}}$

PROBLEM SOLVING

Exercise C Use the formulas $d = rt$, $r = \frac{d}{t}$, and $t = \frac{d}{r}$ to solve these problems, in which d = distance in miles, r = speed in miles per hour, and t = time in hours.

These facts are related to driving each day of a five-day vacation.

Day 1: 45 miles per hour; 5.5 hours

Day 2: $264\frac{1}{2}$ miles; $5\frac{3}{4}$ hours

Day 3: $13\frac{1}{2}$ miles per hour; $10\frac{1}{8}$ miles

Day 4: $2\frac{3}{4}$ hours; 77 miles

Day 5: $97\frac{1}{2}$ miles; 39 miles per hour

36. Find the distance driven on Day 1.

37. Find the average rate of speed on Day 2.

38. Find the time spent driving on Day 3.

39. Find the average rate of speed on Day 4.

40. Find the time spent driving on Day 5.

TRY THIS Simplify this complex fraction:

$$\frac{x}{\frac{a}{b}}$$

Lesson 5 Least Common Multiples and Prime Factors

Recall that you can find the least common multiple (LCM) of two numbers by listing the multiples of each number. You can also find the LCM using prime factors.

EXAMPLE 1 Simplify $\dfrac{\frac{5}{12}}{\frac{3}{10}}$ using prime factors.

Step 1 List the prime factors of 12 and 10.

$12 = 2 \bullet 2 \bullet 3$
$10 = 2 \bullet 5$

Step 2 Count the greatest number of times each prime factor occurs in either factorization.

The greatest number of times the factor 2 appears is twice.

$12 = 2 \bullet 2 \bullet 3$
$10 = 2 \bullet 5$

The greatest number of times the factor 3 appears is once.

$12 = 2 \bullet 2 \bullet 3$

$10 = 2 \bullet 5$

The greatest number of times the factor 5 appears is once.

$12 = 2 \bullet 2 \bullet 3$

$10 = 2 \bullet 5$

Step 3 Find the product of the greatest number of times each factor appears.

$2 \bullet 2 \bullet 3 \bullet 5 = 60$

The LCM of 12 and 10 is 60.

Step 4 Multiply both the numerator and the denominator by 60.

$$\dfrac{\frac{5}{12}}{\frac{3}{10}} \bullet \frac{60}{60} = \dfrac{\frac{300}{12}}{\frac{180}{10}} = \frac{25}{18} = 1\frac{7}{18}$$

Writing About Mathematics

Which method for dividing fractions do you prefer? Why?

$\frac{3}{4} \div \frac{1}{2} = \frac{3}{4} \bullet \frac{2}{1} =$

$\frac{3 \bullet 2}{4 \bullet 1} = \frac{6}{4} = \frac{3}{2} = 1\frac{1}{2}$

or $\frac{3}{4} \div \frac{1}{2} = \frac{\frac{3}{4}}{\frac{1}{2}} =$

$\frac{\frac{3}{4}}{\frac{1}{2}} \bullet \frac{4}{4} = \frac{\frac{3}{4} \bullet \frac{4}{1}}{\frac{1}{2} \bullet \frac{4}{1}} = \frac{3}{2}$

$= 1\frac{1}{2}$

EXAMPLE 2 Simplify $\dfrac{\frac{a}{b^2}}{\frac{c}{bd}}$.

Step 1 Find the LCM of b^2 and bd.

$b^2 = b \bullet b \quad bd = b \bullet d$

The LCM of b^2 and bd is $b \bullet b \bullet d$ or b^2d.

Step 2 Multiply both the numerator and the denominator by b^2d.

$$\frac{\frac{a}{b^2}}{\frac{c}{bd}} \bullet \frac{b^2d}{b^2d} = \frac{\frac{ab^2d}{b^2}}{\frac{cb^2d}{bd}} = \frac{ad}{bc}$$

Exercise A Using prime factorization, find the least common multiple for each pair.

1. 3, 5

2. 2, 8

3. 6, 10

4. 12, 3

5. 7, 28

6. 18, 24

7. 21, 14

8. a^2b^2, a^3bc

9. x^3y^2, x^2y

10. r^3s^2t, r^2t

Exercise B Use factorization to simplify these complex fractions. Write your answer in simplest form.

11. $\dfrac{\frac{2}{3}}{\frac{1}{2}}$

12. $\dfrac{\frac{4}{5}}{\frac{7}{15}}$

13. $\dfrac{\frac{7}{18}}{\frac{5}{27}}$

14. $\dfrac{\frac{9}{20}}{\frac{3}{4}}$

15. $\dfrac{ax}{\frac{x}{b}}$

16. $\dfrac{\frac{yx}{b}}{\frac{x}{bx}}$

17. $\dfrac{\frac{8a^3}{6y^3}}{\frac{2a}{24y^2}}$

18. $\dfrac{\frac{a}{x^2}}{\frac{a^2}{x^3}}$

19. $\dfrac{\frac{mn^2}{mn}}{\frac{x^2}{mn}}$

20. $\dfrac{\frac{4xy^2}{8x^2}}{\frac{xy}{12x^3}}$

Lesson 6 Sums and Differences

Remember, multiplying a number by 1 does not change the value of the number.

Algebra and arithmetic have a great deal in common. For example, to add or subtract arithmetic or algebraic fractions with unlike denominators, you must first find a common denominator.

EXAMPLE 1 Subtract $\frac{1}{10}$ from $\frac{3}{4}$.

Step 1 The denominators are unlike. Find the LCM of 4 and 10.

$4 = 2 \bullet 2$

$10 = 2 \bullet 5$

The LCM of 4 and 10 is $2 \bullet 2 \bullet 5 = 20$.

Step 2 Multiply each fraction by 1 in a form that will make the denominator 20.

$$\frac{3}{4} - \frac{1}{10} = \frac{3}{4} \bullet \left[\frac{5}{5}\right] - \frac{1}{10}\left[\frac{2}{2}\right] = \frac{15}{20} - \frac{2}{20} = \frac{15-2}{20} = \frac{13}{20}$$

Follow the same method when adding or subtracting algebraic fractions.

EXAMPLE 2 Find the sum of $\frac{3}{y} + \frac{2}{y}$.

Because the fractions have like denominators, you can add without rewriting.

$$\frac{3}{y} + \frac{2}{y} = \frac{3+2}{y} = \frac{5}{y}$$

Find the sum of $\frac{3}{x^2y^5} + \frac{2}{xy^3}$.

Step 1 The denominators are unlike. Find the LCM of x^2y^5 and xy^3.

$x^2y^5 = x \bullet x \bullet y \bullet y \bullet y \bullet y \bullet y$

$xy^3 = x \bullet y \bullet y \bullet y$

The LCM of x^2y^5 and xy^3 is $x \bullet x \bullet y \bullet y \bullet y \bullet y \bullet y = x^2y^5$.

Step 2 Multiply each fraction by a form of 1 so that each fraction denominator is x^2y^5.

$$\frac{3}{x^2y^5}\left[\frac{1}{1}\right] + \frac{2}{xy^3}\left[\frac{xy^2}{xy^2}\right] = \frac{3}{x^2y^5} + \frac{2xy^2}{x^2y^5}$$

Step 3 Simplify by adding the fractions.

$$\frac{3}{x^2y^5} + \frac{2xy^2}{x^2y^5} = \frac{3+2xy^2}{x^2y^5}$$

Exercise A Find the LCM, then add or subtract. Write your answer in simplest form.

1. $\frac{3}{4} + \frac{7}{8}$

2. $\frac{3}{4} - \frac{7}{8}$

3. $\frac{7}{8} + \frac{5}{24}$

4. $\frac{7}{8} - \frac{5}{25}$

5. $\frac{3}{10} + \frac{3}{5}$

6. $\frac{4}{9} + \frac{4}{7}$

7. $1\frac{1}{2} - \frac{5}{7}$

8. $-3\frac{2}{3} - \frac{5}{7}$

9. $4\frac{1}{8} + \frac{3}{5}$

10. $\frac{2}{a} + \frac{3}{b}$

11. $\frac{10}{x} - \frac{7}{y}$

12. $\frac{5}{2} + \frac{2}{h}$

13. $\frac{-2}{x^2} + \frac{3}{y}$

14. $\frac{13}{p} - \frac{1}{2r}$

15. $\frac{1}{a} + \frac{3}{a^2}$

16. $\frac{9}{mn} - \frac{2}{np}$

17. $\frac{25}{ab} - \frac{4}{acd}$

18. $\frac{2a}{p^2} + \frac{1}{pq}$

19. $\frac{5x}{c^2d} - \frac{3x}{d^2c}$

20. $\frac{7a}{ab} + \frac{c}{b^2c}$

21. $\frac{3}{a^2b} + \frac{4}{ab^2}$

22. $\frac{5}{x^2y^3} - \frac{7}{xy^2}$

23. $\frac{5y}{ax^2} + \frac{7x}{ay^2}$

24. $\frac{3y}{m^2n} + \frac{3m}{ym}$

25. $\frac{3xy}{4a^2b} + \frac{2a^2b}{7xy}$

Estimation Activity

Estimate: Find the sum of a set of mixed numbers.

$1\frac{1}{8} + 2\frac{3}{4} + 5\frac{1}{3} + 6\frac{2}{3} = ?$

Solution: Round to the nearest whole number. For fractions less than $\frac{1}{2}$, round down. For fractions $\frac{1}{2}$ and higher, round up.

$1 + 3 + 5 + 7 = 16$

The estimated sum is 16.

Lesson 7 Proportions and Fractions in Equations

Recall that two equivalent rational numbers (such as $\frac{1}{2} = \frac{3}{6}$) form a proportion and in that proportion the cross products are equal.

$$(2 \cdot 3) = (1 \cdot 6)$$
$$6 = 6 \qquad \text{True}$$

You can check if $\frac{3}{4} = \frac{75}{100}$.

Using cross products, if (3)(100) is equal to the product (4)(75), the fractions are equivalent. Check if the products are equal.

$$(3)(100) = (4)(75)$$
$$300 = 300 \qquad \text{True}$$

You can use this idea to solve for an unknown in a proportion.

EXAMPLE 1 Solve $\frac{3}{n} = \frac{75}{100}$ for n.

Step 1 Set up the cross products.

$$(75)(n) = (3)(100)$$
$$75n = 300$$

Step 2 Solve for n.

$$\frac{75n}{75} = \frac{300}{75}$$
$$n = 4$$

Step 3 Check. (3)(100) = (4)(75)

$$300 = 300 \qquad \text{True}$$

You can also use this idea to solve for this unknown. Rectangle *A* has a base of 45 m and a height of 30 m. Rectangle *B*, a similar rectangle, has a height of 15 m.

A
30 m
45 m

B
15 m
? m

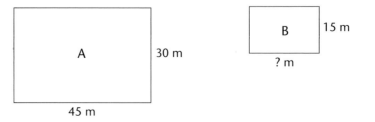

EXAMPLE 2 How long is the base of rectangle *B*?

Step 1 Set up a proportion.

$$\frac{\text{height of rectangle } A}{\text{height of rectangle } B} = \frac{\text{base of rectangle } A}{\text{base of rectangle } B}$$

$$\frac{30 \text{ m}}{15 \text{ m}} = \frac{45 \text{ m}}{\text{base of rectangle } B}$$

Step 2 Set up the cross products. Then solve for the unknown.

$$(30 \text{ m})(\text{base of rectangle } B) = (15 \text{ m})(45 \text{ m})$$

$$(\text{base of rectangle } B) = \frac{(15 \text{ m})(45 \text{ m})}{(30 \text{ m})}$$

$$\text{base of rectangle } B = 22.5 \text{ m}$$

Step 3 Check. $(15 \text{ m})(45 \text{ m}) = (30 \text{ m})(22.5 \text{ m})$

$675 \text{ m} = 675 \text{ m}$ True

Use cross products to solve this equation.

EXAMPLE 3 Solve $\frac{8}{4x - 1} = \frac{3}{x + 3}$ for x.

Step 1 Set up the cross products.

$(8)(x + 3) = (4x - 1)(3)$

Step 2 Solve for x.

$$8(x + 3) = (4x - 1)(3)$$

$$8x + 24 = 12x - 3$$

$$27 = 4x$$

$$x = \frac{27}{4} = 6\frac{3}{4}$$

Step 3 Check. $(8)(x + 3) = (4x - 1)(3)$

$(8)(6\frac{3}{4} + 3) = (27 - 1)(3)$

$78 = 78$ True

Exercise A Solve for the variable. Check your work.

1. $\frac{x}{4} = \frac{75}{100}$

2. $\frac{3}{4} = \frac{x}{100}$

3. $\frac{3}{4} = \frac{75}{x}$

4. $\frac{2y}{3} = 8$

5. $\frac{-4y}{5} = 12$

6. $\frac{5x}{12} = 10$

7. $\frac{5m}{7} = 35$

8. $\frac{h}{6} = \frac{3}{9}$

9. $\frac{d}{7} = \frac{-4}{28}$

10. $\frac{(x+1)}{8} = \frac{-3(x+2)}{4}$

11. $\frac{(x-4)}{25} = \frac{x+2}{9}$

12. $\frac{(x-5)}{6} = \frac{(x+5)}{11}$

13. $\frac{(x+4)}{3} = \frac{(x+4)}{3(x-4)}$

14. $\frac{3}{(y+2)} = \frac{6}{(y+4)}$

15. $\frac{4x}{(x+1)} = \frac{4}{7}$

PROBLEM SOLVING

Exercise B Use what you know about proportions and fractions to solve these problems.

16. The plans for a doghouse are drawn to a scale of 1 in. equals $\frac{3}{4}$ ft. What is the distance from the ground to the top of the roof?

17. There are 10 girls in Mitchell's algebra class of 18 students. Only 5 girls are in his history class, but the ratio of girls to boys is the same as in his algebra class. How many students are in Mitchell's history class?

18. A model railroad is built to $\frac{1}{87}$th the size of a real train. The gauge (track width) for a train is about $\frac{5}{8}$ of an inch. What is the (approximate) actual track width of the railroad?

19. On a map of the United States, Anchorage, Alaska, is 8.1 cm from Olympia, Washington. Denver, Colorado, is the same distance from Charleston, West Virginia. The map scale indicates that 2 cm = 500 km. About how far apart are the cities of Anchorage and Olympia?

20. In order to win a "Guess the Number of Jelly Beans" contest, Jamie bought a jar exactly like the one in the contest. His jar is 12 inches high. He placed 55 jelly beans in the jar. The jelly beans filled $\frac{7}{8}$ in. of the jar. About how many jelly beans will the filled jar hold?

Anchorage, Alaska, is located at the base of the Chugach Mountains.

TRY THIS Consider $3x = 15y$ and $3x = 5 \cdot 6$. Which proportion can you solve and why? Use this information to think about this question. In order to solve a proportion such as $\frac{a}{b} = \frac{c}{d}$, how many constants and how many variables do you need to know? Explain.

Lesson 8 More Solutions to Equations with Fractions

The equation $(\frac{3}{4})x = 15$ can be solved using two different methods.

You can solve the equation using multiplication:

$$(\frac{3}{4})x = 15$$

Multiply both sides of the equation by 4.

$$4 \cdot (\frac{3}{4})x = 4 \cdot 15$$

$$3x = 60$$

$$x = 20$$

Check: $(\frac{3}{4})(20) = \frac{60}{4} = 15$ True

Or, you can solve the equation using division.

$$\frac{3}{4}x = 15$$

Divide both sides of the equation by $\frac{3}{4}$.

$$\frac{\frac{3}{4}}{\frac{3}{4}}\ x = \frac{15}{\frac{3}{4}}$$

$$x = \frac{15}{\frac{3}{4}} = \frac{60}{3} = 20$$

EXAMPLE 1 Solve $(\frac{2}{3})x = -5$ using multiplication and using division.

Solutions:

$$(\frac{2}{3})x = -5 \qquad\qquad (\frac{2}{3})x = -5$$

$$(3) \bullet (\frac{2}{3})x = (3) \bullet (-5) \qquad\qquad \frac{\frac{2}{3}}{\frac{2}{3}}\ x = \frac{-5}{\frac{2}{3}}$$

$$2x = -15$$

$$x = -7\frac{1}{2}x \qquad = \qquad -5[\frac{3}{2}] = \frac{-15}{2} = -7\frac{1}{2}$$

EXAMPLE 2 If you subtract $\frac{1}{2}$ from $\frac{2}{3}$ of a number, the result is 2. What is the number?

Step 1 Let n = the number. Write an equation describing the number.

$(\frac{2}{3})n - \frac{1}{2} = 2$

Step 2 Solve the equation using multiplication or division.

$(\frac{2}{3})n - \frac{1}{2} = 2$

$6 \bullet [(\frac{2}{3})n - \frac{1}{2}] = 6 \bullet 2$

$4n - 3 = 12$

$4n = 15 \quad n = \frac{15}{4}$ or $3\frac{3}{4}$

Step 3 Check.

$(\frac{2}{3})(\frac{15}{4}) - \frac{1}{2} = 2$

$\frac{30}{12} - \frac{6}{12} = 2$

$\frac{24}{12} = 2$ True

Exercise A Solve each equation using multiplication and using division. Check each method you use.

1. $(\frac{3}{4})y = 18$

2. $(\frac{3}{4})x = 33$

3. $(\frac{7}{8})m = 49$

4. $(\frac{9}{15})t = 81$

5. $(\frac{5}{7})h = -35$

6. $(\frac{2}{3})m = 7$

7. $(\frac{5}{9})d = 15$

8. $(\frac{3}{7})p - \frac{1}{3} = 1$

9. $(\frac{4}{9})x = 5 + \frac{1}{9}$

Technology Connection

Computerized Taps

Quarter notes, eighth notes, or half notes? Now buglers don't have to know the difference when they play Taps at a veteran's funeral. Currently, there aren't enough buglers around, and families of veterans do not think playing a recording of Taps on a CD player is dignified. So, the U.S. Pentagon has developed a bugle with a computerized chip insert that plays Taps. Now, buglers only have to press a button, wait five seconds, hold the bugle to their lips, and pretend to blow as Taps plays.

Exercise B Solve using division *or* multiplication. Check your answers.

10. $(\frac{4}{9})m + \frac{1}{9} = 5$

11. $(\frac{6}{7})x - \frac{2}{3} = 4$

12. $4 - (\frac{2}{3})z = \frac{1}{2}$

13. $12 - (\frac{6}{7})y = 5$

14. $(\frac{2}{3})x - \frac{4}{7} = 6$

15. $(\frac{5}{6})m - (\frac{2}{3})m = 14$

16. $(\frac{7}{8})y + (1\frac{1}{2})y = 8$

17. $(\frac{3}{7})x - (\frac{2}{3})x = -6$

Suppose you use pencil and paper to determine that $n = 6$ in the equation $\frac{3}{4}n + \frac{1}{2} = 5$. To check your answer using a calculator, follow these steps.

EXAMPLE 3 Substitute $n = 6$ into the equation $\frac{3}{4}n + \frac{1}{2} = 5$.

$\frac{3}{4}(6) + \frac{1}{2} = 5$

Then press (3 ÷ 4) (6) + (1 ÷ 2) =

The calculator display will read 5.

If you have a calculator with a fraction key $a^{b}/_{c}$, follow these steps:

Press 3 $a^{b}/_{c}$ 4 × 6 + 1 $a^{b}/_{c}$ 2 =

The calculator display will read 5.

Writing About Mathematics

Write a word problem that can be solved using an equation with fractions. Solve it, then challenge a classmate to solve it. (Hint: You can use problems 23, 24, and 25 to help.)

Exercise C Use a calculator to check these computations. If the answer is correct, write *correct.* If the answer is not correct, write *not correct.*

18. $\frac{3}{8}a = 64; a = 24$

19. $\frac{4}{5}b = 105; b = 94$

20. $\frac{1}{10}c + \frac{1}{2} = 1; c = 5$

21. $\frac{2}{3}d + \frac{1}{3} = 18; d = 28$

22. Tell how you might use a calculator to check a computation that has a fraction for an answer.

PROBLEM SOLVING

Exercise D Write and solve equations using division or multplication.

23. Keisha and Jamaal take the same standard math test. The ratio of their scores is 4 to 5. The difference in their scores is 15. What are their scores?

24. Everitt is twice as old as Danny. The difference in their ages is 6 years. How old is Everitt? How old is Danny?

25. Ella scores 54 points in a basketball game. This is $\frac{2}{3}$ of her team's points. How many points does the team score?

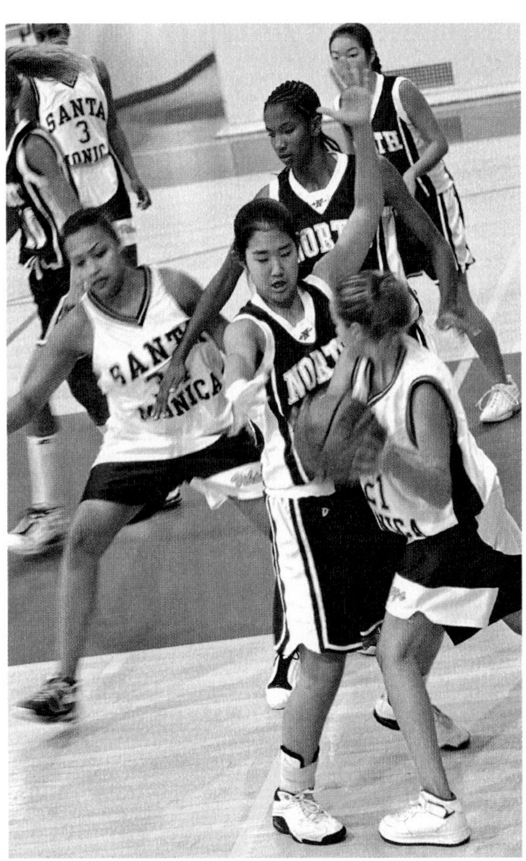

Lesson 9 Denominators and Zero

Undefined

A term used without a specific mathematical definition

Recall that for any rational number $\frac{a}{b}$, $b \neq 0$. You know that $\frac{12}{3} = 4$ because $12 = 3 \cdot 4$. Likewise, $\frac{a}{b} = c$ means $a = bc$. Now, look at $\frac{a}{0} = c$. This means that $a = 0 \cdot c$. But $a = 0$ is false, so division by zero is **undefined** because no quotient works.

> **Rule** The expressions $\frac{1}{0}$ and $\frac{a}{0}$ are undefined because division by zero is not defined.

Therefore, the denominators in algebraic expressions must never be zero.

If $x = 2$ in the expression $\frac{1}{(x-2)}$, then $\frac{1}{(x-2)} = \frac{1}{(2-2)} = \frac{1}{0}$.

Since division by zero is not defined, $\frac{1}{(x-2)}$ can have any value except 2. This is usually written $\frac{1}{(x-2)}$ for $x \neq 2$.

Sometimes a solution is a value that is both positive and negative, such as $x = +2$ and $x = -2$. The solution $x = +2$ and $x = -2$ can be written in a simpler way by just writing $x = \pm 2$.

EXAMPLE 1

For what value of x is $\frac{1}{(x + \frac{1}{2})}$ undefined?

If $x + \frac{1}{2} = 0$, then $x = -\frac{1}{2}$ makes the fraction undefined.

For what values of x is $\frac{1}{(x^2 - 4)}$ undefined?

If $x^2 - 4 = 0$, then the fraction is undefined.

$x^2 = 4$, $x = \pm 2$ makes the fraction undefined.

$x = \pm 2$ makes the fraction undefined.

Algebra in Your Life

When $\frac{1}{4}$ Inch Equals One Foot

When constructing anything from a house to a skyscraper, builders follow an architect's drawings. Architects can't make drawings that are the same size as the buildings, so they make scale drawings. A measurement of one foot of the building might only equal a quarter inch on the plan. Architects have to do the math to "scale down" a building for the drawing. Builders have to "scale up" the plans to know how long to cut a timber or how large a window should be.

Writing About Mathematics

Describe why you cannot divide any number by zero. What would the quotient be?

EXAMPLE 2 For what values of y is $\frac{y}{y(y+1)}$ undefined?

If $y(y + 1) = 0$, then the fraction is undefined.

Either $y = 0$ or $y + 1 = 0$ makes the fraction undefined.

Therefore, both $y = 0$ and $y = -1$ make the fraction undefined.

Exercise A Determine the value(s) for which each expression is undefined.

1. $\frac{1}{x-4}$
2. $\frac{3}{v-3}$
3. $\frac{10}{c+5}$
4. $\frac{-2m}{25m^4}$
5. $\frac{4a}{-7b}$
6. $\frac{-45x^2}{90x^3}$
7. $\frac{13m^2n^3}{-39mn^2}$
8. $\frac{(x-3)}{(x-3)^3}$
9. $\frac{(a^2+4)^2}{(-a^2+4)}$
10. $\frac{(m-6)}{(m^2-36)}$
11. $\frac{-(r-12)}{(r^2-24r+144)}$
12. $\frac{(w^2+14w+49)}{(w+7)}$
13. $\frac{(-n^2+36)}{(n-6)(n^2+12n+36)}$
14. $\frac{(a-4)}{(a^2-6a+8)}$
15. $\frac{(-m-8)}{(m^2+5m-24)}$
16. $\frac{(x^2+2x)}{(x^2+5x+6)}$
17. $\frac{(x^2+7x+12)}{(9-x^2)(x+4)}$
18. $\frac{(x+1)}{(x^2+5x+4)}$
19. $\frac{(b-3)}{(b^2-9b+20)}$
20. $\frac{(2a+1)}{(2a^2-a-1)}$

Application $\pi^2 \Sigma + \Omega \sqrt{x^2}\ \% \neq y \geq n = \nabla 30^\circ \pi$

Working Fractions

One of the most useful applications of rational numbers and fractional equivalents is the work problem. Work problems rely on the fact that work done by one person + work done by a second person = total amount of work completed.

EXAMPLE 1 It takes Steve 3 hours to clear a mile of riverbank. Seela can clear the riverbank in 4 hours. If Steve and Seela work together, how quickly can the riverbank be cleared?

Let x = the time, in hours, for both workers to clear the riverbank.

Because Steve can clear the riverbank in 3 hours, you know that in one hour he can clear $\frac{1}{3}$ of the riverbank, and in x hours $\frac{x}{3}$ of the bank. Because Seela can clear the riverbank in 4 hours, you know that in one hour she can clear $\frac{1}{4}$ of the riverbank, and in x hours $\frac{x}{4}$ of the bank.

Set up an equation that describes the work problem:

part of the bank cleared by Steve in x hours + part of the bank cleared by Seela = 1 (entire riverbank cleared)

$$\frac{x}{3} + \frac{x}{4} = 1$$

Use what you know about fractional equations to solve the equation.

$$\frac{x}{3} + \frac{x}{4} = 1$$

$$12 \bullet \left[\frac{x}{3} + \frac{x}{4}\right] = 12 \bullet 1$$

$$4x + 3x = 12$$

$$7x = 12$$

$$x = \frac{12}{7} \text{ or } 1\frac{5}{7} \text{ hours}$$

Exercise Find the solutions to the following problems.

1. Marc can mow Bobolink Meadow in 7 hours. Earlene can mow it in 6 hours. How long will it take Earlene and Marc, working together, to mow Bobolink Meadow?

2. In 3 hours, Mai can complete a series of water-quality tests. Harry needs $3\frac{1}{2}$ hours to complete the same tests. If they work together, how long will it take them to complete the tests?

3. Emile can survey the East River in 4 hours. Daniel can survey the same area in 5 hours. If they work together, how quickly can they survey the river?

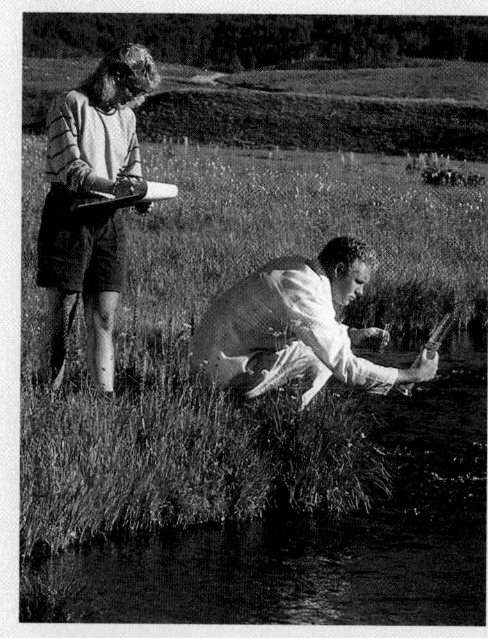

Chapter 8 REVIEW

Write the letter of the correct answer.

1. What is $\frac{48}{72}$ in simplest form?

A $\frac{24}{36}$

B 0.667

C $\frac{2}{3}$

D 24

2. Multiply $2\frac{1}{2} \cdot 4\frac{2}{3}$.

A $11\frac{2}{3}$

B 45

C $23\frac{1}{3}$

D 3

3. Divide $ab^3 \div a^2b$.

A $\frac{ab}{a^2b}$

B $\frac{b^2}{a}$

C $\frac{(ab)^3}{a^2b}$

D $\frac{a}{b^2}$

4. Simplify $\frac{6}{\frac{7}{8}}$.

A $6\frac{6}{7}$

B 48

C $\frac{8}{7}$

D $8\frac{6}{7}$

5. Find the sum of $\frac{3}{x} + \frac{5}{x^2}$.

A $\frac{3x}{x^2}$

B $\frac{3x^2}{5x}$

C $\frac{3x}{5x^2}$

D $\frac{(3x + 5)}{x^2}$

6. Find the difference of $\frac{15}{xy} - \frac{4}{xz}$.

A $\frac{15z}{xyz}$

B $\frac{11}{(y - z)}$

C $\frac{(15z - 4y)}{xyz}$

D $\frac{15}{(xyz - 4)}$

7. Solve for x. $\frac{x}{5} = \frac{80}{100}$

A 4

B $6\frac{1}{4}$

C 160

D 40

Write each fraction in simplest form.

Example: $\frac{8}{10}$ Solution: $\frac{8}{10} = \frac{2 \bullet 2 \bullet 2}{2 \bullet 5}$ GCF = 2 $\frac{8}{10} \div \frac{2}{2} = \frac{4}{5}$

8. $\frac{12}{36}$

9. $\frac{47}{235}$

10. $\frac{13}{-169}$

11. $\frac{x^4}{x^5}$

12. $\frac{225y^9}{25y^5}$

13. $\frac{49mn}{63m^2n^2}$

14. $\frac{36xz^2}{72x^2z}$

15. $\frac{(y^2-9)}{y+3}$

16. $\frac{(x^4 + 7x^3 + 12x^2)}{(x^3 + 8x^2 + 15x)}$

Multiply or divide. Simplify your answers.

Example: $\frac{3}{4} \div \frac{4}{5}$ Solution: $\frac{3}{4} \div \frac{4}{5} = \frac{3}{4} \bullet \frac{5}{4} = \frac{15}{16}$

17. $\frac{1}{(x^2-9)} \bullet \frac{(x-3)}{(x+3)}$

18. $\frac{1}{(y^2-9)} \bullet \frac{(y+3)}{(y-3)}$

19. $\frac{5}{7} \div \frac{2}{3}$

20. $\frac{(z+3)}{(z-3)} \div \frac{1}{(z^2-9)}$

Simplify these complex fractions. Simplify your answers.

Example: $\frac{\frac{3}{5}}{2}$ Solution: $\frac{\frac{3}{5}}{2} = \frac{3}{5} \div 2 = \frac{3}{5} \div \frac{2}{1} = \frac{3}{5} \bullet \frac{1}{2} = \frac{3}{10}$

21. $\frac{\frac{a}{x}}{\frac{x}{b}}$

22. $\frac{\frac{b}{y^2}}{\frac{b^2}{y^3}}$

Solve for the variable. Check your work.

Example: $\frac{6}{a} = \frac{2}{3}$ Solution: $\frac{6}{a} = \frac{2}{3}$ $2a = 6(3)$ $2a = 18$ $a = 9$
Check. $2(9) = 6(3)$ $18 = 18$

23. $\frac{20}{5} = \frac{80}{y}$

24. $\frac{h}{7} = \frac{3}{35}$

25. $\frac{5}{9}h = -45$

26. $\frac{5}{9}m = 4\frac{1}{9}$

27. $\frac{1}{6}x - \frac{2}{3}x = 14$

28. $\frac{3x}{2} = -45$

29. $\frac{(3x-5)}{2} = -45$

30. $\frac{3(x-5)}{2} = -45$

31. $\frac{2}{3} + \frac{5}{6} = 9x$

Find the sum or difference.

Example: $\frac{3}{4} - \frac{1}{8}$ Solution: $\frac{3}{4} - \frac{1}{8} = \frac{3}{4}\left[\frac{2}{2}\right] - \frac{1}{8}\left[\frac{1}{1}\right] = \frac{6}{8} - \frac{1}{8} = \frac{5}{8}$

32. $\frac{3}{(x-1)} + \frac{3}{(x-1)^2}$

33. $\frac{(x+3)}{(x-5)} + \frac{(x-5)}{(x+3)}$

34. $\frac{9a}{ab} - \frac{c}{bc^2}$

35. $\frac{3m}{n^2p} + \frac{5}{p^2n}$

Solve these problems. Write your answer in simplest form.

Example: The scale on a map is 1 cm = 20 miles.
How many cm represent 180 miles?

Solution: $\frac{1}{20} = \frac{x}{180}$ $(1)(180) = (20)(x)$ $180 = 20x$ $x = 9$

36. John won the class election by a margin of 3 to 2. He received 414 votes. How many votes did the other candidate get?

37. Conservationists capture, tag, and release 250 deer in a preserve. Later, 150 deer are caught for observation; 45 of them are already tagged. About how many deer are in the preserve?

38. In four hours, Edgar can collect 100 spittle bugs. Gene collects the same number in $3\frac{1}{2}$ hours. If they work together, how quickly can they catch 100 bugs?

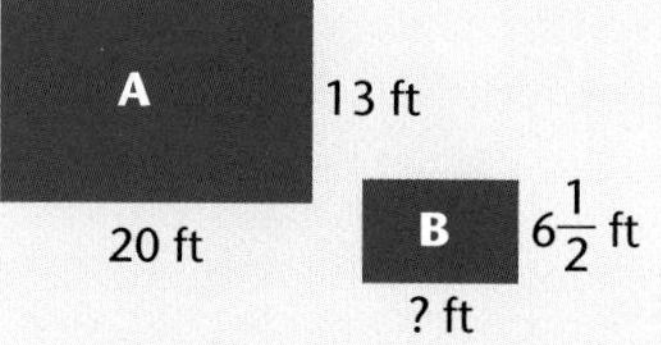

39. Rectangle A has a base of 20 ft and a height of 13 ft. Rectangle B, a similar rectangle, has a height of $6\frac{1}{2}$ ft. How long is the base of rectangle B?

40. One third a number equals 5 less than $\frac{3}{4}$ of the number. What is the number?

Test-Taking Tip

If you have time, compute problems a second time. Then check your original answer.

Chapter

Linear Equations and Inequalities in the Coordinate Plane

Nordic, or cross-country, skiing takes practice and strength. Advanced skiers can ski up steep slopes. To compare the steepness of two hills, you could graph the slope of a ski trail on a coordinate plane. The points in the horizontal line on the *x*-axis represent the flat plane of the earth. Next, you'd plot points in a line on the *y*-axis. This line would be tilted like the slant of the ski trail. Using the formula for slope, you could find the angle between the *x*- and *y*- lines. The wider the angle, the steeper the hill. And the steeper the hill, the more work it takes to reach the top.

In Chapter 9, you will study, create and interpret graphs.

Goals for Learning

- To identify the parts of a graph
- To locate and plot points in the coordinate system
- To solve equations for ordered pairs and graph a line
- To find the *x*-intercept and *y*-intercept of a graph
- To determine the slope of a line
- To write and solve an equation of a straight line
- To identify and evaluate functions
- To determine the range of a function with a given domain
- To graph inequalities
- To interpret and create graphs without numbers

Lesson 1 The Coordinate System

X-axis

The horizontal axis in a coordinate system

Y-axis

The vertical axis in a coordinate system

Origin

The point at which the axes in a coordinate system intersect

Quadrant

Region of a coordinate plane bounded by the x- and y-axes

Ordered pair

Two real numbers that locate a point in the plane

The coordinate system is made up of two number lines that are perpendicular to each other. Using these axes, you can name every point in the plane.

The horizontal number line is known as the ***x*-axis,** and the vertical number line is known as the ***y*-axis.**

The point at which the axes meet, or intersect, is known as the **origin.**

The *x*-axis and the *y*-axis divide the coordinate system into four regions called **quadrants.**

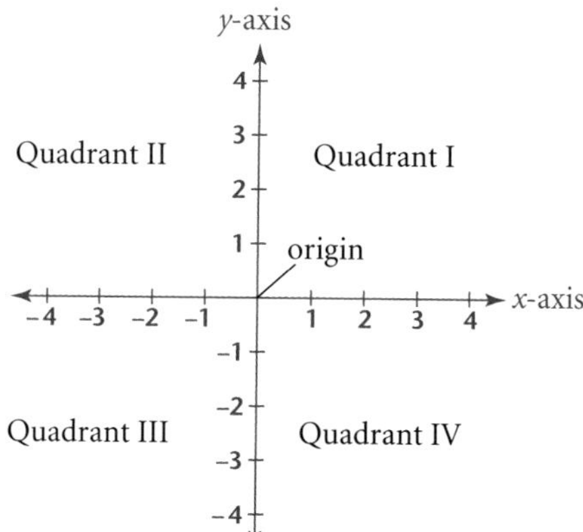

Rule In the coordinate system, any point *P* can be represented by an **ordered pair** of real numbers written in the form (*x*, *y*).

EXAMPLE 1 To locate a point in the coordinate system:

First, determine the *x*-value of the point by drawing or imagining a perpendicular line from the point to the *x*-axis.

Second, determine the *y*-value of the point by drawing or imagining a perpendicular line from the point to the *y*-axis.

Then write the ordered pair in the form (*x*, *y*).

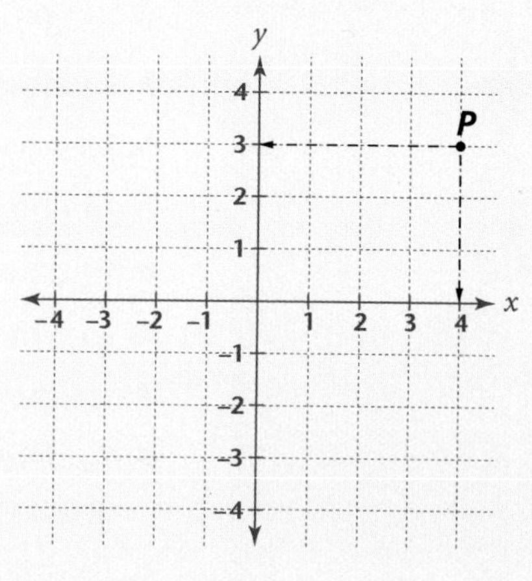

Locate Point *P*. Point *P* is located at (4, 3).

In an ordered pair of real numbers written in the form (*x*, *y*), the *x*-value is always first and the *y*-value is always second.

To *graph* a point on the coordinate system means to draw a *dot* where the point is located.

EXAMPLE 2 Graph $(-3, 2)$.

Recall that in the ordered pair $(-3, 2)$, -3 represents the x-value and 2 represents the y-value.

To graph $(-3, 2)$, begin at the origin and move 3 units to the left. Then move 2 units up.

Draw a dot and label the point $(-3, 2)$.

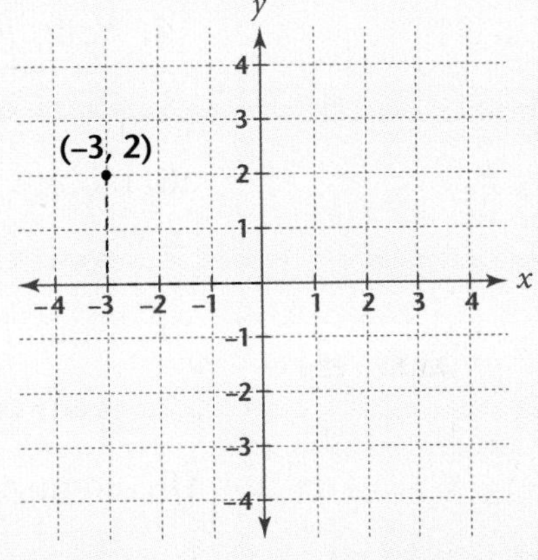

EXAMPLE 3 Graph Point H at $(2, 0)$.

Begin at the origin and move 2 units to the right. Because the y-value is 0, no further movement is required.

Draw a dot and label the point H.

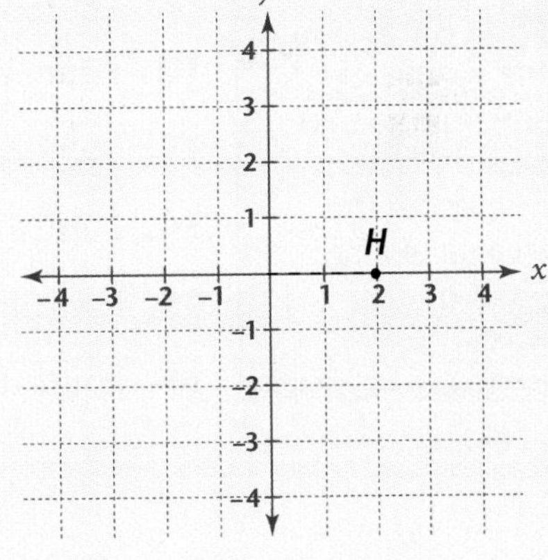

Exercise A Write the ordered pair that represents the location of each point.

1. Point B

2. Point W

3. Point K

4. Point R

5. Point N

6. Point Q

7. Point L

8. Point T

9. Point G

10. Point A

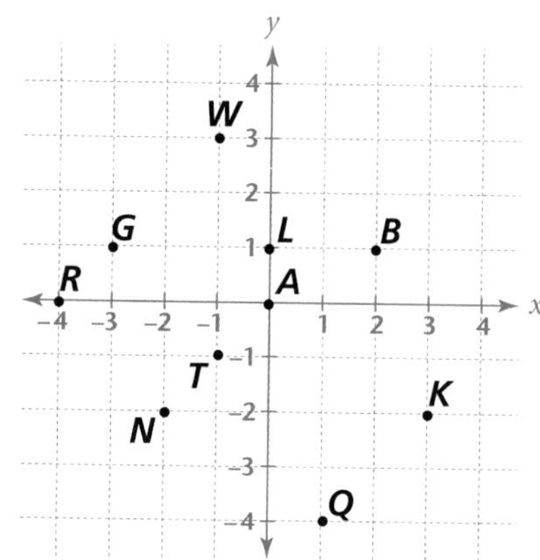

Writing About Mathematics

What is true about the y-value of any point on the x-axis? What is true about the x-value of any point on the y-axis?

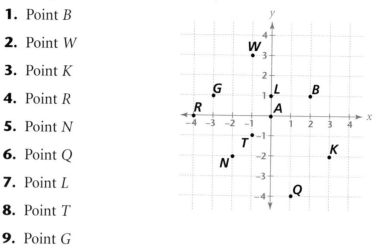

Exercise B Draw a coordinate system like the one shown and graph the following points.

11. Point Y at (1, 2)

12. Point V at (0, −4)

13. Point C at (−3, −1)

14. Point D at (4, 0)

15. Point F at (−2, −4)

16. Point Z at (0, 3)

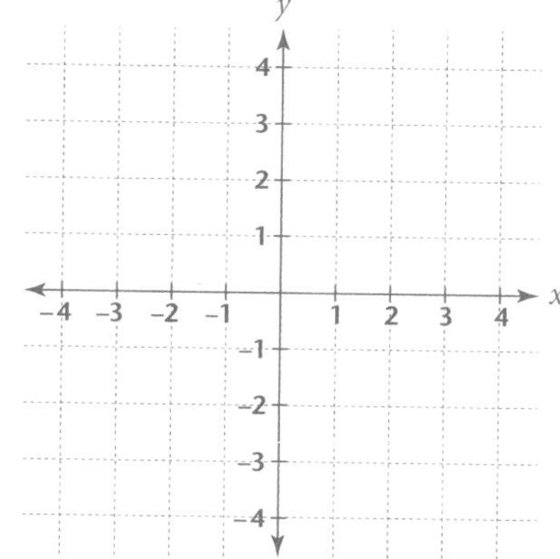

Exercise C Identify the quadrant in which each point is located.

17. (3, 3)

18. (–1, –3)

19. (–2, 1)

20. (2, –1)

21. (–3, 2)

22. (–2, –3)

PROBLEM SOLVING

Exercise D Answer each question.

23. For exercise, Amy walks eight blocks east. After walking four blocks north, twelve blocks west, and four blocks south, she stops to rest. At that time, Amy is how many blocks away from her starting point?

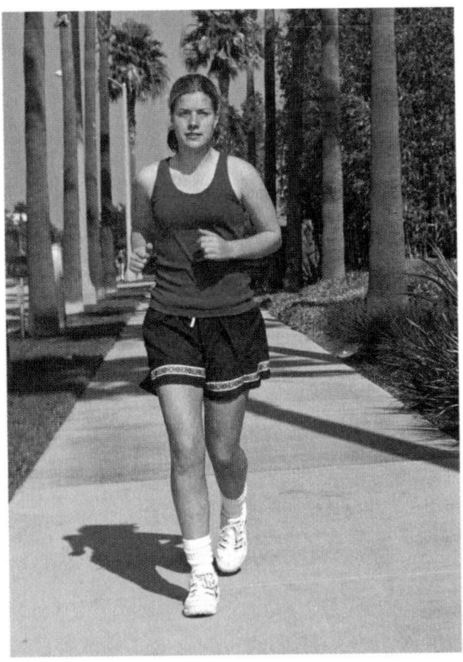

24. Mario is lost and asks two people for directions. The first person says that Mario should drive four blocks west and then five blocks north. The second person says that Mario should drive five blocks west and then four blocks north. Are the directions given by each person the same? Explain.

25. Suppose a north-south line and an east-west line pass through the exact middle of the contiguous United States. If the north-south line represents the y-axis and the east-west line represents the x-axis, in which quadrant of the United States do you live?

Lesson 2 Graphing Equations

Since ordered pairs are represented by (x, y), an equation can be used to represent x and y. You can then substitute numbers for x, solve for y, plot the points (x, y), and graph the line of the equation.

EXAMPLE 1 Graph $y = 2x$.

Step 1 Assign values for x. For example, let $x = -1, 0, 1,$ and 2.

Step 2 Solve $y = 2x$ for y. Display the results in a table.

$y = 2x$	
x	**y**
−1	−2
0	0
1	2
2	4

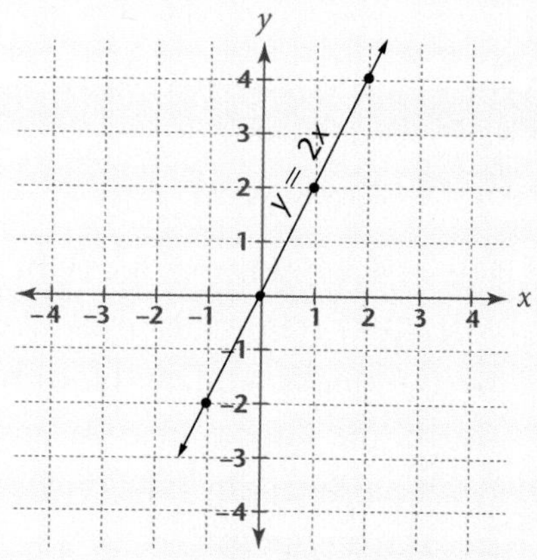

Step 3 Plot the points shown in the table, then graph the line.

The graph of the equation $y = 2x$ forms a straight line.

EXAMPLE 2

Graph $y = 2x - 3$.

Step 1 Assign two values for x. Let $x = -1$ and $x = 1$.

Step 2 Solve for y.

$y = 2x - 3$	$y = 2x - 3$
$y = 2(-1) - 3$	$y = 2(1) - 3$
$y = -2 - 3$	$y = 2 - 3$
$y = -5$	$y = -1$
When $x = -1, y = -5$.	When $x = 1, y = -1$.
$(-1, -5)$	$(1, -1)$

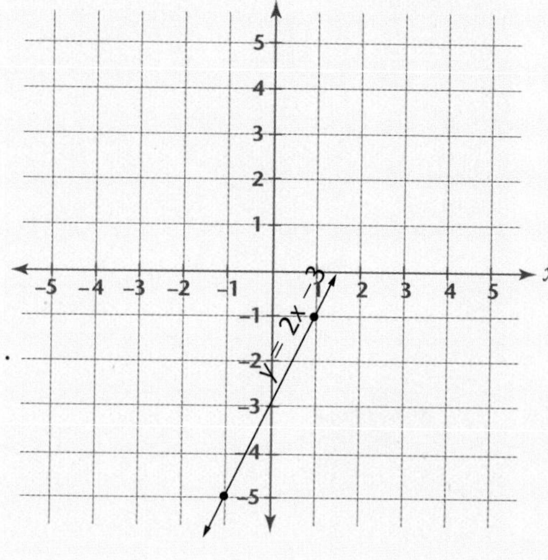

Step 3 Plot the points $(-1, -5)$ and $(1, -1)$. Then graph and label the line.

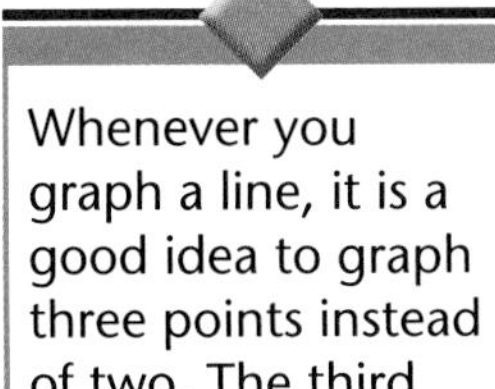

Whenever you graph a line, it is a good idea to graph three points instead of two. The third point will act as a check to be sure the points you chose are correct.

Exercise A Copy and complete the table of values for each equation.

1.

$y = x$	
x	y
–2	
–1	
0	
1	
2	

2.

$y = 3x$	
x	y
–5	
–3	
–1	
1	
3	

3.

$y = 2x + 1$	
x	y
–4	
–2	
0	
2	
4	

Exercise B Copy and complete a table of values for each equation. Then graph and label the line of each equation.

4.

$y = x$	
x	y

5.

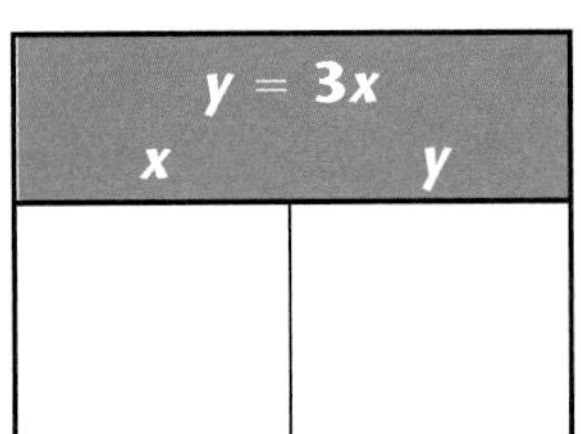

$y = 3x$	
x	y

6.

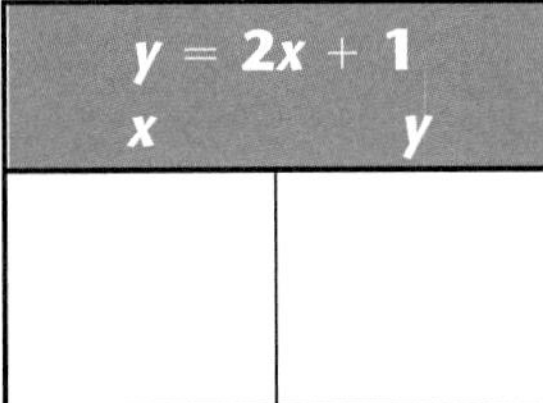

$y = 2x + 1$	
x	y

7.

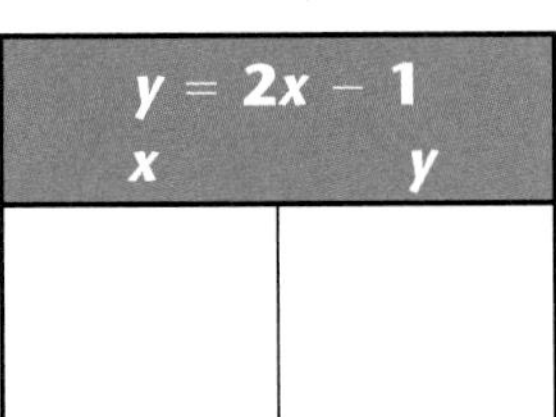

$y = 2x - 1$	
x	y

8.

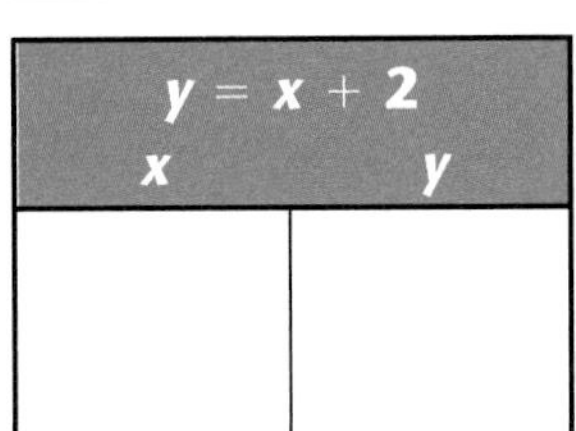

$y = x + 2$	
x	y

9.

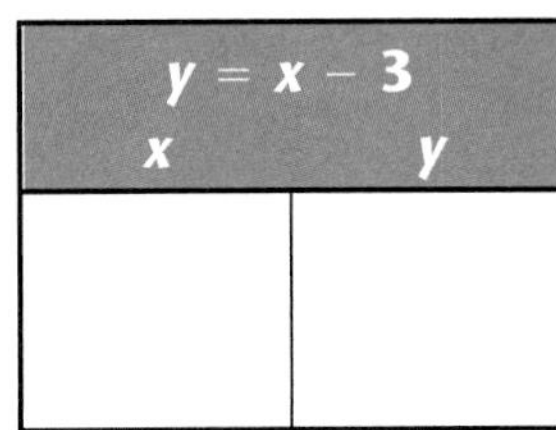

$y = x - 3$	
x	y

10.

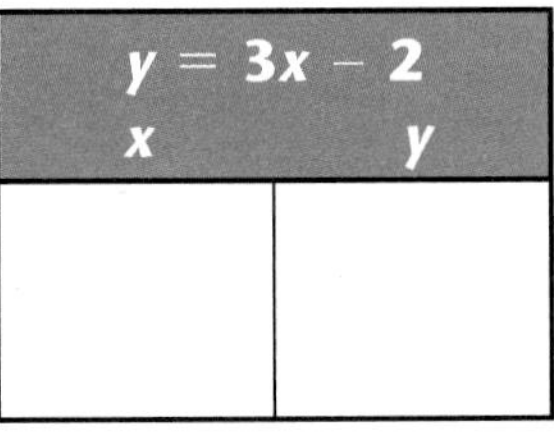

$y = 3x - 2$	
x	y

TRY THIS A straight line passes through (100, 100) and the origin. What is the equation of the line?

Lesson 3 Intercepts of Lines

y-intercept

The point at which a graph intersects the y-axis

In the previous lesson, you explored the graph of $y = 2x + 1$.

The graph passes through the point (0, 1). Since (0, 1) is a point on the y-axis, (0, 1) is called the ***y*-intercept** of the graph.

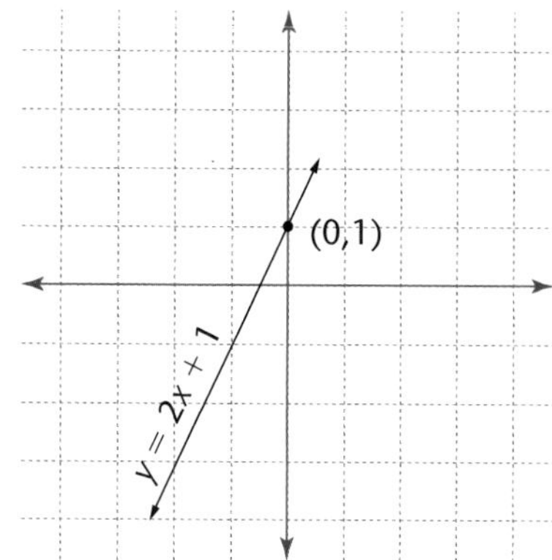

The y-intercept of a graph is the point at which a graph intersects the y-axis.

To find the y-intercept of a graph, substitute $x = 0$ into the equation of the graph and solve for y.

EXAMPLE 1 Find the y-intercept of $y = 3x + 1$.

Step 1 Let $x = 0$.

Step 2 Substitute $x = 0$ into the equation $y = 3x + 1$ and solve for y.

$y = 3x + 1$

$y = 3(0) + 1$

$y = 0 + 1$

$y = 1$

Step 3 Write an ordered pair to represent the y-intercept.

The y-intercept of $y = 3x + 1$ is (0, 1).

x-intercept

The point at which a graph intersects the x-axis

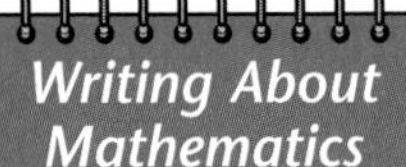

Will every graph have an x-intercept and a y-intercept? Explain.

Look again at the graph of $y = 2x + 1$.

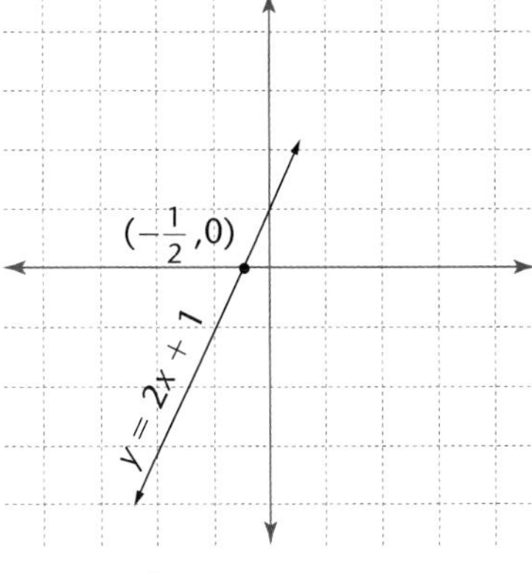

The graph also passes through the point $(-\frac{1}{2}, 0)$. Since $(-\frac{1}{2}, 0)$ is a point on the x-axis, $(-\frac{1}{2}, 0)$ is called the **x-intercept** of the graph.

The x-intercept of a graph is the point at which a graph intersects the x-axis. The x-intercept is also known as the root of the equation. To find the x-intercept of a graph, substitute $y = 0$ into the equation of the graph and solve for x.

EXAMPLE 2 Find the x-intercept of $y = 3x + 1$.

Step 1 Let $y = 0$.

Step 2 Substitute $y = 0$ into the equation $y = 3x + 1$ and solve for x.

$$y = 3x + 1$$
$$0 = 3x + 1$$
$$-1 = 3x$$
$$-\frac{1}{3} = x$$

Step 3 Write an ordered pair to represent the x-intercept. The x-intercept of $y = 3x + 1$ is $(-\frac{1}{3}, 0)$.

Exercise A Answer these questions.

1. Explain how to find the y-intercept of a graph.

2. Explain how to find the x-intercept of a graph.

Exercise B Find the x-intercept and y-intercept of each graph.

3. $y = x + 1$

4. $y = x - 1$

5. $y = x - 3$

6. $y = x + 2$

7. $y = 2x$

8. $y = 3x$

9. $y = 2x - 1$

10. $y = 4x - 4$

11. $y = -x + 1$

12. $y = -2x + 8$

13. $y = -3x - 9$

14. $y = -2x - 5$

Exercise C Answer this question.

15. When are the x-intercept and the y-intercept of a graph identical?

Lesson 4 Slopes of Lines

Slope

A measure of the steepness of a line

Acute

An angle smaller than a 90° angle

Obtuse

An angle larger than a 90° angle and smaller than a 180° angle

Remember, ordered pairs are written in the form (x, y).

The coefficient of x controls the **slope,** or steepness, of a graph.

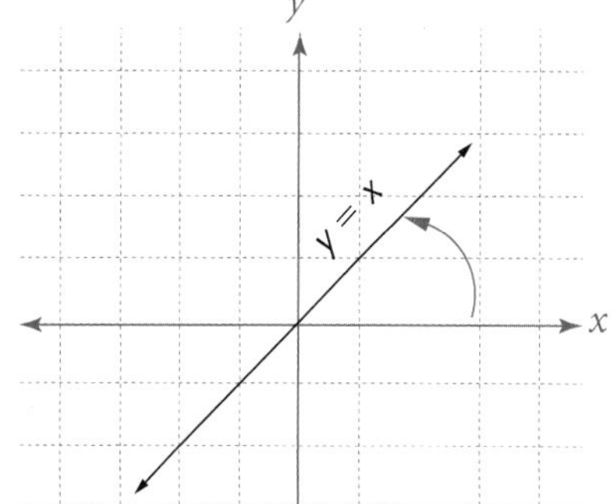

A graph with a *positive* slope creates an **acute** angle with the positive direction of the x-axis.

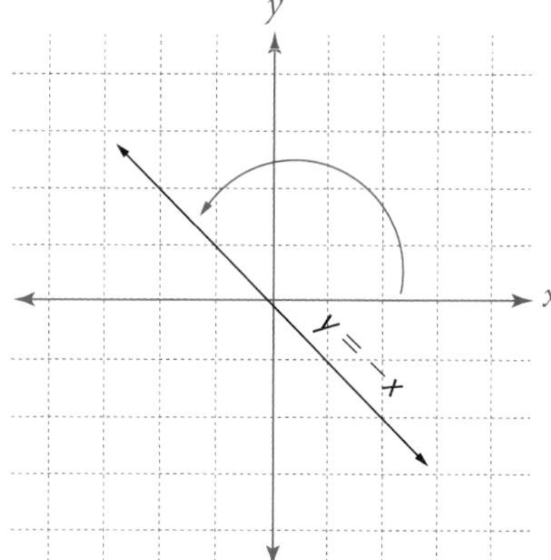

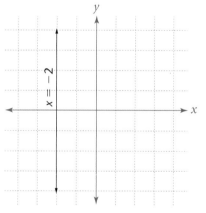

A graph with a *negative* slope creates an **obtuse** angle with the positive direction of the x-axis.

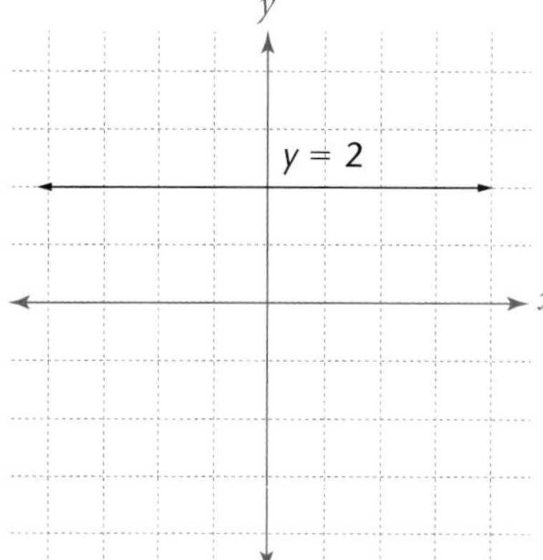

A graph with a *slope of zero* is parallel to the x-axis.

y

$x = -2$

x

A graph with a slope that is *undefined* is parallel to the y-axis.

Roofs have slope. Is the slope of each roof the same or different?

Formula for Slope

If you know two points on a straight line, use the formula $m = \frac{y_2 - y_1}{x_2 - x_1}$ to find the slope of that line. In the formula, m = slope.

EXAMPLE 1 Find the slope of a line that passes through $(-2, 5)$ and $(2, -3)$.

Step 1 Label one ordered pair (x_1, y_1) and label the other (x_2, y_2).

$$\begin{array}{cc} (-2, 5) & (2, -3) \\ \uparrow\uparrow & \uparrow\uparrow \\ (x_1, y_1) & (x_2, y_2) \end{array}$$

Step 2 Substitute the x_1, y_1, x_2, and y_2 values into the formula $m = \frac{y_2 - y_1}{x_2 - x_1}$.

$m = \frac{-3 - 5}{2 - (-2)} = -\frac{8}{4} = -2$ The slope of the line is -2.

EXAMPLE 2 Find the slope of a line that passes through $(1, 0)$ and $(5, 2)$.

Step 1 Label one ordered pair (x_1, y_1) and label the other (x_2, y_2).

$$\begin{array}{cc} (1, 0) & (5, 2) \\ \uparrow\uparrow & \uparrow\uparrow \\ (x_1, y_1) & (x_2, y_2) \end{array}$$

Step 2 Substitute the x_1, y_1, x_2, and y_2 values into the formula $m = \frac{y_2 - y_1}{x_2 - x_1}$.

$m = \frac{2 - 0}{5 - 1} = \frac{2}{4} = \frac{1}{2}$ The slope of the line is $\frac{1}{2}$.

You can label either ordered pair (x_1, y_1) or (x_2, y_2).

EXAMPLE 3 Find the slope of a line that passes through $(1, 0)$ and $(5, 2)$.

Step 1 This time label the second ordered pair (x_1, y_1) and label the first ordered pair (x_2, y_2).

$$\begin{array}{cc} (5, 2) & (1, 0) \\ \uparrow\uparrow & \uparrow\uparrow \\ (x_1, y_1) & (x_2, y_2) \end{array}$$

Step 2 Substitute the x_1, y_1, x_2, and y_2 values into the formula $m = \frac{y_2 - y_1}{x_2 - x_1}$.

$m = \frac{0 - 2}{1 - 5} = \frac{-2}{-4} = \frac{2}{4} = \frac{1}{2}$ The slope of the line is $\frac{1}{2}$.

As you can see, the way that ordered pairs are labeled does not affect the slope of the line.

There are two ways to label ordered pairs when using the formula for slope. $(x_1, y_1) = (1, 0)$ and $(x_2, y_2) = (5, 2)$ or $(x_1, y_1) = (5, 2)$ and $(x_2, y_2) = (1, 0)$ Either way gives the same answer when using the formula for slope.

Exercise A Draw a coordinate system. Use it for this exercise.

1. Draw a line that has a positive slope. Label the line *A*.
2. Draw a line that has a negative slope. Label the line *B*.
3. Draw a line whose slope is neither positive nor negative. Label the line *C*.

Exercise B Describe the slope of each line. Write positive, negative, or neither.

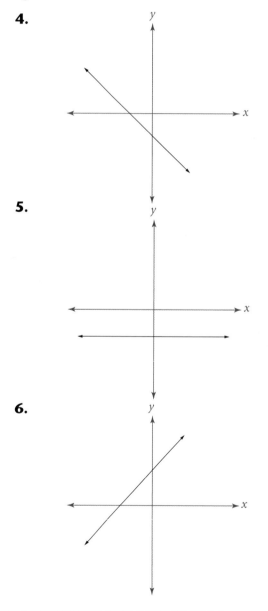

4.

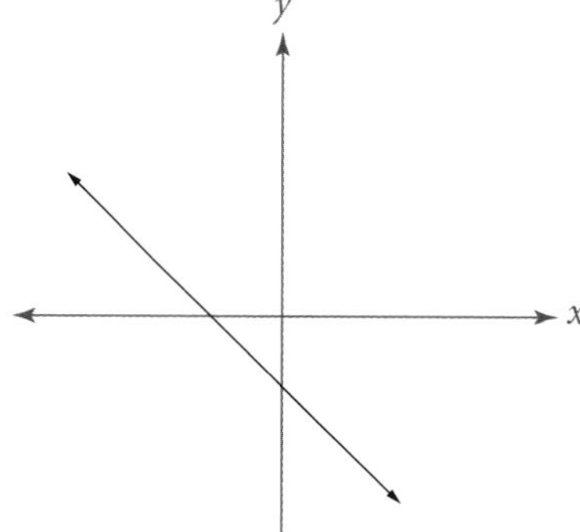

5.

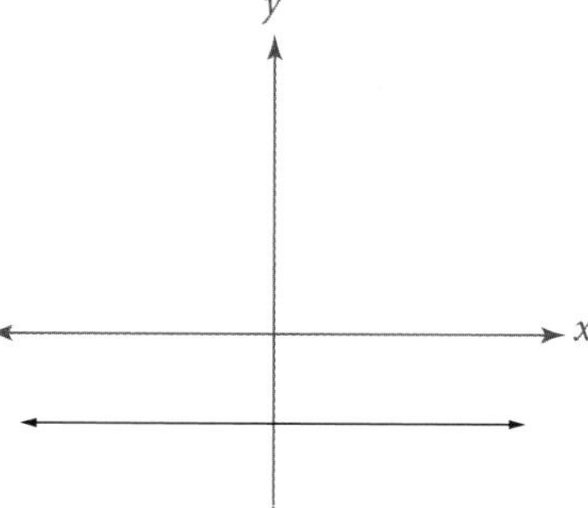

6.

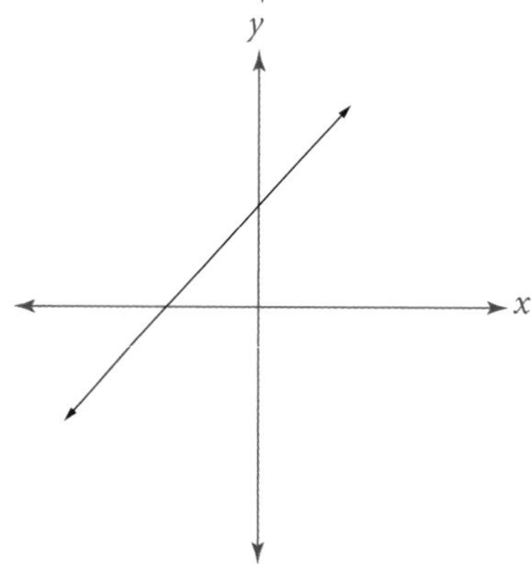

Calculator Practice

You can use a calculator to check your answer whenever you find the slope of a line.

EXAMPLE 4 Suppose the slope formula looks like this after substituting *x*- and *y*-values:

$$\frac{-6-(-2)}{1-5}=1$$

To check, input the entire numerator in a set of parentheses and input the entire denominator in a set of parentheses:

Press: (− 6 − (− 2)) ÷ (1 − 5) =

The calculator will display 1.

Writing About Mathematics

Imagine coasting down a short but steep hill on a bicycle. If the slope of the hill could be measured, would it be closer to $\frac{1}{2}$ or $\frac{2}{1}$? Explain.

Exercise C Use a calculator to compute each slope.

7. $\frac{-1-(-1)}{2-3}$

8. $\frac{-9-5}{-3-4}$

9. $\frac{5-(-3)}{-2-2}$

10. $\frac{-1-(-7)}{-6-(-3)}$

11. How can you use a calculator to check a slope computation that has a fraction or mixed number for an answer?

Exercise D Find the slope of the line that passes through the following points.

12. $(-3, -3)\ (3, 3)$

13. $(1, -6)\ (4, -6)$

14. $(-3, -2)\ (5, 1)$

15. $(2, 6)\ (5, 0)$

16. $(4, 3)\ (2, 2)$

17. $(-1, 5)\ (5, 5)$

PROBLEM SOLVING

Exercise E Use the data given to answer each question.

Bicycle Trail 1: Slope = $\frac{1}{100}$

Bicycle Trail 2: Slope = $\frac{2}{15}$

Bicycle Trail 3: Slope = $-\frac{1}{25}$

18. Elena is making a scale drawing of the trails. Which trail or trails are downhill? Which are uphill?

19. Aaron wants to avoid riding on the steepest trail. Which trail should he avoid?

20. Robby rides the least steep trail almost every day. Which trail does he ride?

Algebra in Your Life

It's All Downhill from Here

Have you ever seen a sign along a roadway that says "Trucks Check Brakes Grade 6%." What does that mean? It means there's a hill ahead. The steepness or slope of the road is called its grade. The grade is measured in percents. It is calculated the same way you find the slope of a line in algebra. If the slope is too steep, the trucker could lose control and wreck. Amazing as it may seem, people use algebra to help prevent traffic accidents!

Lesson 5 Writing Linear Equations

Linear equation

An equation whose graph is a straight line

If the graph of an equation is a straight line, the equation is a **linear equation.** The general form for all linear equations is

$y = mx + b$ where m is the slope of the line and b is the y-intercept

(m ↑ slope, b ↑ y-intercept)

The equation $y = 2x + 1$ is an example of a linear equation.

(2 ↑ slope, 1 ↑ y-intercept)

It has a slope of 2 and a y-intercept of 1.

If you know the values of m and b, you can use the general form $y = mx + b$ to write the equation of a line.

EXAMPLE 1 Write the equation of a line whose slope is 3 and y-intercept is $\frac{1}{2}$.

Solution Given $m = 3$ and $b = \frac{1}{2}$, $y = mx + b$ becomes $y = 3x + \frac{1}{2}$.

If you are given two points through which a line passes, you can write the equation of the line.

EXAMPLE 2 Write the equation of a line that passes through (7, 1) and (−2, 3).

Step 1 Compute the slope. $m = \frac{y_2 - y_1}{x_2 - x_1} = \frac{3 - 1}{-2 - 7} = -\frac{2}{9}$

Step 2 Substitute $-\frac{2}{9}$ for m in $y = mx + b$. $y = -\frac{2}{9}x + b$

Step 3 Compute the y-intercept. Since both points (7, 1) and (−2, 3) are on the line, substitute either point into $y = -\frac{2}{9}x + b$, then solve for b.

Use the point (–2, 3); $x = -2$ and $y = 3$:

$y = -\frac{2}{9}x + b$

$3 = -\frac{2}{9}(-2) + b \quad 3 = \frac{4}{9} + b \quad 2\frac{5}{9} = b$

Step 4 Write the equation of the line by substituting the values you computed for m and b in $y = mx + b$. Since $m = -\frac{2}{9}$ and $b = 2\frac{5}{9}$, $y = mx + b$ becomes $y = -\frac{2}{9}x + 2\frac{5}{9}$.

EXAMPLE 3 Write the equation of a line that has a slope of $\frac{1}{2}$ and passes through $(-1, 2)$.

Step 1 Since the slope is given, substitute $\frac{1}{2}$ for m in $y = mx + b$. $\quad y = \frac{1}{2}x + b$

Step 2 Compute the y-intercept. Substitute the point $(-1, 2)$ into $y = \frac{1}{2}x + b$, then solve for b.
Given the point $(-1, 2)$, $x = -1$ and $y = 2$:
$y = \frac{1}{2}x + b$
$2 = \frac{1}{2}(-1) + b \qquad 2 = -\frac{1}{2} + b \qquad 2\frac{1}{2} = b$

Step 3 Write the equation of the line by substituting the values you computed for m and b in $y = mx + b$.
Since $m = \frac{1}{2}$ and $b = 2\frac{1}{2}$, $y = mx + b$ becomes
$y = \frac{1}{2}x + 2\frac{1}{2}$.

Writing About Mathematics

Can $y = mx + b$ be used to write an equation of a line that passes through (1, 0) and (1, 10)? Explain.

Exercise A Write the equation of each line.

1. $m = 2; b = 1$ **2.** $m = 3; b = -3$ **3.** $m = -2; b = 5$

Exercise B Graph the line that passes through the following points. Then write the equation of each line.

4. $(1, 1)\ (3, 3)$
5. $(0, 0)\ (2, 4)$
6. $(-1, 2)\ (3, -6)$
7. $(5, 0)\ (0, 10)$
8. $(-4, -1)\ (4, 7)$
9. $(-2, 0)\ (-6, -1)$
10. $(1, 8)\ (2, -16)$

Exercise C Write the equation of the line that has the given slope and passes through the given point.

11. $m = 5; (5, 5)$
12. $m = 10; (-1, -4)$
13. $m = \frac{1}{2}; (1, 6)$
14. $m = \frac{3}{4}; (8, 4)$
15. $m = 2; (4, 8)$

Lesson 6 Lines as Functions

Dependent variable

The value of the y variable that depends on the value of x

Independent variable

The value of x that determines the value of y

Function

A rule that associates every x-value with one and only one y-value

Vertical line test

A way of determining whether a graph is a function; if a vertical line intersects a graph in more than 1 point, the graph is not a function

If you make a table of values for the equation $y = \frac{3}{2}x + 7$, you will find that for each value you choose for x, the value of y changes. Because the value of y depends on the value you choose for x, y is known as the **dependent variable** and x is known as the **independent variable**. Another way to describe the same idea is to say that y is a **function** of x.

To use the language of functions, use the symbol $f(x)$ in place of y.

$y = mx + b$ is the same as $f(x) = mx + b$.

(The symbol $f(x)$ is read "the function of x.")

Rewrite $y = \frac{3}{2}x + 7$ as $f(x) = \frac{3}{2}x + 7$

Rule A function is a rule that associates every x-value with one and only one y-value.

All equations of the form $f(x) = mx + b$ are functions. To decide whether the graph of an equation is a function, perform a **vertical line test**—if a vertical line crosses the graph more than once, the graph is not a function because the x-value of the vertical line is associated with more than one y-value.

Example 1 Is the graph at the right a function?

Solution No; a vertical line crosses the graph more than once—for every x-value, there is more than one y-value.

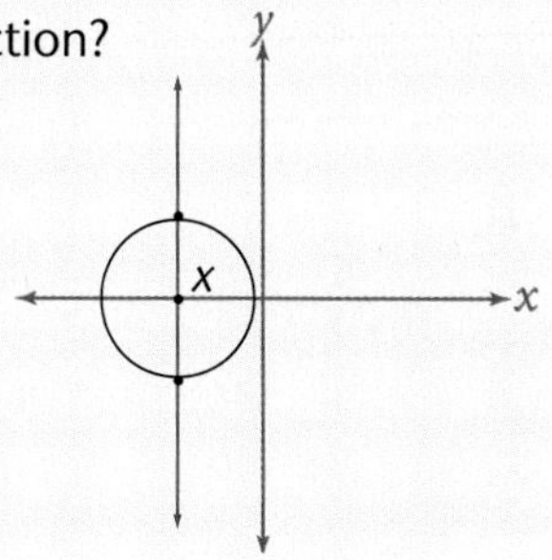

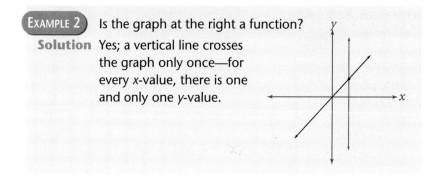

EXAMPLE 2 Is the graph at the right a function?

Solution Yes; a vertical line crosses the graph only once—for every x-value, there is one and only one y-value.

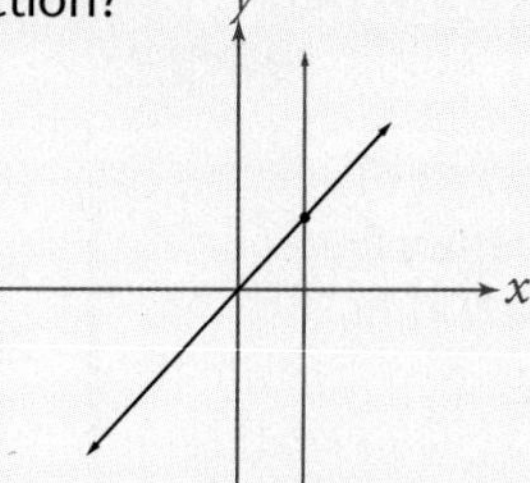

To evaluate a function means to substitute a value for x and solve for $f(x)$.

EXAMPLE 3 Evaluate $f(x) = x^2 + x - 1$ given $x = 3$.

Solution $f(x) = x^2 + x - 1$

$f(3) = 3^2 + 3 - 1$

$f(3) = 11$

Exercise A Is each graph an example of a function? Write yes or no.

1.

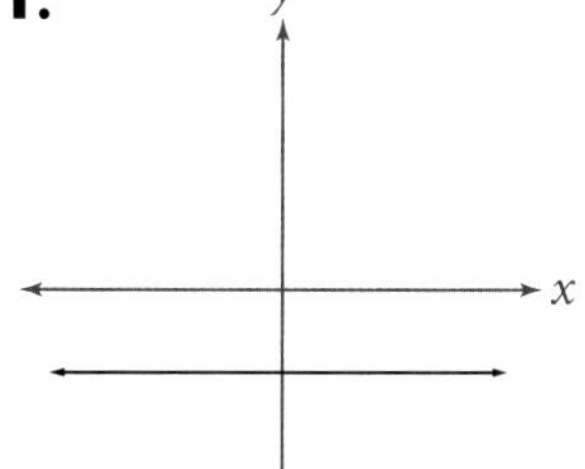

2.

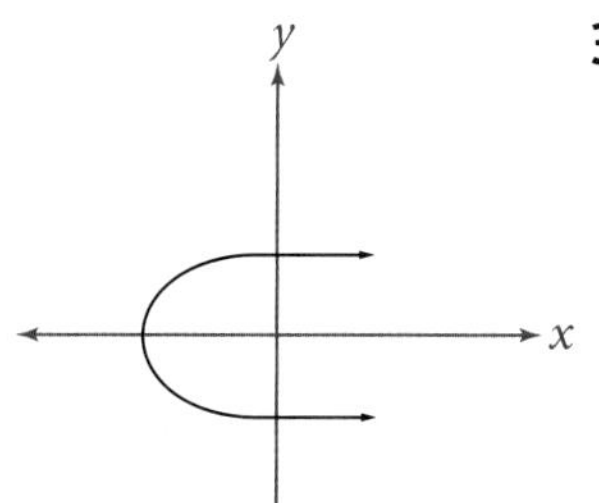

3.

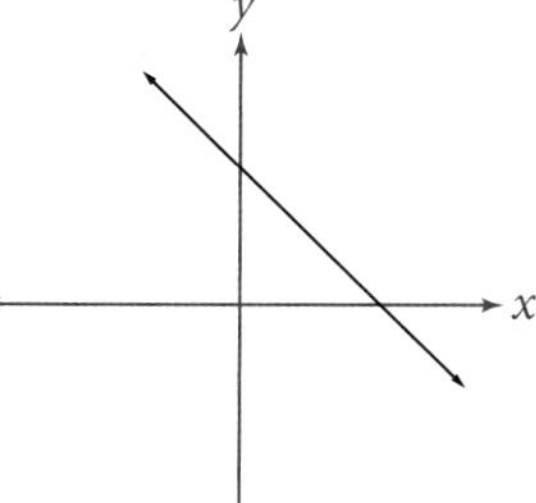

4.

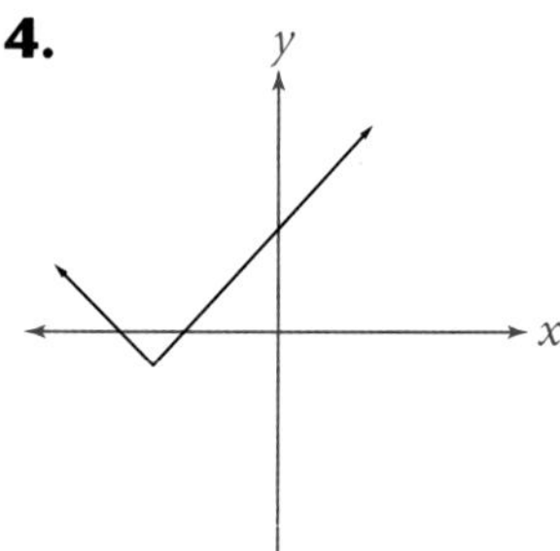

5.

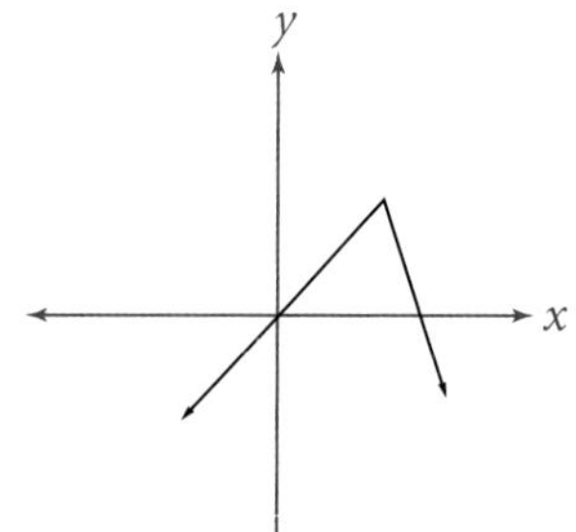

6.

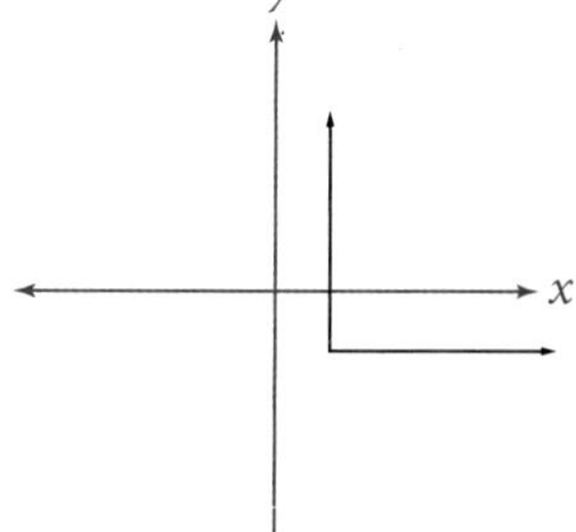

Writing About Mathematics

In your local newspaper, find a line graph. Is this graph an example of a function? Explain why or why not.

Exercise B Evaluate each function two times. Use $x = 2$ and $x = -4$.

7. $f(x) = x^2 + x$

8. $f(x) = x^2 - x$

9. $f(x) = 4x^2 - x$

10. $f(x) = -2x^2 + x$

11. $f(x) = -x^2 + 3x$

12. $f(x) = x^2 - 6x$

13. $f(x) = -3x^2 + x - 1$

14. $f(x) = 4x^2 - x - 4$

15. $f(x) = 1.5x^2 + 3x$

Lesson 7 Domain and Range of a Function

Domain
The independent variables, or set of x–values, of a function

Range
The dependent variables, or set of y–values, of a function

The set of x-values, the independent variables that are used in a function, is called the **domain** of the function. The corresponding set of y-values, the dependent variables, is called the **range** of the function.

Example 1 $y = f(x) = 2x - 1$

Let the domain be $-1, 0, 2, 5$.

Determine the range.

Substitute the domain values in $f(x)$ to determine the range.

$x = -1$ $y = f(-1) = 2(-1) - 1 = -3$ so $y = -3$

$x = 0$ $y = f(0) = 2(0) - 1 = -1$ so $y = -1$

$x = 2$ $y = f(2) = 2(2) - 1 = 3$ so $y = 3$

$x = 5$ $y = f(5) = 2(5) - 1 = 9$ so $y = 9$

The range is $-3, -1, 3, 9$.

Example 2 Look at the graph for $f(x) = x - 1$ for $1 \leq x \leq 4$

What is the range?

Find the endpoints of the range by evaluating $f(1)$ and $f(4)$.

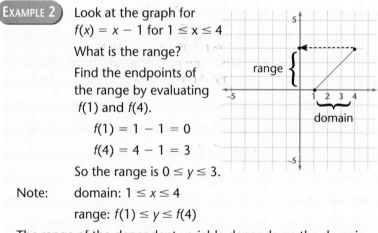

$f(1) = 1 - 1 = 0$

$f(4) = 4 - 1 = 3$

So the range is $0 \leq y \leq 3$.

Note: domain: $1 \leq x \leq 4$

range: $f(1) \leq y \leq f(4)$

The range of the dependent variable depends on the domain.

EXAMPLE 3 Use the graph at the right to determine the domain and range of the graphed function.

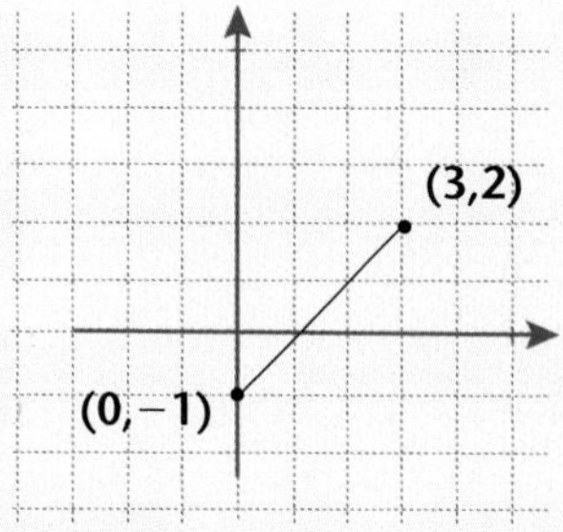

The ordered pairs $(0, -1)$ and $(3, 2)$ give the endpoints of the intervals of domain and range.

$(0, -1)$ and $(3, 2)$

domain

range

domain: $0 \leq x \leq 3$

range: $-1 \leq y \leq 2$

Remember:

1. The domain includes all the x-values needed to define the function. The domain is found on the x-axis. You can choose the domain. It is independent.
2. The range includes all the y-values, which depend directly on the domain-values substituted in the function. The range is found on the y-axis. It is dependent on the domain.

Exercise A Determine the range for each function with the given domain.

1. $f(x) = 2x - 5$ domain: $-1, 0, 3, 7, 10$

2. $f(x) = -x^2$ domain: $-1, 0, 5, 9, 100$

3. $f(x) = \frac{1}{2}x + 2$ domain: $-\frac{1}{2}, 0, 2, 3, 4$

4. $f(x) = x^2 + 2x + 3$ domain: $-2, 0, 1, 2, 3$

5. $f(x) = 2x + 6$ domain: $-4, -3, -\frac{1}{2}, 1, 8$

Exercise B Determine the range for each function, given the domain and the graph.

6. $f(x) = -x + 2$ for $-2 \leq x \leq 4$

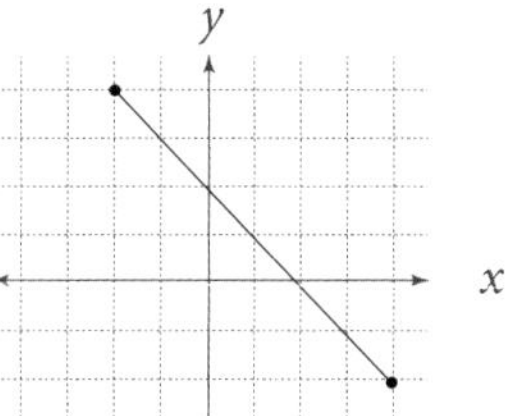

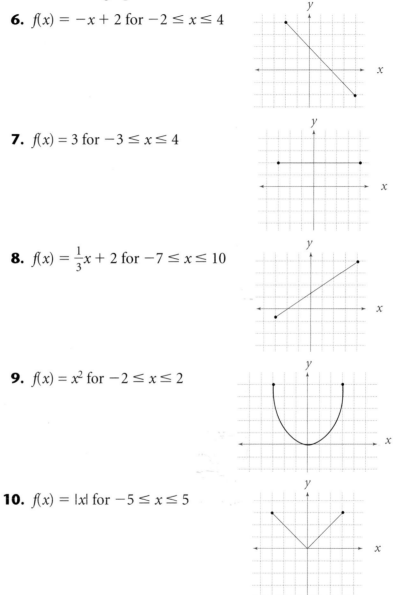

7. $f(x) = 3$ for $-3 \leq x \leq 4$

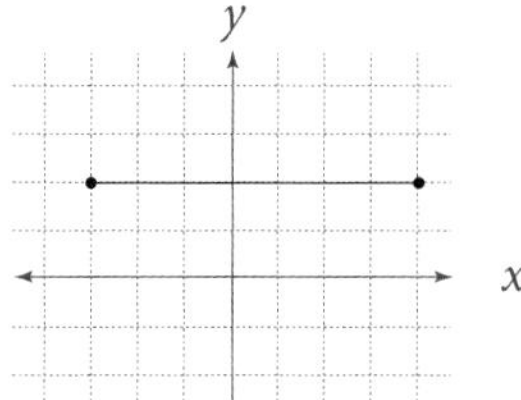

8. $f(x) = \frac{1}{3}x + 2$ for $-7 \leq x \leq 10$

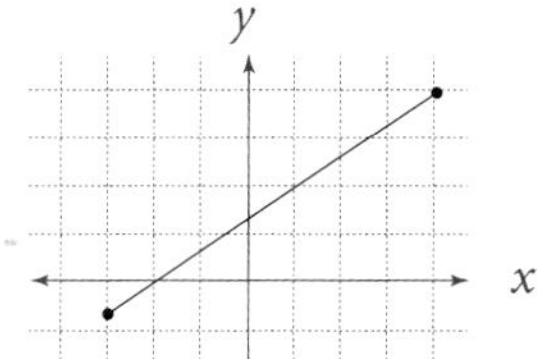

9. $f(x) = x^2$ for $-2 \leq x \leq 2$

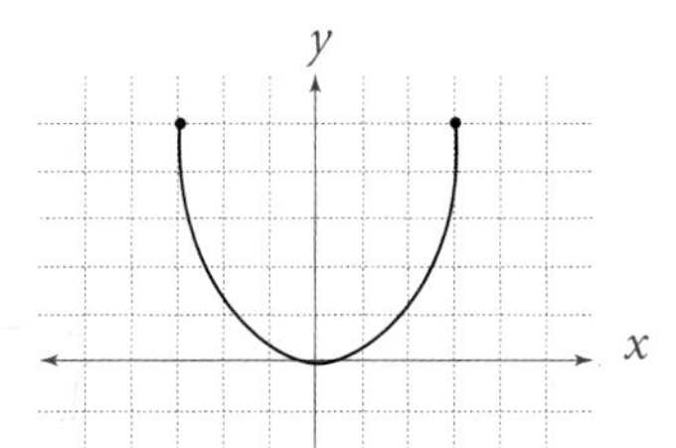

10. $f(x) = |x|$ for $-5 \leq x \leq 5$

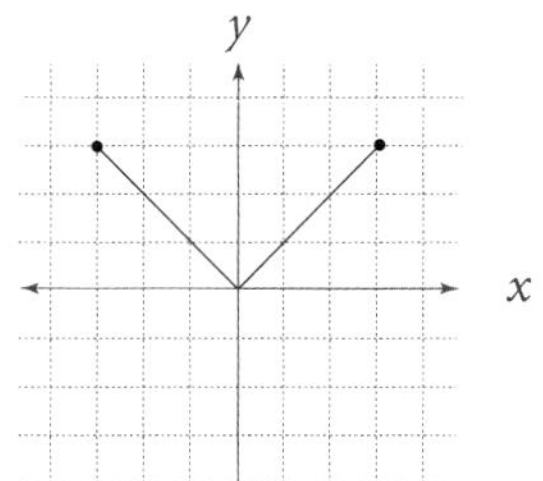

Exercise C Determine the domain and the range from the graph and the given ordered pairs.

11.

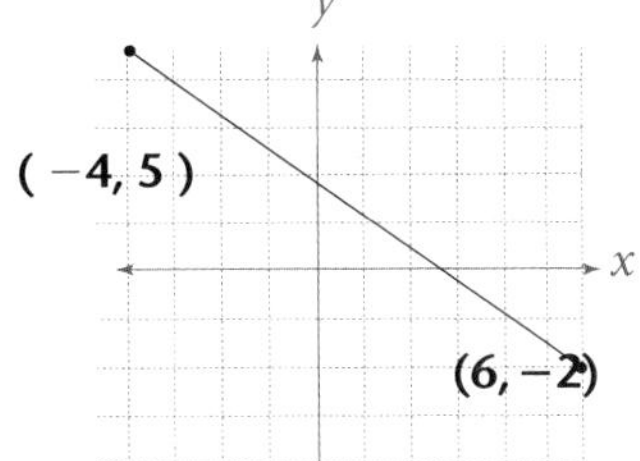

12.

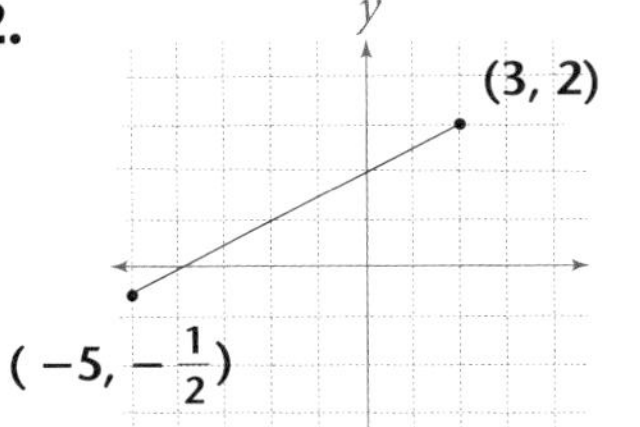

13.

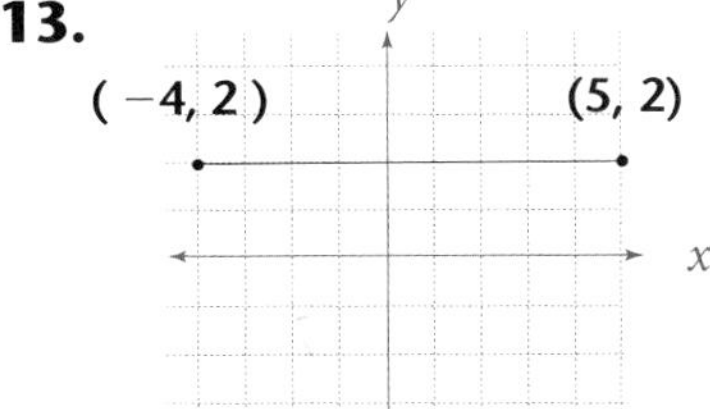

14.

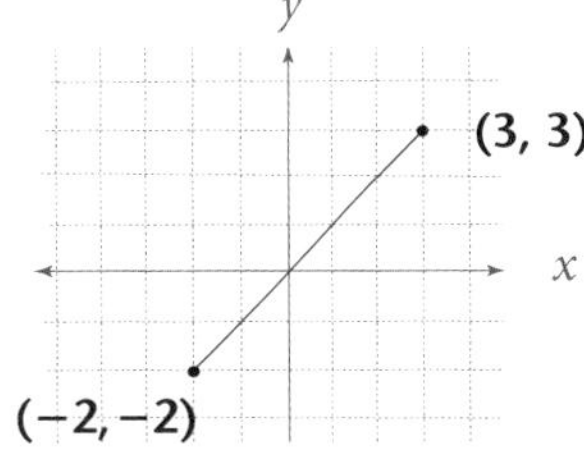

15.

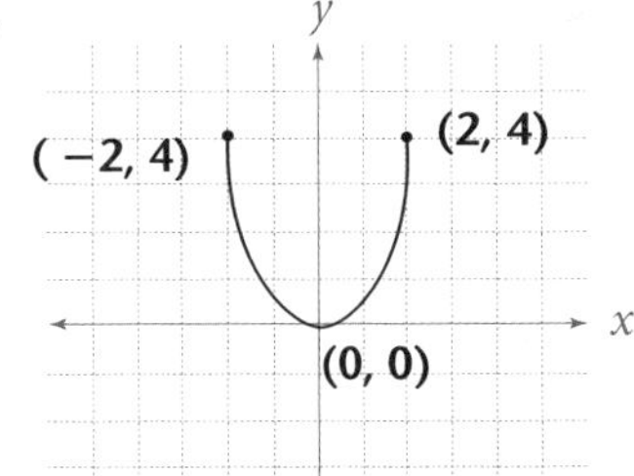

Technology Connection

Graphing Tools

If you have access to the Internet, there are lots of graphing tools available. Go to a search engine, type in the words "online graphing tools," and you'll find several you can download for free. (There are many you can buy them, as well.) Computer spreadsheet and even word-processing programs are capable of making graphs, too. All these graphing tools function the same way. You plug in a formula or data, and the tool will display the resulting graph.

Lesson 8 Graphing Inequalities: $y < mx + b$, $y > mx + b$

A line in a plane divides a plane into three parts: the points on the line, the points above the line, and the points below the line.

For any point (x, y), three possibilities exist:

1. (x, y) is on $y = x + 1$
   Example $(0, 1) \rightarrow y = x + 1 \rightarrow 1 = 0 + 1 \rightarrow 1 = 1$
   True, (0,1) is on the line.

2. (x, y) is above $y = x + 1$
   Example $(-2, 5) \rightarrow y = x + 1 \rightarrow 5 = -2 + 1 \rightarrow 5 = -1$
   False, $(-2, 5)$ is *not* on the line.
   However $(-2, 5) \rightarrow y > x + 1 \rightarrow 5 > -2 + 1 \rightarrow 5 > -1$ True
   Conclusion $y > x + 1$ represents the region above $y = x + 1$.

3. (x, y) is below $y = x + 1$
   Example $(5, -2) \rightarrow y = x + 1 \rightarrow -2 = 5 + 1 \rightarrow -2 = 6$
   False, $(5, -2)$ is *not* on the line.
   However $(5, -2) \rightarrow y < x + 1 \rightarrow -2 < 5 + 1 \rightarrow -2 < 6$ True
   Conclusion $y < x + 1$ represents the region below $y = x + 1$.

This graph shows all three possibilities.

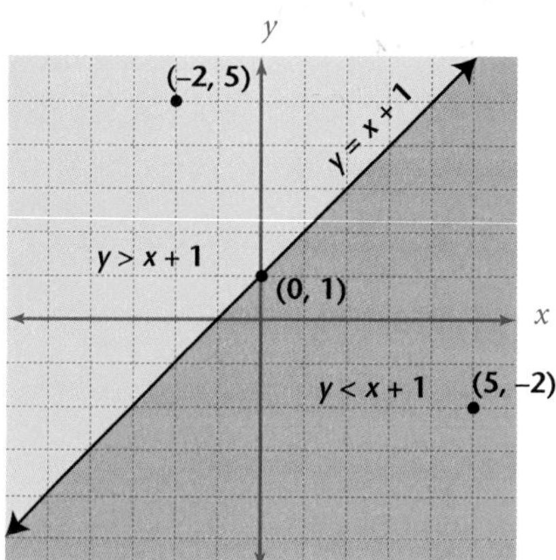

Whenever you graph inequalities, begin by sketching the equality, then decide whether you need to shade the region above or below the line.

EXAMPLE 1 Graph the region represented by $y < 3x + 1$.

Step 1 Use $y = 3x + 1$ and substitution to find two points on the line. Plot the points and then draw a broken line and label the line $y < 3x + 1$.

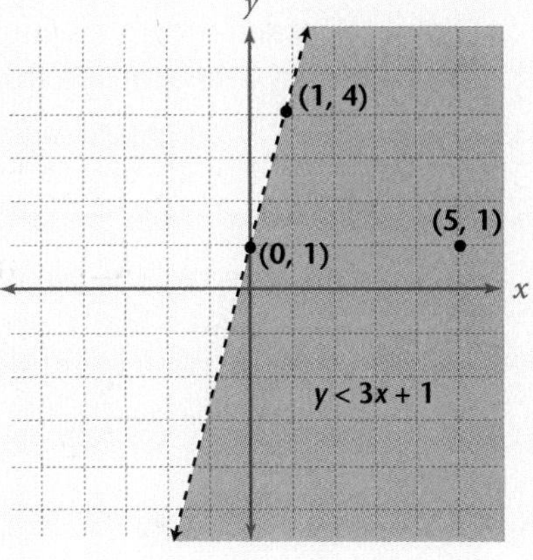

Step 2 $y < 3x + 1$ represents the region below the broken line. Check by choosing a point such as (5, 1) that is located below the broken line.

$y < 3x + 1$

$1 < 3(5) + 1$

$1 < 16$ True

Step 3 Shade the region below the broken line without touching the broken line.

EXAMPLE 2 Graph the region represented by $y > 3$.

Step 1 All ordered pairs having a y-value of 3 are on a horizontal line that passes through $y = 3$. So $y > 3$ is parallel to the x-axis. Draw a broken line and label the line $y > 3$.

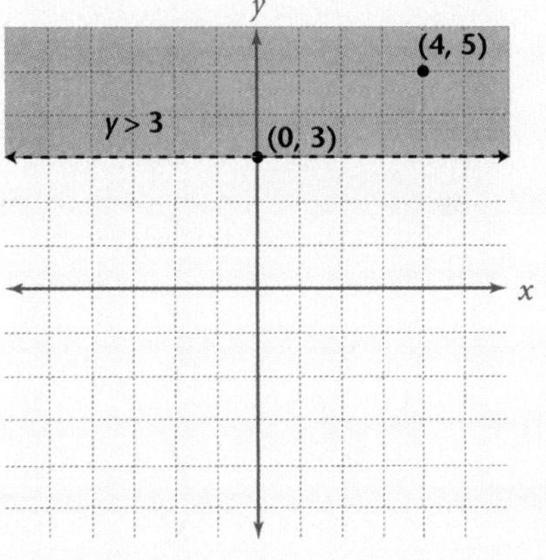

Step 2 $y > 3$ represents the region above the broken line. Check by choosing a point such as (4, 5) that is located above the broken line.

$y > 3$

$5 > 3$ True

Step 3 Shade the region above the broken line without touching the broken line.

EXAMPLE 3 Graph the region represented by $x < -1$.

Step 1 All ordered pairs having an x-value of -1 are on a vertical line that passes through $x = -1$. So $x < -1$ is perpendicular to the y-axis. Draw a broken line and label the line $x < -1$.

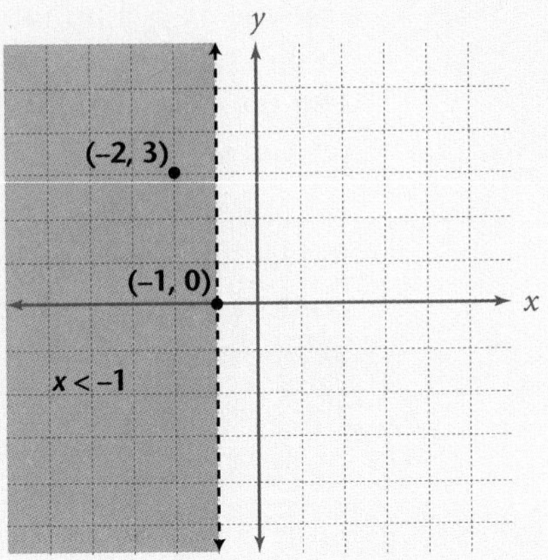

Step 2 $x < -1$ represents the region to the left of the broken line. Check by choosing a point such as $(-2, 3)$ that is located to the left of the broken line.

$x < -1$

$-2 < -1$ True

Step 3 Shade the region to the left of the broken line without touching the broken line.

Exercise A Graph the region represented by each line.

1. $y > 3x + 1$
2. $y > 4x - 1$
3. $y < 2x + 3$
4. $y < x - 2$
5. $y > 5x$
6. $y < 2$
7. $x > 6$
8. $x < -3$
9. $y > 1$
10. $y < -1$
11. $y > x + 4$
12. $y < 4x$
13. $y > -2$
14. $x < 4$
15. $x > -1$

Estimation Activity

Estimate: The graph shows the population growth in Johnsonville. If the population grows the same amount as it did between 1970 and 1980, what will the population of Johnsonville be in 2010?

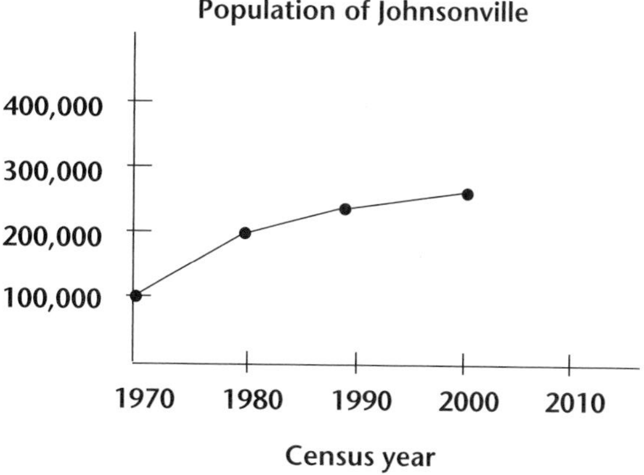

Solution: Look at the information on the graph and use it to solve the problem.

Between 1970 and 1980, the population grew from 100,000 to 200,000, an increase of 100,000. The last population data on the graph shows the population at 250,000. So, you can estimate that the population in 2100 will be 350,000.

Lesson 9 Graphing Inequalities: $y \leq mx + b$, $y \geq mx + b$

Graphs of inequalities also include inequalities such as $y \leq x + 1$ and $y \geq x + 1$. In these cases, you must *include* equality in the graphs of these regions.

EXAMPLE 1 Graph the region represented by $y \leq x + 1$.

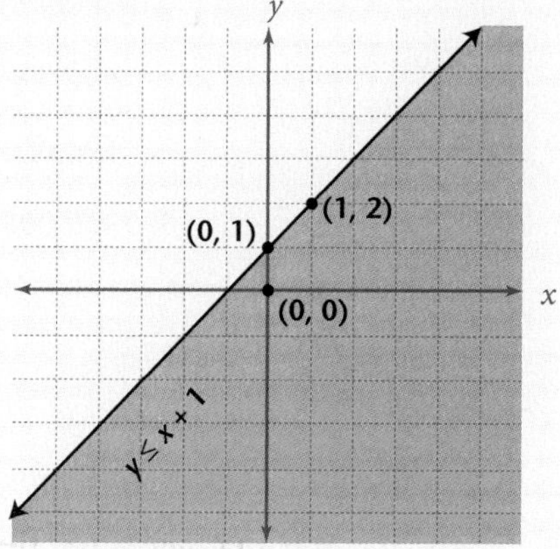

Step 1 Use $y = x + 1$ and substitution to find two points on the line. Plot the points and then draw a solid line and label the line $y \leq x + 1$.

Step 2 $y \leq x + 1$ represents the region below the solid line. Check by choosing a point such as (0, 0) that is located below the solid line.

$y \leq x + 1$
$0 \leq 0 + 1$
$0 \leq 1$ True

Step 3 Shade the region *below* the solid line. Include the line in your shading.

EXAMPLE 2 Graph the region represented by $y \geq x + 1$.

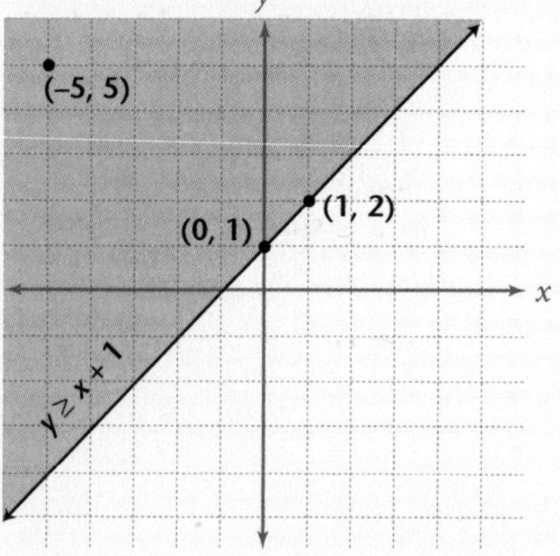

Step 1 Use $y = x + 1$ and substitution to find two points on the line. Plot the points and then draw a solid line and label the line $y \geq x + 1$.

Step 2 $y \geq x + 1$ represents the region above the solid line. Check by choosing a point such as $(-5, 5)$ that is located above the solid line.

$y \geq x + 1$
$5 \geq -5 + 1$
$5 \geq -4$ True

Step 3 Shade the region above the solid line. Include the line in your shading.

You can write the algebraic inequality represented by a graph if you are given a graph and the equation of the line of the graph.

EXAMPLE 3 Write the inequality that describes the shaded region.

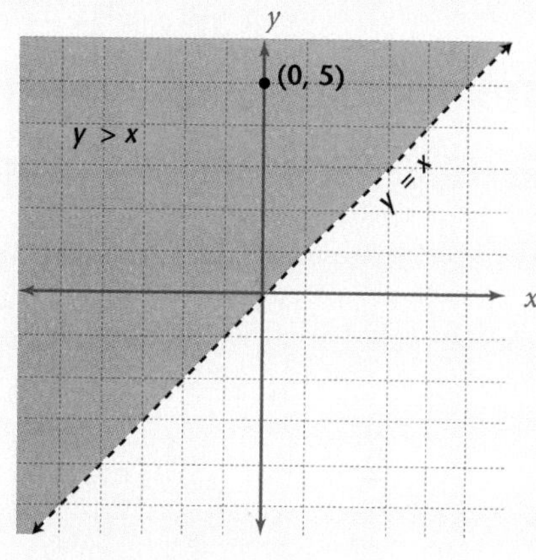

Step 1 Since the shaded region is defined by a broken line, the inequality does not include =. Since the shaded region is above $y = x$, the inequality is >, and $y > x$ is the inequality that describes the shaded region.

Step 2 Check by choosing a point such as (0, 5) that is located in the shaded region.

$y > x$

$5 > 0$ True

EXAMPLE 4 Write the inequality that describes the shaded region.

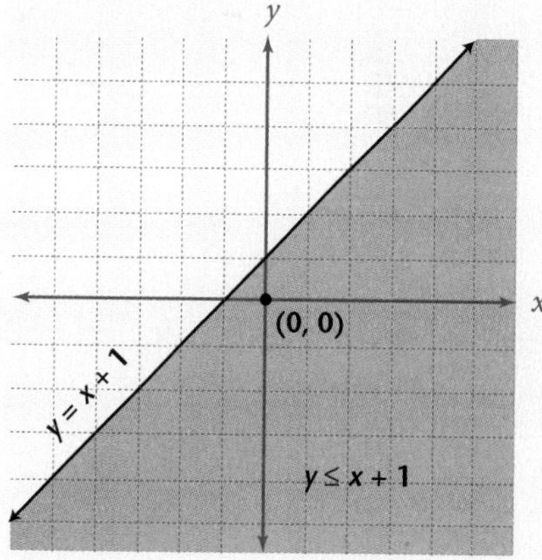

Step 1 Since the shaded region is defined by a solid line, the inequality includes =. Since the shaded region is *below* $y = x + 1$, the inequality is <, and $y \leq x + 1$ is the inequality that describes the shaded region.

Step 2 Check by choosing a point such as (0, 0) that is located in the shaded region.

$y \leq x + 1$

$0 \leq 0 + 1$

$0 \leq 1$ True

Exercise A Graph the region represented by each line.

1. $y \geq x + 2$

2. $y \leq x + 2$

3. $y \leq 2x - 1$

4. $y < 3x + 3$

5. $y \geq -2x$

6. $y \leq 5x$

7. $y > -1$

8. $y \leq 4$

9. $x > 2$

10. $x \geq -3$

Exercise B Write the inequality that describes each shaded region.

11.

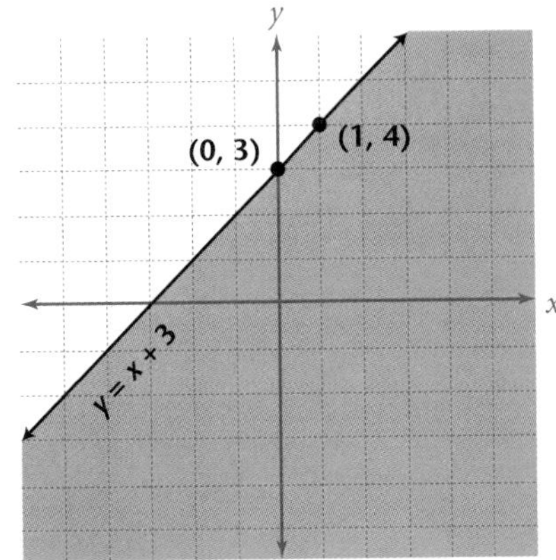

12.

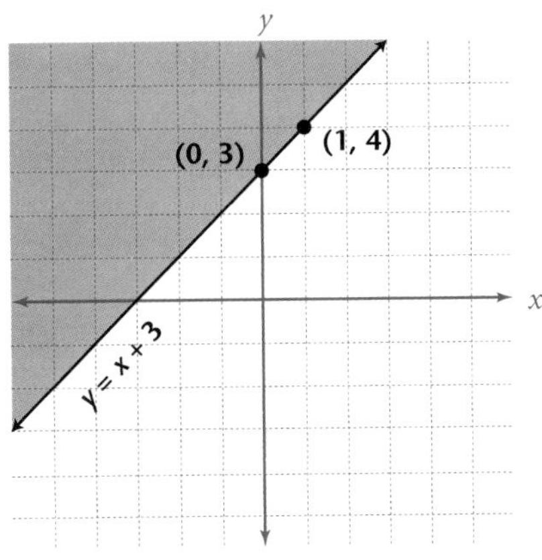

13.

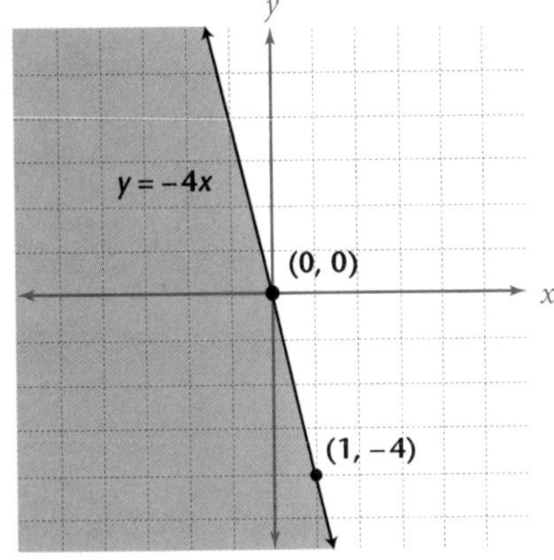

14.

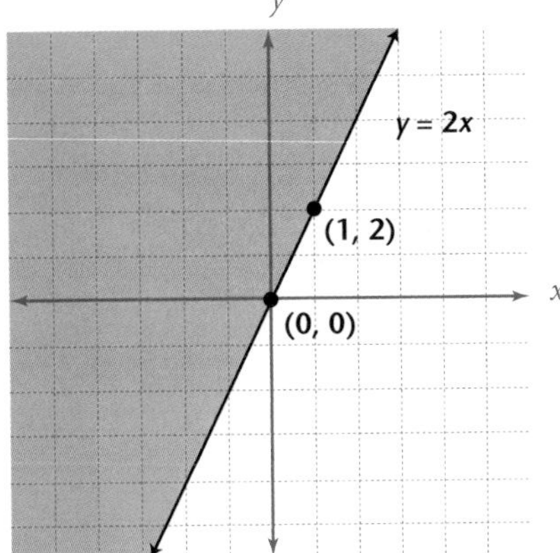

15.

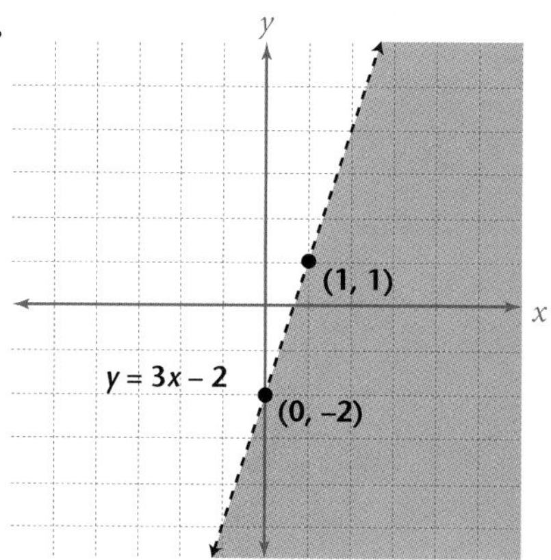

16.

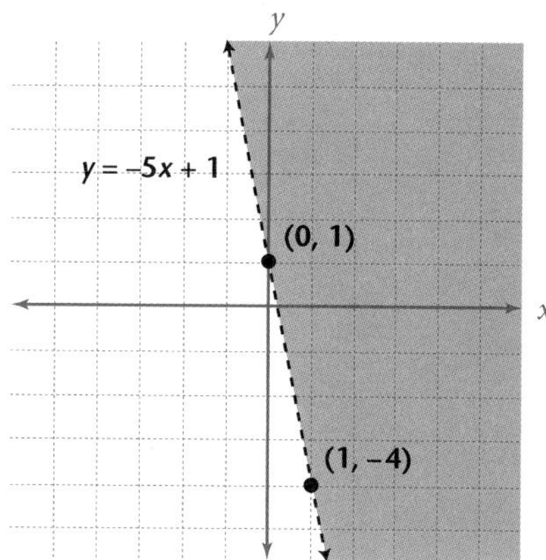

17.

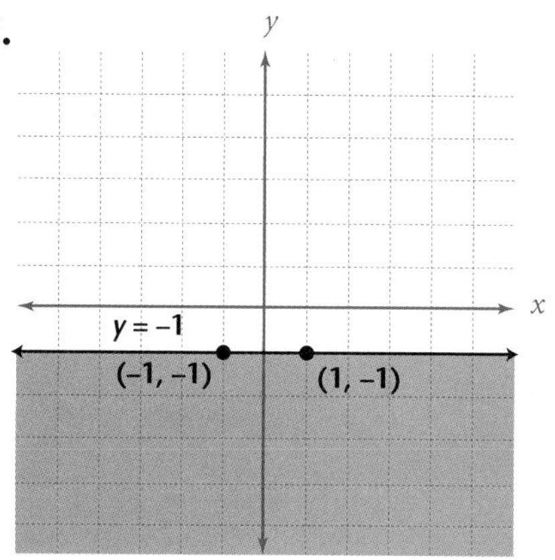

18.

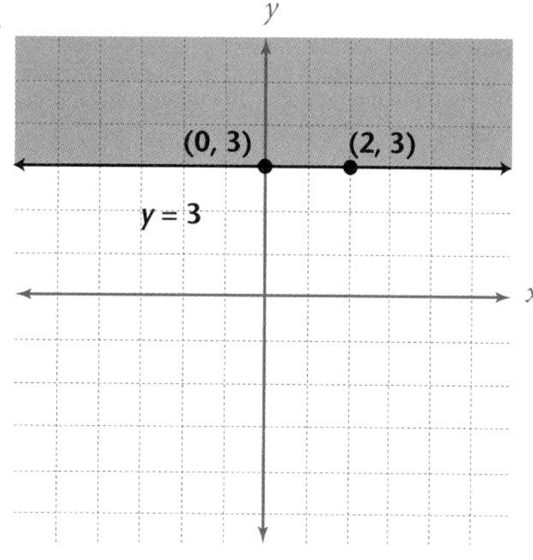

19.

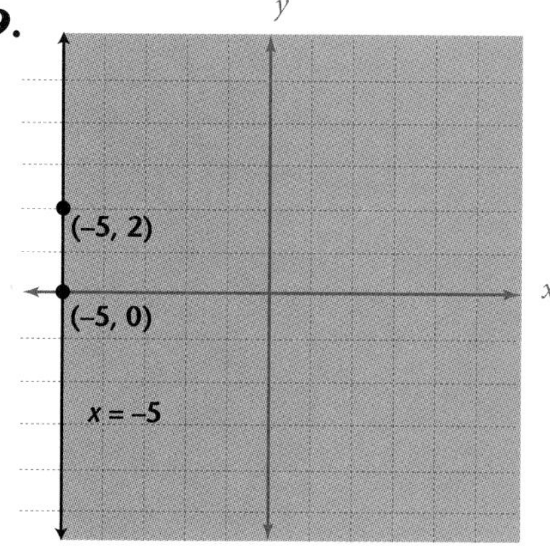

20.

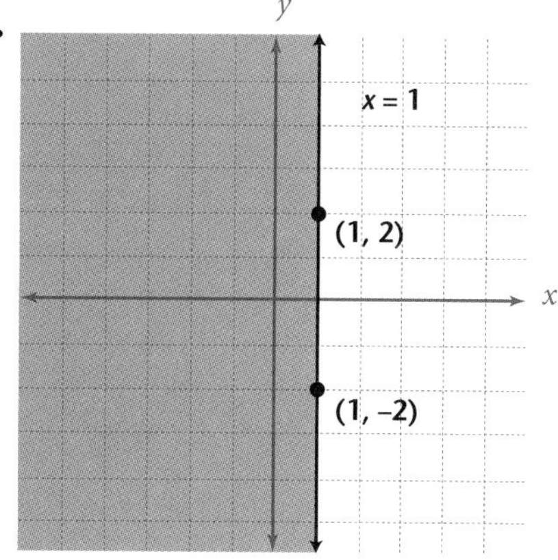

Lesson 10 Graphs Without Numbers

Every graph is a picture of something that has happened sometime in the past or is happening now.

Look at the graph at the right. It tells a story. Use your imagination—what story might it be telling?

Possible solution:
Suppose the horizontal axis, or x-axis, represents time, and the vertical axis, or y-axis, represents height above ground. The graph shows how a balloon filled with helium rises until it bursts and falls to the ground.

Note that the graph shows only the first quadrant. This makes both axes positive and you can assume the origin of the graph is (0, 0).

Look at the graph at the right. It too tells a story. Again use your imagination—what story might it be telling?

Possible solution:
Suppose the x-axis represents time and the y-axis represents speed. The graph shows how an automobile driver accelerates from 0 miles per hour to the speed limit. The driver maintains a steady speed for a while and then slows and stops for a stop sign. The process then repeats itself.

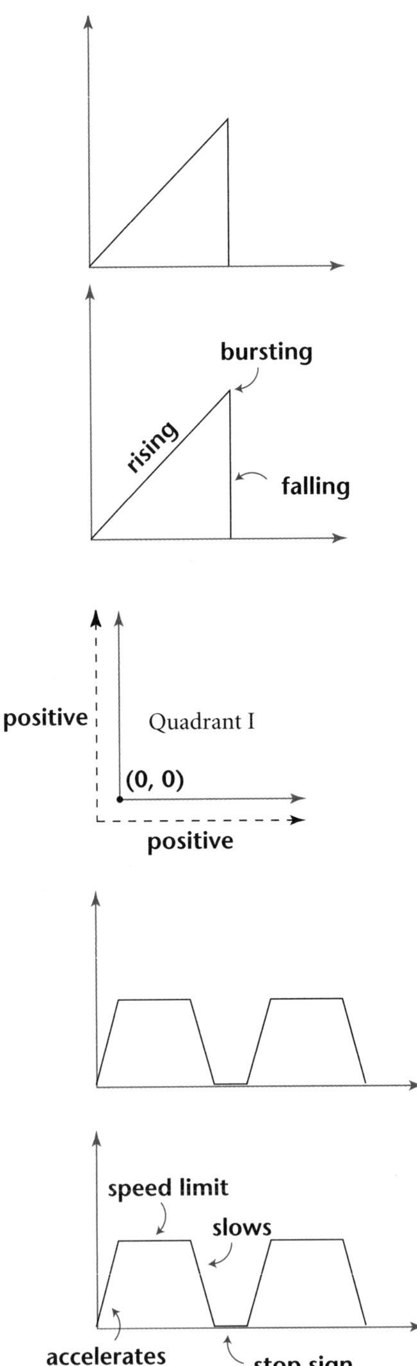

Exercise A What story might each of these graphs be telling?

1.

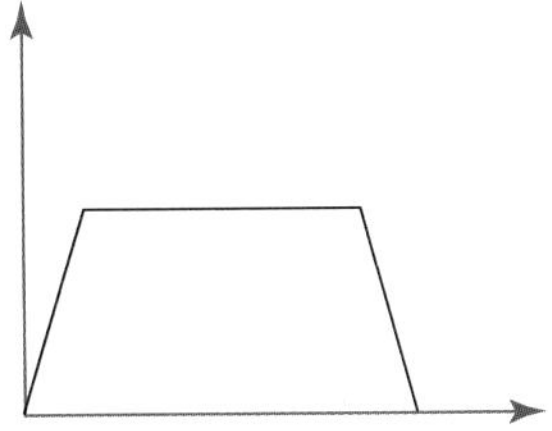

2.

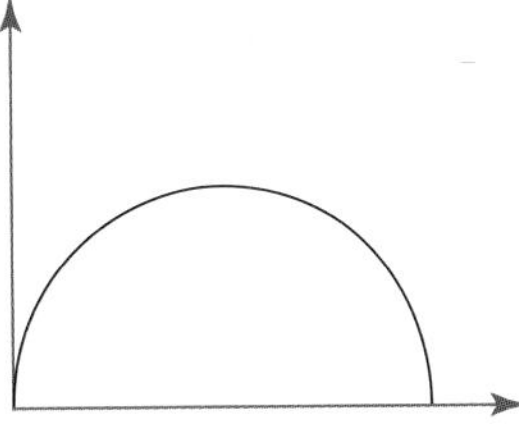

3.

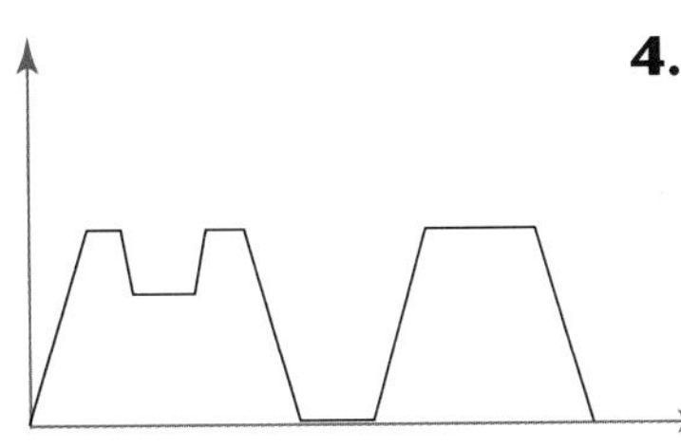

4.

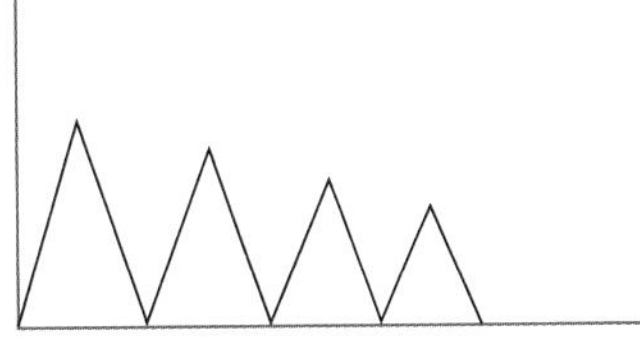

Exercise B

5. Create a graph of your own design. Invite another student to tell a story about it.

Application $\pi^2 \Sigma + \Omega \sqrt{x^2} \% \neq y \geq n = \nabla 30^\circ \pi$

Graphing

In the coordinate system, you can connect points with line segments to form polygons and other figures. For example, the points (2, 1), (6, 1), and (3, 3) form a triangle when connected with line segments.

EXAMPLE 1 To graph any point in the coordinate system:

Step 1 Locate the x-value of the pair by starting at the origin and moving left or right the appropriate number of units on the x-axis.

Step 2 Locate the y-value of the point by moving up or down the appropriate number of units from the x-value.

Step 3 Mark the point.

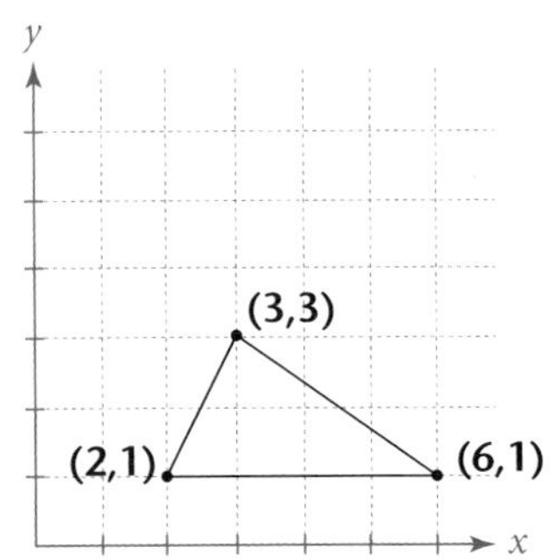

Exercise Make each graph to find the answer.

1. Graph these points: (0, 0), (5, 0), (0, −3). Then draw a line from (0, 0) to (5, 0), from (5, 0) to (0, −3), and from (0, −3) to (0, 0). What shape is the figure?

2. Graph these points: (2, 6), (4, 6), (0, 4), (6, 4), (4, 2), (2, 2). Connect the points using line segments. What figure is formed?

3. Name four points in the coordinate system that form a rectangle when connected.

4. Name five points in the coordinate system that form a pentagon, or five-sided figure, when connected.

5. Name four points in the coordinate system that form a square when connected.

Chapter 9 REVIEW

Use the graph at the left for questions 1 and 2.
Write the letter of the correct answer.

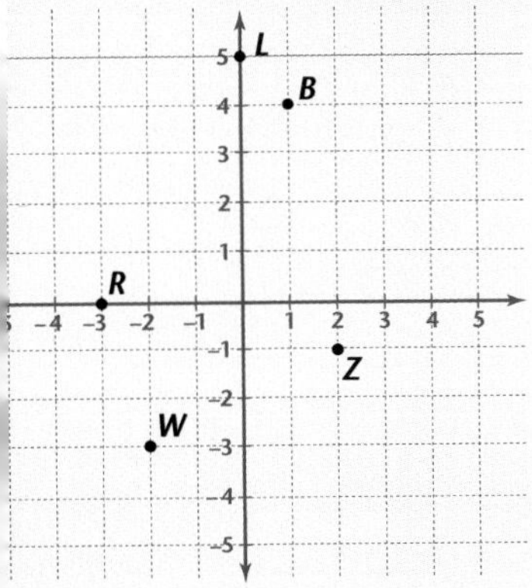

1. Find the ordered pair that represents the location of point R.

   A $(0, -3)$ C $(-3, 0)$

   B $(3, 0)$ D $(-1, -3)$

2. Find the ordered pair that represents the location of point Z.

   A $(2, -1)$ C $(-1, 2)$

   B $(-1, 0)$ D $(2, 1)$

Write the letter of the correct answer.

3. What is the x-intercept and the y-intercept of the graph $y = x + 3$?

   A x-intercept $= (0, 0)$, y-intercept $= (0, 3)$

   C x-intercept $= (-3, 0)$, y-intercept $= (0, 3)$

   B x-intercept $= (-3, 0)$, y-intercept $= (0, 0)$

   D x-intercept $= (3, 0)$, y-intercept $= (0, 3)$

4. What is the x-intercept and the y-intercept of the graph $y = 4x - 1$?

   A x-intercept $= (-4, 0)$, y-intercept $= (0, 1)$

   C x-intercept $= (4, 0)$, y-intercept $= (0, -1)$

   B x-intercept $= (\frac{1}{4}, 0)$, y-intercept $= (0, -1)$

   D x-intercept $= (-\frac{1}{4}, 0)$, y-intercept $= (0, 1)$

5. Find the slope (m) of the line that passes through the points $(-1, -1)$ $(2, 2)$.

   A $m = -1$ C $m = 1$

   B $m = -3$ D $m = 2$

6. What is the equation of the line with $m = 4$ that passes through the point $(2, 8)$?

   A $y = 8x + 4$ C $y = x + 2$

   B $y = 4x$ D $y = 2x + 8$

Draw a coordinate system and graph the following points.

Example: Point *A* at (1, 3)
Solution: Move 1 unit to the right.
Then move up 3 units. Draw the point.

7. Point *M* at (1, 2)

8. Point *S* at (0, –4)

9. Point *H* at (–3, –1)

10. Point *Q* at (4, 0)

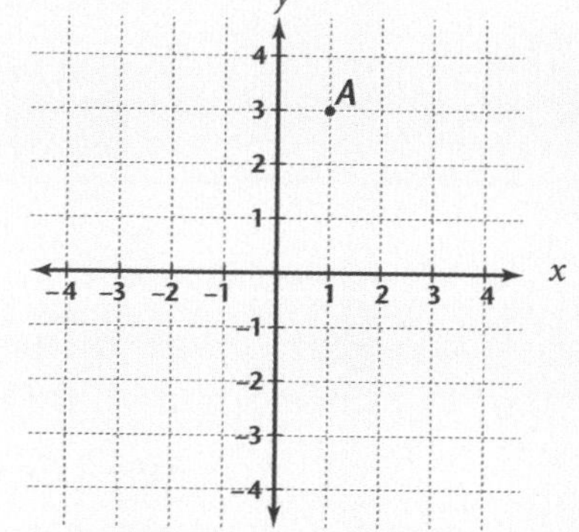

Find the slope of the line that passes through the following points.

Example: (1, 0) (−1, 2) Solution: $m = \frac{y_2 - y_1}{x_2 - x_1} = \frac{2 - 0}{-1 - 1} = \frac{2}{-2} = -1$

11. (3, −6) (−1, −2)

12. (−8, 1) (4, −1)

13. (0, 4) (8, 0)

Graph the line that passes through the following points.
Then write the equation of each line.

Example: (1, 1) (3, 2) Solution: $m = \frac{y_2 - y_1}{x_2 - x_1}$

$m = \frac{2 - 1}{3 - 1}$ $m = \frac{1}{2}$

$y = mx + b$ $y = \frac{1}{2}(3) + b$

$2 = \frac{3}{2} + b$ $\frac{1}{2} = b$

$y = \frac{1}{2}x + \frac{1}{2}$

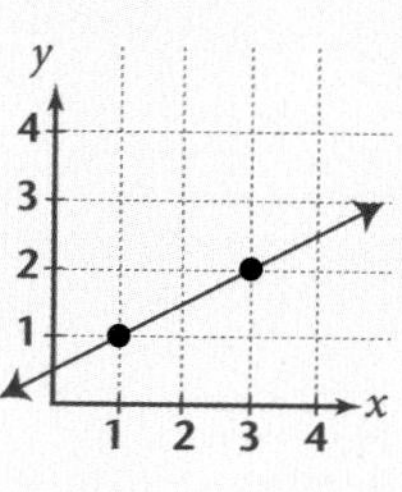

14. (2, 2) (5, 5)

15. (−3, −7) (1, 1)

16. (0, 4) (8, 0)

17. (−2, −1) (−4, −4)

Is each graph an example of a function? Write *yes* or *no*.

Example: Solution: no

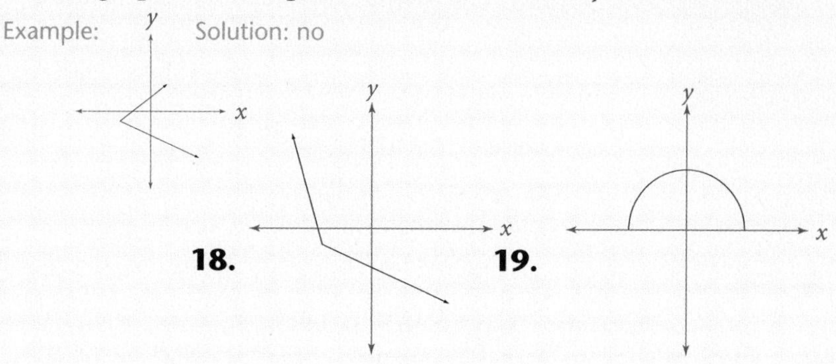

Evaluate each function two times. Use $x = -1$ and $x = 2$.

Example: $f(x) = x + 1$ Solution: $f(-1) = -1 + 1$ $f(-1) = 0$ $f(2) = 2 + 1$ $f(2) = 3$

20. $f(x) = x^2 + x$ **21.** $f(x) = x^2 - x$ **22.** $f(x) = -x^2 - x$

Graph the region represented by each line.

Example: $y > x + 1$ Solution: Find two points: (1, 2) (2, 3)
Check using (0, 5). $y > x + 1$
$5 > 0 + 1$ True

23. $y < 2x + 1$

24. $y > 4$

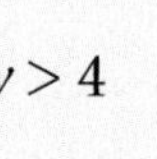

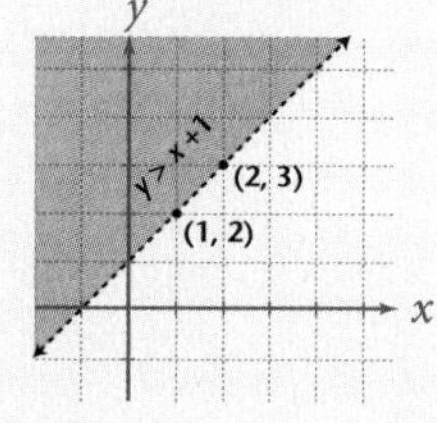

Write the inequality that describes the shaded region.

Example:

Solution: $y \geq 3x$

25.

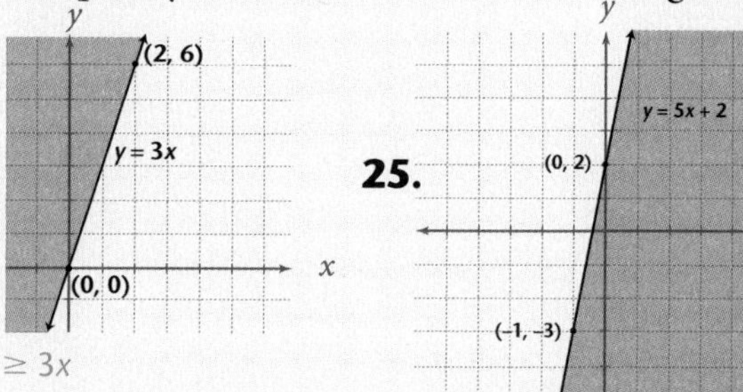

Test-Taking Tip

When you create a graph from a chart of data, check the number of facts you are supposed to record from the chart.

Chapter

Systems of Linear Equations

As the city of Chicago grew larger, city planners developed a flat graph to create a street system. The easiest design called for straight roads that were parallel and perpendicular to each other. We graph straight lines by solving a series of equations, called linear equations. To be parallel, lines (as well as streets) must have the same slope. Each linear equation determines a point on the graph. With a list of four or five points, we can draw a straight line. Systems of equations are used for graphing two or more lines, including parallel and intersecting lines. City planners use equation systems when designing new communities or neighborhoods.

In Chapter 10, you will learn about systems of linear equations.

Goals for Learning

- To write and solve equations for parallel lines
- To determine whether a system of equations has a common solution
- To use substitution or elimination to find the common solution for a system of equations
- To graph equations to find the common solution
- To evaluate conjunctions
- To solve problems using systems of linear equations
- To add, subtract, and multipy matrices

Lesson 1 Parallel Lines

Parallel lines

Lines that have the same slope

In Chapter 9, you saw that an equation such as $y = mx + b$ or $f(x) = mx + b$ describes a straight line. You also saw that the coefficient of the x-term, m, tells you the slope of the line.

EXAMPLE 1

$y = 3x$	slope $m = 3$
$y = 3x + 2$	slope $m = 3$
$y = 3x + 4$	slope $m = 3$
$y = 3x - 2$	slope $m = 3$

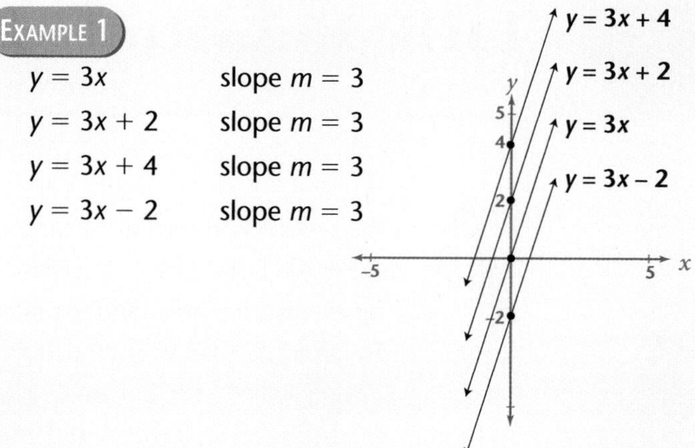

All these lines have the same slope, and all these lines are **parallel lines.**

Rule Two lines are parallel to one another if and only if they have the same slope.

There are some special cases of parallel lines that are useful to remember.

All lines defined by the equation $y =$ constant are horizontal lines. They are all parallel to the x-axis and parallel to each other.

All horizontal lines

- are parallel to each other,
- are parallel to the x-axis,
- have slope $m = 0$,
- have an equation of the form $y = 0(x) +$ constant.

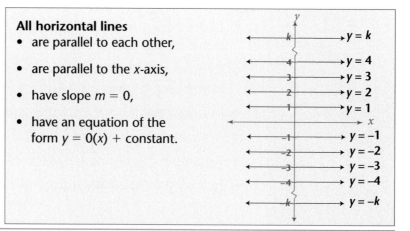

Recall the point (0, y) is a point on the y-axis. This is called the y-intercept for the line $y = mx + b$.

All lines defined by the equation $x =$ constant are parallel to the y-axis and parallel to each other.

All vertical lines

- are parallel to each other,
- are parallel to the y-axis,
- have undefined slope,
- have an equation of the form $x =$ constant.

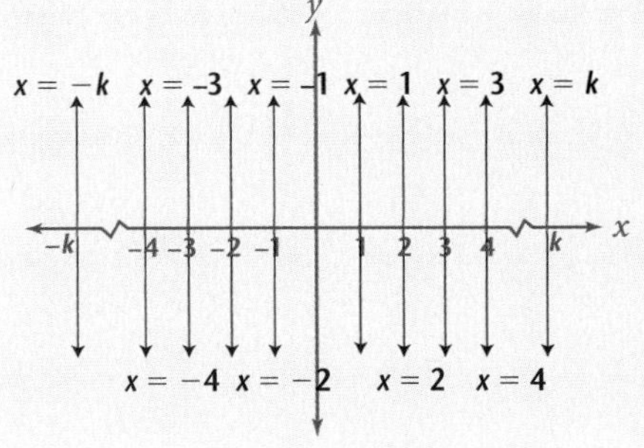

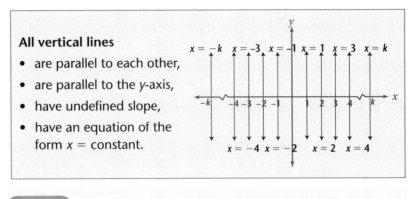

EXAMPLE 2 Find the equation of a line parallel to the line $y = -\frac{3}{4}x + 2$ and passing through the y-intercept (0, −2).

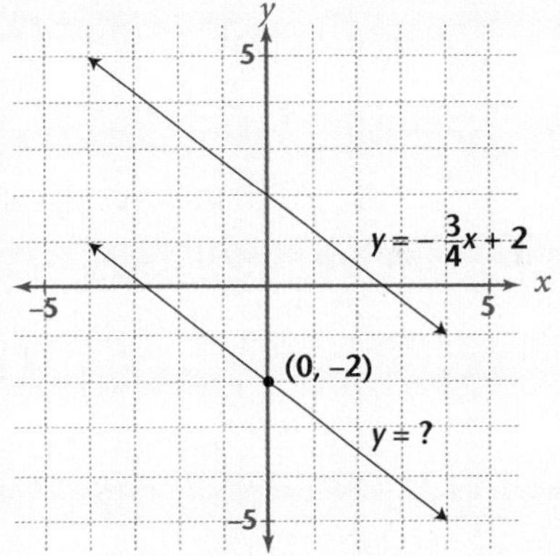

Step 1 Write the equation of the parallel line in the form $y = mx + b$. You will find values for m (slope) and b (y-intercept).

Step 2 Determine the slope of the parallel line. Because the slope of parallel lines is the same, the slope of the second line must be $-\frac{3}{4}$, so $m = -\frac{3}{4}$.

$$y = -\frac{3}{4}x + b$$

Step 3 Because the line passes through the y-intercept (0, −2), $y = -2$ when $x = 0$, so $b = -2$. Substitute −2 for b.

$$y = -\frac{3}{4}x - 2$$

The parallel lines are $y = -\frac{3}{4}x + 2$ and $y = -\frac{3}{4}x - 2$.

EXAMPLE 3 Find the equation of a line parallel to the line $3x = 4y + 4$ and passing through the y-intercept $(0, 3)$.

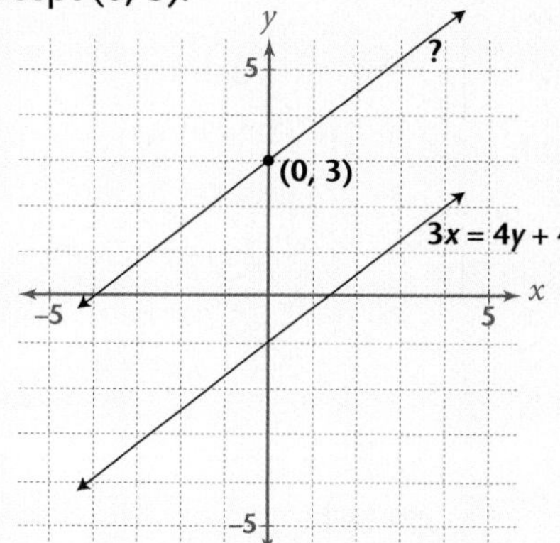

Step 1 Rewrite $3x = 4y + 4$ so that it is in the form $y = mx + b$.

$3x = 4y + 4$

$4y = 3x - 4$

$y = \frac{3}{4}x - 1$

Step 2 Determine the slope of the parallel line. Because the slope of parallel lines is the same, the slope of the second line must be $\frac{3}{4}$, so $m = \frac{3}{4}$.

$y = \frac{3}{4}x + b$

Step 3 Because the line passes through the y-intercept $(0, 3)$, $y = 3$ when $x = 0$, so $b = 3$. Substitute 3 for b.

$y = \frac{3}{4}x + 3$

The equations for the parallel lines are $y = \frac{3}{4}x - 1$ and $y = \frac{3}{4}x + 3$ or $3x = 4y + 4$ and $3x = 4y - 12$.

Exercise A Find the slope of a line parallel to each line.

1. $y = 2x - 3$

2. $y = \frac{1}{3}x - 4$

3. $y = -\frac{4}{9}x + 1$

4. $8y = -7x + 16$

5. $-5x = 10 - 2y$

Writing About Mathematics

Write a general statement about the direction of parallel lines that have a negative slope.

Exercise B Write the equation of the line parallel to the given line and passing through the given point, which is the y-intercept. Check your answer by graphing the lines.

6. $y = 2x - 4; (0, 4)$

7. $y = 3x - 5; (0, -2)$

8. $y = -\frac{3}{5}x + 2; (0, 6)$

9. $y = -\frac{1}{2}x; (0, -3)$

Exercise C Rewrite each equation in the form $y = mx + b$. Then write the equation of the line parallel to the given line and passing through the given point, which is the y-intercept.

10. $2y = x + 2; (0, 3)$

11. $3y = 3x + 3; (0, 3)$

12. $9x - 3y = 12; (0, 2)$

PROBLEM SOLVING

Exercise D Answer the following questions.

13. Antonio says that the greatest and least slope of a line that lies only in Quadrants I and II is the same as the greatest and least slope of a line that lies only in Quadrant III and Quadrant IV. Is he correct?

14. Antonio decides to use a number line to show the possible slope of a line that lies in Quadrant I and Quadrant III of a graph. What does his number line look like?

15. Carrie uses a number line to show the possible slope of a line that lies in Quadrant II and Quadrant IV of a graph. Does her number line look like Antonio's?

TRY THIS Show why lines of the form x = constant have an undefined slope. HINT: Plot two points along the line and then look at the value for $m = \frac{y_2 - y_1}{x_2 - x_1}$.

Lesson 2 Describing Parallel Lines

In Lesson 1, you wrote equations for parallel lines with different y-intercepts. Now you'll explore how to write equations for parallel lines passing through any point (x, y) using the same linear equation: $y = mx + b$.

EXAMPLE 1 Write the equation of a line that is parallel to the line $y = -2x + 5$ and passes through the point $(-3, 4)$.

Step 1 For the lines to be parallel, the slope of the second line must be the same as the slope of the first:
$y = -2x + 5$, so $m = -2$
$y = -2x + b$

Step 2 Because the line passes through $(-3, 4)$, you know that $y = -2x + b$ must be true when $x = -3$ and $y = 4$.
$(-3, 4)$ is on line $y = -2x + b$

Step 3 Substitute the values for y and x in the equation and solve for b.
$(-3, 4)$ is on line $y = -2x + b$, so
$4 = -2(-3) + b$
$-2 = b$

Step 4 Place the value for b in the equation of the parallel line.
$y = -2x = b, b = -2,$
$y = -2x + (-2)$
Therefore, $y = -2x + (-2)$ is parallel to $y = -2x + 5$ and passes through $(-3, 4)$.

EXAMPLE 2 Write the equation of a line that is parallel to the line $2y - 3x = 6$ and passes through the point $(2, 4)$.

Step 1 Rewrite $2y - 3x = 6$ in the form $y = mx + b$.
$2y - 3x = 6$ becomes $y = \frac{3}{2}x + 3$

Step 2 Because they are parallel, the slope of the second line must be the same as the slope of the first:
$y = \frac{3}{2}x + 3$, so $m = \frac{3}{2}$
$y = \frac{3}{2}x + b$

> **Writing About Mathematics**
>
> How many lines are parallel to the line $y = 3x + 1$? How would you write an equation for all the lines?

EXAMPLE 2 *(continued)*

Step 3 Because the line passes through (2, 4), you know that $y = \frac{3}{2}x + b$ must be true when $x = 2$ and $y = 4$.

(2, 4) is on line $y = \frac{3}{2}x + b$, so

$4 = \frac{3}{2}(2) + b$

$4 = 3 + b$

$1 = b$

Step 4 Place the value for b in the equation of the parallel line.

$y = \frac{3}{2}x + 1$

Therefore, $y = \frac{3}{2}x + 1$ is parallel to $2y - 3x = 6$ and passes through (2, 4).

Exercise A Write the equation of the line parallel to the given line and passing through the given point.

1. $y = 2x - 4$; (6, 2)

2. $y = 3x - 5$; (4, −3)

3. $y = -\frac{3}{5}x + 2$; (0, 2)

4. $y = -\frac{3}{5}x + 2$; $(-\frac{3}{2}, 1)$

5. $y = -\frac{1}{2}x$; (3, −2)

6. $y = 2x$; (−2, 5)

7. $y = -2x$; (5, −2)

8. $y = -(\frac{2}{5})x + 3$; $(\frac{5}{4}, 1)$

9. $y = 2x - 4$; (1, 1)

Exercise B Rewrite each equation in the form $y = mx + b$. Then write an equation for a line parallel to the first and passing through the given point.

10. $2y = x + 2$; (1, 2)

11. $3y = 3x + 3$; (3, 5)

12. $\frac{y}{2} = -2x - 3$; (4, 2)

13. $4y - 2x = 5$; (0, 0)

14. $10 = y - 2x$; (−1, −3)

15. $9x = 3y - 12$; (4, 1)

TRY THIS Given a line $y = mx + b$, write the equation for a line parallel to the line and passing through point (c, d).

Lesson 3 Intersecting Lines—Common Solutions

> ***System of equations***
> *Equations describing two or more lines*
>
> ***Intersecting lines***
> *Lines with one point in common*
>
> ***Common solution***
> *The ordered pair of real numbers that two intersecting lines share*

The equations describing two or more lines are called a **system of equations.** In Lessons 1 and 2, you examined parallel lines in a graph. In this lesson, you will examine **intersecting lines** in a graph. Intersecting lines are lines that share one point in the graph.

Two Parallel Lines

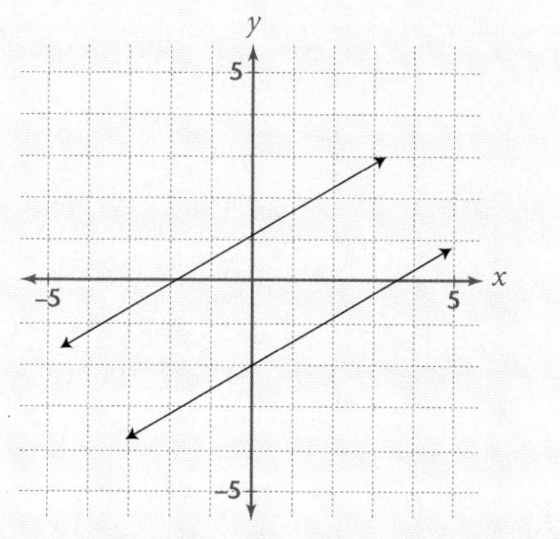

NO COMMON POINTS

Therefore, there is no common solution.

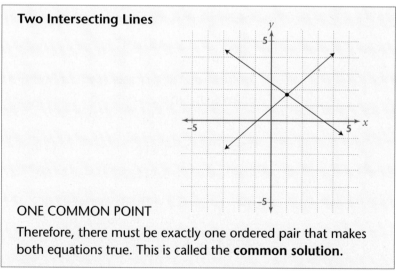

Two Intersecting Lines

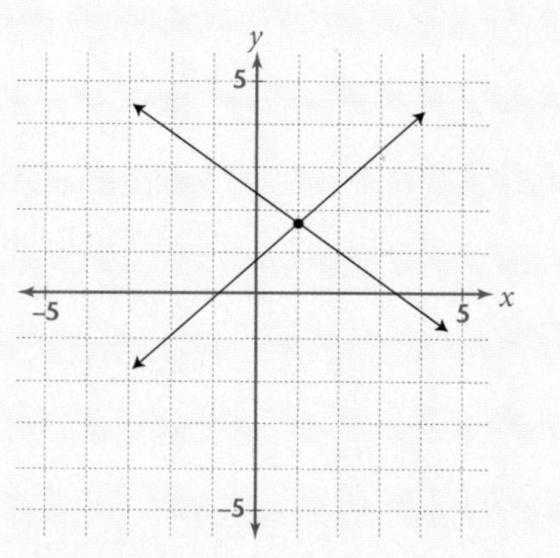

ONE COMMON POINT

Therefore, there must be exactly one ordered pair that makes both equations true. This is called the **common solution.**

Intersecting lines have a common solution. Parallel lines do not have a common solution.

EXAMPLE 1 Does the system of equations have a common solution?

system: $y = 2x + 2$

$y = 2x - 1$

The slopes are equal; $m = 2$ for both equations. Therefore, the lines are parallel and there is no common solution.

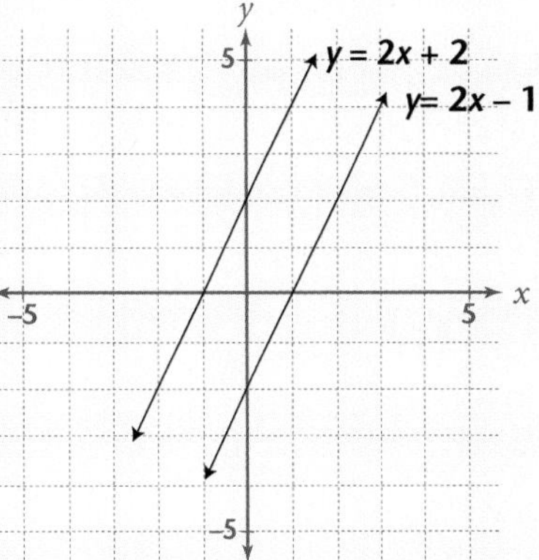

system: $y = x$

$y = -x + 2$

The slopes are not equal. The lines intersect and have a common solution.

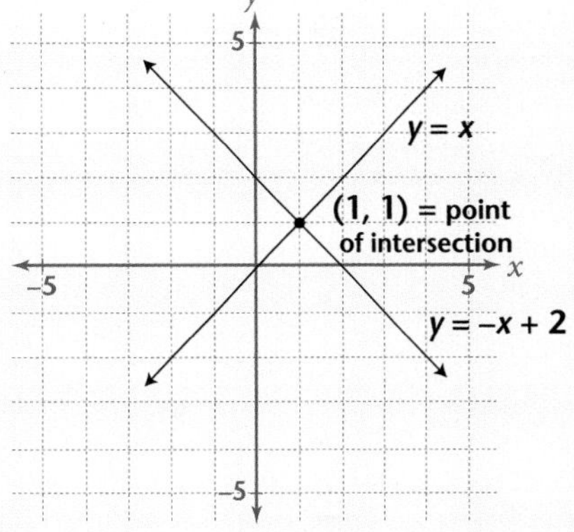

You can determine whether a system has a common solution by looking at the algebraic expressions. You do not need to make or look at a graph of the line.

EXAMPLE 2 Does the system of equations have a common solution?

system: $y = 5x + 1$

$y = 5x - \frac{1}{2}$

Since the slopes are equal, $m = 5$ for both equations. The lines are parallel and they do not intersect. Therefore, they have no common solution.

system: $y = -3x + 1$

$y = x + 2$

Since the slopes $m = -3$ and $m = 1$ are not equal, the lines intersect and there is a common solution.

Exercise A Do these systems of equations have a common solution? Give a reason for your answer.

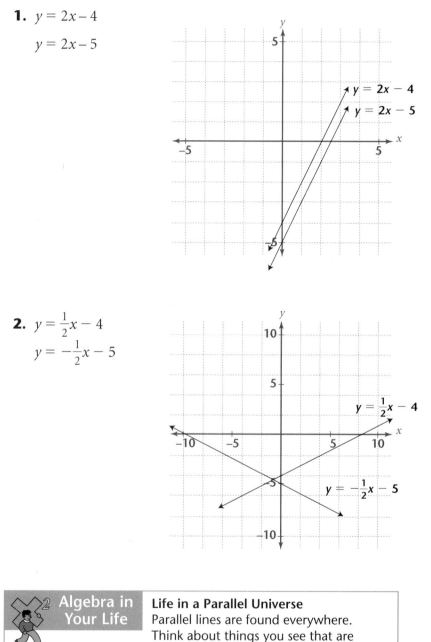

1. $y = 2x - 4$

$y = 2x - 5$

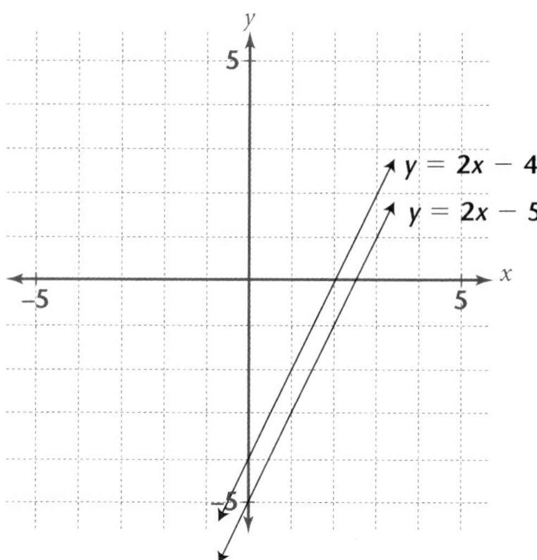

2. $y = \frac{1}{2}x - 4$

$y = -\frac{1}{2}x - 5$

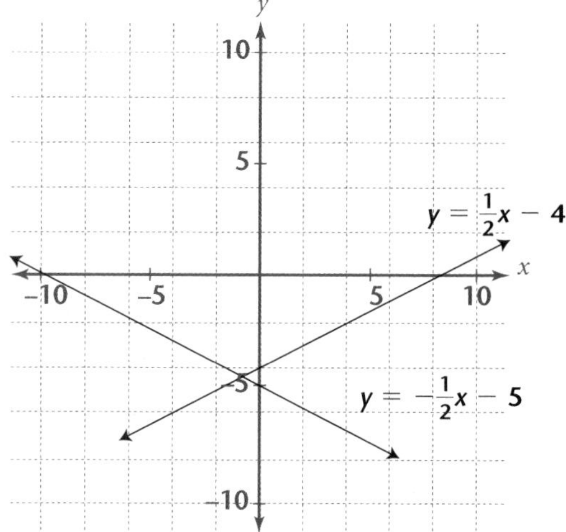

Algebra in Your Life

Life in a Parallel Universe
Parallel lines are found everywhere. Think about things you see that are shaped like rectangles. Homes, windows, and doors all have parallel lines. So do skyscrapers or roads. Look around you—what else can you find that is an example of parallel lines?

Exercise B Do these systems of equations have a common solution? Tell why or why not.

3. $y = -\frac{4}{9}x + 1$

$y = -\frac{9}{4}x + 1$

4. $y = -\frac{3}{5}x + 2$

$y = -\frac{3}{5}x$

5. $y = -\frac{3}{5}x + 2$

$y = -\frac{5}{3}x + 2$

The boards on this fence are parallel to each other. Parallel lines have no common solutions.

Lesson 4 Solving Linear Equations—Substitution

You can find the common solution for a system of linear equations algebraically. Remember, a common solution is an ordered pair of real numbers that, when substituted in each equation, makes each equation a true statement.

EXAMPLE 1 Find the common solution for the system:

$y = 3x + 1$

$y = x + 5$

Step 1 Notice that in the second equation, y is expressed in terms of x. That is, $y = x + 5$. Substitute this value of y into the first equation.

$y = 3x + 1$ $\qquad x + 5 = 3x + 1$

Step 2 Solve the equation for x.

$x + 5 = 3x + 1$

$5 = 3x - 1x + 1$

$4 = 2x$

$2 = x$

Step 3 Substitute this value of x in either equation to find the value of y.

$y = x + 5$

$y = 2 + 5 = 7$ $\qquad$ The common solution is the ordered pair (2, 7).

Step 4 Check your work. Substitute (2, 7) for x and y in each equation. Determine whether the statements are true.

$y = 3x + 1$	$y = x + 5$
$7 = 3(2) + 1$	$7 = 2 + 5$
$7 = 7$ True	$7 = 7$ True

EXAMPLE 2 Find the common solution for the system:

$2x - 3y = 15$

$x + y = 6$

Step 1 You can use either equation to solve for either x or y. Solve $x + y = 6$ for x. Substitute this value of x in the first equation.

$x + y = 6$, solving for x gives $x = -y + 6$

$$2x - 3y = 15$$

$$2(-y + 6) - 3y = 15$$

Step 2 Solve the equation for y.

$$2(-y + 6) - 3y = 15$$

$$-2y + 12 - 3y = 15$$

$$-5y = 3$$

$$y = -\frac{3}{5}$$

Step 3 Substitute this value of y into either equation to find the value of x.

$$x + y = 6$$

$$x - \frac{3}{5} = 6$$

$$x = 6 + \frac{3}{5} = 6\frac{3}{5} \text{ or } \frac{33}{5}$$

The common solution is the ordered pair $(\frac{33}{5}, -\frac{3}{5})$.

Step 4 Check. Substitute $(\frac{33}{5}, -\frac{3}{5})$ for x and y in each equation. Determine whether the statements are true.

$$2x - 3y = 15$$

$$2(\tfrac{33}{5}) - 3(-\tfrac{3}{5}) = 15$$

$$\frac{66}{5} + \frac{9}{5} = 15$$

$$\frac{75}{5} = 15 \quad \text{True}$$

$$x + y = 6$$

$$-\frac{3}{5} + \frac{33}{5} = 6$$

$$\frac{30}{5} = 6 \quad \text{True}$$

Exercise A Find the common solution for each system of equations. Check your solution.

1. $y + x = 5$
   $2x + y = 6$
2. $6 + 2x = y$
   $y = x + 2$
3. $2x = 3y + 2$
   $5y + 10 = x$
4. $\frac{x + y}{2} = \frac{7}{4}$
   $4x + 2y = 12$
5. $x = 2y$
   $3x = y - 10$
6. $6 + x = y + 4$
   $2x + 3y = 6$
7. $3x + 2y = 7$
   $4x + 3y = 9$
8. $x + 2y = 7$
   $3y + 2x = -31$

Intersecting lines have common solutions. These roads are an example of intersecting lines.

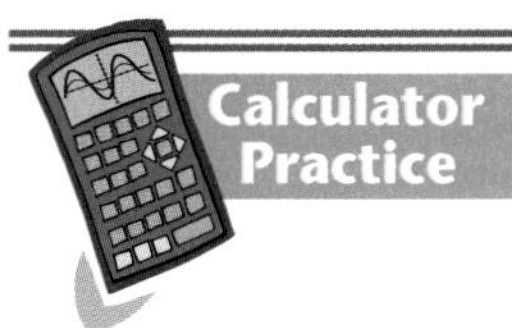

Suppose that you determine the common solution for the equations $4x + 6y = 12$ and $x - y = -2$ is $x = 0$ and $y = 2$. Use a calculator to check.

EXAMPLE 3

Step 1 Choose one equation and substitute for x and y.
$4x + 6y = 12 = 4(0) + 6(2) = 12$

Step 2 Input the $4(0) + 6(2) =$ portion of the equation.
Press 4 [×] 0 [+] 6 [×] 2 [=]
If the calculator gives an answer of 12, your x and y solutions for that equation are correct.

Step 3 Repeat the procedure for the other equation.

Exercise B Use a calculator to check each common solution. If the solution is correct, write *correct.* If the solution is not correct, write *not correct.*

9.	$x = 4y$	$6x = 2y - 20$	(56, 14)
10.	$x + y = 10$	$4x + 2y = 12$	(−4, 14)

Estimation Activity

Estimate: Which has a greater slope: a rise of 3 meters per kilometer or 3 inches per foot?

Solution: Use the slope formula and compare the fractions. The larger fraction will have the greater slope.

$$\text{slope} = \frac{\text{rise}}{\text{run}}$$

$$\frac{3\text{ m}}{1\text{ km}} = \frac{3\text{ m}}{1000\text{ m}} = \frac{3}{1000}$$

$$\frac{3''}{1'} = \frac{3''}{12''} = \frac{1}{4}$$

$$\frac{1}{4} > \frac{3}{1000}$$

The slope of 3 inches per foot has the greater slope.

Lesson 5 Solving Linear Equations—Elimination

There is another way to find the common solution for a system of equations. You can use your knowledge of linear equations to eliminate one of the variables.

EXAMPLE 1 Find the common solution for the system: $x + 2y = 5$
$-x + y = 13$

Step 1 Add the two equations to eliminate the x term.

$$\begin{array}{r} x + 2y = 5 \\ -x + y = 13 \\ \hline 0 + 3y = 18 \end{array} \text{ or } y = 6$$

Step 2 Substitute the value of y into either equation.

$$x + 2y = 5$$
$$x + 2(6) = 5$$
$$x = 5 - 12 \text{ or } x = -7$$

The common solution, or the point of intersection, is $(-7, 6)$.

Step 3 Check your work. Substitute $(-7, 6)$ for x and y in each equation. Determine whether the statements are true.

$$\begin{array}{rl} x + 2y = 5 & \\ (-7) + 2(6) = 5 & \\ -7 + 12 = 5 & \\ 5 = 5 & \text{True} \end{array} \qquad \begin{array}{rl} -x + y = 13 & \\ -(-7) + 6 = 13 & \\ 7 + 6 = 13 & \\ 13 = 13 & \text{True} \end{array}$$

EXAMPLE 2 Find the common solution for the system: $2y + 5x = 10$
$-y + x = 2$

Step 1 Multiply the second equation by 2. Then add to eliminate the y-term.

$$\begin{array}{r} 2y + 5x = 10 \\ -2y + 2x = 4 \\ \hline 0 + 7x = 14 \end{array} \text{ or } x = 2$$

Step 2 Substitute the value of x into either equation.

$$2y + 5x = 10$$
$$2y + 5(2) = 10$$
$$2y = 10 - 10$$
$$2y = 0 \text{ or } y = 0$$

The common solution, or the point of intersection, is $(2, 0)$.

EXAMPLE 2 *(continued)*

Step 3 Check your work. Substitute (2, 0) for x and y in each equation. Determine whether the statements are true.

$$\begin{aligned} 2y + 5x &= 10 \\ 2(0) + 5(2) &= 10 \\ 0 + 10 &= 10 \\ 10 &= 10 \quad \text{True} \end{aligned} \qquad \begin{aligned} -y + x &= 2 \\ -(0) + 2 &= 2 \\ 2 &= 2 \quad \text{True} \end{aligned}$$

EXAMPLE 3 Find the common solution for the system: $2y + x = 4$
$3y + x = 6$

Step 1 Multiply the second equation by -1. Then add to eliminate the x-term.

$$\begin{aligned} 2y + x &= 4 \\ -3y - x &= -6 \\ \hline -y + 0 &= -2 \text{ or } y = 2 \end{aligned}$$

Step 2 Substitute the value of y in either equation.

$$\begin{aligned} 2y + x &= 4 \\ 2(2) + x &= 4 \\ x &= 4 - 4 \text{ or } x = 0 \end{aligned}$$

The common solution, or the point of intersection, is (0, 2).

Step 3 Check your work. Substitute (0, 2) for x and y in each equation. Determine whether the statements are true.

$$\begin{aligned} 2y + x &= 4 \\ 2(2) + 0 &= 4 \\ 4 + 0 &= 4 \\ 4 &= 4 \quad \text{True} \end{aligned} \qquad \begin{aligned} 3y + x &= 6 \\ 3(2) + 0 &= 6 \\ 6 + 0 &= 6 \\ 6 &= 6 \quad \text{True} \end{aligned}$$

Writing About Mathematics

Which method do you prefer to use—substitution or elimination? Why?

Exercise A Find the common solution for each system of equations using elimination. Check your solution.

1. $2y + x = 4$
   $3y - x = 6$
2. $y + x = 5$
   $2x + y = 6$
3. $6 + 2x = y$
   $y = x + 2$
4. $x + \frac{y}{2} = 3$
   $2x + 2y = 7$
5. $x = 2y$
   $3x = y - 10$
6. $3x + 2y = 6$
   $6x + 2y = 10$
7. $\frac{3}{4}x + y = 14$
   $3x + 2y = 52$
8. $3x - y = 10$
   $4x + y = 15$
9. $4x + 2y = 8$
   $4y - 4x = 10$
10. $4x - 3y = 1$
    $2x + 3y = 2$

Lesson 6 Graphing Systems of Linear Equations

Another way you can find the common solution for two intersecting lines is to graph the lines. Occasionally, the graph's solution may not be as precise as an algebraic solution. Even so, the graph will give you a picture of the lines and an approximation of the point of intersection.

EXAMPLE 1 Use a graph to find the common solution for

$x + y = 6$
$x - y = 4$

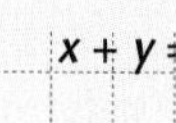

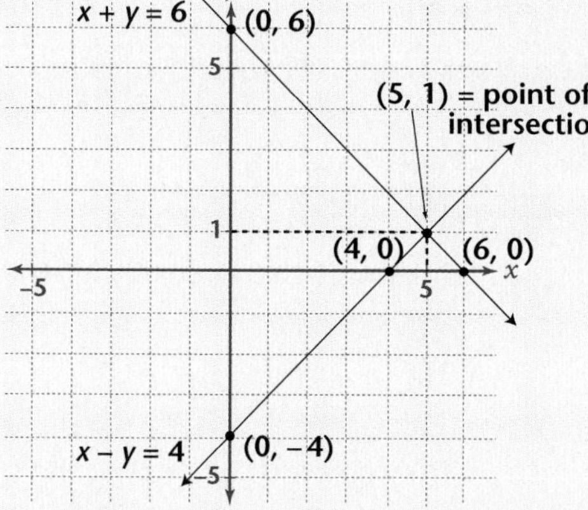

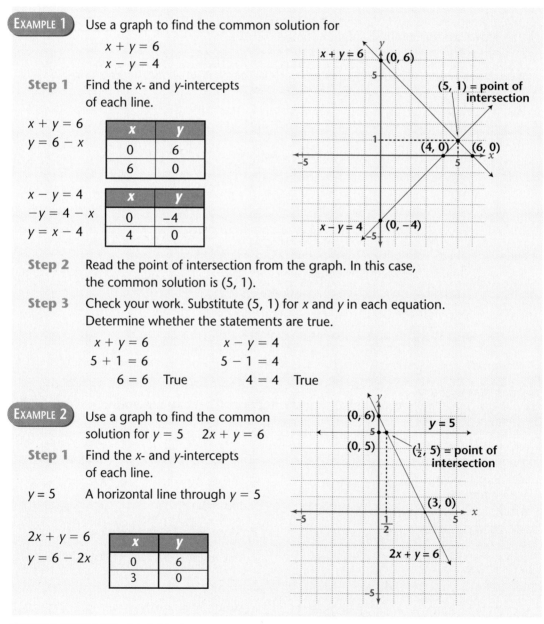

Step 1 Find the x- and y-intercepts of each line.

$x + y = 6$
$y = 6 - x$

x	y
0	6
6	0

$x - y = 4$
$-y = 4 - x$
$y = x - 4$

x	y
0	−4
4	0

Step 2 Read the point of intersection from the graph. In this case, the common solution is (5, 1).

Step 3 Check your work. Substitute (5, 1) for x and y in each equation. Determine whether the statements are true.

$x + y = 6$
$5 + 1 = 6$
$6 = 6$ True

$x - y = 4$
$5 - 1 = 4$
$4 = 4$ True

EXAMPLE 2 Use a graph to find the common solution for $y = 5$ $2x + y = 6$

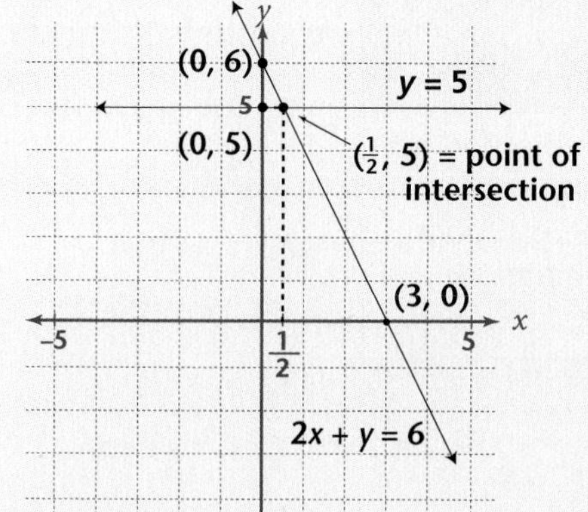

Step 1 Find the x- and y-intercepts of each line.

$y = 5$ A horizontal line through $y = 5$

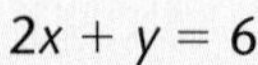

$2x + y = 6$
$y = 6 - 2x$

x	y
0	6
3	0

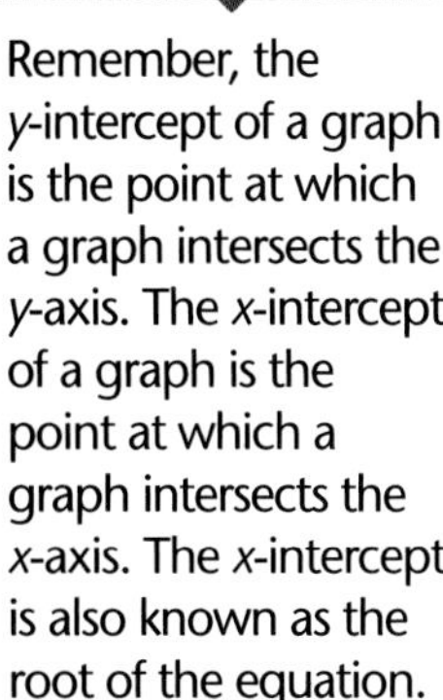

Remember, the y-intercept of a graph is the point at which a graph intersects the y-axis. The x-intercept of a graph is the point at which a graph intersects the x-axis. The x-intercept is also known as the root of the equation.

EXAMPLE 2 *(continued)*

Step 2 Read the point of intersection from the graph.

In this case, the common solution is $(\frac{1}{2}, 5)$.

Step 3 Check your work. Substitute $(\frac{1}{2}, 5)$ for x and y in each equation. Determine whether the statements are true.

$y = 5$	$x + y = 6$
$5 = 5$ True	$2(\frac{1}{2}) + 5 = 6$
	$1 + 5 = 6$ True

A special case of intersection includes those lines that are parallel to the x-axis and y-axis.

EXAMPLE 3 Find the points of intersection for these systems of equations.

$x = 1$	$x = -1$	$x = 3$
$y = 5$	$y = 0$	$y = -2$

Graph each line using the given values of x and y.
Then read the common solution from the point of intersection.

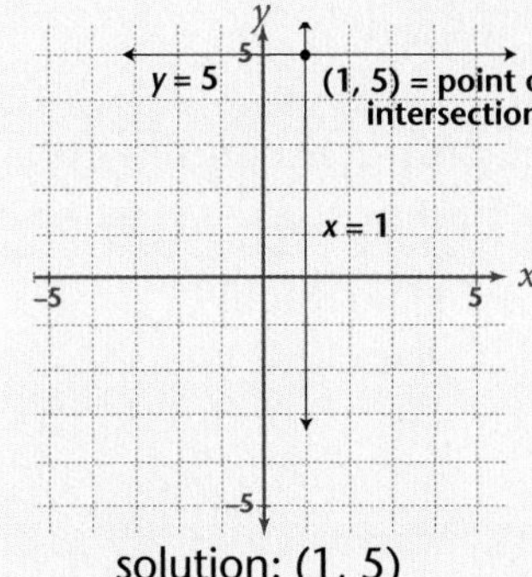

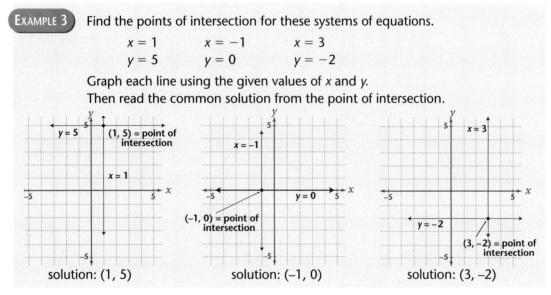

solution: (1, 5)

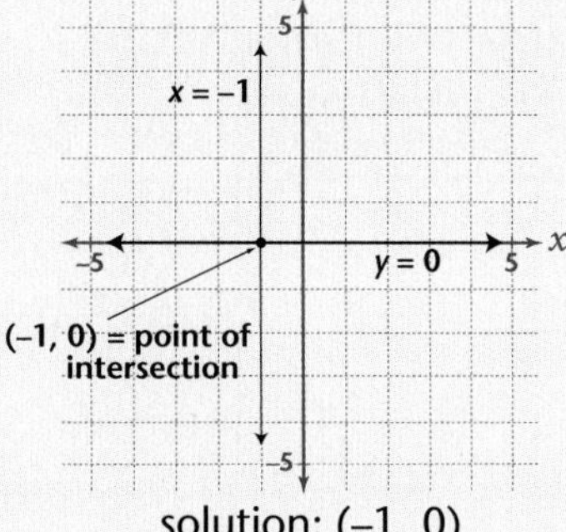

solution: (–1, 0)

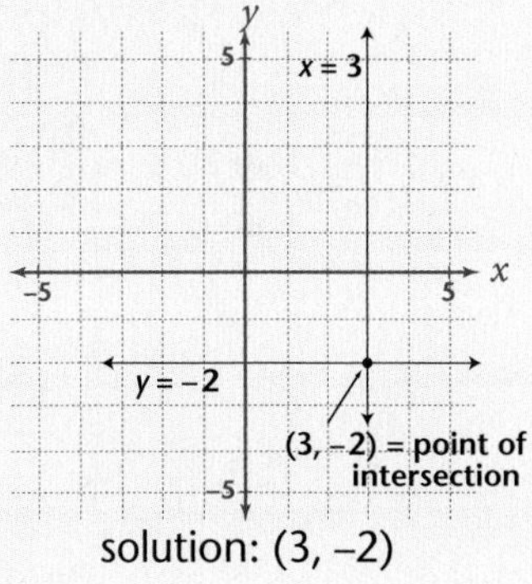

solution: (3, –2)

Exercise A Graph each system of equations. Find the point of intersection.

1. $x = 2$
$y = -3$

2. $x = 4$
$y = 4$

3. $x = 3$
$y = -3$

4. $x = 1$
$y = 3$

5. $x = 2$
$2x + y = 4$

6. $y = -3$
$3y = 4 - x$

7. $y = 2$
$4x + 2y = 7$

8. $x = -3$
$3y + 2x = 4$

9. $-x + 2y = 4$
$x + 5y = 10$

10. $-3x + 2y = 10$
$4y + 3x = 20$

11. $4x + 2y = 12$
$3x - 2y = 9$

12. $4x + y = 10$
$3y - 23 = 2x$

13. $x + 5y = 6$
$x + 2y = 9$

14. $2x - y = 6$
$4x + y = 18$

15. $3x + 6 = y$
$2x - 3y = 10$

Lesson 7 *And* Statements—Conjunctions

Conjunction

Two or more simple statements connected by "and"

In Lesson 6, you learned that the common solution for a system of linear equations is the point of intersection—the single point that is on each of the lines. In other words, the point must belong to the first line *and* the second line. The statement "the point must belong to the first line *and* the second line" is an example of a **conjunction**. Two simple statements connected by *and* are called a conjunction.

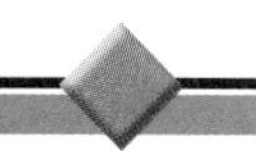

A truth table is a table of true (T) and false (F) values.

Rule for Conjunctions

A conjunction is TRUE whenever both simple statements are true. All other conjunctions are FALSE.

You can let *p* and *q* stand for simple sentences that can be either true or false. You can use the symbol ^ to stand for *and*. Then you can use this information to make a truth table to show when the conjunction is true and when it is false.

Truth Table for Conjunctions

p	q	$p \wedge q$
T	T	T
T	F	F
F	T	F
F	F	F

Note that the only true conjunction occurs when both *p* and *q* are true. If one statement is false, the conjunction is false.

EXAMPLE 1

Graph the lines $y = 2$ and $x = 4$. Refer to the graph to check the truth-value of each statement and the truth-value of each conjunction. Use the truth table at the top of page 307.

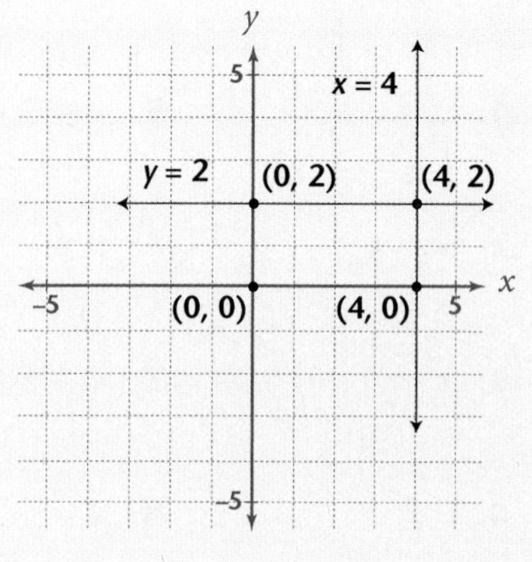

p	^	q	p ^ q
(4, 2) is on the line $y = 2$ T	and	(4, 2) is on the line $x = 4$ T	T
(0, 2) is on the line $y = 2$ T	and	(0, 2) is on the line $x = 4$ F	F
(4, 0) is on the line $y = 2$ F	and	(4, 0) is on the line $x = 4$ T	F
(0, 0) is on the line $y = 2$ F	and	(0, 0) is on the line $x = 4$ F	F

EXAMPLE 2 Tell whether the following conjunctions are true or false. Give a reason.

$2 + 2 = 4$ and $3^2 = 9$ True

T T

Both statements are true. The conjunction is true.

$2 \cdot 2 = 4$ and squares are circles False

T F

Only one statement is true. The conjunction is false.

$\sqrt{9} = 3$ and $3 \neq 5$ True

T T

Both statements are true. The conjunction is true.

Is p ^ q true or false when $p = 2 + 3 = 5$ and $q = 15 \div 3 \neq 5$?

Evaluate each statement:

$2 + 3 = 5$ is true, so p is true.

$15 \div 3 \neq 5$ is false, so q is false.

Therefore, by the rule of conjunctions, p ^ q is false.

Writing About Mathematics

If you know that p is true, what must be the truth-value of q in order for $p \wedge q$ to be true? Give an example.

Exercise A Tell whether the following conjunctions are true or false. Explain why.

1. $2 + 2 = 4$ and $2^2 = 4$

2. $2^3 = 8$ and $8 = 2 \cdot 2 \cdot 2$

3. $4 \div 0 = 0$ and $4 \cdot 0 = 0$

4. $4 \div 4 = 1$ and $4 \cdot 1 \neq 5$

5. $6 \cdot 0 = 0$ and $6 + 0 = 6$

6. Angles in a triangle add up to 360°, and there are four right angles in a square.

7. All parallel lines have the same slope, and all vertical lines have a slope of 1.

8. Dividing by $\frac{3}{4}$ is the same as multiplying by $-\frac{4}{3}$, and $3\frac{1}{2}$ has the same value as $\frac{14}{4}$.

9. $2^2 + 2^3 = 2^5$ and $a^2 + a^2 = 2a^2$

10. $-x = 12$ is the same as $x = -12$ and $3^3 = 27$

11. $\frac{42}{7} = 6$ and $6 + 7 = 15$

12. $4\frac{2}{7} = 30$ and $\frac{3}{2}x = (1\frac{1}{2})x$

Truth Table for Conjunctions

p	q	$p \wedge q$
T	T	T
T	F	F
F	T	F
F	F	F

Writing About Mathematics

If p is false, is it possible to make $p \wedge q$ true? Explain.

Exercise B What is the truth-value of $p \wedge q$ in the following exercises?

13. $p = 4^3 = 64, q = 23 - 15 = 8$

14. $p = 2 + 6 = 8, q = 4 + 4 = 8$

15. $p =$ Parallel lines have the same slope.

$q = 0 \div 0$ is undefined.

16. $p =$ All triangles have one right angle.

$q =$ All circles have $4 \cdot 90°$.

17. $p =$ All squares have four sides.

$q =$ All rectangles have a perimeter.

18. $p =$ All numbers greater than 100 are prime.

$q =$ Some numbers greater than 100 are prime.

19. $p = x^2 \cdot x^3 = x^5$

$q =$ for all lines, slope $(m) > 0$

20. $p = x^6 \div x^2 = x^3$

$q = a^2 + b^2 = (ab)^2$

Technology Connection

Search Engines

Many Internet search engines use *and statements* to help limit and focus a search. Try this: type a word into a search engine. Notice the number of Web sites that show up. Add a second word to your search phrase (separated from the first by a comma), and you get fewer sites. Type a third word, and you get even fewer sites. That's because you get only the Web sites with all three words—word 1 AND word 2 AND word 3.

Lesson 8 Problem Solving Using Linear Equations

You can solve certain word problems by setting up and then solving systems of equations.

Example 1 The sum of two numbers is 10 and the difference of the same two numbers is 4. What are the numbers?

Step 1 Let x = one number, let y = the other number. Write an equation for each condition.

$x + y = 10$ The sum is 10.

$x - y = 4$ The difference is 4.

Step 2 Solve the system of equations. In this case, elimination works well.

$$\begin{array}{r} x + y = 10 \\ + \; x - y = 4 \\ \hline 2x + 0y = 14 \\ 2x = 14 \\ x = 7 \end{array}$$

Substitute 7 for x in either equation.

$x + y = 10$

$7 + y = 10$

$y = 3$

You found that $x = 7$ and $y = 3$. The two numbers are 7 and 3.

Step 3 Check.

$x + y = 10$	$x - y = 4$
$7 + 3 = 10$	$7 - 3 = 4$
$10 = 10$ True	$4 = 4$ True

Remember to answer the question in the problem after you find the values for x and y.

Notice there are three steps to solve these problems. First, decide which variable in the problem will be x and which variable will be y. Write an equation for each condition using the variables x and y. Second, solve the system of equations. Third, check your answer. Substitute the value for x and y in your equations. Also, reread the problem and decide if your answer makes sense.

EXAMPLE 2 A father's age is three less than two times the son's age. The difference in their ages is 30 years. Find the ages of father and son.

Step 1 Let x = father's age and let y = son's age. Write an equation for each condition.

$x = 2y - 3$ Three less than twice son's age.

$x - y = 30$ The difference is 30.

Step 2 Solve the system of equations. In this case, substitution works well.

$x = 2y - 3$

$x - y = 30$ becomes

$(2y - 3) - y = 30$

$y - 3 = 30$

$y = 30 + 3$ or $y = 33$

Substitute 33 for y in either equation.

$x = 2y - 3$ becomes

$x = 2(33) - 3$

$x = 66 - 3$ or $x = 63$

The father's age is 63, the son's age is 33.

Step 3 Check.

$x - y = 30$	$x = 2y - 3$
$63 - 33 = 30$	$63 = 2(33) - 3$
$30 = 30$ True	$63 = 66 - 3$
	$63 = 63$ True

Writing About Mathematics

Write a word problem of your own. Exchange problems with a partner and solve one another's problems. (Be sure you solve and check your own problem first.)

EXAMPLE 3 Rosa's best time in a race is 2 seconds faster than her second-best time. Her second-best time is $1\frac{1}{4}$ times her best time. What is her best time? What is her second-best time?

Step 1 Let x = second-best time, let y = best time.
Write an equation for each condition.

best time: $x - y = 2$ (two seconds faster than second-best time)

second-best time: $x = 1\frac{1}{4}y$ ($1\frac{1}{4}$ times the best time)

Step 2 Solve the system of equations. In this case, substitution works well.

$$x = \frac{5}{4}y$$

$x - y = 2$ becomes

$$\frac{5}{4}y - y = 2$$

$$\frac{1}{4}y = 2 \text{ or } y = 8$$

Substitute 8 for y in either equation.

$x - y = 2$ becomes

$$x - 8 = 2$$

$$x = 2 + 8 \text{ or } x = 10$$

Rosa's second-best time is 10 seconds, and her best time is 8 seconds.

Step 3 Check.

$x - y = 2$	$x = \frac{5}{4}y$
$10 - 8 = 2$	$10 = \frac{5}{4}(8)$
$2 = 2$ True	$10 = \frac{5 \cdot 8}{4}$
	$10 = 10$ True

PROBLEM SOLVING

Exercise A Set up and solve a system of equations to find the answers. Check your answers.

1. The sum of two numbers is 24 and the difference of the same two numbers is 8. What are the numbers?

2. A mother's age is three less than three times her daughter's age. The sum of their ages is 45. Find the ages of the mother and daughter.

3. This week Leah earned three times as much as she earned last week. During both weeks, Leah earned \$72. How much did she earn each week?

4. While walking for exercise, Mia is able to walk only $\frac{3}{4}$ as far on Saturday as she walked on Friday. On Saturday she walks $1\frac{1}{2}$ miles. How many miles did she walk on Friday?

5. Christopher's best time in a race is 4 seconds faster than his second-best time. His second-best time is $1\frac{1}{3}$ times slower than his best time. What is his best time? What is his second-best time?

Exercise B Set up and solve a system of equations to answer the questions. Check your answers.

6. In a 50-question test, the highest score in class is three times the lowest score minus four. The difference between the highest and the lowest scores is 30. What are the highest and lowest scores?

7. In one game, the Amityville football team scores $\frac{3}{5}$ as many points as the Johnstown team. Johnstown wins the game by 16 points. What is each team's score?

8. Mark and Miguel compare paychecks. Miguel makes \$13.50 more than Mark. Their combined wages for the week are \$125.50. How much does each earn?

9. DaWayne is $1\frac{1}{2}$ times as old as his younger sister Shavonne. DaWayne is also 14 years older than Shavonne. What are their ages?

10. At Makita's Market, this month's electric bill is $\frac{1}{3}$ as much as the market's highest bill. This bill is also \$40 less than the highest bill. How much is this month's bill? How much is the highest bill?

Lesson 9 Introduction to Matrices: Addition and Subtraction

Matrix

Any rectangular arrangement of numbers or symbols

A **matrix** is any rectangular arrangement of numbers or symbols. The plural of matrix is **matrices**. A matrix of m rows and n columns is a matrix with dimensions $m \times n$, which is read "m by n."

EXAMPLE 1 This is a 2×3 matrix.

$$\begin{array}{r} \text{Row 1} \rightarrow \\ \text{Row 2} \rightarrow \end{array} \begin{bmatrix} -2 & 5 & 7 \\ \pi & \frac{1}{2} & 0 \end{bmatrix}$$

$$\begin{array}{ccc} \uparrow & \uparrow & \uparrow \\ \text{Column} & \text{Column} & \text{Column} \\ 1 & 2 & 3 \end{array}$$

EXAMPLE 2 This is a 3×3 matrix.

This is a square matrix. In a square matrix, the number of rows equals the number of columns, $m = n$.

$$\begin{array}{r} \rightarrow \\ \text{Rows} \rightarrow \\ \rightarrow \end{array} \begin{bmatrix} 5 & -1 & \frac{1}{2} \\ \pi & \sqrt{2} & 1 \\ 1 & 0 & 7 \end{bmatrix}$$

$$\begin{array}{ccc} \uparrow & \uparrow & \uparrow \\ 1 & 2 & 3 \\ & \text{Columns} & \end{array}$$

EXAMPLE 3 This is a 2×1 matrix.

$$\begin{array}{r} \text{Row 1} \rightarrow \\ \text{Row 2} \rightarrow \end{array} \begin{bmatrix} x \\ -10 \end{bmatrix}$$

$$\begin{array}{c} \uparrow \\ 1 \\ \text{Column} \end{array}$$

EXAMPLE 4 This is a 3×3 matrix.

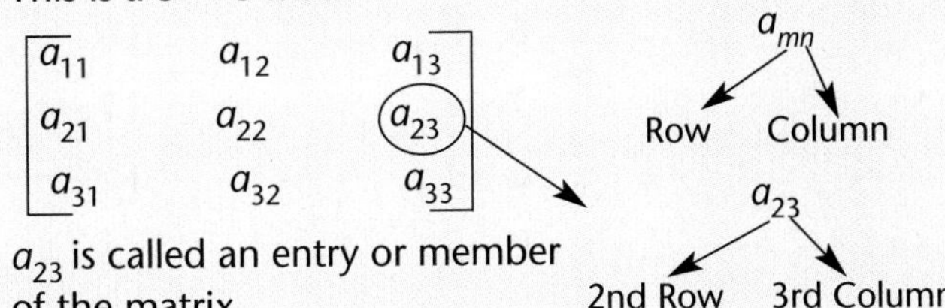

a_{23} is called an entry or member of the matrix.

Rule To add or subtract matrices, you add or subtract corresponding entries or members. The two matrices must have the same dimensions.

EXAMPLE 5 Add.

$$\begin{bmatrix} 2 & 3 & 1 \\ 5 & 3 & -6 \end{bmatrix} + \begin{bmatrix} 10 & 5 & -1 \\ 6 & 3 & -2 \end{bmatrix}$$

$$\begin{bmatrix} 2+10 & 3+5 & 1+(-1) \\ 5+6 & 3+3 & -6+(-2) \end{bmatrix} = \begin{bmatrix} 12 & 8 & 0 \\ 11 & 6 & -8 \end{bmatrix}$$

EXAMPLE 6 Subtract.

$$\begin{bmatrix} 2 & 3 & 1 \\ 5 & 3 & -6 \end{bmatrix} - \begin{bmatrix} 10 & 5 & -1 \\ 6 & 3 & -2 \end{bmatrix}$$

$$\begin{bmatrix} 2-10 & 3-5 & 1-(-1) \\ 5-6 & 3-3 & -6-(-2) \end{bmatrix} = \begin{bmatrix} -8 & -2 & 2 \\ -1 & 0 & -4 \end{bmatrix}$$

Exercise A Write the dimension of each matrix.

1. $\begin{bmatrix} a & b \\ c & d \end{bmatrix}$

2. $\begin{bmatrix} x & 1 & 2 \\ 7 & 3 & -\frac{1}{2} \end{bmatrix}$

3. $\begin{bmatrix} 1 & 9 & \sqrt{2} & \pi \end{bmatrix}$

4. $\begin{bmatrix} x & y \\ 3 & 5 \\ -1 & 2 \end{bmatrix}$

5. $\begin{bmatrix} a_{11} & a_{12} & a_{13} & a_{14} \\ a_{21} & a_{22} & a_{23} & a_{24} \end{bmatrix}$

Exercise B Give the row and column of each entry.

6. a_{22}
7. a_{51}
8. a_{64}
9. a_{99}
10. a_{63}
11. a_{17}
12. a_{11}
13. a_{28}
14. a_{44}
15. a_{72}

Exercise C Add.

16. $\begin{bmatrix} 1 & 2 \\ 3 & 4 \end{bmatrix} + \begin{bmatrix} -1 & 0 \\ 5 & -3 \end{bmatrix}$

17. $\begin{bmatrix} 5 & 1 & 6 \\ 2 & -1 & 0 \end{bmatrix} + \begin{bmatrix} 5 & 1 & 7 \\ 2 & -3 & -5 \end{bmatrix}$

18. $\begin{bmatrix} 3x & 3x & y \\ 7 & 6 & -3 \end{bmatrix} + \begin{bmatrix} x & -x & 2y \\ 6 & -7 & -5 \end{bmatrix}$

19. $\begin{bmatrix} 2 & \frac{1}{2} & 7 \\ 6 & 3 & 5 \\ 1 & 2 & 1 \end{bmatrix} + \begin{bmatrix} a & x & y \\ -7 & 4 & -5 \\ 2 & 3 & 7 \end{bmatrix}$

20. $\begin{bmatrix} 5 & 1 & 6 \\ \sqrt{2} & 7 & 3 \\ 9 & 1 & 6 \end{bmatrix} + \begin{bmatrix} 0 & 0 & 0 \\ 0 & 0 & 0 \\ 0 & 0 & 0 \end{bmatrix}$

Exercise D Subtract.

21. $\begin{bmatrix} 2 & 4 \\ 6 & 8 \end{bmatrix} - \begin{bmatrix} 3 & -1 \\ -2 & 0 \end{bmatrix}$

22. $\begin{bmatrix} -1 & 0 & 1 \\ -2 & 1 & -3 \end{bmatrix} - \begin{bmatrix} 4 & -1 & 1 \\ 0 & -1 & 3 \end{bmatrix}$

23. $\begin{bmatrix} x & 2x & y \\ 4 & 8 & 1 \end{bmatrix} - \begin{bmatrix} 2x & x & -y \\ 2 & -1 & 3 \end{bmatrix}$

24. $\begin{bmatrix} 3 & 1 & 6 \\ 0 & -5 & 2 \\ -3 & 2 & 4 \end{bmatrix} - \begin{bmatrix} a & b & c \\ 1 & 4 & -2 \\ 0 & 1 & 0 \end{bmatrix}$

25. $\begin{bmatrix} 8 & 9 & 20 & -6 \\ 0 & 23 & -15 & 4 \end{bmatrix} - \begin{bmatrix} 8 & -9 & 4 & 7 \\ 31 & 75 & 18 & 20 \end{bmatrix}$

Lesson 10 Multiplication of Matrices

To multiply a matrix by a number, simply multiply each entry by that number.

EXAMPLE 1 Let $A = \begin{bmatrix} 2 & 1 \\ 10 & -1 \end{bmatrix}$ Find $3A$.

$$③\begin{bmatrix} 2 & 1 \\ 10 & -1 \end{bmatrix} = ③A = \begin{bmatrix} ③ \cdot 2 & ③ \cdot 1 \\ ③ \cdot 10 & ③(-1) \end{bmatrix} = \begin{bmatrix} 6 & 3 \\ 30 & -3 \end{bmatrix}$$

EXAMPLE 2

$$t \begin{bmatrix} a_{11} & a_{12} & a_{13} \cdots\cdots a_{1n} \\ a_{21} & a_{22} & a_{23} \cdots\cdots a_{2n} \\ a_{31} & a_{32} & a_{33} \cdots\cdots a_{3n} \\ \cdot & \cdot & \cdot & \cdot \\ \cdot & \cdot & \cdot & \cdot \\ \cdot & \cdot & \cdot & \cdot \\ \cdot & \cdot & \cdot & \cdot \\ a_{m1} & a_{m2} & a_{m3} \cdots\cdots a_{mn} \end{bmatrix} = \begin{bmatrix} ta_{11} & ta_{12} & ta_{13} \cdots\cdots ta_{1n} \\ ta_{21} & ta_{22} & ta_{23} \cdots\cdots ta_{2n} \\ ta_{31} & ta_{32} & ta_{33} \cdots\cdots ta_{3n} \\ \cdot & \cdot & \cdot & \cdot \\ \cdot & \cdot & \cdot & \cdot \\ \cdot & \cdot & \cdot & \cdot \\ \cdot & \cdot & \cdot & \cdot \\ ta_{m1} & ta_{m2} & ta_{m3} \cdots ta_{mn} \end{bmatrix}$$

To multiply a matrix by another matrix, you use row × column multiplication. Two matrices, *A* and *B* can be multiplied if the number of columns in *A* is the same as the number of rows in *B*. All square matrices of the same dimension can be multiplied.

EXAMPLE 3 Multiply.

$$\begin{bmatrix} 3 & 2 \\ 5 & 1 \end{bmatrix} \times \begin{bmatrix} 2 & 4 \\ 6 & 7 \end{bmatrix} = \begin{bmatrix} \text{Row 1} \times \text{Column 1*} & \text{Row 1} \times \text{Column 2} \\ \text{Row 2} \times \text{Column 1} & \text{Row 2} \times \text{Column 2} \end{bmatrix}$$

$$= \begin{bmatrix} 3 \cdot 2 + 2 \cdot 6 & 3 \cdot 4 + 2 \cdot 7 \\ 5 \cdot 2 + 1 \cdot 6 & 5 \cdot 4 + 1 \cdot 7 \end{bmatrix}$$

$$= \begin{bmatrix} 6 + 12 & 12 + 14 \\ 10 + 6 & 20 + 7 \end{bmatrix} = \begin{bmatrix} 18 & 26 \\ 16 & 27 \end{bmatrix}$$

* Multiply corresponding entries and add all products.

EXAMPLE 4 Multipy.

$$A_{23} \times B_{32} = \begin{bmatrix} 2 & x & y \\ -1 & 0 & 5 \end{bmatrix} \times \begin{bmatrix} 1 & x \\ 2 & y \\ 3 & z \end{bmatrix}$$

$$= \begin{bmatrix} \text{Row 1} \times \text{Column 1*} & \text{Row 1} \times \text{Column 2} \\ \text{Row 2} \times \text{Column 1} & \text{Row 2} \times \text{Column 2} \end{bmatrix}$$

$$= \begin{bmatrix} 2 \bullet 1 + x \bullet 2 + y \bullet 3 & 2 \bullet x + x \bullet y + y \bullet z \\ -1 \bullet 1 + 0 \bullet 2 + 5 \bullet 3 & -1 \bullet x + 0 \bullet y + 5 \bullet z \end{bmatrix}$$

$$= \begin{bmatrix} 2 + 2x + 3y & 2x + xy + yz \\ -1 + 0 + 15 & -x + 0 + 5z \end{bmatrix}$$

$$= \begin{bmatrix} 2 + 2x + 3y & 2x + xy + yz \\ 14 & -x + 5z \end{bmatrix}$$

* Multiply corresponding entries and add all products.

Note: A_{23} times $B_{32} = C_{22}$ $A_{23} \times B_{32} = C_{22}$

Product Matrix

In general: A_{mn} times $B_{np} = C_{mp}$ $A_{mn} \times B_{np} = C_{mp}$

Product Matrix

Each entry in a matrix contains two pieces of information:

- First, a number or a symbol.
- Second, a location within the matrix.

A business can use this information to evaluate its inventory.

EXAMPLE 5 The price of canned goods per one can is given in matrix A. The number of cans of each product on the shelf is shown in matrix B. $A \times B$ = Total dollar value of the items on the shelf.

A_{13} = [\$1.29/can of peas \$2.19/can of carrots \$0.98/can of lentils]

$= [\ 1.29 \quad 2.19 \quad 0.98\ ]$

$$B_{31} = \begin{bmatrix} \text{10 cans of peas} \\ \text{15 cans of carrots} \\ \text{25 cans of lentils} \end{bmatrix} = \begin{bmatrix} 10 \\ 15 \\ 25 \end{bmatrix}$$

Note: the position denotes the correct price.

Example 5 *Continued*

$A_{13} \times B_{31}$ = Product Matrix_{11} which will give the total dollar value of the three types of canned vegetables on the shelf.

$$[1.29\ \ 2.19\ \ 0.98] \times \begin{bmatrix} 10 \\ 15 \\ 25 \end{bmatrix} = [(1.29)(10) + (2.19)(15) + (0.98)(25)]$$

$$= 12.90 + 32.85 + 24.50$$

$$= 70.25$$

The total value of the canned goods is $70.25.

Exercise A Multiply.

1. $3\begin{bmatrix} 16 & 0 \\ 5 & 1 \end{bmatrix}$

2. $x\begin{bmatrix} 3 & 5 & x \\ 1 & 2 & y \end{bmatrix}$

3. $7\begin{bmatrix} x & y \\ 3 & 15 \end{bmatrix}$

4. $(ab)\begin{bmatrix} 1 & x & a \\ -3 & y & 0 \\ b & z & -a \end{bmatrix}$

5. $y^2\begin{bmatrix} 3x & -x & a \\ 4 & 14 & 0 \\ -6 & 10 & -y^2 \\ y & 1 & xy \end{bmatrix}$

Exercise B Multiply.

6. $\begin{bmatrix} a & b \\ c & d \end{bmatrix} \times \begin{bmatrix} 2 & 3 \\ 4 & 5 \end{bmatrix}$

7. $\begin{bmatrix} 1 & 0 & 2 \\ 1 & 1 & 6 \\ 3 & 2 & 1 \end{bmatrix} \times \begin{bmatrix} 1 & 0 & 0 \\ 0 & 1 & 0 \\ 0 & 0 & 1 \end{bmatrix}$

8. $\begin{bmatrix} 3 & -2 & x \\ \frac{1}{2} & 5 & 6 \\ 7 & 10 & y \end{bmatrix} \times \begin{bmatrix} x & 4 & -1 \\ 11 & 5 & 3 \\ 20 & y & \frac{1}{4} \end{bmatrix}$

PROBLEM SOLVING

Exercise C

9. Show that $A \times B \neq B \times A$.

Let $A = \begin{bmatrix} 1 & 2 \\ 3 & 4 \end{bmatrix}$ $B = \begin{bmatrix} 1 & 0 \\ -1 & 1 \end{bmatrix}$

10. Al sells three different brands of sparkplugs. Quick Start sparkplugs cost $11.60 per box. Power Up sparkplugs cost $18.50 per box. Ultimate sparkplugs cost $42.00 per box. There are 17 boxes of Quick Start sparkplugs on the top shelf, 20 boxes of Power Up sparkplugs on the middle shelf, and 8 boxes of Ultimate spark plugs on the bottom shelf. Set up a matrix for the price of the sparkplugs and another matrix for the number of boxes and location of the sparkplugs. Multiply the two matrices to find the value of Al's sparkplug inventory.

Application $\pi^2 \Sigma + \Omega \sqrt{x^2} \% \neq y \geq n = \nabla 30^\circ \pi$

Using Venn Diagrams

Venn diagrams represent one of the most common applications of conjunction and disjunction. A Venn diagram is a way to illustrate ideas in logic.

EXAMPLE 1 A Venn diagram consists of a universal set and various subsets. In this Venn diagram, the universal set U contains the integers 1–7. Subset A contains the integers 1, 3, and 4. Subset B contains the integers 2, 3, and 5.

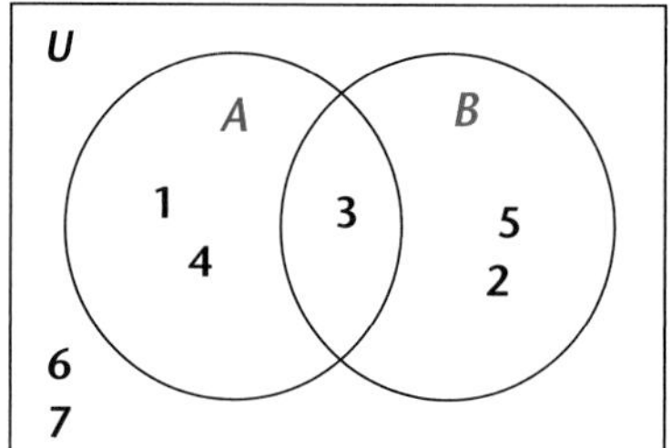

The union of sets A and B is written $A \cup B$ and represents the set of all elements in A or in B or in both A and B. In this Venn diagram, $A \cup B = \{1, 2, 3, 4, 5\}$.

The intersection of sets A and B is written $A \cap B$ and represents the set of all elements common to both A and B. In this Venn diagram, $A \cap B = \{3\}$.

A set that contains no elements is called an *empty set*, or *null set*. The symbol $\varnothing$ or { } is used to designate the empty set.

Exercise Find the answer to each problem.

1. Use the Venn diagram to find U, $A \cup B$, and $A \cap B$.

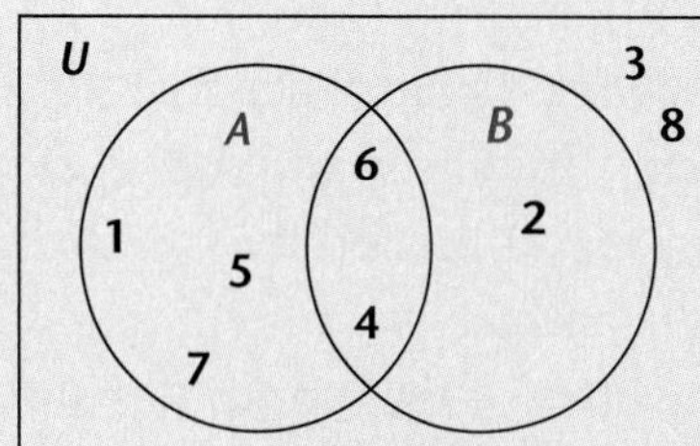

2. Draw a Venn diagram that displays these elements: $U = \{2, 4, 6, 8, 10\}$, $A \cup B = \{2, 6, 10\}$, and $A \cap B = \varnothing$.

3. How many different Venn diagrams can be drawn to show $U = \{1, 2, 3\}$, $A \cup B = \{1, 2, 3\}$, and $A \cap B = \varnothing$?

4. A survey of 24 high school freshmen found that 13 of the students surveyed were taking mathematics and science courses, 0 students were taking science and no mathematics, and 9 students were taking mathematics and no science. How many students were not taking a science or a mathematics course?

5. Given A = the set of all the letters in your first name, and B = all the letters in your last name, what is U? $A \cup B$? $A \cap B$?

Chapter 10 REVIEW

Find the point of intersection for each pair of equations. Write the letter of the correct answer.

1. $y = 2x - 2$ $y = x + 1$

A $(4, 3)$ C $(3, 4)$

B $(1, 2)$ D $(0, 0)$

2. $y = x + 4$ $y = 3x$

A $(-2, 3)$ C $(0, -2)$

B $(2, 6)$ D $(3, 2)$

3. $y = 2x + 1$ $y = x + 1$

A $(\frac{-1}{2}, 0)$ C $(0, 1)$

B $(0, 2)$ D $(-2, 2)$

Set up and solve a system of equations to answer the questions. Write the letter of the correct answer.

4. One number is six more than another number. Four times the smaller number is the same as three times the larger number. What are the unknown numbers?

A 18 and 24 C 3 and 4

B 9 and15 D 18 and 10

5. Two angles are supplementary. (Their sum = 180°.) The larger angle is 90° more than the smaller angle. What are the measurements of the angles?

A 45° and 45° C 90° and 45°

B 65° and 115° D 135° and 45°

6. Andy is three years younger than Bobby. When their ages are added together, the sum is 23. How old is Bobby?

A 10 years old C 13 years old

B 12 years old D 23 years old

Write the equation of the line parallel to the given line and passing through the given point. Check your answer by graphing the lines.

Example: $y = 3x + 2$; $(0, 5)$ Solution: $y = mx + b$, $5 = 3(0) + b$, $b = 5$, so parallel line is $y = 3x + 5$

7. $y = 2x - 5$; $(0, 10)$

8. $y = -\frac{1}{3}x$; $(0, -3)$

9. $2y = x + 2$; $(0, 4)$

10. $y = 2x - 3$; $(6, 2)$

11. $y = 3x$; $(3, 6)$

12. $y = 2x - 6$; $(1, 1)$

Find a common solution for each system.

Example: $y = 2x + 4$, $y = x - 2$

Solution:

$x - 2 = 2x + 4$ $\quad y = 2x + 4$

$-2 = x + 4$ $\quad y = 2(-6) + 4$

$-6 = x$ $\quad y = -12 + 4$

$y = -8$

$(-6, -8)$

13. $y = x - 2$

$y = \frac{1}{2}x$

14. $8 + 2x = y$

$y = x + 2$

15. $x = 3y$

$3x = y + 8$

16. $3y = x - 1$

$6y = x$

17. $x = 5y + 5$

$x + 2y = 10$

18. $2y = 5x - 1$

$3x = y + 3$

Tell whether the following conjunctions are true or false. Explain.

Example: Two dimes = 30¢, and two pennies = 2¢.
Solution: False, the first statement is false. Two dimes = 20¢.

19. All parallel lines have the same slope, and all vertical lines have a slope of 1.

20. Dividing by $\frac{6}{7}$ is the same as multiplying by $\frac{7}{6}$, and $3\frac{1}{2}$ has the same value as $\frac{14}{4}$.

21. $x^a \cdot x^b = x^{a \cdot b}$, and $4\frac{1}{3}$ has the same value as $\frac{5}{3}$.

22. All weeks have seven days, and all months have 30 days.

Set up and solve a system of equations to answer questions 23–25. Check your answers.

Example: Tom is 2 times plus 1 year older than his sister. The difference in their ages is 5 years. How old is Tom? How old is his sister?
Solution: Let x = the sister's age and y = Tom's age.

$y = 2x + 1$
$y - x = 5$ or $y = 5 + x$
$5 + x = 2x + 1$
$4 = x$

The sister is 4 years old so Tom is $2(4) + 1 = 9$ years old.
Check: $9 - 4 = 5$. True $9 = 2 \cdot 4 + 1$ True

23. The difference between two complementary angles is 34°. What are the angles? (Complementary angles are angles whose sum = 90°.)

24. The perimeter of a rectangle is 200 ft. The width of the rectangle is 20 ft less than the length. What is the length and width of the rectangle?

25. Markette is 4 years older than Earlene. Earlene's age is $\frac{4}{5}$ Markette's age. What are their ages?

Test-Taking Tip

When you read word problems, watch for numbers that are written in word form.

Chapter

Irrational Numbers and Radical Expressions

Suppose you needed eight paper squares for a huge box kite. You want each square to have an area of 16 square feet. What length should the sides of the squares be? You need a number that multiplied by itself equals 16. For 16, that number is its square root, 4. Four is a rational number that can be written as the fraction $\frac{4}{1}$. Not all square roots come out so neatly. Some numbers are irrational. They cannot be written as fractions. For instance, the square root of 2 is 1.414213... The number goes on and on. Let's just say it's somewhere between 1 and 2 on the number line.

In Chapter 11, you will investigate irrational numbers and radicals.

Goals for Learning

- To distinguish rational and irrational numbers
- To find the rational number equivalents of decimal expansions
- To find the roots of radicals
- To simplify radical expressions
- To add, subtract, multiply, and divide radicals
- To rationalize the denominator of a fraction
- To solve equations with radicals and exponents
- To use a graph to find square root

Lesson 1 Rational Numbers as Decimals

Irrational number

A real number, such as $\sqrt{2}$, that cannot be written in the form $\frac{a}{b}$ in which a and b are whole numbers and $b \neq 0$

The set of real numbers contains those numbers you can find on the number line.

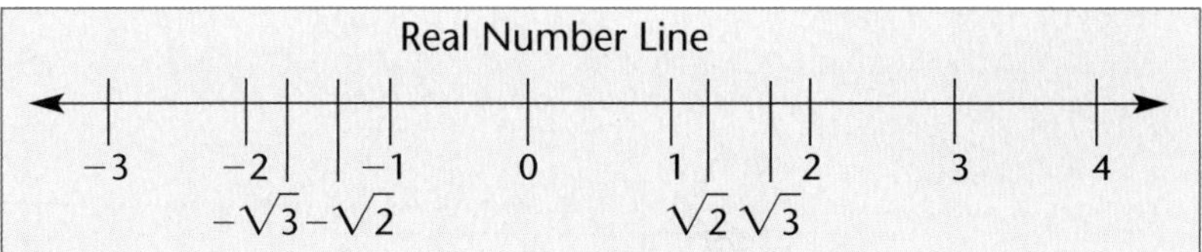

For every point on the real number line, there is one and only one real number. For every real number, there is one and only one point on the number line.

The set of real numbers can be grouped into two distinct subsets:

rational numbers such as $1, \frac{2}{3}, -\frac{7}{8}$, and so on,

and **irrational numbers** such as $\sqrt{2}, \sqrt{3}, \sqrt[3]{2}$, and so on.

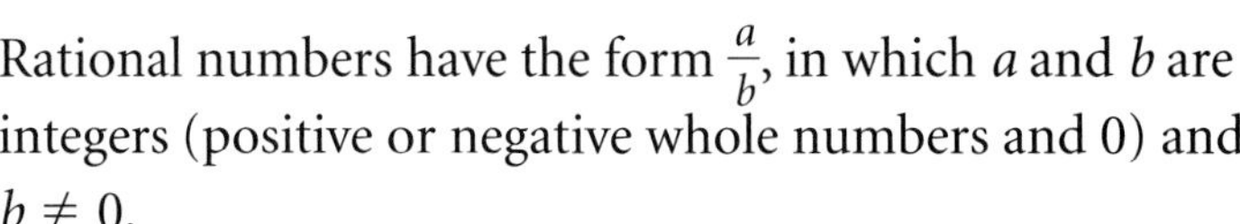

Rational numbers have the form $\frac{a}{b}$, in which a and b are integers (positive or negative whole numbers and 0) and $b \neq 0$.

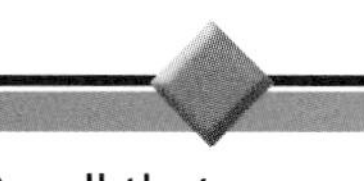

Recall that a rational number is any number that is expressed as an integer or as a ratio between two integers when 0 does not serve as the denominator.

All integers are rational numbers because they can be written in the form $\frac{a}{b}$ where $b = 1$. For instance,

$$5 = \frac{5}{1}, -7 = -\frac{7}{1}, 0 = \frac{0}{1}, \text{ and so on.}$$

One way to identify a rational number that is not an integer is to look at the number written as a decimal. To write a rational number as a decimal, divide the numerator by the denominator.

Decimal expansion

Writing a number, such as a fraction, as a decimal

Terminating decimal expansion

A decimal sequence that ends in all 0s

Repeating decimal expansion

A decimal sequence in which the numbers repeat in exactly the same order

EXAMPLE 1 Write $\frac{2}{5}$ as a decimal.

$\frac{2}{5}$ is the same as $2 \div 5$ or $5\overline{)2.0}$ with quotient 0.4

$\frac{2}{5} = 0.4$ The decimal places after 4 are all occupied by 0s.

So, $\frac{2}{5} = 0.4000....$ This can be written as $0.4\overline{0}$.

$0.4\overline{0}$ is called the **decimal expansion** of $\frac{2}{5}$.

A decimal expansion ending in all zeroes is called a **terminating decimal expansion.**

EXAMPLE 2 Write $\frac{1}{3}$ as a decimal.

$\frac{1}{3}$ is the same as $1 \div 3$ or $3\overline{)1.0}$ with quotient 0.33

$\frac{1}{3} = 0.333...$ or $0.\overline{3}$.

The 3 repeats an infinite number of times in the decimal.

EXAMPLE 3 Write $\frac{1}{7}$ as a decimal.

$\frac{1}{7}$ is the same as $1 \div 7$ or $7\overline{)1.0}$ with quotient 0.142

Use a calculator to find this decimal expansion.

Press 1 [÷] 7 [=] 0.142857

↑ ↑

repeating pattern

$\frac{1}{7} = 0.142857142857... = 0.\overline{142857}$

↑ ↑

repeating pattern

A decimal expansion in which one or more digits repeat in exactly the same order is called a **repeating decimal expansion.** Rational numbers have either terminating or repeating decimal expansions.

Exercise A Write the decimal expansions for these rational numbers. Tell whether the expansions are terminating or repeating.

1. $\frac{3}{5}$

2. $\frac{2}{9}$

3. $\frac{5}{9}$

4. $\frac{7}{9}$

5. $\frac{2}{11}$

6. $\frac{3}{11}$

7. $\frac{7}{11}$

8. $\frac{5}{7}$

9. $\frac{5}{33}$

10. $\frac{28}{33}$

11. $\frac{3}{25}$

12. $\frac{7}{25}$

13. $\frac{5}{12}$

14. $\frac{1}{12}$

15. $\frac{11}{15}$

Use your calculator to change fractions to expanded decimals.

EXAMPLE 4 Change $\frac{5}{9}$ to a decimal.

Press 5 ÷ 9 =

The display reads 0.555555555 or 0.555555556 because of rounding.

You can write the repeating decimal expansion as $0.\overline{5}$.

Exercise B Use your calculator to find the expanded decimal for each fraction in the chart. Copy the chart onto a sheet of paper. Use long division to check any repeating expansions.

16.

Rational Number	$\frac{1}{1}$	$\frac{1}{2}$	$\frac{1}{3}$	$\frac{1}{4}$	$\frac{1}{5}$	$\frac{1}{6}$	$\frac{1}{7}$	$\frac{1}{8}$	$\frac{1}{9}$	$\frac{1}{10}$
Decimal Expansion										

17.

Rational Number	$\frac{1}{1}$	$\frac{1}{2}$	$\frac{2}{3}$	$\frac{3}{4}$	$\frac{4}{5}$	$\frac{5}{6}$	$\frac{6}{7}$	$\frac{7}{8}$	$\frac{8}{9}$	$\frac{9}{10}$
Decimal Expansion										

PROBLEM SOLVING

Rational and irrational numbers can be used to describe much of the world in which you live. For example, to change degrees Celsius to degrees Fahrenheit or to change degrees Fahrenheit to degrees Celsius, use one of these formulas:

$$°F = (\frac{9}{5})(°C) + 32 \qquad °C = (\frac{5}{9})(°F - 32)$$

In these formulas, $\frac{9}{5}$ is a rational number and $\frac{5}{9}$ is an irrational number.

TRY THIS

What is the normal temperature of the human body in degrees Celsius?

Exercise C Suppose you visit distant countries and experience the following temperatures in degrees Celsius. Change the temperatures to degrees Fahrenheit.

18. 34°C

19. −18°C

20. 25°C

21. −4°C

Suppose a tourist visiting the United States experiences the following temperatures in degrees Fahrenheit. Change the temperatures to degrees Celsius.

22. 104°F

23. 46°F

24. −10°F

25. 70°F

Algebra in Your Life

The Square of the Hypotenuse
Roofing contractors use the Pythagorean theorem to figure out the length of the rafters in a building. Rafters run parallel to one another. They are the diagonal boards on which the roof of a building is laid. A rafter represents the unknown hypotenuse of a right triangle. To find the length of a rafter you need to find the square root of the triangle's hypotenuse. If roofing contractors couldn't calculate square roots, they wouldn't be able to measure rafters correctly.

Lesson 2 Rational Number Equivalents

You can use what you know about solving equations to find the rational number that represents a repeating or terminating decimal expansion.

EXAMPLE 1 What rational number is equal to $0.45\overline{0}$?

Because $0.45\overline{0}$ is a terminating decimal expansion, you can write it as $0.45 = \frac{45}{100}$.

Simplify.

$\frac{45}{100} = \frac{9}{20}$, so $\frac{45}{100} = \frac{9}{20} = 0.450$

EXAMPLE 2 What rational number is equal to $0.\overline{3}$?

Step 1 For a repeating decimal expansion, let x = the expansion written as a repeating decimal.
In this case, $x = 0.333...$

Step 2 Multiply both sides of the equation to place the repeating digit(s) to the left of the decimal.
In this case, multiply by 10.

$$10(x) = (10)0.3333...$$
$$10x = 3.333...$$

Step 3 Subtract the repeating decimal.

$$\begin{aligned} 10x &= 3.333... \\ -\quad x &= 0.333... \\ \hline 9x &= 3.000... \\ 9x &= 3 \end{aligned}$$

(The repeating part of the decimal subtracts to 0.)

Step 4 Simplify.

$x = \frac{3}{9} = \frac{1}{3}$, so $\frac{1}{3} = 0.\overline{3}$

EXAMPLE 3 What rational number is equal to $1.0\overline{51}$?

Step 1 Let $x = 1.0515151...$

Step 2 Multiply both sides of the equation to place the repeating digit(s) to the left of the decimal.
In this case, multiply by 1,000.

$$1{,}000(x) = (1{,}000)1.0515151...$$
$$1{,}000x = 1{,}051.51...$$

EXAMPLE 3 *(continued)*

Step 3 Multiply both sides of $x = 1.0515151...$ so the repeating part of the expansion immediately follows the decimal. In this case, multiply by 10.

$$(10)x = (10)1.05151...$$
$$10x = 10.5151...$$

Step 4 Subtract the products from one another.

$$\begin{array}{rl} 1{,}000x = & 1{,}051.5151... \\ -\quad 10x = & 10.5151... \\ \hline 990x = & 1{,}041.0000... \\ 990x = & 1{,}041 \end{array}$$

(The repeating part of the decimal subtracts to 0.)

Step 5 Simplify.

$$x = \frac{1041}{900} = \frac{347}{330}$$

$$\text{so } \frac{347}{330} = 1.0\overline{51}$$

Exercise A Find the rational number equivalents for these decimal expansions. Write your answers in lowest terms.

1. $0.4\overline{0}$

2. $0.75\overline{0}$

3. $0.36\overline{0}$

4. $0.52\overline{0}$

5. $0.\overline{81}$

6. $0.\overline{09}$

7. $0.0\overline{75}$

8. $0.5\overline{3}$

Exercise B Find the rational number equivalents for these decimal expansions.

9. $0.7\overline{3}$

10. $0.\overline{07}$

11. $0.\overline{13}$

12. $0.15\overline{90}$

13. $0.\overline{153846}$

14. $1.\overline{153846}$

15. $0.0\overline{0495}$

Technology Connection

Software Programs Use Formulas

Balancing your checkbook is easy when you use a software program. Just enter the amounts of your checks and deposits in the right place. The software calculates your balance for you. In the same way, other software programs help businesses to do payroll. They also help insurance companies to figure out premiums, and scientists to calculate the growth of bacteria and viruses. These software programs all use formulas with variables!

Lesson 3 Irrational Numbers as Decimals

Radical

A number that is written with the radical sign

Radical sign

The mathematical symbol ($\sqrt{\ }$) placed before a number or algebraic expression to indicate that the root should be found

Recall that the set of real numbers can be grouped into two distinct subsets—rational numbers and irrational numbers.

Irrational numbers include the square root, cube root, and *n*th root of many numbers. These numbers are sometimes called roots, or **radicals**, because they are written with the **radical sign** ($\sqrt{\ }$). For example, $\sqrt{2}$, $\sqrt{3}$, $\sqrt[3]{2}$, and so on.

It is important to note that not all radicals or roots are irrational. For instance, $\sqrt{4} = 2$, $\sqrt[3]{-8} = -2$, and $\sqrt[5]{32} = 2$. In each case, the root is an integer. You know that integers are also rational numbers, so these roots are *not* irrational.

Use your calculator to find the decimal expansion of irrational numbers.

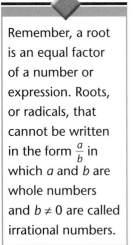

Remember, a root is an equal factor of a number or expression. Roots, or radicals, that cannot be written in the form $\frac{a}{b}$ in which a and b are whole numbers and $b \neq 0$ are called irrational numbers.

EXAMPLE 1 Write the decimal expansion for $\sqrt{2}$.

Use a calculator to find the decimal expansion of $\sqrt{2}$.

Press 2 [$\sqrt{\ }$]. (On many calculators, the answer will be displayed after the [$\sqrt{\ }$] is pressed. On some calculators, you will have to press [=] for the answer to be displayed.)

The display reads *1.4142136*.

This expansion does *not* end in zeroes and it does *not* have a repeating pattern. Therefore, $\sqrt{2}$ is *not* a rational number. Because the display of some calculators is limited to 8 digits, $\sqrt{2} = 1.4142136\ldots$ is an approximation of the complete decimal expansion. This is often written using "$\approx$," a symbol standing for *approximately equal.*

So $\sqrt{2} \approx 1.4142136$, which is an irrational number.

The decimal expansion of an irrational number is nonterminating and nonrepeating.

Example 2 Write a decimal expansion for $\sqrt[3]{2}$. Tell whether it is rational or irrational.

Use a calculator to find the cube root. Note that the cube root key may look like $\sqrt[3]{x}$, $\sqrt[3]{\ }$, or $\sqrt[x]{y}$ depending on the calculator.

Press 2 $\sqrt[3]{x}$. The display shows 1.259921.

The decimal is not terminating and not repeating, so $\sqrt[3]{2}$ is irrational.

The area of a square is 30 cm². What is the length of one side (s) of the square?

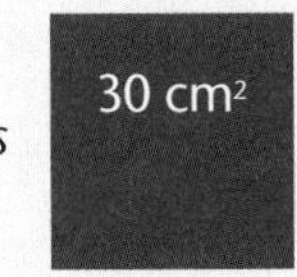

Area $= s^2$, so $\sqrt{\text{area}} = s$

You can estimate the length of one side by comparing the area to known squares:

$\sqrt{25} < \sqrt{30} < \sqrt{36}$ so $5 < s < 6$

Use a calculator to make a closer approximation.

Press 30 $\sqrt{\ }$. The display shows 5.477225.

Exercise A Use your calculator to find the roots for these radicals. Tell whether they are rational or irrational.

1. $\sqrt[3]{400}$
2. $\sqrt[4]{400}$
3. $\sqrt[5]{400}$
4. $\sqrt[3]{512}$
5. $\sqrt[3]{45}$
6. $\sqrt[9]{512}$
7. $\sqrt[10]{1024}$
8. $\sqrt[2]{30}$
9. $\sqrt[8]{256}$
10. $\sqrt{55}$

PROBLEM SOLVING

Exercise B Answer the following questions.

11. Hisako is building a square birdhouse with a 36 in.² floor. How long will each side of the birdhouse be?
12. Sharon wants to make a square poster with an area of about 500 cm². What will be the length of each side of the square, rounded to the nearest hundredth?
13. Jesse's room has an area of 160 ft². What is the length of one side of the square room? Round to the nearest hundredth.
14. A store has a square floor space with an area of 1,600 ft². Can you find the exact length of a side of this square? Explain.
15. A building is divided into four square offices with each having 49 square units. What is the area of the building (larger square)? What is the length of a side of the larger square?

49 sq. units	
	49 sq. units

Lesson 4 Products and Quotients of Radicals

The rules for multiplying or dividing radicals can be illustrated by the following examples.

EXAMPLE 1 Find the product of $\sqrt{4} \bullet \sqrt{25}$.

$$\sqrt{4} \bullet \sqrt{25} = (2) \bullet (5) = 10$$

$$\sqrt{100} = 10$$

$$\text{so } \sqrt{4} \bullet \sqrt{25} = \sqrt{4 \bullet 25} = \sqrt{100} = 10$$

Find the product of $\sqrt{4} \bullet \sqrt{9}$.

$$\sqrt{4} \bullet \sqrt{9} = (2) \bullet (3) = 6$$

$$\sqrt{36} = 6$$

$$\text{so } \sqrt{4} \bullet \sqrt{9} = \sqrt{4 \bullet 9} = \sqrt{36} = 6$$

These examples form the first rule of radicals.

Rule $\sqrt{a} \bullet \sqrt{b} = \sqrt{a \bullet b}$, for $a > 0$ and $b > 0$

A similar rule exists for working with expressions that contain radicals in both the numerator and the denominator. Consider these examples.

EXAMPLE 2 Find the quotient of $\frac{\sqrt{16}}{\sqrt{4}}$

$$\frac{\sqrt{16}}{\sqrt{4}} = \frac{(4)}{(2)} = 2$$

$$\sqrt{\frac{16}{4}} = \sqrt{4} = 2$$

$$\text{so } \frac{\sqrt{16}}{\sqrt{4}} = \sqrt{\frac{16}{4}} = \sqrt{4} = 2$$

Find the quotient of $\frac{\sqrt{36}}{\sqrt{4}}$.

$$\frac{\sqrt{36}}{\sqrt{4}} = \frac{(6)}{(2)} = 3$$

$$\sqrt{\frac{36}{4}} = \sqrt{9} = 3$$

$$\text{so } \frac{\sqrt{36}}{\sqrt{4}} = \sqrt{\frac{36}{4}} = \sqrt{9} = 3$$

These examples demonstrate the rule of radicals for fractions.

Rule $\frac{\sqrt{a}}{\sqrt{b}} = \sqrt{\frac{a}{b}}$, where $a \geq 0$ and $b > 0$

You can use these rules to simplify some types of radicals.

Example 3 Simplify $\sqrt{200}$.

Factor 200 using the largest possible perfect squares:
$\sqrt{200} = \sqrt{100 \bullet 2} = \sqrt{100} \bullet \sqrt{2} = 10\sqrt{2}$.
Check: $(10\sqrt{2})^2 = 200 \quad 100 \bullet 2 = 200$ True
You cannot factor 2 any further—you are finished simplifying.

Suppose you had factored 200 as $8 \bullet 25$? You would then have $\sqrt{200} = \sqrt{25 \bullet 8} = \sqrt{25} \bullet \sqrt{8} = 5\sqrt{8}$.
But 8 can be factored further, leading to
$5\sqrt{8} = 5\sqrt{4 \bullet 2} = 5 \bullet \sqrt{4} \bullet \sqrt{2} = 5 \bullet 2 \bullet \sqrt{2} = 10\sqrt{2}$.

Simplify $\sqrt{(16x^3)}$.
$\sqrt{(16x^3)} = \sqrt{16} \bullet \sqrt{x^3} = \sqrt{16} \bullet \sqrt{x^2} \bullet \sqrt{x} = 4 \bullet x \bullet \sqrt{x}$
Check. $(4x\sqrt{x})^2 = 16x^3 \quad 16x^2 \bullet x = 16x^3$ True

Simplify $\sqrt{\frac{25y^6}{x^3}}$, $\sqrt{\frac{25y^6}{x^3}} = \frac{(\sqrt{25} \bullet \sqrt{y^6})}{\sqrt{x^3}} = \frac{\sqrt{25} \bullet \sqrt{y^3 \bullet y^3}}{\sqrt{x^2 \bullet x}} = \frac{5y^3}{x\sqrt{x}}$

Check. $(\frac{5y^3}{x\sqrt{x}})^2 = \frac{25y^6}{x^3} \quad \frac{25y^6}{x^2x} = \frac{25y^6}{x^3}$ True

TRY THIS

Simplify these expressions.
$\sqrt[3]{\frac{27y^6}{64z^3}}$ and $\sqrt[4]{\frac{256y^4}{16x^8}}$

Exercise A Simplify the following radicals. Be sure to check your answers.

1. $\sqrt{2500}$
2. $\sqrt{500}$
3. $\sqrt{196}$
4. $\sqrt{441}$
5. $\sqrt{25a^2}$
6. $\sqrt{27y^3}$
7. $\sqrt{25x^4y^5}$
8. $\sqrt{225z^7}$
9. $\sqrt{90x^5}$
10. $\sqrt{72t^2}$
11. $\sqrt{1{,}089m^2n^4}$
12. $\sqrt{288y^3z^5}$

Exercise B Simplify the following expressions. Check your work.

13. $\sqrt{\frac{16}{81}}$
14. $\sqrt{\frac{81}{225}}$
15. $\sqrt{\frac{75}{36}}$
16. $\sqrt{\frac{36x^6}{y^4}}$
17. $\sqrt{\frac{27}{y^3}}$
18. $\sqrt{\frac{x^2}{25y^3}}$
19. $\sqrt{\frac{16y^2}{25x^4}}$
20. $\sqrt{\frac{49x^3}{100y^4}}$
21. $\sqrt{\frac{81h^6}{27y^2}}$
22. $\sqrt{\frac{441j^2}{9h^4}}$
23. $\sqrt{\frac{243x^6}{90y^2}}$
24. $\sqrt{\frac{48m^3}{56n^5}}$
25. $\sqrt{\frac{36d^2}{24t^4}}$

Lesson 5 Sums and Differences of Radicals

You already know that the sum of $a + 2a$ is $3a$. In much the same way, the sum of $\sqrt{3} + 2\sqrt{3}$ is $3\sqrt{3}$. You can show why this is true if you factor the expressions.

$$\sqrt{3} + 2\sqrt{3} = 1\sqrt{3} + 2\sqrt{3} = (1 + 2)\sqrt{3} = 3\sqrt{3}.$$

However, you cannot add expressions in which the radicals are different. For example, the terms $2\sqrt{5}$ and $5\sqrt{2}$ have different radicals and cannot be added or subtracted.

In some cases, you can simplify radicals so that the resulting terms can be added or subtracted.

Numbers under the $\sqrt{\ }$ are equal	Numbers under the $\sqrt{\ }$ are *not* equal
$2\sqrt{5} + \sqrt{5} = 3\sqrt{5}$ $3\sqrt{7} - \sqrt{7} = 2\sqrt{7}$ $5\sqrt{3} - 2\sqrt{3} = 3\sqrt{3}$ These radicals can be added or subtracted.	$\sqrt{5} + \sqrt{2}$ $2\sqrt{7} - \sqrt{5}$ $5\sqrt{2} - 5\sqrt{3}$ These radicals *cannot* be added or subtracted.

Rule Like radicals can be added or subtracted; unlike radicals cannot.

EXAMPLE 1 Find the sum of $\sqrt{2} + \sqrt{8}$.

First, simplify the terms of the expression.

$\sqrt{2} + \sqrt{8} = \sqrt{2} + \sqrt{(4 \bullet 2)}$

$= \sqrt{2} + (\sqrt{4} \bullet \sqrt{2})$. Then factor and add:

$= (1)\sqrt{2} + (2)\sqrt{2}$

$= 3\sqrt{2}$

Subtract $\sqrt{27} - \sqrt{3}$

Simplify. $\sqrt{27} - \sqrt{3} = \sqrt{(9 \bullet 3)} - \sqrt{3}$

$= (\sqrt{9} \bullet \sqrt{3}) - \sqrt{3}$. Factor and subtract:

$= (3)\sqrt{3} - (1)\sqrt{3}$

$= 2\sqrt{3}$

Writing About Mathematics

Is the square root of a number always less than the number itself? In symbol form, is $\sqrt{x} < x$ true for all positive, real numbers? Try some examples. Explain your answer.

EXAMPLE 2 Subtract $2\sqrt{8} - \sqrt{32}$

Simplify. Then factor and subtract:

$$2\sqrt{8} - \sqrt{32} = 2(\sqrt{4} \bullet \sqrt{2}) - (\sqrt{16} \bullet \sqrt{2})$$
$$= 2(2 \bullet \sqrt{2}) - 4(\sqrt{2})$$
$$= 4\sqrt{2} - 4\sqrt{2} = 0$$

Exercise A If possible, find the sum or difference.

1. $\sqrt{2} + 5\sqrt{2}$
2. $\sqrt{2} - 5\sqrt{2}$
3. $3\sqrt{7} - 2\sqrt{7}$
4. $2\sqrt{7} + 7\sqrt{2}$
5. $\sqrt{64} + \sqrt{16}$
6. $\sqrt{13} - \sqrt{11}$
7. $3\sqrt{75} - 4\sqrt{27}$
8. $2\sqrt{28} + 4\sqrt{112}$
9. $5\sqrt{8} - \sqrt{2}$
10. $\sqrt{27} + \sqrt{3}$
11. $\sqrt{52} - 2\sqrt{13}$
12. $\sqrt{21} - 2\sqrt{23}$

Exercise B Simplify, then add or subtract.

13. $\sqrt{24} + \sqrt{36}$
14. $2\sqrt{108} + 3\sqrt{36}$
15. $\sqrt{24} + 3\sqrt{48}$
16. $2\sqrt{7} + 3\sqrt{28}$
17. $4\sqrt{40} + 6\sqrt{60}$
18. $4\sqrt{125} - 3\sqrt{25}$
19. $6\sqrt{36x^4} - \sqrt{25x^4}$
20. $4\sqrt{64x^2} - 3\sqrt{16x^2}$

TRY THIS Simplify, then factor and subtract this expression: $2\sqrt{64x^2} - 3\sqrt{49x^2}$

Lesson 6 Radicals and Fractions

Rationalizing the denominator

Changing a fraction with an irrational number to an equivalent fraction with a rational number

Conjugate

A factor that when multiplied rationalizes (or simplifies) an expression

Remember that $\sqrt{\frac{1}{4}} = \frac{\sqrt{1}}{\sqrt{4}} = \frac{1}{2}$ and that, in general, $\sqrt{\frac{a}{b}} = \frac{\sqrt{a}}{\sqrt{b}}$ when $b \neq 0$. And, you can evaluate $\frac{\sqrt{2}}{2}$ by rewriting it as $\sqrt{2} \div 2$. How would you evaluate $\frac{2}{\sqrt{2}}$? You know that $\frac{2}{\sqrt{2}}$ is the same as $2 \div \sqrt{2}$. But what value can you assign to the denominator? A value of 1.4? 1.41? 1.414?

You can avoid choosing a value by multiplying the fraction by 1 in the form of $\frac{\sqrt{2}}{\sqrt{2}}$. Remember, multiplying by 1 does not change the value of a number or expression.

$$\frac{2}{\sqrt{2}} = \frac{2}{\sqrt{2}} \cdot \left[\frac{\sqrt{2}}{\sqrt{2}}\right] = \frac{2\sqrt{2}}{2} = \sqrt{2}$$

↑ irrational number ↑ [1] ↑ rational number

You have now changed the denominator from an irrational number to a rational number.

The process of changing a fraction with an irrational denominator to an equivalent fraction with a rational denominator is called **rationalizing the denominator.**

EXAMPLE 1 Rationalize the denominators of $\frac{1}{\sqrt{3}}$, $\frac{2\sqrt{2}}{\sqrt{3}}$, and $\frac{\sqrt{2}}{2\sqrt{5}}$.

$\frac{1}{\sqrt{3}}$	$\frac{2\sqrt{2}}{\sqrt{3}}$	$\frac{\sqrt{2}}{2\sqrt{5}}$
$= \frac{1}{\sqrt{3}} \bullet \left[\frac{\sqrt{3}}{\sqrt{3}}\right]$	$= \frac{2\sqrt{2}}{\sqrt{3}} \bullet \left[\frac{\sqrt{3}}{\sqrt{3}}\right]$	$= \frac{\sqrt{2}}{2\sqrt{5}} \bullet \left[\frac{\sqrt{5}}{\sqrt{5}}\right]$
$= \frac{\sqrt{3}}{(\sqrt{3} \bullet \sqrt{3})}$	$= \frac{(2\sqrt{2} \bullet \sqrt{3})}{(\sqrt{3} \bullet \sqrt{3})}$	$= \frac{(\sqrt{2} \bullet \sqrt{5})}{(2 \bullet \sqrt{5} \bullet \sqrt{5})}$
$= \frac{\sqrt{3}}{3}$	$= \frac{2\sqrt{6}}{3}$	$= \frac{\sqrt{10}}{10}$

You can use the same process to rationalize a denominator such as $3 + \sqrt{2}$. Notice in the following example that you will multiply $(3 + \sqrt{2})$ by $(3 - \sqrt{2})$ to rationalize the denominator. The terms $(3 + \sqrt{2})$ and $(3 - \sqrt{2})$ are called **conjugates** of one another.

Remember, if you multiply the numerator and denominator by the same number, the value of the fraction does not change.

EXAMPLE 2 Rationalize the denominator of $\frac{2}{(3 + \sqrt{2})}$.

In this case, you will need to multiply by 1 in the form of $[\frac{3 - \sqrt{2}}{(3 - \sqrt{2})}]$.

$$\frac{2}{(3 + \sqrt{2})} \bullet [\frac{3 - \sqrt{2}}{(3 - \sqrt{2})}] = \frac{(2)(3 - \sqrt{2})}{(3 + \sqrt{2})(3 - \sqrt{2})}$$

$$= \frac{(2)(3 - \sqrt{2})}{3(3 - \sqrt{2}) + \sqrt{2}(3 - \sqrt{2})} = \frac{(2)(3 - \sqrt{2})}{9 - 3\sqrt{2} + 3\sqrt{2} - 2}$$

$$= \frac{6 - 2\sqrt{2}}{9 - 0 - 2} = \frac{6 - 2\sqrt{2}}{7}$$

In general, this multiplication follows the pattern of the difference between two perfect squares.

$$(a + \sqrt{b})(a - \sqrt{b}) = a^2 - (\sqrt{b})^2 = a^2 - b$$

Rule To rationalize a denominator of the form $a + \sqrt{b}$ or $a - \sqrt{b}$, multiply both the numerator and the denominator by the conjugate of the denominator.

EXAMPLE 3 Rationalize the denominator of $\frac{2}{(3 - \sqrt{5})}$.

Multiply $(3 - \sqrt{5})$ by its conjugate, $(3 + \sqrt{5})$.

$$\frac{2}{(3 - \sqrt{5})} = \frac{2}{(3 - \sqrt{5})} \bullet \frac{(3 + \sqrt{5})}{(3 + \sqrt{5})}$$

$$= \frac{(6 + 2\sqrt{5})}{(9 - 5)} = \frac{(6 + 2\sqrt{5})}{4} = \frac{(3 + \sqrt{5})}{2}$$

Exercise A Rationalize the denominator of each fraction. Be sure your answer is in simplest form.

1. $\frac{(4)\sqrt{3}}{\sqrt{2}}$

2. $\frac{(6)\sqrt{8}}{\sqrt{3}}$

3. $\frac{(3\sqrt{7})}{\sqrt{5}}$

4. $\frac{(3\sqrt{5})}{(3\sqrt{15})}$

5. $\frac{(2\sqrt{12})}{(3\sqrt{6})}$

6. $\frac{(3\sqrt{21})}{(2\sqrt{7})}$

7. $\frac{(5\sqrt{35})}{(3\sqrt{7})}$

8. $\frac{(4\sqrt{14})}{(2\sqrt{28})}$

Exercise B Use a conjugate to rationalize the denominator of each fraction. Be sure your answer is in simplest form.

9. $\frac{2}{(2 + \sqrt{2})}$

10. $\frac{6}{(3 + \sqrt{3})}$

11. $\frac{5}{(2 + \sqrt{5})}$

12. $\frac{\sqrt{3}}{(1 + \sqrt{2})}$

13. $\frac{3\sqrt{5}}{(3 + \sqrt{5})}$

14. $\frac{3\sqrt{x^3}}{(3 + \sqrt{x^3})}$

15. $\frac{3y}{(3 - \sqrt{y^3})}$

Lesson 7 Radicals in Equations

Suppose you were asked to solve this puzzle: "The square root of a number is 10. What is the number?" You could solve the puzzle by letting n equal the number and writing the puzzle in terms of an equation:

$$\sqrt{n} = 10$$

You already know that you can multiply each side of an equation by an equivalent of 1 without changing the value of the equation. In this case, you can "square" both sides of the equation:

$$(\sqrt{n})^2 = (10)^2$$

And then solve for n: $n = 100$

EXAMPLE 1 Find x when $(\sqrt{3x}) = 4$.

First, square both sides of the equation.

$(\sqrt{3x})^2 = 4^2$ Then solve for x.

$3x = 16$

$x = \frac{16}{3}$

Check: $\sqrt{[3(\frac{16}{3})]} = 4$

$\sqrt{16} = 4$ True

EXAMPLE 2 Find x when $[\sqrt{x - 1}] = 5$.

Square both sides of the equation, then solve for x.

$[\sqrt{(x - 1)}]^2 = 5^2$

$x - 1 = 25$

$x = 26$

Check: $\sqrt{(26 - 1)} = 5$

$\sqrt{25} = 5$ True

EXAMPLE 3 Find x when $12 - \sqrt{3x} = 4$.

Step 1 In this case, you must first isolate the variable. Place the term with the variable on one side of the equation and place all other terms on the opposite side of the equation.

$12 - \sqrt{3x} = 4$ is the same as $-\sqrt{3x} = -8$.

EXAMPLE 3 *(continued)*

Step 2 Square both sides of the equation and solve for x.

$$-\sqrt{3x} = -8$$
$$(-\sqrt{3x})^2 = (-8)^2$$
$$3x = 64$$
$$x = \frac{64}{3}$$

Check: $12 - \sqrt{3x} = 4$

$$12 - \sqrt{3(\tfrac{64}{3})} = 4$$
$$12 - \sqrt{64} = 4$$
$$12 - 8 = 4 \quad \text{True}$$

You may also need to use radicals when presented with some formulas.

EXAMPLE 4 What is the length of the side of a square whose area is A?

Write the question in equation form: $A = s^2$. Then solve for s. Your answer is in simplified radical form.

$$A = s^2, \sqrt{A} = s \text{ or } s = \sqrt{A}$$

A s s

What is the length of the side of a square whose area is 25 cm^2?

$$s = \sqrt{A}$$
$$s = \sqrt{25} \text{ or } 5 \text{ cm}$$

What is the radius of a circle whose area is A?

Write the question in equation form: $A = \pi r^2$.

Isolate r^2 on one side of the equation.

$$A = \pi r^2 \text{ is the same as } \frac{A}{\pi} = r^2.$$

A r

Solve for r.

$$\sqrt{(\tfrac{A}{\pi})} = r \text{ or } r = \sqrt{(\tfrac{A}{\pi})}$$

What is the radius of a circle whose area is 12 cm^2? Let $\pi \approx 3$.

$$r = \sqrt{(\tfrac{A}{\pi})}$$
$$r = \sqrt{\tfrac{12}{3}}$$
$$r = \sqrt{4} \text{ or } 2 \text{ cm}$$

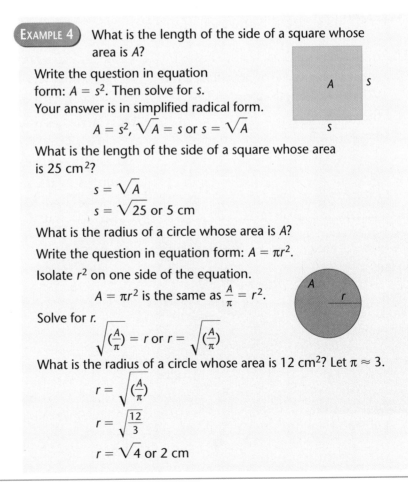

Exercise A Solve each equation for the unknown.

1. $\sqrt{n} = 7$
2. $\sqrt{x} = 4$
3. $\sqrt{2y} = 6$
4. $\sqrt{4m} = 8$
5. $\sqrt{5y} = 35$
6. $\sqrt{z} = \frac{3}{2}$
7. $\sqrt{3x} = 7$
8. $\sqrt{4x} = 6$

Exercise B Solve each equation for x. Check your answers.

9. $13 - \sqrt{x} = 5$
10. $29 - \sqrt{x} = 13$
11. $43 - \sqrt{x} = 18$
12. $\sqrt{x} - 9 = 16$
13. $\sqrt{(2x - 1)} = 16$

PROBLEM SOLVING

Exercise C Solve each problem.

14. In the new mall, each store has a square floor space of 36 square units. What is the length of one side of the store?

$A = 36$ sq. units

s

s

15. Gina rides her bike around a square park that has 49 square units. What is the length of one side of the park?

16. Carrie has drawn a right triangle. She asks you to determine the lengths of the sides of the triangle by using the formula $a^2 + b^2 = c^2$. Solve for a, b, and c.

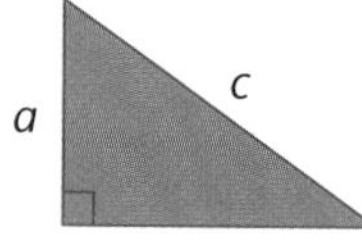

$a^2 + b^2 = c^2$

The formula for the area of a circle with radius r is $A = \pi r^2$. Use this formula for Problems 17 and 18.

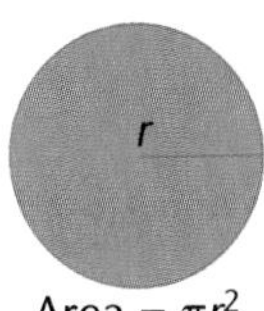

Area = πr^2

17. The small, circular area rug in Jackson's room has an area of 1,200 square inches. What is the length of the rug's radius? (Use $\pi \approx 3$.) You may use radicals in your answer.

18. Juanita draws a chalk circle on the sidewalk after tying the chalk to a length of string and taping the string to the ground. The length of the string is equal to the radius of the circle. How long is her string if the circle has an area of 81 square units? (Use $\pi \approx 3$.)

The formula for the volume of a cylinder with radius r is $V = \pi r^2 h$. Use this formula for Problems 19 and 20.

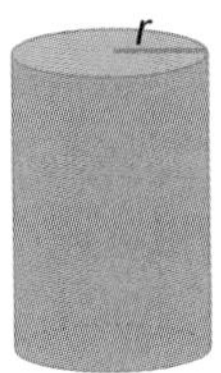

$V = \pi r^2 h$

19. Cal is making a lid for a can shaped like a cylinder. What is the radius of the circle Cal must make for the lid? The volume (V) of the cylinder is 600 cubic units and its height is 200 units. What is its radius? (Use $\pi \approx 3$.)

20. An auto mechanic pours used oil into a cylindrical drum. What is the radius of the lid of the drum if the drum's volume is 1,200 cubic units and its height is 16 units? (Use $\pi \approx 3$.)

Estimation Activity

Estimate: Predict the nature of the roots from the graphed solution.

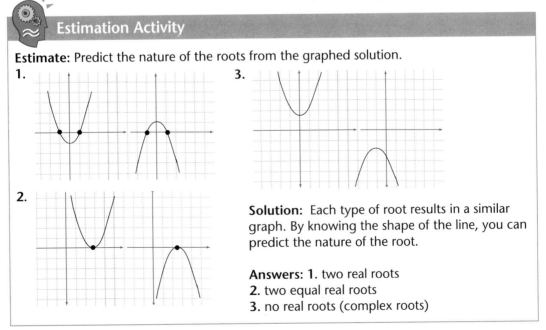

1.

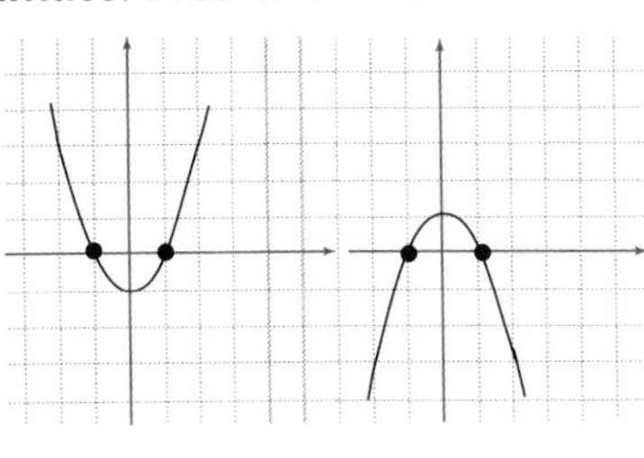

2.

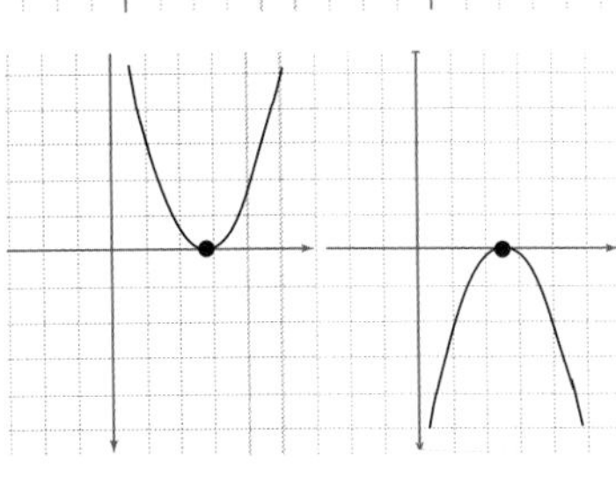

3.

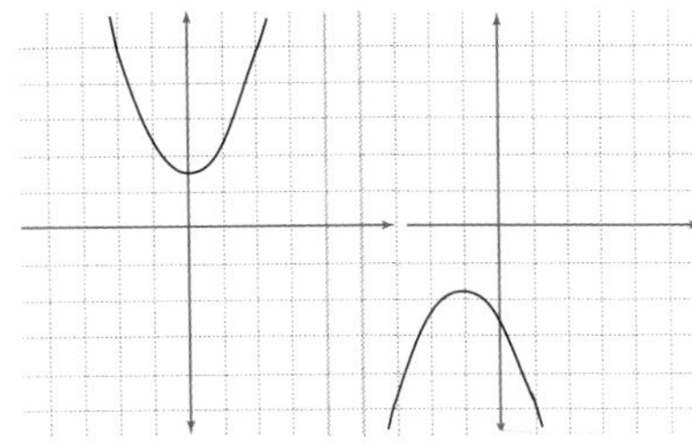

Solution: Each type of root results in a similar graph. By knowing the shape of the line, you can predict the nature of the root.

Answers: 1. two real roots
2. two equal real roots
3. no real roots (complex roots)

Lesson 8 Radicals and Exponents

Radicand

A number under the radical sign ($\sqrt{\ }$)

Recall that $x \cdot x^2 = x^3$, $y^2 \cdot y^3 = y^5$, and, in general, $n^a \cdot n^b = n^{(a+b)}$.

In algebra, you will sometimes need to find products of terms containing radicals, such as $x \cdot \sqrt{x}$ and $(y^2)\sqrt[3]{y}$. To find these products, you will need to rewrite the radicals using exponents.

> The nth root of x is written $x^{\frac{1}{n}}$.
>
> Using symbols, $\sqrt[n]{x} = x^{\frac{1}{n}}$.

To write the radical using exponents, you need to write the **radicand** as the base raised to a power.

$\sqrt[2]{x} = x^{\frac{1}{2}}$ $\quad$ $\sqrt[3]{x} = x^{\frac{1}{3}}$ $\quad$ $\sqrt[6]{x} = x^{\frac{1}{6}}$

↑ radicand $\quad$ ↑ base $\quad$ ↑ power

The $\sqrt{x}$ represents the square or second root of x. The 2 is understood and not usually written.

$\sqrt{x} = \sqrt[2]{x}$.

Recall that

$$\sqrt{(a \cdot b)} = \sqrt{a} \cdot \sqrt{b}$$

$$(a \cdot b)^{\frac{1}{2}} = a^{\frac{1}{2}} \cdot b^{\frac{1}{2}}$$

> In general,
>
> $\sqrt[n]{(a \bullet b)} = \sqrt[n]{a} \bullet \sqrt[n]{b}$, and $(a \bullet b)^{\frac{1}{n}} = a^{\frac{1}{n}} \bullet b^{\frac{1}{n}}$.

EXAMPLE 1 Write $\sqrt[5]{xy}$ using exponents.

$$\sqrt[5]{xy} = x^{\frac{1}{5}} \bullet y^{\frac{1}{5}}$$

Write $\sqrt[3]{4x}$ using exponents.

$$\sqrt[3]{4x} = 4^{\frac{1}{3}} \bullet x^{\frac{1}{3}}$$

Write $x \bullet \sqrt{x}$ with exponents and simplify.

$$x \bullet \sqrt{x} = x \bullet x^{\frac{1}{2}} = x^{(1+\frac{1}{2})} = x^{\frac{3}{2}}$$

Write $y^2 \bullet \sqrt[3]{y}$ with exponents and simplify.

$$y^2 \bullet \sqrt[3]{y} = y^2 \bullet y^{\frac{1}{3}} = y^{(2+\frac{1}{3})} = y^{(2\frac{1}{3})}$$

You can find square roots, cube roots, and even *n*th roots by rewriting and simplifying radical expressions.

EXAMPLE 2 $\sqrt[3]{x^3} = \sqrt[3]{(x \bullet x \bullet x)} = x^{\frac{1}{3}} \bullet x^{\frac{1}{3}} \bullet x^{\frac{1}{3}} = x^{(\frac{1}{3} + \frac{1}{3} + \frac{1}{3})} = x^1 = x$

And, $\sqrt[3]{x^3}$ can be written as $(x^3)^{\frac{1}{3}}$, which equals $x^{(3 \bullet \frac{1}{3})} = x^1 = x$.

$$\sqrt[n]{x^m} = (x^m)^{\frac{1}{n}}$$

Simplify $\sqrt[3]{8^2}$.

$\sqrt[3]{8^2} = (8^2)^{\frac{1}{3}} = 8^{\frac{2}{3}}$

In words, $8^{\frac{2}{3}}$ means the cube root of 8, squared, or 2^2, which is 4.

$\sqrt[3]{8^2} = 2^2 = 4$ or cube root of 8 squared, or $\sqrt[3]{8^2} = \sqrt[3]{64} = 4$

Rewrite $\sqrt[4]{x^5}$ using exponents.

$\sqrt[4]{x^5} = (x^5)^{\frac{1}{4}} = x^{(5 \bullet \frac{1}{4})} = x^{\frac{5}{4}}$

Exercise A Rewrite the following using exponents.

1. $\sqrt[3]{y}$
2. $\sqrt[5]{m}$
3. $\sqrt[3]{4y}$
4. $\sqrt[6]{2x}$

Exercise B Simplify using exponents. Then find the products.

5. $x \cdot \sqrt[3]{x}$
6. $y^2 \cdot \sqrt[3]{y}$
7. $z \cdot \sqrt[3]{z}$
8. $m^2 \cdot \sqrt[5]{m}$

Exercise C Rewrite these expressions using exponents.

9. $\sqrt[3]{x^2}$
10. $\sqrt[5]{y^3}$
11. $\sqrt[4]{x^4}$
12. $\sqrt[3]{k^4}$

Calculator Practice

You can use a calculator to find the square root or cube root of a number. The cube root key may look like $\sqrt[3]{\ }$, $\sqrt[3]{x}$, or $\sqrt[x]{y}$, depending on your calculator.

EXAMPLE 3 $\sqrt[3]{8^2} = 8^{\frac{2}{3}}$

Press 8 x^2. Display reads 64. Then press $\sqrt[3]{\ }$. Display reads 4. $\sqrt[3]{8^2} = 4$.

You could also press 8 × 8. Display reads 64. Then press $\sqrt[3]{\ }$. Display reads 4.

Exercise D Use a calculator to find the square root or cube root of a number.

13. $\sqrt{2^4}$
14. $\sqrt[3]{3^3}$
15. $\sqrt{10^4}$

Lesson 9 Drawing and Using a Square Root Graph

You have used a calculator to approximate square roots that are irrational numbers. You can also find these square roots using a graph. Use the following steps to draw your own square root graph.

EXAMPLE 1

Step 1 On graph paper, draw the first quadrant of the *xy* coordinate system. Mark the location of $x = 0, 1, 2, 3, 4,$ and 5 along the *x*-axis.

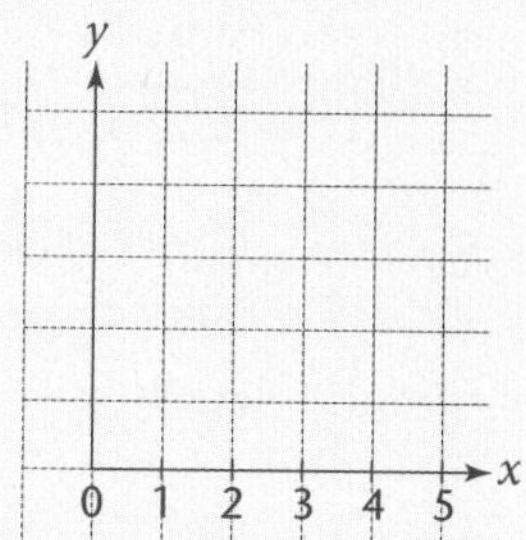

Step 2 On the *y*-axis, mark the values $y = 0, 5, 10, 15, 20,$ and 25. These values will represent the squares of the numbers along the *x*-axis.

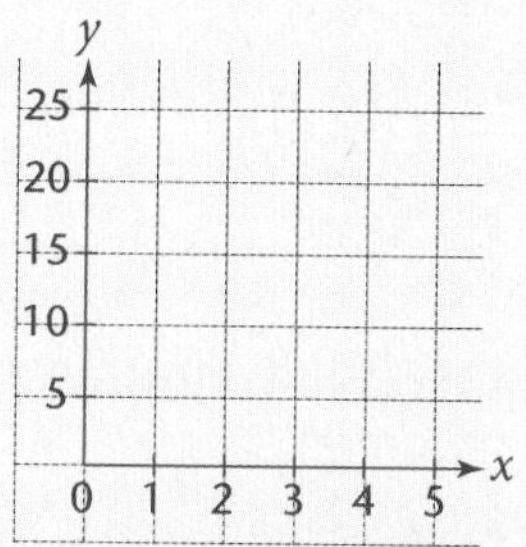

Step 3 On a separate sheet of paper, complete the following chart. Then find and label the ordered pairs (x, x^2).

x	0	$\frac{1}{2}$	1	$1\frac{1}{2}$	2	$2\frac{1}{2}$	3	$3\frac{1}{2}$	4	$4\frac{1}{2}$	5
x^2	0	$\frac{1}{4}$	1								

Step 4 Connect the points you have plotted. This will produce a graph of $y = x^2$. Any point along the line has the coordinates (x, x^2).

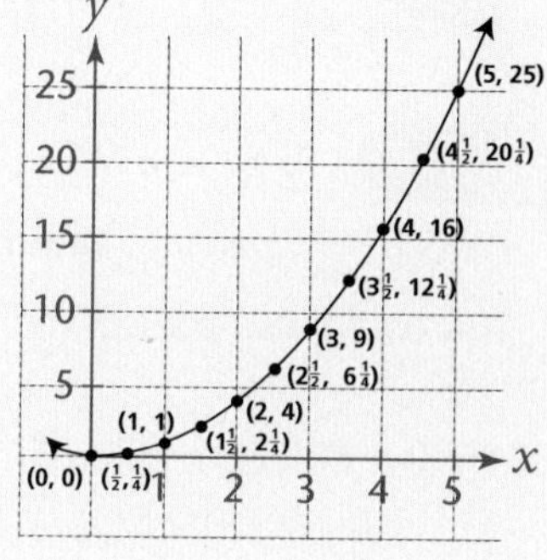

To use the graph on page 348, complete the steps shown in the following example.

EXAMPLE 2 Find the value of x when $x^2 = 15$.

Recall that if $x^2 = 15$, then $x = \sqrt{15}$. You can approximate the value of $x = \sqrt{15}$ using a square root graph.

Step 1 Find $y = 15$ on the y-axis. Draw a horizontal line to the graph. The point at which the line meets the square root graph will be $(x, 15)$ where $15 = x^2$.

Step 2 Draw a perpendicular line from $(x, 15)$ to the x-axis. The perpendicular line will intersect the x-axis at the value $x = \sqrt{15}$. You can read the value of x from the graph. In this case, the value is approximately 3.9, so $x = \sqrt{15} \approx 3.9$.

Step 3 Compare this value to the calculator value.
Press 15 [√]. Display reads 3.8729833.
So 3.9 from the graph approximates the calculator value of 3.8729833 rounded to nearest tenth.

Exercise A Follow these steps to make a square root graph.

Step 1 Use the long side of a sheet of graph paper as the x-axis. Label these values of x: $0, \frac{1}{2}, 1, 1\frac{1}{2}, 2, 2\frac{1}{2}, \ldots$ to $x = 10$.

Step 2 Label the y-axis, making the values by 10s, so that $y = 0$, 10, 20, 30, … and so on to $y = 100$.

Step 3 Find and label the ordered pairs $(0,0)$, $(\frac{1}{2}, \frac{1}{4})$, $(1,1)$, … and so on to $(10, 100)$.

Step 4 Connect the ordered pairs to graph the line $y = x^2$. Use your graph to approximate the following square roots. Confirm your graph value with a calculator value.

1. $\sqrt{10}$

2. $\sqrt{30}$

3. $\sqrt{50}$

4. $\sqrt{60}$

5. $\sqrt{70}$

6. $\sqrt{80}$

7. $\sqrt{90}$

8. $\sqrt{75}$

9. $\sqrt{85}$

10. $\sqrt{55}$

Application $\pi^2 \Sigma + \Omega \sqrt{x^2} \% \neq y \geq n = \nabla 30^\circ \pi$

Falling Objects

You might be surprised to know that "radical" is just the right description for falling objects. In the sixteenth and seventeenth centuries, Galileo Galilei did several experiments with falling objects. He found that the farther an object falls, the faster its velocity when it reaches the ground.

The velocity, v, of a falling object can be computed using the following expression: $v = \sqrt{2gh}$ in which h is the distance the object has fallen, and g is the acceleration due to gravity. On Earth, the acceleration due to gravity is about 32 feet per second squared, 32 ft/s^2.

EXAMPLE 1 Find the velocity of an object after it has fallen 10 feet.

Use the expression $v = \sqrt{2gh}$.

In this example, $h = 10$ feet. (Use $g = 32$ ft/s^2.)

$$\begin{aligned} v &= \sqrt{2gh} \\ &= \sqrt{2(32)(10)} \\ &= \sqrt{640} \\ &= 25.3 \text{ feet per second} \end{aligned}$$

You can find the velocity of falling lea[ves] by using a formula.

Exercise Find the solutions.

1. Find the velocity of a falling object after it has fallen 50 feet.
2. What is a falling object's velocity after it has fallen 100 meters? (Use $g = 9.8$ m/s^2.)
3. Find the velocity of a falling object after it has fallen 1,000 meters. (Use $g = 9.8$ m/s^2.)
4. Find the velocity of a falling object after it has fallen 300 feet.
5. Find the velocity of a falling object after it has fallen 2,500 feet.

Chapter 11 REVIEW

Write the letter of the correct answer.

1. Find the decimal expansion of the number $\frac{5}{17}$, and identify it as a rational or irrational number.

A 0.2941177 is irrational

B 0.20 is rational

C 0.32941177 is irrational

D 2.94128 is rational

2. Find the decimal expansion of the number $\sqrt{73}$, and identify it as a rational or irrational number.

A 4.85 and rational

B 8.54 and rational

C 8.54 and irrational

D 6.08 and irrational

3. Find the rational number equivalent in lowest terms for the number 0.5625.

A $\frac{16}{9}$

B $\frac{15}{9}$

C $\frac{9}{16}$

D $\frac{18}{32}$

4. Find the rational number equivalent in lowest terms for the number $0.4\overline{6}$.

A $\frac{15}{7}$

B $\frac{7}{15}$

C $\frac{21}{45}$

D $\frac{14}{30}$

5. Simplify the expression $\sqrt{600}$.

A $10\sqrt{6}$

B $5\sqrt{6}$

C 60

D 20

6. Simplify the expression $\sqrt{25x^4}$.

A $2x^5$

B $5x^5$

C $5x$

D $5x^2$

7. A square has an area of 16,900 ft^2. What is the length of one side of the square?

A 103.5 ft

B 105.3 ft

C 310 ft

D 130 ft

Find the decimal expansions of these numbers. Identify each number as rational or irrational and tell why it is rational or irrational.

Example: $\frac{1}{4}$ Solution: $1.00 \div 4 = 0.25\overline{0}$ rational, terminating

8. $\frac{1}{5}$

9. $\frac{23}{37}$

10. $\sqrt{289}$

11. $\sqrt{625}$

Add or subtract these radicals.

Example: $\sqrt{9} + \sqrt{16}$ Solution: $3 + 4 = 7$

12. $\sqrt{3} + 6\sqrt{3}$

13. $3\sqrt{5} + 5\sqrt{3}$

14. $4\sqrt{8} - \sqrt{2}$

15. $2\sqrt{48} - 3\sqrt{72}$

Rationalize the denominators of these fractions.

Example: $\frac{1}{\sqrt{5}}$ Solution: $\frac{1}{\sqrt{5}} = \frac{1}{\sqrt{5}} \bullet \frac{\sqrt{5}}{\sqrt{5}} = \frac{\sqrt{5}}{(\sqrt{5})(\sqrt{5})} = \frac{\sqrt{5}}{5}$

16. $\frac{(5\sqrt{35})}{(3\sqrt{7})}$

17. $\frac{(4\sqrt{7})}{(4 + \sqrt{7})}$

18. $\frac{8\sqrt{x}}{\sqrt{2x}}$

19. $3x \div \frac{\sqrt{3x}}{4}$

Rewrite using exponents.

Example: $\sqrt[3]{x^4}$ Solution: $\sqrt[3]{x^4} = (x^4)^{\frac{1}{3}} = x^{(4 \bullet \frac{1}{3})} = x^{\frac{4}{3}}$

20. $\sqrt[6]{x^5}$

21. $\sqrt{2}$

22. $\sqrt{11^3}$

23. $\sqrt[4]{13^3}$

Answer each of the following questions.

Example: The square root of a number is 5. What is the number?
Solution: $\sqrt{x} = 5 \qquad x = 5^2 = 25$

24. The square root of a number is 15. What is the number?

25. The volume of a cylinder is 240 cubic units. The height of the cylinder is 5 units. What is the radius? (Use $V = \pi r^2 h$, $\pi \approx 3$.)

26. The square root of a number is $16y^2$. What is the number?

27. The area of a circle is 243 square units. What is the approximate radius of the circle? (Use $A = \pi r^2$, $\pi \approx 3$.)

28. The area of a square is 810 units. What is the length of a side of the square? Can you find the exact length of the side? Explain.

Make and use a square root graph to approximate the following square roots. Label the x-axis with these values of x: $0, \frac{1}{2}, 1, 1\frac{1}{2}$, and so on to 10. Label the y-axis with the squares of the x values: $0, \frac{1}{4}, 1, 2.25, 4, 6.25$, and so on to 100. Find and label the ordered pairs $(0, 0)$, $(\frac{1}{2}, \frac{1}{4})$ $(1, 1)$, and so on to $(10, 100)$.

29. $\sqrt{40}$

30. $\sqrt{85}$

Test-Taking Tip

When you read decimal numbers, get in the habit of reading them as mathematical language. For example, read 0.61 as "sixty-one hundredths" instead of "point 61."

Chapter

Geometry

Skyscrapers can provide geometry lessons about shapes, angles, and intersecting lines. The ancient Greeks believed everything in the universe was made from five basic shapes, called the "Platonic solids." They built a special rectangle called the Golden Section. The sides of this "golden" rectangle had a ratio of 1:1.6. The Greeks used this special rectangle in the Parthenon and other buildings. People thought it was pleasing to look at. Architects still use this 1:1.6 ratio for modern buildings. Architects use angles and lines to make pleasing geometric shapes a part of their buildings.

In Chapter 12, you will relate algebra to geometry.

Goals for Learning

- To name and determine the measure of angles
- To identify how lines are related in planes and space
- To use theorems to help solve problems involving triangles
- To name triangles by their characteristics
- To determine the measures of angles in quadrilaterals
- To use theorems to determine whether triangles are congruent or similar
- To use trigonometric ratios to solve problems

Lesson 1 Angles and Angle Measure

Ray
A set of points that is part of a line. It has one endpoint and extends infinitely in one direction.

Angle
A geometric figure made up of two rays with a common endpoint called a vertex

Vertex
A point common to both sides of an angle

Adjacent angle
An angle that shares a vertex and a common side with another angle

Geometric figures exist in many shapes and sizes. Two such figures are rays and angles. A **ray** is a set of points that is a part of a line. It has one endpoint and extends infinitely in one direction. An **angle** is a geometric figure formed by two rays that share a common endpoint called the **vertex.**

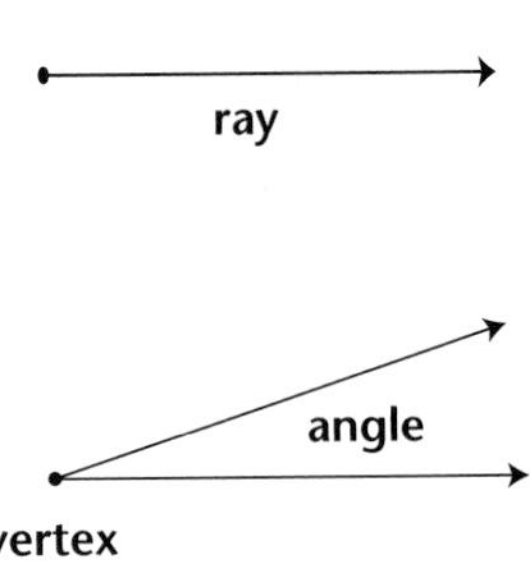

The symbol ∠ is used to designate an angle. Any angle can be read or named two ways. The angle at the right can be named $\angle ABC$ or $\angle CBA$. Note that the vertex, *B*, is always the middle letter.

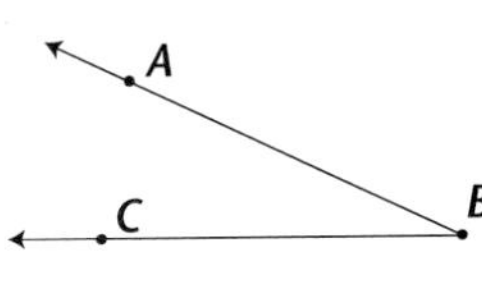

Angles are sometimes named by one letter or number.

$\angle 1$ and $\angle 2$ $\angle a$ and $\angle b$

The basic unit of angle measure is the degree (°).

The measure of an angle is used to classify angles.

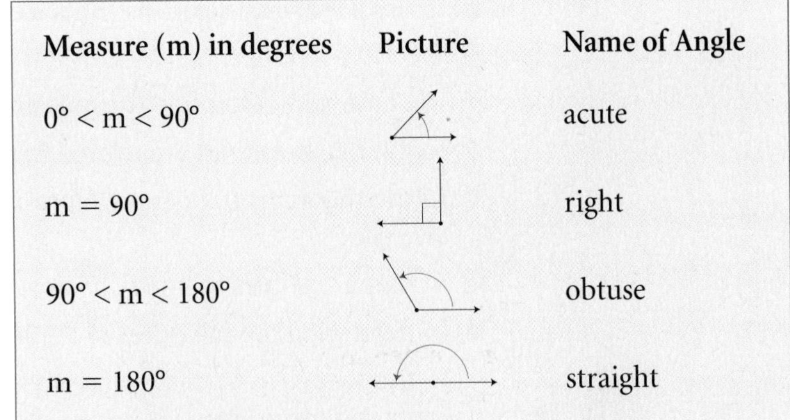

Measure (m) in degrees	Picture	Name of Angle
$0° < m < 90°$		acute
$m = 90°$		right
$90° < m < 180°$		obtuse
$m = 180°$		straight

Angles that share a common vertex and a common side are called **adjacent angles.**

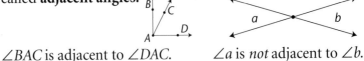

$\angle BAC$ is adjacent to $\angle DAC$. $\angle a$ is *not* adjacent to $\angle b$.

Vertical angles are opposite pairs of angles formed when two lines intersect.

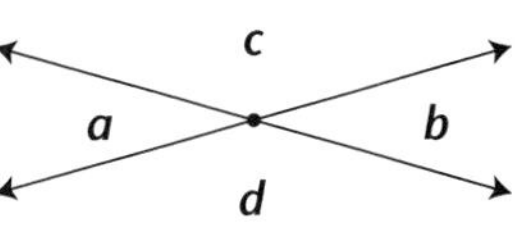

$\angle a$ and $\angle b$ are vertical angles. $\angle c$ and $\angle d$ are vertical angles.

It is possible to compute angle measures.

Vertical angles

Pairs of opposite angles formed by intersecting lines. Vertical angles have the same measure.

Complementary angles

Two angles whose sum of their measures is 90°

EXAMPLE 1 Given $m\angle a = 20°$, find the measure (m) of $\angle b$, $\angle c$, and $\angle d$.

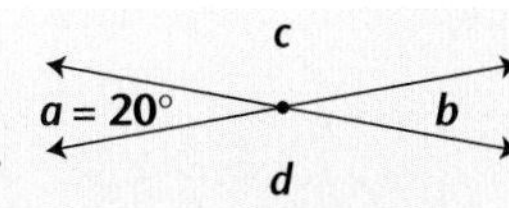

Step 1 Find the measure of $\angle c$. Recall that the measure of a straight angle is 180°. Since $\angle a$ and $\angle c$ are adjacent and form a straight angle, $m\angle a + m\angle c = 180°$.

$20° + m\angle c = 180°$
$m\angle c = 180° - 20°$
$m\angle c = 160°$

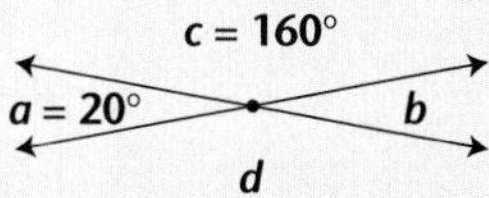

The measure of a circle is 360°.
The measure of a straight line is 180°.

Step 2 Find the measure of $\angle d$. Since $\angle a$ and $\angle d$ are adjacent and form a straight angle, $m\angle a + m\angle d = 180°$.

$20° + m\angle d = 180°$
$m\angle d = 180° - 20°$
$m\angle d = 160°$

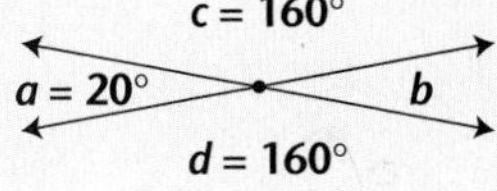

Step 3 Find the measure of $\angle b$. Since $\angle d$ and $\angle b$ are adjacent and form a straight angle, $m\angle d + m\angle b = 180°$.

$160° + m\angle b = 180°$
$m\angle b = 180° - 160°$
$m\angle b = 20°$

c = 160°
a = 20°
b = 20°
d = 160°

Recall that $\angle a$ and $\angle b$ are vertical angles. So are $\angle c$ and $\angle d$. Vertical angles have the same measure.

If the sum of the measures of two angles is 90°, the angles are **complementary angles**. Angles do not have to be adjacent to be complementary.

Examples of Complementary Angles

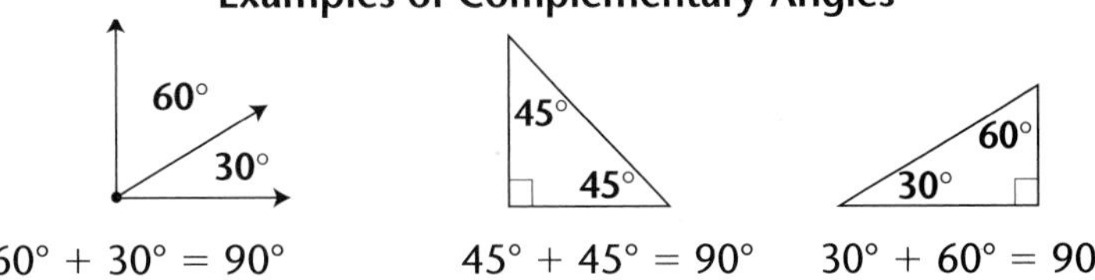

$60° + 30° = 90°$ $45° + 45° = 90°$ $30° + 60° = 90°$

EXAMPLE 2 Suppose that the measure of one complementary angle is five times greater than the measure of the other. What is the measure of each angle?

Step 1 Let $x =$ the measure of the lesser angle.

Let $5x =$ the measure of the greater angle.

Step 2 Since the sum of the measures of complementary angles is 90°, use the equation $x + 5x = 90°$ and solve for x.

$x + 5x = 90°$

$6x = 90°$

$x = 15°$

Since $x = 15°$, $5x = 5(15°)$ or 75°. The angles measure 15° and 75°.

Step 3 Check. $15° + 75° = 90°$

Supplementary angles

Two angles whose sum of their measures is 180°

If the sum of the measures of two angles is 180°, the angles are **supplementary angles.** Angles do not have to be adjacent to be supplementary.

Examples of Supplementary Angles

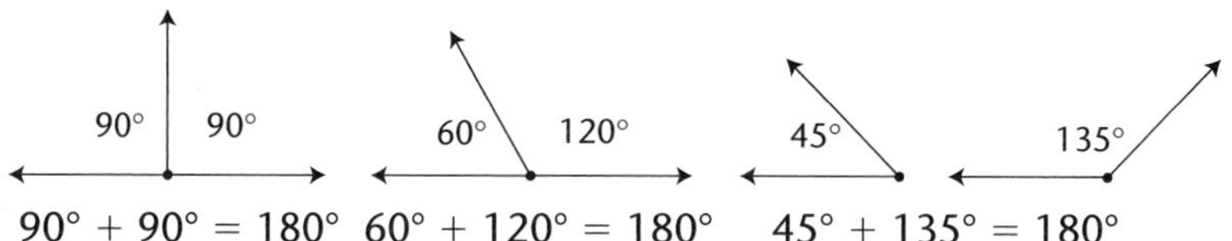

$90° + 90° = 180°$ $60° + 120° = 180°$ $45° + 135° = 180°$

EXAMPLE 3 Suppose that the measure of one supplementary angle is $3\frac{1}{2}$ times greater than the measure of the other. What is the measure of each angle?

Step 1 Let $x =$ the measure of the lesser angle.

Let $3\frac{1}{2}x =$ the measure of the greater angle.

Step 2 Since the sum of the measures of supplementary angles is 180°, use the equation $x + 3\frac{1}{2}x = 180°$ and solve for x.

$x + 3\frac{1}{2}x = 180°$

$4\frac{1}{2}x = 180°$

$\frac{9}{2}x = 180°$

$x = 180°(\frac{2}{9})$

$x = (\frac{360°}{9})$

$x = 40°$

Since $x = 40°$, $3\frac{1}{2}(40°) = 140°$. The angles measure 40° and 140°.

Step 3 Check. $40° + 140° = 180°$

Writing About Mathematics

A square contains four right angles. Make a list of the different pairs of supplementary angles that can be formed. Explain how you know you have listed all such pairs.

Exercise A Classify each angle. Write *acute, right, obtuse,* or *straight.*

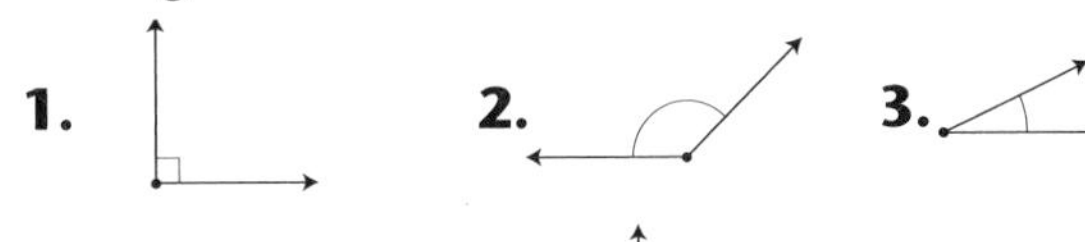

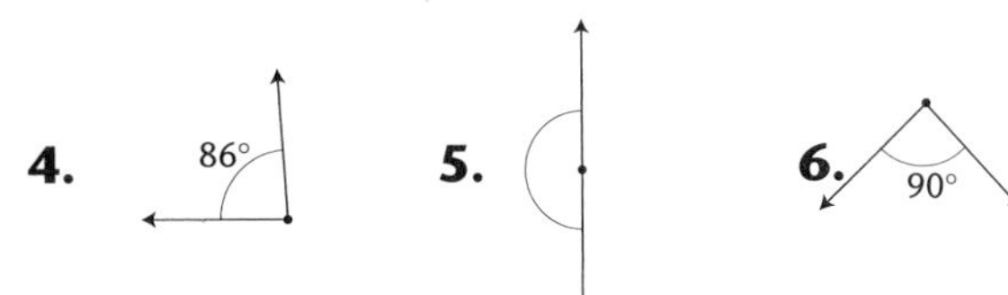

Exercise B Classify each pair of angles using the figure at the right. Write *vertical* or *adjacent.*

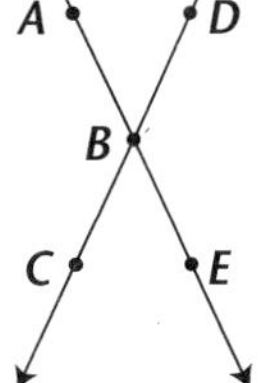

7. $\angle ABC$ and $\angle CBE$

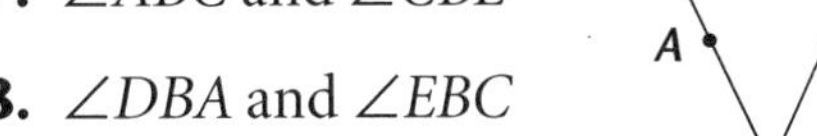

8. $\angle DBA$ and $\angle EBC$

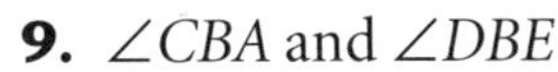

9. $\angle CBA$ and $\angle DBE$

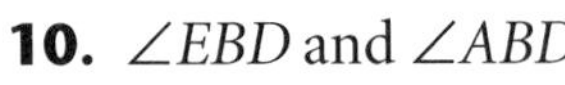

10. $\angle EBD$ and $\angle ABD$

Exercise C Use the figure at the right.

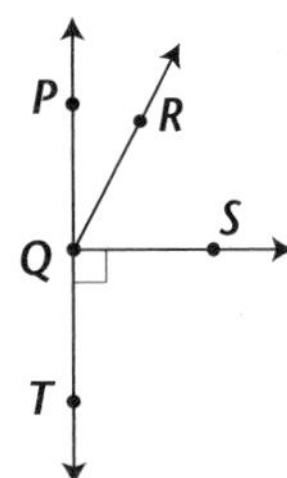

11. Which angles are complementary?

12. Which angles are supplementary?

Exercise D Answer each question.

13. The measure of one supplementary angle is 2 times greater than the measure of the other. What is the measure of each angle?

14. The measure of one complementary angle is 3 times greater than the measure of the other. What is the measure of each angle?

15. The measure of one complementary angle is $\frac{1}{4}$ as large as the measure of the other. What is the measure of each angle?

Technology Connection

Computer-Generated Tessellations

Have you seen the art of M. C. Escher? He is famous for his tessellations. Tessellations are repeating geometric forms in interesting patterns. Computer drawing programs let you make your own tessellations. Select a pattern. Then copy and paste your pattern, fitting it next to your original like pieces of a jigsaw puzzle. For some examples, type "computer-generated tessellations" into an Internet search engine. While you're at it, see if you can find some examples of M. C. Escher's art.

Lesson 2 Pairs of Lines in a Plane and in Space

Plane

A two-dimensional flat surface

Transversal

A line that intersects two or more lines

A **plane** can be thought of as a two-dimensional flat surface. Pairs of lines in a plane can exist in two different ways.

Lines in a Plane

Intersecting lines in a plane meet at exactly one point *P*.

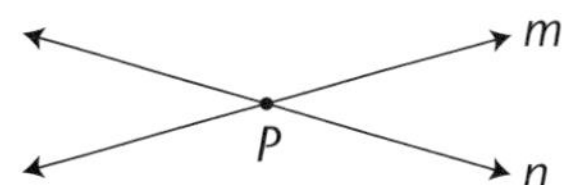

Parallel lines in a plane never meet or intersect.

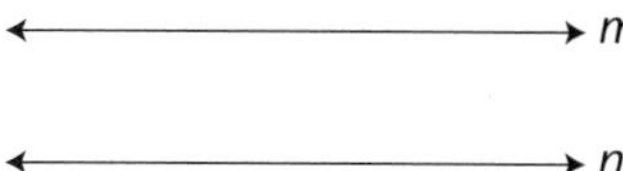

The symbol for parallel is $||$; $m||n$ is read "*m* is parallel to *n*."

Space is three-dimensional. Pairs of lines in space can exist in three different ways.

Lines in Space

Intersecting lines form a plane and meet in that plane.

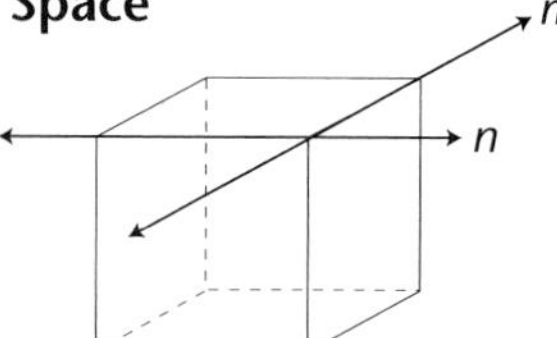

Parallel lines form a plane and do not meet.

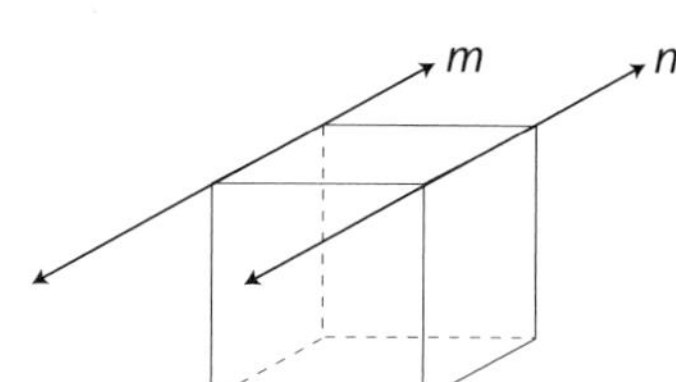

Skew lines are not parallel and do not intersect. Skew lines do not determine a plane.

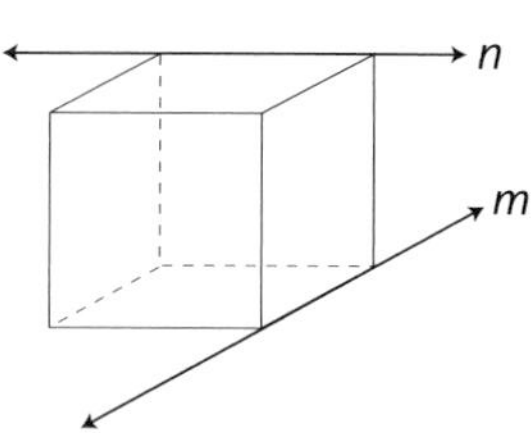

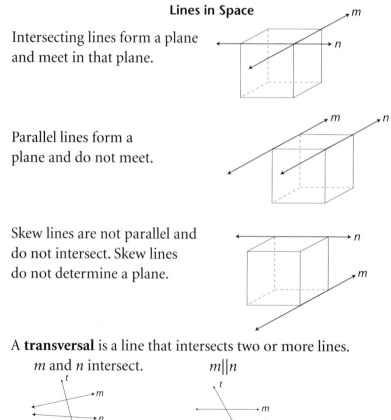

A **transversal** is a line that intersects two or more lines.

m and *n* intersect.

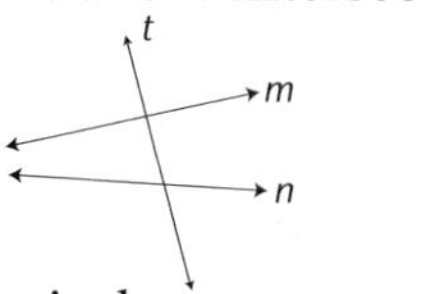

t is the transversal.

$m||n$

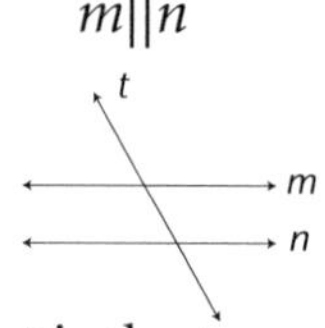

t is the transversal.

Exterior angles

Angles that are formed outside two lines cut by a transversal

Interior angles

Angles that are formed inside, or between, two lines cut by a transversal

Corresponding angles

Interior and exterior angles on the same side of a transversal cutting through parallel lines

Theorem

A statement that can be proven

Angles formed by transversals have special names.

Exterior angles are those angles outside lines cut by a transversal.

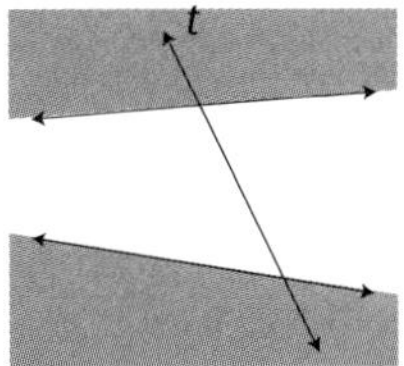

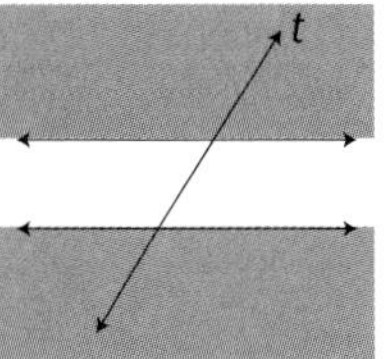

Interior angles are those angles inside, or between, lines cut by a transversal.

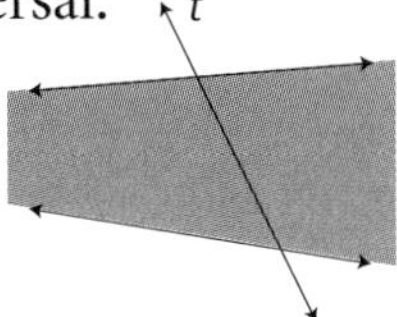

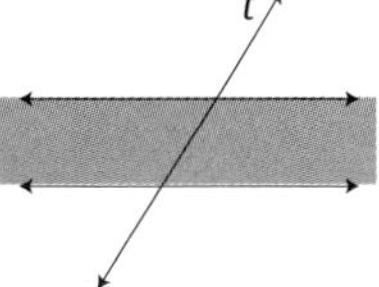

When parallel lines are cut by a transversal, certain angles will always be equal and others supplementary. Here is an example of $l \| m$, t is the transversal.

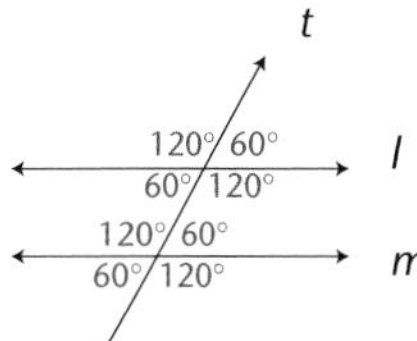

Alternate interior angles are equal:

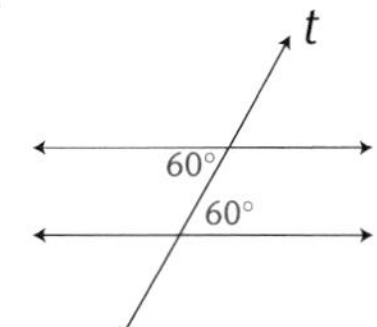

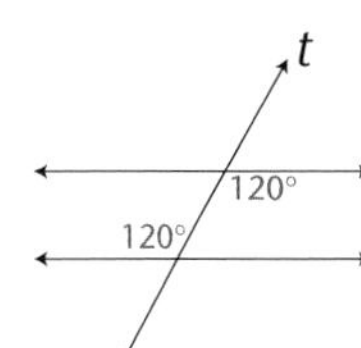

Interior angles on the same side of the transversal are supplementary:

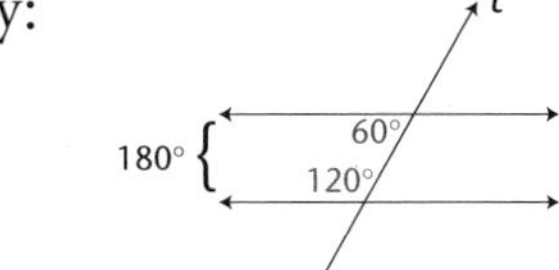

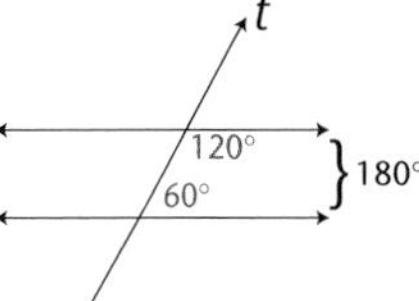

Corresponding angles are equal:

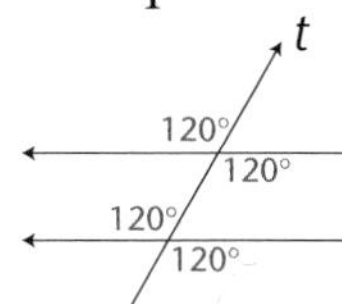

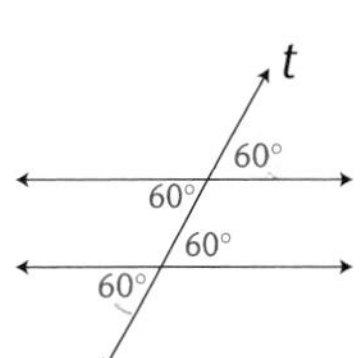

Each fact illustrated here is a **theorem** from geometry. This means these angles are always equal or supplementary as long as they are in the positions as shown in the diagrams.

In this figure, $p \parallel q$ and t is a transversal.

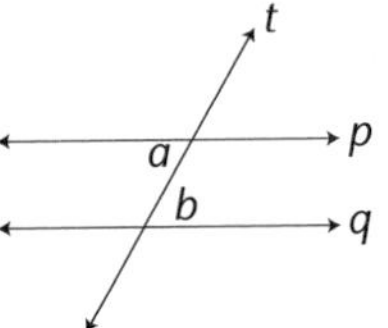

If you would measure $\angle a$ and $\angle b$, you would find that $m\angle a = m\angle b$. $\angle a$ and $\angle b$ are alternate interior angles. Whenever a transversal cuts two parallel lines, the alternate interior angles that are formed are equal.

EXAMPLE 1 In the following figure, $p \parallel q$ and $m\angle a = 30°$. Find $m\angle b$, $m\angle c$, and $m\angle d$.

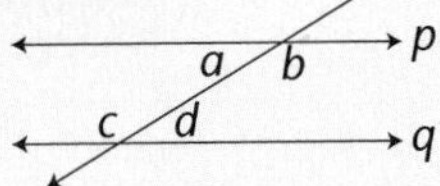

Step 1 If $p \parallel q$ and t is a transversal, then $m\angle a = m\angle d$ and $m\angle b = m\angle c$. This statement is true because it is a theorem from geometry.

Step 2 Since $m\angle a = 30°$, $m\angle d = 30°$ because alternate interior angles have the same measure.

Step 3 Recognize that $\angle a$ and $\angle b$ are supplementary angles because they form a straight line. Find $m\angle b$.

$m\angle a + m\angle b = 180°$
$30° + m\angle b = 180°$
$m\angle b = 180° - 30°$
$m\angle b = 150°$

Step 4 Since $m\angle b = 150°$, $m\angle c = 150°$ because alternate interior angles have the same measure.

In this figure, $p \parallel q$ and t is a transversal.

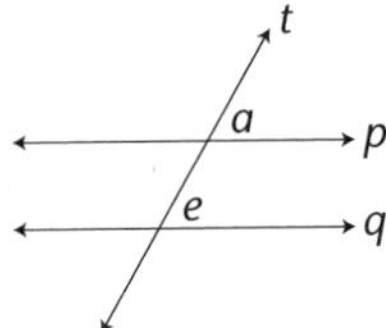

If you would measure $\angle a$ and $\angle e$, you would find that $m\angle a = m\angle e$. $\angle a$ and $\angle e$ are corresponding angles. Whenever a transversal cuts two parallel lines, the corresponding angles that are formed on the same side of the transversal are equal.

Exercise A Identify the lines shown in each figure. Write *intersecting*, *parallel*, or *skew*.

1. 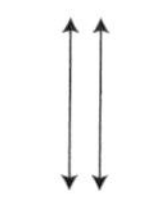

2. 

3. 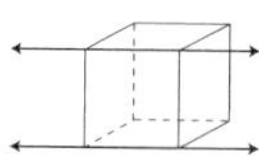

4. 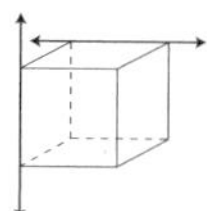

5. 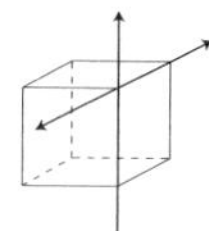

6. 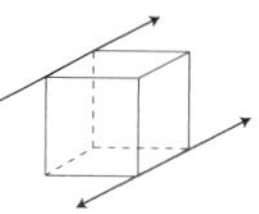

Exercise B Identify the angles shown in this figure. Write *interior* or *exterior*.

7. $\angle 1$

8. $\angle 7$

9. $\angle 4$

10. $\angle 3$

11. $\angle 8$

12. $\angle 5$

13. $\angle 2$

14. $\angle 6$

Exercise C In this figure, $p \| q$ and t is a transversal. Identify the following pairs of angles. Write *supplementary, alternate interior,* or *corresponding*.

15. $\angle e$ and $\angle f$

16. $\angle d$ and $\angle h$

17. $\angle b$ and $\angle g$

18. $\angle d$ and $\angle f$

19. $\angle d$ and $\angle e$

20. $\angle b$ and $\angle f$

21. $\angle b$ and $\angle c$

22. $\angle e$ and $\angle c$

23. $\angle a$ and $\angle e$

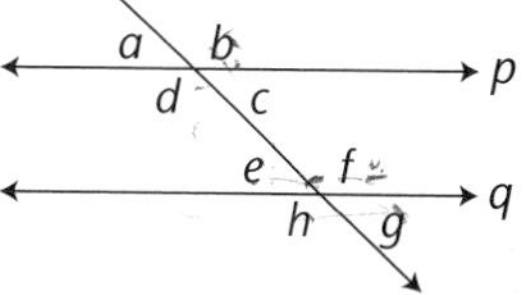

Exercise D In this figure, $p \| q$, t is a transversal, and $m\angle h = 72°$. Find the measure (m) of each of the following angles.

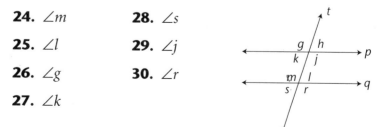

24. $\angle m$

25. $\angle l$

26. $\angle g$

27. $\angle k$

28. $\angle s$

29. $\angle j$

30. $\angle r$

Lesson 3 Angle Measures in a Triangle

Any triangle is made up of three sides and three angles. The sides and angles of triangles share relationships that can be proven. For example, one way to discover the sum of the measures of the angles in any triangle is to do this experiment.

1. Draw any triangle.

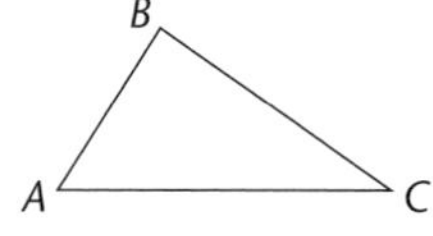

2. Using scissors, cut off each angle of the triangle.

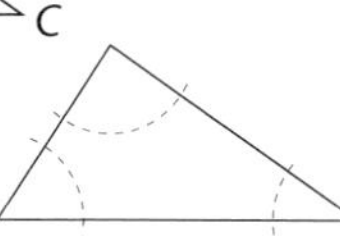

3. Place the angles adjacent to each other along a straight line.

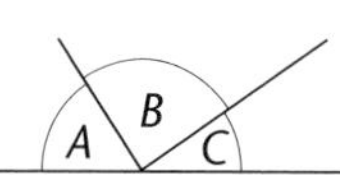

Since the exterior sides of the angles form a supplementary angle and the measure of a supplementary angle is 180°,

$m\angle A + m\angle B + m\angle C = 180°$.

You can also prove this as a theorem. This is an example of a proof.

EXAMPLE 1 **Theorem:** The sum of the measures of the angles in any triangle is 180°.

Prove $m\angle A + m\angle B + m\angle C$ in $\triangle ABC = 180°$.

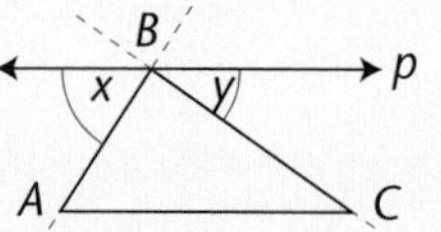

Step 1 $\triangle ABC$ is a triangle. Given.

Step 2 Draw Line $p \| AC$ through Point B. By construction.

Step 3 AB is a transversal of p and AC, so $m\angle x = m\angle A$ because alternate interior angles are equal.

Step 4 BC is a transversal of p and AC, so $m\angle y = m\angle C$ because alternate interior angles are equal.

Step 5 $\angle x + \angle B + \angle y$ are adjacent and form a straight angle. Since the measure of a straight angle is 180°, $m\angle x + m\angle B + m\angle y = 180°$ and by substitution $m\angle A + m\angle B + m\angle C = 180°$.

You can use this angle-sum theorem to solve problems like the following example.

EXAMPLE 2 One angle in a triangle measures 60°. Another measures 85°. What is the measure of the third angle?

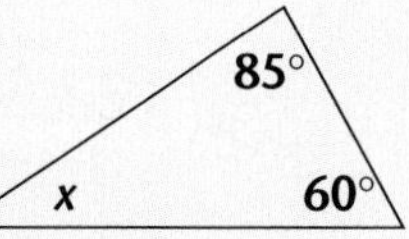

Step 1 Since the sum of the measures of the angles in any triangle is 180°, $x + 60° + 85° = 180°$.

Step 2 Solve $x + 60° + 85° = 180°$ for x.

$$x + 60° + 85° = 180°$$
$$x = 180° - 60° - 85°$$
$$x = 35°$$

Step 3 Check.

$$\begin{array}{r} 60° \\ 85° \\ +\ 35° \\ \hline 180° \end{array}$$

Other relationships exist in any triangle. For example, an exterior angle of a triangle is formed by extending one side of a triangle at any vertex.

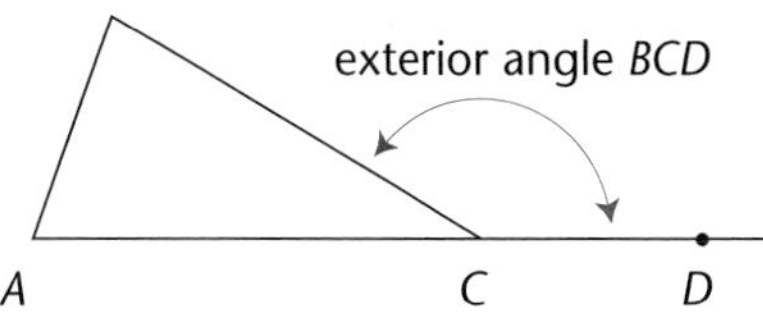

$\angle BCD$ is an exterior angle.

Any exterior angle of a triangle is supplementary to the adjacent interior angle.

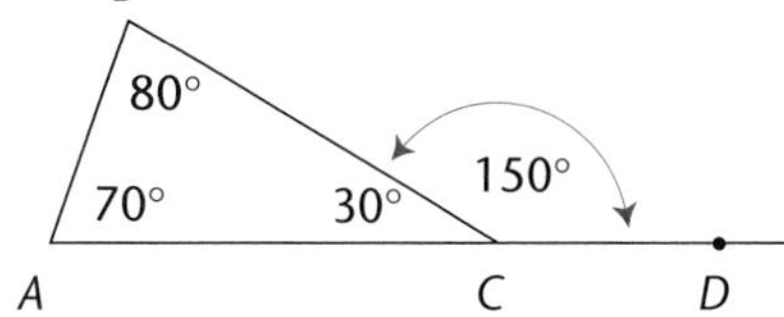

$\angle BCA$ is supplementary to $\angle BCD$, so

$$m\angle BCA + m\angle BCD = 180°$$
$$30° + m\angle BCD = 180°$$
$$m\angle BCD = 180° - 30°$$
$$m\angle BCD = 150°$$

In this example, note that the sum $m\angle A + m\angle B$ is equal to $m\angle BCD$. In other words, the sum of the measures of the two non-adjacent interior angles in any triangle is equal to the measure of the exterior angle.

Here is another example of a proof.

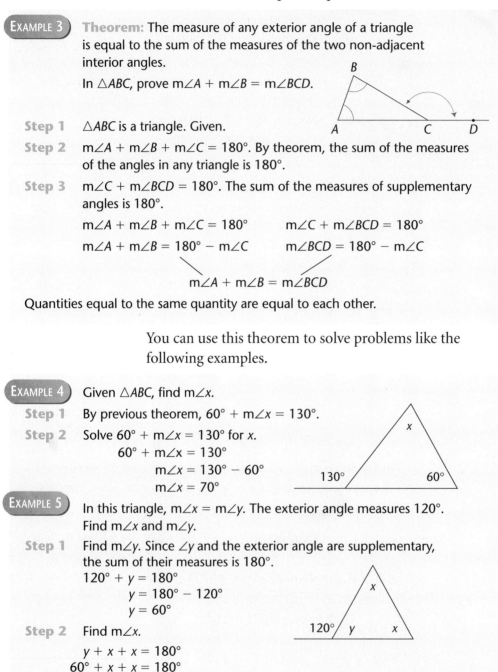

Example 3 **Theorem:** The measure of any exterior angle of a triangle is equal to the sum of the measures of the two non-adjacent interior angles.

In $\triangle ABC$, prove $m\angle A + m\angle B = m\angle BCD$.

Step 1 $\triangle ABC$ is a triangle. Given.

Step 2 $m\angle A + m\angle B + m\angle C = 180°$. By theorem, the sum of the measures of the angles in any triangle is 180°.

Step 3 $m\angle C + m\angle BCD = 180°$. The sum of the measures of supplementary angles is 180°.

$$m\angle A + m\angle B + m\angle C = 180° \qquad m\angle C + m\angle BCD = 180°$$

$$m\angle A + m\angle B = 180° - m\angle C \qquad m\angle BCD = 180° - m\angle C$$

$$m\angle A + m\angle B = m\angle BCD$$

Quantities equal to the same quantity are equal to each other.

You can use this theorem to solve problems like the following examples.

Example 4 Given $\triangle ABC$, find $m\angle x$.

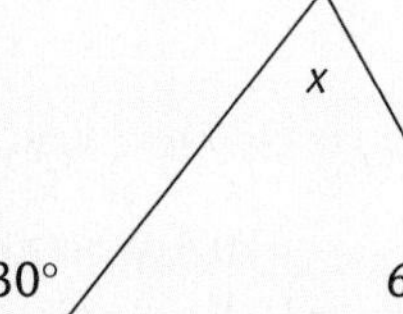

Step 1 By previous theorem, $60° + m\angle x = 130°$.

Step 2 Solve $60° + m\angle x = 130°$ for x.

$$60° + m\angle x = 130°$$
$$m\angle x = 130° - 60°$$
$$m\angle x = 70°$$

Example 5 In this triangle, $m\angle x = m\angle y$. The exterior angle measures 120°. Find $m\angle x$ and $m\angle y$.

Step 1 Find $m\angle y$. Since $\angle y$ and the exterior angle are supplementary, the sum of their measures is 180°.

$$120° + y = 180°$$
$$y = 180° - 120°$$
$$y = 60°$$

Step 2 Find $m\angle x$.

$$y + x + x = 180°$$
$$60° + x + x = 180°$$
$$x + x = 180° - 60°$$
$$2x = 120°$$
$$x = 60°$$

Step 3 Check. $60° + 60° + 60° = 180°$

Exercise A Find m$\angle x$.

1. 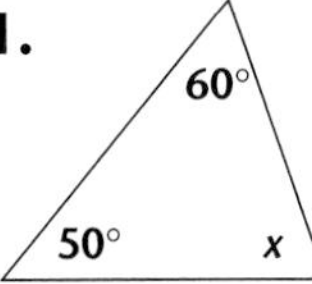

2. 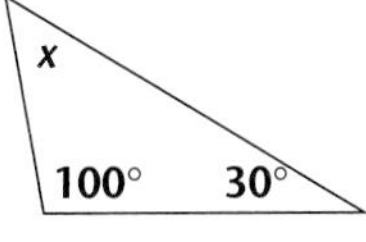

3. 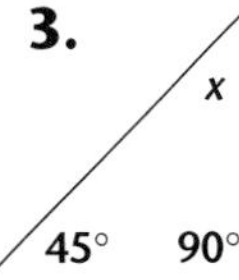

4. 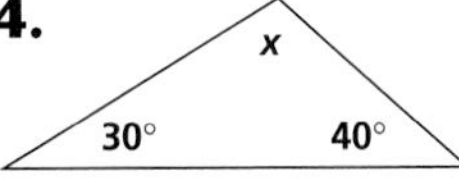

5. 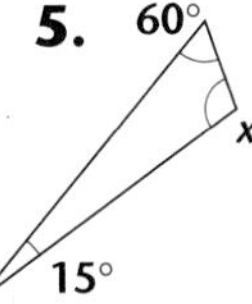

Exercise B Find m$\angle y$.

6. 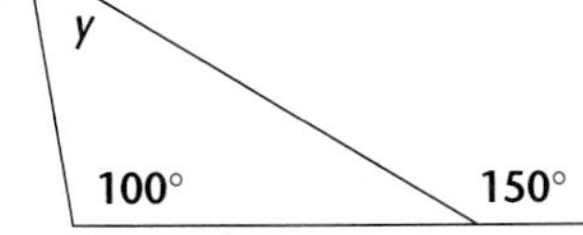

7. 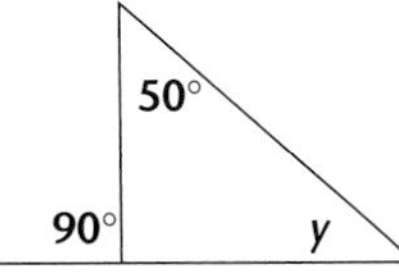

8. 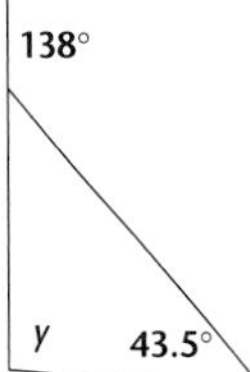

9. 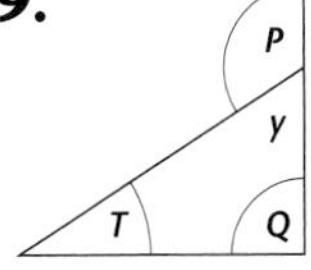

Exercise C Answer this question.

10. If the sum of the measures of the angles in any triangle is 180°, what is the sum of the measures of the angles in any four-sided figure? Give a reason for your answer.

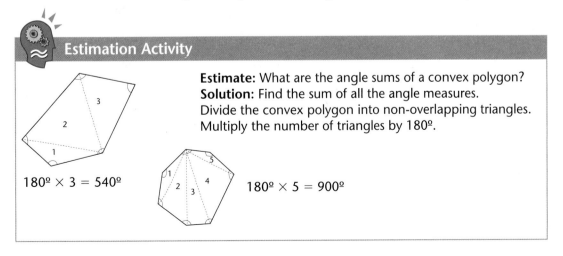

Estimation Activity

Estimate: What are the angle sums of a convex polygon?
Solution: Find the sum of all the angle measures.
Divide the convex polygon into non-overlapping triangles.
Multiply the number of triangles by 180º.

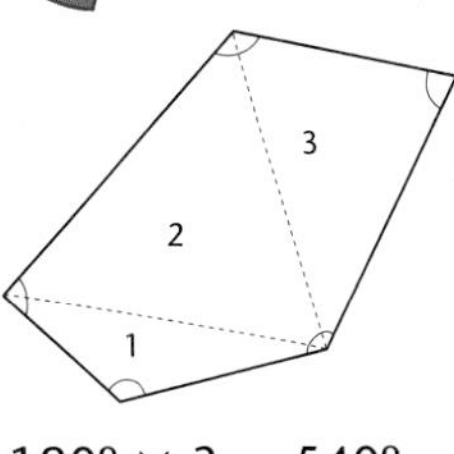

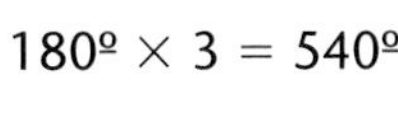

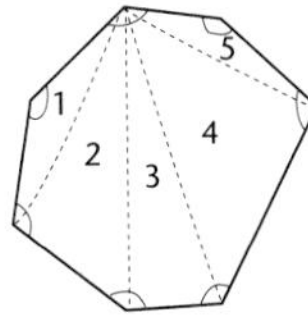

180º × 5 = 900º

Lesson 4 Naming Triangles

Acute triangle

A triangle with three acute angles

Equiangular triangle

A triangle with three angles, each measuring 60°

Obtuse triangle

A triangle with one obtuse angle

Scalene triangle

A triangle with no equal sides

Isosceles triangle

A triangle with two sides of equal length

Lines may be used to mark the sides of a figure. A single line represents one side length, double lines another, and triple lines a third. For example, a triangle that has a single line marking each side has three sides of equal length.

Triangles are named by their angles and by their sides.

Triangles Named by Their Angles

Acute

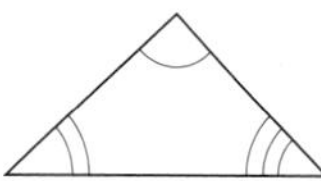

Each angle of an **acute triangle** measures less than 90°.

Equiangular

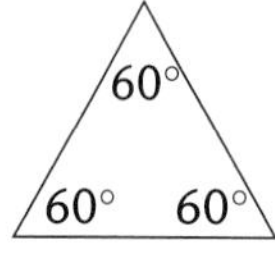

All of the angles of an **equiangular triangle** measure 60°.

Obtuse

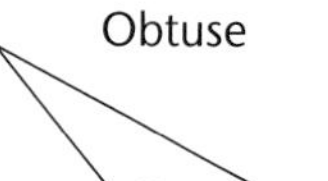

One angle of an **obtuse triangle** measures more than 90°.

Right

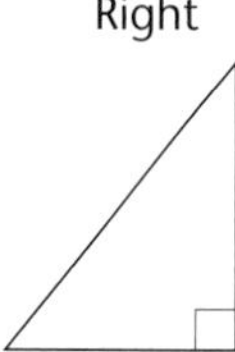

One angle of a right triangle measures 90°.

Triangles Named by Their Sides

Scalene

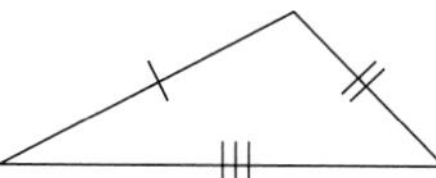

Each side of a **scalene triangle** is a different length.

Isosceles

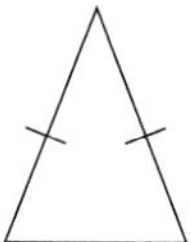

Two sides of an **isosceles triangle** have the same length.

Equilateral

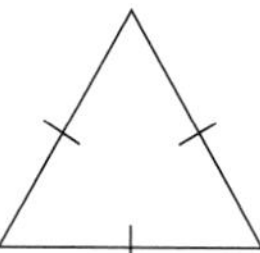

All of the sides of an equilateral triangle have the same length.

Arcs are used like lines to show angles. On a triangle that has two angles marked with a single arc, those two angles are of equal measure.

You can use these characteristics of triangles to name triangles.

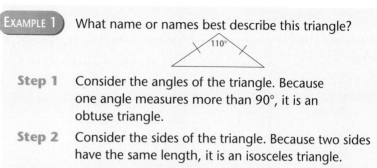

EXAMPLE 1 What name or names best describe this triangle?

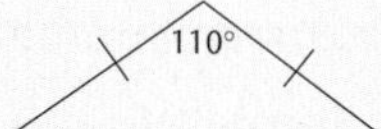

Step 1 Consider the angles of the triangle. Because one angle measures more than 90°, it is an obtuse triangle.

Step 2 Consider the sides of the triangle. Because two sides have the same length, it is an isosceles triangle.

Step 3 Name the triangle: The triangle is *obtuse isosceles*.

TRY THIS

Find triangles used as graphs, illustrations, or decorations in newspapers and magazines. Measure the lengths of the sides and use lines to compare the sides of each triangle. Name the triangles by the lengths of their sides.

Exercise A Name each triangle.

1. 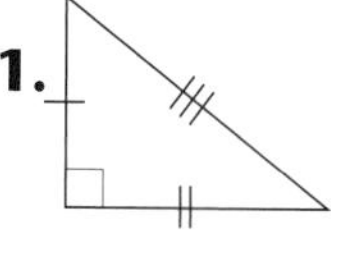

2.

3. 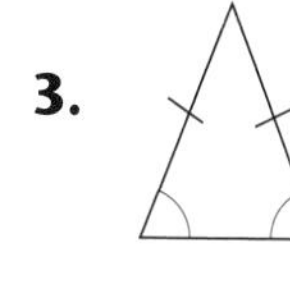

4. 

5. 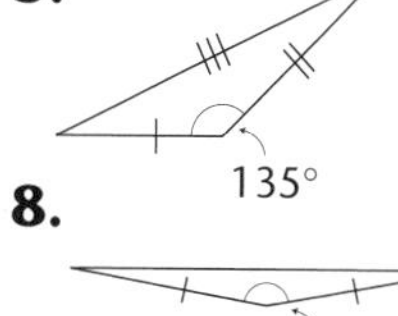

6. 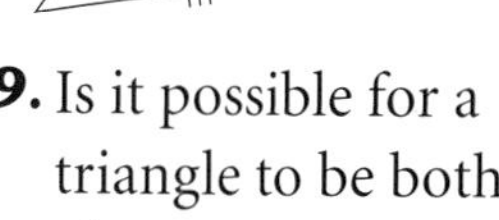

7.

8.

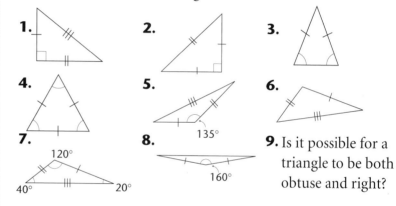

9. Is it possible for a triangle to be both obtuse and right?

PROBLEM SOLVING

Exercise B In this figure, a televison antenna is attached to the top of a rigid mast. The mast is attached to the roof of a home. Guy wires help prevent the mast and antenna from flowing over.

Determine the following angle measures.

10. m∠ b

11. m∠ w

12. m∠ y

13. m∠ c

14. m∠ x

15. m∠ z

In the figure, m∠ a = 60°, m∠ b = m∠ c, m∠ y = m∠ z, and $\frac{1}{2}$m∠ y = m∠ w

Lesson 5 Quadrilaterals

Parallelogram
A four-sided polygon with two pairs of equal and parallel sides

Trapezoid
A four-sided polygon with one pair of parallel sides and one pair of sides that are not parallel

Rectangle
A four-sided polygon with four right angles and the opposite sides equal

Square
A polygon with four equal sides and four right angles

Rhombus
A four-sided polygon with four parallel sides the same length

Quadrilaterals are polygons. In general, a quadrilateral has four sides, four angles, and two diagonals. The sum of the angle measures in any quadrilateral is 360°. This is shown by the fact that a triangle has 180° and two triangles make up every quadrilateral.

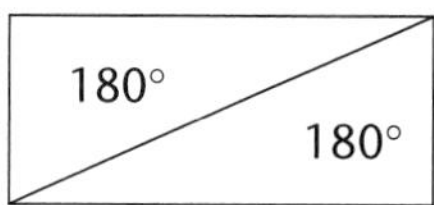

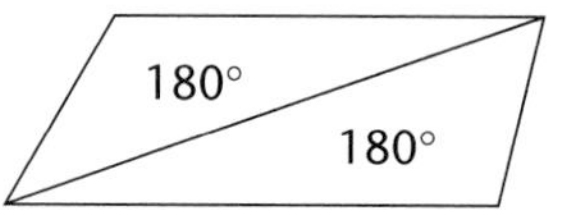

Quadrilaterals have special names.

Parallelogram

A quadrilateral with both pairs of opposite sides the same length and parallel

Rectangle

A parallelogram with four right angles

Square

A rectangle with all sides the same length

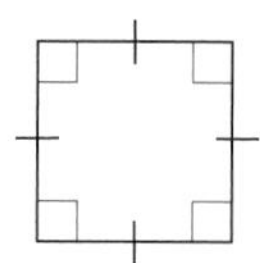

Rhombus

A parallelogram with all sides the same length

Trapezoid

A quadrilateral with only one pair of parallel sides

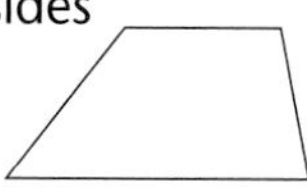

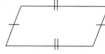

Right trapezoid

A quadrilateral with one pair of parallel sides and two right angles

Isosceles trapezoid

A quadrilateral with one pair of parallel sides and two sides the same length

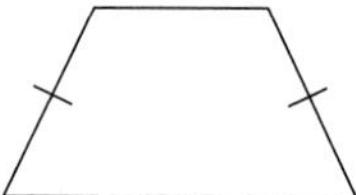

The angle measures of a quadrilateral can be computed.

EXAMPLE 1 In parallelogram *ABCD*, $m\angle A = 70°$.

Find $m\angle B$, $m\angle C$, and $m\angle D$.

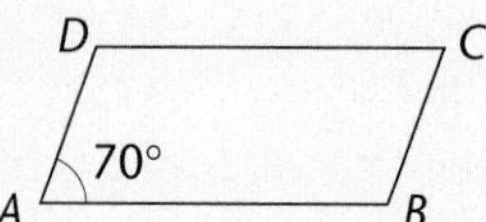

EXAMPLE 1 *(continued)*

Step 1 Because $\overline{AB} \| \overline{CD}$, $\angle A$ and $\angle D$ are supplementary. Find $m\angle D$.

$$\begin{aligned} m\angle A + m\angle D &= 180° \\ 70° + m\angle D &= 180° \\ m\angle D &= 180° - 70° \\ m\angle D &= 110° \end{aligned}$$

Step 2 Because $\overline{AD} \| \overline{BC}$, $\angle C$ and $\angle D$ are supplementary. Find $m\angle C$.

$$\begin{aligned} m\angle C + m\angle D &= 180° \\ m\angle C + 110° &= 180° \\ m\angle C &= 180° - 110° \\ m\angle C &= 70° \end{aligned}$$

Step 3 Because $\overline{AB} \| \overline{CD}$, $\angle B$ and $\angle C$ are supplementary. Find $m\angle B$.

$$\begin{aligned} m\angle B + m\angle C &= 180° \\ m\angle B + 70° &= 180° \\ m\angle B &= 180° - 70° \\ m\angle B &= 110° \end{aligned}$$

Exercise A Find the measures of the angles.

1. In right trapezoid $ABCD$, $\overline{AB} \| \overline{DC}$. Find $m\angle D$ and $m\angle C$.

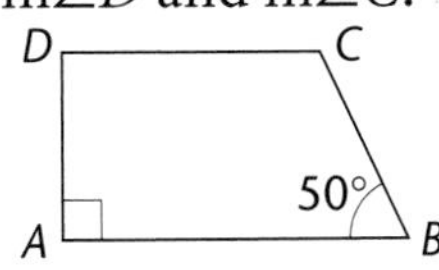

2. In rhombus $ABCD$, $\overline{AB} \| \overline{CD}$, $\overline{BC} \| \overline{AD}$, and $m\angle B = 142°$. Find $m\angle A$, $m\angle C$, and $m\angle D$.

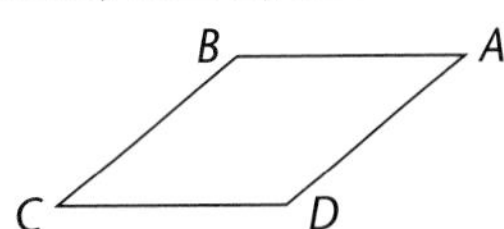

Exercise B Draw each figure on graph paper. Then compute the measure of each unknown angle.

3. Draw rectangle $ABCD$. Draw each diagonal of the rectangle. What is the sum of the measures of the angles that are formed at the intersection of the diagonals?

4. Draw square $ABCD$. Draw each diagonal of the square. What is the measure of each angle that is formed at the intersection of the diagonals?

5. Draw a quadrilateral that has one pair of parallel sides and no sides the same length.

Lesson 6 Congruent and Similar Triangles

Congruent

Figures that have the same size and shape

Figures that have exactly the same size and shape are **congruent.** The symbol for *congruent* is $\cong$. $\triangle ABC \cong \triangle DEF$ is read "Triangle *ABC* is congruent to triangle *DEF*."

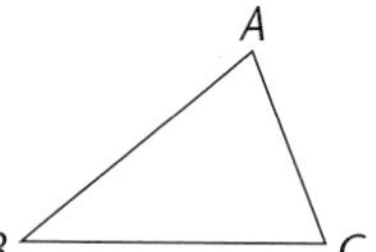

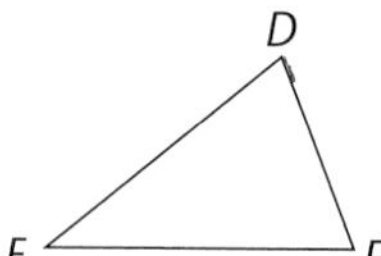

A diagonal divides each of these quadrilaterals into two triangles. Two triangles are congruent if their corresponding sides and angles are equal.

square

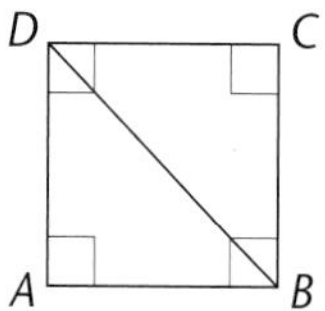

$\triangle ABD \cong \triangle CBD$.
If you fold the square along the diagonal, the triangles would match exactly.

rectangle

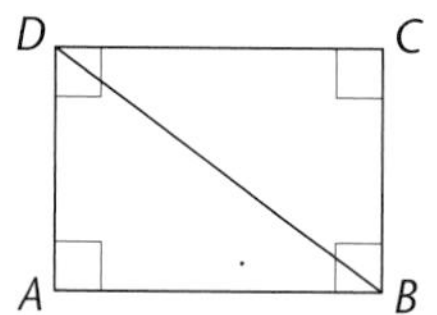

$\triangle ABD \cong \triangle CDB$.
If you cut along the diagonal and make two triangles, one triangle could be moved and placed exactly on top of the other.

right trapezoid

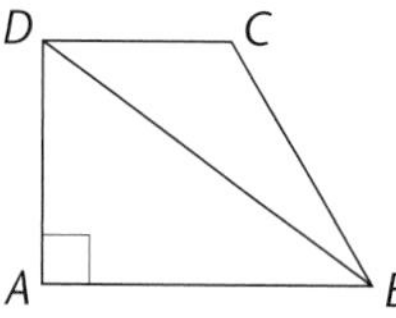

$\triangle ABD$ and $\triangle CBD$ are not congruent.
$\triangle ABD \ncong \triangle CBD$.
$\triangle ABD$ is a right triangle.
$\triangle CBD$ is not a right triangle.

Three theorems can help you determine whether two triangles are congruent.

The Side-Angle-Side Theorem (SAS)

If two sides and the included angle of two triangles are equal, then the triangles are congruent.

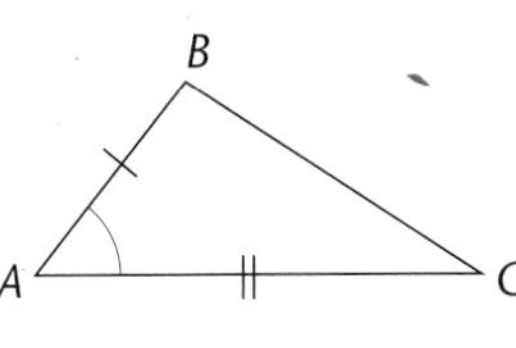

$$\overline{AB} = \overline{DE}$$
$$\overline{AC} = \overline{DF}$$
$$m\angle A = m\angle D$$
$$\downarrow$$
$$\triangle ABC \cong \triangle DEF$$

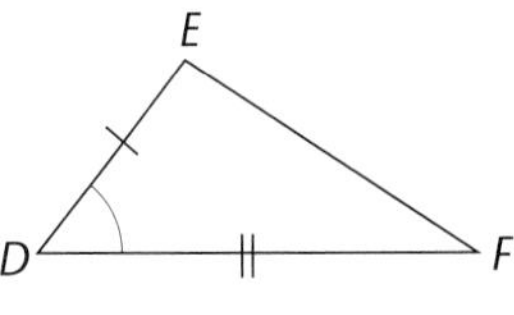

The Side-Side-Side Theorem (SSS)

If the corresponding sides of two triangles are equal, then the triangles are congruent.

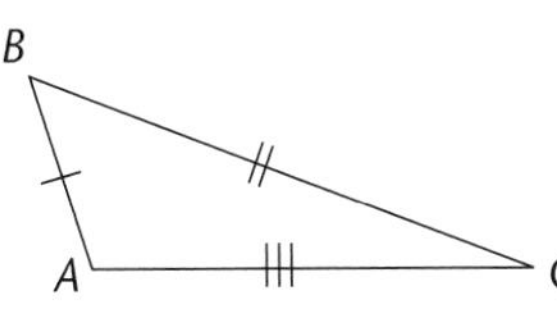

$$\overline{AB} = \overline{DE}$$
$$\overline{BC} = \overline{EF}$$
$$\overline{AC} = \overline{DF}$$
$$\downarrow$$
$$\triangle ABC \cong \triangle DEF$$

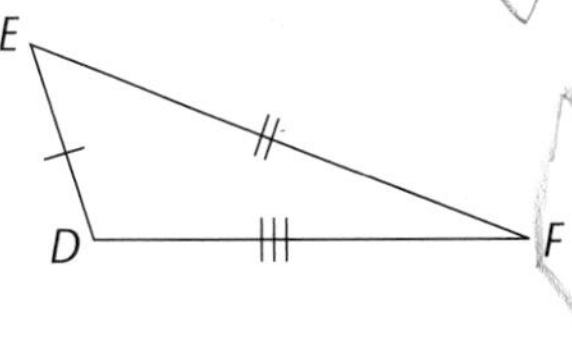

The Angle-Side-Angle Theorem (ASA)

If two angles and the included side of two triangles are equal, then the triangles are congruent.

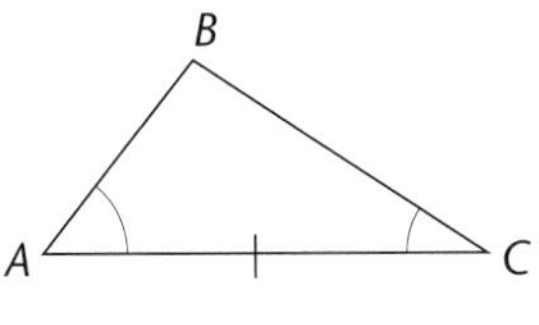

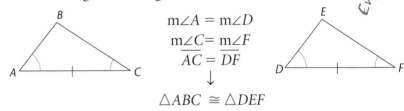

$$m\angle A = m\angle D$$
$$m\angle C = m\angle F$$
$$\overline{AC} = \overline{DF}$$
$$\downarrow$$
$$\triangle ABC \cong \triangle DEF$$

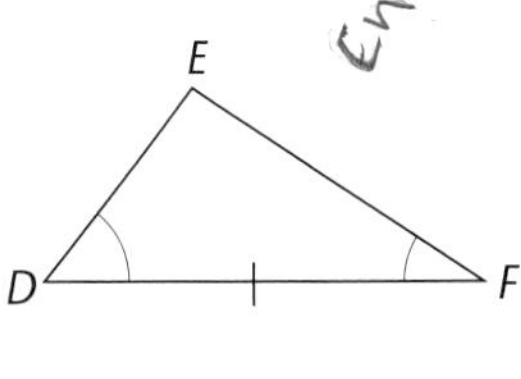

EXAMPLE 1 Given $\triangle ABC$ and $\triangle DEF$ with $m\angle A = m\angle D$, $AB = DE$, and $AC = DF$, determine whether the triangles are congruent. If the triangles are congruent, name the theorem that proves congruence.

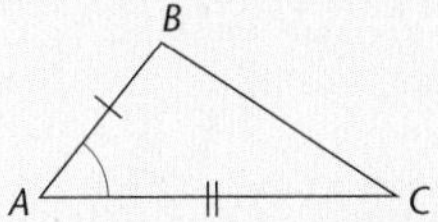

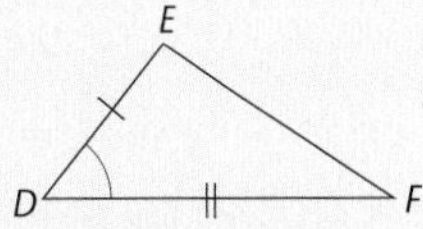

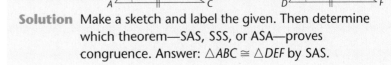

Solution Make a sketch and label the given. Then determine which theorem—SAS, SSS, or ASA—proves congruence. Answer: $\triangle ABC \cong \triangle DEF$ by SAS.

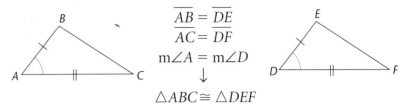

EXAMPLE 2 Given $\triangle ABC$ and $\triangle DEF$ with $m\angle B = m\angle E$, $m\angle C = m\angle F$, and $\overline{BC} = \overline{EF}$, determine whether the triangles are congruent. If the triangles are congruent, name the theorem that proves congruence.

Solution Make a sketch and label the given. Then determine which theorem—SAS, SSS, or ASA—proves congruence. Answer: $\triangle ABC \cong \triangle DEF$ by ASA.

EXAMPLE 3 Given $\triangle ABC$ and $\triangle DEF$ with $m\angle A = m\angle D$, $\overline{BC} = \overline{EF}$, and $\overline{AB} = \overline{DE}$, determine whether the triangles are congruent. If the triangles are congruent, name the theorem that proves congruence.

Solution Make a sketch and label the given. Then determine which theorem—SAS, SSS, or ASA—proves congruence. Answer: Because the given does not satisfy SAS, SSS, or ASA, $\triangle ABC$ is not congruent to $\triangle DEF$.

Similar

Figures that have the same shape but not the same size

Figures that have the same shape but not the same size are **similar.** The symbol for *similar* is $\sim$. $\triangle ABC \sim \triangle DEF$ is read "Triangle *ABC* is similar to triangle *DEF*."

Similar triangles have equal corresponding angles but not equal corresponding sides. These triangles are similar because their corresponding angles are equal.

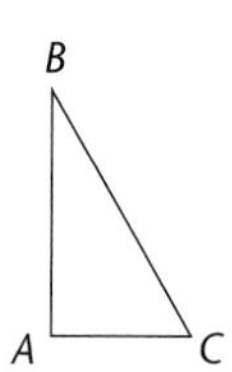

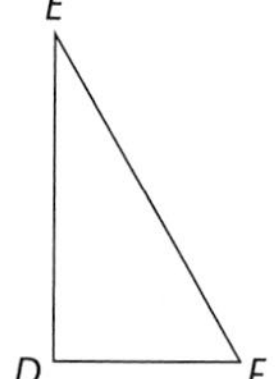

EXAMPLE 4

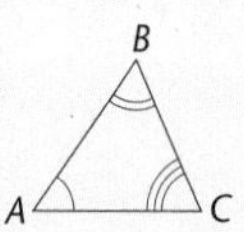

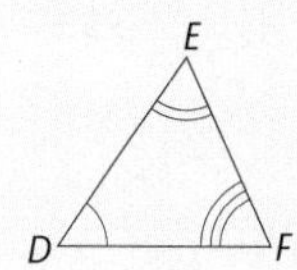

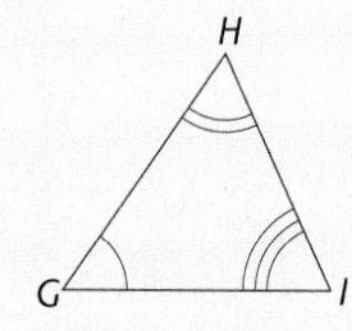

$\angle A = \angle D = \angle G$ $\quad\angle B = \angle E = \angle H$ $\quad\angle C = \angle F = \angle I$

Given $\triangle ABC \sim \triangle DEF$, $m\angle A = 55°$, and $m\angle B = 60°$, find $m\angle F$.

Step 1 Find $m\angle C$.

$m\angle A + m\angle B + m\angle C = 180°$

$55° + 60° + m\angle C = 180°$

$m\angle C = 180° - 55° - 60°$

$m\angle C = 65°$

Step 2 Find $m\angle F$.

Since the triangles are similar, their corresponding angles are equal, and $m\angle C = m\angle F$. So $m\angle F = 65°$.

TRY THIS

Draw three rectangles. Make two of the rectangles similar and make one that is not similar. Tell why the rectangles are similar or not similar.

Exercise A Name the theorem that proves congruence.

1.

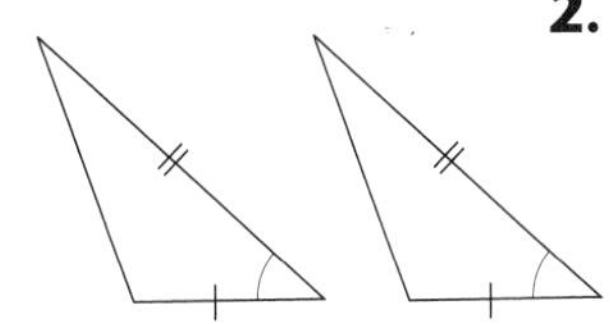

2.

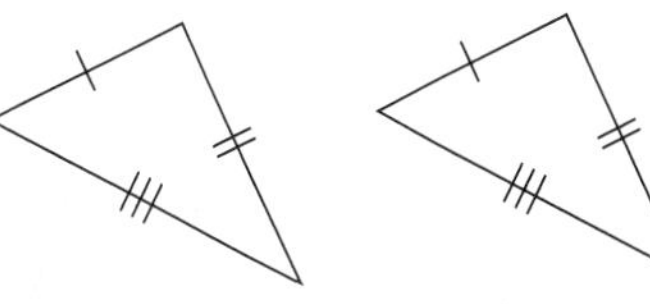

3.

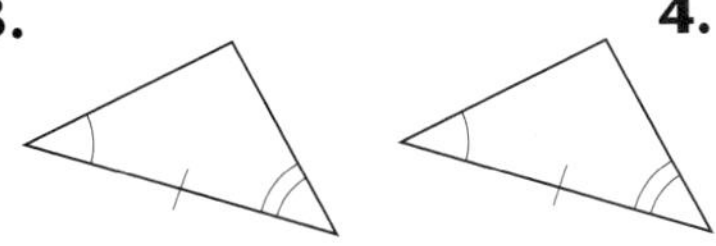

4.

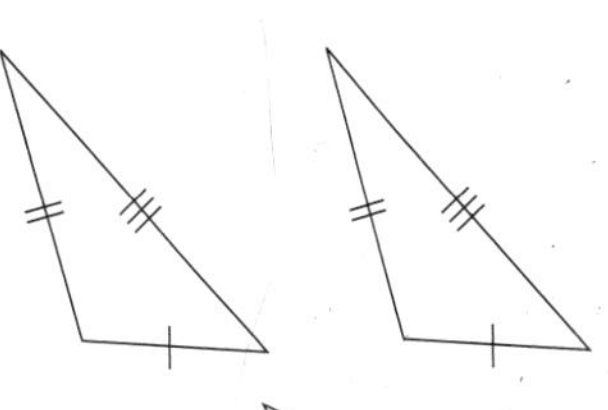

5.

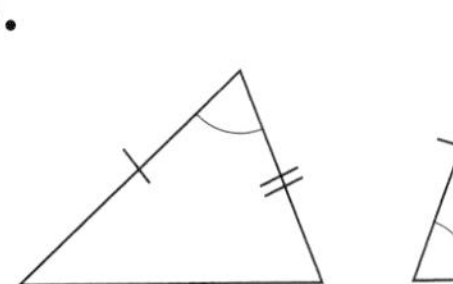

6.

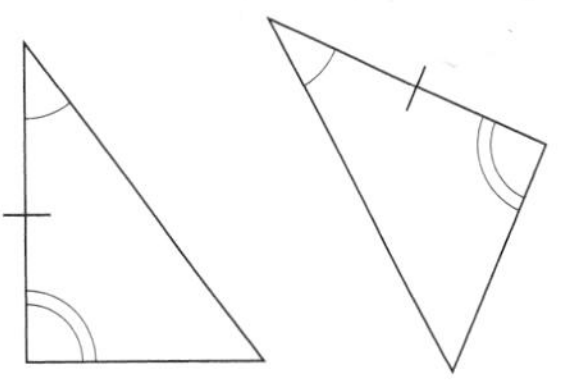

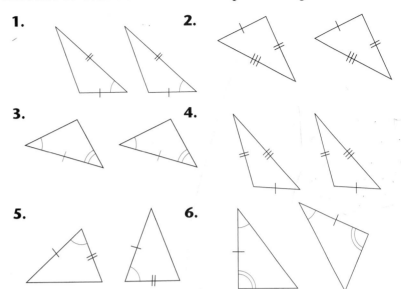

Exercise B Find the measures of the angles.

7. Given $\triangle ABC \sim \triangle DEF$, $m\angle A = 88°$, and $m\angle B = 29°$, find $m\angle F$.

8. Given $\triangle ABC \sim \triangle DEF$, $m\angle B = 30°$, and $m\angle C = 107°$, find $m\angle D$.

Exercise C Answer these questions.

9. Are all isosceles triangles similar? Tell why or why not.

10. Which triangles are always similar?

Algebra in Your Life

The Golden Rectangle

The "golden rectangle" is considered the most pleasing of all geometric shapes. It uses a height-to-width ratio of 1:1.6. A 3×5 index card has ratio that is close to a golden rectangle. Architects and artists have used the golden rectangle for centuries. The ancient Greek temple, the Parthenon, fits almost perfectly inside a golden rectangle. Leonardo da Vinci's (1452–1519) painting, *Mona Lisa*, contains many golden rectangles. Today, package designers and advertisers often use the golden rectangle because of its appeal to consumers.

Lesson 7 Trigonometric Ratios

Trigonometric ratios

Angles measured by ratios of the sides of a right triangle

In right triangle *ABC*, the hypotenuse is *AC*, the side adjacent to $\angle A$ is *AB*, and the side opposite $\angle A$ is *BC*.

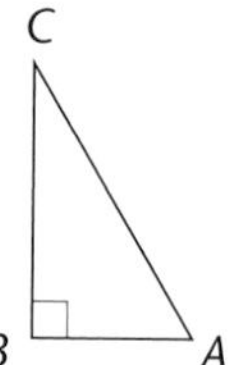

From the measures of the lengths of these sides, **trigonometric ratios** can be established.

Trigonometric ratios include

$$\text{sine ratio of } \angle A = \frac{\text{the length of the side opposite } \angle A}{\text{the length of the hypotenuse}}$$

The sine of $\angle A$ is written sin *A*.

$$\text{cosine ratio of } \angle A = \frac{\text{the length of the side adjacent to } \angle A}{\text{the length of the hypotenuse}}$$

The cosine of $\angle A$ is written cos *A*.

$$\text{tangent ratio of } \angle A = \frac{\text{the length of the side opposite } \angle A}{\text{the length of the side adjacent to } \angle A}$$

The tangent of $\angle A$ is written tan *A*.

Trigonometric ratios can be used in different ways to solve problems.

EXAMPLE 1 In right triangle *ABC*, find sin *A*, cos *A*, and tan *A*.

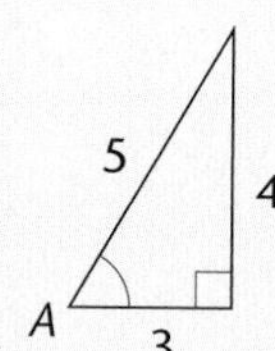

Step 1 $\sin A = \frac{\text{the length of the side opposite } \angle A}{\text{the length of the hypotenuse}} = \frac{4}{5} = 0.8$

Step 2 $\cos A = \frac{\text{the length of the side adjacent to } \angle A}{\text{the length of the hypotenuse}} = \frac{3}{5} = 0.6$

Step 3 $\tan A = \frac{\text{the length of the side opposite } \angle A}{\text{the length of the side adjacent to } \angle A} = \frac{4}{3} = 1.\overline{3}$

EXAMPLE 2 In the right triangle shown here, find x. Round your answer to the nearest hundredth.

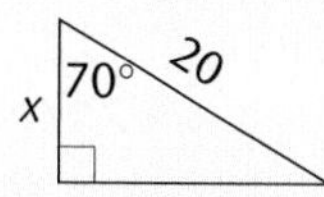

Step 1 Decide which trigonometric ratio to use. Since the measure of the hypotenuse is given and you need to find the length of the side adjacent to the 70° angle, use the cosine ratio and a calculator.

Step 2 $\cos A = \dfrac{\text{the length of the adjacent side}}{\text{the length of the hypotenuse}}$

$$\cos 70^\circ = \frac{x}{20}$$
$$(20)\cos 70^\circ = x$$
$$(20)(0.3420201) = x$$
$$6.840402 = x$$
$$6.84 = x \text{ (rounded to the nearest hundredth)}$$

EXAMPLE 3 Suppose you are standing 100 feet from the foot of a flagpole. The angle of elevation from the ground on which you are standing to the top of the flagpole is 20°. Find the height of the flagpole to the nearest foot.

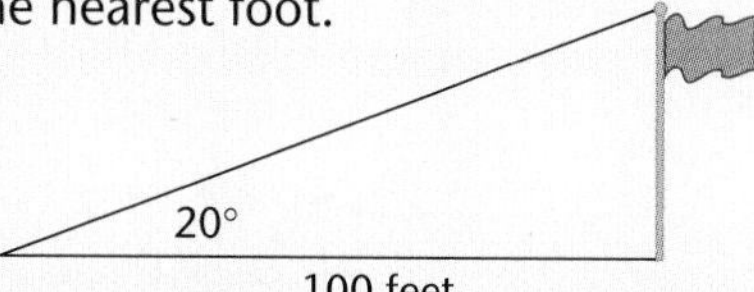

Step 1 You know that the length of the side adjacent to the 20° angle is 100 feet, and you are trying to find x, the side opposite. Use the tangent ratio:

$$\tan A = \frac{\text{opposite side}}{\text{adjacent side}}$$

Step 2 Find x.

$$\tan A = \frac{\text{the length of the opposite side}}{\text{the length of the adjacent side}}$$
$$\tan 20^\circ = \frac{x}{100}$$
$$(100)(\tan 20^\circ) = x$$
$$(100)(0.3639702) = x$$
$$36.39702 = x$$
$$36 \text{ feet} = x \text{ (rounded to the nearest foot)}$$

EXAMPLE 4 A 30-foot-long ladder leaning against a house forms a 70° angle with the ground. To the nearest foot, how far above the ground does the ladder touch the house?

Step 1 You know the length of the hypotenuse and want to find the side opposite of the 70° angle.

Use the sine ratio: $\sin A = \frac{\text{opposite side}}{\text{hypotenuse}}$

Step 2 Find x.

$$\sin A = \frac{\text{opposite side}}{\text{hypotenuse}}$$
$$\sin 70° = \frac{x}{30}$$
$$(30)(\sin 70°) = x$$
$$(30)(0.9396926) = x$$
$$28.190779 = x$$
$$28 \text{ feet} = x \text{ (rounded to the nearest foot)}$$

Calculator Practice Using a calculator can help you find trigonometric ratios easily.

EXAMPLE 5 Angle A of a right triangle is 50°. The measure of the hypotenuse is 5. You want to know the length of the side opposite to the 50° angle.

$\sin 50° = \frac{x}{5}$

$5(\sin 50°) = x$

Use your calculator to find the answer.

Press 50 [SIN]. The display reads 0.766044. Press [×] 5 [=].

The display reads 3.83022.

Round to the nearest hundredth. 3.83 is the length of the side opposite the 50° angle.

Exercise A Use a calculator to find the following values. Round your answers to the nearest hundredth.

1. sin 15° **2.** cos 15° **3.** tan 15°

Exercise B Use a calculator to find the following values.

4. sin C

5. cos C

6. tan C

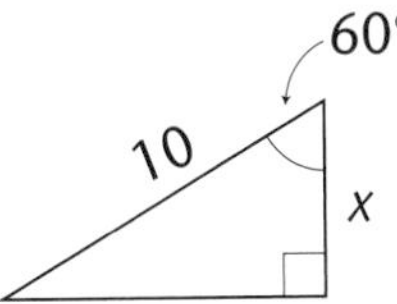

Exercise C Use a calculator to find the value for x. Round your answers to the nearest hundredth.

7.

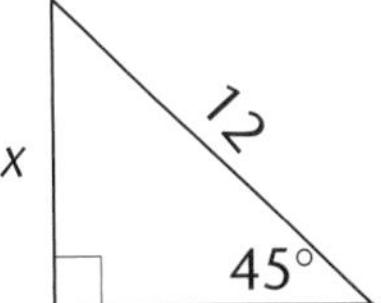

8.

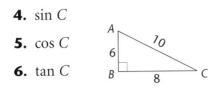

PROBLEM SOLVING

Exercise D Answer these questions.

9. On the shore of a pond, $\overline{AC}$ measures 100 feet, $\angle A = 90°$, and $\angle C = 60°$.

To the nearest foot, find the distance from A to B.

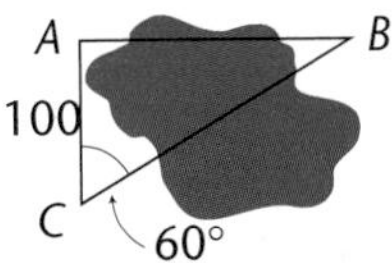

10. Suppose you are standing 2 miles away from a tall building and you see the lights on the top of the building. The angle of elevation from you to the lights is 25°.

To the nearest 100 feet, how far above ground are the lights?

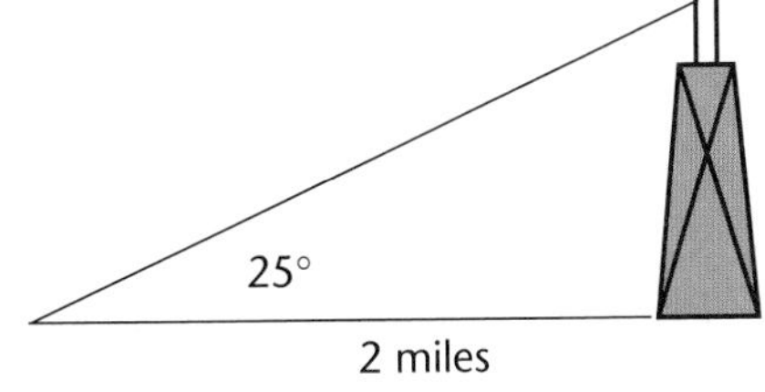

Surveyors use line and angle measures to determine distances and areas.

Using Geometric Shapes

Geometric figures exist in an infinite variety of shapes and sizes.

In some geometric figures, diagonals can be drawn.

EXAMPLE 1 Two different diagonals can be drawn in a square.

No diagonals can be drawn in a triangle.

In a pentagon, five diagonals can be drawn.

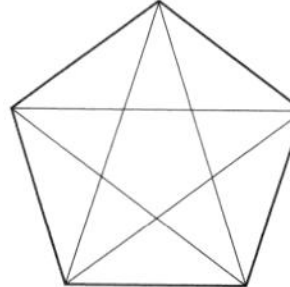

Exercise Determine the number of diagonals that can be drawn in each figure.

1. a hexagon

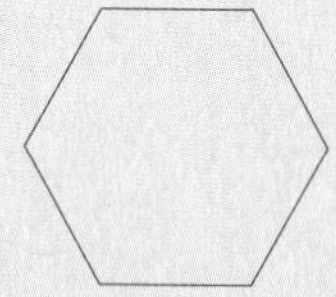

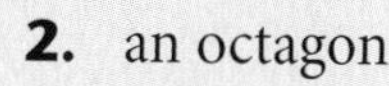

2. an octagon

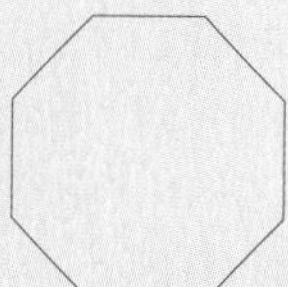

The number of diagonals that can be drawn in these geometric figures is predictable. Think again about the number of diagonals that can be drawn in a triangle (three sides), square (four sides), pentagon (five sides), hexagon (six sides), and octagon (eight sides). Find a pattern. Then use the pattern to predict the number of diagonals that can be drawn in the following shapes.

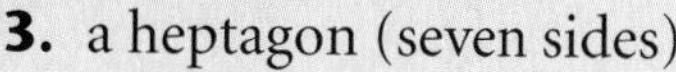

3. a heptagon (seven sides)

4. a decagon (ten sides)

5. a dodecagon (12 sides)

Chapter 12 REVIEW

Use this figure and the information that $p \parallel q$, t is a transversal, and $m\angle c = 52.4^\circ$ for questions 1 through 4. Write the letter of the correct answer.

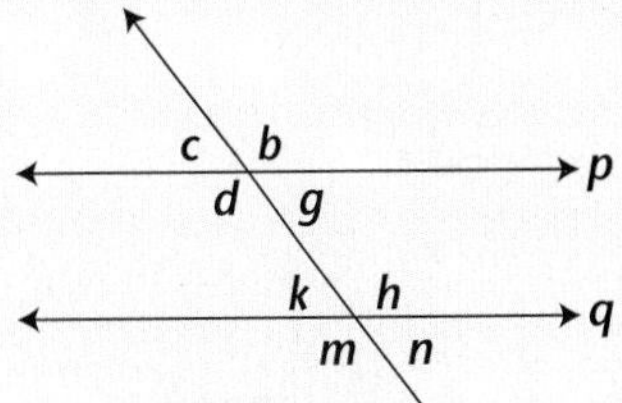

1. Find the measure of $\angle d$.

   A $\angle d = 128.6^\circ$

   B $\angle d = 52.4^\circ$

   C $\angle d = 128.4^\circ$

   D $\angle d = 127.6^\circ$

2. Find the measure of $\angle h$.

   A $\angle h = 127.6^\circ$

   B $\angle h = 90^\circ$

   C $\angle h = 52.4^\circ$

   D $\angle h = 180^\circ$

3. Find the measure of $\angle k$.

   A $\angle k = 45^\circ$

   B $\angle k = 52.4^\circ$

   C $\angle k = 227.4^\circ$

   D $\angle k = 108.4^\circ$

4. Find the measure of $\angle n$.

   A $\angle n = 127.6^\circ$

   B $\angle n = 90^\circ$

   C $\angle n = 52.4^\circ$

   D $\angle n = 45^\circ$

Write the letter of the correct answer.

5. Find $m\angle x$.

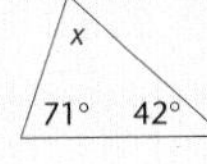

   A $m\angle x = 129^\circ$

   B $m\angle x = 67^\circ$

   C $m\angle x = 88^\circ$

   D $m\angle x = 113^\circ$

6. Find $m\angle x$.

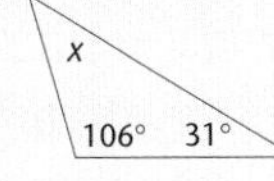

   A $m\angle x = 53^\circ$

   B $m\angle x = 43^\circ$

   C $m\angle x = 137^\circ$

   D $m\angle x = 40^\circ$

7. Find $m\angle x$.

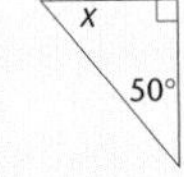

   A $m\angle x = 40^\circ$

   B $m\angle x = 30^\circ$

   C $m\angle x = 50^\circ$

   D $m\angle x = 130^\circ$

Classify each angle or pair of angles. Line $m||n$. Write *acute, right, obtuse, straight, adjacent, complementary, supplementary, interior, exterior, alternate interior,* or *corresponding*. For any angle or pair of angles, more than one name may apply.

Example: $\angle p$ Solution: $\angle p$, interior, right angle

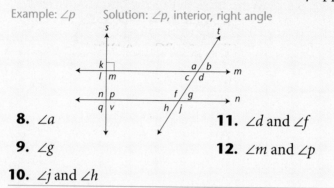

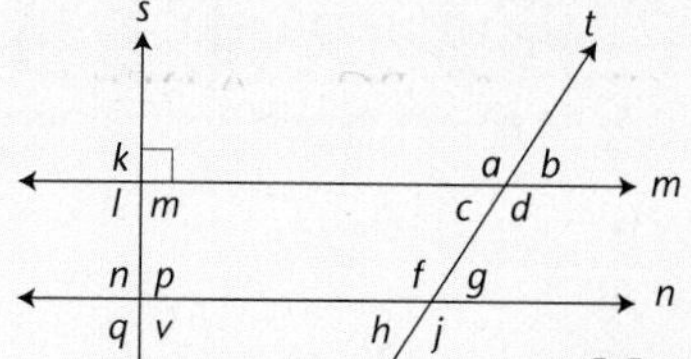

8. $\angle a$

9. $\angle g$

10. $\angle j$ and $\angle h$

11. $\angle d$ and $\angle f$

12. $\angle m$ and $\angle p$

Find each angle.

Example: In parallelogram $ABCD$, $\overline{AB}||\overline{CD}$, $\overline{AD}||\overline{BC}$, and $m\angle A = 75°$. Find $m\angle B$, $m\angle C$, and $m\angle D$.
Solution: $\angle A$ and $\angle D$ are supplementary.
$m\angle D + 75° = 180°$, $m\angle D = 180° - 75°$,
$m\angle D = 105°$; $\angle D$ and $\angle C$ are supplementary.
$m\angle C + 105° = 180°$, $m\angle C = 180° - 105°$,
$m\angle C = 75°$; $\angle C$ and $\angle B$ are supplementary.
$m\angle B + 75° = 180°$, $m\angle B = 180° - 75°$, $m\angle B = 105°$

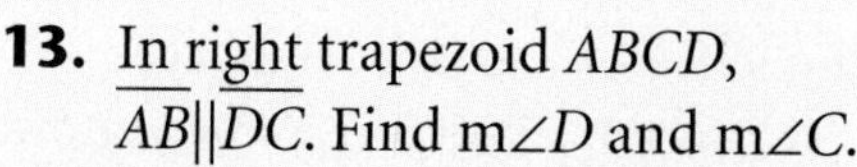

13. In right trapezoid $ABCD$, $\overline{AB}||\overline{DC}$. Find $m\angle D$ and $m\angle C$.

14. In rhombus $ABCD$, $\overline{AB}||\overline{CD}$, $\overline{BC}||\overline{AD}$, and $m\angle B = 146°$. Find $m\angle A$, $m\angle C$, and $m\angle D$.

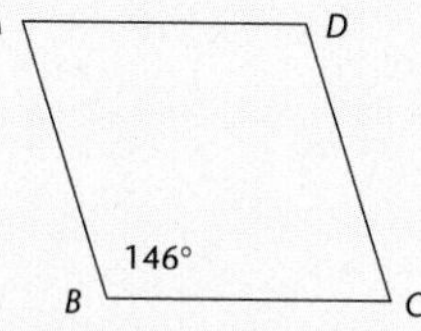

Name the theorem that proves congruence.

Example:
Solution: The Side-Side-Side Theorem

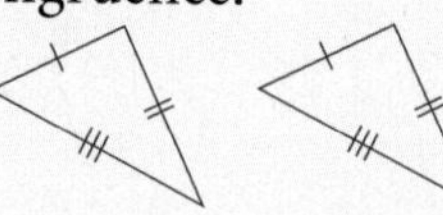

15.

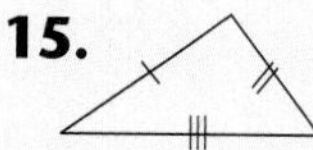

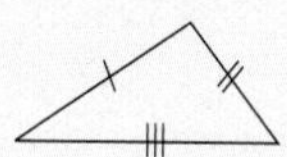

16.

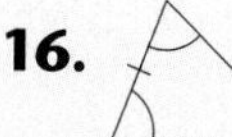

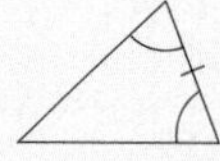

Find each angle.

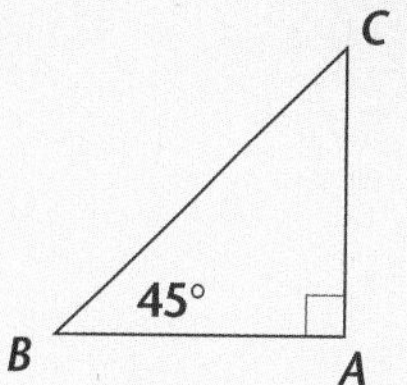

Example: Given $\triangle ABC \sim \triangle DEF$, $m\angle A = 90°$, and $m\angle B = 45°$, find $m\angle F$. Solution: Find $m\angle C$. $m\angle A + m\angle B + m\angle C = 180°$, $m\angle C + 90° + 45° = 180°$, $m\angle C = 180° - 135°$, $m\angle C = 45°$, $m\angle C = m\angle F = 45°$

17. Given $\triangle ABC \sim \triangle DEF$, $m\angle A = 73°$, and $m\angle B = 31°$, find $m\angle F$.

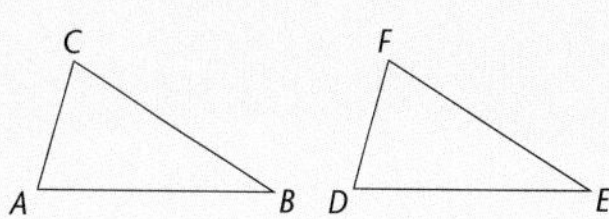

18. Given $\triangle ABC \sim \triangle DEF$, $m\angle B = 28°$, and $m\angle F = 38°$, find $m\angle A$.

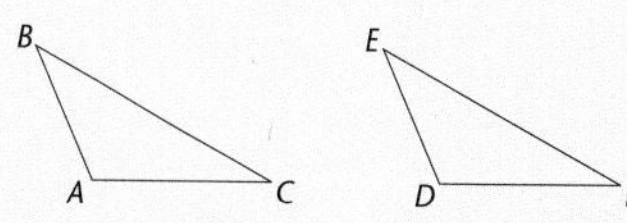

Answer these questions. You may use a calculator.

Example: Suppose that you are planting flowers along one side of a flower bed that is in the shape of a right triangle. You know that the hypotenuse of the triangle is 30 feet and that the angle opposite to the side you want to plant is 50°. What is the length of the side you are going to plant? Round to the nearest foot.

Solution: $\sin 50° = \frac{x}{30}$, $30(\sin 50°) = (30)0.766 = 22.9813 = 23$ feet

19. Suppose you are standing 150 feet away from a tree and you see a hawk hovering directly above that tree. The angle of elevation from you to the hawk is 21°. To the nearest foot, how far above ground is the hawk?

20. Suppose that a painter has leaned a 3-meter ladder against a wall so that the ladder forms a 70° angle with the floor. To the nearest tenth of a meter, how far above the floor does the ladder touch the wall?

Test-Taking Tip

Drawing pictures and diagrams is one way to help you understand and solve problems.

22

Chapter

Quadratic Equations

Satellite dishes are everywhere, including backyards! These dishes are antennas designed to send and receive signals. The signals are bounced off of satellites orbiting the earth. The dish shape is an arc, or parabola. You create parabolas when you pitch a baseball or turn on a drinking fountain. To plot parabolas on a graph, we use quadratic equations. You've plotted straight lines using linear equations to the power of one. Soon you'll be able to graph a curved line by using an equation with a second power or exponent. The direction your parabola opens depends upon the type of quadratic equation you use.

In Chapter 13, you will solve and graph quadratic equations.

Goals for Learning

- To solve quadratic equations by factoring
- To write quadratic equations from their roots
- To solve quadratic equations by completing the square
- To use the quadratic formula to solve quadratic equations
- To graph quadratic equations

Lesson 1 Solutions by Factoring

Set of roots
The set of numbers that make an equation true

Recall that a quadratic equation is of the form $ax^2 + bx + c = 0$, where a, b, and c are real numbers, and $a \neq 0$.

The root of an equation is the value of the variable that makes the equation true. The **set of roots** for an equation forms the solution set for the equation.

Some quadratic equations can be solved by factoring.

EXAMPLE 1 Find the roots, or the solution set, of $x^2 + 3x + 2 = 0$.

Step 1 Factor the equation.

$$x^2 + 3x + 2 = 0$$
$$(x + 2)(x + 1) = 0$$

Step 2 Remember, $ab = 0$ if and only if $a = 0$ or $b = 0$.

Therefore, for $(x + 2)(x + 1) = 0$ to be true, either $x + 2 = 0$ or $x + 1 = 0$.

Set each factor equal to zero, and solve for x.

$x + 2 = 0$ or $x + 1 = 0$

$x = -2$ or $x = -1$

Step 3 Check.

Let $x = -2$	Let $x = -1$
$x^2 + 3x + 2 \stackrel{?}{=} 0$	$x^2 + 3x + 2 \stackrel{?}{=} 0$
$(-2)^2 + 3(-2) + 2 \stackrel{?}{=} 0$	$(-1)^2 + 3(-1) + 2 \stackrel{?}{=} 0$
$4 - 6 + 2 \stackrel{?}{=} 0$	$1 - 3 + 2 \stackrel{?}{=} 0$
$0 = 0$	$0 = 0$
True	True

The solution set is -2 and -1.

When you check an open statement, use $\stackrel{?}{=}$ until you reach the answer. If the equality holds, write *True.* If the equality does not hold, write *False.*

EXAMPLE 2 Find the roots, or the solution set, of

$2x^2 + 7x = 15.$

Step 1 Write the equation so that the sum of the terms equals zero.

$2x^2 + 7x - 15 = 0$

Step 2 Factor the equation.

$$2x^2 + 7x - 15 = 0$$
$$(2x - 3)(x + 5) = 0$$

Step 3 Because $ab = 0$ if and only if $a = 0$ or $b = 0$,

either $2x - 3 = 0$ or $x + 5 = 0.$

$x = \frac{3}{2}$ or $x = -5$

Step 4 Check.

Let $x = \frac{3}{2}$

$$2x^2 + 7x - 15 \stackrel{?}{=} 0$$
$$2(\tfrac{3}{2})^2 + 7(\tfrac{3}{2}) - 15 \stackrel{?}{=} 0$$
$$\frac{18}{4} + \frac{21}{2} - 15 \stackrel{?}{=} 0$$
$$\frac{9}{2} + \frac{21}{2} - 15 \stackrel{?}{=} 0$$
$$\frac{30}{2} - 15 \stackrel{?}{=} 0$$
$$0 = 0$$

True

Let $x = -5$

$$2x^2 + 7x - 15 \stackrel{?}{=} 0$$
$$2(-5)^2 + 7(-5) - 15 \stackrel{?}{=} 0$$
$$50 - 35 - 15 \stackrel{?}{=} 0$$
$$0 = 0$$

True

The roots are $\frac{3}{2}$ and -5.

Estimation Activity

Estimate: The pond on Li's farm is an odd shape. He has a scale drawing of the farm that shows the pond. How can Li estimate the area of the pond?

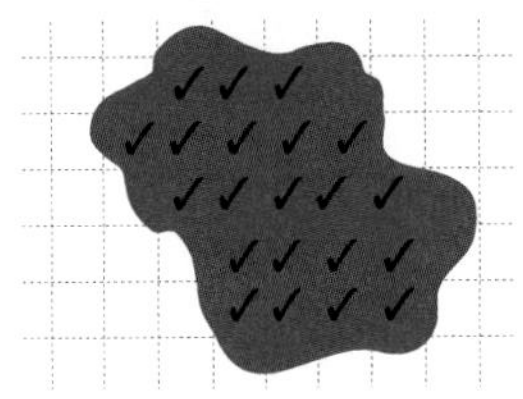

Solution: Draw a grid to a known scale over the scale drawing. Count the number of squares and estimate the area of the partial squares. Checked squares on the grid are totally within the area of the pond. Other units must be estimated.

You can use what you know about quadratic equations to solve some problems.

EXAMPLE 3 The product of two consecutive integers is 72. What are the integers?

Step 1 Write the problem as an equation. Let x represent the first integer, and let $x + 1$ represent the next integer.

$(x)(x + 1) = 72$

Step 2 Multiply and rearrange terms so the equation is in the form $ax^2 + bx + c = 0$.

$x^2 + x - 72 = 0$

Step 3 Factor, then solve for x.

$(x - 8)(x + 9) = 0$

either $x - 8 = 0$ or $x + 9 = 0$

If $x = 8$, the integers are 8 and 9.

If $x = -9$, the integers are -9 and -8.

Step 4 Check.

Let $x = 8$			Let $x = -9$		
$x(x + 1)$	$\stackrel{?}{=}$	72	$x(x + 1)$	$\stackrel{?}{=}$	72
$8 \bullet 9$	$\stackrel{?}{=}$	72	$-9(-8)$	$\stackrel{?}{=}$	72
72	$=$	72	72	$=$	72
	True			True	

Exercise A Find the roots of these equations by factoring. Check your answers.

1. $x^2 + 5x + 6 = 0$

2. $x^2 + 5x = 0$

3. $y^2 + 11y + 30 = 0$

4. $x^2 - 8x + 16 = 0$

5. $x^2 + 6x + 5 = 0$

6. $3x^2 + x - 2 = 0$

7. $6x^2 - 4x - 10 = 0$

8. $2y^2 + 12y + 10 = 0$

9. $12x^2 + 5x - 2 = 0$

10. $-x^2 + 12x = 0$
(Hint: Multiply both sides by -1.)

Writing About Mathematics

Choose one of the problems from Exercise B. Explain the steps you used to factor the equation.

Exercise B Rewrite these equations in the form $ax^2 + bx + c = 0$. Then find the roots.

11. $t^2 + 6t = -9$

12. $3x^2 - 12 = 5x$

13. $3x^2 = 9x + 30$

14. $4x^2 + 4x = 48$

15. $5y^2 = 7y$

16. $3x^2 - 7x = 20$

17. $14 = x^2 - 5x$

18. $m^2 - 5m = 18 + 2m$

19. $3z^2 - 2 = -z$

20. $x^2 + 5x = 36$

PROBLEM SOLVING

Exercise C Answer each problem.

21. The area of a rectangular floor is 36 square units. The length is 4 times greater than its width. What are the length and width of the floor?

22. The product of Miguel's and Maria's ages is 108. Miguel is 3 years older than Maria. What are their ages?

23. Mai can install one more computer chip every hour than Tom can. The product of the number of computer chips Mai installs in an hour and the number of computer chips Tom installs in an hour is 420. How many computer chips does Mai install in an hour? How many chips does Tom install?

24. Janet is one year older than her best friend. Their ages multiplied together equal 56. How old is Janet? How old is her friend?

25. Jesse is 2 years older than Kristen. The product of their ages is 48. How old is Jesse? How old is Kristen? (Hint: Let one integer be x and the other be $x + 2$.)

Lesson 2 Writing the Equations from Their Roots

> Remember, if $a = 0$ and $b = 0$, then $ab = 0$. Multiply. Then write in general form.

You can factor to find the roots of a quadratic equation. You can also reverse the process of factoring—if you know the roots of a quadratic equation, you can find the equation itself. For example, suppose the roots of an equation are

$$x = 1 \quad \text{or} \quad x = -2.$$

You can find the factors of the equation by setting each root equation equal to zero.

$$x = 1 \quad \text{or} \quad x = -2$$
$$x - 1 = 0 \quad \text{or} \quad x + 2 = 0$$
$$(x - 1)(x + 2) = 0$$
$$x^2 + x - 2 = 0$$

> r_1 and r_2 are the roots of the quadratic equation
> $(x - r_1)(x - r_2) = 0.$

EXAMPLE 1 The roots of a quadratic equation are 1 and 2. What is the general form of the equation?

Step 1 The roots are values of x that satisfy the equation, so $x = 1$ or $x = 2$.

Step 2 Set each factor equal to zero.

$(x - 1) = 0$ or $(x - 2) = 0$

Step 3 Multiply the factors.

$(x - 1)(x - 2) = 0$

Step 4 Use the distributive property to place the equation in general form. $x^2 - 3x + 2 = 0$

EXAMPLE 2 The roots of a quadratic equation are $\frac{2}{3}$ and -2. What is the general form of the equation?

Step 1 If the roots are $\frac{2}{3}$ and -2, then $x = \frac{2}{3}$ or $x = -2$.

Step 2 Set each factor equal to zero.

$(x - \frac{2}{3}) = 0$ or $(x + 2) = 0$

Step 3 Multiply each side of the first equation by 3 to remove the fraction.

$3(x - \frac{2}{3}) = 3 \bullet 0$ or $3x - 2 = 0$

EXAMPLE 2 *(continued)*

Step 4 Multiply the factors.

$(3x - 2)(x + 2) = 0$

Step 5 Use the distributive property to place the equation in general form.

$3x^2 + 4x - 4 = 0$

Exercise A Find the quadratic equation that has these roots.

1. $-2, -3$
2. $2, 4$
3. $6, 4$
4. $-6, 4$
5. $6, -4$
6. $-6, -4$
7. $-7, 4$
8. $6, -7$
9. $8, 11$
10. $-3, -7$
11. $2, -5$
12. $-2, 5$
13. $3, 5$
14. $\frac{2}{3}, 3$
15. $\frac{4}{5}, 5$
16. $\frac{3}{4}, 1$
17. $-\frac{3}{2}, -1$
18. $-\frac{4}{3}, 1$
19. $-\frac{4}{3}, 2$
20. $-\frac{3}{5}, 3$
21. $\frac{1}{2}, 3$
22. $0, \frac{2}{3}$
23. $\frac{4}{7}, 7$

PROBLEM SOLVING

Exercise B Solve each problem.

24. Denise says that it is impossible for one of the roots of a quadratic equation to be zero. Is she correct? If not, give an example. If yes, tell why.

25. Nate wants to prove that both roots of a quadratic equation could be zero. Write the quadratic equation to determine whether Nate is correct. Explain your answer.

TRY THIS Write two roots of an equation. Ask a classmate to write the quadratic equation for those roots. Solve the equation to check that it was done correctly.

Lesson 3 Solving by Completing the Square

Completing the square

Finding the roots of a perfect square trinomial

One method you can use to solve a quadratic equation is called **completing the square.**

Completing the square works because $(x + b)^2 = x^2 + 2bx + b^2$, and $x^2 + 2bx + b^2$ is a perfect square trinomial. You can find the roots of a perfect square trinomial by finding the square root of each side of the equation.

EXAMPLE 1 Find the roots of $x^2 + 4x + 1 = 0$.

Step 1 Rewrite the equation so that the variable is on one side of the equation, and the constant is on the other.

$x^2 + 4x + 1 = 0$ becomes $x^2 + 4x = -1$.

Step 2 Add a constant to each side of the equation so that the expression on the left is a perfect square trinomial. $x^2 + 4x + \blacksquare^2 = -1 + \blacksquare^2$

Step 3 Find the value of the constant, $\blacksquare$. Remember, the model perfect square trinomial is

$x^2 + 2bx + b^2 = (x + b)^2$ In this case, $2bx = 4x$.

$x^2 + 4x + \blacksquare^2 = -1 + \blacksquare^2$ so $2 \bullet \blacksquare = 4$, and $\blacksquare = 2$.

Step 4 Rewrite the equation with the value $\blacksquare = 2$, $\blacksquare^2 = 4$.

$$x^2 + 4x + \blacksquare^2 = -1 + \blacksquare^2 \text{ becomes}$$

$$x^2 + 4x + 4 = -1 + 4.$$

Step 5 Factor the perfect square trinomial, then find the square root of each side of the equation.

$$\begin{aligned} x^2 + 4x + 4 &= -1 + 4 \\ (x + 2)^2 &= 3 \\ \sqrt{(x + 2)^2} &= \sqrt{3} \\ x + 2 &= \pm\sqrt{3} \\ x &= -2 \pm \sqrt{3} \end{aligned}$$

The roots of the equation are $-2 + \sqrt{3}$ and $-2 - \sqrt{3}$.

Step 6 Check.

Let $x = -2 + \sqrt{3}$

$$\begin{aligned} x^2 + 4x + 1 &\stackrel{?}{=} 0 \\ (-2 + \sqrt{3})^2 + 4(-2 + \sqrt{3}) + 1 &\stackrel{?}{=} 0 \\ (4 - 4\sqrt{3} + 3) - 8 + 4\sqrt{3} + 1 &\stackrel{?}{=} 0 \\ 0 &= 0 \end{aligned}$$

True

Let $x = -2 - \sqrt{3}$

$$\begin{aligned} x^2 + 4x + 1 &\stackrel{?}{=} 0 \\ (-2 - \sqrt{3})^2 + 4(-2 - \sqrt{3}) + 1 &\stackrel{?}{=} 0 \\ (4 + 4\sqrt{3} + 3) - 8 - 4\sqrt{3} + 1 &\stackrel{?}{=} 0 \\ 0 &= 0 \end{aligned}$$

True

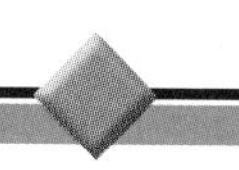

Recall that a quadratic equation is of the form $ax^2 + bx + c = 0$, where a, b, and c are real numbers and $a \neq 0$.

EXAMPLE 2 Find the roots of $x^2 + 6x + 1 = 0$ by completing the square.

Step 1 Rewrite the equation so that the variable is on one side of the equation, the constant on the other.

$x^2 + 6x + 1 = 0$ becomes $x^2 + 6x = -1$.

Step 2 Add a constant to each side of the equation so that the expression on the left is a perfect square trinomial.

$x^2 + 6x + \blacksquare^2 = -1 + \blacksquare^2$

Step 3 Find the value of the constant, $\blacksquare$. Remember, the model perfect square trinomial is

$x^2 + 2bx + b^2 = (x + b)^2$ In this case, $2bx = 6x$

$x^2 + 6x + \blacksquare^2 = -1 + \blacksquare^2$ so $2 \bullet \blacksquare = 6$, and $\blacksquare = 3$.

Step 4 Rewrite the equation using the value $\blacksquare = 3$, $\blacksquare^2 = 9$.

$x^2 + 6x + \blacksquare^2 = -1 + \blacksquare^2$ becomes

$x^2 + 6x + 9 = -1 + 9$.

Step 5 Factor the perfect square trinomial, then find the square root of each side of the equation.

$$\begin{aligned} x^2 + 6x + 9 &= -1 + 9 \\ (x + 3)^2 &= 8 \\ \sqrt{(x + 3)^2} &= \sqrt{8} \\ x + 3 &= \pm 2\sqrt{2} \\ x &= -3 \pm 2\sqrt{2} \end{aligned}$$

The roots of the equation are $-3 + 2\sqrt{2}$ and $-3 - 2\sqrt{2}$.

Step 6 Check.

Let $x = -3 + 2\sqrt{2}$

$$\begin{aligned} x^2 + 6x + 1 &\stackrel{?}{=} 0 \\ (-3 + 2\sqrt{2})^2 + 6(-3 + 2\sqrt{2}) + 1 &\stackrel{?}{=} 0 \\ (9 - 12\sqrt{2} + 8) + (-18 + 12\sqrt{2}) + 1 &\stackrel{?}{=} 0 \\ 0 &= 0 \end{aligned}$$

True

Let $x = -3 - 2\sqrt{2}$

$$\begin{aligned} x^2 + 6x + 1 &\stackrel{?}{=} 0 \\ (-3 - 2\sqrt{2})^2 + 6(-3 - 2\sqrt{2}) + 1 &\stackrel{?}{=} 0 \\ (9 + 12\sqrt{2} + 8) - (18 - 12\sqrt{2}) + 1 &\stackrel{?}{=} 0 \\ 0 &= 0 \end{aligned}$$

True

Exercise A Find the roots of these equations by completing the square.

1. $x^2 + 6x + 5 = 0$
2. $y^2 - 3y = 18$
3. $2x^2 + 6x = 0$
4. $m^2 + 4m - 12 = 0$
5. $x^2 - 4x = 5$
6. $z^2 - 8z + 15 = 0$
7. $x^2 + 2x = 15$
8. $t^2 + 9t = -18$
9. $x^2 - 6x + 8 = 0$
10. $x^2 - 2x - 4 = 0$

The First American Indian Astronaut John Bennett Herrington became interested in mathematics when he worked as a surveyor's assistant. The surveyor showed him how to use mathematics to convert instrument sightings into useful information for road construction. After high school, Herrington earned a degree in applied mathematics, joined the Navy, and became a test pilot. In the Navy, he earned a master's degree in aeronautical engineering and joined NASA. On his first flight into space, Herrington carried with him several objects honoring his heritage.

Exercise B Find the roots of these equations by completing the square.

11. $x^2 - 12 = 4x$

12. $y^2 + 2y - 6 = 0$

13. $x^2 = -6x - 5$

14. $d^2 - 3d = 6$

15. $2m^2 + 4m = 6$

16. $3x^2 - 6x - 24 = 0$

17. $2y^2 - 3y = 3$

18. $3x^2 + 33x + 72 = 0$

19. $x^2 - 6x - 17 = 0$

20. $4x^2 + 28x = 32$

Technology Connection

Without a Calculator

Graphing a quadratic equation on a calculator takes seconds. Graphing it on paper can take a minute or so. Imagine having to do thousands of calculations and graphs with almost no technological help. Buckminster Fuller, developer of the geodesic dome, didn't even have a calculator. In the 1940s, Fuller had a mechanical adding machine that could only add and subtract. So it took him *two years* to complete the calculations he needed to build his first dome in 1948.

Lesson 4 Solving Using the Quadratic Formula

In addition to factoring and completing the square, there is another tool you can use to find the roots of a quadratic equation. The steps below show how this tool is derived.

Step 1: Start with the general form of the quadratic equation. Divide by a so that the coefficient of x^2 is 1.

$$ax^2 + bx + c = 0 \text{ becomes}$$
$$x^2 + \frac{b}{a}x + \frac{c}{a} = 0$$

Step 2: Rewrite so that the variables are on one side of the equation, constants on the other.

$$x^2 + \frac{b}{a}x = -\frac{c}{a}$$

Step 3: Add a constant to each side of the equation to complete the square.

$$x^2 + \frac{b}{a}x + \blacksquare = -\frac{c}{a} + \blacksquare$$

To find the value of the constant, $\blacksquare$, look again at the model perfect square trinomial.

$$x^2 + 2cx + c^2 = (x + c)^2$$

In this case, $2cx = \frac{b}{a}x$, so $2c = \frac{b}{a}$, and $c = \frac{b}{2a}$, $c^2 = \frac{b^2}{4a^2}$.

Step 4: Rewrite the equation using the value $c = \frac{b}{2a}$, $c^2 = \frac{b^2}{4a^2}$.

$$x^2 + \frac{b}{a}x + \blacksquare = -\frac{c}{a} + \blacksquare \text{ becomes}$$
$$x^2 + \frac{b}{a}x + [\frac{b^2}{4a^2}] = -\frac{c}{a} + [\frac{b^2}{4a^2}].$$

Factor the left side. Place the right side over the common denominator $4a^2$.

$$(x + \frac{b}{2a})^2 = \frac{b^2 - 4ac}{4a^2}$$ Take the square root of each side.

$$(x + \frac{b}{2a}) = \pm\sqrt{\frac{b^2 - 4ac}{4a^2}}$$ Simplify. Take the square root of $4a^2$.

$$x + \frac{b}{2a} = \pm\frac{\sqrt{b^2 - 4ac}}{2a}$$ Rearrange terms.

$$x = -\frac{b}{2a} \pm \frac{\sqrt{b^2 - 4ac}}{2a}$$ Place over common denominator.

$$x = \frac{-b \pm \sqrt{b^2 - 4ac}}{2a}$$ This is the quadratic formula.

Quadratic formula

The formula that can be used to find the roots of any quadratic equation

$x = \frac{-b \pm \sqrt{b^2 - 4ac}}{2a}$

This value of x is true for any quadratic equation and is called the **quadratic formula.** You can use the formula to find the roots of any quadratic equation by substituting the coefficients a and b and the constant c.

EXAMPLE 1 Use the quadratic formula to find the roots of $x^2 - 8x = -15$.

Step 1 Compare the equation with the model $ax^2 + bx + c = 0$. Determine the values of a, b, and c.

In $x^2 - 8x + 15 = 0$, $a = 1$, $b = -8$, and $c = 15$.

Step 2 Substitute the values for a, b, and c in the general quadratic formula.

$$x = \frac{-b \pm \sqrt{b^2 - 4ac}}{2a} = \frac{-(-8) \pm \sqrt{(8)^2 - 4(1)(15)}}{2(1)} =$$

$$\frac{8 \pm \sqrt{64-60}}{2} = \frac{8 \pm \sqrt{4}}{2} = \frac{8+2}{2} \text{ and } \frac{8-2}{2}$$

The roots are 5 and 3.

Step 3 Check.

Let $x = 5$	Let $x = 3$
$x^2 - 8x + 15 \stackrel{?}{=} 0$	$x^2 - 8x + 15 \stackrel{?}{=} 0$
$25 - 8(5) + 15 \stackrel{?}{=} 0$	$9 - 8(3) + 15 \stackrel{?}{=} 0$
$25 - 40 + 15 \stackrel{?}{=} 0$	$9 - 24 + 15 \stackrel{?}{=} 0$
$40 - 40 \stackrel{?}{=} 0$	$24 - 24 \stackrel{?}{=} 0$
$0 = 0$	$0 = 0$
True	True

Remember to begin by writing the equation in standard form.
$x^2 - 8x + 15 = 0$

Exercise A Find the roots of these equations. Remember to write the equation in standard form first.

1. $x^2 + 2x - 8 = 0$

2. $x^2 - 8x + 16 = 0$

3. $m^2 + 2 = 3m$

4. $x^2 - 13x = -36$

5. $y^2 - 9 = 0$

6. $x^2 - 25 = 0$

7. $-x^2 - 2x = -8$

8. $6r^2 + r - 1 = 0$

9. $-2x^2 + 11x = 15$

10. $5y^2 - 8y + 3 = 0$

11. $3x^2 + 2x - 7 = 0$

12. $2z^2 + 4z = 5$

13. $2x^2 + 7x + 3 = 0$

14. $x^2 - 10x = -22$

Exercise B

15. Check that $\frac{(1 + \sqrt{7})}{3}$ and $\frac{(1 - \sqrt{7})}{3}$ are the roots of $3x^2 = 2x + 2$.

Lesson 5 Graphing Quadratic Equations

Parabola

A plane curve generated by a point that moves so that its distance from a fixed point is always the same as its distance from a fixed line

Recall that the graph of a linear equation (such as $y = x + 1$) is a straight line. Because a quadratic equation contains a second power, the graph of a quadratic equation is not a straight line. This means you will need to plot more than two points in order to determine the shape of the graph.

EXAMPLE 1 Graph $y = x^2 - 1$.

Step 1 Make a table of values. Substitute values for x to find the values of y.

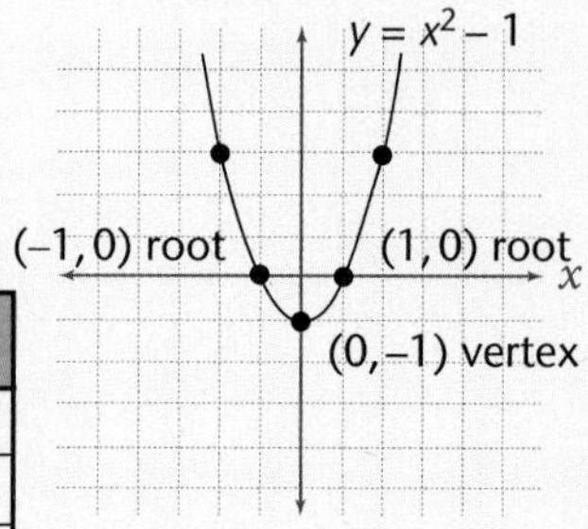

x	$y = x^2 - 1$	(x, y)
0	$0 - 1 = -1$	(0, –1)
1	$1 - 1 = 0$	(1, 0) ROOT
–1	$(-1)^2 - 1 = 0$	(–1, 0) ROOT
2	$4 - 1 = 3$	(2, 3)
–2	$(-2)^2 - 1 = 3$	(–2, 3)

$y = x^2 - 1$

(–1,0) root

(1,0) root

x

(0,–1) vertex

Step 2 Plot points along the graph using the coordinates from the table. Connect the points starting with the least value of x and continuing to the greatest value.

The shape of the graph of $x^2 - 1 = y$ is known as a **parabola.** This particular parabola opens upward or "holds water." The turning point of a parabola, in this case, the point $(0, -1)$, is called the vertex.

EXAMPLE 2 Graph $y = -x^2 + 1$.

Step 1 Make a table of values for x and y.

x	$y = -x^2 + 1$	(x, y)
0	$0 + 1 = 1$	(0, 1)
1	$-(1^2) + 1 = 0$	(1, 0) ROOT
–1	$-(-1)^2 + 1 = 0$	(–1, 0) ROOT
2	$-(2^2) + 1 = -3$	(2, –3)
–2	$-(-2)^2 - 1 = -3$	(–2, –3)

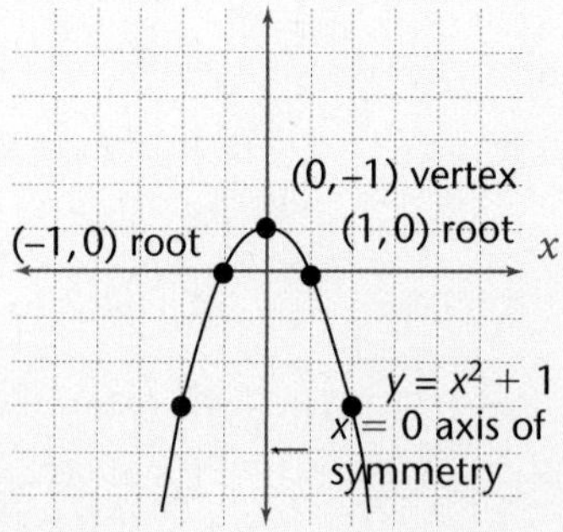

(0,–1) vertex

(–1,0) root

(1,0) root

x

$y = x^2 + 1$

$x = 0$ axis of symmetry

Step 2 Plot points along the graph using the coordinates from the table. Connect the points starting with the least value of x and continuing to the greatest value.

Symmetry

The exact agreement of parts on opposite sides of a line

Axis of symmetry

A perpendicular line that passes through the midpoint between the roots

As in the first example, the shape of the graph of $-x^2 + 1 = y$ is also a parabola. However, the vertex of this parabola is (0, 1) and the parabola opens downward or "spills water."

If you look closely at each parabola, you will notice that it has **symmetry** about a line through the vertex. In other words, if you fold the graph along an imaginary line halfway between the two roots, the two halves of the graph will match exactly. This imaginary line is called the **axis of symmetry**. In these two examples, the line of symmetry is the y-axis.

Axis of Symmetry

The axis of symmetry is a perpendicular line that passes through the midpoint between the roots.

You can compute the x-value of the axis of symmetry using the quadratic formula.

$$x = \frac{-b \pm \sqrt{b^2 - 4ac}}{2a} = \frac{-b}{2a} \pm \frac{\sqrt{b^2 - 4ac}}{2a}$$

We can place these values along a number line:

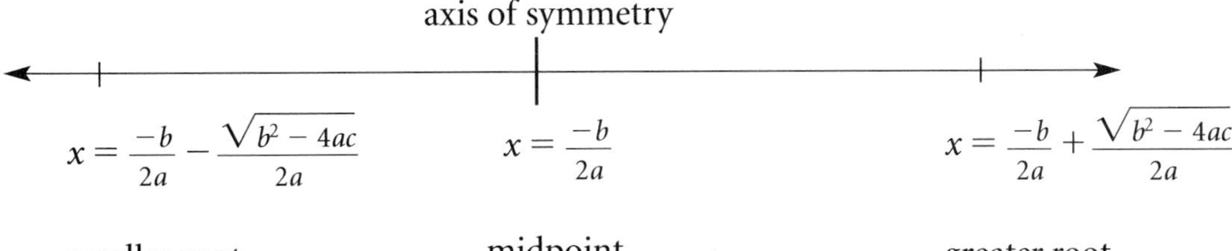

The number line shows that the x-value of the axis of symmetry is $x = \frac{-b}{2a}$.

Nature provides an example of symmetry. Both sides of the leaf match exactly.

EXAMPLE 3 Graph $y = x^2 + 2x - 3$ and identify its line of symmetry.

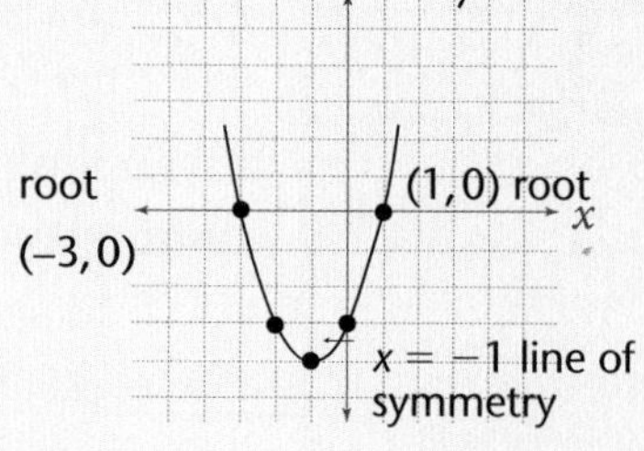

Step 1 To graph the line of symmetry, compare the equation $y = x^2 + 2x - 3$ with the model, $ax^2 + bx + c = 0$. In this case, $a = 1$ and $b = 2$. Substitute these values in the expression for the line of symmetry.

$x = \frac{-b}{2a}$ becomes $x = \frac{-2}{2(1)} = -1$.

The line of symmetry is the line $x = -1$.

Step 2 To graph the equation, make a table of values for x and y.

x	$y = x^2 + 2x - 3$	(x, y)
0	$0 + 0 - 3 = -3$	$(0, -3)$
1	$1^2 + 2(1) - 3 = 0$	$(1, 0)$ ROOT
−1	$(-1)^2 + 2(-1) - 3 = -4$	$(-1, -4)$
−2	$(-2)^2 + 2(-2) - 3 = -3$	$(-2, -3)$
−3	$(-3)^2 + 2(-3) - 3 = 0$	$(-3, 0)$ ROOT

Step 3 Plot points along the graph using the coordinates from the table. Connect the points using the axis of symmetry as a guide.

Exercise A Graph the following equations. The axis of symmetry and the roots for each are given.

1. $y = x^2, x = 0; (0, 0)$

2. $y = -(x^2), x = 0; (0, 0)$

3. $y = x^2 - 1, x = 0; (1, 0), (-1, 0)$

Exercise B Find the axis of symmetry using the expression $x = \frac{-b}{2a}$. Find the roots of the equation, then graph the equation.

4. $y = 2x^2 - 2$

5. $y = x^2 - 8x + 16$

6. $y = x^2 - 7x + 12$

If you have a graphing calculator, you can use it to graph linear or quadratic equations.

EXAMPLE 4 Graph $y = x^2 - 5$.

Step 1 Press GRAPH.

Step 2 Press $y(x)$ to go to the equation screen. Press CLEAR to remove any equations that may have been left in the calculator's memory.
You will see this screen.

Y1 =
Y2 =
Y3 =
Y4 =
Y5 =

Step 3 Move the cursor to Y1 =, then press × ^ 2 − 5.

Step 4 Press GRAPH. The screen will display this graph.

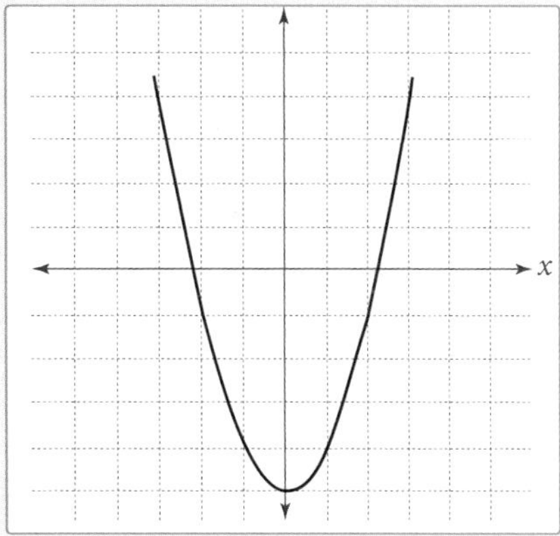

Exercise C Graph these equations. Use a graphing calculator if you have one.

7. $y = x^2 + 3$

8. $y = x^2 - 3$

9. $y = x^2 + 2x + 1$

10. $y = x^2 - 3x - 1$

Application

Using Quadratic Equations

The quadratic equation can be used to model the path of a rocket in flight.

EXAMPLE 1 A model rocket is launched vertically with a starting velocity of 100 feet per second. After how many seconds will the rocket be 50 feet above the ground?

Step 1 Use the vertical motion formula $h = -16t^2 + vt + s$.

h = height above ground in feet
t = time in seconds
v = starting velocity in feet per second
s = starting height in feet

$$h = -16t^2 + vt + s$$
$$(50) = -16t^2 + 100(t) + 0$$
$$0 = -16t^2 + 100t - 50$$

Step 2 Use the quadratic formula to find t.

$$x = \frac{-b \pm \sqrt{b^2 - 4ac}}{2a}$$
$$t = \frac{-100 \pm \sqrt{(100)^2 - (4)(-16)(-50)}}{2(-16)}$$
$$t = \frac{-100 \pm \sqrt{6800}}{-32}$$

$t = 0.55$ seconds and 5.70 seconds, rounded to the nearest hundredth.

The rocket will be 50 feet above the ground after 0.55 seconds and 5.70 seconds.

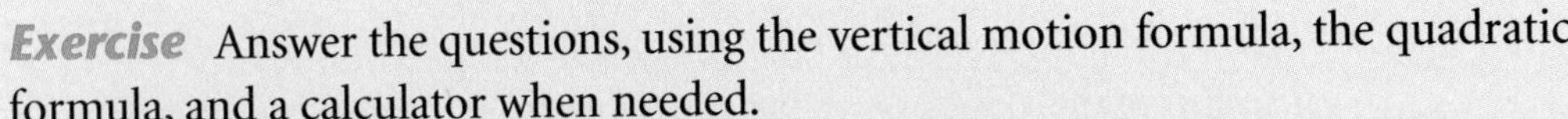

Exercise Answer the questions, using the vertical motion formula, the quadratic formula, and a calculator when needed.

1. After how many seconds will the rocket in the example be 100 feet above the ground?
2. After how many seconds will the rocket be 150 feet above the ground?
3. Look again at the example. Why is the model rocket 50 feet above the ground at two different times?
4. Explain how you could estimate the total flight time of the rocket.
5. Estimate the total flight time of the rocket.

Chapter 13 REVIEW

Write the letter of the correct answer.

1. Find the roots of this quadratic equation by factoring.
$3x^2 - 2x - 21 = 0$

A $3, 7$
B $7, -3$
C $\frac{7}{3}, -3$
D $-\frac{7}{3}, 3$

2. Find the roots of this quadratic equation by factoring.
$x^2 + 2x - 15 = 0$

A $-5, -3$
B $3, -5$
C $15, 1$
D $-1, 15$

3. What is the equation for the roots $\frac{3}{8}, -1$?

A $8x^2 + 3x - 5 = 0$
B $8x^2 + 5x - 5 = 0$
C $8x^2 + 5x - 3 = 0$
D $8x^2 - 5x + 3 = 0$

4. What is the equation for the roots $1, -2$?

A $x^2 + x - 2 = 0$
B $2x^2 + x - 2 = 0$
C $x^2 + 2x - 1 = 0$
D $x^2 + x - 1 = 0$

5. Solve the equation $x^2 - 4x - 21 = 0$ by completing the square.

A $-3, -7$
B $7, -3$
C $3, -7$
D $3, 7$

6. Solve the equation $x^2 + 6x = -5$ by completing the square.

A $1, 5$
B $-1, -5$
C $1, -5$
D $-1, 5$

7. Use the quadratic formula to find the roots of the equation: $3x^2 - 8x + 4 = 0$.

A $\frac{2}{3}, -2$
B $2, -\frac{2}{3}$
C $-\frac{2}{3}, -2$
D $\frac{2}{3}, 2$

Find the roots of these quadratic equations by factoring.

Example: $x^2 - x - 12 = 0$ Solution: $x^2 - x - 12 = 0$, $(x + 3)(x - 4) = 0$
$x + 3 = 0$. $x - 4 = 0$, $x = -3$, $x = 4$

8. $x^2 - 5x + 6 = 0$

9. $-x^2 + 8x = 0$

10. $x^2 - 2x - 24 = 0$

11. $x^2 + 4x = 21$

Find the equations for these roots.

Example: $-2, 5$ Solution: $(x + 2)(x - 5) = x^2 - 5x + 2x - 10$
$= x^2 - 3x - 10$

12. $-3, -8$ **13.** $3, -6$ **14.** $-3, 6$ **15.** $\frac{3}{4}, 3$

Solve these equations by completing the square. Check your answers.

Example: $y^2 + 8y + 2 = 0$ Solution:

$$y^2 + 8y + 2 = 0$$
$$y^2 + 8y = -2$$
$$y^2 + 8y + 16 = -2 + 16$$
$$y^2 + 8y + 16 = 14$$
$$(y + 4)^2 = 14$$
$$\sqrt{(y + 4)} = \pm\sqrt{14}$$
$$y + 4 = \pm\sqrt{14}$$
$$y = -4 + \sqrt{14} \quad \text{or} \quad y = -4 - \sqrt{14}$$

16. $y^2 + 4y - 6 = 0$

17. $x^2 + 6x - 16 = 0$

18. $d^2 - 8d = 0$

19. $2x^2 + 24x = 8$

Use the quadratic formula to find the roots to these equations. Check your answers.

Example: $6x^2 + 7x - 5$ Solution:

$$x = \frac{-b \pm \sqrt{b^2 - 4ac}}{2a}$$
$$x = \frac{-7 \pm \sqrt{(7)^2 - 4(6)(-5)}}{2(6)}$$
$$x = \frac{-7 \pm \sqrt{169}}{12}$$
$$x = \frac{-7 + 13}{12} \quad \text{or} \quad x = \frac{-7 - 13}{12}$$
$$x = \frac{6}{12} \text{ or } \frac{1}{2} \quad \text{or} \quad x = \frac{-20}{12} \text{ or } -1.6\overline{6}$$

20. $4x^2 - 7 = 0$

21. $2x^2 - 7x - 9 = 0$

22. $y^2 + 4y - 5 = 0$

23. $x^2 - 9x = -20$

Find the axis of symmetry and the roots for these equations. Then graph the equation.

Example: $y = x^2 + x$ Solution: $x = -\frac{1}{2}$, (0, 0), (−1, 0)

24. $y = -x^2 + 2x$

25. $y = -2x^2 - 4x + 1$

26. $y = 2x^2 - 4x - 16$

27. $y = x^2 + 9x + 18$

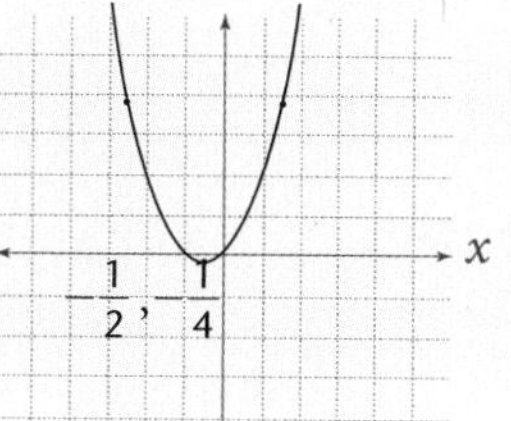

Answer these questions.

Example: The product of two consecutive integers is 72. What are the integers?

Solution: $x(x + 1) = 72$

$x^2 + x - 72 = 0$

$(x - 8)(x + 9) = 0$

$x - 8 = 0$ or $x + 9 = 0$

If $x = 8$, the integers are 8 and 9.

If $x = -9$, the integers are −8 and −9.

28. The product of two consecutive positive integers is 56. What are the integers?

29. The product of two consecutive positive integers is 156. What are the integers?

30. The product of two brothers' ages is 35. They are two years apart. How old are they?

Test-Taking Tip

Whenever you solve an open sentence and find the value of a variable, always check your answer. Substitute the value you found for the variable in the equation. Then evaluate each side of the equation and check that the two sides are equal.

Chapter 1 Supplementary Problems

Write *true* or *false* for each statement.

1. $6 + 3 = 18$

2. $2 \cdot 6 = 12$

3. $\frac{40}{8} = 32$

4. $25 - 13 = 38$

5. $21 \div 3 = 7$

Classify each expression, name the operation, and identify any variables.

6. $20 + 4$

7. $8y$

8. $2d - 14$

9. $n \div 3$

10. $4 \cdot 6$

Find the absolute value.

11. $|5|$

12. $|-22|$

13. $|+18|$

14. $|-16|$

15. $|25|$

Find each sum.

16. $-8 + 15$

17. $9 + 12$

18. $-5 + (-11)$

19. $3 + (-10)$

20. $-4 + 7$

Find each difference.

21. $5 - (-6)$

22. $7 - 9$

23. $-3 - 4$

24. $-2 - (-8)$

25. $+10 - 1$

Find each product.

26. $(7)(4)$

27. $(6)(-5)$

28. $(-3)(-9)$

29. $(11)(-3)$

30. $(-12)(2)$

Find each quotient.

31. $36 \div (-6)$

32. $-72 \div (-9)$

33. $27 \div 3$

34. $-80 \div 10$

35. $-49 \div (-7)$

Simplify each expression.

36. $3n + n$

37. $4v - 14 + 12v$

38. $-5x + 3 + 10x$

39. $b + 4b - 8$

40. $6g + (-8g) - 18$

Combine like terms to simplify each expression.

41. $2y + 3y + 4 + 6c$

42. $7r - 4f + 8 + 6r - 3f$

43. $t + 4t - 9 + 2b - 4b$

44. $3x + (-5b) + (-2x) + 15 + 5b$

45. $6 + d - 8s - 4d + 5$

Simplify each expression.

46. $a^5 \cdot a^4$

47. $c^7 \cdot c \cdot c^3$

48. $m^{10} \div m^5$

49. $z^9 \cdot z \cdot z^5 \cdot z^3$

50. $\frac{y^{15}}{y^2}$

Solve each problem using a formula.

51. Perimeter formula for a square: $P = 4s$. Find the perimeter, when $s = 12$ cm.

52. Perimeter formula for a regular nonagon: $P = 9s$. Find the perimeter, when $s = 13$ m.

53. Perimeter formula for a regular decagon: $P = 10s$. What is the length of each side, when the perimeter is 120 km?

54. Perimeter formula for an equilateral triangle: $P = 3s$. What is the length of each side, when the perimeter is 72 dm?

55. Perimeter formula for a triangle: $P = a + b + c$. What is the length of side b, when the perimeter is 132 mm, $a = 38$ mm, and $c = 59$ mm?

Chapter 2 Supplementary Problems

Find each sum using expanded notation.

1. $6y + 9y$

2. $15a - 2a$

3. $x + 4x$

4. $13n + 21n$

5. $7j + 7j$

Rewrite each expression showing the commutative property of multiplication.

6. mq

7. $(2s)(5c)$

8. $3(6t)$

9. $(7k)(10e)$

10. $(12v)(i)$

Rewrite each expression showing the associative property of addition.

11. $(5 + 4z) + 3$

12. $(3d + f) + 7$

13. $25g + (2w + 14)$

14. $(8 + r) + k$

15. $6b + (9c + 11e)$

Copy the problems. Find the products by multiplying the factors in parentheses first.

16. $(4 \cdot 25)3 = 4(25 \cdot 3)$

17. $40(2 \cdot 5) = (40 \cdot 2)5$

18. $(9 \cdot 2)50 = 9(2 \cdot 50)$

19. $6\,(2 \cdot 10) = (6 \cdot 2)10$

20. $5(5 \cdot 4) = (5 \cdot 5)4$

Use the distributive property to simplify each expression.

21. $3(x - j)$

22. $4(7w + -5)$

23. $-6(2 + z)$

24. $8(-f + -g)$

25. $-2(-k + 4)$

Use the distributive property to factor each expression.

26. $15m + 5y$

27. $-9n - 7n$

28. $mc - mh$

29. $qy^4 + qs^2$

30. $-wr - wh^3$

Copy and fill in the missing number or letter.

31. $6 + \blacksquare = 0$

32. $9 - \blacksquare = 0$

33. $-c^3 + \blacksquare = 0$

34. $u + \blacksquare = 0$

35. $-2 + \blacksquare = 0$

What is the reciprocal of each term? Check by multiplying.

36. 4

37. $\frac{1}{p}$

38. m^5

39. $\frac{1}{h}$

40. 15

Use your calculator to find the square root of each term.

41. $\sqrt{5.0625}$

42. $\sqrt{985.96}$

43. $\sqrt{335.9889}$

44. $\sqrt{320.41}$

45. $\sqrt{27.3529}$

Use your calculator to simplify each term.

46. $(3u)^4$

47. $(-5y)^3$

48. $(2a)^6$

49. $(-16d)^2$

50. $(-11n)^3$

Use the order of operations to simplify.

51. $4x + 3x(4)$

52. $3h(4 + 7) - 6h$

53. $10s - s(4) + 7s$

54. $g^3 + 6(g^3 + 2g^3)$

55. $5m^2 + (3m)(2m)$

Chapter 3 Supplementary Problems

Find the root of each equation by writing T (true) or F (false) for each value.

1. $5p = 25$ $p = 4, 5, 8, 20$

2. $7n = 42$ $n = 6, 10, 25, 42$

3. $3x = 12$ $x = 1, 3, 4, 9$

4. $8k = 40$ $k = 2, 3, 4, 5$

5. $6y = 18$ $y = 2, 3, 12, 18$

Find the solution for each equation.

6. $a - 3 = 15$

7. $p - 20 = 39$

8. $w - (-6) = 5$

9. $f - 13 = 20$

10. $n - (-8) = 6$

11. $g + 15 = 23$

12. $y + 2.4 = 8$

13. $u + (-6) = 17$

14. $c + 16.9 = 29.7$

15. $t + (-13) = 42$

16. $5h = 35$

17. $2q = 48$

18. $-8.6v = 77.4$

19. $-19.3i = -115.8$

20. $7.6d = 60.8$

21. $\frac{3}{4}j = 6$

22. $\frac{8}{9}j = 16$

23. $-\frac{2}{5}c = -10$

24. $\frac{7}{16}m = -21$

25. $\frac{1}{8}b = 2$

26. $3f - 2 = 13$

27. $2y - 10 = 14$

28. $\frac{5}{7}r + (-6) = 29$

29. $8t + 0 = 0$

30. $\frac{2}{3}m - (-4) = 8$

31. $P = 5s$ for s

32. $V = lwh$ for l

33. $C = 2\pi r$ for r

34. $s = \frac{P}{10}$ for P

35. $A = \frac{1}{2}(bh)$ for h

Use the Pythagorean theorem to solve each problem.

36. $a = 6, b = \blacksquare, c = 10$

37. $a = 15, b = 20, c = \blacksquare$

38. $a = \blacksquare, b = 40, c = 50$

39. $a = 18, b = \blacksquare, c = 30$

40. $a = \blacksquare, b = 28, c = 35$

Graph each of the equalities or inequalities on a number line.

41. $x > 0$

42. $x \leq 2$

43. $-2 \leq x \leq 2$

44. $x \geq -4$

45. $x \neq 1$

Solve each inequality.

46. $b + 3 < 6$

47. $\frac{3}{5}e \geq 9$

48. $t + (-9) > -3$

49. $-4m < 16$

50. $-\frac{1}{5}g \leq 3$

Chapter 4 Supplementary Problems

Write an equation and solve each question.

1. Five times a number decreased by 4 is 26. What is the number?

2. The sum of two consecutive integers is –21. What are the integers?

3. The sum of three consecutive odd integers is 51. What are the integers?

4. Sixty subtracted from eight times some number is 4. What is the number?

Use the 1% solution to solve each problem.

5. Aaron earns \$3,000 a month. He invests \$45 a month in a mutual fund. What percent of his income is invested in a mutual fund?

6. Sarah wants to buy a CD player that costs \$300. She has already saved \$231. What percent of the total has she saved?

7. Juan has an annual income of \$42,000. He saves 4% of his income. How much does he save?

8. Linda has 24 classical music CDs in her collection. 12% of her CDs are classical music. How many CDs does she have in her collection?

Find the percent of each number.

9. 26% of 88

10. 37% of 950

11. 64% of 25

12. 81% of 515

Solve each problem using kilometers or miles.

13. Michelle rides her bike for $3\frac{1}{3}$ hours at a speed of $15\frac{1}{2}$ kilometers per hour. How far does she travel?

14. DeNorris drives $162\frac{1}{2}$ miles in $2\frac{1}{2}$ hours. What is his average speed?

15. Maria and Patty jog for $1\frac{3}{4}$ hours at a rate of 18 kilometers per hour. How many kilometers do they jog?

16. Eliza and Mike walk at a rate of 4 miles per hour for $1\frac{1}{2}$ hours and 6 miles per hour for $\frac{1}{2}$ hour. What is their average speed?

Use your calculator to tell how many nickels and dimes are in each problem.

17. \$1.75, three times more dimes than nickels

18. \$3.00, three times more nickels than dimes

19. \$11.25, four times more dimes than nickels

20. \$1.20, six times more nickels than dimes

Find the interest, principal, or rate of interest. ($I = prt$)

	Principal	Rate	Time	Interest
21.	Principal: \$2,500	Rate: 6%	Time: 2 years	Interest: ■
22.	Principal: ■	Rate: 8%	Time: 4 years	Interest: \$200
23.	Principal: \$900	Rate: ■	Time: 3 years	Interest: \$135
24.	Principal: \$800	Rate: 13%	Time: 5 years	Interest: ■

Solve each problem.

25. Cashews cost \$3 per pound and peanuts cost \$2.50 a pound. Three pounds of cashews and three pounds of peanuts are mixed. What is the cost for one pound of the mixture?

26. Walnuts cost \$6 per pound and peanuts cost \$3.50 a pound. Four pounds of walnuts and three pounds of peanuts are mixed. What is the cost for one pound of the mixture?

27. A mixture of peanuts and walnuts sells for \$3.00 per pound. How many pounds of peanuts at \$1.50 per pound should be mixed with 12 pounds of walnuts at \$4.00 per pound?

28. The price for one pound of a mixture of cashews and walnuts is \$5.75. The total cost of the mixture is \$34.50. What is the total number of pounds in the mixture?

Find the missing term in each proportion

29. $\frac{3}{x} = \frac{18}{24}$

30. $\frac{6}{9} = \frac{14}{y}$

31. $\frac{m}{8} = \frac{20}{32}$

32. $\frac{4}{7} = \frac{32}{w}$

33. $\frac{z}{20} = \frac{6}{12}$

34. $\frac{12}{c} = \frac{24}{64}$

35. $\frac{6}{18} = \frac{b}{36}$

Chapter 5 Supplementary Problems

Show why these statements are true.

1. $(y^3)^3 = y^9$

2. $(a^2)^4 = a^8$

3. $[(x + y)^3]^2 = (x + y)^6$

Find the quotient.

4. $(9^9) \div (9^6)$

5. $\frac{7^8}{7^4}$

6. $\frac{n^5}{n^3}, n \neq 0$

7. $(5g + 3y)^{10} \div (5g + 3y)^4, 5g + 3y \neq 0$

8. $\frac{(h - i)^8}{(h - i)^3}, h - i \neq 0$

Write the following numbers in scientific notation.

9. 0.00000000554

10. 9,000,000

11. 0.00000078

Write the following numbers in standard notation.

12. $2.6(10^5)$

13. $3.14(10^{-3})$

14. $5.21(10^6)$

Find the sum, difference, product, or quotient. Be sure your answers are in scientific notation.

15. $2.7(10^{-3}) + 3.4(10^{-3})$

16. $8.3(10^8) - 4.9(10^8)$

17. $1.3(10^{-2}) \cdot 2.1(10^{-6}) \cdot 2(10^{10})$

18. $1.6(10^3) \div 3.2(10^{-8})$

19. $2.2(10^{-7}) \cdot 2.1(10^{-3}) \cdot 4.0(10^8)$

Find the sum and difference for each pair of polynomials.

20. $2x^2 + 5x + 1$

$-2x^2 + 6x + 3$

21. $c^4 + c^2 + 3c + 1$

$2c^4 + 3c^2 + c + 5$

22. $-3w^5 - 6w^4 - 2w^3 - w^2 - w - 5$

$w^5 + 6w^4 + 2w^3 + w^2 - w + 5$

23. $k^5 + k^3 + 3$

$k^4 + w^2 + 5$

24. $n^5 + n^3 + n - 3$

$n^7 + n^2$

25. $8d^7 + 3d^6 + 9d^3$

$d^2 + d - 8$

Find the product.

26. $(y + 4)(y + 3)$

27. $(b - 4)(b + 4)$

28. $3n^3(n^2 + 2n - 8)$

29. $(-4x^2 - 5)(x^2 - 5)$

30. $(c^3 + c^2)^2$

31. $(3z + 1)(z - 2)$

32. $(u^3 + 3)(2u^2 + 5u + 4)$

33. $(3y^3 - 6)(4y^5 - y)$

Find the quotients. Identify any remainder. Use multiplication to check your answer.

34. $\frac{(24x^2 + 32x - 24)}{8}$

35. $\frac{(30y^3 - 36y^2 + 42y + 48)}{-6}$

36. $\frac{(h^2 - 2h)^2}{(h^2 - 2h)}$

37. $\frac{(4s^2 - 12s)}{2s(s - 3)}$

38. $(42t^3 + 70t^2 - 21t) \div 7t$

39. $(2y^2 + 2y) \div (y + 1)$

40. $(25x^3 - 5x^2 + x - 2)(7x^3 - 4x^2) \div (7x^3 - 4x^2)$

Chapter 6 Supplementary Problems

Find the GCF for these groups.

1. 25, 75

2. 22, 121

3. 36, 27

4. $16x, 20x^2, 12x^3$

5. $15a^3d, 25ad^3$

Find the GCF for these expressions.

6. $20j^4 + 10$

7. $18x^3 + 24x^2 + 42x$

8. $25c^4 - 35c^3 - 45c^2 - 55$

9. $-21x^5y^5 - 63x^4y^2 - 56x^2y^2 + 14xy^2$

10. $13w^3t^2 - 26wt$

Factor the following expressions. Check by multiplying.

11. $x^2 - x - 56$

12. $c^2 + 6c + 9$

13. $y^2 - y - 12$

14. $3m^2 + 24m + 36$

15. $5x^4 + 5x^3 - 60x^2$

16. $6e^2 + 33e + 42$

17. $12n^2 - 26n + 10$

18. $3z^2 + 35z - 52$

19. $10s^2 + 17s + 6$

20. $3v^4 + 15v^3 + 18v^2$

21. $b^2 - 81$

22. $q^2 - 400$

23. $36g^2 - 49$

24. $81r^2 - 16$

25. $25w^4 - 9x^2$

Find the factors of these perfect square trinomials.

26. $i^2 - 26i + 169$

27. $y^2 + 16y + 64$

28. $k^2 - 20k + 100$

29. $p^2 + 22p + 121$

30. $m^2 - 44m + 484$

Find the value of the variable in each expression.

31. $3d = 0$

32. $6(x + 4) = 0$

33. $(h - 4)(h + 6) = 0$

34. $(2y - 4)(3y + 6) = 0$

35. $6(3b - 12)(b + 9) = 0$

Solve each of these quadratic equations. Be sure to check your work.

36. $x^2 + 10x + 24 = 0$

37. $y^2 - 9y + 18 = 0$

38. $b^2 + 11b + 28 = 0$

39. $6s^2 - 12s + 6 = 0$

40. $10x^2 + 60x + 80 = 0$

Chapter 7 Supplementary Problems

Use the following words to fill in the ■: *box-and-whiskers plot, dependent, frequency, fundamental principle of counting, histogram, impossible, independent, mean, mode, probability, range, sample space,* and *stem-and-leaf plot.*

1. A ■ table is a method used to summarize data.

2. When data is organized and displayed using stems and leaves, it is called a ■.

3. A bar graph that uses intervals is called a ■.

4. The difference between the highest and lowest values is the ■ of data.

5. The sum of the values in a set of data divided by the total number of values is called the ■.

6. The value that occurs the most is called the ■.

7. To show the concentration and spread of data in a set, one uses a ■.

8. The chance that an outcome will occur is called ■.

9. An event that has a probability of zero is called an ■ event.

10. The set of all possible outcomes of an experiment is called a ■.

11. The outcome of one event affects the outcome of another event in ■ events.

12. The outcome of one event has no effect on the outcome of another event in ■ events.

13. A general rule that states you can multiply the numbers of choices to find the total number of choices is called the ■.

Use the chart on English test scores for problems 14–21.

English Test Scores							
59	73	87	59	90	80	58	69
60	63	78	96	59	68	81	85
90	73	64	98	97	75	77	91

14. Display the data in a stem-and-leaf plot.

15. How many students had scores lower than 60?

16. How many students scored 75 or higher?

17. What score occurred the most?

18. What was the lowest score?

19. What was the highest score?

20. How many students received scores between 62 and 76?

21. Display the data in a histogram using intervals of 10.

Use this data set {$3.39, $4.77, $9.07, $1.40, $6.23, $7.25, $2.23, $4.77, $5.01} for problems 22–25.

22. Find the range.

23. Find the mean.

24. Find the median.

25. Find the mode.

Use the box-and-whiskers plot for problems 26–30.

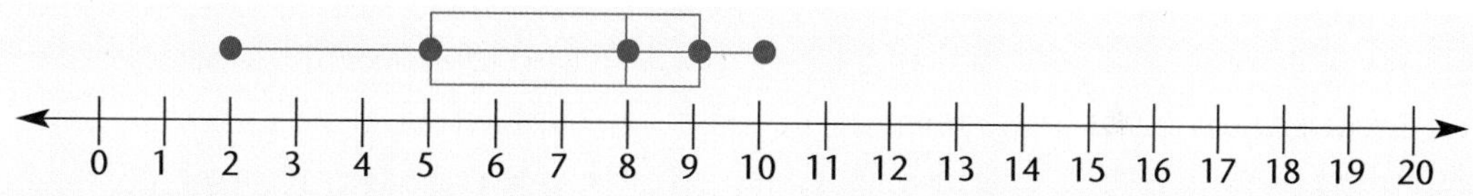

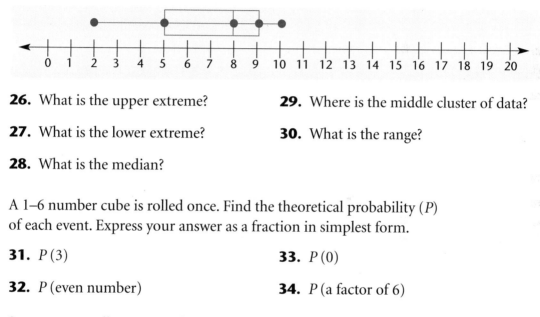

26. What is the upper extreme?

27. What is the lower extreme?

28. What is the median?

29. Where is the middle cluster of data?

30. What is the range?

A 1–6 number cube is rolled once. Find the theoretical probability (P) of each event. Express your answer as a fraction in simplest form.

31. $P(3)$

32. P(even number)

33. $P(0)$

34. P(a factor of 6)

Suppose you roll a 1–6 number cube and toss a coin. Use a tree diagram to determine the probability of each event.

35. P(heads and 2)

36. P(tails and a number less than 4)

37. P(not heads and not 3)

A bag contains 10 marbles of equal size. One marble is blue, one is white, three are yellow, and five are red. A marble is taken from the bag two times. Each time a marble is taken, it is not replaced.

38. Find P(red and red)

39. Find P(blue and white)

40. Find P(yellow and blue)

Chapter 8 Supplementary Problems

Reduce each fraction to its lowest terms.

1. $\frac{35}{45}$

2. $\frac{200}{250}$

3. $\frac{16}{24}$

4. $-\frac{12}{144}$

5. $\frac{21}{42}$

6. $\frac{c^8}{c^3}$

7. $\frac{24s^7}{6s^2}$

8. $\frac{45hg^3}{63h^4g^5}$

9. $\frac{18x^5y^3}{81x^5y}$

10. $\frac{(p^2 - 16)}{(p + 4)}$

11. $\frac{(y^2 + 7y + 12)}{(y + 4)}$

12. $\frac{(m + 6)}{(m^2 + 2m - 24)}$

13. $\frac{(x^4 + 15x^3 + 56x^2)}{(2x^3 + 30x^2 + 112x)}$

Multiply or divide. Reduce your answers to lowest terms.

14. $5\frac{1}{3} \cdot 6\frac{2}{9}$

15. $\frac{7}{8} \div \frac{2}{5}$

16. $\frac{1}{(y^2 - 16)} \cdot \frac{(y + 4)}{(y - 4)}$

17. $\frac{(d + 6)}{(d - 6)} \div \frac{(d + 6)}{(d^2 - 36)}$

18. $e^2f^3 \div ef^2$

19. $3\frac{3}{4} \cdot \frac{7}{8}$

Simplify these complex fractions. Write your answers in lowest terms.

20. $\frac{9}{\frac{3}{4}}$

21. $\frac{\frac{3}{16}}{\frac{15}{16}}$

22. $\frac{\frac{c}{u}}{\frac{u}{d}}$

23. $\frac{\frac{x^2}{w^3}}{\frac{x^3}{w^2}}$

Find each sum or difference.

24. $(\frac{5}{8}) - (\frac{5}{16})$

25. $(\frac{2}{y}) + (\frac{y}{3^2})$

26. $\frac{5}{(b - 1)} + \frac{4}{(b - 1)^2}$

27. $\frac{2}{(k + 2)} - \frac{1}{(k - 3)}$

28. $\frac{3x}{(x - 8)} - \frac{6x}{(x + 8)}$

29. $\frac{9}{(v^2 - 9)} - \frac{3}{(v + 3)}$

Solve for each variable.

30. $\frac{n}{16} = \frac{75}{80}$

31. $\frac{g}{8} = \frac{72}{64}$

32. $\frac{13}{11} = \frac{p}{65}$

33. $\frac{5}{7}a = -35$

34. $3\frac{1}{2}t = 5\frac{1}{4}$

35. $\frac{7}{8}x - \frac{3}{4}x = 15$

36. $\frac{3}{2}d = -9$

37. $\frac{(2c - 6)}{3} = 7$

38. $\frac{2(r - 4)}{5} = -3$

39. $\frac{1}{2} + \frac{9}{16} = \frac{n}{4}$

40. $\frac{3}{8} - \frac{5}{8} = \frac{q}{3}$

Solve these problems. Make sure your answers are in lowest terms.

41. Gloria received four-fifths of the election votes. 385 students voted. How many votes did Gloria receive?

42. The Washington High School football team's winning ratio is 4 to 3. They won 12 games. How many games did they lose?

43. George has $\frac{3}{4}$ pounds of raspberries. Each jelly recipe needs $\frac{3}{16}$ pounds of raspberries. How many recipes can he make?

44. The scale drawing of Jefferson Park reads 2 cm : 7 km. The width of the park is $3\frac{9}{10}$ cm. How many kilometers wide is the park?

45. Jenny's survey reveals that $\frac{5}{8}$ of the students at Washington High School watch $2\frac{1}{2}$ hours of television on Friday night. There are 648 students at the high school. How many hours of television do they watch altogether on Friday night?

Chapter 9 Supplementary Problems

Write the ordered pair that represents the location of each point.

1. Point B

2. Point D

3. Point A

4. Point E

5. Point C

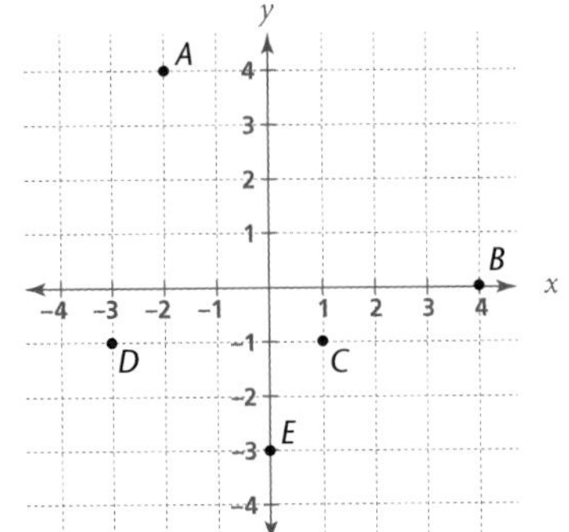

Draw a coordinate system and graph the following points.

6. Point X at $(2, -1)$

7. Point V at $(-4, 1)$

8. Point S at $(0, 4)$

9. Point M at $(-3, -5)$

Copy and complete the table of values for each equation.

10.

$y = x - 2$	
x	y
−1	
0	
1	

11.

$y = 3x + 1$	
x	y
−1	
0	
1	

Find the x-intercept and the y-intercept of each graph.

12. $y = x + 1$

13. $y = x - 4$

14. $y = -2x + 3$

15. $y = 5x - 2$

Find the slope of the line that passes through the following points.

16. $(3, 6)(-2, -4)$

17. $(2, 5)(-1, -4)$

18. $(0, 2)(-6, 8)$

19. $(2, -2)(1, -3)$

Graph the line that passes through the following points. Then write the equation of each line.

20. $(0, -3)(2, -1)$

21. $(5, -3)(-1, 3)$

22. $(4, 3)(-2, 0)$

23. $(0, 0)(-2, 4)$

Write the equation of the line that has the given slope and passes through the given point.

24. $m = 3; (2, 7)$

25. $m = -1; (4, -5)$

26. $m = 4; (3, 8)$

27. $m = \frac{1}{2}; (-4, -1)$

Is each graph an example of a function? Write *yes* or *no*.

28.

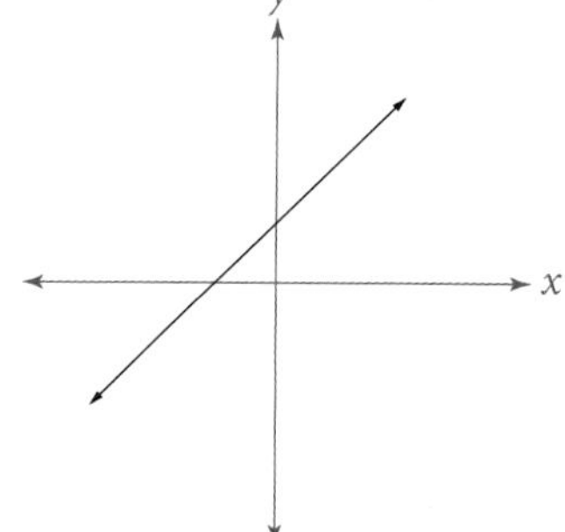

29.

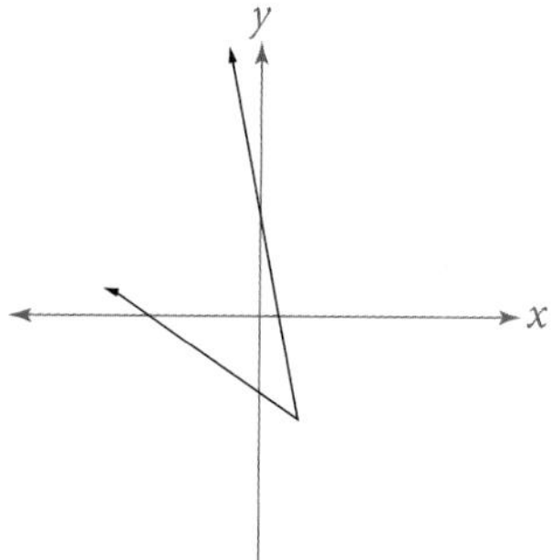

Evaluate each function two times. Use $x = 3$ and $x = -2$.

30. $f(x) = -x^2 + x$

31. $f(x) = 2x^2 + x$

32. $f(x) = x^2 + 2x$

Graph the region represented by each line.

33. $y > -3x$

34. $y \leq x - 3$

35. $y < x - 1$

Chapter 10 Supplementary Problems

Write the equation of the line parallel to the given line and passing through the given point. Check your answer by graphing the lines.

1. $y = 3x - 2; (3, 9)$

2. $y = x + 4; (2, 2)$

3. $2y = 8x - 8; (1, 6)$

4. $y - 5 = -2x; (0, 0)$

5. $2y = x - 4; (6, 5)$

6. $8x - 2y = -10; (2, 5)$

7. $3y - 3x = 18; (3, -5)$

8. $6x = -2y + 16; (0, 1)$

9. $2y + 16 = 6x; (1, 7)$

10. $4y - 8x = -12; (2, 5)$

Find a common solution for the systems that have one.
Write *none* if the system does not have a common solution.

11. $y = 3x - 2$
$y = x + 4$

12. $y = 5x - 3$
$9x + 3 = 3y$

13. $2y = x + 2$
$3y = x + 6$

14. $-4x = -y - 3$
$-2x = -y - 5$

15. $y = 4x + 6$
$y - 3x = 4$

16. $y + 2x = -1$
$y + x = 3$

17. $y - x = -7$
$y = 3x - 11$

18. $2x = y - 5$
$2y = 4x - 14$

19. $5y - 5x = -5$
$y = 2x - 5$

20. $2y + x = 4$
$y + 12 = 3x$

Graph each system of equations on the same set of axes.
Name the point of intersection.

21. $y = x + 1$
$y = 2x - 1$

22. $y = 3x + 1$
$y = x + 3$

23. $y = 3x$
$y = x + 4$

Tell whether the following conjunctions are true or false. Explain.

24. All intersecting lines have the same slope, and all vertical lines have slopes that are equal to zero.

25. Subtracting four is the same as adding negative four, and 2 is the same as $\frac{22}{11}$.

26. $3(6b + 2) = 18b + 2$, and the reciprocal of $\frac{3}{8}$ is $\frac{8}{3}$.

27. There are 12 eggs in a dozen, and there are 169 eggs in 12 dozen.

Graph each four-sided figure. Write the equations of the lines that form the figure.

28. A square with the vertices at (2, 3), (4, 1), (2, 1), (4, 3)

29. A square with the vertices at (1, 4), (2, 5), (1, 5), (2, 4)

30. A rectangle with the vertices at (3, –2), (–5, 4), (3, 4), (–5, –2)

Set up and solve a system of equations to answer the questions.

31. One number is 36 more than the second number. Seven times the smaller number is the larger number. What are the numbers?

32. The difference between two supplementary angles is 130 degrees. What are the angles? (Supplementary angles are two angles whose sum equals 180 degrees.)

33. The difference between two supplementary angles is 20 degrees. What are the angles?

34. Two angles are complementary. The larger angle is eight times the smaller angle. What are the angles? (Complementary angles are two angles whose sum equals 90 degrees.)

35. The perimeter of a rectangle is 300 feet. The width of the rectangle is 10 feet more than the length. What are the length and width of the rectangle?

Chapter 11 Supplementary Problems

Write the decimal expansions for these rational numbers. Tell whether the expansions are terminating or repeating.

1. $\frac{7}{8}$

2. $\frac{2}{3}$

3. $\frac{1}{16}$

4. $\frac{4}{11}$

5. $\frac{5}{8}$

Find the rational number equivalents for these decimal expansions. Be sure your answer is in lowest terms.

6. $0.6\overline{0}$

7. $0.8\overline{3}$

8. $0.9375\overline{0}$

9. $0.15625\overline{0}$

10. $0.\overline{2}$

Use your calculator to find the roots for these radicals. Tell whether they are rational or irrational.

11. $\sqrt[8]{6{,}561}$

12. $\sqrt[7]{1{,}024}$

13. $\sqrt[5]{243}$

14. $\sqrt[3]{900}$

15. $\sqrt[4]{2{,}100}$

Simplify the following radicals. Be sure to check your answers.

16. $\sqrt{1{,}296}$

17. $\sqrt{2{,}704x^6y^2}$

18. $\sqrt{\frac{64}{81}}$

19. $\sqrt{\frac{25g^4}{36a^2}}$

20. $\sqrt{\frac{49t^6}{121b^8}}$

Simplify, then add or subtract.

21. $\sqrt{100} + \sqrt{25}$

22. $3\sqrt{18} - 3\sqrt{2}$

23. $2\sqrt{75} + 8\sqrt{3}$

24. $4\sqrt{48} - 4\sqrt{27}$

25. $2\sqrt{12x^2} + \sqrt{48x^2}$

Rationalize or conjugate the denominator of each fraction. Be sure your answer is in simplest form.

26. $3\frac{\sqrt{2}}{\sqrt{5}}$

27. $\frac{6\sqrt{28}}{2\sqrt{7}}$

28. $\frac{5\sqrt{35}}{2\sqrt{7}}$

29. $\frac{2}{(2 + \sqrt{3})}$

30. $\frac{2\sqrt{5}}{(4 + \sqrt{5})}$

Solve each equation for the unknown.

31. $\sqrt{n} = 64$

32. $\sqrt{2x} = 4$

33. $\sqrt{c} = \frac{5}{6}$

34. $\sqrt{x} + 4 = 10$

35. $25 - \sqrt{y} = 8$

Simplify using exponents, then find the products.

36. $y^3 \cdot \sqrt[5]{y}$

37. $m \cdot \sqrt{m}$

38. $\sqrt[3]{w} \cdot w^3$

39. $q^5 \cdot \sqrt[4]{q}$

40. $d^3 \cdot \sqrt[7]{d}$

Chapter 12 Supplementary Problems

Classify each angle or pairs of angles. Write *acute, right, obtuse, straight, adjacent, complementary, supplementary, interior, exterior, alternate interior, vertical,* or *corresponding*. For any angle or pair of angles, more than one name may apply. Line $x \parallel y$.

1. $\angle i$

2. $\angle n$

3. $\angle b$ and $\angle i$

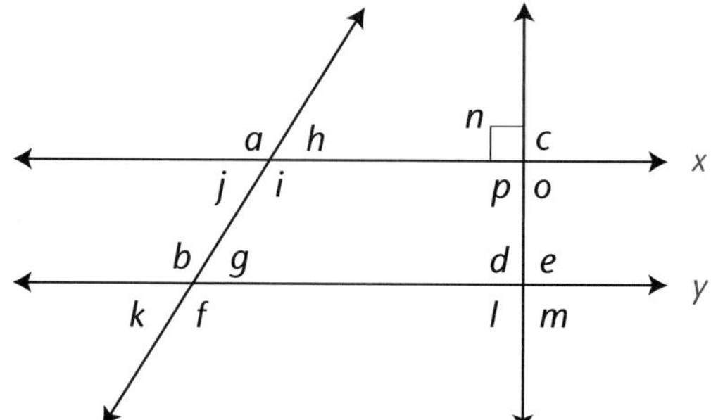

4. $\angle c$ and $\angle e$

5. $\angle k$ and $\angle f$

6. $\angle h$ and $\angle j$

7. $\angle p$ and $\angle o$

8. $\angle a$ and $\angle b$

9. $\angle d$ and $\angle n$

10. $\angle h$ and $\angle k$

In this figure, line $a \parallel$ line b, c is the transversal, and measure of angle $x = 65.7°$. Find the measure (m) of each of the following angles.

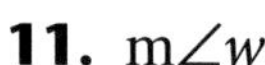

11. m$\angle w$

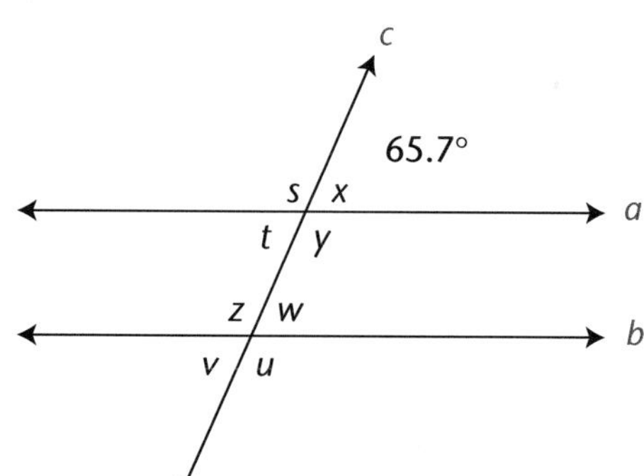

12. m$\angle t$

13. m$\angle y$

14. m$\angle s$

15. m$\angle u$

16. m$\angle v$

17. m$\angle z$

In each triangle, find m∠x.

18. 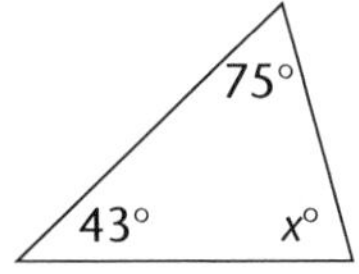

20. 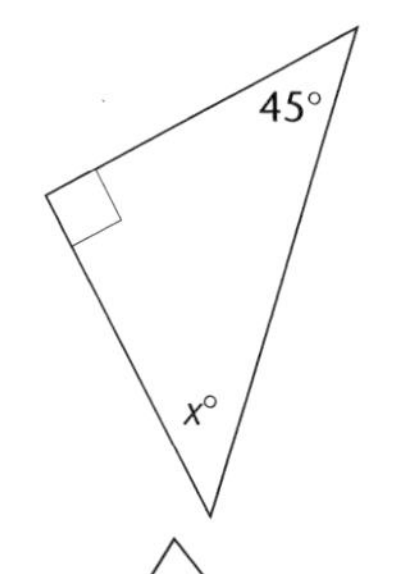

22. 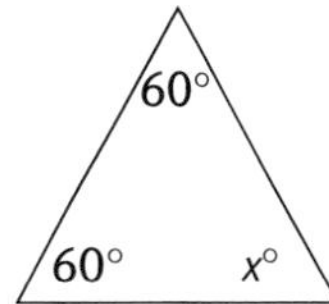

19. 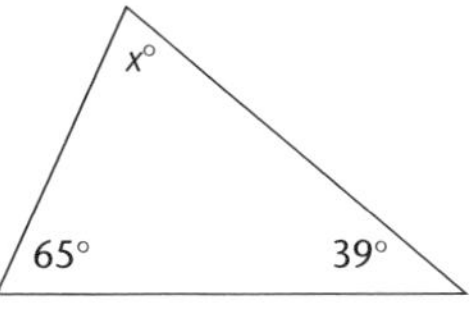

21. 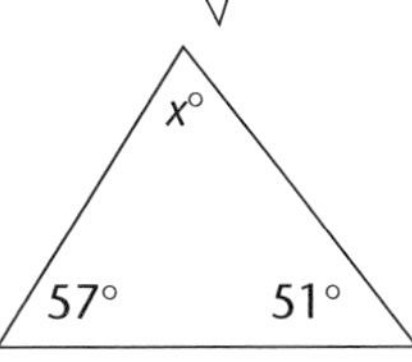

Name the theorem that proves congruence.

23. 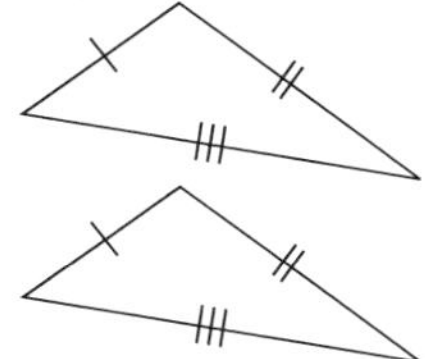

24. 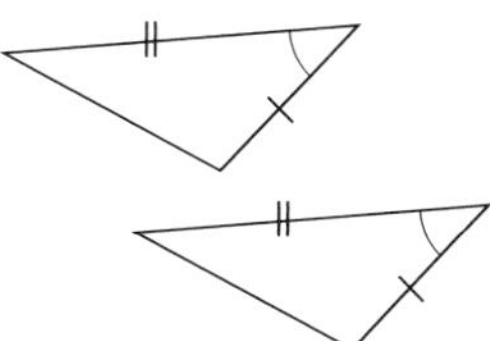

25. 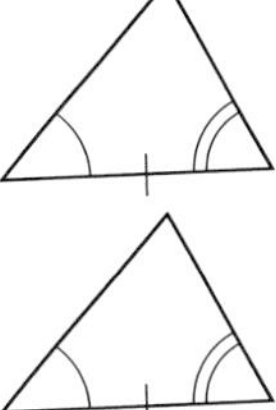

Use your calculator to find the following values.

26. tan 45°

27. sin 90°

28. cos 60°

29. cos 90°

30. sin 30°

31. Mildred stands 45 feet from a tree to measure the angle to the top of the tree. The angle measures 65°. How tall is the tree to the nearest foot?

32. A 25-foot guy wire is attached to the top of a telephone pole. The guy wire forms a 45° angle with the ground. How tall is the telephone pole to the nearest foot?

33. On a particular day, when the sun was setting, it caused the Bryan Library to cast a shadow at an angle of 32° The shadow was 100 feet long. How tall is the Bryan Library to the nearest foot?

34. Angle A of a right triangle is 38°. The hypotenuse is 6 feet. What is the length of the opposite side to the nearest tenth?

35. Angle A of a right triangle is 52°. The hypotenuse is 41 meters. What is the length of the adjacent side to the nearest tenth?

Chapter 13 Supplementary Problems

Find the roots of these quadratic equations by factoring.

1. $x^2 - 10x = -21$

2. $x^2 - x - 30 = 0$

3. $2x^2 + 4x = 0$

4. $x^2 + 11x + 24 = 0$

5. $5x^2 - 9x = 2$

6. $x^2 - 16x + 55 = 0$

Find the equations for these roots.

7. $-4, 3$

8. $6, 7$

9. $8, -2$

10. $\frac{1}{2}, 3$

11. $4, -\frac{2}{3}$

12. $1, -6$

Solve these equations by completing the square.

13. $m^2 + 6m + 2 = 0$

14. $c^2 + 8c - 10 = 0$

15. $v^2 + 4v - 11 = 0$

16. $x^2 - 14x = -10$

17. $4d^2 + 8d = 2$

18. $y^2 - 10y = -20$

Use the quadratic formula to find the roots to these equations. Check your answers.

19. $2x^2 + 7x - 4 = 0$

20. $y^2 + 14y + 33 = 0$

21. $2x^2 + 3x - 2 = 0$

22. $y^2 + 6y - 16 = 0$

23. $y^2 - 2y - 15 = 0$

24. $2x^2 - 11x + 14 = 0$

Find the axis of symmetry and the roots for these equations. Then graph the equation.

25. $y = x^2 + 6x + 8$

26. $y = 2x^2 - 5x - 3$

27. $y = -x^2 + 10x - 24$

28. $y = x^2 - 12x + 27$

29. $y = x^2 + x - 2$

30. $y = 2x^2 + 5x + 3$

Answer these questions.

31. The product of two consecutive positive integers is 182. What are the integers?

32. The product of two consecutive odd integers is 255. What are the integers?

33. The product of two consecutive even integers is 288. What are the integers?

34. The product of two sisters' ages is 72. They are one year apart. How old are they?

35. Trixie is 8 years older than her brother. The product of their ages is 33. How old is Trixie? How old is her brother?

Selected Answers and Solutions

CHAPTER 1

Lesson 1, page 3

1. 12 = 12 true **3.** 12 = 12 true **5.** 7 = 8 false **7.** 24 = 22 false **9.** 36 = 36 true **11.** true **13.** false **15.** true **17.** open **19.** true **21.** 7 = 10 false **23.** 10 = 10 true **25.** 45 = 40 false **27.** 2 = 4 false **29.** 4 = 4 true

Lesson 2, pages 4–5

1. algebraic because it includes a variable and an operation, division **3.** algebraic, addition **5.** numerical, subtraction **7.** algebraic, addition and multiplication **9.** algebraic, multiplication and multiplication **11.** *d*, the value of *d* is unknown **13.** *e* **15.** *k* **17.** *y* **19.** *n* **21.** multiplication, 2*x* means 2 times some unknown number *x* **23.** multiplication and subtraction **25.** multiplication and division **27.** multiplication **29.** multiplication **31.** numerical because it contains only numbers, addition **33.** algebraic, multiplication, *x* **35.** algebraic, multiplication and addition, *y* **37.** numerical, multiplication **39.** algebraic, multiplication and addition, *m* **41.** 3 • 7, there are seven days in one week **43.** 3 + 18 **45.** 3 • *n*

Lesson 3, page 7

1. −4; on a number line, −4 and 4 are the same distance from zero **3.** −6 **5.** −11 **7.** 24 **9.** −9 **11.** 2, the distance of −2 from 0 is 2 **13.** 4 **15.** 6 **17.** 3 **19.** 8 **21.** +15 yards, −8 yards; a gain is + and a loss is − ; the team is 7 yards from where it started. **23.** 4° warmer **25.** Use a number line to indicate the time.

Try This

Answers will vary. Sample answer: −2 because a countdown usually begins with a negative real number and ends at zero.

Lesson 4, page 9

1. 5 + 8 = 13 **3.** 4 **5.** −8 **7.** −2 **9.** −4 **11.** −6 **13.** −4 **15.** 0 **16.** −5°F + 4°F = −1°F **17.** –2°F **19.** 0°F **21.** 8°F **23.** 10°F **25.** −5°C + (−5°C) = −5°C − 5°C = −10°C **27.** 6°C **29.** −11°C **31.** −170 **33.** 231 **35.** −493

Lesson 5, page 11

1. 5 + −4; 1 **3.** −5 + 6; 1 **5.** −7 + −5; −12 **7.** −3 + 10; 7 **9.** 8 + 1; 9 **11.** −6 + −2; −8 **13.** 9 + −6 = 3 **15.** 8 + 8 = 16 **17.** 12 + 3 = 15 **19.** 7 + −9 = −2 **21.** 3 + −6 = −3 **23.** 5 + −8 = −3 **25.** 6 + 9 = 15 **27.** 8 + −2 = 6 **28.** 153°F, add the absolute value of each number **29.** 18°F

Lesson 6, page 13

1. 56, (positive) • (positive) = (positive) **3.** −30 **5.** 81 **7.** 60 **9.** −60 **11.** 63 **13.** 24 **15.** 30 **17.** −50 **19.** −20 **21.** positive, (negative) • (negative) = (positive) **23.** positive **25.** zero **27.** positive **29.** 12 feet, (4)(3) = 12

Lesson 7, page 15

1. 7, (positive) ÷ (positive) = (positive) **3.** −4 **5.** 9 **7.** 6 **9.** −8 **11.** 0 **13.** 10 **15.** 7 **17.** 8 **19.** 3 **21.** negative, (positive) ÷ (negative) = (negative) **23.** negative **25.** positive **27.** negative **29.** +, (positive) ÷ (positive) = (positive)

Lesson 8, pages 16–17

1. $2m$, $1m + 1m = 2m$ **3.** $3v$ **5.** $4c$ **6.** $3m$, $2m + 1m = 3m$ **7.** $10h$ **9.** $8k$ **11.** $5p + 8p + 6 = 13p + 6$ **13.** $10y - 4$ **15.** $9 + 4c$ **17.** $6q - 2q - 3 = 4q - 3$ **19.** $20v + 9v + 9 = 29v + 9$ **21.** $-5g$ **23.** $-12m$ **25.** $28x$ **27.** $2r - 18r + 18 = -16r + 18$ **29.** $15u - 17u - 18 = -2u - 18$ **31.** $9c$, $1c + 9c = 10c$ **33.** $-6e$ **35.** $-10z$ **36.** $4x + 20$, a sum is the result of addition **37.** $2n - 30$ or $30 - 2n$ **39.** $4p - 3$

Lesson 9, pages 18–19

1. $8x + 4 + 7b$, the like terms are $5x$ and $3x$ **3.** $16 + 2a + 9u$ **5.** $7y + 17y + 10p + 10p + 18 = 24y + 20p + 18$ **7.** $m + 2m + 10 + 7t = 3m + 10 + 7t$ **9.** $8w - 4w - 13 + y = 4w - 13 + y$ **11.** $8u - 4u + 7b + 2b + 17 = 4u + 9b + 17$ **13.** $9g - 7g + 2 + 15 + 16r - 13r = 2g + 17 + 3r$ **15.** $3m - m + 7y - 6y + 5 = 2m + y + 5$ **16.** $-9t - 14 + (-5c)$ or $-9t - 14 - 5c$, the like terms are $7t$ and $-16t$, and $9c$ and $-14c$ **17.** $8 + (-16c) + (-16b)$ or $8 - 16c - 16b$ **19.** $3x + 3x + (-17) + 21f - (-21f) = 6x + (-17) + 42f$ **21.** $y - 2y - 14 + 30c + 16c = -y - 14 + 46c$ **23.** $40j + (-32m) + 16$ or $40j - 32m + 16$ **25.** $9m - 6m + 14 + 4r + 12r = 3m - 14 + 16r$ **26.** false, the expression simplifies to $-2m + 15c - 4$ **27.** false, $44x + 9 + 6m$ **29.** false, $7 + 6y + 8m$

Lesson 10, page 21

1. true, $23 = 2 \cdot 2 \cdot 2 = 8$ **3.** false, m^7 **5.** true **7.** true **9.** false, a^{20} **11.** $w^{8+7} = w^{15}$ **13.** $b^{2+1} = b^3$ **15.** $v^{7+7} = v^{14}$ **17.** $d^{4+3+1} = d^8$ **19.** $t^{1+8+10} = t^{19}$ **21.** $x^{3+1+5+4} = x^{13}$ **23.** $g^{14-3} = g^{11}$ **25.** $v^{2+2+8+7} = v^{19}$ **26.** 4 **27.** $4 + 3 = 7$ **29.** $1 + 2 = 3$ **31.** $12 - 6 = 6$ **33.** 3 **35.** 15 **36.** 390,625 **37.** 16.81 **39.** 0.0001

Lesson 11, pages 22–25

1. $P = s + s + s + s$, $P = 4s$ **3.** 40 m **5.** $P = a + b + c$ **7.** 90 cm **9.** $P = l + w + l + w$ or $P = 2l + 2w$ **11.** 38 cm **13.** $P = s + s + s + s + s$, $P = 5s$ **15.** 40 cm **17.** $P = s + s + s + s = 4s$ **19.** 32 km **21.** square **22.** $P = s + s + s + s + s + s$, $P = 6s$ **23.** 60 mm **25.** 12 m

Chapter 1 Application, page 26

1. 175 mph − 53 mph = 122 mph **3.** 155 mph + 15 mph = 170 mph **5.** 305 mph − 41 mph = 264 mph

Chapter 1 Review, pages 27–29

1. 2 **3.** 5 **5.** a^9b^6 **7.** algebraic expression **9.** algebraic expression **11.** numerical expression **13.** 3 **15.** 14 **17.** −4; +4 and −4 are the same distance from zero **19.** 1.5 **21.** $-\frac{3}{4}$ **23.** 28 **25.** 8 **27.** −1 **29.** −5 **31.** −60 **33.** 0 **35.** −10 **37.** 0 **39.** $-5y + 15$ **41.** $-2.2k$ **43.** $-22v + 8r$ **45.** n^8 **47.** e^5g^5 **49.** n^6 **51.** j^6 **53.** 45 km **55.** 16 m

CHAPTER 2

Lesson 1, page 33

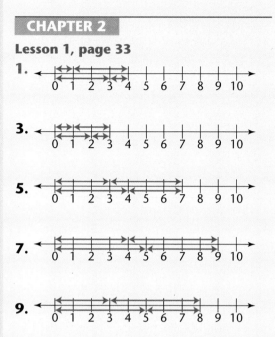

1. 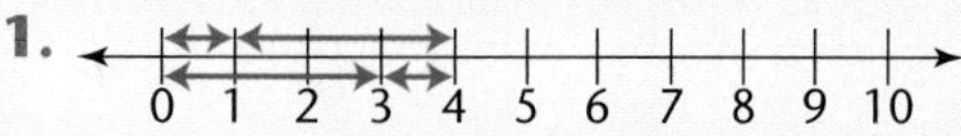

3.

5.

7.

9.

11. $x + x + x + x + x + x = 6x$ **13.** $t + t + t + t + t + t = 6t$ **15.** $m + m + m + m + m + m + m = 7m$ **17.** $y + y + y = 3y$ **19.** $3 + a$ **21.** $y + x$ **23.** $8g + 5g$ **25.** $7r + 4r$ **27.** $y + 2x$ **29.** $7p + 6p$ **31.** $2q + 16q$ **33.** $10 + x$ **35.** $y + 5y$

Lesson 2, page 35

1.

3.

5.

7. Factors: 5 and 3. Product: $5 \cdot 3 = 15$.
9. Factors: 3 and 2. Product: $3 \cdot 2 = 6$.
11. ba **13.** wz **15.** $(2)(3z)$ **17.** $(9w)h$ **19.** yes; because the pizza contains all three ingredients, the order of the ingredients is not important **21.** yes **23.** no **25.** no

Lesson 3, page 37

1. $25 = 25$; $(4 + 6) + 15 = (10) + 15 = 25$; $4 + (6 + 15) = 4 + (21) = 25$ **3.** $27 = 27$ **5.** $37 = 37$ **7.** $63 = 63$ **9.** $72 = 72$
11. $(x + y) + z = x + (y + z)$; the associative property of addition is used to group sums in different ways
13. $(g + h) + j = g + (h + j)$ **15.** $(w + 4c) + p = w + (4c + p)$ **17.** $(4f + 9y) + 2x = 4f + (9y + 2x)$ **19.** $(21k + 13u) + 16s = 21k + (13u + 16s)$ **21.** $(3 + 6) + z$; the associative property of addition is used to group sums in different ways
23. $(2b + 3c) + 8$ **25.** $5s + (3d + 28)$

Try This

No. The order of the numbers cannot be changed in subtraction without changing the result.

Lesson 4, pages 39–41

1. $300 = 300$; $(3 \cdot 5)20 = (15)20 = 300$; $3(5 \cdot 20) = 3(100) = 300$ **3.** $260 = 260$ **5.** $135 = 135$ **7.** $170 = 170$ **9.** $400 = 400$
For problems 11 and 13, other answers are possible. **11.** $(3 \cdot 5)4 = 60$ cubic units and $3(5 \cdot 4) = 60$ cubic units **13.** $(7 \cdot 4)3 = 84$ cubic units and $7(4 \cdot 3) = 84$ cubic units **15.** $(1w)h = 1(wh)$; the associative property of multiplication is used to group factors in different ways **17.** $(fp)n = f(pn)$ **19.** $(mk)s = m(ks)$

Lesson 5, page 43

1. 10; 5; the 4 outside the parentheses is distributed using multiplication to each number inside the parentheses **3.** b; 14 **5.** 6; 7 **7.** 29; n **9.** $4a + 4b$; the 4 outside the parentheses is distributed using multiplication to each variable inside the parentheses **11.** $-2d + -2k$ **13.** $-4a + -4b$ **15.** $9v + -81$ **17.** $8z + 32$ **19.** $-3x + -12$ **20.** 77; $7(6 + 5) = 7(6) + 7(5) = 42 + 35 = 77$ square units **21.** $10(5) + 10(4) = 90$ square units **23.** $n(8) + n(4) = 12n$ square units **25.** $x(y) + x(z) = xy + xz$ square units

Lesson 6, page 45

1. a is the common factor; it is common to both $2a$ and $3a$ **3.** x **5.** $2b$ **7.** $-z$ **9.** a **11.** $4(x + y)$; 4 is the common factor **13.** $3(j - p)$ **15.** $6(y + z)$ **17.** $-4(m + y)$ **19.** $a(x - y)$ **21.** $a(-s + j)$ **23.** $-u(v + m)$ **25.** $b(x^2 + y^2)$ **27.** $w(x^4 + m^2)$ **29.** $9(b + c)$; 9 is the common factor of $9b$ and $9c$

Lesson 7, page 47

1. 3 **3.** x^2 **5.** 5 **7.** $-a$ **9.** 0; the product of any number and zero is zero **11.** 0 **13.** 0 **14.** Possible answer: They are opposites. **15.** $5°F - (-5°F) = 10°F$

Lesson 8, page 49

1. $\frac{5}{5}, \frac{1}{2} \cdot \frac{5}{5} = \frac{5}{10}$ **3.** $\frac{2}{2}$ **5.** $\frac{4}{4}$ **7.** $\frac{k}{k}$ **9.** $\frac{3}{3}$ **11.** 3; $(\frac{1}{3})(\frac{3}{1}) = 1$; the product of any nonzero number and its reciprocal is 1 **13.** $\frac{1}{c}$; $(c)(\frac{1}{c}) = 1$ **15.** $\frac{1}{n^2}$; $(n^2)(\frac{1}{n^2}) = 1$ **17.** d; $(\frac{1}{d})(d) = 1$ **19.** 4 ; $4(\frac{1}{4}) = 1$

Lesson 9, pages 52–53

1. $\sqrt{36} = 6$; $62 = 36$ **3.** $3 < \sqrt{15} < 4$; $\sqrt{15}$ is between $\sqrt{9}$, which is 3, and $\sqrt{16}$, which is 4 **5.** $2 < \sqrt{7} < 3$ **7.** $9 < \sqrt{83} < 10$ **9.** 25.6 **11.** 1.75

Lesson 10, page 55

1. 7 and -7; $(7)^2 = 49$ and $(-7)^2 = 49$ **3.** b^3 or $-b^3$ **5.** -2 **7.** $-x^2$ **9.** 8 and -8; $\sqrt{64} = +8$ and -8 **11.** 2 and -2 **13.** 4 and -4 **15.** $-125x^3$ **17.** $256m^4$ **19.** $256w^2$ **21.** $-243n^5$ **23.** $729v^6$ **25.** $1{,}296a^4$

Lesson 11, page 57

1. -7; multiply first, then subtract **3.** $5 + 4 = 9$ **5.** $2 \cdot 2 = 4$ **7.** $-39 + -3 = -42$ **9.** $10 - 30 = -20$ **11.** $8 + 3 = 11$ **13.** $4c$; multiply first, then subtract **15.** $8k + 6k + 12k = 26k$ **17.** $25y + (-18y) = 7y$ **19.** $4b^2 + 3b^2 = 7b^2$ **21.** $5z^2 - z^2 = 4z^2$ **23.** 2($10) + $5 − $5 = $20 profit; profit = money earned − cost **25.** $5.00 + 3($8.00) = $29.00

Chapter 2 Application, page 58

1. 10 blocks; $\sqrt{100} = 10$ **3.** 18 blocks **5.** 32 blocks

Chapter 2 Review, pages 59–61

1. $(3y)(5n)$ **3.** 140 **5.** 49 **7.** $37n$ **9.** $b + 3x$ **11.** $8a + 14g$ For problems 13–17, other answers are possible: **13.** $h + (t + s)$ **15.** $2m + (6n + s)$ **17.** $4b + (x + 2)$ **19.** $100 = 100$ **21.** $6m + 6n$ **23.** $-2x + 2z$ **25.** $-7h + -7p$ **27.** $5(n + s)$ **29.** $b(2 + 3)$ **31.** -8 **33.** $-w$ **35.** 5 **37.** 8 **39.** c **41.** 8 and -8 **43.** 216 **45.** $-27y^3$ **47.** $16m^4$ **49.** $49j^2$

CHAPTER 3

Lesson 1, pages 64–65

1. $9x = 36$; represent an unknown such as "some number" with a variable such as x **3.** $9x - 18 = 0$ **5.** $5x + 3 = 28$ **7.** $3x = 27$ **9.** $10x - 13 = 47$ **11.** $x - 6 = 25$ **13.** $x - 4 = 10$ **15.** $2(5) = 14$ F, $2(6) = 14$ F, $2(7) = 14$ T, $2(8) =$ F **17.** F, F, F, T **19.** F, F, T, F **21.** T, F, F, F **23.** T, F, F, F **25.** F, F, T, F

Try This

Methods will vary; $y = 39$

Lesson 2, page 67

1. $x = 16$; add 7 to both sides of the equation; $x + 7 = 9 + 7$ **3.** 11 **5.** 23 **7.** 37 **9.** 47 **11.** 55 **13.** 92 **15.** $m = 7$; rewrite the equation as $m + (+2) = 9$, then subtract 2 from both sides **17.** 0 **19.** -6 **21.** $x =$ \$9.50; solve the equation $x -$ \$4.50 = \$5.00 **23.** \$21.33 **25.** \$6.24

Lesson 3, page 69

1. $x = 6$; subtract 4 from both sides of the equation **3.** 3 **5.** 5 **7.** 13 **9.** 14 **11.** 9 **13.** 0 **15.** 7 **17.** 2.4 **19.** 4.4 **21.** $c = 12$; add $+3$ to each side of the equation **23.** 14 **25.** 45 **27.** \$8.77; \$13.99 − \$5.22 = \$8.77 **29.** \$72.00

Lesson 4, page 71

1. $x = 5$; divide both sides of the equation by 5 **3.** 4 **5.** 10 **7.** 9 **9.** 2 **11.** 2 **13.** 4 **15.** 6 **17.** -50 **19.** 6 **21.** -2 **23.** 9 **25.** -11 **27.** $x = 4$; write the equation $13x = 52$, then divide each side by 13 **29.** $-6g = 66$; $g = -11$

Lesson 5, page 73

1. $x = 6$; multiply each side by $\frac{2}{1}$, the reciprocal of $\frac{1}{2}$ **3.** 35 **5.** 20 **7.** 15 **9.** 7 **11.** 32 **13.** 16 **15.** 40 **17.** -40 **19.** 50 **21.** -20 **23.** 60 **25.** 36 **27.** $x = 24$ students; solve the equation $\frac{2}{3}x = 16$ by multiplying each side by $\frac{3}{2}$, the reciprocal of $\frac{2}{3}$ **29.** 18 questions

Lesson 6, page 75

1. $x = 4$; add 6 to each side of the equation, then divide each side of the equation by 3 **3.** 5 **5.** 6 **7.** 1 **9.** 8 **11.** 5 **13.** 10 **15.** 0 **17.** $b = 6$; subtract 20 from each side of the equation, then divide each side of the equation by -6 **19.** 0 **21.** -8 **23.** 6 **25.** -7 **26.** $s =$ 442 square miles; follow the order of operations—multiply first, then add **27.** 573 square miles **29.** 71 square miles

Lesson 7, page 77

1. $x = \frac{b}{-a}$; isolate the variable x by dividing each side of the equation by $-a$ **3.** $x = \frac{a}{b}$ **5.** $x = \frac{-a}{b}$ **7.** $x = \frac{-c}{(b + a)}$ **9.** $x = \frac{-b}{c}$ **11.** $x = \frac{c}{(b - a)}$ **13.** $x = \frac{a}{(c - b)}$ **15.** $x = \frac{-a}{(c + b)}$ **17.** $x = \frac{c}{(b + a)}$ **19.** $x = \frac{-b}{(c + a)}$

Lesson 8, page 79

1. $h = \frac{A}{b}$; isolate the variable h by dividing each side of the equation by b **3.** $s = \frac{P}{3}$ **5.** $d = \frac{W}{f}$ **7.** $b = \frac{A}{\text{h}}$ **9.** $s = \frac{P}{5}$ **11.** $r = \frac{d}{t}$ **13.** $F = \frac{W}{d}$ **15.** $h = \frac{(b_1 + b_2)}{2A}$ **17.** $a = P - c$ **19.** $d = An$ **21.** $s = \frac{1}{2A}$ **23.** $a = sP$ **25.** $A = (\frac{c}{d}) - b$

Lesson 9, pages 81–83

1. $a^2 = 50$; solve $a^2 + 50 = 100$ for a^2 by subtracting 50 from each side of the equation **3.** 26 **5.** 51 **6.** $c = 41$; solve $a^2 + b^2 = c^2$ when $a = 9$ and $b = 40$ **7.** 8 **9.** 53.1 **11.** 26.6 **12.** $c = 5$ blocks; sketch a diagram; in the diagram, the path Martin walked represents the legs of a right triangle. Use $a^2 + b^2 = c^2$ to find the hypotenuse. **13.** 8 feet **15.** 26 feet

Lesson 10, pages 86–87

1. $x = 6$; the closed dot means 6 is a solution; no other solutions are shown **3.** $x \neq 9$ **5.** $x \neq -5$ **7.** $x > 1$ **8.** open dot on 2, arrow left; the open dot means do not include the number 2, and the left arrow means include all of the numbers less than 2 **9.** closed dot on 2 **11.** closed dot on -3, arrow left **13.** open dot on -4, arrow right **15.** open dots on 1 and 4, line connecting 1 and 4 **17.** closed dots on -8 and 8, line connecting -8 and 8 **19.** open dot on 3, arrow right, arrow left **20.** T; on a number line, 1 is to the left of 10, so 1 is less than 10 **21.** T **23.** T **25.** F

Lesson 11, page 89

1. $x > 6$; solve for x by subtracting 4 from each side of the inequality **3.** $w > 7$ **5.** $g \leq 20$ **7.** $m < -14$ **9.** $c > -4$; solve for c by dividing each side of the inequality by -5 **11.** $t \leq 10$ **13.** $x < -4$ **15.** $m \geq -3$ **17.** $p < 95$; use the symbol $<$ to represent "less than" **19.** $i < 2{,}500$

Chapter 3 Application, page 90

1. 548 feet **3.** 948 feet **5.** 448 feet

Chapter 3 Review, pages 91–93

1. $m = 7$ **3.** $x = 32$ **5.** $h = -2$ **7.** $x = \frac{b}{(c + a)}$ **9.** $14x + 5 = 33$ **11.** $8x = 24$ **13.** $A = wh$ **15.** $A = \frac{bh}{2}$ **17.** $c = 10$ **19.** $c = 20$ **21.** closed dot at -2 **23.** open dot at 6, arrow left, arrow right **25.** closed dots at -9 and 2, connected by darkened line segment **27.** $b \geq 18$ **29.** $v < 9$

CHAPTER 4

Lesson 1, page 97

1. $n + 1$; on a number line, the next consecutive integer is 1 greater than any previous integer **3.** $n - 2$ **4.** 3; write and solve the equation $7n - 2 = 19$ **5.** -8 **7.** 10, 12, 14 **9.** Responses will vary. Possible answer: $2n + 2m = 2(n + m)$; use variables such as n and m to represent two unknown integers

Lesson 2, page 99

1. 34%; write and solve the equation for "\$850 is what percent of \$2,500?" **3.** 32,800 seats are filled. **5.** 6 people **7.** 500 books **9.** 24 stations

Lesson 3, pages 101–103

1. 10; to find a percent of a number, change the percent to a decimal, then multiply **3.** 41 **5.** $331\frac{1}{2}$ **7.** 135 **9.** $13\frac{1}{2}$ **11.** 100%; a whole is represented by 100% **13.** $37\frac{1}{2}$% **15.** 100 freshmen

16. to find a percent of a number, change the percent to a decimal, then multiply

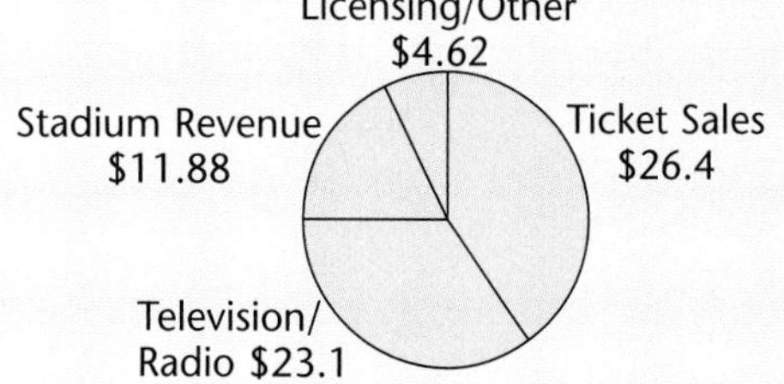

17.

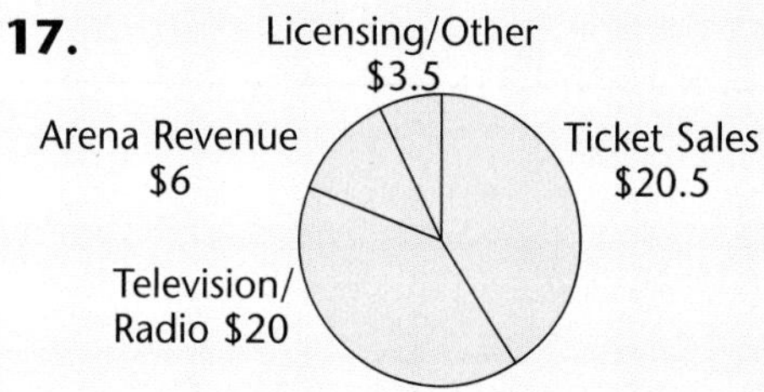

19.

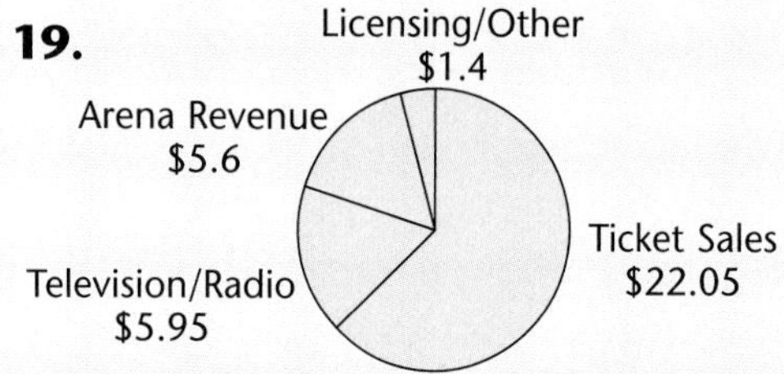

Lesson 4, pages 105–107

1. 3 hours; use the formula $t = \frac{d}{r}$ when $d = 165$ and $r = 55$ **3.** $d = 39\frac{7}{8}$ *km*; use the formula $d = rt$ when $r = 2\frac{3}{4}$ and $t = 14\frac{1}{2}$ **5.** $8\frac{1}{2}$ *km* per hour

Lesson 5, pages 109–110

1. a) 24 of each coin; let $5x$ represent the number of nickels and $10x$ represent the number of dimes, then solve $5x + 10x = \$3.60$ for x b) $2x = 48$; 48 coins **3.** a) 12 dimes and 24 half-dollars b) 36 coins **5.** 12 dimes and 24 nickels; let $2x(5¢)$ represent the number of nickels and $1x(10¢)$ represent the number of dimes, then solve $2x(5¢) + 1x(10¢) = \$2.40$ for x **7.** 20 nickels and 80 dimes **9.** 2 nickels and 16 dimes

Lesson 6, pages 112–113

1. $165; use the formula $I = prt$ when $p = \$3{,}000$, $r = 5.5\%$, and $t = 1$ year, change the percent to a decimal and solve for I **3.** $2,300 **4.** $\frac{640}{(.04 \cdot 1)} = \$16{,}000$ **5.** $5,600 **7.** $1,312.50; use the formula $I = prt$ when $p = \$4{,}200$, $r = 6.25\%$, and $t = 5$ years, change the percent to a decimal and solve for I **9.** $48

Lesson 7, page 115

1. $3.25; add the cost of the cashews ($\$4 \cdot 4$) to the cost of the peanuts ($\$2.50 \cdot 4$), then divide by 8, the number of pounds in the mixture **3.** 24 pounds of peanuts, 16 pounds of walnuts **5.** $1.00

Try This

Possible response: $V = \frac{C}{A}$

Lesson 8, page 117

1. a) $\frac{64}{40} = \frac{8}{5}$; express a ratio as a fraction, then write the fraction in simplest form b) $\frac{40}{64} = \frac{5}{8}$ c) $\frac{40}{104} = \frac{5}{13}$ d) $\frac{64}{104} = \frac{8}{13}$ **3.** a) $\frac{3}{2}$ b) $\frac{2}{3}$ c) $\frac{1}{8}$ d) $\frac{1}{12}$ **4.** $n = 6$; solve a proportion by setting the cross products equal to each other, then solve for the unknown; $(2)(9) = (3)(n)$ **5.** $y = 3$ **7.** $n = 9$ **9.** $x = 5$ **11.** $y = 3$ **13.** $n = 40$ **15.** $x = 40$

Chapter 4 Application, page 118

1. 90 laps **3.** \$11.88 **5.** $9\frac{1}{3}$ inches

Chapter 4 Review, pages 119–121

1. 45 **3.** 450 **5.** \$3.75 **7.** 37, 38, 39 **9.** 400 **11.** 1,200 **13.** 19 nickels, 38 dimes **15.** 8 nickels, 2 dimes, and 6 quarters **17.** $x = 3$ **19.** $26\frac{2}{3}$ mph

CHAPTER 5

Lesson 1, page 125

1. $(3 \cdot 3)(3 \cdot 3)(3 \cdot 3) = 9 \cdot 9 \cdot 9 = 729$ or $3^6 = 729$ **3.** $x^{3 \cdot 4} = x^{12}$ **5.** $m^{4 \cdot 4} = m^{16}$ **7.** $(2x + 3y)^{4 \cdot 2} = (2x + 3y)^8$ **8.** $(3^5) \div (3^3) = 3^{5-3} = 3^2 = 9$ **9.** 4 **11.** y^2 **13.** $(x + y)^3$ **15.** $\frac{3 \cdot 3 \cdot 3 \cdot 3 \cdot 3}{3 \cdot 3 \cdot 3 \cdot 3 \cdot 3} = 1, 3^{5-5} = 3^0 = 1$ **17.** $x^{7-7} = x^0 = 1, \frac{1}{1} = 1$ **19.** $(p + q)^{3-3} = 1, \frac{1}{1} = 1$

Lesson 2, pages 127–128

1. $\frac{4 \cdot 4 \cdot 4 \cdot 4 \cdot 4}{4 \cdot 4 \cdot 4 \cdot 4 \cdot 4 \cdot 4 \cdot 4 \cdot 4 \cdot 4} = \frac{1}{4^4} = 4^{-4}$ **3.** 10^{-5} **5.** 10^{-10} **7.** 15^{-2} **9.** 203^{-4} **11.** $x^{5-7} = x^{-2}$ **13.** $(x + 2y)^{-4}$ **15.** $(x + y)^{-3}$ **17.** $(-3m - 9)^{-3}$ **19.** $3^{-2} = \frac{1}{3^2}$ **21.** $\frac{1}{10^{23}}$ **23.** $\frac{2}{y^6}$ **25.** $\frac{1}{4^2}$

Lesson 3, page 130

1. $1.86 \cdot 105$ **3.** $2.76 \cdot 10^{11}$ **5.** $1.34254 \cdot 10^3$ **7.** $1 \cdot 10^{-10}$ **9.** $9.3542 \cdot 10^8$ **11.** 0.00328 **13.** 186 **15.** 5,280 **17.** 0.0000000000000000000000000016 **19.** 11,122

Lesson 4, pages 132–133

1. $(1.4 \cdot 6.3)(10^{3-4}) = 8.82 \cdot 10^{-1}$ **3.** $6.4481201 \cdot 10^7$ **5.** $3.6712 \cdot 10^{13}$ **7.** $5.12 \cdot 10^4$ **9.** $9.711765 \cdot 10^{-15}$ **11.** $(6.8 \div 3.4)(10^{2-6}) = 2.0 \cdot 10^{-4}$ **13.** $4 \cdot 10^7$ **15.** $5.45 \cdot 10^3$ **17.** $1.25 \cdot 10^{-13}$ **19.** $1.29 \cdot 10^{-2}$

Lesson 5, page 135

1. binomial in y **3.** trinomial in x **5.** polynomial in p **7.** trinomial in y **9.** polynomial in b **11.** 2 **13.** 4 **15.** 3 **17.** 7 **19.** 3 **21.** $x^3 + x + 1$ **23.** $b^5 + 1$ **25.** $4r^n$ **26.** Responses will vary. Possible answer: negative exponent **27.** is not a sum or difference **29.** is not a sum or difference

Lesson 6, page 137

1. $4y^6 + 2y^5 + 2y^3 - 4y^2 + 28$ **3.** $-2b^4 - 4b^2 + 5b - 5$ **5.** $4x^4 + 11x^3 + 17x^2 + 17x + 4$ **7.** $-5x^7 + 6x^6 - 6x^5 - 7x^3 + 2x^2 - 9x + 6$ **9.** $2x^7 - 6x^6 + x^5 - 3x^3 - 2x^2 + 16x - 16$ **11.** $-4y^6 + 2y^5 + 4y^2 + 14y + 38$ **13.** $4b^4 + 2b^3 + 9b - 5$ **15.** $6x^6 + x^5 + 12$ **17.** $4x^4 + 3x^3 + 13x^2 - 17x + 4$ **19.** $(x + 5) + (x + 5) + (x^2) + (x^2) = 2x^2 + 2x + 10$

Lesson 7, page 139

1. $(x + 2)(8x - 2) = (8x^2 - 2x) + (16x - 4) = 8x^2 + 14x - 4$ **3.** $b^8 + 2b^7 + b^6$ **5.** $60x^5 - 239x^3 - 68x$ **7.** $2x^6 + 4x^5 + 2x^4 - x^3 - 2x^2 - x$ **9.** $10m^5 + 50m^4 + 4m^3 + 10m^2 - 50m$ **11.** $(a + 2b) \cdot (a + 2b) = a^2 + 2ab + 2ba + 4b^2 = a^2 + 4ab + 4b^2$ **13.** $x^2 + 4x + 3$ **15.** $3x^2 + 12x + 9$

Try This

$(ax + ay + az) + (bx + by + bz) + (cx + cy + cz)$

Lesson 8, page 141

1. $(x + y)^2 = x^2 + 2xy + y^2$ **3.** $m^2 - n^2$ **5.** $x^2 + 4x + 4$ **7.** $z^2 - 9$ **9.** $x^2 - 25$ **11.** $x^2 + 6x + 9$ **12.** $(z + 4)(z + 4)(z + 4) = z^3 + 12z^2 + 48z + 64$

13. $x^3 + 6x^2 = 11x + 6$ **15.** $m^3 - m^2n - mn^2 + n^3$

Try This

$a^4 + 4a^3b + 6a^2b^2 + 4ab^3 + b^4$

Lesson 9, page 143

1. $(16x^2 \div 4) + (4 \div 4) = 4x^2 + 1$ **3.** $-4x^3 + 3x^2 - 2x + 1$ **5.** $m^2 - m + 1$ **7.** $26x^2 + 4x$ **9.** $23x^4 - 41x^2 + 31$ **11.** $25x^5 - 14x - 9$ **13.** $15y^4 + y^3 + 5y^2 - 17y + 1$ **15.** $-a^4 + 12a^3 + 18a^2 + 20$

Lesson 10, pages 146–147

1. $x - 4$ **3.** $x - 2$ **5.** $x + 10$ **7.** $x + 4$ **9.** $x - 2$ **11.** $x - 5$ r1 **13.** $x + 2$ r-5 **15.** $x - 6$ r2 **16.** $5m^2 - 2$ **17.** $-4m + 3$ r-31 **19.** $3y^2 - 5$ **21.** $x^2 + 5x - 2$ **23.** $y^2 - 4y + 6$ r21 **25.** $5z$ r1

Lesson 11, page 149

1. $P(0, -1) = 1$ **3.** $P(\frac{1}{2}, -4) = 14\frac{1}{4}$ **5.** $P(\frac{1}{3}, 9) = 84\frac{1}{9}$ **7.** $P(-1, -1) = -1$ **9.** $P(9, 1) = 819$ **11.** $P(1, 1, 1) = 4$ **13.** $P(2, -1, 2) = 34$ **15.** $P(1, -2, -3) = 25$

Chapter 5 Application, page 150

1. \$1,050.63 **3.** \$1,104.49 **5.** \$1,268.24

Chapter 5 Review, pages 151–153

1. $(x \cdot x \cdot x \cdot x \cdot x \cdot x) \cdot (x \cdot x \cdot x \cdot x \cdot x \cdot x) \cdot (x \cdot x \cdot x \cdot x \cdot x \cdot x)$ **3.** 4 **5.** $4.0(10^9)$ **7.** $7.3(10^{-4})$ **9.** $1.0374(10^{-7})$ **11.** $2.5(10^{-9})$ **13.** $5x^4 + x^3 - 6x^2 + 8x + 17$; $-x^4 - 9x^3 - 6x^2 + 8x + 3$ **15.** $m^5 + m^4 + m^3 + m^2$; $m^5 - m^4 + m^3 - m^2 - 10$ **17.** $18x^4 + 2x^3 - 14x^2$ **19.** $-12y^3 - 12y^2 - 12y - 12$ **21.** $4x^2 - 5x - 6$ **23.** $2m^7 - 3m^6 + 2m^4 + 10m^3 + 15m^2 + 10$ **25.** $6x^3 - 5x^2 + 4x - 2$ **27.** 3 **29.** $(x^2 - 7x)$ or $x(x - 7)$

CHAPTER 6

Lesson 1, pages 158–159

1. $2^2 \cdot 3^2, 36 = 2 \cdot 2 \cdot 3 \cdot 3$ and $72 = 2 \cdot 2 \cdot 2 \cdot 3 \cdot 3$ **3.** 3 **5.** $2^2 \cdot 3$ **7.** $3 \cdot 11$ **9.** 5^2 **11.** $3x$; $3x^2 = 3 \cdot x \cdot x$ and $3x = 3 \cdot x$ **13.** m^2 **15.** $4x$ **17.** $7xy$ **19.** $4xy$ **21.** 47; 48, 49 composite numbers **23.** 33 **25.** since $180 = 20 \cdot 9$, $180 = (22 \cdot 5)(32)$ or $22 \cdot 32 \cdot 5$ **26.** 72 **27.** 1,125 **29.** 3,705,625

Lesson 2, page 161

1. $3(x^2 + 1)$; 3 is common to $3x^2$ and to 3 **3.** $m^2(n^2 + 3)$ **5.** $6(x^3 + 3x^2 + 4)$ **7.** $8(2m^3 + 3m^2 + 2)$ **9.** $16x(2x^4 + 4x^3 + 1)$ **11.** $a^4(-3a^2 - 4a - 1)$ or $-a^4(3a^2 + 4a + 1)$ **13.** $6y(-4x^2 + x^2y + 5y)$ **15.** $3xy^2(-5x^2 - 15x - 11)$ or $-3xy^2(5x^2 + 15x + 11)$ **17.** $17xy(x - 2)$ **19.** $5t(-8t + ts + 4s^2)$

Lesson 3, page 163

1. $(x + 2)(x + 3)$; the expression $x^2 + 5x + 6$ has no common factors **3.** $(a - 2)(a - 4)$ **5.** $(y + 6)(y - 3)$ **7.** $(t - 5)(t + 4)$ **9.** $(x - 1)(x + 17)$ **10.** $x^2(x^2 + 7x + 12) = x^2(x + 4)(x + 3)$ **11.** $2b(b^2 + 5b + 4) = 2b(b + 4)(b + 1)$ **13.** $(a^2 + 3)(a^2 + 4)$ **14.** $(2x + 1)(3x - 2)$; $6x^2 - x - 2 = (2x + 1)(3x - 2)$ **15.** $2(x + 1) + 2(x + 3) = 4x + 8$

Lesson 4, page 165

1. $(3y + 2)(y + 4)$; the expression $3x^2 + 14y + 8$ has no common factors **3.** $(2c + 3)(3c + 5)$ **5.** $(2m + 4)(10m + 5)$ **7.** $(20y + 1)(y + 20)$ **9.** $(7x - 3)(x + 1)$; the expression $7x^2 + 4x - 3$ has no common factors **11.** $(7x - 2)(7x + 3)$ **13.** $(3y + 4)(2y - 6)$ **15.** $(3x - 7)(2x - 4)$

17. $(3x - 8)(x + 2)$ **18.** $4x(x + 4)(x + 1)$; $4x^3 + 20x^2 + 16x = 4x(x^2 + 5x + 4) = 4x(x + 4)(x + 1)$ **19.** $2x^2(3x + 8)(2x - 1)$

Lesson 5, page 167

1. 44 **3.** 11 **5.** 40 **7.** $(y + 7)(y - 7)$; the expression $y^2 - 49$ has no common factors **9.** $(p + 11)(p - 11)$ **11.** $(z + 15)(z - 15)$ **13.** $(7x + 1)(7x - 1)$; the expression $49x^2 - 1$ has no common factors **15.** $(6t^2 + 11)(6t^2 - 11)$ **17.** $(5r^4 + 1)(5r^4 - 1)$ **19.** $(7x^2 - 5y)(7x^2 + 5y)$; the expression $49x^4 - 25y^2$ has no common factors **21.** $(6ab + 1)(6ab - 1)$ **23.** $(9m + 8n^5)(9m - 8n^5)$ **25.** 319 m^2; subtract the area of the fountain from the area of the plaza $(20 \cdot 20) - (9 \cdot 9) = 400 - 81 = 319$ m^2

Lesson 6, pages 169–171

1. I $= 2 \cdot 2$ or 4 sq. units, II $= 2 \cdot 8$ or 16 sq. units, III $= 8 \cdot 8$ or 64 sq. units, IV $= 8 \cdot 2$ or 16 sq. units, total $= 100$ sq. units **3.** I $= 25$ sq. units, II $= 10$ sq. units, III $= 4$ sq. units, IV $= 10$ sq. units, total $= 49$ sq. units **4.** $(m - 12)^2$; $m^2 - 24m + 144 = (m - 12)(m - 12)$ **5.** $(x + 12)^2$ **7.** $(t + 9)^2$ **9.** $(x + 13)^2$ **10.** $(2m + 12)^2$; $4m^2 + 48m + 144 = (12m + 12)(2m + 12)$ **11.** $(2r - 12)^2$ **13.** $(9p^3 + 5)^2$ **15.** $(5x^2 + 5)^2$ **17.** $(12b^2 - 1)^2$ **19.** I $= 7 \cdot 7$, II $= 7 \cdot 3$, III $= 7 \cdot 3$, IV $= 3 \cdot 3$; to have an area of 100 square units, the new room must measure $10 \cdot 10$

Lesson 7, page 173

1. $m = 0$; any number times zero is zero **3.** $y = 0$ **5.** $x^2 = 0, x = 0$ **7.** $b^4 = 0, b = 0$ **9.** $x^3 = 0, x = 0$ **11.** $x = 5$; $17(5 - 5) = 17(0) = 0$ **13.** $m = -21$ **15.** $n = 12$ or $n = -4$ **17.** $m = 4$ **19.** $x = \frac{6}{4} = 1\frac{1}{2}$ or $x = -6$ **21.** $z = -\frac{1}{2}$ or $z = 2$ **23.** $x = -2$ or $x = 5$ **25.** $p = 1$ or $p = -\frac{27}{13}$

Try This

$(2x^2 - 32) = 0$ or $(x - 9) = 0$ if $(2x^2 - 32) = 0$, then $2x^2 = 32$, $x^2 = 16$ and $x = 4$ or $x = -4$; if $x - 9 = 0$, $x = 9$

Lesson 8, pages 176–177

1. $-2, -3$; $x^2 + 5x + 6 = (x + 2)(x + 3)$ **3.** $+2, +4$ **5.** $-6, +3$ **7.** $+5, -4$ **9.** $+1, -17$ **11.** $-3, -4$ **13.** $8, -2$ **15.** $\frac{-3}{2}, -5$ **16.** $(2n - 12)(4n + 4) = 0$, solutions are $6, -1$ **17.** $3, -5$ **19.** $1\frac{1}{2}, -6$ **21.** $3(b^2 + 5b + 4) = 3(b + 4)(b + 1)$, solutions are $-4, -1$ **23.** $6(2x^2 + 3x + 1) = 6(2x + 1)(x + 1)$, solutions are $-\frac{1}{2}, -1$ **25.** $12(c^2 + 5c + 6) = 12(c + 3)(c + 2)$, solutions are $-2, -3$ **26.** C **27.** C **29.** B

Chapter 6 Application, page 178

1. $\frac{1}{2}$ ft or 6 in. **3.** 6 ft

Chapter 6 Review, pages 179–181

1. $3 \cdot 22$ **3.** $8(3m^2 - 1)$ **5.** $(p - 9)(p + 9)$ **7.** $m = -6$ **9.** $x = -\frac{1}{2}$ or $x = -4$ **11.** $x = 0$ or $x = -2$ **13.** $y = 1$ or $y = \frac{3}{2}$ **15.** $z = -\frac{3}{2}$ or $z = \frac{3}{2}$ **17.** $y = +11$ or $y = -11$ **19.** $c = 0$ or $c = -9$ **21.** $a^2 - b^2$ **23.** I = length and width = 8; II = length 4, width 8, III = length and width = 4, IV = length 8, width 4 **25.** $9a^2 + 6ab + b^2$ **27.** width = 5 units, length = 12 units **29.** 7 cm

CHAPTER 7

Lesson 1, pages 186–187

1. In each data value, use the digit in the tens place for the stem and the digit in the ones place for the leaf. Write each tens digit only once.

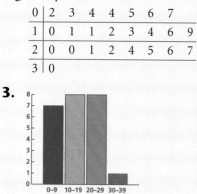

0	2	3	4	4	5	6	7	
1	0	1	1	2	3	4	6	9
2	0	0	1	2	4	5	6	7
3	0							

3.

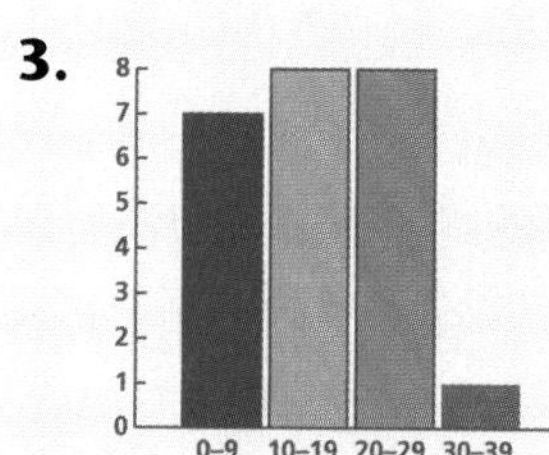

For problems 5 and 9, other answers are possible and, in some cases, likely.

5. Sample answer: They all give a visual display of the data. **7.** 4, 11, and 20 occur most often. 2, 3, 5, 6, 7, 10, 12, 13, 14, 16, 19, 21, 22, 24, 25, 26, 27, and 30 occur least often. **9.** Sample answer: frequency table

Lesson 2, pages 190–191

1. 14 – 1.01 = 12.99; to compute the range, subtract the least value in the set from the greatest 3. 3.005 5. Answers will vary. 6. Answers will vary. 7, 9. Answers will vary. 11. 18.5; find the sum of the values in the set, then divide by 4; 74 ÷ 4 = 18.5 13. 118 15. 661.812

Lesson 3, pages 194–195

1. 39, 40, 41, 42, 44, 44, 45, 45, 47, 48, 49, 49, 51; upper extreme 51 **3.** median 45

5.

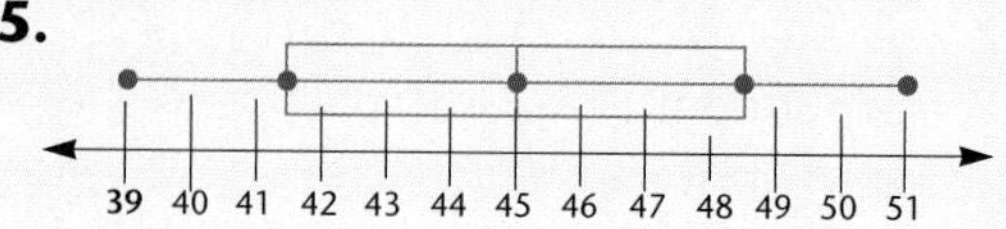

7. lower extreme 12 **9.** upper quartile 21; lower quartile 15

Lesson 4, pages 198–199

1. $\frac{1}{6}$; the number cube has 6 possible outcomes; there is 1 favorable outcome of rolling a 2 **3.** $\frac{3}{6} = \frac{1}{2}$ **5.** $\frac{3}{6} = \frac{1}{2}$ **7.** $\frac{2}{6} = \frac{1}{3}$; two of the six sides of the cube are yellow **9.** $\frac{1}{6}$ **11.** $\frac{0}{6}$ or 0 **13, 15, 17, 19.** Answers will vary.

Lesson 5, pages 202–203

1. certain; a coin has 2 possible outcomes; a toss of heads or tails represents 2 favorable outcomes; $P = \frac{2}{2}$ or $P = 1$ **3.** more likely **5.** more likely **7.** not likely **9.** $\frac{1}{2}$; divide the spinner into 8 equal parts; 4 of those parts are yellow; $\frac{4}{8} = \frac{1}{2}$ **11.** $\frac{1}{8}$ **13.** $\frac{3}{4}$ **15.** $\frac{1}{4}$ **17.** $\frac{5}{8}$ **19.** $\frac{1}{\text{(number of students in the class.}}$; there is only 1 favorable outcome in this experiment—your name being chosen

Lesson 6, page 205

1. $(\frac{1}{2})(\frac{1}{4}) = \frac{1}{8}$; find the product of the probability of each event **3.** $\frac{1}{8}$ **5.** $\frac{3}{8}$ **7.** 1 **8.** $(\frac{1}{5})(\frac{1}{6}) = \frac{1}{30}$; find the product of the probability of each event **9.** $\frac{1}{10}$ **11.** $\frac{4}{15}$ **13.** $\frac{2}{5}$ **15.** $\frac{2}{15}$

Try This

36 different outcomes; $\frac{1}{36}$

Lesson 7, pages 208–209

1. Independent events, any toss does not affect the previous toss or the next toss of the coin **3.** These are independent events; the next outcome will be 1, 2, 3, 4, 5, or 6 **4.** $(\frac{2}{6})(\frac{1}{6}) = \frac{1}{18}$; find the product of the probability of each event **5.** $\frac{1}{12}$ **7.** $(\frac{2}{8})(\frac{1}{7}) = \frac{1}{28}$; find the product of the probability of each event; in the second event; there will only be 7 marbles left in the bag because the marble taken during the first event was not replaced **9.** $\frac{5}{56}$

Try This

3%

Lesson 8, pages 212–213

1. 2; if, for example, you choose the letters *A* and *B*, the letters can be arranged two ways—*A*, *B* or *B*, *A* **3.** 120 **5.** 36 **6.** 58,500; the first letter in the password has 26 possibilities, the second letter has 25 possibilities; the first digit has 10 possibilities (0 – 9) and the second digit has 9 possibilities; 26 • 25 • 10 • 9 = 58,500 **7.** 1,024 **9.** 10,000

Chapter 7 Application, page 214

1. third, $\frac{1}{100} < \frac{1}{10}$ **3.** $\frac{1}{10{,}000}$ **5.** 100, sample explanation:

$$\frac{1 \text{ failure}}{10{,}000 \text{ launches}} = \frac{100 \text{ failures}}{1{,}000{,}000 \text{ launches}}$$

Chapter 7 Review, pages 215–217

1. 35 **3.** 80 **5.** 255 and 272 **7.** 251 and 279 **9.** $P = 0$ **11.** $P = 1$ **13.** $P = 0$ **15.** $P = \frac{1}{6}$ **17.** $P = \frac{1}{4}$ **19.** $P = \frac{2}{25}$ **21.** Answers will vary. Sample answer: The spinner will land on black. **23.** 720 ways **25.** 24 ways

CHAPTER 8

Lesson 1, page 221

1. $\frac{1}{7}$; the GCF of 9 and 63 is 9; $\frac{9}{63} \div \frac{9}{9} = \frac{1}{7}$ **3.** $\frac{-1}{4}$ **5.** $\frac{1}{4}$ **7.** $\frac{1}{12}$ **9.** $\frac{2}{9}$ **11.** $\frac{21}{32}$ **13.** $\frac{3}{8}$ **15.** $\frac{11}{81}$; the GCF of 121 and 891 is 11; $\frac{121}{89} \div \frac{11}{11} = \frac{11}{81}$ **17.** $\frac{1}{-5}$ **19.** $\frac{2}{3}$ **21.** $\frac{3}{8}$ **23.** $\frac{5}{-21}$ **25.** $\frac{1}{5}$

Lesson 2, page 223

1. $\frac{1}{m}$; the GCF of m^5 and m^6 is m^5; $\frac{m^5}{m^6} \div \frac{m^5}{m^5} = \frac{1}{m^1}$ or $\frac{1}{m}$ **3.** $5x$ **5.** $5x^2$ **7.** $\frac{2}{3xy^2}$ **9.** $(\frac{xyz^2}{-2})$ **11.** $\frac{-1}{(a^2 + 4)}$ **13.** $(x - 5)$ **15.** $(-x + 5)$; $\frac{(-x^2 + 25)}{(x + 5)} = \frac{-(x^2 - 25)}{(x + 5)} = \frac{-(x^2 - 5)(x + 5)}{(x + 5)} = \frac{-(x - 5)}{1}$ or $-x + 5$ **17.** $(w + 7)$ **19.** $\frac{1}{(a - 2)}$

Lesson 3, page 225

1. $\frac{5}{8}$; $\frac{3}{4} \cdot \frac{5}{6} = \frac{15}{24} \div \frac{3}{3} = \frac{5}{8}$ **3.** $2\frac{2}{3}$ **5.** $\frac{a}{x}$ **7.** $\frac{1}{(a - 5)^2}$ **9.** $\frac{(1 - x)}{(bx - 1)}$ **11.** $\frac{9}{10}$; $\frac{3}{4} \div \frac{5}{6} = \frac{3}{4} \cdot \frac{6}{5} = \frac{18}{20} = \frac{9}{10}$ **13.** $4\frac{1}{6}$ **15.** $\frac{x^3}{a^5}$ **17.** $\frac{1}{(a + 5)^2}$ **19.** $\frac{(x - 1)(x + 1)^2}{(bx - 1)(bx + 1)^2}$

Lesson 4, pages 228–229

1. 12; 12 is the first common multiple of 3 and 4 **3.** 56 **5.** 36 **7.** 21 **9.** 18 **11.** $8n$ **13.** $20r$ **15.** $99b$ **16.** $1\frac{2}{3}$; $1 \div \frac{3}{5}1 = 1 \cdot \frac{5}{3} = \frac{5}{3} = 1\frac{2}{3}$ **17.** 8 **19.** $\frac{5}{18}$ **21.** $4\frac{4}{11}$ **23.** $\frac{3}{40}$ **25.** $\frac{9}{16}$ **27.** $\frac{8}{9}$ **29.** $\frac{5}{9}$ **31.** $\frac{8}{25}$ **33.** $\frac{3}{5}$ **35.** $\frac{9}{16h}$ **36.** 247.5 mi.; $d = rt$, $d = 45 \cdot 5.5$, $d = 247.5$ **37.** 46 mph **39.** 28 mph

Try This

$\frac{xb}{a}$

Lesson 5, page 231

1. 15; 15 is the first common multiple of 3 and 5 **3.** 30 **5.** 28 **7.** 42 **9.** x^3y^2 **11.** $1\frac{1}{3}$; $\frac{2}{3} \div \frac{1}{2} = \frac{2}{3} \cdot \frac{2}{1} = \frac{4}{3} = 1\frac{1}{3}$ **13.** $2\frac{1}{10}$ **15.** ab **17.** $\frac{16a^2}{y}$ **19.** $\frac{mn^2}{x^2}$

Lesson 6, page 233

1. $1\frac{5}{8}$; $\frac{3}{4} + \frac{7}{8} = \frac{6}{8} + \frac{7}{8} = \frac{13}{8} = 1\frac{5}{8}$ **3.** $1\frac{1}{12}$ **5.** $\frac{9}{10}$ **7.** $\frac{11}{14}$ **9.** $4\frac{29}{40}$ **11.** $\frac{10y - 7x}{xy}$ **13.** $\frac{3x^2 - 2y}{x^2y}$ **15.** $\frac{a + 3}{a^2}$ **17.** $\frac{25cd - 4b}{abcd}$ **19.** $\frac{5dx - 3cx}{c^2d^2}$ **21.** $\frac{3b + 4a}{a^2b^2}$ **23.** $\frac{5y^3 + 7x^3}{ax^2y^2}$ **25.** $\frac{21x^2y^2 + 8a^4b^2}{28a^2bxy}$

Lesson 7, pages 236–237

1. 3; set the cross products equal to each other, then solve for x; $100x = 300$, so $x = 3$ **3.** 100 **5.** -15 **7.** 49 **9.** -1 **11.** $-5\frac{3}{8}$ **13.** 5, -4 **15.** $\frac{1}{6}$ **16.** $2\frac{5}{8}$ feet; solve $\frac{1 \text{ in.}}{\frac{3}{4} \text{ ft}} = \frac{3\frac{1}{2} \text{ in.}}{x}$ for x

17. 9 students **19.** 2,025 km

Try This

$3x = 5 \cdot 6$; if a proportion has three constants and one unknown, it can be solved; the expression $3x = 15y$ has two unknowns

Lesson 8, pages 239–241

1. 24; multiply both sides of the equation by $\frac{4}{3}$, the reciprocal of $\frac{3}{4}$ **3.** 56 **5.** -49 **7.** 27 **9.** $11\frac{1}{2}$ **10.** 11; subtract $\frac{1}{9}$ from both sides, then multiply both sides by $\frac{9}{4}$, the reciprocal of $\frac{4}{9}$ **11.** $5\frac{4}{9}$ **13.** $8\frac{1}{6}$ **15.** 84 **17.** $25\frac{1}{5}$ **18.** not correct **19.** not correct **21.** not correct **23.** Their scores are 75 and 60. **25.** 81 points

Lesson 9, page 243

1. $x = 4$; if $x = 4$, the denominator is undefined because $4 - 4 = 0$ **3.** $c = -5$ **5.** $b = 0$ **7.** $m = 0$ and/or $n = 0$ **9.** $a = +2$ or $a = -2$ **11.** $r = 12$ **13.** $n = +6$ or $n = -6$ **15.** $m = -8$ or $m = +3$ **17.** $x = -3$ or $x = -4$ or $x = +3$ **19.** $b = +5$ or $b = +4$

Chapter 8 Application, page 244

1. $3\frac{1}{13}$ hours **3.** $2\frac{2}{9}$ hours

Chapter 8 Review, pages 245–247

1. $\frac{2}{3}$ **3.** $\frac{b^2}{a}$ **5.** $\frac{(3x + 5)}{x^2}$ **7.** $x = 4$ **9.** $\frac{1}{5}$ **11.** $\frac{1}{x}$ **13.** $\frac{7}{9mn}$ **15.** $(y - 3)$ **21.** $\frac{ab}{x^2}$ **23.** 20 **25.** -81 **27.** -28 **29.** $-28\frac{1}{3}$ **31.** $13\frac{1}{2}$ **33.** $\frac{(x + 3)^2 + (x - 5)^2}{(x + 3)(x - 5)}$ **35.** $\frac{3mp + 5n}{n^2p^2}$ **37.** about 833 deer **39.** 10 feet

CHAPTER 9

Lesson 1, pages 252–253

1. (2, 1); point B is located 2 units right and 1 unit up **3.** (3, –2) **5.** (–2, –2) **7.** (0, 1) **9.** (–3, 1) **11.** To plot any point, move left or right first, then move up or down. **13, 15.**

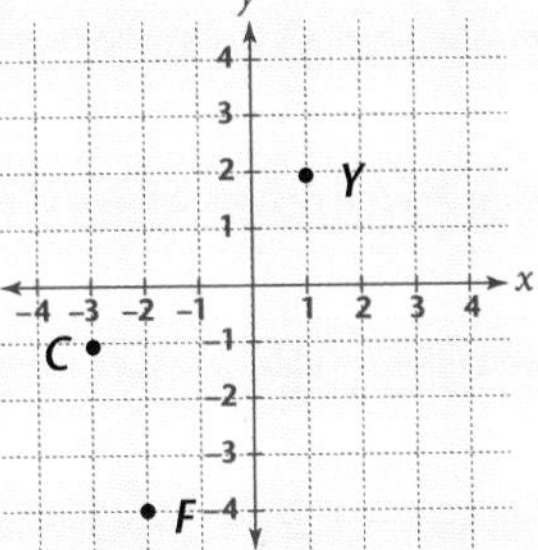

17. Quadrant I; point (3, 3. is three units to the right of the origin and 3 units up. **19.** Quadrant II **21.** Quadrant II **23.** 4 blocks; make a diagram on grid paper. Write north at the top of the page, south at the bottom, east at the right, and west at the left. **25.** Answers will vary.

Lesson 2, page 255

1. $y = x$ x $-2, -1, 0, 1, 2$ y $-2, -1, 0, 1, 2$; choose a value for x, then substitute that value into the equation and solve for y **3.** $y = 2x + 1$ x $-4, -2, 0, 2, 4$ y $-7, -3, 1, 5, 9$ For problems 4–9, choose a value for x, then substitute that value into the equation and solve for y **4.** $y = x$ x $-1, 0, 1$ y $-1, 0, 1$ The graph should pass through the points (0, 0) and (1, 1) **5.** $y = 3x$, x $-1, 0, 1$ y $-3, 0, 3$ The graph should pass through the points (0, 0) and (1, 3) **7.** $y = 2x - 1$ x $-1, 0, 1$ y $-3, -1, 1$ The graph should pass through the points (0, -1) and (1, 1) 9. $y = x - 3$ x $-1, 0, 1$ y $-4, -3, -2$ The graph should pass through the points (0, -3) and (1, -2)

Try This

$y = x$

Lesson 3, page 257

1. Substitute $x = 0$ into the equation of the graph and solve for y. Write an ordered pair in the form (x, y). **3.** x-intercept $= -1$; y-intercept $= 1$. To find the y-intercept, substitute $x = 0$ into the equation and solve for y. To find the x-intercept, substitute $y = 0$ into the equation and solve for x. **5.** x-intercept $= 3$; y-intercept $= -3$ **7.** x-intercept $= 0$; y-intercept $= 0$ **9.** x-intercept $= \frac{1}{2}$; y-intercept $= -1$ **11.** x-intercept $= 1$; y-intercept $= 1$ **13.** x-intercept $= -3$; y-intercept $= -9$ **15.** Sample answer: when the graph passes through the origin

Lesson 4, pages 260–262

1. The graph should create an acute angle with the positive direction of the x-axis; a line with a positive slope moves upward when read from left to right. **3.** The graph must be parallel to either the x- or y-axis. **4.** negative; a line with a negative slope moves downward when read from left to right. **5.** neither **7.** $m = 0; \frac{-1-(-1)}{2-3} = \frac{-1+1}{2-3} = \frac{0}{-1}$ or 0 **9.** $m = -2$ **11.** Change the fraction or mixed number to a decimal. Use a calculator to check the slope calculation. Then compare decimal answers. **12.** $m = 1$; to find the slope of a line, use the formula $\frac{y_2 - y_1}{x_2 - x_1}$ **13.** $m = 0$ **15.** $m = -2$

17. $m = 0$ **18.** Trail 3; Trails 1 and 2; a negative slope is downhill. A positive slope is uphill. **19.** Trail 2

Lesson 5, page 264

1. $y = 2x + 1$; substitute $m = 2$ and $b = 1$ into $y = mx + b$, the general form for any linear equation **3.** $y = -2x + 5$

4. The graph should pass through (1, 1) and (3, 3); $y = x$; first use $\frac{y_2 - y_1}{x_2 - x_1}$ to find the slope of the line. Then substitute the slope and either point into $y = mx + b$ and solve for b. Substitute m and b into $y = mx + b$ to find the equation of the line. **5.** The graph should pass through (0, 0) and (2, 4); $y = 2x$ **7.** The graph should pass through (5, 0) and (0, 10); $y = -2x + 10$ **9.** The graph should pass through (−2, 0) and (−6, −1); $y = \frac{1}{4}x + \frac{1}{2}$ **11.** $y = 5x - 20$; substitute the slope and the point into $y = mx + b$ to find b. Then substitute m and b into $y = mx + b$ to find the equation of the line.

13. $y = \frac{x + 11}{2}$ or $y = \frac{1}{2}x + \frac{11}{2}$ **15.** $y = 2x$

Lesson 6, pages 266–267

1. yes; a vertical line intersects the graph only once **3.** yes **5.** yes **7.** $f(2) = 6$; $f(-4) = 12$; to evaluate a function, substitute the given values into the function one at a time, and solve for $f(x)$ **9.** $f(2) = 14$; $f(-4) = 68$ **11.** $f(2) = 2$; $f(-4) = -28$ **13.** $f(2) = -11$; $f(-4) = -53$ **15.** $f(2) = 12$; $f(-4) = 12$

Lesson 7, pages 269–271

1. Range: $-7 \leq y \leq 15$ **3.** Range: $1 \leq y \leq 4$ **5.** Range: $-2 \leq y \leq 24$

6. Range: $-2 \leq y \leq 4$ **7.** Range: $y = 3$

9. Range: $y = 4$ **11.** Domain: $-4 \leq x \leq -2$ Range: $-2 \leq y \leq 5$ **13.** Domain: $-4 \leq x \leq 5$ Range: $y = 2$

Lesson 8, page 274

1.

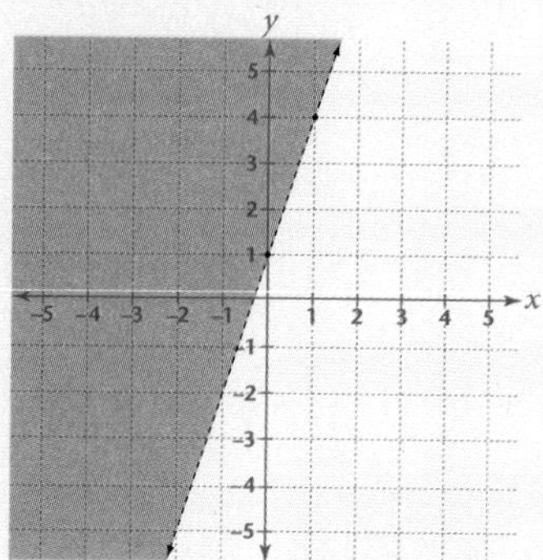

3.

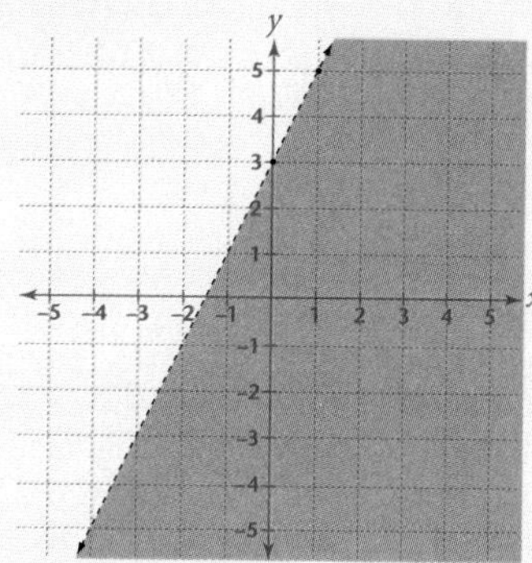

5.

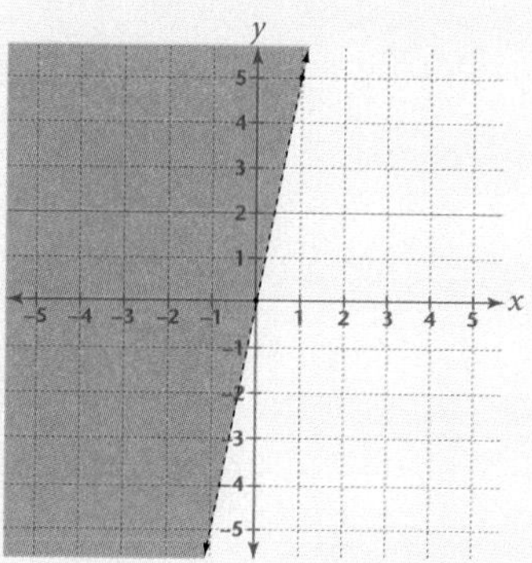

7.

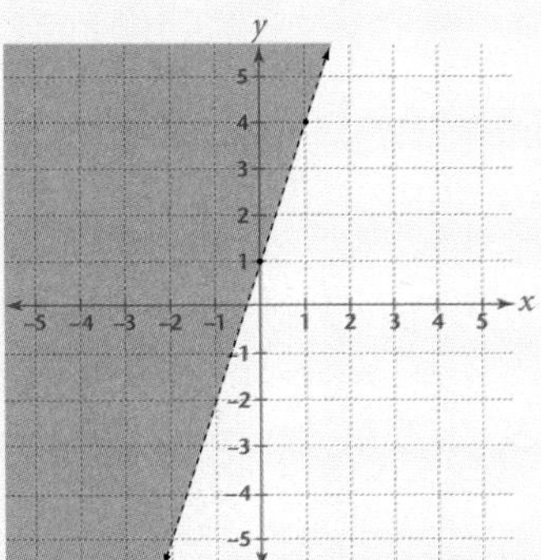

9.

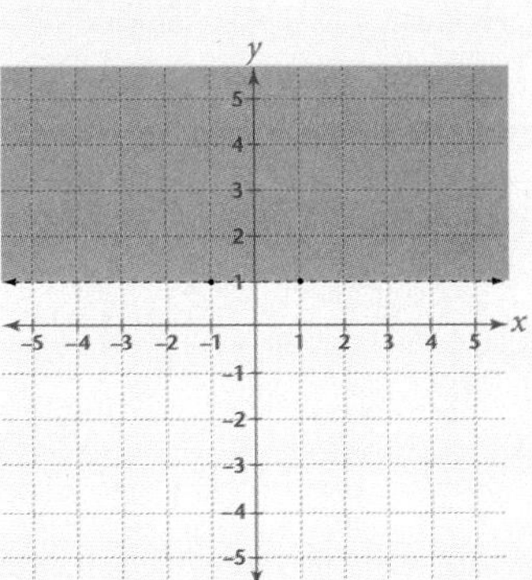

11.

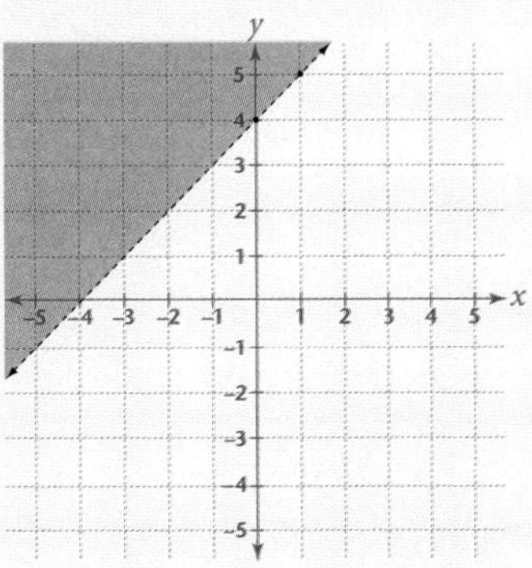

13.

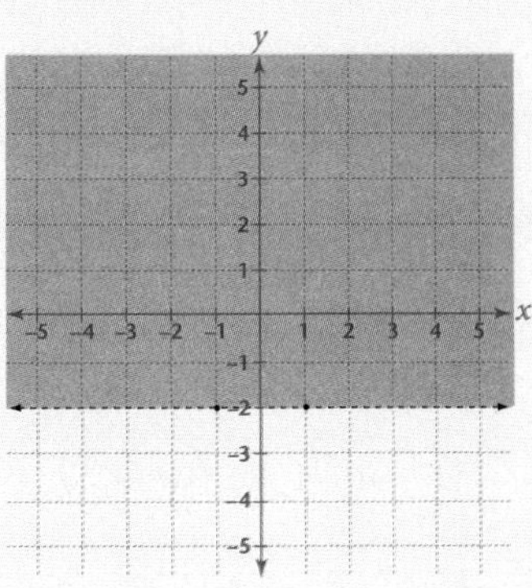

15.

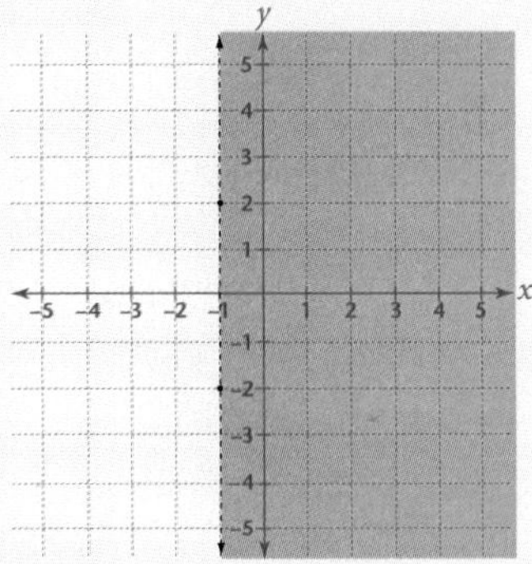

Lesson 9, pages 278–279

1. Choose a value for x, solve the equation for y, and write an ordered pair. Repeat. Graph the line connecting the points with a solid line because the inequality is $\geq$ or $\leq$. Choose a point to help decide which area to shade.

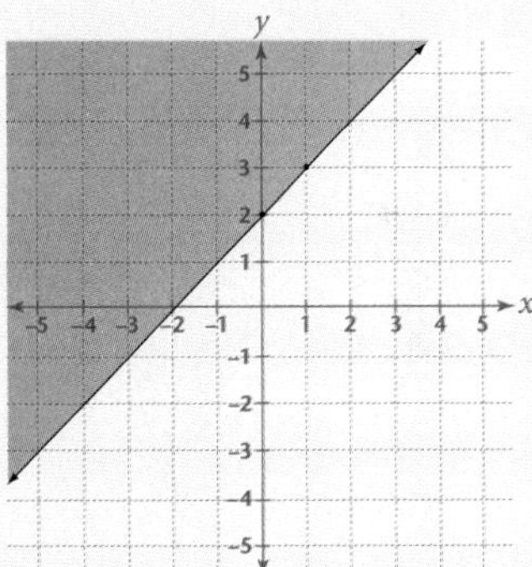

3.

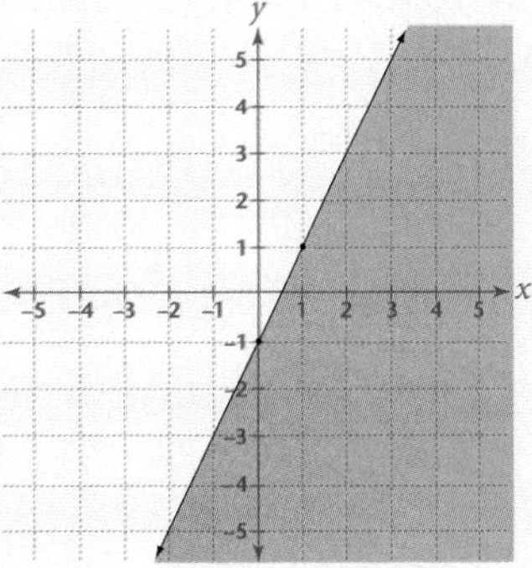

5.

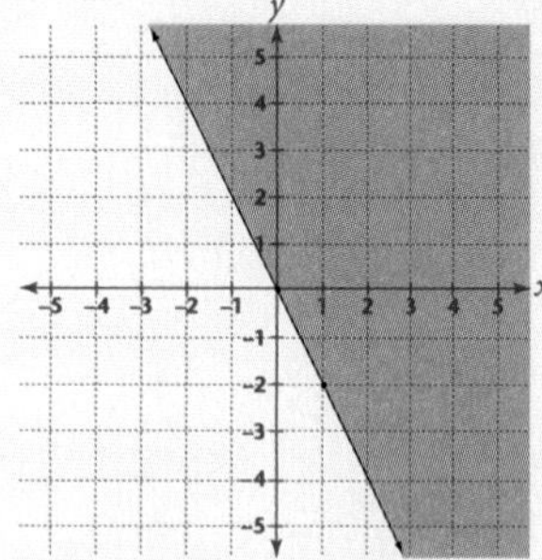

7.

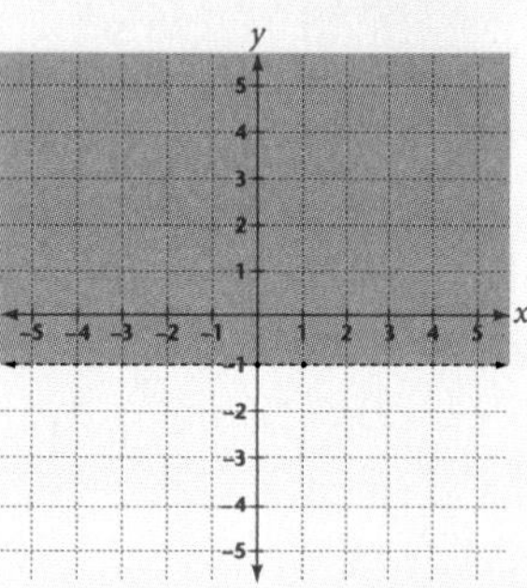

9.

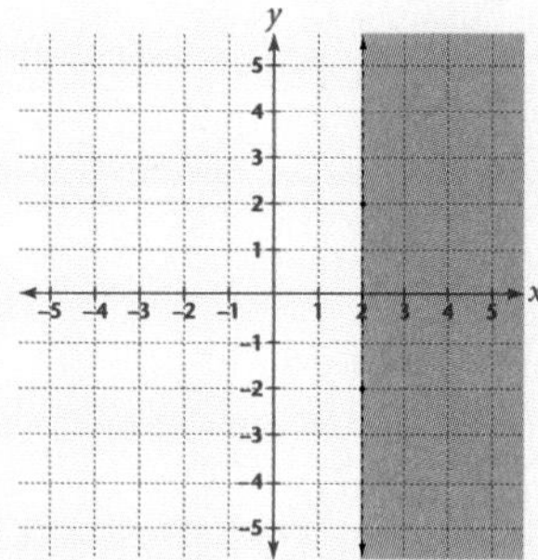

11. $y \leq x + 3$; Choose a point in the shaded region. Substitute that point into the equation of the line. Choose $\geq$ or $\leq$ if the graph is a solid line, or $<$ or $>$ if the graph is a broken line. **13.** $y \leq -4x$ **15.** $y < 3x - 2$ **17.** $y \leq -1$ **19.** $x \geq -5$

Lesson 10, page 281

1. Answers will vary. The graph increases, remains flat for some period of time, then decreases at the same rate it increased. **3.** Answers will vary. **5.** Graphs and stories will vary.

Chapter 9 Application, page 282

1. triangle **3.** Sample answer: (1, 1), (3, 1), (1, 4), (3, 4) **5.** Sample answer: (0, 0), (2, 0), (2, 2), (0, 2)

Chapter 9 Review, pages 283–285

1. (–3, 0) **3.** *x*-intercept = (−3, 0); *y*-intercept = (0, 3) **5.** $m = 1$ **7., 9.**

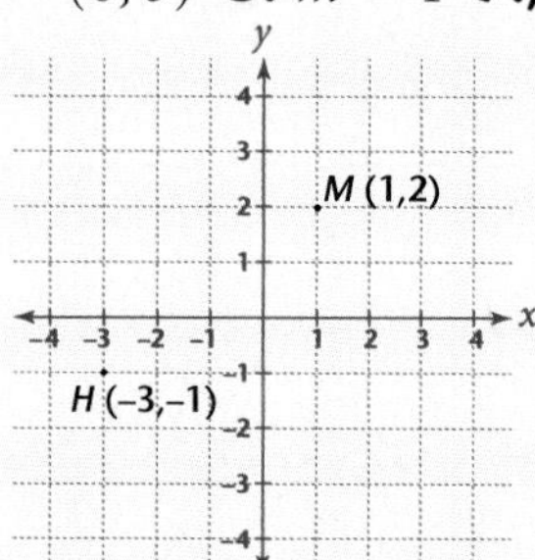

11. $m = -1$ **13.** $m = -\frac{1}{2}$ **15.** The graph should pass through (1, 1) and (−3, −7); $y = 2x - 1$ **17.** The graph should pass through (−2, −1) and (−4, −4); $y = \frac{3}{2}x + 2$ **19.** yes **21.** $f(-1) = 2$; $f(2) = 2$ **23.** The graph should be a broken line passing through (0, 1) and (1, 3). The region to the right of the broken line should be shaded. **25.** $y \leq 5x + 2$

CHAPTER 10

Lesson 1, pages 290–291

1. $m = 2$; the slope of a line is written in the form $y = mx + b$ **3.** $m = \frac{4}{9}$ **5.** $m = \frac{5}{2}$ or $m = 2\frac{1}{2}$; the slope of a line parallel to a given line is the same as the given line. The *y*-intercept of the parallel line is 4 because a point on that line is (0, 4) and because when $x = 0$, $y = b$. **6.** $y = 2x + 4$ **7.** $y = 3x - 2$ **9.** $y = -\frac{1}{2}x - 3$ **10.** rewrite as $y = 2x + 1$; $y = 2x + 3$; divide each side of the given equation by 2 to rewrite the equation in the form $y = mx + b$ **11.** rewrite as $y = x + 1$; $y = x + 3$ **13.** yes; the only lines on a graph that can lie only in Quadrants I and II, and only in Quadrants III and IV, are lines that are parallel to the x-axis. Since the slope of the x-axis of any graph is zero, the slope of any line parallel to the x-axis is also zero. **15.** no

Try This

Lines of the form $x =$ constant or $x =$ any number means the line is vertical and parallel to the y-axis. The slope of any two points on the line gives a zero for the $x_2 - x_1$ portion of the slope formula. Division by zero is undefined.

Lesson 2, page 293

1. $y = 2x - 10$; substitute $(6, 2)$ into $y = mx + b$ to find the y-intercept of the line. The line must also have the same slope (2) of the given line. **3.** $y = -\frac{3}{5}x + 2$ **5.** $y = -\frac{1}{2}x - \frac{1}{2}$ **7.** $y = -2x + 8$ **9.** $y = 2x - 1$ **10.** $y = \frac{x}{2} + 1$; $y = \frac{x}{2} + \frac{3}{2}$; divide each side of the given equation by 2 to find $y = \frac{x}{2} + 1$. Then substitute $(1, 2)$ into $y = mx + b$ to find the y-intercept of a line that has the same slope as the given line. **11.** rewrite as $y = x + 1$; $y = x + 2$ **13.** rewrite as $y = \frac{x}{2} + \frac{5}{4}$; $y = \frac{x}{2}$ **15.** rewrite as $y = 3x + 4$; $y = 3x - 11$

Try This

Sample answers: $y = mx + (d - mc)$ or $y = mx + (c - md)$

Lesson 3, pages 296–297

1. no; $m = 2$ for each, parallel; in order for a system of equations to have a solution, two or more lines in that system must intersect **3.** yes, slopes not equal, lines intersect; a common solution for a system of equations is the point or points of intersection of the lines in that system **5.** yes, slopes not equal, lines intersect

Lesson 4, pages 300–301

1. $(1, 4)$; solve $y + x = 5$ for x: $x = 5 - y$. Substitute $x = 5 - y$ into $2x + y = 6$ to find that $y = 4$. Substitute $y = 4$ into either equation to find that $x = 1$. Check. **3.** $(-\frac{20}{7}, -\frac{18}{7})$ **5.** $(-4, -2)$ **7.** $(3, -1)$ **9.** not correct

Lesson 5, page 303

1. $(0, 2)$; add the equations to eliminate the x term. Substitute the value of y into either equation. Check your work by substituting the point into both equations. If both equations are true, then the common solution is correct. **3.** $(-4, -2)$ **5.** $(-4, -2)$ **7.** $(16, 2)$ **9.** $(\frac{1}{2}, 3)$

Lesson 6, page 305

1. $(2, -3)$ Create a table of values to find the x- and y-intercepts of each line. Use the points in the table to graph the lines. Identify the point of intersection, then check by substituting the x- and y-value for the point into each equation. **3.** $(3, -3)$ **5.** $(2, 0)$ **7.** $(\frac{3}{4}, 2)$ **9.** $(0, 2,)$ **11.** $(3, 0)$ **13.** $(11, -1)$ **15.** $(-4, -6)$

Lesson 7, pages 308–309

1. True, both are true **3.** False, $4 \div 0 = 0$ is false **5.** True, both are true **7.** False, all vertical lines have a slope of 1 is false **9.** False, $2^2 + 23 = 25$ is false **11.** False, $6 + 7 = 15$ is false **13.** True, both are true **15.** True, both are true **17.** True, both are true **19.** False, q is false

Lesson 8, page 313

1. 8 and 16; solve $x + y = 24$ or $x - y = 8$ for x or y. Then substitute to find the other value. **3.** this week \$54, last week \$18 **5.** 12 seconds, 16 seconds **7.** Amityville 24 points, Johnstown 40 points; let a = Amityville's score and j = Johnstown's score. Solve $\frac{3}{5}j = a$ and $a + 16 = j$ for a and j. **9.** Shavonne is 28 and DaWayne is 42.

Lesson 9, pages 315–317

1. 2×2 **3.** 1×4 **5.** 2×4 **6.** row 2, column 2 **7.** row 5, column 1 **9.** row 9, column 9 **11.** $\begin{bmatrix} 0 & 2 \\ 8 & 1 \end{bmatrix}$ **13.** $\begin{bmatrix} 10x & 2x & 3y \\ 13 & -1 & -8 \end{bmatrix}$

15. $\begin{bmatrix} 5 & 1 & 6 \\ \sqrt{2} & 7 & 3 \\ 9 & 1 & 6 \end{bmatrix}$ **16.** $\begin{bmatrix} -1 & 5 \\ 8 & 8 \end{bmatrix}$

17. $\begin{bmatrix} -5 & 1 & 0 \\ -2 & 2 & -6 \end{bmatrix}$ **19.** $\begin{bmatrix} 3-a & 1-b & 6-c \\ -1 & -9 & -4 \\ -3 & 1 & 4 \end{bmatrix}$

Lesson 10, pages 320–321

1. $\begin{bmatrix} 48 & 0 \\ 15 & 3 \end{bmatrix}$ **3.** $\begin{bmatrix} 7x & 7y \\ 21 & 105 \end{bmatrix}$

5. $\begin{bmatrix} 3xy^2 & -xy^2 & ay^2 \\ 4y^2 & 14y^2 & 0 \\ -6y^2 & 10y^2 & -y^4 \\ y^3 & y^2 & xy^3 \end{bmatrix}$

7. $\begin{bmatrix} 1 & 0 & 2 \\ 1 & 1 & 6 \\ 3 & 2 & 1 \end{bmatrix}$

Chapter 10 Application, page 322

1. $U = \{1, 2, 3, 4, 5, 6, 7, 8\}$; $A \cup B = \{1, 2, 4, 5, 6, 7\}$; $A \cap B = \{4, 6\}$ **3.** 8 **5.** Answers will vary.

Chapter 10 Review, pages 323–325

1. (3, 4) **3.** (0, 1) **5.** 135° and 45° **7.** $y = 2x + 10$ **9.** $y = \frac{x}{2} + 4$ or $2y = x + 8$ **11.** $y = 3x - 3$ **13.** (4, 2) **15.** (3, 1) **17.** $(8\frac{4}{7}, \frac{5}{7})$ **19.** False, the second statement is not true **21.** False, both statements are false **23.** 62° and 28° **25.** Markette is 20 and Earlene is 16.

CHAPTER 11

Lesson 1, pages 330–331

1. $0.6\overline{0}$, terminating; $\frac{3}{5} = 3 \div 5 = 0.6 = 0.6\overline{0}$ **3.** $0.\overline{5}$, repeating **5.** $0.\overline{18}$, repeating **7.** $0.\overline{63}$, repeating **9.** $0.\overline{15}$, repeating **11.** $0.12\overline{0}$, terminating **13.** $0.41\overline{6}$, repeating **15.** $0.7\overline{3}$; repeating

16. Decimal Expansion 1 0.5 $0.\overline{3}$ 0.25 0.2 $0.1\overline{6}$ $0.\overline{142857}$ 0.125 $0.\overline{1}$ 0.1

17. Decimal Expansion 1 0.5 $0.\overline{6}$ 0.75 0.8 $0.8\overline{3}$ $0.\overline{857142}$ 0.875 $0.\overline{8}$ 0.9

18. 93.2°F; $°F = (\frac{9}{5})(34) + 32$; $°F = \frac{306}{5} + 32$; $°F = 61.2 + 32$; $°F = 93.2$

19. −0.4°F **21.** 24.8°F **22.** 40°C; $°C = (\frac{5}{9})(104 - 32)$; $°C = (\frac{5}{9})(72)$; $°C = \frac{360}{9}$; $°C = 40$ **23.** $7.\overline{7}$°C **25.** $21.\overline{1}$°C

Try This

37°C

Lesson 2, page 333

1. $\frac{2}{5}$; $0.4\overline{0} = \frac{4}{10} \div \frac{2}{2} = \frac{2}{5}$ **3.** $\frac{9}{25}$ **5.** $\frac{9}{11}$

7. $\frac{5}{66}$ **9.** $\frac{11}{15}$; let $x = 0.7\overline{3}$; $10x = 7.\overline{3}$ and $100x = 73.\overline{3}$; $(100x = 73.\overline{3}) - (10x = 7.\overline{3}) = 90x = 66$; $x = \frac{66}{90}$ or $\frac{11}{15}$ **11.** $\frac{13}{99}$

13. $\frac{2}{13}$ **15.** $\frac{1}{202}$

Lesson 3, page 335

1. 7.368 irrational **3.** 3.314 irrational **5.** 3.557 irrational **7.** 2 rational **9.** 2 rational **11.** 6 in.; since the area of a square is (side)2, finding the square root of the area will give you the length of a side of the square **13.** 12.65 ft **15.** 196 square units; 14 units

Lesson 4, page 337

1. $\sqrt{25} \cdot \sqrt{100} = 5 \cdot 10 = 50$ **3.** $\sqrt{49} \cdot \sqrt{4} = 7 \cdot 2 = 14$ **5.** $\sqrt{5a \cdot 5a} = 5a$

7. $\sqrt{25} \cdot \sqrt{x^4} \cdot \sqrt{y^4} \cdot \sqrt{y} = 5x^2y^2 \cdot \sqrt{y}$

9. $\sqrt{9} \cdot \sqrt{10} \cdot \sqrt{x^4} \cdot \sqrt{x} = 3 \cdot \sqrt{10} \cdot x^2\sqrt{x} = 3x^2\sqrt{(10x)}$ **11.** $\sqrt{121} \cdot \sqrt{9} \cdot \sqrt{m^2} \cdot \sqrt{n^4} = 11 \cdot 3 \cdot mn^2 = 33mn^2$

13. $\frac{\sqrt{16}}{\sqrt{18}} = \frac{4}{9}$ **15.** $\frac{\sqrt{25} \cdot \sqrt{3}}{\sqrt{36}} = \frac{5\sqrt{3}}{6}$

17. $\frac{\sqrt{27}}{\sqrt{y^3}} = \frac{\sqrt{9} \cdot \sqrt{3}}{\sqrt{y^2} \cdot \sqrt{y}} = \frac{3\sqrt{3}}{y\sqrt{y}}$

19. $\frac{\sqrt{(16y^2)}}{\sqrt{(25x^4)}} = \frac{4y}{5x^2}$ **21.** $\frac{\sqrt{81h^6}}{\sqrt{27y^2}} =$

$\frac{9h^3}{\sqrt{9} \cdot \sqrt{3} \cdot \sqrt{y^2}} = \frac{9h^3}{3y \cdot \sqrt{3}} = \frac{3h^3}{y\sqrt{3}}$

23. $\frac{(\sqrt{81} \cdot \sqrt{3} \cdot \sqrt{x^6})}{(\sqrt{9} \cdot \sqrt{10} \cdot \sqrt{y^2})} = \frac{9 \cdot \sqrt{3} \cdot x^3}{3 \cdot \sqrt{10} \cdot y} =$

$\frac{3x^3\sqrt{3}}{y\sqrt{10}}$ **25.** $\frac{\sqrt{4} \cdot \sqrt{9} \cdot \sqrt{d^2}}{\sqrt{4} \cdot \sqrt{6} \cdot \sqrt{t^4}} = \frac{3d}{t^2\sqrt{6}}$

Try This

$$\frac{\sqrt[3]{(27y^6)}}{\sqrt[3]{(64z^3)}} = \frac{3y^2}{4z} = \frac{\sqrt[4]{(256y^4)}}{\sqrt[4]{(16x^8)}} = \frac{4y}{2x^2} = \frac{2y}{x^2}$$

Lesson 5, page 339

1. $6\sqrt{2}$; $\sqrt{2} + 5\sqrt{2} = 1\sqrt{2} + 5\sqrt{2} = 6\sqrt{2}$ **3.** $\sqrt{7}$ **5.** 12 **6.** cannot be simplified or subtracted **7.** $3\sqrt{3}$

9. $9\sqrt{2}$ **11.** 0 **13.** $2\sqrt{6} + 6$; $\sqrt{24} + \sqrt{36} = \sqrt{6 \cdot 4} + \sqrt{36} = 2\sqrt{6} + 6$

15. $2\sqrt{6} + 12\sqrt{3}$ **17.** $8\sqrt{10} + 12\sqrt{15}$ **19.** $31x^2$

Try This

$-5x$

Lesson 6, page 341

1. $2\sqrt{6}$; $\frac{(4\sqrt{3} \cdot \sqrt{2})}{(\sqrt{2} \cdot \sqrt{2})} = \frac{4\sqrt{6}}{2} = 2\sqrt{6}$

3. $\frac{(3\sqrt{35})}{5}$ **5.** $\frac{(2\sqrt{2})}{3}$ **7.** $\frac{(5\sqrt{5})}{3}$

9. $2 - \sqrt{2}$; $\frac{2}{(2 + \sqrt{2})} \cdot \frac{(2 - \sqrt{2})}{(2 - \sqrt{2})} =$

$\frac{4 - 2\sqrt{2}}{4 - 2} = \frac{4 - 2\sqrt{2}}{2} = 2 - 2\sqrt{2}$

11. $5\sqrt{5} - 10$ or $-5(2 - \sqrt{5})$

13. $\frac{(9\sqrt{5} - 15)}{4}$ **15.** $\frac{[3y(3 + y^3)]}{9 - y^3}$

Lesson 7, pages 344–345

1. $n = 49$ **3.** $y = 18$ **5.** $y = 245$

7. $x = 16\frac{1}{3}$ **9.** $x = 64$ **11.** $x = 625$

13. $x = 128\frac{1}{2}$ **14.** 6 units; since the area of a square is $(\text{side})^2$, finding the square root of the area will give you the length of a side of the square **15.** 7 units

17. 20 inches **19.** 1 unit

Lesson 8, page 347

1. $y^{\frac{1}{3}}$ **3.** $4^{\frac{1}{3}} \cdot y^{\frac{1}{3}}$ **5.** $x^{\frac{4}{3}}; x \cdot \sqrt[3]{x} = x \cdot x^{\frac{1}{3}} = x^{(1+\frac{1}{3})} = x^{\frac{4}{3}}$ **7.** $z^{\frac{4}{3}}$ **9.** $x^{\frac{2}{3}}; \sqrt[3]{x^2} = (x^2)^{\frac{1}{3}} = (x)^{2 \cdot \frac{1}{3}} = x^{\frac{2}{3}}$ **11.** x **13.** 4 **15.** 100

Lesson 9, page 349

Approximate answers shown for **1–10.**
1. 3.2 **3.** 7.1 **5.** 8.4 **7.** 9.5 **9.** 9.2

Chapter 11 Application, page 350

1. 56.6 feet per second **3.** 140 meters per second **5.** 400 feet per second

Chapter 11 Review, pages 351–353

1. 0.2941177; irrational, nonrepeating nonterminating **3.** $\frac{9}{16}$ **5.** $10\sqrt{6}$
7. 130 ft **9.** $0.\overline{621}$; rational, repeating
11. 25; rational, terminating **13.** cannot be added **15.** $8\sqrt{3} - 18\sqrt{2}$
17. $\frac{(16\sqrt{7} - 28)}{9}$ **19.** $4\sqrt{3x}$ **21.** $2^{\frac{1}{2}}$
23. $13^{\frac{3}{4}}$ **25.** $r \approx 4$ units **27.** $r \approx 9$ units

29.

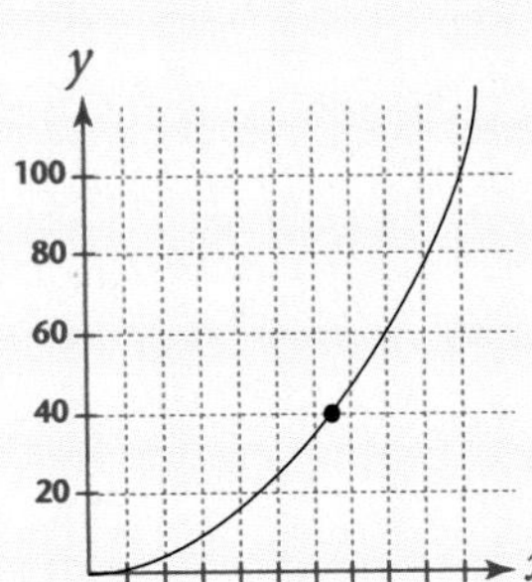

CHAPTER 12

Lesson 1, page 359

1. right; an angle that measures exactly 90° is a right angle **3.** acute **5.** straight **7.** adjacent; angles that share a common side are adjacent **9.** vertical **11.** $\angle PQR$ and $\angle SQR$; the sum of the measures of complementary angles is 90° **13.** 60°; 120°; the sum of the measures of supplementary angles is 180° **15.** 18°; 72°

Lesson 2, page 363

1. parallel; parallel lines never intersect **3.** parallel **5.** intersecting **7.** exterior; an exterior angle opens away, or toward the outside, of a figure **9.** interior
11. exterior **13.** exterior
15. supplementary; the sum of the measures of supplementary angles is 180°
17. supplementary **19.** supplementary
21. supplementary **23.** corresponding
24. 108°; 180° − 72° = 108° **25.** 72°
27. 72° **29.** 108°

Lesson 3, page 367

1. 70°; $x = 180° - 50° - 60°$ or $x = 70°$
3. 45° **5.** 105° **7.** 40°; find the measure of the angle adjacent to the 90° angle; 180° − 90° or 90°. Then find y: $y = 180° - 90° - 50° = 40°$. **9.** $m\angle Y = 180° - m\angle P$ or $180° - m\angle Q + m\angle T$ **10.** 360°; since there are four 90° angles in a square, the sum of the measures of the angles in a four-sided figure is (4)(90°) or 360°

Lesson 4, page 369

1. right scalene; in the triangle, one angle measures 90°, and none of the sides of the triangle have the same measure

3. isosceles **5.** obtuse scalene **7.** obtuse scalene **9.** No. Sample explanation: The sum of the angles in any triangle is 180°. If one angle in that triangle is right, the sum of the measures of the other angles in the triangle is 180° − 90° or 90°. Since the measure of an obtuse angle is greater than 90°, neither of the remaining angles in the triangle can be obtuse. **10.** 150°; the sum of the measures of $\angle a$, $\angle b$, and $\angle c$ is 360°; since the measure of $\angle a$ is 60°, the sum of the measures of $\angle b$ and $\angle c$ is 360° − 60° or 300° **11.** 10° **13.** 150° **15.** 20°

Lesson 5, page 371

1. $m\angle C = 130°$; $m\angle D = 90°$; since the measure of $\angle D$ is 90°, the measure of $\angle C = 360° - 90° - 90° - 50°$ or 130°

3. 360°; the sum of the measures of the angles forms a circle **5.** Check your drawing.

Lesson 6, page 375

1. SAS; in the triangles, the corresponding sides are adjacent to the same angle **3.** ASA **5.** SAS

7. 63°; in any triangle, the sum of the angle measures is 180° **9.** No; isosceles triangles can have different sizes and different shapes

Try This

Answers will vary.

Lesson 7, pages 378–379

1. 0.26 **3.** 0.27 **4.** 0.6 **5.** 0.8 **7.** $x = 5$; use the cosine ratio because the length of the hypotenuse is known and you are trying to find the length of the adjacent side **9.** 173 feet; use the tangent ratio because the length of the adjacent side is known and you are trying to find the length of the opposite side

Chapter 12 Application, page 380

1. 9 **3.** 14 **5.** 54

Chapter 12 Review, pages 381–383

1. m $\angle d = 127.6°$ **3.** m $\angle k = 52.4°$ **5.** m $\angle x = 67°$ **7.** m $\angle x = 40°$ **9.** acute; interior **11.** obtuse; interior; alternate interior **13.** m $\angle D = 90°$ **15.** SSS **17.** m $\angle f = 76°$ **19.** 58 feet

CHAPTER 13

Lesson 1, pages 388–389

1. −2, −3; $(x + 3)(x + 2) = 0$; $x + 3 = 0$, $x = -3$; $x + 2 = 0$; $x = -2$ **3.** −5, −6 **5.** −1, −5 **7.** $\frac{5}{3}$, −1 **9.** $-\frac{2}{3}, \frac{1}{4}$ **11.** −3; $t^2 + 6t + 9 = 0$; $(t + 3)(t + 3) = 0$; $t + 3 = 0$, $t = -3$ **13.** −2, 5 **15.** 0, $\frac{7}{5}$ **17.** 7, −2 **19.** $\frac{2}{3}$, −1 **21.** length 12, width 3; since the area of a rectangle is found using the formula $A = lw$, use the equation $(x)(4x) = 36$. Solve for x, then solve for $4x$. **23.** Mai puts in 21 chips; Tom puts in 20 **25.** Kristen is 6; Jesse is 8

Lesson 2, page 391

1. $x^2 + 5x + 6 = 0$; since $x = -2$ and $x = -3$, $x + 2 = 0$ and $x + 3 = 0$; $(x + 2)(x + 3) = x^2 + 5x + 6$ **3.** $x^2 - 10x + 24 = 0$ **5.** $x^2 - 2x - 24 = 0$ **7.** $x^2 + 3x - 28 = 0$ **9.** $x^2 - 19x + 88 = 0$

11. $x^2 + 3x - 10 = 0$ **13.** $x^2 - 8x + 15 = 0$ **15.** $5x^2 - 29x + 20 = 0$ **17.** $2x^2 + 5x + 3 = 0$ **19.** $3x^2 - 2x - 8 = 0$

21. $2x^2 - 7x + 3 = 0$ **23.** $7x^2 - 53x + 28 = 0$ **24.** No; for example, in the equation $x^2 - 8x = 0$, the roots are 0 and 8 **25.** No; you could only have one root, and it would equal zero: $x^2 = 0$

Lesson 3, pages 394–395

1. $-1, -5$; rewrite $x^2 + 6x + 5 = 0$ as $x^2 + 6x = -5$. Add the constant $+9$ to each side of the equation: $x^2 + 6x + 9 = 9 - 5$. Factor: $(x + 3)2 = 4$. Find the square root of each side: $\sqrt{(x+3)^2} = \sqrt{4}$; $x + 3 = \pm 2$. Find the roots: $x = -3 \pm 2$, or $x = -3 + 2$ and $x = -3 - 2$. **3.** $0, -3$ **5.** $5, -1$ **7.** $3, -5$ **9.** $2, 4$ **11.** $6, -2$ **13.** $-1, -5$ **15.** $1, -3$ **17.** $\frac{(3 \pm \sqrt{33})}{4}$ **19.** $3 \pm \sqrt{26}$

Lesson 4, page 397

1. $2, -4$; use the quadratic formula and substitute 1 for a, 2 for b, and -8 for c. **3.** $2, 1$ **5.** $3, -3$ **7.** $2, -4$ **9.** $\frac{5}{2}, 3$ **11.** $\frac{(-1 \pm \sqrt{22})}{3}$ **13.** $-3, -\frac{1}{2}$

15. Substitute $x = \frac{1 + \sqrt{7}}{3}$ in $3x^2 - 2x - 2 = 0$; $3(\frac{1 + \sqrt{7}}{3})^2 - 2(\frac{1 + \sqrt{7}}{3}) - 2 = 0$;

$3(\frac{1 + 2\sqrt{7} + 7}{9}) - 2(\frac{1 + \sqrt{7}}{3}) - 2 = 0$;

$\frac{8 + 2\sqrt{7}}{3} - 2(\frac{1 + \sqrt{7}}{3}) - 2 = 0$;

$\frac{(8 + 2\sqrt{7} - 2 - 2\sqrt{7})}{3} - 2 = 0$; $\frac{6}{3} - 2 = 0$;

$0 = 0$. Check for $x = \frac{1 - \sqrt{7}}{3}$ is similar.

Lesson 5, pages 400–401

1.

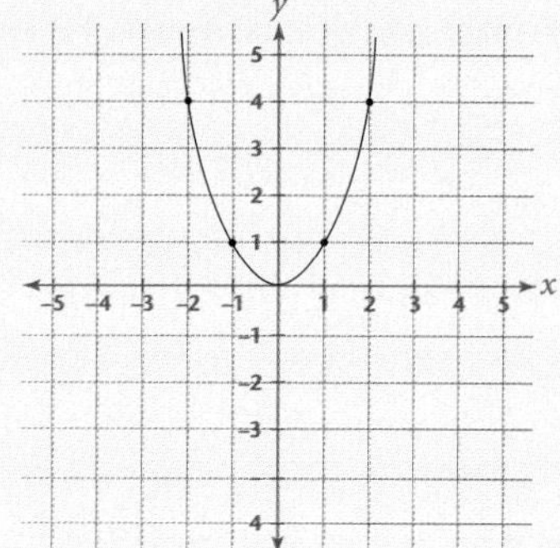

Make a table of values for the equation $y = x^2$. Points on the graph include $(0, 0)$, $(1, 1)$, $(-1, 1)$, $(2, 4)$, $(-2, 4)$, $(3, 9)$, $(-3, 9)$, $(4, 16)$, and $(-4, 16)$

3.

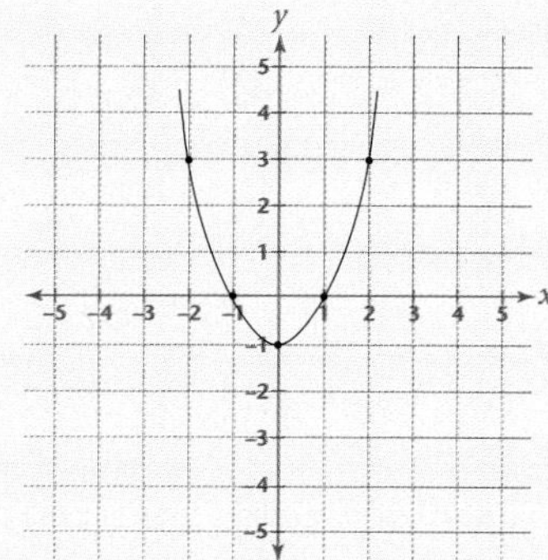

4.

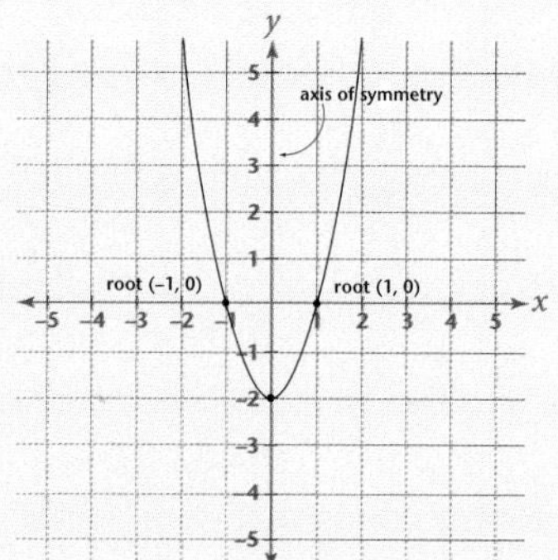

$x = 0$; $(-1, 0)$, $(1, 0)$; In the equation $x = \frac{-b}{2a}$, substitute 2 for a and 0 for b; the axis of symmetry is $\frac{-0}{2(2)} = \frac{0}{4} = 0$, or $x = 0$. To find the roots of the equation, set the equation equal to zero and solve.

5.

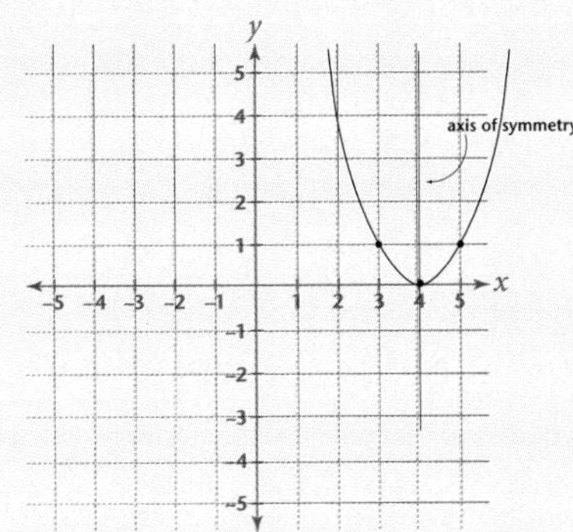

$x = 4$; $(4, 0)$

7.

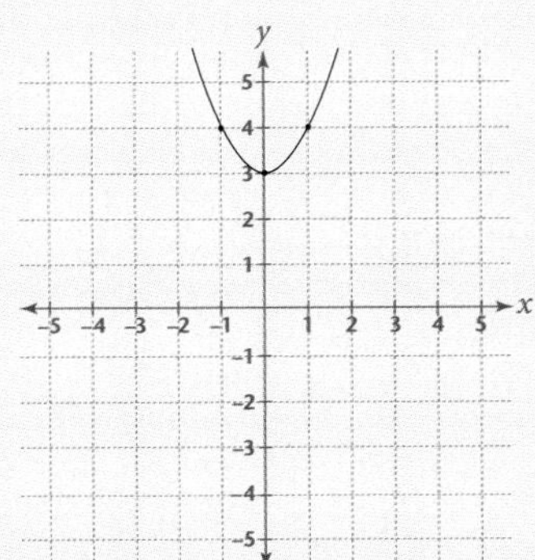

9.

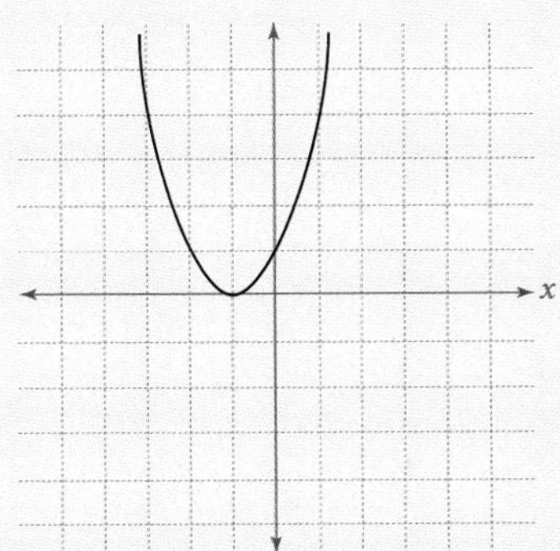

Chapter 13 Application, page 402

1. 1.25 seconds and 5 seconds

3. The model rocket is at any height above ground twice—once on its way up and once on its way down. **5.** A good estimate is 6.25 seconds.

Chapter 13 Review, pages 403–405

1. $-\frac{7}{3}, 3$ **3.** $8x^2 + 5x - 3 = 0$ **5.** 7, −3 **7.** $x = 2$ or $x = \frac{2}{3}$ **9.** $x = 0$ or $x = 8$ **11.** $x = -7$ or $x = 3$ **13.** $x^2 + 3x - 18 = 0$ **15.** $4x^2 - 15x + 9 = 0$ **17.** $x = -8$ or $x = 2$ **19.** $x = -6 \pm 2\sqrt{10}$ **21.** $x = \frac{9}{2}$ or $x = -1$ **23.** $x = 5$ or $x = 4$ **25.** $x = -1$, $(\frac{2 + \sqrt{6}}{-2}, 0)$, and $(\frac{2 - \sqrt{6}}{-2}, 0)$

27. $x = \frac{-9}{2}$, $(-6, 0)$ and $(-3, 0)$

29. 12 and 13

Supplementary Problems

CHAPTER 1

Pages 406–407

1. false, $6 + 3 = 9$ **2.** true **3.** false, $\frac{40}{8} = 5$
4. false, $25 - 13 = 12$ **5.** true
6. numerical, addition **7.** algebraic, multiplication, y **8.** algebraic, multiplication and subtraction, d
9. algebraic, division, n **10.** numerical, multiplication **11.** 5 **12.** 22 **13.** 18
14. 16 **15.** 25 **16.** 7 **17.** 21 **18.** -16
19. -7 **20.** 3 **21.** 11 **22.** -2 **23.** -7
24. 6 **25.** 9 **26.** 28 **27.** -30 **28.** 27
29. -33 **30.** -24 **31.** -6 **32.** 8 **33.** 9
34. -8 **35.** 7 **36.** $4n$ **37.** $16v - 14$
38. $5x + 3$ **39.** $5b - 8$ **40.** $-2g - 18$
41. $5y + 4 + 6c$ **42.** $13r - 7f + 8$
43. $5t - 9 + (-2b)$ **44.** $x + 15$ **45.** $11 + (-3d) - 8s$ **46.** a^9 **47.** c^{11} **48.** m^5
49. z^{18} **50.** y^{13} **51.** 48 cm **52.** 117 m
53. 12 km **54.** 24 dm **55.** 35 mm

CHAPTER 2

Pages 408–409

1. $15y$ **2.** $13a$ **3.** $5x$ **4.** $34n$ **5.** $14j$
6. qm **7.** $(5c)(2s)$ **8.** $(6t)^3$ **9.** $(10e)(7k)$
10. $(i)(12v)$ **11.** $5 + (4z + 3)$ **12.** $3d + (f + 7)$ **13.** $(25g + 2w) + 14$ **14.** $8 + (r + k)$ **15.** $(6b + 9c) + 11e$ **16.** $300 = 300$ **17.** $400 = 400$ **18.** $900 = 900$
19. $120 = 120$ **20.** $100 = 100$ **21.** $3x - 3j$ **22.** $28w + (-20)$ **23.** $-12 + (-6z)$
24. $-8f + (-8g)$ **25.** $2k + (-8)$
26. $5(3m + y)$ **27.** $-n(9 + 7)$ **28.** $m(c - h)$ **29.** $q(y^4 + s^2)$ **30.** $-w(r + h^3)$
31. -6 **32.** 9 **33.** c^3 **34.** $-u$ **35.** 2
36. $\frac{1}{4}$; $(4)(\frac{1}{4}) = 1$ **37.** p; $(\frac{1}{p})(p) = 1$
38. $\frac{1}{m^5}$; $(\frac{1}{m^5})(m^5) = 1$ **39.** h; $(\frac{1}{h})(h) = 1$
40. $\frac{1}{15}$; $(15)(\frac{1}{15}) = 1$ **41.** 2.25 **42.** 31.4
43. 18.33 **44.** 17.9 **45.** 5.23 **46.** $81u^4$
47. $-125y^3$ **48.** $64a^6$ **49.** $256d^2$
50. $-1{,}331n^3$ **51.** $16x$ **52.** $27h$ **53.** $13s$
54. $19g^3$ **55.** $11m^2$

CHAPTER 3

Pages 410–411

1. F, T, F, F **2.** T, F, F, F **3.** F, F, T, F
4. F, F, F, T **5.** F, T, F, F **6.** 18 **7.** 59
8. -1 **9.** 33 **10.** -2 **11.** 8 **12.** 5.6
13. 23 **14.** 12.8 **15.** 55 **16.** 7 **17.** 24
18. -9 **19.** 6 **20.** 8 **21.** 8 **22.** 18
23. 25 **24.** -48 **25.** 16 **26.** 5 **27.** 12
28. 49 **29.** 0 **30.** 6 **31.** $s = \frac{P}{5}$
32. $1 = (\frac{V}{wh})$ **33.** $r - \frac{C}{2\pi}$ **34.** $P = 10s$
35. $h = \frac{2A}{b}$ **36.** 8 **37.** 25 **38.** 30
39. 24 **40.** 21

41.

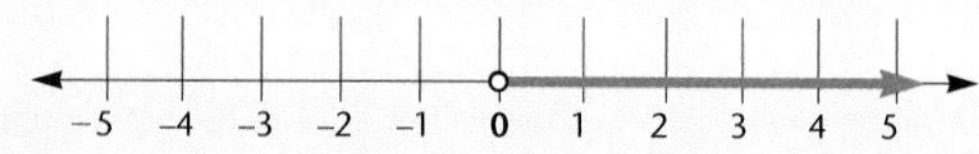

42.

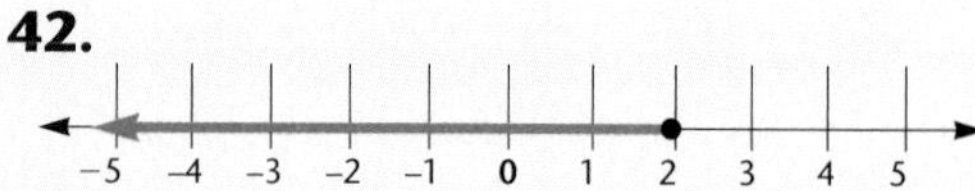

43.

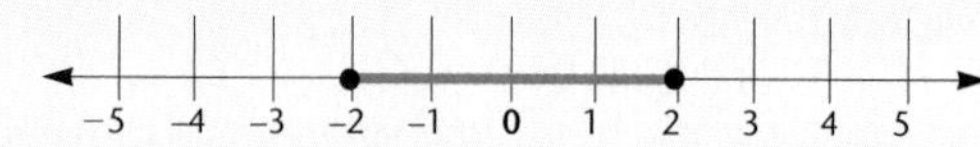

44.

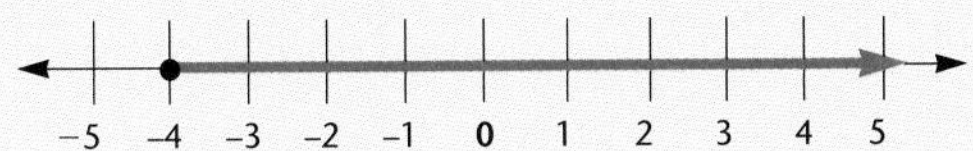

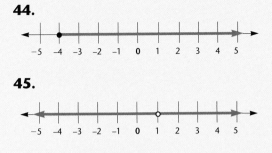

45.

46. $b < 3$ **47.** $e \geq 15$ **48.** $t > 6$ **49.** m > -4 **50.** $g \geq -15$

CHAPTER 4

Pages 412–413

1. $5 \cdot x - 4 = 26$; 6 **2.** $x + (x + 1) = -21$; -10, -11 **3.** $x + (x + 2) + (x + 4) = 51$; 15, 17, 19 **4.** $8x - 60 = 4$; 8 **5.** 1.5% **6.** 77% **7.** \$1,680 **8.** 200 CDs **9.** 22.88 **10.** 351.5 **11.** 16 **12.** 417.15 **13.** $51\frac{2}{3}$ km **14.** 65 mph **15.** $31\frac{1}{2}$ km **16.** $4\frac{1}{2}$ miles per hour **17.** 5 nickels and 15 dimes **18.** 36 nickels and 12 dimes **19.** 25 nickels and 100 dimes **20.** 18 nickels and 3 dimes **21.** \$300 **22.** \$625 **23.** 5% **24.** \$520 **25.** \$2.75 **26.** \$4.93 **27.** 8 pounds **28.** 6 pounds **29.** 4 **30.** 21 **31.** 5 **32.** 56 **33.** 10 **34.** 32 **35.** 12

CHAPTER 5

Pages 414–415

1. $(y \cdot y \cdot y)(y \cdot y \cdot y)(y \cdot y \cdot y) = y^9$ **2.** $(a \cdot a)(a \cdot a)(a \cdot a)(a \cdot a) = a^8$ **3.** $(x + y)(x + y)(x + y)(x + y)(x + y)(x + y) = (x + y)^6$ **4.** 93 **5.** 74 **6.** n^2 **7.** $(5g + 3y)^6$ **8.** $(h - i)^5$ **9.** $5.54 \cdot 10^{-9}$ **10.** $9 \cdot 106$ **11.** $7.85 \cdot 10^{-7}$ **12.** 260,000 **13.** 0.00314 **14.** 5,210,000 **15.** $6.1(10^{-3})$ **16.** $3.4(10^8)$ **17.** $5.46 \cdot 102$ **18.** $5 \cdot 10^{-5}$ **19.** $1.848 \cdot 10^{-1}$ **20.** $11x + 4$; $4x^2 - x - 2$ **21.** $3c^4 + 4c^2 + 4c + 6$; $-c^4 - 2c^2 + 2c - 4$ **22.** $-2w^5 - 2w$; $-4w^5 - 12w^4 - 4w^3 - 2w^2 - 10$ **23.** $k^5 + k^4 + k^3 + w^2 + 8$; $k^5 - k^4 + k^3 - w^2 - 2$ **24.** $n^7 + n^5 + n^3 + n^2 + n - 3$; $-n^7 + n^5 + n^3 - n^2 + n - 3$ **25.** $8d^7 + 3d^6 + 9d^3 + d^2 + d - 8$; $8d^7 + 3d^6 + 9d^3 - d^2 - d + 8$ **26.** $y^2 + 7y + 12$ **27.** $b^2 - 16$ **28.** $3n^5 + 6n^4 - 24n^3$ **29.** $-4x^4 + 15x^2 + 25$ **30.** $c^6 + 2c^5 + c^4$ **31.** $3z^2 - 5z - 2$ **32.** $2u^5 + 5u^4 + 4u^3 + 6u^2 + 15u + 12$ **33.** $12y^8 - 24y^5 - 3y^4 + 6y$ **34.** $3x^2 + 4x - 3$ **35.** $-5y^3 + 6y^2 - 7y - 8$ **36.** $(h^2 + 2h)$ **37.** 2 **38.** $6t^2 + 10t - 3$ **39.** $2y$ **40.** $(25x^3 - 5x^2 + x - 2)$

CHAPTER 6

Pages 416–417

1. 25 **2.** 11 **3.** 9 **4.** $4x$ **5.** $5ad$ **6.** 10 **7.** $6x$ **8.** 5 **9.** $7xy^2$ **10.** $13wt$ **11.** $(x + 7)(x - 8)$ **12.** $(c + 3)(c + 3)$ **13.** $(y - 4)(y + 3)$ **14.** $3(m + 2)(m + 6)$ **15.** $5x^2(x - 3)(x + 4)$ **16.** $3(2e + 7)(e + 2)$ **17.** $2(2n - 1)(3n - 5)$ **18.** $(z + 13)(3z - 4)$ **19.** $(2s + 1)(5s + 6)$ **20.** $3v^2(v + 2)(v + 3)$ **21.** $(b - 9)(b + 9)$ **22.** $(q - 20)(q + 20)$ **23.** $(6g - 7)(6g + 7)$ **24.** $(9r - 4)(9r + 4)$ **25.** $(5w^2 - 3x)(5w^2 + 3x)$ **26.** $(i - 13)(i - 13)$ **27.** $(y + 8)(y + 8)$ **28.** $(k - 10)(k - 10)$ **29.** $(p + 11)(p + 11)$ **30.** $(m - 22)(m - 22)$ **31.** 0 **32.** -4 **33.** 4 and -6 **34.** 2 and -2 **35.** 4 and -9 **36.** -4 and -6 **37.** 3 and 6 **38.** -4 and -7 **39.** 1 **40.** -2 and -4

CHAPTER 7

Pages 418–419

1. frequency **2.** stem-and-leaf plot **3.** histogram **4.** range **5.** mean **6.** mode **7.** box-and-whiskers plot **8.** probability **9.** impossible **10.** sample space **11.** dependent **12.** independent **13.** fundamental principle of counting

14.

Stem	Leaves
5	8 9 9 9
6	0 3 4 8 9
7	3 3 5 7 8
8	0 1 5 7
9	0 0 1 6 7 8

15. 4 **16.** 13 **17.** 59 **18.** 58 **19.** 98 **20.** 7

21.

frequency

8 7 6 5 4 3 2 1 0

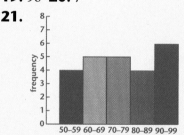

50–59 60–69 70–79 80–89 90–99

22. \$7.67 **23.** \$4.90 **24.** \$4.77 **25.** \$4.77 **26.** 10 **27.** 2 **28.** 8 **29.** between 5 and 9 **30.** 8 **31.** $\frac{1}{6}$

32. $\frac{1}{2}$ **33.** 0 **34.** $\frac{2}{3}$ **35.** $\frac{1}{12}$ **36.** $\frac{1}{4}$ **37.** $\frac{5}{12}$ **38.** $\frac{2}{9}$ **39.** $\frac{1}{90}$ **40.** $\frac{1}{30}$

CHAPTER 8

Pages 420–421

1. $\frac{7}{9}$ **2.** $\frac{4}{5}$ **3.** $\frac{2}{3}$ **4.** $-\frac{1}{12}$ **5.** $\frac{1}{2}$ **6.** c^5 **7.** $4s^5$ **8.** $\frac{5}{7h^3g^2}$ **9.** $\frac{2y^2}{9}$ **10.** $(p - 4)$ **11.** $(y + 3)$ **12.** $\frac{1}{(m-4)}$ **13.** $\frac{x}{2}$ **14.** $33\frac{5}{27}$ **15.** $2\frac{3}{16}$ **16.** $\frac{1}{(y-4)^2}$ **17.** $(d + 6)$ **18.** ef **19.** $3\frac{9}{32}$

20. 12 **21.** $\frac{1}{5}$ **22.** $\frac{cd}{u^2}$ **23.** $\frac{1}{xw}$ **24.** $\frac{5}{16}$ **25.** $\frac{18 + y^2}{9y}$ **26.** $\frac{5b - 1}{(b-1)^2}$ **27.** $\frac{(k-8)}{(k-3)(k+2)}$ **28.** $\frac{-3x(x-24)}{(x+8)(x-8)}$ **29.** $\frac{-3}{(v+3)(v-3)}$ **30.** 15 **31.** 9 **32.** 76.8 **33.** -49 **34.** $1\frac{1}{2}$ **35.** 120 **36.** -6 **37.** 13.5 **38.** $-3\frac{1}{2}$ **39.** $4\frac{1}{4}$ **40.** $-\frac{3}{4}$ **41.** 308 votes **42.** 9 games **43.** 4 jelly recipes **44.** $13\frac{13}{20}$ km **45.** $1{,}012\frac{1}{2}$ hours of television

CHAPTER 9

Pages 422–423

1. (4, 0) **2.** (−3, −1) **3.** (−2, 4) **4.** (0, −3) **5.** (1, −1)

6.–9.

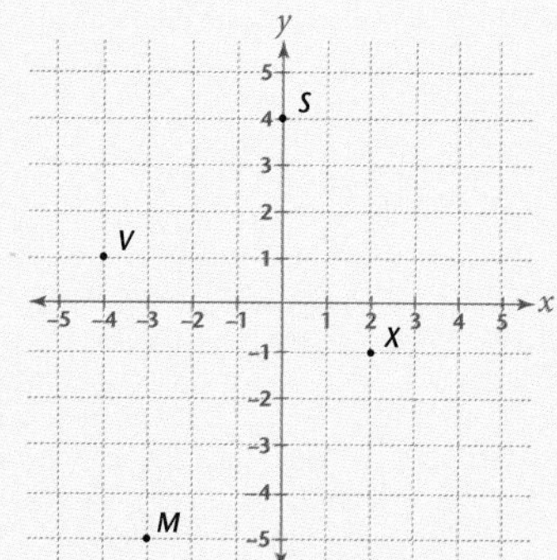

10.

$y = x - 2$	
x	**y**
−1	−3
0	−2
1	−1

11.

$y = 3x + 1$	
x	**y**
−1	−2
0	1
1	4

12. x-intercept $= (-1, 0)$; y-intercept $= (0, 1)$ **13.** x-intercept $= (4, 0)$; y-intercept $= (0, -4)$ **14.** x-intercept $= (3, 0)$; y-intercept $= (0, 3)$ **15.** x-intercept $= (\frac{2}{5}, 0)$; y-intercept $= (0, -2)$ **16.** $m = 2$ **17.** $m = 3$ **18.** $m = -1$ **19.** $m = 1$

20.

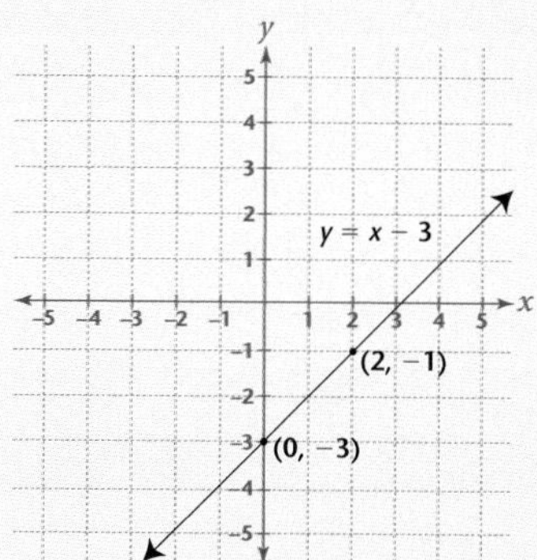

21.

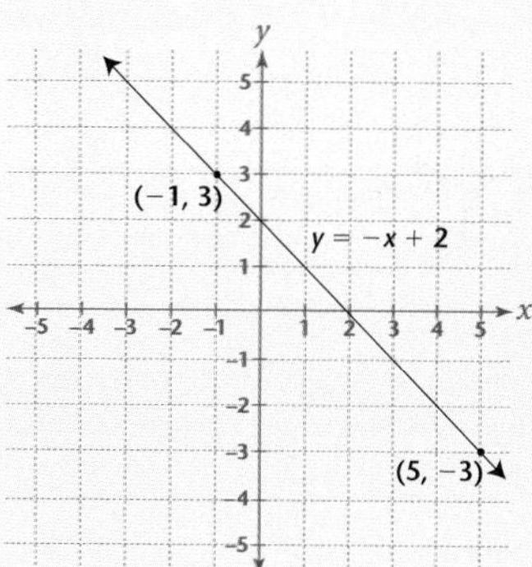

22.

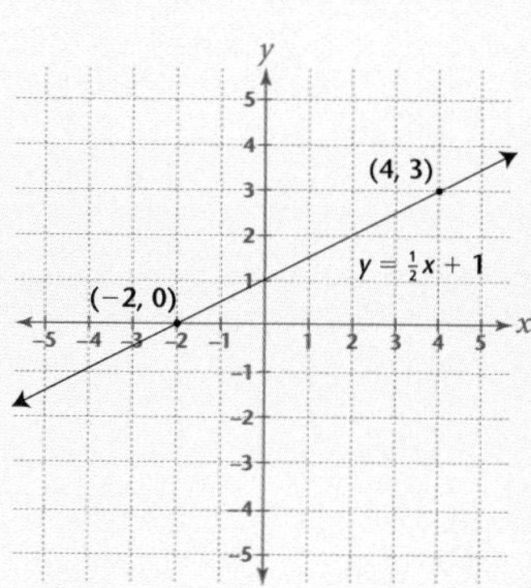

23.

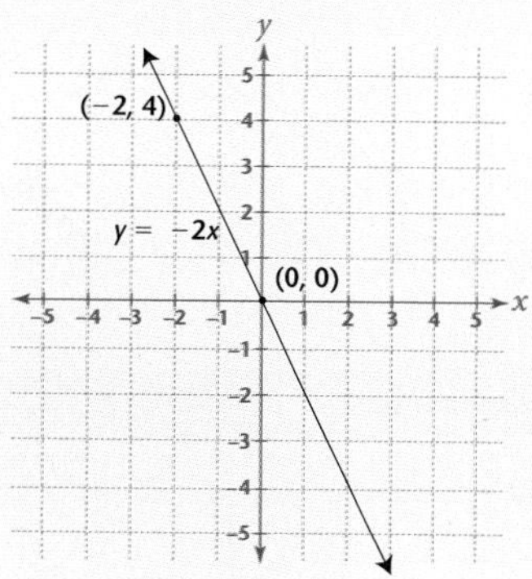

24. $y = 3x + 1$ **25.** $y = -x - 1$ **26.** $y = 4x - 4$ **27.** $y = \frac{1}{2}x + 1$ **28.** yes **29.** no **30.** -6; -6 **31.** 21; 6 **32.** 15; 0

33.

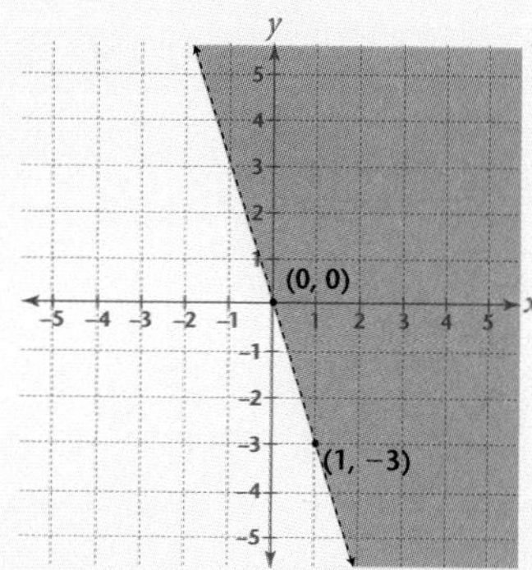

34.

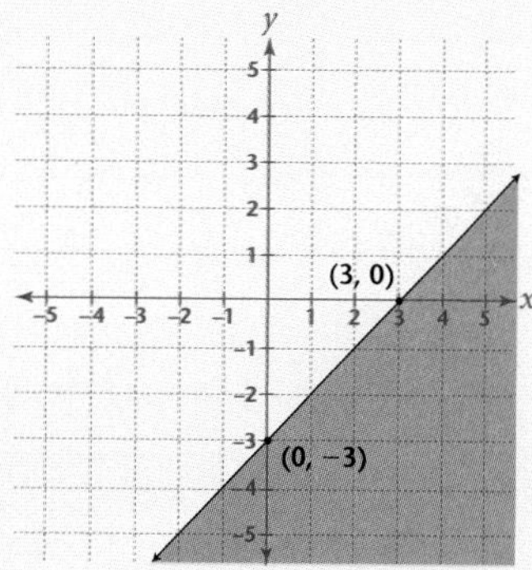

35.

CHAPTER 10

Pages 424–425

1.

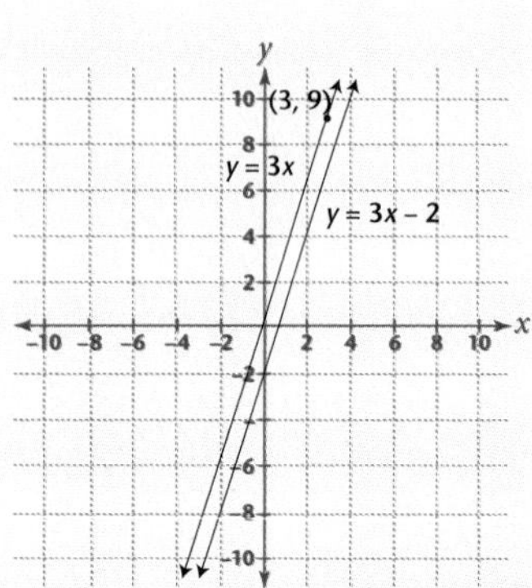

2.

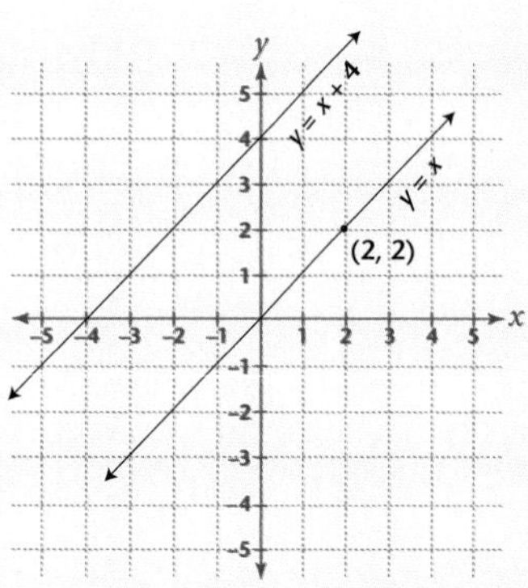

3.

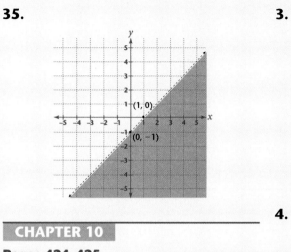

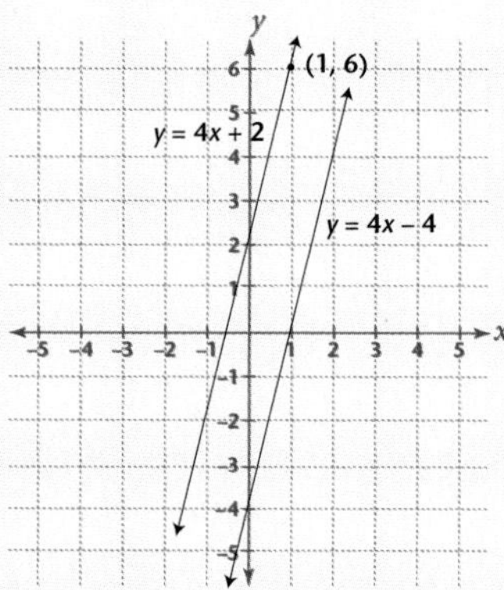

4.

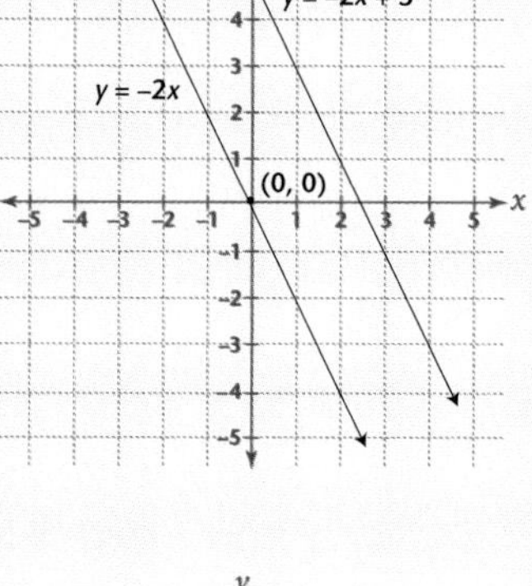

5.

6.

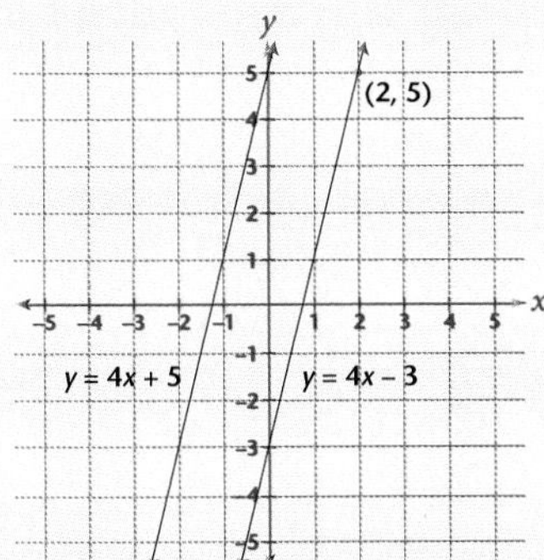

7.

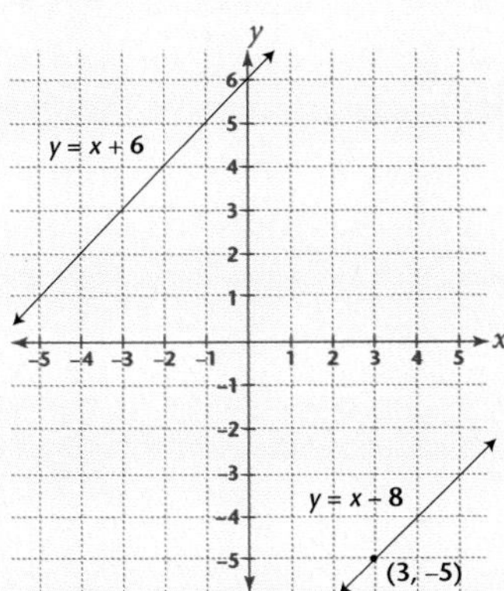

8.

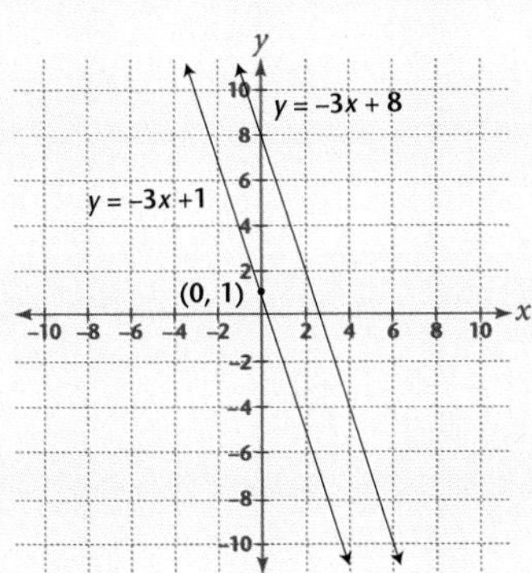

9.

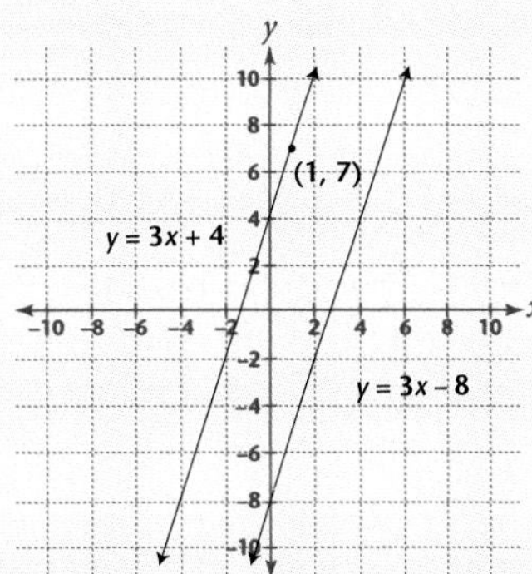

10.

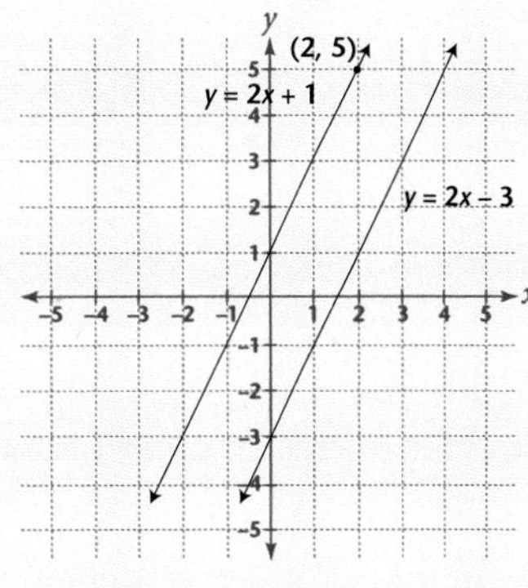

11. (3, 7) **12.** (2, 7) **13.** (6, 4)
14. (−1, −7) **15.** (−2, −2)
16. (−4, 7) **17.** (2, −5) **18.** none
19. (4, 3) **20.** (4, 0)
21. (2, 3)

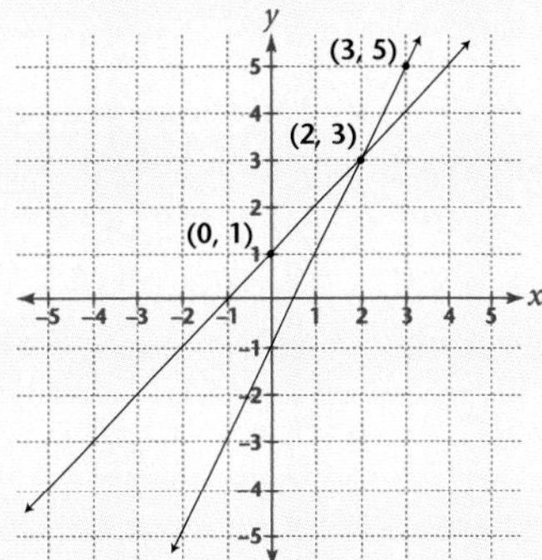

22. (1, 4)

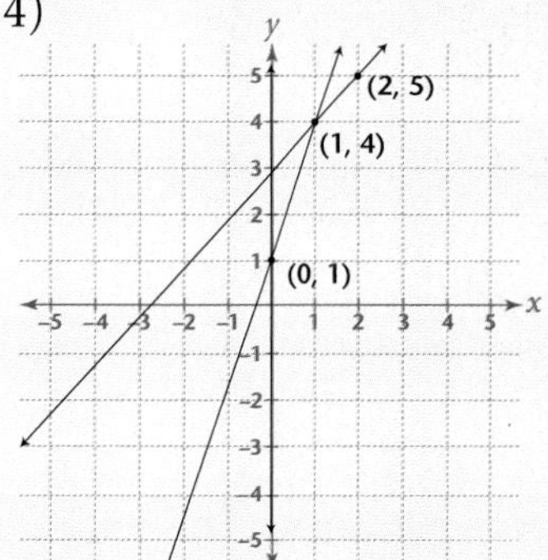

23. (2, 6)

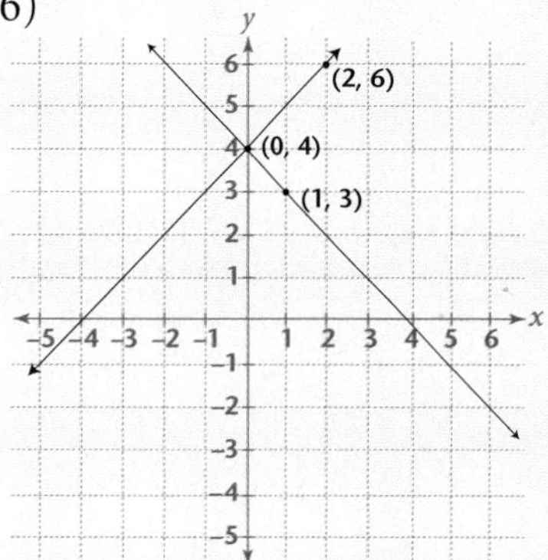

24. False, all parallel lines have the same slope **25.** True **26.** False, $3(6b + 2) = 18b + 3$ **27.** False, there are 144 eggs in 12 dozen

28. $x = 2, x = 4, y = 1, y = 3$

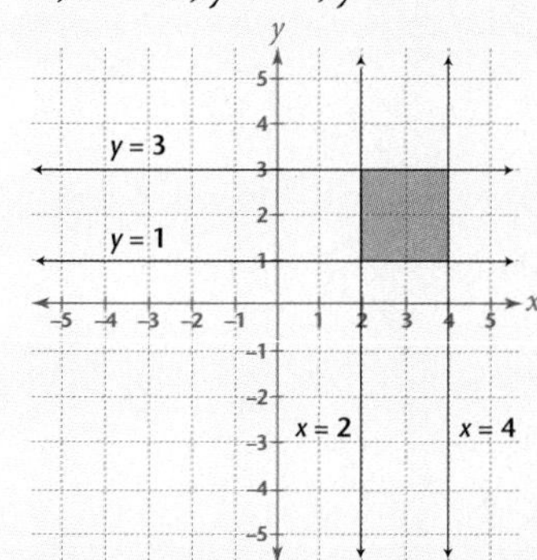

29. $x = 2, x = 1, y = 5, y = 4$

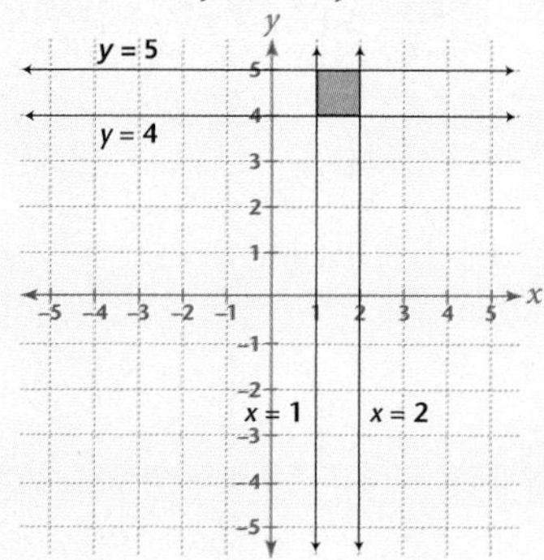

30. $x = 3, x = -5, y = -2, y = 4$

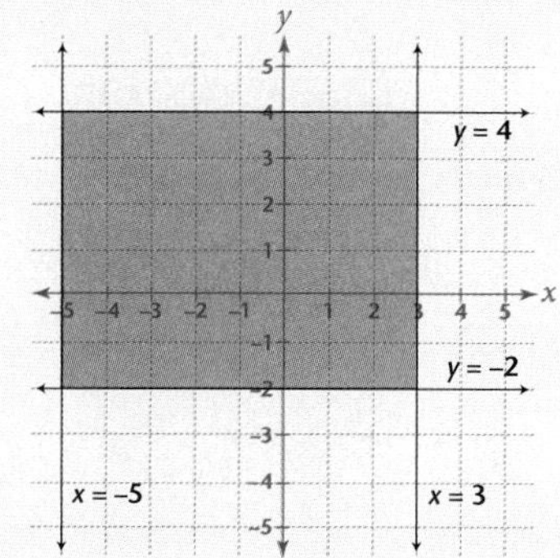

31. 6 and 42
32. 25 degrees and 155 degrees
33. 80 degrees and 100 degrees
34. 10 degrees and 80 degrees
35. length = 70 feet; width = 80 feet

CHAPTER 11

Pages 426–427

1. $0.875\overline{0}$, terminating **2.** $0.\overline{6}$, repeating **3.** $0.0625\overline{0}$, terminating **4.** $0.\overline{36}$, repeating **5.** $0.625\overline{0}$, terminating **6.** $\frac{3}{5}$ **7.** $\frac{5}{6}$ **8.** $\frac{15}{16}$ **9.** $\frac{5}{32}$ **10.** $\frac{2}{9}$ **11.** 3; rational **12.** 2.6918004; irrational **13.** 3; rational **14.** 9.6548938; irrational **15.** 6.7694724; irrational **16.** 36 **17.** $52x^3y$ **18.** $\frac{8}{9}$ **19.** $\frac{5g^2}{6a}$ **20.** $\frac{7t^3}{11b^4}$ **21.** 15 **22.** $6\sqrt{2}$ **23.** $18\sqrt{3}$ **24.** $4\sqrt{3}$

25. $8x\sqrt{3}$ **26.** $3\sqrt{\frac{10}{5}}$ **27.** 6 **28.** $\frac{5\sqrt{5}}{2}$ **29.** $(4 - 2\sqrt{3})$ **30.** $\frac{8\sqrt{5}-10}{11}$ **31.** 8 **32.** 8 **33.** $\frac{25}{36}$ **34.** 36 **35.** 289 **36.** $y^{3\frac{1}{5}}$ **37.** $m^{1\frac{1}{2}}$ **38.** w **39.** $q^{5\frac{1}{4}}$ **40.** $d^{3\frac{1}{7}}$

CHAPTER 12

Pages 428–429

1. obtuse and interior **2.** right and exterior **3.** alternate interior and obtuse **4.** right and corresponding **5.** supplementary and exterior **6.** acute and vertical **7.** supplementary and interior **8.** obtuse and corresponding **9.** right and corresponding **10.** acute and exterior **11.** 65.7° **12.** 65.7° **13.** 114.3° **14.** 114.3° **15.** 114.3° **16.** 65.7° **17.** 114.3° **18.** 62° **19.** 76° **20.** 45° **21.** 72° **22.** 60° **23.** SSS **24.** SAS **25.** ASA **26.** 1 **27.** 1 **28.** 0.5 **29.** 0 **30.** 0.5 **31.** 97 feet **32.** 18 feet **33.** 62 feet **34.** 3.7 feet **35.** 25.2 meters

CHAPTER 13

Pages 430–431

1. $x = 7, x = 3$ **2.** $x = 6, x = -5$ **3.** $x = 0, x = -2$ **4.** $x = -3, x = -8$ **5.** $x = -\frac{1}{5}, x = 2$ **6.** $x = 5, x = 11$ **7.** $x^2 + x - 12$ **8.** $x^2 - 13x + 42$ **9.** $x^2 - 6x - 16$ **10.** $2x^2 - 7x + 3$ **11.** $3x^2 - 10x - 8$ **12.** $x2 + 5x - 6$ **13.** $m = -3 + \sqrt{7}$ or $-3 - \sqrt{7}$ **14.** $c = -4 + \sqrt{26}$ or $-4 - \sqrt{26}$ **15.** $v = -2 + \sqrt{15}$ or $-2 - \sqrt{15}$ **16.** $x = 7 + \sqrt{39}$ or $7 - \sqrt{39}$ **17.** $d = -1 + \sqrt{\frac{3}{2}} - 1 - \sqrt{\frac{3}{2}} = \frac{-1 + \sqrt{3}}{2}$ or $\frac{-1 - \sqrt{3}}{2}$ **18.** $y = 5 + \sqrt{5}$ or $5 - \sqrt{5}$ **19.** $x = -4$ or $x = \frac{1}{2}$ **20.** $y = -3$ or $y = -11$ **21.** $x = -2$ or $x = \frac{1}{2}$ **22.** $y = -8$ or $y = 2$ **23.** $y = -3$ or $y = 5$ **24.** $x = \frac{7}{2}$ or $x = 2$ **25.** $x = -3, (-4, 0), (-2, 0)$

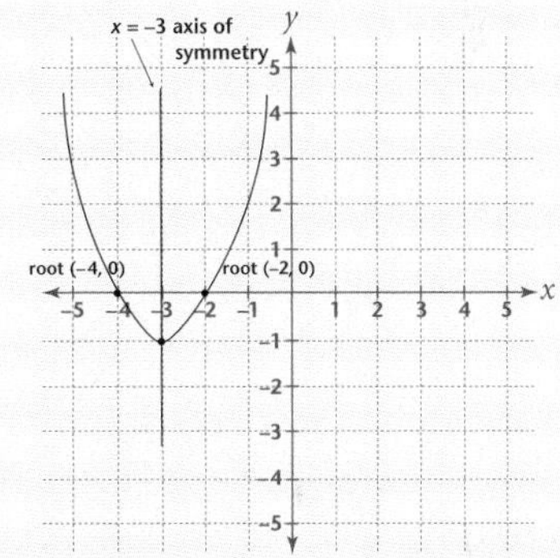

26. $x = \frac{5}{4}. (-\frac{1}{2}, 0), (3, 0)$

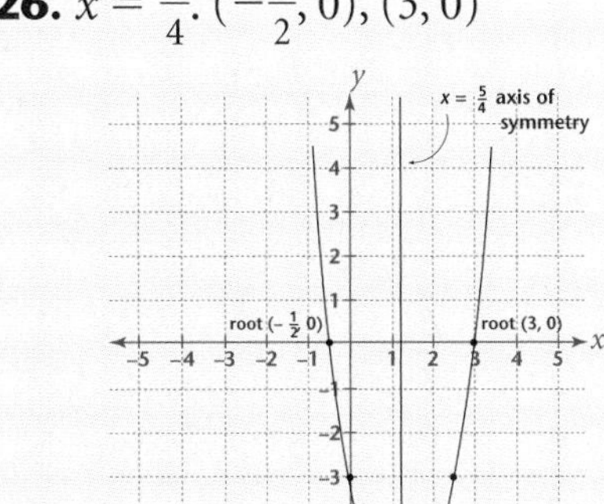

27. $x = 5, (4, 0), (6, 0)$

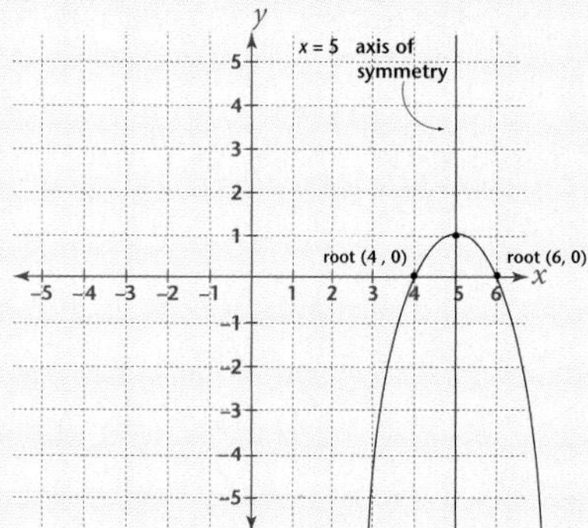

28. $x = 6, (3, 0), (9, 0)$

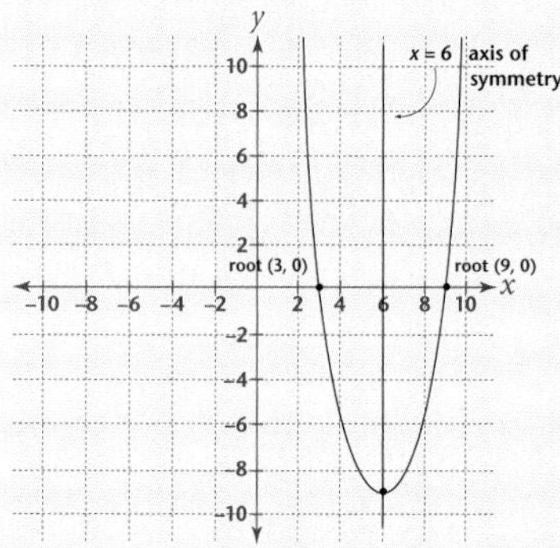

29. $x = -\frac{1}{2}, (-2, 0), (1, 0)$

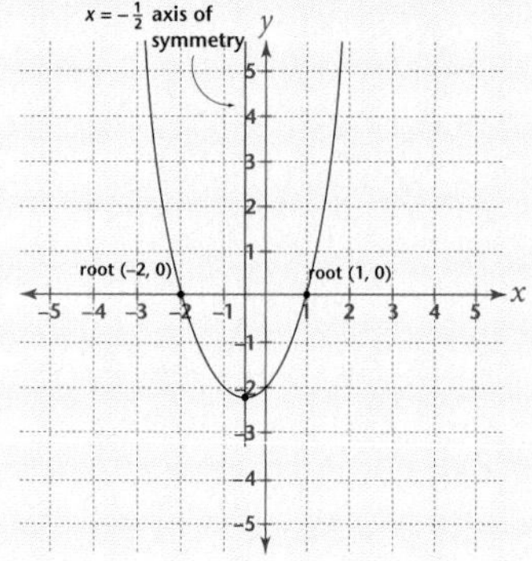

30. $x = -\frac{5}{4}, (-\frac{3}{2}, 0), (-1, 0)$

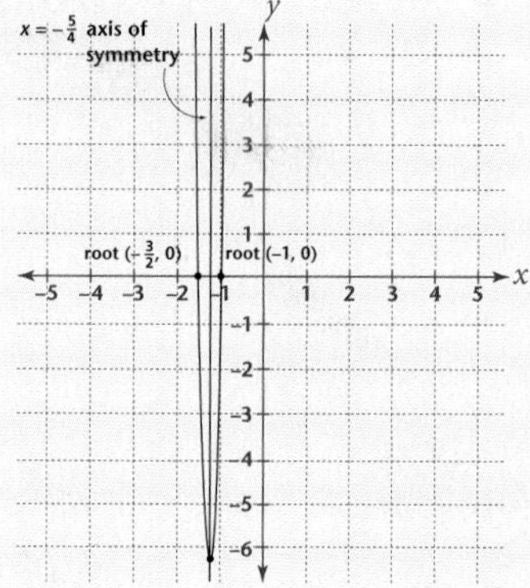

1. 13, 14 **32.** 15, 17 or −15, −17 **33.** 16, 18 or −16, −18 **34.** 8 and 9 years old **35.** Trixie is 11 years old. Her brother is 3 years old.

Review of Basic Skills

Review of Basic Skills 1, page 470

1. ones **2.** tens **3.** hundreds **4.** hundreds **5.** tens **6.** ones **7.** thousands **8.** hundreds **9.** tens **10.** ones **11.** hundreds **12.** thousands **13.** ones **14.** ten-thousands **15.** ten-thousands **16.** hundred-thousands **17.** thousands **18.** millions **19.** hundred-thousands **20.** hundred-millions

Review of Basic Skills 2, page 471

1. 10 **2.** 20 **3.** 190 **4.** 360 **5.** 1,890 **6.** 2,390 **7.** 4,020 **8.** 55,490 **9.** 63,560 **10.** 250,960 **11.** 100 **12.** 100 **13.** 300 **14.** 600 **15.** 800 **16.** 8,700 **17.** 13,400 **18.** 64,800 **19.** 267,500 **20.** 416,300 **21.** 1,000 **22.** 1,000 **23.** 5,000 **24.** 9,000 **25.** 10,000 **26.** 21,000 **27.** 46,000 **28.** 148,000 **29.** 250,000 **30.** 864,000

Review of Basic Skills 3, page 472

1. 6 **2.** 9 **3.** 8 **4.** 15 **5.** 19 **6.** 27 **7.** 113 **8.** 510 **9.** 1,017 **10.** 36 **11.** 118 **12.** 112 **13.** 377 **14.** 43,888 **15.** 110,682 **16.** 104,248 **17.** 256,818 **18.** 1,050 **19.** 2,107 **20.** 6,628

Review of Basic Skills 4, page 473

1. 4 **2.** 5 **3.** 10 **4.** 11 **5.** 32 **6.** 37 **7.** 141 **8.** 160 **9.** 404 **10.** 506 **11.** 309 **12.** 411 **13.** 736 **14.** 950 **15.** 40,736 **16.** 49,654 **17.** 1,692 **18.** 4,052 **19.** 873 **20.** 80,033 **21.** 59,960 **22.** 17,785 **23.** 493,000 **24.** 490,000 **25.** 400,000

Review of Basic Skills 5, page 474

1. 2, 4, 6, 8, 10, 12, 14, 16, 18, 20
2. 3, 6, 9, 12, 15, 18, 21, 24, 27, 30
3. 4, 8, 12, 16, 20, 24, 28, 32, 36, 40
4. 5, 10, 15, 20, 25, 30, 35, 40, 45, 50
5. 6, 12, 18, 24, 30, 36, 42, 48, 54, 60
6. 7, 14, 21, 28, 35, 42, 49, 56, 63, 70
7. 8, 16, 24, 32, 40, 48, 56, 64, 72, 80
8. 9, 18, 27, 36, 45, 54, 63, 72, 81, 90
9. 10, 20, 30, 40, 50, 60, 70, 80, 90, 100
10. 138 **11.** 182 **12.** 315 **13.** 252 **14.** 576 **15.** 162 **16.** 1,610 **17.** 987 **18.** 1,443 **19.** 3,312 **20.** 2,997 **21.** 3,087 **22.** 2,163 **23.** 6,768 **24.** 21,298 **25.** 48,020

Review of Basic Skills 6, page 475

1. 30 **2.** 500 **3.** 7,000 **4.** 60 **5.** 1,000 **6.** 1,400 **7.** 12,000 **8.** 270 **9.** 2,700 **10.** 27,000 **11.** 430 **12.** 4,300 **13.** 43,000 **14.** 2,670 **15.** 26,700 **16.** 267,000 **17.** 3,490 **18.** 34,900 **19.** 349,000 **20.** 3,490,000 **21.** 830 **22.** 8,300 **23.** 83,000 **24.** 5,860 **25.** 58,600 **26.** 586,000 **27.** 41,840 **28.** 418,400 **29.** 4,184,000 **30.** 41,840,000

Review of Basic Skills 7, page 476

1. 8 **2.** 7 **3.** 2 **4.** 4 **5.** 10 **6.** 6 **7.** 7 **8.** 7 **9.** 6 **10.** 9 **11.** 9 **12.** 9 **13.** 9 **14.** 7 **15.** 6 **16.** 23 **17.** 53 **18.** 123 **19.** 121 **20.** 207 **21.** 47 **22.** 17 **23.** 15 **24.** 50 **25.** 57

Review of Basic Skills 8, page 477

1. $27\frac{3}{14}$ **2.** $15\frac{1}{39}$ **3.** $45\frac{6}{7}$ **4.** $9\frac{7}{71}$
5. $24\frac{7}{20}$ **6.** 591.52 **7.** 423.10
8. 2,838.33 **9.** 7,467.47 **10.** 17,082.15

Review of Basic Skills 9, page 478

1. 170 **2.** 304 **3.** 120 **4.** 460 **5.** 360
6. 502 **7.** 610 **8.** 6,011 **9.** 21,100
10. 4,300

Review of Basic Skills 10, page 479

1. 9 **2.** 16 **3.** 25 **4.** 36 **5.** 49 **6.** 64
7. 81 **8.** 100 **9.** 32 **10.** 625 **11.** 16
12. 27 **13.** 125 **14.** 1,000 **15.** 64
16. 900 **17.** 8,000 **18.** 121
19. 1,000,000 **20.** 1,000,000 **21.** 23
22. 24 **23.** 33 **24.** 92 **25.** 75 **26.** 105
27. 43 **28.** 923 **29.** 464 **30.** 106 **31.** 43
32. 44 **33.** 63 **34.** 65 **35.** 905 **36.** 433
37. 58 **38.** 364 **39.** 944 **40.** 1005

Review of Basic Skills 11, page 480

1. 7 **2.** 6 **3.** 12 **4.** 8 **5.** 23 **6.** 1 **7.** 8
8. 8 **9.** 5 **10.** 35 **11.** 43 **12.** 15 **13.** 25
14. 159 **15.** 22 **16.** 23 **17.** 45 **18.** 0
19. 10 **20.** 3

Review of Basic Skills 12, page 481

1. 47.4 **2.** 64.2 **3.** 53.2 **4.** 70.7 **5.** 62.7
6. 50.7 **7.** 61.7 **8.** 53.7 **9.** 68.6 **10.** 51.6
11. 103.5 **12.** 54.7 **13.** 95.3 **14.** 42.7
15. 41.2

Review of Basic Skills 13, page 482

1. $<$ **2.** $>$ **3.** $<$ **4.** $<$ **5.** $<$ **6.** $>$ **7.** $<$
8. $<$ **9.** $<$ **10.** $>$ **11.** $<$ **12.** $<$ **13.** $>$
14. $<$ **15.** $<$ **16.** $>$ **17.** $<$ **18.** $<$ **19.** $>$
20. $<$

Review of Basic Skills 14, page 483

1. $\frac{15}{30}$ **2.** $\frac{10}{24}$ **3.** $\frac{9}{21}$ **4.** $\frac{12}{18}$ **5.** $\frac{21}{36}$ **6.** $\frac{27}{39}$
7. $\frac{20}{35}$ **8.** $\frac{15}{40}$ **9.** $\frac{30}{35}$ **10.** $\frac{90}{100}$ **11.** $\frac{9}{33}$
12. $\frac{18}{39}$ **13.** $\frac{25}{60}$ **14.** $\frac{18}{45}$ **15.** $\frac{36}{64}$ **16.** $\frac{15}{65}$
17. $\frac{15}{51}$ **18.** $\frac{12}{38}$ **19.** $\frac{30}{550}$ **20.** $\frac{14}{630}$

Review of Basic Skills 15, page 484

1. $\frac{1}{2}$ **2.** $\frac{1}{23}$ **3.** $\frac{5}{11}$ **4.** $\frac{1}{5}$ **5.** $\frac{1}{3}$ **6.** $\frac{28}{29}$
7. $\frac{7}{9}$ **8.** $\frac{1}{9}$ **9.** $\frac{1}{7}$ **10.** $\frac{3}{4}$ **11.** $\frac{1}{5}$ **12.** $\frac{1}{4}$
13. $\frac{1}{2}$ **14.** $\frac{2}{11}$ **15.** $\frac{1}{2}$ **16.** $\frac{1}{4}$ **17.** $\frac{1}{3}$
18. $\frac{5}{22}$ **19.** $\frac{5}{26}$ **20.** $\frac{1}{2}$

Review of Basic Skills 16, page 485

1. $3\frac{3}{5}$ **2.** 6 **3.** $3\frac{1}{6}$ **4.** $4\frac{2}{3}$ **5.** $5\frac{3}{4}$ **6.** 6
7. $7\frac{3}{5}$ **8.** 6 **9.** $5\frac{1}{11}$ **10.** $3\frac{4}{5}$ **11.** $1\frac{5}{8}$
12. $6\frac{7}{8}$ **13.** $4\frac{2}{3}$ **14.** 8 **15.** 30 **16.** $7\frac{3}{4}$
17. $8\frac{1}{3}$ **18.** $8\frac{2}{7}$ **19.** $10\frac{1}{5}$ **20.** $12\frac{1}{3}$

Review of Basic Skills 17, page 486

1. $\frac{17}{5}$ **2.** $\frac{32}{5}$ **3.** $\frac{31}{6}$ **4.** $\frac{86}{12}$ **5.** $\frac{13}{6}$ **6.** $\frac{19}{2}$
7. $\frac{37}{9}$ **8.** $\frac{90}{11}$ **9.** $\frac{17}{3}$ **10.** $\frac{25}{3}$ **11.** $\frac{88}{13}$ **12.** $\frac{50}{3}$
13. $\frac{59}{8}$ **14.** $\frac{47}{3}$ **15.** $\frac{191}{14}$ **16.** $\frac{29}{3}$ **17.** $\frac{61}{10}$
18. $\frac{62}{3}$ **19.** $\frac{341}{21}$ **20.** $\frac{89}{8}$

Review of Basic Skills 18, page 487

1. $\frac{1}{3}$ **2.** $\frac{1}{2}$ **3.** $\frac{21}{51}$ **4.** $\frac{2}{15}$ **5.** $\frac{3}{7}$ **6.** $\frac{6}{55}$ **7.** $\frac{4}{63}$
8. $\frac{5}{44}$ **9.** $\frac{1}{27}$ **10.** $\frac{5}{24}$ **11.** $\frac{1}{22}$ **12.** $\frac{8}{45}$
13. $\frac{1}{14}$ **14.** $\frac{13}{112}$ **15.** $\frac{1}{6}$ **16.** $\frac{5}{104}$ **17.** $\frac{1}{8}$
18. $\frac{5}{9}$ **19.** $\frac{1}{2}$ **20.** $\frac{1}{8}$

Review of Basic Skills 19, page 488

1. $\frac{5}{6}$ **2.** $\frac{3}{5}$ **3.** $\frac{8}{21}$ **4.** $\frac{8}{35}$ **5.** $2\frac{2}{5}$ **6.** $1\frac{2}{15}$ **7.** $1\frac{39}{56}$ **8.** $1\frac{1}{4}$ **9.** 3 **10.** $3\frac{3}{25}$ **11.** $6\frac{1}{14}$ **12.** $11\frac{11}{35}$ **13.** $6\frac{1}{5}$ **14.** $2\frac{4}{9}$ **15.** $2\frac{41}{56}$ **16.** $17\frac{7}{8}$ **17.** $4\frac{1}{5}$ **18.** $5\frac{5}{8}$ **19.** 8 **20.** $5\frac{7}{8}$

Review of Basic Skills 20, page 489

1. $1\frac{2}{5}$ **2.** $2\frac{1}{2}$ **3.** $2\frac{2}{7}$ **4.** $4\frac{4}{5}$ **5.** $\frac{12}{35}$ **6.** $\frac{3}{4}$ **7.** $\frac{24}{25}$ **8.** $1\frac{1}{9}$ **9.** $2\frac{1}{12}$ **10.** 5 **11.** $1\frac{3}{5}$ **12.** $\frac{1}{2}$ **13.** $\frac{9}{10}$ **14.** $1\frac{1}{3}$ **15.** $\frac{2}{3}$ **16.** $1\frac{2}{3}$ **17.** $1\frac{7}{48}$ **18.** $\frac{35}{48}$ **19.** $\frac{7}{10}$ **20.** 2 **21.** $1\frac{7}{9}$ **22.** $\frac{7}{8}$ **23.** $2\frac{1}{6}$ **24.** $1\frac{1}{3}$ **25.** 1

Review of Basic Skills 21, page 490

1. 3 **2.** $7\frac{1}{3}$ **3.** $2\frac{2}{5}$ **4.** $3\frac{1}{4}$ **5.** $\frac{1}{10}$ **6.** $\frac{26}{45}$ **7.** $2\frac{1}{10}$ **8.** 10 **9.** 7 **10.** $4\frac{1}{2}$ **11.** 2 **12.** $3\frac{1}{2}$ **13.** 8 **14.** 6 **15.** 7 **16.** $8\frac{1}{3}$ **17.** $4\frac{1}{7}$ **18.** $7\frac{1}{9}$ **19.** $13\frac{1}{2}$ **20.** $15\frac{4}{5}$ **21.** $\frac{2}{3}$ **22.** $2\frac{1}{6}$ **23.** $1\frac{4}{5}$ **24.** $5\frac{2}{3}$ **25.** $2\frac{8}{11}$ **26.** $5\frac{2}{3}$ **27.** $1\frac{16}{19}$ **28.** $2\frac{16}{21}$ **29.** $1\frac{1}{4}$ **30.** $2\frac{22}{27}$

Review of Basic Skills 22, page 491

1. 3 **2.** $5\frac{1}{2}$ **3.** 8 **4.** 13 **5.** $7\frac{2}{3}$ **6.** $8\frac{1}{4}$ **7.** 10 **8.** $8\frac{1}{2}$ **9.** $8\frac{5}{16}$ **10.** $3\frac{1}{2}$ **11.** $11\frac{1}{2}$ **12.** $4\frac{13}{16}$ **13.** $6\frac{3}{16}$ **14.** $9\frac{4}{5}$ **15.** $7\frac{15}{16}$ **16.** 9 **17.** 4 **18.** 17 **19.** 7 **20.** 12

Review of Basic Skills 23, page 492

1. $\frac{3}{4}$ **2.** $\frac{8}{15}$ **3.** $1\frac{1}{4}$ **4.** $\frac{7}{10}$ **5.** $\frac{11}{12}$ **6.** $\frac{17}{30}$ **7.** $\frac{19}{30}$ **8.** $\frac{3}{4}$ **9.** $\frac{13}{14}$ **10.** $\frac{2}{3}$ **11.** $3\frac{5}{6}$ **12.** $7\frac{5}{6}$ **13.** $5\frac{1}{4}$ **14.** $5\frac{11}{12}$ **15.** $6\frac{7}{10}$ **16.** $5\frac{5}{12}$ **17.** $4\frac{5}{6}$ **18.** $10\frac{4}{5}$ **19.** $12\frac{11}{24}$ **20.** $12\frac{1}{32}$

Review of Basic Skills 24, page 493

1. $\frac{1}{4}$ **2.** $\frac{3}{7}$ **3.** $3\frac{1}{4}$ **4.** $4\frac{1}{4}$ **5.** $1\frac{2}{5}$ **6.** $2\frac{1}{2}$ **7.** $1\frac{1}{6}$ **8.** $2\frac{1}{4}$ **9.** $3\frac{1}{5}$ **10.** $3\frac{1}{2}$ **11.** $2\frac{1}{8}$ **12.** $\frac{1}{4}$ **13.** $1\frac{1}{8}$ **14.** $2\frac{1}{4}$ **15.** $3\frac{2}{5}$ **16.** 1 **17.** $2\frac{1}{17}$ **18.** $5\frac{11}{39}$ **19.** $2\frac{1}{5}$ **20.** $2\frac{1}{2}$

Review of Basic Skills 25, page 494

1. $\frac{1}{8}$ **2.** $\frac{1}{4}$ **3.** $1\frac{1}{8}$ **4.** $2\frac{1}{4}$ **5.** $4\frac{7}{20}$ **6.** $1\frac{1}{6}$ **7.** $3\frac{1}{8}$ **8.** $4\frac{1}{8}$ **9.** $3\frac{27}{100}$ **10.** $1\frac{31}{100}$ **11.** $7\frac{5}{8}$ **12.** $2\frac{1}{2}$ **13.** $4\frac{4}{9}$ **14.** $3\frac{1}{10}$ **15.** 7

Review of Basic Skills 26, page 495

1. $3\frac{3}{4}$ **2.** $3\frac{1}{4}$ **3.** $7\frac{1}{2}$ **4.** $2\frac{2}{3}$ **5.** $1\frac{1}{3}$ **6.** $2\frac{2}{5}$ **7.** $2\frac{3}{4}$ **8.** $2\frac{4}{7}$ **9.** $4\frac{7}{10}$ **10.** $4\frac{7}{9}$ **11.** $3\frac{1}{2}$ **12.** $3\frac{2}{3}$ **13.** $4\frac{3}{5}$ **14.** $1\frac{5}{6}$ **15.** $1\frac{7}{8}$ **16.** $4\frac{3}{4}$ **17.** $2\frac{5}{6}$ **18.** $6\frac{5}{6}$ **19.** $4\frac{1}{2}$ **20.** $4\frac{3}{5}$

Review of Basic Skills 27, page 496

1. tenths **2.** thousandths **3.** ten-thousandths **4.** thousandths **5.** hundred-thousandths **6.** millionths **7.** thousandths **8.** hundreds **9.** hundredths **10.** hundred-thousandths **11.** $>$ **12.** $<$ **13.** $<$ **14.** $<$ **15.** $>$ **16.** $<$ **17.** $>$ **18.** $<$ **19.** $>$ **20.** $<$

Review of Basic Skills 28, page 497

1. 2.1, 2.06, 2.063 **2.** 0.1, 0.09, 0.089 **3.** 1.0, 1.04, 1.035 **4.** 0.2, 0.15, 0.155 **5.** 32.7, 32.70, 32.704 **6.** 7.6, 7.63, 7.630 **7.** 19.8, 19.81, 19.809 **8.** 34.0, 34.00, 34.004 **9.** 2.1, 2.06, 2.061 **10.** 139.4, 139.42, 139.418

Review of Basic Skills 29, page 498

1. \$18.03 **2.** \$13.73 **3.** \$18.20 **4.** \$13.42 **5.** \$18.64 **6.** \$15.78 **7.** \$33.09 **8.** \$26.26 **9.** \$26.25 **10.** \$29.93 **11.** 15.32 **12.** 20.13 **13.** 12.11 **14.** 31.383 **15.** 64.403 **16.** 18.099 **17.** 11.617 **18.** 24.098 **19.** 86.0991 **20.** 28.8514

Review of Basic Skills 30, page 499

1. \$16.33 **2.** \$3.11 **3.** \$11.35 **4.** \$10 **5.** \$2.11 **6.** \$27.18 **7.** \$8.26 **8.** \$8.28 **9.** \$13.37 **10.** \$5.19 **11.** 5.09 **12.** 0.66 **13.** 1.09 **14.** 5.29 **15.** 5.79 **16.** 74.51 **17.** 21.81 **18.** 35.13 **19.** 36.73 **20.** 80.63

Review of Basic Skills 31, page 500

1. 2.8 **2.** 12 **3.** 18.9 **4.** 14.7 **5.** 33.5 **6.** 3.12 **7.** 15.86 **8.** 15.99 **9.** 8.04 **10.** 58.48 **11.** 3.159 **12.** 17.748 **13.** 7.408 **14.** 26.568 **15.** 14.094 **16.** 11.993 **17.** 36.036 **18.** 8.838 **19.** 27.434 **20.** 55.188

Review of Basic Skills 32, page 501

1. $2.9 \cdot 10^3$ **2.** $3.6 \cdot 10^3$ **3.** $8.75 \cdot 10^3$ **4.** $6.32 \cdot 10^3$ **5.** $33.5 \cdot 10^4$ **6.** $4.6 \cdot 10^4$ **7.** $7.11 \cdot 10^4$ **8.** $4 \cdot 10^5$ **9.** $4 \cdot 10^6$ **10.** $1.7 \cdot 10^9$ **11.** $3.8 \cdot 10^{-4}$ **12.** $39 \cdot 10^{-2}$ **13.** $41 \cdot 10^{-2}$ **14.** $72 \cdot 10^{-3}$ **15.** $7.2 \cdot 10^{-3}$ **16.** 8.1 • 10–3 **17.** 7.4 • 10–4 **18.** $1.2 \cdot 10^{-5}$ **19.** $1.23 \cdot 10^{-3}$ **20.** $2.46 \cdot 10^{-4}$

Review of Basic Skills 33, page 502

1. 2.35 **2.** 0.26 **3.** 0.25 **4.** 3.17 **5.** 6.5 **6.** 3.1 **7.** 7.1 **8.** 0.21 **9.** 7.1 **10.** 2.1 **11.** 3.1 **12.** 3.3 **13.** 20.5 **14.** 9.09 **15.** 6.1 **16.** 1.202 **17.** 6.1 **18.** 0.51 **19.** 1.02 **20.** 0.5

Review of Basic Skills 34, page 503

1. 7.2 **2.** 12.3 **3.** 11 **4.** 14.9 **5.** 55.7 **6.** 37.4 **7.** 96.7 **8.** 427 **9.** 0.002 **10.** 210.5 **11.** 210.5 **12.** 6,460 **13.** 810 **14.** 81 **15.** 8.1 **16.** 707 **17.** 33 **18.** 6,620 **19.** 532 **20.** 0.98

Review of Basic Skills 35, page 504

1. $\frac{14}{100}, \frac{7}{50}$ **2.** $\frac{15}{100}, \frac{3}{20}$ **3.** $\frac{75}{100}, \frac{3}{4}$ **4.** $\frac{36}{100}, \frac{9}{25}$ **5.** $\frac{79}{100}$ **6.** $\frac{15}{100}, \frac{3}{20}$ **7.** $\frac{159}{1000}$ **8.** $\frac{375}{1000}, \frac{3}{8}$ **9.** $\frac{875}{1000}, \frac{7}{8}$ **10.** $\frac{999}{1000}$ **11.** $\frac{42}{100}, \frac{21}{50}$ **12.** $\frac{65}{100}, \frac{13}{20}$ **13.** $\frac{60}{100}, \frac{3}{5}$ **14.** $\frac{45}{100}, \frac{9}{20}$ **15.** $\frac{50}{100}, \frac{1}{2}$ **16.** $\frac{168}{1000}, \frac{21}{125}$ **17.** $\frac{22}{100}, \frac{11}{50}$ **18.** $\frac{98}{100}, \frac{49}{50}$ **19.** $\frac{568}{1000}, \frac{71}{125}$ **20.** $\frac{72}{100}, \frac{18}{25}$

Review of Basic Skills 36, page 505

1. 0.1 **2.** 0.2 **3.** 0.5 **4.** 0.12 **5.** 0.18 **6.** 0.35 **7.** 0.36 **8.** 0.006 **9.** 0.024 **10.** 0.118 **11.** 0.4285714 **12.** 0.7142857 **13.** 0.6666666 **14.** 0.2222222 **15.** 0.3846153 **16.** 0.117647 **17.** 0.1578947 **18.** 0.2173913 **19.** 0.2068965 **20.** 0.1612903

Review of Basic Skills 1

Place Value of Whole Numbers

Recall that 1,234 means 1 thousand + 2 hundreds + 3 tens + 4 ones.
So the place value of 1 is thousands, 2 is hundreds, 3 is tens, and 4 is ones.

EXAMPLE 1 Write the place value of the underlined digit.

$\underline{4},301$ thousands

$4,\underline{3}01$ hundreds

$4,3\underline{0}1$ tens

$4,30\underline{1}$ ones

Exercise Write the place value of the underlined digit.

1. $35\underline{6}$

2. $3\underline{5}6$

3. $\underline{3}56$

4. $\underline{9}81$

5. $9\underline{8}1$

6. $98\underline{1}$

7. $\underline{3},401$

8. $3,\underline{4}01$

9. $3,4\underline{0}1$

10. $3,40\underline{1}$

You may use this place value chart for larger numbers.

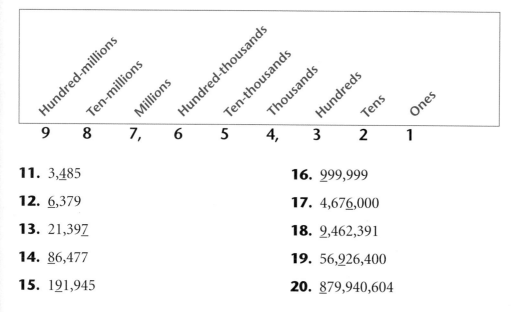

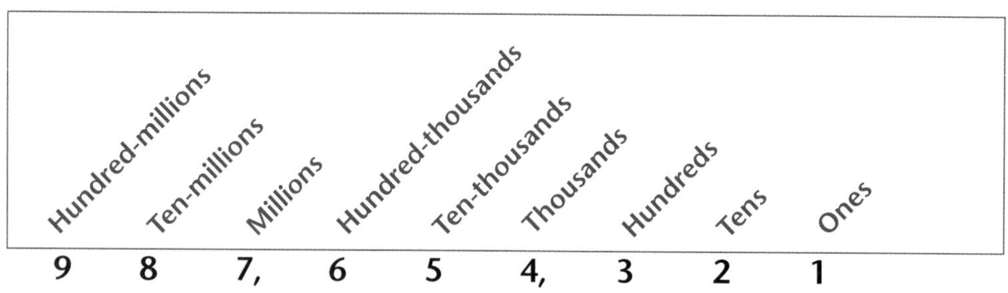

11. $3,\underline{4}85$

12. $\underline{6},379$

13. $21,39\underline{7}$

14. $\underline{8}6,477$

15. $1\underline{9}1,945$

16. $\underline{9}99,999$

17. $4,67\underline{6},000$

18. $\underline{9},462,391$

19. $56,\underline{9}26,400$

20. $\underline{8}79,940,604$

Review of Basic Skills 2

Rounding Whole Numbers

Example 1

	Round to the nearest:	Ten	Hundred	Thousand
Step 1	Find the place to be rounded.	1,582	1,582	1,582
Step 2	If the digit to the right is 5 or larger, add 1 to the place to be rounded.	1,582 ↑	1,582 ↑	1,582 ↑
Step 3	Change all digits to the right of the rounded place to 0s.	1,580	1,600	2,000

Exercise Round to the nearest ten.

1. 9
2. 16
3. 191
4. 356
5. 1,888
6. 2,394
7. 4,017
8. 55,487
9. 63,561
10. 250,960

Round to the nearest hundred.

11. 89
12. 51
13. 284
14. 561
15. 840
16. 8,696
17. 13,401
18. 64,789
19. 267,476
20. 416,313

Round to the nearest thousand.

21. 787
22. 806
23. 5,350
24. 8,634
25. 9,500
26. 21,435
27. 46,187
28. 147,831
29. 250,011
30. 864,217

Review of Basic Skills 3

Adding Whole Numbers

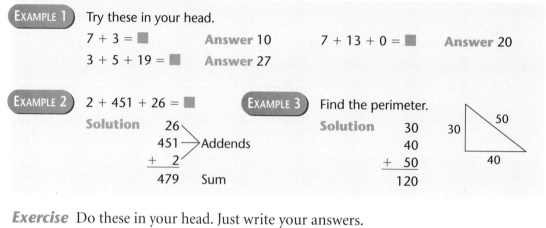

EXAMPLE 1 Try these in your head.

7 + 3 = ■ **Answer** 10

7 + 13 + 0 = ■ **Answer** 20

3 + 5 + 19 = ■ **Answer** 27

EXAMPLE 2 2 + 451 + 26 = ■

Solution

```
  26 \
 451 --> Addends
+  2 /
 479    Sum
```

EXAMPLE 3 Find the perimeter.

Solution

```
   30
   40
+  50
  120
```

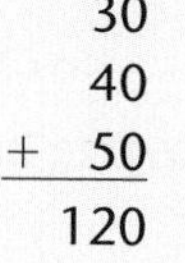

Exercise Do these in your head. Just write your answers.

1. 2 + 4

2. 2 + 4 + 3

3. 2 + 5 + 1 + 0

4. 2 + 0 + 3 + 10

5. 3 + 7 + 5 + 4

6. 6 + 7 + 4 + 10

7. 2 + 5 + 6 + 100

8. 500 + 2 + 7 + 1

9. 3 + 5 + 9 + 1,000

Write in vertical form, then add.

10. 9 + 27

11. 3 + 29 + 86

12. 7 + 14 + 91

13. 2 + 69 + 5 + 301

14. 26,487 + 17,401

15. 37,091 + 73,591

16. 100,847 + 3,401

17. 217,401 + 39,417

Find the perimeters.

18.

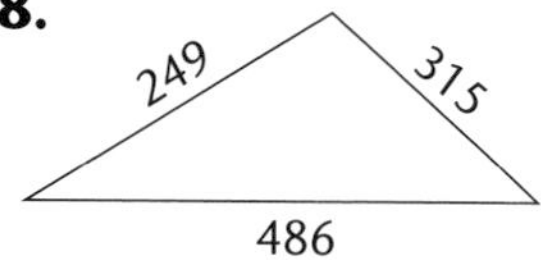

19.

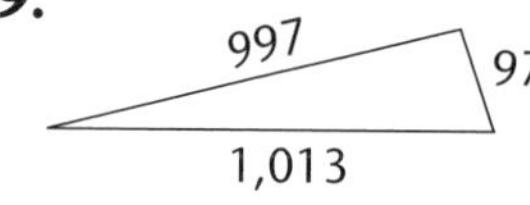

20.

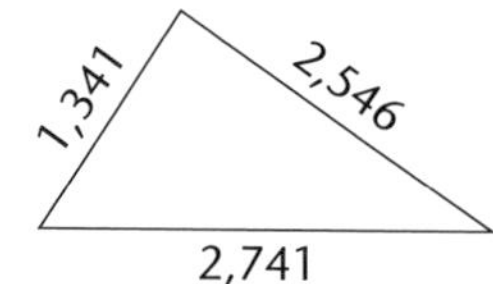

Review of Basic Skills 4

Subtracting Whole Numbers

Example 1 Try these in your head.

7 − 3 = ■ **Answer** 4

28 − 10 = ■ **Answer** 18

13 − 3 + 0 = ■ **Answer** 10

Example 2 Subtract 26 from 235.

Solution

```
  235   Minuend
−  26   Subtrahend
  209   Difference
```

Check.

```
   26
+ 209
  235
```

Example 3 208 − 35

Solution

```
  208
−  35
  173
```

Check.

```
  173
+  35
  208
```

Exercise Do these in your head. Just write the answers.

1. 9 − 5
2. 8 − 3
3. 14 − 4
4. 19 − 8
5. 42 − 10
6. 57 − 20
7. 143 − 2
8. 167 − 7
9. 409 − 5
10. 536 − 30

Write in vertical form, then subtract.

11. subtract 26 from 335
12. subtract 39 from 450
13. subtract 48 from 784
14. subtract 341 from 1,291
15. subtract 481 from 41,217
16. subtract 346 from 50,000

Write in vertical form, then subtract.

17. 2,113 − 421
18. 8,101 − 4,049
19. 6,714 − 5,841
20. 81,573 − 1,540
21. 72,451 − 12,491
22. 63,456 − 45,671
23. 493,146 − 146
24. 493,146 − 3,146
25. 493,146 − 93,146

Review of Basic Skills 5

Multiplying Whole Numbers

Multiplication is repeated addition.

$6 \cdot 3$ means 6 threes. $\underbrace{3 + 3 + 3 + 3 + 3 + 3}_{18}$

$6 \cdot 3 = 18$

You may want to practice your times tables before doing these problems.

EXAMPLE 1 $23 \bullet 6 = \blacksquare$

Solution

$$\begin{array}{r} 23 \\ \times \ \ 6 \\ \hline 138 \end{array}$$

23 and 6 — Factors; 138 — Product

EXAMPLE 2 $46 \bullet 35 = \blacksquare$

Solution

$$\begin{array}{r} 46 \\ \times 35 \\ \hline 230 \\ +1\,38 \\ \hline 1{,}610 \end{array}$$

46 and 35 — Factors; 1,610 — Product

Exercise Do these in your head. Just write your answers.

1. $1 \cdot 2, 2 \cdot 2, 3 \cdot 2, 4 \cdot 2, 5 \cdot 2, 6 \cdot 2, 7 \cdot 2, 8 \cdot 2, 9 \cdot 2, 10 \cdot 2$
2. $1 \cdot 3, 2 \cdot 3, 3 \cdot 3, 4 \cdot 3, 5 \cdot 3, 6 \cdot 3, 7 \cdot 3, 8 \cdot 3, 9 \cdot 3, 10 \cdot 3$
3. $1 \cdot 4, 2 \cdot 4, 3 \cdot 4, 4 \cdot 4, 5 \cdot 4, 6 \cdot 4, 7 \cdot 4, 8 \cdot 4, 9 \cdot 4, 10 \cdot 4$
4. $1 \cdot 5, 2 \cdot 5, 3 \cdot 5, 4 \cdot 5, 5 \cdot 5, 6 \cdot 5, 7 \cdot 5, 8 \cdot 5, 9 \cdot 5, 10 \cdot 5$
5. $1 \cdot 6, 2 \cdot 6, 3 \cdot 6, 4 \cdot 6, 5 \cdot 6, 6 \cdot 6, 7 \cdot 6, 8 \cdot 6, 9 \cdot 6, 10 \cdot 6$
6. $1 \cdot 7, 2 \cdot 7, 3 \cdot 7, 4 \cdot 7, 5 \cdot 7, 6 \cdot 7, 7 \cdot 7, 8 \cdot 7, 9 \cdot 7, 10 \cdot 7$
7. $1 \cdot 8, 2 \cdot 8, 3 \cdot 8, 4 \cdot 8, 5 \cdot 8, 6 \cdot 8, 7 \cdot 8, 8 \cdot 8, 9 \cdot 8, 10 \cdot 8$
8. $1 \cdot 9, 2 \cdot 9, 3 \cdot 9, 4 \cdot 9, 5 \cdot 9, 6 \cdot 9, 7 \cdot 9, 8 \cdot 9, 9 \cdot 9, 10 \cdot 9$
9. $1 \cdot 10, 2 \cdot 10, 3 \cdot 10, 4 \cdot 10, 5 \cdot 10, 6 \cdot 10, 7 \cdot 10, 8 \cdot 10, 9 \cdot 10, 10 \cdot 10$

Multiply.

10. $23 \cdot 6$
11. $26 \cdot 7$
12. $35 \cdot 9$
13. $63 \cdot 4$
14. $72 \cdot 8$
15. $54 \cdot 3$
16. $46 \cdot 35$
17. $47 \cdot 21$
18. $37 \cdot 39$
19. $46 \cdot 72$
20. $81 \cdot 37$
21. $49 \cdot 63$
22. $309 \cdot 7$
23. $423 \cdot 16$
24. $926 \cdot 23$
25. $196 \cdot 245$

Review of Basic Skills 6

Multiplying Whole Numbers by Powers of 10

Example 1 267 • 10 = ■

Solution

$$\begin{array}{r} 267 \\ \times\ 10 \\ \hline 2{,}670 \end{array}$$

$\times$ 10 ← One zero
2,670 ← One zero

Example 2 342 • 100 = ■

Solution

$$\begin{array}{r} 342 \\ \times\ 100 \\ \hline 34{,}200 \end{array}$$

$\times$ 100 ← Two zeros
34,200 ← Two zeros

Exercise Do these in your head. Just write the answers.

1. 3 • 10

2. 5 • 100

3. 7 • 1,000

4. 3 • 20

5. 5 • 200

6. 7 • 200

7. 6 • 2,000

8. 9 • 30

9. 9 • 300

10. 9 • 3,000

Multiply.

11. 43 • 10

12. 43 • 100

13. 43 • 1,000

14. 267 • 10

15. 267 • 100

16. 267 • 1,000

17. 349 • 10

18. 349 • 100

19. 349 • 1,000

20. 349 • 10,000

21. 83 • 10

22. 83 • 100

23. 83 • 1,000

24. 586 • 10

25. 586 • 100

26. 586 • 1,000

27. 4,184 • 10

28. 4,184 • 100

29. 4,184 • 1,000

30. 4,184 • 10,000

Review of Basic Skills 7

Division of Whole Numbers

Division is repeated subtraction:

$21 \div 3 = 7$ because $21 - 3 = 18$, $18 - 3 = 15$, $15 - 3 = 12$, $12 - 3 = 9$,

$9 - 3 = 6$, $6 - 3 = 3$, $3 - 3 = 0$ There are 7 threes in 21.

You may want to practice basic division facts through $\div$ 9 before doing these problems.

Division of Whole Numbers with Zero Remainders

EXAMPLE 1 $576 \div 12 = n$

Solution

$$\begin{array}{r} 48 \\ 12\overline{)576} \\ -\underline{48} \\ 96 \\ -\underline{96} \\ 0 \end{array} = \text{Remainder}$$

Check.

$$\begin{array}{r} 48 \\ \underline{\times 12} \\ 96 \\ \underline{+48} \\ 576 \end{array}$$

Exercise Do these in your head. Just write the answers.

1. $24 \div 3$

2. $14 \div 2$

3. $14 \div 7$

4. $12 \div 3$

5. $30 \div 3$

6. $24 \div 4$

7. $35 \div 5$

8. $49 \div 7$

9. $48 \div 8$

10. $18 \div 2$

11. $45 \div 5$

12. $63 \div 7$

13. $81 \div 9$

14. $56 \div 8$

15. $54 \div 9$

Divide.

16. $138 \div 6$

17. $371 \div 7$

18. $369 \div 3$

19. $484 \div 4$

20. $621 \div 3$

21. $564 \div 12$

22. $323 \div 19$

23. $540 \div 36$

24. $4{,}100 \div 82$

25. $1{,}539 \div 27$

Review of Basic Skills 8

Division of Whole Numbers with Fractional Remainders

EXAMPLE 1 $3{,}191 \div 25 = \blacksquare$

Solution

$$\begin{array}{r} 127\frac{16}{25} \\ 25\,\overline{)\,3{,}191} \\ \underline{-\,2\,5} \\ 69 \\ \underline{-\,50} \\ 191 \\ \underline{-\,175} \\ 16 \end{array}$$

Write the remainder over the divisor.

Check.

$$\begin{array}{r} 127 \\ \underline{\times\ \ 25} \\ 635 \\ \underline{+\ 254} \\ 3{,}175 \\ \underline{+\ \ \ 16} \\ 3{,}191 \end{array}$$

(16: Remainder)

Exercise Divide. Write remainders as fractions. (These cannot be done with a calculator.)

1. $381 \div 14$

2. $586 \div 39$

3. $963 \div 21$

4. $646 \div 71$

5. $487 \div 20$

Estimate the quotients to the nearest thousand first, then use a calculator. Copy the calculator answer to the nearest hundreth.

6. $19{,}520 \div 33$

7. $30{,}040 \div 71$

8. $51{,}090 \div 18$

9. $126{,}947 \div 17$

10. $341{,}643 \div 20$

Review of Basic Skills 9

Division of Whole Numbers with Zeros in the Quotient

EXAMPLE 1 2,380 ÷ 14 = ■

Solution

$$\begin{array}{r} 170 \\ 14\,\overline{)\,2,380} \\ -1\,4 \\ \hline 98 \\ -98 \\ \hline 00 \end{array}$$

Check.

$$\begin{array}{r} 170 \\ \times\ 14 \\ \hline 680 \\ +\,1\,70 \\ \hline 2,380 \end{array}$$

EXAMPLE 1 4,864 ÷ 16 = ■

Solution

$$\begin{array}{r} 304 \\ 16\,\overline{)\,4,864} \\ -4\,8 \\ \hline 064 \\ -\ 64 \\ \hline 0 \end{array}$$

Check.

$$\begin{array}{r} 304 \\ \times\ 16 \\ \hline 1,824 \\ +\,3\,04 \\ \hline 4,864 \end{array}$$

Exercise Divide. Do not use a calculator.

1. 2,380 ÷ 14

2. 4,864 ÷ 16

3. 2,040 ÷ 17

4. 5,980 ÷ 13

5. 16,200 ÷ 45

6. 31,626 ÷ 63

7. 19,520 ÷ 32

8. 138,253 ÷ 23

9. 738,500 ÷ 35

10. 103,200 ÷ 24

Review of Basic Skills 10

Numbers with Exponents

2^4 means $2 \cdot 2 \cdot 2 \cdot 2$.
So $2^4 = 2 \cdot 2 \cdot 2 \cdot 2 = 16$.

2^4 — Base, Exponent

2 is the base, 4 is the exponent.

EXAMPLE 1 Find the value of 3^4.

Solution $3^4 = 3 \bullet 3 \bullet 3 \bullet 3$

$3^4 = 81$

EXAMPLE 2 Write with an exponent $2 \bullet 2 \bullet 2$.

Solution $2 \bullet 2 \bullet 2 = 2^3$

Exercise Find the value of each.

1. 3^2
2. 4^2
3. 5^2
4. 6^2
5. 7^2
6. 8^2
7. 9^2
8. 10^2
9. 2^5
10. 25^2
11. 2^4
12. 3^3
13. 5^3
14. 10^3
15. 4^3
16. 30^2
17. 20^3
18. 11^2
19. $1{,}000^2$
20. 10^6

Write with an exponent.

21. $2 \cdot 2 \cdot 2$
22. $2 \cdot 2 \cdot 2 \cdot 2$
23. $3 \cdot 3 \cdot 3$
24. $9 \cdot 9$
25. $7 \cdot 7 \cdot 7 \cdot 7 \cdot 7$
26. $10 \cdot 10 \cdot 10 \cdot 10 \cdot 10$
27. $81 \cdot 81$
28. $92 \cdot 92 \cdot 92$
29. $46 \cdot 46 \cdot 46 \cdot 46$
30. $10 \cdot 10 \cdot 10 \cdot 10 \cdot 10 \cdot 10$
31. $4 \cdot 4 \cdot 4$
32. $4 \cdot 4 \cdot 4 \cdot 4$
33. $6 \cdot 6 \cdot 6$
34. $6 \cdot 6 \cdot 6 \cdot 6 \cdot 6$
35. $90 \cdot 90 \cdot 90 \cdot 90 \cdot 90$
36. $43 \cdot 43 \cdot 43$
37. $5 \cdot 5 \cdot 5 \cdot 5 \cdot 5 \cdot 5 \cdot 5 \cdot 5$
38. $36 \cdot 36 \cdot 36 \cdot 36$
39. $94 \cdot 94 \cdot 94 \cdot 94$
40. $100 \cdot 100 \cdot 100 \cdot 100 \cdot 100$

Review of Basic Skills 11

Using the Order of Operations

Rule

1. Evaluate exponents first.
2. Multiply and divide from left to right in order.
3. Add and subtract from left to right in order.

EXAMPLE 1 $2 + 3 \cdot 4 - 8 \div 4 = \blacksquare$

Solution

$$2 + 3 \cdot 4 - 8 \div 4 =$$
$$\downarrow \qquad \downarrow$$
$$2 + 12 - 2 = 12$$

EXAMPLE 2 $2^3 + 3 \cdot 4 \div 2 - 48 \div 4^2 = \blacksquare$

Solution

$$8 + 3 \cdot 4 \div 2 - 48 \div 16 =$$
$$\downarrow \qquad \downarrow$$
$$12 \div 2 \qquad 3 =$$
$$\downarrow \qquad \downarrow$$
$$8 + 6 - 3 = 11$$

Exercise Use the rules for the order of operations. Find the answers.

1. $3 + 8 \cdot 2 \div 4$

2. $5 + 9 \cdot 4 \div 12 - 2$

3. $8 - 8 \div 4 + 3 \cdot 2$

4. $13 - 16 \cdot 3 \div 12 - 1$

5. $9 + 6 \cdot 3 - 8 \cdot 2 \div 4$

6. $1 + 16 \cdot 3 \div 12 - 4$

7. $14 + 32 \div 16 - 4 \cdot 2$

8. $32 \div 16 + 9 \div 3 \cdot 2$

9. $5 - 16 \div 4 + 1 + 3$

10. $35 - 25 \cdot 4 \div 20 + 5$

11. $2^3 + 8 \cdot 2^2 + 3$

12. $8 - 6^2 \div 12 + 2 \cdot 5$

13. $15 + 8^2 \div 4 - 6$

14. $25 + 11^2 + 8 \cdot 2 - 3$

15. $39 \div 13 + 12^2 \div 6 - 5$

16. $52 + 12 \div 2^2 - 82 \div 2 + 3^2$

17. $35 + 2^5 \div 2^4 \cdot 3^2 - 2^3$

18. $18 \div 3^2 + 6 \cdot 8 \div 4^2 - 5$

19. $4 \cdot 3 \cdot 5 \div 10 + 8 \cdot 2^3 \div 2^4$

20. $9 - 16 \cdot 3 \div 12 + 8 \div 2^2 - 2^2$

Review of Basic Skills 12

Finding an Average (Mean)

The word *mean* is sometimes used for *average.*

Rule

1. Add the numbers whose average or mean you want.
2. Divide the sum by the number of addends. The quotient is the average or mean.

EXAMPLE 2 Find the average of 98, 88, 80, and 60.

Solution Add the numbers.

$$\left.\begin{array}{r} 98 \\ 88 \\ 80 \\ +\ 60 \end{array}\right\} \text{4 addends}$$

$$\begin{array}{r} \underline{} \\ 326 \end{array}$$

Then divide.

$$\begin{array}{r} 81.5 \\ 4\,\overline{)\,326.0} \\ \underline{-\ 32} \\ 06 \\ \underline{-\ \ 4} \\ 20 \\ \underline{-\ 20} \\ 0 \end{array}$$

Answer The average is 81.5.

Exercise Find the average for each set of numbers. Round to the nearest tenth.

1. 25, 63, 48, 52, 49

2. 98, 53, 42, 56, 72

3. 39, 40, 39, 62, 53, 86

4. 95, 83, 39, 42, 88, 77

5. 88, 62, 42, 53, 96, 35

6. 53, 60, 72, 43, 35, 39, 53

7. 91, 62, 39, 50, 42, 88, 60

8. 36, 19, 41, 63, 72, 64, 81

9. 39, 41, 62, 73, 96, 81, 92, 65

10. 40, 49, 51, 73, 29, 86, 29, 56

11. 100, 103, 96, 105, 105, 97, 102, 120

12. 36, 42, 85, 92, 30, 33, 88, 29, 62, 50

13. 109, 156, 95, 108, 90, 83, 45, 80, 90, 98, 93, 96

14. 40, 42, 43, 40, 41, 42, 43, 48, 44, 42, 45, 42

15. 40, 38, 37, 35, 42, 43, 36, 49, 48, 53, 42, 39, 34

Review of Basic Skills 13

Comparing Fractions

Comparing fractions with *like* denominators—

Rule

Compare numerators: the larger the numerator, the larger the fraction.

Example 1 Compare $\frac{5}{8}$ and $\frac{7}{8}$.

Solution The denominators are alike.

$5 < 7$, therefore $\frac{5}{8} < \frac{7}{8}$.

Comparing fractions with *unlike* denominators—

Rule

Change each fraction to a decimal. You may use a calculator. Compare decimals.

Example 2 Compare $\frac{5}{8}$ and $\frac{3}{4}$.

Solution $\frac{5}{8}$ is

$$\begin{array}{r} 0.625 \\ 8\overline{)5.0} \\ -4\,8 \\ \hline 20 \\ -16 \\ \hline 40 \\ -40 \\ \hline 0 \end{array}$$

$\frac{3}{4}$ is

$$\begin{array}{r} 0.75 \\ 4\overline{)3.0} \\ -2\,8 \\ \hline 20 \\ -20 \\ \hline 0 \end{array}$$

$0.625 < 0.75$, therefore $\frac{5}{8} < \frac{3}{4}$.

Exercise Compare the fractions. Write < or >.

1. $\frac{1}{8}$ $\frac{3}{8}$
2. $\frac{6}{7}$ $\frac{5}{7}$
3. $\frac{3}{8}$ $\frac{5}{8}$
4. $\frac{7}{3}$ $\frac{11}{3}$
5. $\frac{5}{4}$ $\frac{7}{4}$
6. $\frac{5}{3}$ $\frac{2}{3}$
7. $\frac{8}{5}$ $\frac{9}{5}$
8. $\frac{1}{3}$ $\frac{2}{3}$
9. $\frac{4}{7}$ $\frac{5}{7}$
10. $\frac{11}{13}$ $\frac{9}{13}$
11. $\frac{3}{4}$ $\frac{7}{8}$
12. $\frac{3}{5}$ $\frac{3}{4}$
13. $\frac{6}{7}$ $\frac{5}{8}$
14. $\frac{3}{8}$ $\frac{5}{9}$
15. $\frac{6}{10}$ $\frac{7}{11}$
16. $\frac{3}{10}$ $\frac{3}{11}$
17. $\frac{9}{13}$ $\frac{11}{12}$
18. $\frac{6}{11}$ $\frac{7}{9}$
19. $\frac{7}{13}$ $\frac{8}{15}$
20. $\frac{9}{13}$ $\frac{6}{7}$

Review of Basic Skills 14

Changing Fractions to Higher Terms

EXAMPLE 1 Write $\frac{5}{6}$ as a fraction with 30 as the new denominator.

Step 1 $\frac{5}{6} = \frac{■}{30}$

Step 2 Divide 30 by 6. $\quad 6\overline{)30}$ = 5

Step 3 Multiply $\frac{5}{6}$ by $\frac{5}{5}$. $\quad \frac{5 \bullet 5}{6 \bullet 5} = \frac{25}{30}$

Exercise Write each fraction with a new denominator.

1. $\frac{3}{6} = \frac{■}{30}$

2. $\frac{5}{12} = \frac{■}{24}$

3. $\frac{3}{7} = \frac{■}{21}$

4. $\frac{6}{9} = \frac{■}{18}$

5. $\frac{7}{12} = \frac{■}{36}$

6. $\frac{9}{13} = \frac{■}{39}$

7. $\frac{4}{7} = \frac{■}{35}$

8. $\frac{3}{8} = \frac{■}{40}$

9. $\frac{6}{7} = \frac{■}{35}$

10. $\frac{9}{10} = \frac{■}{100}$

11. $\frac{3}{11} = \frac{■}{33}$

12. $\frac{6}{13} = \frac{■}{39}$

13. $\frac{5}{12} = \frac{■}{60}$

14. $\frac{6}{15} = \frac{■}{45}$

15. $\frac{9}{16} = \frac{■}{64}$

16. $\frac{3}{13} = \frac{■}{65}$

17. $\frac{5}{17} = \frac{■}{51}$

18. $\frac{6}{19} = \frac{■}{38}$

19. $\frac{6}{110} = \frac{■}{550}$

20. $\frac{7}{315} = \frac{■}{630}$

Review of Basic Skills 15

Renaming Fractions in Simplest Terms

Simplest terms means using the *smallest* numbers in both the numerator and the denominator of a fraction.

EXAMPLE 1 Rename $\frac{75}{100}$ in simplest terms.

Solution $\frac{75 \div 25}{100 \div 25} = \frac{3}{4}$

Choose a number that divides both the numerator and the denominator. If you do not use the largest common divisor, you may have to divide more than once.

EXAMPLE 2 Rename $\frac{24}{30}$ in simplest terms.

Solution $\frac{24 \div 3}{30 \div 3} = \frac{8}{10}$

The division process may occur more than once if the divisor is not large enough in the first step.

$\frac{8 \div 2}{10 \div 2} = \frac{4}{5}$

Answer $\frac{24}{30} = \frac{4}{5}$

Exercise Rename these fractions in simplest terms.

1. $\frac{24}{48}$

2. $\frac{10}{230}$

3. $\frac{45}{99}$

4. $\frac{5}{25}$

5. $\frac{13}{39}$

6. $\frac{56}{58}$

7. $\frac{63}{81}$

8. $\frac{6}{54}$

9. $\frac{16}{112}$

10. $\frac{39}{52}$

11. $\frac{12}{60}$

12. $\frac{16}{64}$

13. $\frac{18}{36}$

14. $\frac{22}{121}$

15. $\frac{53}{106}$

16. $\frac{18}{72}$

17. $\frac{5}{15}$

18. $\frac{55}{242}$

19. $\frac{10}{52}$

20. $\frac{48}{96}$

Review of Basic Skills 16

Renaming Improper Fractions as Mixed Numbers

EXAMPLE 1 Rename $\frac{13}{5}$ as a mixed number.

Solution Divide numerator by denominator.

Write the remainder as a fraction.

$$\begin{array}{r} 2 \\ 5\overline{)13} \\ -10 \\ \hline 3 \end{array} \quad \text{Remainder}$$

Answer $2\frac{3}{5}$ Write the remainder over the divisor.

Mixed Numbers in Lowest Terms

Write mixed numbers in lowest terms.
This means to write the fraction part of a mixed number in lowest terms.

EXAMPLE 2 Write $3\frac{5}{15}$ in lowest terms.

Solution Rename $\frac{5}{15}$ in lowest terms.

$\frac{5 \div 5}{15 \div 5} = \frac{1}{3}$, so $3\frac{5}{15} = 3\frac{1}{3}$

Exercise Rename as mixed numbers in lowest terms or whole numbers.

1. $\frac{18}{5}$

2. $\frac{18}{3}$

3. $\frac{19}{6}$

4. $\frac{14}{3}$

5. $\frac{23}{4}$

6. $\frac{12}{2}$

7. $\frac{38}{5}$

8. $\frac{66}{11}$

9. $\frac{56}{11}$

10. $\frac{19}{5}$

11. $\frac{52}{32}$

12. $\frac{55}{8}$

13. $\frac{28}{6}$

14. $\frac{32}{4}$

15. $\frac{90}{3}$

16. $\frac{62}{8}$

17. $\frac{50}{6}$

18. $\frac{58}{7}$

19. $\frac{52}{10}$

20. $\frac{37}{3}$

Review of Basic Skills 17

Renaming Mixed Numbers as Improper Fractions

Example 1 Write $2\frac{3}{4}$ as an improper fraction.

Step 1 Multiply the whole number by the denominator.

$2 \cdot 4 = 8$

Step 2 Add the numerator to the product from Step 1.

$3 + 8 = 11$

Step 3 Write the sum over the old denominator.

$\frac{11}{4}$

Answer $2\frac{3}{4} = \frac{11}{4}$

Exercise Rename these mixed numbers as improper fractions.

1. $3\frac{2}{5}$

2. $6\frac{2}{5}$

3. $5\frac{1}{6}$

4. $7\frac{2}{12}$

5. $2\frac{1}{6}$

6. $9\frac{1}{2}$

7. $4\frac{1}{9}$

8. $8\frac{2}{11}$

9. $5\frac{2}{3}$

10. $8\frac{1}{3}$

11. $6\frac{10}{13}$

12. $16\frac{2}{3}$

13. $7\frac{3}{8}$

14. $15\frac{2}{3}$

15. $13\frac{9}{14}$

16. $9\frac{2}{3}$

17. $5\frac{11}{10}$

18. $20\frac{2}{3}$

19. $16\frac{5}{21}$

20. $11\frac{1}{8}$

Review of Basic Skills 18

Multiplying Fractions

To multiply fractions, follow this simple rule.

Rule

To multiply two fractions, multiply numerator times numerator and denominator times denominator.

Example 1 $\frac{5}{6} \bullet \frac{3}{4} = \blacksquare$

Solution $\frac{5 \bullet 3}{6 \bullet 4} = \frac{15}{24}$

$\frac{15}{24} = \frac{5}{8}$

Answer $\frac{5}{8}$

Example 2 $7 \bullet \frac{4}{5} = \blacksquare$

Solution $\frac{7 \bullet 4}{1 \bullet 5} = \frac{28}{5}$

$\frac{28}{5} = 5\frac{3}{5}$

Answer $5\frac{3}{5}$

Exercise Multiply. Write your answers in lowest terms.

1. $\frac{1}{2} \bullet \frac{2}{3}$

2. $\frac{3}{5} \bullet \frac{5}{6}$

3. $\frac{7}{8} \bullet \frac{6}{13}$

4. $\frac{2}{9} \bullet \frac{3}{5}$

5. $\frac{6}{7} \bullet \frac{1}{2}$

6. $\frac{3}{11} \bullet \frac{2}{5}$

7. $\frac{2}{7} \bullet \frac{2}{9}$

8. $\frac{5}{11} \bullet \frac{1}{4}$

9. $\frac{1}{6} \bullet \frac{2}{9}$

10. $\frac{5}{6} \bullet \frac{1}{4}$

11. $\frac{3}{11} \bullet \frac{2}{12}$

12. $\frac{4}{5} \bullet \frac{2}{9}$

13. $\frac{4}{7} \bullet \frac{1}{8}$

14. $\frac{3}{16} \bullet \frac{13}{21}$

15. $\frac{5}{21} \bullet \frac{7}{10}$

16. $\frac{5}{24} \bullet \frac{3}{13}$

17. $\frac{6}{28} \bullet \frac{7}{12}$

18. $\frac{2}{3} \bullet \frac{5}{6}$

19. $\frac{12}{21} \bullet \frac{7}{8}$

20. $\frac{13}{32} \bullet \frac{8}{26}$

Review of Basic Skills 19

Multiplying Mixed Numbers

To multiply mixed numbers

1. Change them to improper fractions.
2. Multiply the fractions.
3. Reduce to lowest terms.

EXAMPLE 1 $3\frac{2}{3} \bullet 1\frac{1}{2} = \blacksquare$

Solution $3\frac{2}{3} \bullet 1\frac{1}{2} = \frac{11}{\cancel{3}_1} \bullet \frac{\cancel{3}^1}{2} = \frac{11}{2} = 5\frac{1}{2}$

Answer $3\frac{2}{3} \bullet 1\frac{1}{2} = 5\frac{1}{2}$

Exercise Multiply. Write your answers in lowest terms.

1. $2\frac{1}{2} \cdot \frac{1}{3}$

2. $\frac{1}{2} \cdot 1\frac{1}{5}$

3. $\frac{2}{7} \cdot 1\frac{1}{3}$

4. $\frac{1}{5} \cdot 1\frac{1}{7}$

5. $3\frac{1}{5} \cdot \frac{3}{4}$

6. $5\frac{2}{3} \cdot \frac{1}{5}$

7. $\frac{5}{7} \cdot 2\frac{3}{8}$

8. $1\frac{1}{2} \cdot \frac{15}{18}$

9. $4\frac{5}{7} \cdot \frac{7}{11}$

10. $2\frac{3}{5} \cdot 1\frac{1}{5}$

11. $2\frac{3}{7} \cdot 2\frac{1}{2}$

12. $5\frac{1}{7} \cdot 2\frac{1}{5}$

13. $5\frac{1}{6} \cdot 1\frac{1}{5}$

14. $1\frac{5}{6} \cdot 1\frac{1}{3}$

15. $1\frac{2}{7} \cdot 2\frac{1}{8}$

16. $6\frac{1}{2} \cdot 2\frac{3}{4}$

17. $2\frac{2}{5} \cdot 1\frac{3}{4}$

18. $4\frac{1}{2} \cdot 1\frac{1}{4}$

19. $3\frac{3}{7} \cdot 2\frac{1}{3}$

20. $5\frac{2}{9} \cdot 1\frac{1}{8}$

Review of Basic Skills 20

Dividing Fractions

Rule

To divide one fraction by another fraction, invert the divisor and multiply.

Example 1

$\frac{4}{7} \div \frac{1}{2} = \blacksquare$

$\frac{4}{7} \div \frac{1}{2} = \blacksquare$ ← Invert the divisor. Then multiply.

$\frac{4}{7} \bullet \frac{2}{1} = \frac{8}{7}$

$\frac{8}{7} = 1\frac{1}{7}$

Answer $1\frac{1}{7}$

Exercise Divide. Write your answers in lowest terms.

1. $\frac{2}{5} \div \frac{2}{7}$

2. $\frac{5}{6} \div \frac{1}{3}$

3. $\frac{2}{7} \div \frac{1}{8}$

4. $\frac{4}{5} \div \frac{1}{6}$

5. $\frac{2}{7} \div \frac{5}{6}$

6. $\frac{3}{8} \div \frac{1}{2}$

7. $\frac{4}{5} \div \frac{5}{6}$

8. $\frac{8}{9} \div \frac{4}{5}$

9. $\frac{5}{6} \div \frac{2}{5}$

10. $\frac{5}{11} \div \frac{2}{22}$

11. $\frac{8}{11} \div \frac{5}{11}$

12. $\frac{5}{12} \div \frac{5}{6}$

13. $\frac{3}{8} \div \frac{5}{12}$

14. $\frac{2}{11} \div \frac{3}{22}$

15. $\frac{8}{13} \div \frac{24}{26}$

16. $\frac{3}{9} \div \frac{1}{5}$

17. $\frac{11}{12} \div \frac{24}{30}$

18. $\frac{5}{7} \div \frac{48}{49}$

19. $\frac{1}{2} \div \frac{5}{7}$

20. $\frac{5}{7} \div \frac{5}{14}$

21. $\frac{8}{9} \div \frac{3}{6}$

22. $\frac{3}{4} \div \frac{6}{7}$

23. $\frac{13}{14} \div \frac{3}{7}$

24. $\frac{8}{15} \div \frac{2}{5}$

25. $\frac{1}{2} \div \frac{1}{2}$

Review of Basic Skills 21

Dividing Mixed Numbers

Rule

Rename the mixed numbers as improper fractions. Invert the divisor and multiply.

Example 1 $2\frac{3}{4} \div 3\frac{1}{3} = \blacksquare$

Solution $2\frac{3}{4} \div 3\frac{1}{3} = \blacksquare$

$\frac{11}{4} \div \frac{10}{3} = \blacksquare$ ← Rename as improper fractions.

$\frac{11}{4} \bullet \frac{3}{10} = \blacksquare$ ← Invert the divisor and multiply.

$\frac{11 \bullet 3}{4 \bullet 10} = \frac{33}{40}$

Answer $\frac{33}{40}$

Exercise Divide. Write your answer in lowest terms.

1. $1\frac{1}{2} \div \frac{1}{2}$
2. $3\frac{2}{3} \div \frac{1}{2}$
3. $1\frac{1}{5} \div \frac{1}{2}$
4. $2\frac{1}{6} \div \frac{2}{3}$
5. $\frac{3}{12} \div 2\frac{1}{2}$
6. $\frac{13}{15} \div 1\frac{1}{2}$
7. $1\frac{2}{5} \div \frac{2}{3}$
8. $1\frac{3}{7} \div \frac{1}{7}$
9. $3\frac{1}{2} \div \frac{1}{2}$
10. $1\frac{1}{2} \div \frac{1}{3}$
11. $1\frac{5}{7} \div \frac{6}{7}$
12. $2\frac{1}{3} \div \frac{2}{3}$
13. $3\frac{1}{5} \div \frac{2}{5}$
14. $4\frac{1}{2} \div \frac{3}{4}$
15. $2\frac{5}{8} \div \frac{3}{8}$
16. $6\frac{1}{4} \div \frac{3}{4}$
17. $3\frac{5}{8} \div \frac{7}{8}$
18. $5\frac{1}{3} \div \frac{3}{4}$
19. $6\frac{3}{4} \div \frac{1}{2}$
20. $7\frac{9}{10} \div \frac{1}{2}$
21. $1\frac{1}{2} \div 2\frac{1}{4}$
22. $3\frac{1}{4} \div 1\frac{1}{2}$
23. $2\frac{1}{4} \div 1\frac{1}{4}$
24. $6\frac{3}{8} \div 1\frac{1}{8}$
25. $7\frac{1}{2} \div 2\frac{3}{4}$
26. $8\frac{1}{2} \div 1\frac{1}{2}$
27. $4\frac{3}{8} \div 2\frac{3}{8}$
28. $7\frac{1}{4} \div 2\frac{5}{8}$
29. $6\frac{3}{7} \div 5\frac{1}{7}$
30. $9\frac{1}{2} \div 3\frac{3}{8}$

Review of Basic Skills 22

Adding Mixed Numbers with Like Denominators

Example 1 $3\frac{1}{8} + 2\frac{3}{8}$ **Solution**

$$\begin{array}{r} 3\frac{1}{8} \\ +\ 2\frac{3}{8} \\ \hline 5\frac{4}{8} \end{array}$$

Step 1 Write in vertical form.

Step 2 Add numerators. $1 + 3 = 4$

Step 3 Add whole numbers. $3 + 2 = 5$

Answer $5\frac{1}{2}$ **Step 4** Reduce fraction.

Example 2 Add the sides to get the perimeter of the rectangle. Measurements are in feet.

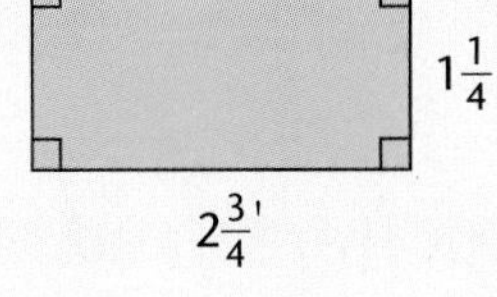

Solution $1\frac{1}{4} + 1\frac{1}{4} + 2\frac{3}{4} + 2\frac{3}{4}$ Add the four sides.

Step 1 Add numerators.

$1 + 1 + 3 + 3 = 8$ $\frac{8}{4}$

Step 2 Add whole numbers.

$1 + 1 + 2 + 2 = 6$

Step 3 Simplify. $\frac{8}{4} = 2$ $6 + 2 = 8$ **Answer** 8'

Exercise Add the mixed numbers.

1. $1\frac{1}{2} + 1\frac{1}{2}$

2. $3\frac{1}{4} + 2\frac{1}{4}$

3. $6\frac{3}{4} + 1\frac{1}{4}$

4. $5\frac{1}{2} + 7\frac{1}{2}$

5. $3\frac{1}{3} + 4\frac{1}{3}$

6. $7\frac{1}{8} + 1\frac{1}{8}$

7. $3\frac{1}{4} + 6\frac{3}{4}$

8. $7\frac{3}{8} + 1\frac{1}{8}$

9. $5\frac{1}{16} + 3\frac{4}{16}$

10. $1\frac{1}{8} + 2\frac{3}{8}$

11. $5\frac{1}{16} + 6\frac{7}{16}$

12. $3\frac{5}{16} + 1\frac{8}{16}$

13. $4\frac{17}{32} + 1\frac{21}{32}$

14. $8\frac{9}{15} + 1\frac{3}{15}$

15. $6\frac{19}{32} + 1\frac{11}{32}$

Find the perimeter of the rectangles.

16.

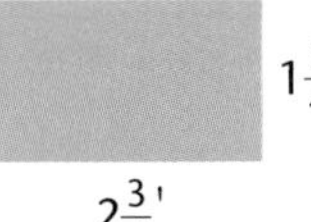

17.

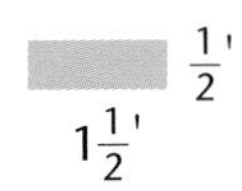

18.

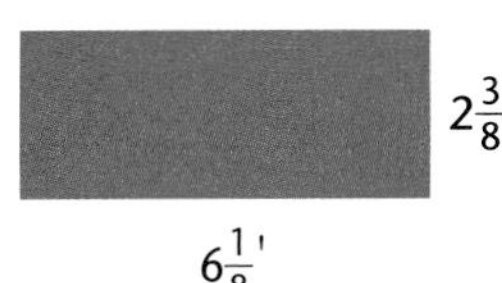

19.

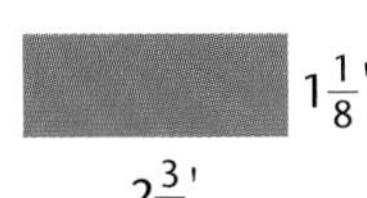

20.

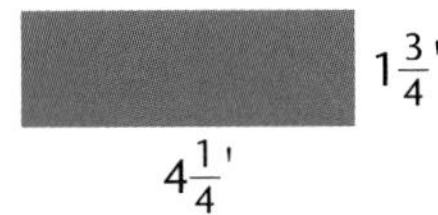

Review of Basic Skills 23

Adding Fractions with Unlike Denominators

To add fractions with *unlike* denominators, you must first rewrite the fractions so that they have *like* denominators. Then you can add.

Example 1 $\frac{2}{3} + \frac{1}{5} = \blacksquare$ $\qquad 3 \bullet 5 = 15$ is a common denominator

Solution

$$\begin{array}{rl} \frac{2}{3} = \frac{2 \bullet 5}{3 \bullet 5} = & \frac{10}{15} \\ + \frac{1}{5} = \frac{1 \bullet 3}{5 \bullet 3} = & \frac{3}{15} \\ \hline \text{Add} & \frac{13}{15} \end{array}$$

Answer $\frac{13}{15}$

Adding Mixed Numbers with Unlike Denominators

Example 2 $1\frac{1}{2} + 2\frac{1}{3} = \blacksquare$

Solution

$$\begin{array}{rl} 1\frac{1}{2} & \frac{1}{2} = \frac{1 \bullet 3}{2 \bullet 3} = \frac{3}{6} \\ + 2\frac{1}{3} & \frac{1}{3} = \frac{1 \bullet 2}{3 \bullet 2} = \frac{2}{6} \\ \hline \end{array}$$

$1\frac{3}{6}$ Rewrite with common denominators.

$+ 2\frac{2}{6}$ Add.

$3\frac{5}{6}$ Simplify if needed.

Answer $3\frac{5}{6}$

Exercise Add the fractions. Watch for unlike denominators.

1. $\frac{1}{2} + \frac{1}{4}$
2. $\frac{1}{3} + \frac{1}{5}$
3. $\frac{3}{4} + \frac{1}{2}$
4. $\frac{3}{5} + \frac{1}{10}$
5. $\frac{7}{12} + \frac{1}{3}$
6. $\frac{1}{10} + \frac{7}{15}$
7. $\frac{3}{10} + \frac{1}{3}$
8. $\frac{7}{12} + \frac{1}{6}$
9. $\frac{3}{7} + \frac{1}{2}$
10. $\frac{3}{8} + \frac{7}{24}$
11. $1\frac{1}{2} + 2\frac{1}{3}$
12. $6\frac{1}{2} + 1\frac{1}{3}$
13. $3\frac{3}{4} + 1\frac{1}{2}$
14. $3\frac{1}{4} + 2\frac{2}{3}$
15. $5\frac{2}{5} + 1\frac{3}{10}$
16. $3\frac{7}{12} + 1\frac{5}{6}$
17. $1\frac{1}{12} + 3\frac{3}{4}$
18. $4\frac{2}{5} + 6\frac{8}{15}$
19. $5\frac{1}{2} + 6\frac{23}{24}$
20. $5\frac{17}{32} + 6\frac{1}{2}$

Review of Basic Skills 24

Subtracting Mixed Numbers with Like Denominators

EXAMPLE 1

$$\begin{array}{r} 14\frac{5}{11} \\ -\ 6\frac{2}{11} \\ \hline 8\frac{3}{11} \end{array}$$

Step 1 Subtract numerators 2 from 5. $5 - 2 = 3$

Step 2 Keep the denominator.

Step 3 Subtract the whole numbers. $14 - 6 = 8$

Answer $8\frac{3}{11}$

Exercise Subtract and write in lowest terms.

1. $\frac{3}{8} - \frac{1}{8}$

2. $\frac{5}{7} - \frac{2}{7}$

3. $4\frac{3}{8} - 1\frac{1}{8}$

4. $5\frac{7}{8} - 1\frac{5}{8}$

5. $3\frac{7}{10} - 2\frac{3}{10}$

6. $5\frac{3}{4} - 3\frac{1}{4}$

7. $6\frac{7}{12} - 5\frac{5}{12}$

8. $7\frac{15}{32} - 5\frac{7}{32}$

9. $9\frac{41}{100} - 6\frac{21}{100}$

10. $5\frac{99}{100} - 2\frac{49}{100}$

11. $6\frac{5}{16} - 4\frac{3}{16}$

12. $\frac{3}{4} - \frac{2}{4}$

13. $2\frac{5}{8} - 1\frac{4}{8}$

14. $5\frac{3}{4} - 3\frac{2}{4}$

15. $6\frac{3}{5} - 3\frac{1}{5}$

16. $2\frac{1}{2} - 1\frac{1}{2}$

17. $3\frac{2}{17} - 1\frac{1}{17}$

18. $10\frac{18}{39} - 5\frac{7}{39}$

19. $3\frac{3}{10} - 1\frac{1}{10}$

20. $4\frac{3}{4} - 2\frac{1}{4}$

Review of Basic Skills 25

Subtracting with Unlike Denominators

EXAMPLE 1 Rewrite fractions with a like denominator.

$$\begin{array}{r} 8\frac{2}{3} \\ -\ 5\frac{1}{2} \\ \hline \end{array} \qquad \frac{2}{3} = \frac{2 \cdot 2}{3 \cdot 2} = \frac{4}{6} \qquad \frac{1}{2} = \frac{1 \cdot 3}{2 \cdot 3} = \frac{3}{6} \qquad \begin{array}{r} 8\frac{4}{6} \\ -\ 5\frac{3}{6} \\ \hline 3\frac{1}{6} \end{array}$$

Subtract numerators and whole numbers.

Answer $3\frac{1}{6}$

Exercise Subtract and write in lowest terms.

1. $\frac{5}{8} - \frac{1}{2}$

2. $\frac{3}{4} - \frac{1}{2}$

3. $2\frac{5}{8} - 1\frac{1}{2}$

4. $5\frac{3}{4} - 3\frac{1}{2}$

5. $6\frac{3}{5} - 2\frac{1}{4}$

6. $2\frac{1}{2} - 1\frac{1}{3}$

7. $4\frac{3}{8} - 1\frac{1}{4}$

8. $6\frac{7}{8} - 2\frac{3}{4}$

9. $9\frac{3}{10} - 6\frac{3}{100}$

10. $7\frac{51}{100} - 6\frac{1}{5}$

11. $7\frac{3}{4} - \frac{1}{8}$

12. $2\frac{6}{11} - \frac{1}{22}$

13. $5\frac{7}{9} - 1\frac{1}{3}$

14. $3\frac{1}{5} - 1\frac{1}{10}$

15. $8\frac{1}{19} - 1\frac{2}{38}$

Review of Basic Skills 26

Subtracting with Renaming

Example 1

$$\begin{array}{r} 12 \\ -\ 3\frac{1}{4} \\ \hline \end{array}$$

You need to rename 12 to $11\frac{4}{4}$ first.
Then you can subtract the fractions and the whole numbers.

$$\begin{array}{r} 12 \\ -\ 3\frac{1}{4} \\ \hline \end{array} = 11 + 1 = \begin{array}{r} 11\frac{4}{4} \\ -\ 3\frac{1}{4} \\ \hline 8\frac{3}{4} \end{array}$$

Answer $8\frac{3}{4}$

Example 2

$$\begin{array}{r} 5\frac{1}{4} \\ -\ 1\frac{3}{4} \\ \hline \end{array}$$

You need to rename $5\frac{1}{4}$ to $4\frac{5}{4}$ first.
Then you can subtract the fractions and the whole numbers.

$$\begin{array}{r} 5\frac{1}{4} \\ -\ 1\frac{3}{4} \\ \hline \end{array} = 4 + 1 + \frac{1}{4} = 4 + \frac{4}{4} + \frac{1}{4} = \begin{array}{r} 4\frac{5}{4} \\ -\ 1\frac{3}{4} \\ \hline 3\frac{2}{4} \end{array}$$

Simplify.

Answer $3\frac{1}{2}$

Exercise Subtract and write in lowest terms.

1. $5 - 1\frac{1}{4}$

2. $6 - 2\frac{3}{4}$

3. $9 - 1\frac{1}{2}$

4. $6 - 3\frac{1}{3}$

5. $7 - 5\frac{2}{3}$

6. $4 - 1\frac{3}{5}$

7. $8 - 5\frac{1}{4}$

8. $9 - 6\frac{3}{7}$

9. $10 - 5\frac{3}{10}$

10. $15 - 10\frac{2}{9}$

11. $5\frac{1}{4} - 1\frac{3}{4}$

12. $6\frac{1}{3} - 2\frac{2}{3}$

13. $6\frac{3}{10} - 1\frac{7}{10}$

14. $4\frac{5}{12} - 2\frac{7}{12}$

15. $8\frac{5}{8} - 6\frac{3}{4}$

16. $7\frac{1}{2} - 2\frac{3}{4}$

17. $5\frac{1}{3} - 2\frac{1}{2}$

18. $9\frac{1}{2} - 2\frac{2}{3}$

19. $10\frac{1}{5} - 5\frac{7}{10}$

20. $11\frac{1}{2} - 6\frac{9}{10}$

Review of Basic Skills 27

Identifying Place Value with Decimals

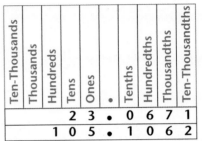

EXAMPLE 1 Write the place value of the underlined digits.

1. $23.0\underline{6}71$ Hundredths

2. $105.106\underline{2}$ Ten-Thousandths

Ten-Thousands	Thousands	Hundreds	Tens	Ones	•	Tenths	Hundredths	Thousandths	Ten-Thousandths
			2	3	•	0	6	7	1
		1	0	5	•	1	0	6	2

EXAMPLE 2 Compare 2.38 and 2.4.
Use the symbol < or >.
< is "less than." > is "more than."

Insert zeros to give each decimal the same number of places.

1. 2.38 and 2.4

2. 2.38 and 2.40 (after inserting zero)

Since 38 is less than 40, then $2.38 < 2.40$.

Exercise Write the place name for each underlined digit.

1. $35.\underline{0}6$

2. $0.52\underline{6}03$

3. $5.681\underline{1}$

4. $1.06\underline{1}1$

5. $0.5811\underline{1}$

6. $0.40101\underline{5}$

7. $0.00\underline{2}731$

8. $\underline{2}76.03$

9. $2.0\underline{8}35$

10. $0.2850\underline{1}$

Write < or >.

11. 2.38 ■ 2.37

12. 6.19 ■ 6.91

13. 3.7 ■ 3.71

14. 6.8 ■ 6.81

15. 9.73 ■ 9.3

16. 4.03 ■ 4.3

17. 6.76 ■ 6.7

18. 4.801 ■ 4.81

19. 6.73 ■ 6.703

20. 8.701 ■ 8.71

Rounding Decimals

EXAMPLE 1 Round 2.7017 to the nearest thousandth.

Solution 2.7017 Number (7) to the right of the thousandths place is 5 or more, so add 1 to the thousandths place and drop all digits to the right.

Answer $2.7017 \approx 2.702$ ($\approx$ means "approximately equal to.")

EXAMPLE 2 Round 8.1649 to the nearest hundredth.

Solution 8.1649 Number (4) to the right of the hundredth place is less than 5, so drop all digits to the right of 6.

Answer $8.1649 \approx 8.16$

Exercise Round each decimal to the places named.

	Tenths	Hundredths	Thousandths
1. 2.063	________	________	________
2. 0.0891	________	________	________
3. 1.0354	________	________	________
4. 0.15454	________	________	________
5. 32.70391	________	________	________
6. 7.63	________	________	________
7. 19.808964	________	________	________
8. 34.00354	________	________	________
9. 2.061155	________	________	________
10. 139.4181891	________	________	________

Review of Basic Skills 29

Adding Decimals

Rule

Remember to line up all decimal points, then add.

EXAMPLE 1 $13.11 + $2 + $1.91

Solution

```
  $13.11
   $2.00  ←  Insert zeros
+  $1.91
  $17.02
```

EXAMPLE 2 23 + .62 + 1.9

Solution

```
  23.00  ←  Insert zeros
    .62
+  1.90  ←  Insert zero
  25.52
```

Exercise Write in vertical form, then add.

1. $13.10 + $3 + $1.93

2. $5.10 + $1 + $7.63

3. $6.03 + $7.17 + $5

4. $3.41 + $4.01 + $6

5. $3 + $14.63 + $1.01

6. $4.63 + $5 + $6.15

7. $9 + $18 + $6.09

8. $16.09 + $7.17 + $3

9. $10 + $0.05 + $16.20

10. $14 + $6.37 + $9.56

11. 4.3 + 6.02 + 5

12. 6.37 + 4 + 9.76

13. 5 + 3.01 + 4.1

14. 6.37 + 6 + 19.013

15. 41 + 16.1 + 7.303

16. 6.1 + 7.23 + 4.769

17. 4 + 3.01 + 4.607

18. 16.1 + 3.23 + 4.768

19. 19.02 + 4 + 63.0791

20. 16.778 + 3 + 9.0734

Review of Basic Skills 30

Subtracting Decimals

Rule

Remember to line up the decimal points first, then subtract.

EXAMPLE 1 \$29.48 − \$5.15 — Write in vertical form.

Solution

\$29.48		Line up decimals.
− \$ 5.15		Subtract.
\$24.33		

EXAMPLE 2 \$12 − \$3.74 — Write in vertical form.

Solution

\$12.00	←	Insert zeros.
− \$3.74		Subtract.
\$8.26		

EXAMPLE 3 6.5 − 1.41 — Write in vertical form.

Solution

6.50	←	Insert zero.
− 1.41		Subtract.
5.09		

Exercise Write in vertical form, then subtract.

1. \$21.48 − \$5.15

2. \$13.41 − \$10.30

3. \$16.71 − \$5.36

4. \$14.70 − \$4.70

5. \$18.41 − \$16.30

6. \$41.86 − \$14.68

7. \$12.00 − \$3.74

8. \$15.00 − \$6.72

9. \$19.00 − \$5.63

10. \$15.00 − \$9.81

11. 6.5 − 1.41

12. 3.6 − 2.94

13. 6.7 − 5.61

14. 8.96 − 3.67

15. 10.46 − 4.67

16. 91.14 − 16.63

17. 41.62 − 19.81

18. 98.14 − 63.01

19. 43.1 − 6.37

20. 84.73 − 4.1

Review of Basic Skills 31

Multiplying Decimals

By adding the decimal places in the factors, you know exactly how many decimal places are in the product.

Example 1 $1.3 \cdot 2 = \blacksquare$

Solution	1.3	one place	
	$\times$ 2	no decimal	
Answer	2.6	one place	$1 + 0 = 1$

Example 2 $1.3 \cdot 2.43 = \blacksquare$

Solution	1.3	one place	
	$\times$ 2.43	two places	
	39		
	52		
	+ 26		
Answer	3.159	three places	$1 + 2 = 3$

Exercise Write in vertical form, then multiply.

1. 1.4 • 2

2. 2.4 • 5

3. 6.3 • 3

4. 4.9 • 3

5. 6.7 • 5

6. 1.3 • 2.4

7. 6.1 • 2.6

8. 3.9 • 4.1

9. 6.7 • 1.2

10. 8.6 • 6.8

11. 1.3 • 2.43

12. 6.8 • 2.61

13. 4.63 • 1.6

14. 9.84 • 2.7

15. 4.86 • 2.9

16. 6.7 • 1.79

17. 7.8 • 4.62

18. 4.91 • 1.8

19. 9.46 • 2.9

20. 6.3 • 8.76

Review of Basic Skills 32

Scientific Notation

Scientific notation expresses any number as a product of a number 1 or greater but less than 10 and a power of ten.

EXAMPLE 1 Express 2,800 in scientific notation.

Solution $2{,}800 = 2.8 \bullet 10^3$ Move the decimal point 3 places to the left.

Answer $2.8 \bullet 10^3$

EXAMPLE 2 Express 0.00039 in scientific notation.

Solution $0.00039 = 3.9 \bullet 10^{-4}$ Move the decimal point 4 places to the right.

Use the negative sign ($^{-4}$) when the decimal is moved to the right.

Answer $3.9 \bullet 10^{-4}$

Exercise Write these numbers in scientific notation.

1. 2,900

2. 3,600

3. 8,750

4. 6,320

5. 35,000

6. 46,000

7. 71,100

8. 400,000

9. 4,000,000

10. 1,700,000,000

11. 0.00038

12. 0.39

13. 0.41

14. 0.072

15. 0.0072

16. 0.0081

17. 0.00074

18. 0.000012

19. 0.00123

20. 0.000246

Review of Basic Skills 33

Dividing Decimals by Whole Numbers

Example 1 $0.168 \div 14 = \blacksquare$

Solution

$$\begin{array}{r} .012 \\ 14\overline{).168} \\ -\underline{14} \\ 28 \\ -\underline{28} \\ 0 \end{array}$$

Place the decimal point in the quotient directly above the one in the dividend.

Example 2 $68.6 \div 28 = \blacksquare$

Solution

$$\begin{array}{r} 2.45 \\ 28\overline{)68.60} \\ -\underline{56} \\ 12\,6 \\ -\underline{11\,2} \\ 1\,40 \\ -\underline{1\,40} \\ 0 \end{array}$$

Add a zero to complete the division.

Exercise Divide each decimal by the whole number.

1. $4.7 \div 2$

2. $0.78 \div 3$

3. $1.25 \div 5$

4. $6.34 \div 2$

5. $19.5 \div 3$

6. $21.7 \div 7$

7. $35.5 \div 5$

8. $1.68 \div 8$

9. $42.6 \div 6$

10. $18.9 \div 9$

11. $12.4 \div 4$

12. $23.1 \div 7$

13. $184.5 \div 9$

14. $36.36 \div 4$

15. $42.7 \div 7$

16. $8.414 \div 7$

17. $36.6 \div 6$

18. $25.5 \div 50$

19. $25.5 \div 25$

20. $12.5 \div 25$

Review of Basic Skills 34

Dividing Decimals by Decimals

Example 1 $8.04 \div 0.6 = \blacksquare$

Solution

$$\begin{array}{r} 13.4 \\ 6\overline{)80.4} \\ -6 \\ \hline 20 \\ -18 \\ \hline 2\,4 \\ -2\,4 \\ \hline 0 \end{array}$$

Step 1 Make the divisor a whole number. Multiply both divisor and dividend by ten.
$8.04 \bullet 10 \div 0.6 \bullet 10 = 80.4 \div 6$

Step 2 Divide. Place the decimal point straight up into the quotient.

Answer 13.4

Exercise Divide each decimal. Watch where you put the decimal point.

1. $1.44 \div 0.2$

2. $3.69 \div 0.3$

3. $5.50 \div 0.5$

4. $13.41 \div 0.9$

5. $16.71 \div 0.3$

6. $14.96 \div 0.4$

7. $1.934 \div 0.02$

8. $21.35 \div 0.05$

9. $0.0014 \div 0.7$

10. $6.315 \div 0.03$

11. $42.10 \div 0.2$

12. $32.30 \div 0.005$

13. $56.7 \div 0.07$

14. $5.67 \div 0.07$

15. $5.67 \div 0.7$

16. $636.3 \div 0.9$

17. $13.2 \div 0.4$

18. $132.4 \div 0.02$

19. $159.6 \div 0.3$

20. $7.938 \div 8.1$

Review of Basic Skills 35

Rewriting Decimals as Fractions

EXAMPLE 1 Rewrite 0.13 as a fraction.

Solution 0.1 3 means 13 hundredths.

↑ ↑

tenths hundredths

so $0.13 = \frac{13}{100}$ **Answer** $\frac{13}{100}$

Exercise Write these decimals as fractions. Then write the fractions in lowest terms.

1. 0.14

2. 0.15

3. 0.75

4. 0.36

5. 0.79

6. 0.150

7. 0.159

8. 0.375

9. 0.875

10. 0.999

11. 0.42

12. 0.65

13. 0.60

14. 0.45

15. 0.50

16. 0.168

17. 0.22

18. 0.98

19. 0.568

20. 0.72

Review of Basic Skills 36

Renaming Fractions as Decimals

Write decimals with denominators 10, 100, 1,000, and 10,000 or use a calculator to divide numerator by denominator.

EXAMPLE 1 Rewrite $\frac{2}{5}$ as a decimal.

Solution $\frac{2}{5} = \frac{2 \cdot 2}{5 \cdot 2} = \frac{4}{10}$ Rewrite with a denominator of 10.

$\frac{4}{10} = 0.4$ **Answer** 0.4

EXAMPLE 2 Rewrite $\frac{2}{7}$ as a decimal.

Solution Since 7 cannot be made into 10 or a multiple of 10, use your calculator.

2 [÷] 7 [=] 0.2857142 **Answer** 0.2857142

Exercise Write as decimals.

1. $\frac{1}{10}$
2. $\frac{1}{5}$
3. $\frac{1}{2}$
4. $\frac{3}{25}$
5. $\frac{9}{50}$
6. $\frac{7}{20}$
7. $\frac{9}{25}$
8. $\frac{3}{500}$
9. $\frac{6}{250}$
10. $\frac{59}{500}$

Use a calculator. Copy the display.

11. $\frac{3}{7}$
12. $\frac{5}{7}$
13. $\frac{2}{3}$
14. $\frac{2}{9}$
15. $\frac{5}{13}$
16. $\frac{2}{17}$
17. $\frac{3}{19}$
18. $\frac{5}{23}$
19. $\frac{6}{29}$
20. $\frac{5}{31}$

Measurement Conversion Factors

Metric Measures

Length

1,000 meters (m) = 1 kilometer (km)
100 centimeters (cm) = 1 m
10 decimeters (dm) = 1 m
1,000 millimeters (mm) = 1 m
10 cm = 1 decimeter (dm)
10 mm = 1 cm

Area

100 square millimeters (mm^2) = 1 square centimeter (cm^2)
10,000 cm^2 = 1 square meter (m^2)
10,000 m^2 = 1 hectare (ha)

Volume

1,000 cubic meters (m^3) = 1 cubic centimeter (cm^3)
100 cm^3 = 1 cubic decimeter (dm^3)
1,000,000 cm^3 = 1 cubic meter (m^3)

Capacity

1,000 milliliters (mL) = 1 liter (L)
1,000 L = 1 kiloliter (kL)

Mass

1,000 kilograms (kg) = 1 metric ton (t)
1,000 grams (g) = 1 kg
1,000 milligrams (mg) = 1 g

Temperature Degrees Celsius (°C)

0°C = freezing point of water
37°C = normal body temperature
100°C = boiling point of water

Time

60 seconds (sec) = 1 minute (min)
60 min = 1 hour (hr)
24 hr = 1 day

Customary Measures

Length

12 inches (in.) = 1 foot (ft)
3 ft = 1 yard (yd)
36 in. = 1 yd
5,280 ft = 1 mile (mi)
1,760 yd = 1 mi
6,076 feet = 1 nautical mile

Area

144 square inches (sq in.) = 1 square foot (sq ft)
9 sq ft = 1 square yard (sq yd)
43,560 sq ft = 1 acre (A)

Volume

1,728 cubic inches (cu in.) = 1 cubic foot (cu ft)
27 cu ft = 1 cubic yard (cu yard)

Capacity

8 fluid ounces (fl oz) = 1 cup (c)
2 c = 1 pint (pt)
2 pt = 1 quart (qt)
4 qt = 1 gallon (gal)

Weight

16 ounces (oz) = 1 pound (lb)
2,000 lb = 1 ton (T)

Temperature Degrees Fahrenheit (°F)

32°F = freezing point of water
98.6°F = normal body temperature
212°F = boiling point of water

Measurement Conversion Factors

To change	To	Multiply by
centimeters	inches	0.3937
centimeters	feet	0.03281
cubic feet	cubic meters	0.0283
cubic meters	cubic feet	35.3145
cubic meters	cubic yards	1.3079
cubic yards	cubic meters	0.7646
feet	meters	0.3048
feet	miles (nautical)	0.0001645
feet	miles (statute)	0.0001894
feet/second	miles/hour	0.6818
gallons (U.S.)	liters	3.7853
grams	ounces avdp	0.0353
grams	pounds	0.002205
hours	days	0.04167
inches	millimeters	25.4000
inches	centimeters	2.5400
kilograms	pounds avdp	2.2046
kilometers	miles	0.6214
liters	gallons (U.S.)	0.2642
liters	pecks	0.1135
liters	pints (dry)	1.8162
liters	pints (liquid)	2.1134
liters	quarts (dry)	0.9081
liters	quarts (liquid)	1.0567

To change	To	Multiply by
meters	feet	3.2808
meters	miles	0.0006214
meters	yards	1.0936
metric tons	tons (long)	0.9842
metric tons	tons (short)	1.1023
miles	kilometers	1.6093
miles	feet	5,280
miles (statute)	miles (nautical)	0.8684
miles/hour	feet/minute	88
millimeters	inches	0.0394
ounces avdp	grams	28.3495
ounces	pounds	0.0625
pecks	liters	8.8096
pints (dry)	liters	0.5506
pints (liquid)	liters	0.4732
pounds avdp	kilograms	0.4536
pounds	ounces	16
quarts (dry)	liters	1.1012
quarts (liquid)	liters	0.9463
square feet	square meters	0.0929
square meters	square feet	10.7639
square meters	square yards	1.1960
square yards	square meters	0.8361
yards	meters	0.9144

Glossary

A

Absolute value (ab´ sə lüt val´ yü) the distance from zero of a number on a number line (p. 6)

$|-4|$ is read "the absolute value of negative 4."

$|-4| = 4$, 4 units from 0.

$|4| = 4$, 4 units from 0.

Acute angle (ə kyüt´ ang gəl) an angle which measures between 0° and 90° (p. 258)

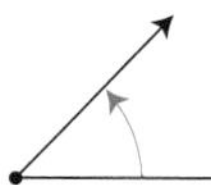

Acute triangle (ə kyüt´ trī´ ang gəl) a triangle with three acute angles (p. 368)

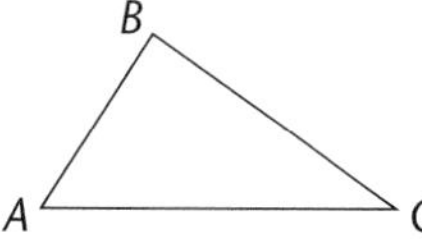

Addend (əd´ end) number to be added to another (p. 8)

$4 + 2 = 6$ The numbers 4 and 2 are addends.

Addition (ə dish´ ən) the arithmetic operation of combining two or more numbers to find a total (p. 8)

$3 + 5 = 8$

Addition property of zero (ə dish´ ən prop´ ər tē ov zir´ ō) a number does not change if 0 is added or subtracted (p. 46)

$2 + 0 = 2$ $\quad 2 - 0 = 2$

Additive inverses (ad´ ə tiv in´ vėrs es) numbers that equal 0 when added together; also called opposites (p. 46)

$6 + (-6) = 0$

$-6 + 6 = 0$

Adjacent angle (ə jā´ snt ang´ gəl)an angle that shares a vertex and a common side with another angle (p. 356)

∠CAD is adjacent to ∠BAC.

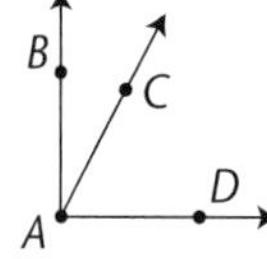

Algebra (al´ jə brə) the branch of mathematics that uses both letters and numbers to show relations between quantities (p. 2)

Algebraic expression (al´ jə brā´ ik ek spresh´ ən)—a mathematical sentence that includes at least one operation and a variable (p. 4)

$2x + 5$ $\quad m \cdot 3$

Algebraic fraction (al´ jə brā´ ik frak´ shən) a single algebraic term divided by a single algebraic term (p. 222)

$\frac{x}{y}$ $\quad \frac{a^2}{3b}$

Angle (ang´ gəl) a geometric figure made up of two rays with a common endpoint called a vertex (p. 356)

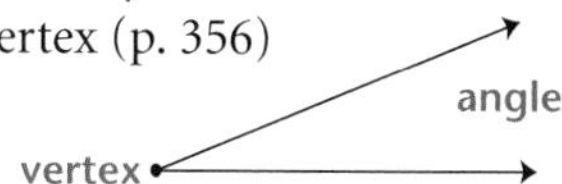

Arithmetic (ə rith´ mə tik) the study of the properties of numbers, using four basic operations—addition, subtraction, multiplication, and division (p. 2)

Associative property of addition (ə so´ shē ā tiv prop´ ər tē ov ə dish´ ən) the same terms added in different groupings result in the same answer (p. 34)

$(3 + 5) + 2 = 3 + (5 + 2)$

Associative property of multiplication (ə so´ shē ā tiv prop´ ər tē ov mul tə plə kā´ shən)the same terms multiplied in different groupings result in the same answer (p. 38)

$(3 \cdot 5)4 = 3(5 \cdot 4)$

Axis of symmetry of a parabola(ak´ sis ov sim´ ə trē) a perpendicular line that passes through the midpoint between the roots (p. 399)

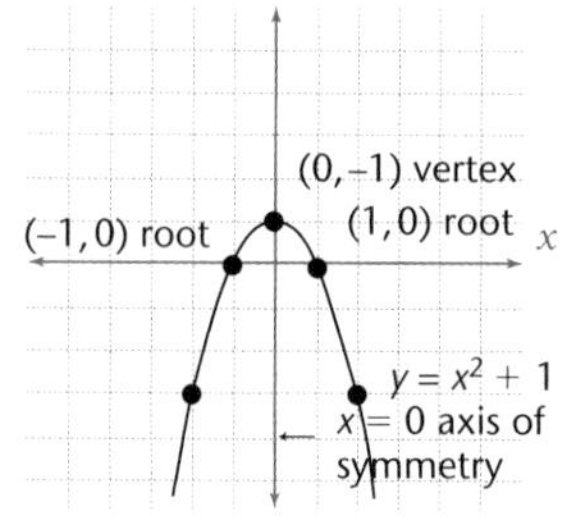

B

Bar graph(bär graf) a way of showing how information can be compared using rectangular bars (p. 185)

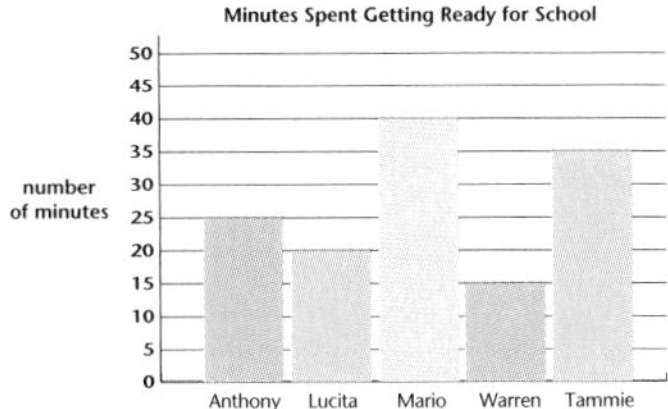

Base (b)(bās) the number being multiplied; a factor (p. 20) *a* is the base. a^2

Box-and-whiskers plot (boks and wis´ kərz plot) a way to describe the concentration and the spread of data in a set (p. 192)

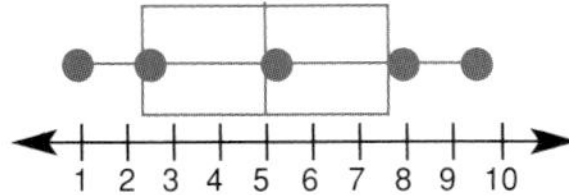

C

Circle graph (sėr´ kəl graf) a graphic way to present information using the parts of a circle (p. 101)

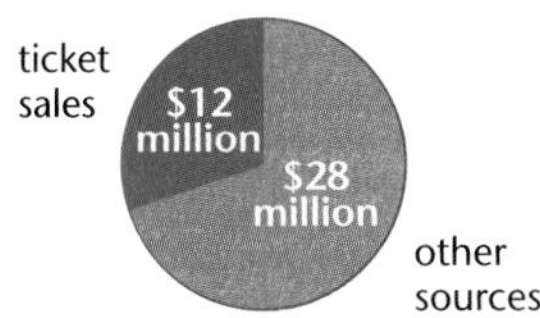

Coefficient (ko ə fish´ ənt) the number that multiplies the variable (p. 4)

$3x$ **3 is the coefficient.**

Common factor (kom´ ən fak´ tər) a multiplier shared by the terms in an expression (p. 44)

$4b + 3b$ ***b* is the common factor.**

Common solution (kom´ ən sə lü´shən)the ordered pair of real numbers that two intersecting lines share (p. 294)

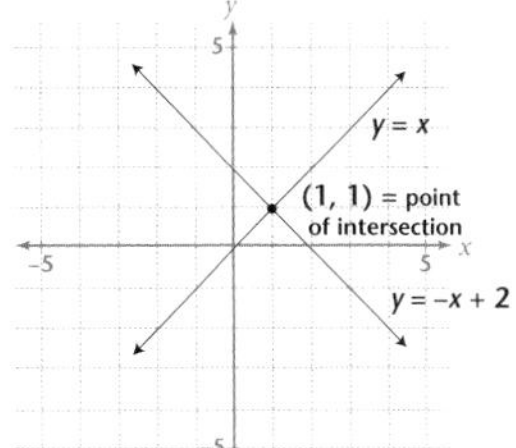

Commutative property of addition (kom´ yə tā tiv prop´ ər tē ov ə dish´ ən) the order in which two numbers are added does not change their sum (p. 32)

$3 + 4 = 4 + 3$

Commutative property of multiplication (kom´ yə tā tiv prop´ ər tē ov mul tə plə kā´ shən)the order in which two numbers are multiplied does not change their product (p. 34)

$3 \cdot 2 = 2 \cdot 3$

Complement of a probability event (kom plə ment´ ov ā prob ə bil´ə tē i vent´) the set of outcomes that are not in the event (p. 201)

Complementary angles (kom plə men´ tər ē ang´ gelz) two angles whose sum of their measures is 90 degrees (p. 357)

Completing the square (kəm plēt´ ing thə skwâr) a method of finding the roots of a perfect square trinomial (p. 392)

Complex fraction (kəm pleks´ frak´ shən) a fraction in which the numerator, the denominator, or both the numerator and the denominator are fractions (p. 226)

$$\frac{\frac{3}{8}}{5} \qquad \frac{10}{\frac{3}{5}} \qquad \frac{\frac{2}{3}}{\frac{1}{2}}$$

a hat	e let	ī ice	ô order	u̇ put	sh she	ə	a in about
ā age	ē equal	o hot	oi oil	ü rule	th thin		e in taken
ä far	ėr term	ō open	ou out	ch child	ᴛʜ then		i in pencil
â care	i it	ȯ saw	u cup	ng long	zh measure		o in lemon
							u in circus

Composite number (kəm poz´ it num´ bər) an integer that is not a prime number (p. 156)

$2 \cdot 2 \cdot 2 \cdot 2 = 16$ **16 is a composite number.**

Congruent (kən grü´ ənt) figures that have the same size and shape (p. 372)

Conjugate (kon´ jə git) a factor that when multiplied rationalizes (or simplifies) an expression (p. 340)

$(2 + \sqrt{3})$ and $(2 - \sqrt{3})$ **are conjugates**

Conjunction (kən jungk´ shən) two or more simple sentences connected by *and* (p. 306)

Consecutive (kən sek´ yə tiv) following one after the other in order (p. 96)

Constant (kon´ stənt) specific real number (p. 76)

$ax - by = c$ ***a, b,* and *c* are constants.**

Corresponding angles (kôr ə spon´ ding ang´ gəlz) interior and exterior angles on the same side of a transversal cutting through parallel lines (p. 361)

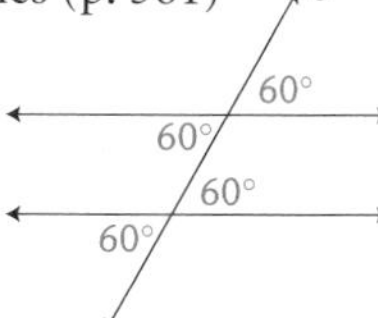

Cross products (krȯs prod´ əkts) the result of multiplying the denominator of one fraction with the numerator of another (p. 116)

$\frac{1}{2} \cdot \frac{2}{3}$ $2 \cdot 2 = 4$ $1 \cdot 3 = 3$

D

Data (dā´ tə) information given in numbers (p. 184)

Decimal expansion (des´ ə məl ek span´ shən) writing a number, such as a fraction, as a decimal (p. 329)

$\frac{3}{5} = 0.6\overline{0}$

Degree of a polynomial (di grē´ ov ā pol ē no´ mē əl) greatest power of the variable (p. 134)

$2y^3 + 3y^2 + 2$ **degree 3**

Dependent event (di pen´ dənt i vent´) in a probability experiment, the outcome of one event is affected by the outcome of any other event (p. 207)

Dependent variable (di pen´ dənt vâr´ ē bəl) the value of the *y* variable that depends on the value of *x* (p. 265)

Difference (dif´ ər əns) the answer to a subtraction problem (p. 10)

$5 - 2 = 3$ **3 is the difference.**

Disjunction (dis jungk´ shən) a compound statement that uses the word *or* to connect two simple statements (p. 84)

Distributive property (dis trib´ yə tiv prop´ ər tē) numbers within parentheses can be multiplied by the same factor (p. 42)

$4(2 + 1) = 4 \cdot 2 + 4 \cdot 1$

Dividend (div´ ə dend) a number that is divided (p. 14)

$6 \div 3 = 2$ **6 is the dividend.**

Division (də vizh´ ən) the arithmetic operation that finds how many times a number is contained in another number (p. 14)

$12 \div 3 = 4$

Divisor (də vī´ zər) the number by which you are dividing (p. 14)

$10 \div 5 = 2$ **5 is the divisor.**

Domain (dō mān´) the independent variables, or set of *x*-values, of a function (p. 268)

E

Equality (i kwol´ ə tē) the state of being equal; shown by the equal sign (p. 84)

$2 \cdot 2 = 4 \cdot 1$

Equation (i kwā´ zhən) a mathematical sentence stating that two quantities are equal and written as two expressions separated by an equal sign (p. 64)

$4n + 4n = 8n$ $3x = 15$

Equiangular triangle (ē kwē ang´ gyə lər trī´ ang gəl) a triangle with three angles, each measuring 60 degrees (p. 368)

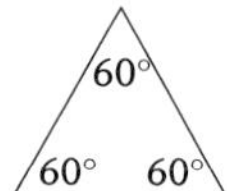

Equilateral triangle (ē kwə lat´ ər əl trī´ ang gəl) a triangle with three equal sides (p. 22)

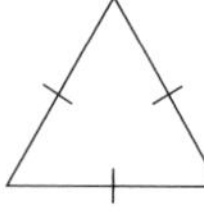

Expanded notation (ek spand´ əd nō tā´ shən) an algebraic expression written to show its smallest terms (p. 32)

$2a + 3a = 5a$

$a \cdot a + a \cdot a \cdot a = a \cdot a \cdot a \cdot a \cdot a$

Exponent (ek spō´ nənt) number that tells the times another number is a factor (p. 20)

Exterior angles (ek stir´ ē ər ang´ gelz) angles that are formed outside two lines cut by a transversal (p. 361)

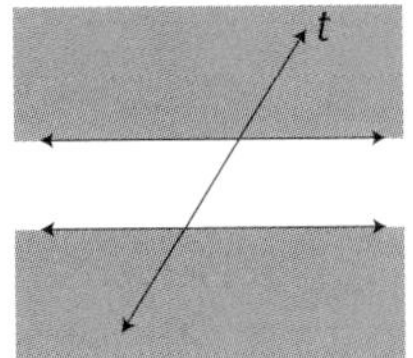

F

Factorial notation (fak tôr´ ē əl nō tā´ shən)the product of all positive integers from a given integer to 1 represented by the symbol [!] (p. 211)

$5! = 5 \cdot 4 \cdot 3 \cdot 2 \cdot 1 = 120$

Factoring (fak´ tər ing) using the distributive property to separate the common factor from the terms in the expression (p. 44)

$4x + 4y = 4(x + y)$

Factoring completely (fak´ tər ing kəm plēt´ lē) expressing an integer as a product of only prime numbers (p. 156)

$20 = 5 \cdot 2 \cdot 2$

Factor (fak´ tər) a number that is multiplied in a multiplication problem (p. 12)

$4 \cdot 3 = 12$ **4 and 3 are the factors.**

Frequency table (frē´ kwən sē tā´ bəl) a way of showing the count of items or number of times in different groups or categories (p. 184)

Frequency Table		
Interval	Tally	Frequency
0–9		0
10–19		0
20–29	𝍸 I	6

Function (fungk´ shən)a rule that associates every x-value with one and only one y-value (p. 265)

Fundamental principle of counting (fun də men´ tl prin´ sə pəl ov koun´ ting) a general rule that states that if one task can be completed p different ways, and a second task can be completed q different ways, the first task followed by the second task can be completed $p \cdot q$, or pq, different ways (p. 210)

G

Geometry (jē om´ ə trē) the study of points, lines, angles, surfaces, and solids (p. 34)

Graphing (graf´ ing) showing on a number line the relationship of a set of numbers or a plane (p. 84)

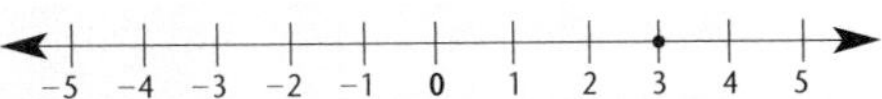

Greatest common factor (GCF) (grāt´ est kom´ fak´ tər) the largest factor of two or more numbers or terms (p. 157)

$10 = 5 \cdot 2$ **The GCF of 10 and 15**

$15 = 5 \cdot 3$ **is 5.**

H

Histogram (his´ te gram) a way of showing the frequency of data using rectangular bars and the area they contain (p. 186)

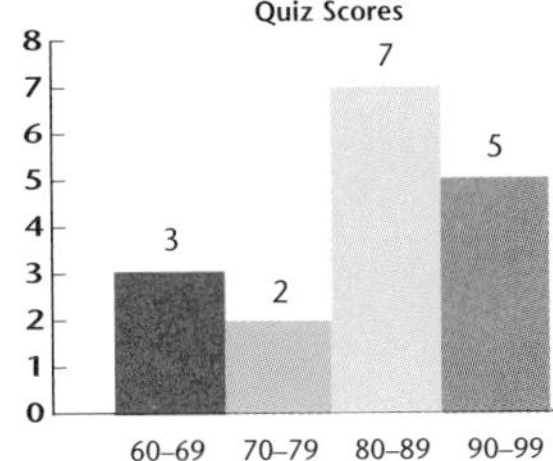

Hypotenuse (hī pot´ n üs) the longest side in a right triangle (p. 80)

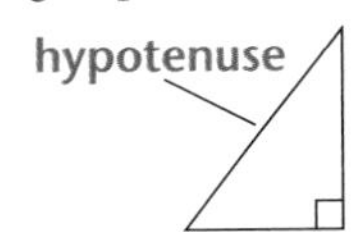

a hat	e let	ī ice	ô order	ů put	sh she	ə a in about	
ā age	ē equal	o hot	oi oil	ü rule	th thin	e in taken	
ä far	ėr term	ō open	ou out	ch child	ᴛʜ then	i in pencil	
â care	i it	ò saw	u cup	ng long	zh measure	o in lemon	
						u in circus	

I

Independent event (in di pen´ dənt i vent´) in a probability experiment, the outcome of any event does not affect the outcome of any other event (p. 208)

Independent variable (in di pen´ dənt vâr´ ē bəl) the value of x that determines the value of y (p. 265)

Inequality (in i kwol´ ə tē) the state of being unequal; shown by the less than, greater than, and unequal to signs (p. 84)

$5 > 2 \quad 5 < 7 \quad 5 \neq 4$

Integer (in´ tə jər) a whole number or its opposite, including 0 (... −2, −1, 0, 1, 2, ...) (p. 6)

Interest (in´ tər ist) the amount of money paid or received for the use of borrowed money (p. 111)

Interior angles (in tir´ ē ər ang´ gəlz) angles that are formed inside, or between, two lines cut by a transversal (p. 361)

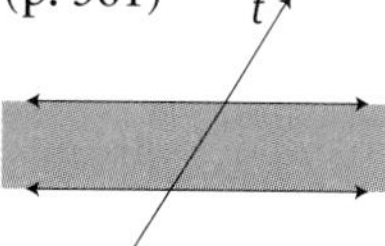

Intersecting lines (in´ tər sekt´ ing līnz) lines with one point in common (p. 294)

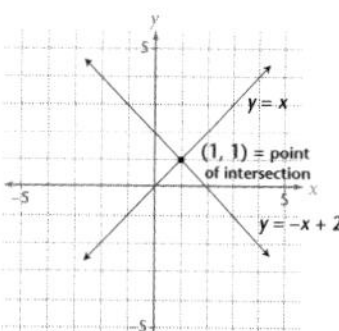

Irrational number (i rash´ ə nəl num´ bər) a real number, such as $\sqrt{2}$, that cannot be written in the form $\frac{a}{b}$ in which a and b are whole numbers and $b \neq 0$ (p. 328)

Isosceles triangle (ī sos´ ə lēz trī´ ang gəl) a triangle with two sides of equal length (p. 368)

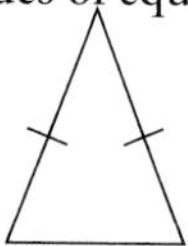

L

Least common multiple (LCM) (lēst kom´ ən mul´ tə pəl) the smallest number that two or more numbers can divide into without leaving a remainder (p. 226)

4: 4, 8, 12, . . . The LCM of 4 and 6
6: 6, 12, . . . is 12.

Like terms (līk tėrmz) terms that have the same variable (p. 16)

Linear equation(lin´ ē ər i kwā´ zhən) an equation whose graph is a straight line (p. 263)

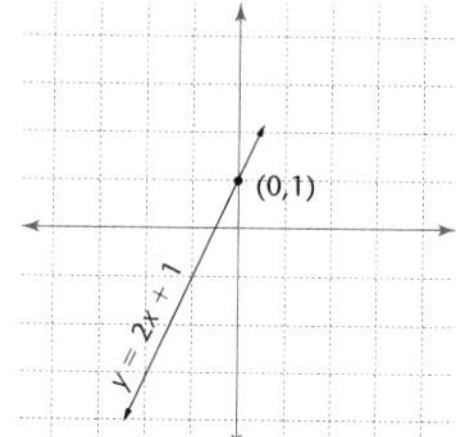

Literal equation (lit´ ər əl i kwā´ zhən) an equation that has only letters (p. 76)

$a + b + c = d$

Lower quartile (lō´ ər kwȯr´ tīl) the median of the scores below the median (p. 192)

{2, 3, 5, 6, 8, 9, 11} **3 is the lower quartile.**

M

Matrix (mā´ triks) any rectangular arrangement of numbers or symbols (p. 314)

Mean (mēn) the sum of the values in a set of data divided by the number of pieces of data in the set (p. 188)

{2, 3, 5, 6, 8, 9, 11} **6.3 is the mean.**

Measures of central tendency (mezh´ ərz ov sen´ trəl ten´ dən sē) the mean, median, and mode of a set of data (p. 190)

Median (mē´ dē ən) the middle value in an ordered set of data (p. 189)

{2, 3, 5, 6, 8, 9, 11} **6 is the median.**

Mode (mōd) the value or values that occur most often in a set of data (p. 190)

{2, 3, 5, 2} **2 is the mode.**

Monomial (mon ō´ mē əl) a single term that is a number, a variable, or the product of a number and one or more variables (p. 134)

$4 \quad x \quad 5b \quad 6y^2$

Multiplication (mul tə plə kā´ shən) the arithmetic operation of adding a number to itself many times (p. 12)

$3 \cdot 5 = 15 \qquad 5 + 5 + 5 = 15$

Multiplication property of 1 (mul tə plə kā´ shən prop´ ər tē ov wun) a number or term does not change when multiplied by 1 (p. 48)

$4 \cdot 1 = 4 \qquad 1x = x$

Multiplication property of zero (mul tə plə kā′ shən prop′ ər tē ov zir′ ō) zero times any number is zero (p. 47)

$4 \cdot 0 = 0 \qquad x \cdot 0 = 0$

Multiplicative inverses (mul tə plik′ ə tiv in′ vėrs es) any two numbers or terms whose product equals 1 (p. 48)

$3 \cdot \frac{1}{3} = 1 \qquad x \cdot \frac{1}{x} = 1, x \neq 0$

Negative exponent (neg′ ə tiv ek spō nənt) for any nonzero integers a and n,

$a^{-n} = \frac{1}{a^n}$ (p. 126)

Negative integer (neg′ ə tiv in′ tə jər) a whole number less than zero (p. 6)... $-3, -2, -1$

Numerical expression (nü mer′ ə kəl ek spresh′ ən) a mathematical sentence that includes operations and numbers (p. 4)

$3 + 2 \qquad 6 - 4 \qquad 12 \div 3 \qquad 5 \cdot 2$

O

Obtuse (əb tüs′) an angle with a measure between 90 and 180 degrees (p. 258)

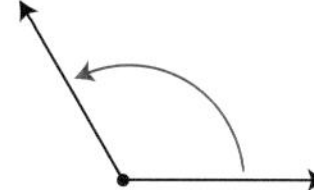

Obtuse triangle (əb tüs′ trī′ ang gəl) a triangle with one obtuse angle (p. 368)

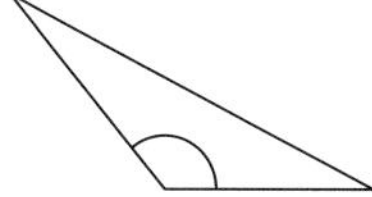

Open statement (ō′ pən stāt′ mənt) a sentence that is neither true nor false (p. 2)

$6a = 30 \qquad 30 \div n = 5$

Operation (op ə rā′ shən) the mathematical processes of addition, subtraction, multiplication, and division (p. 4)

Opposites (op′ ə zits) numbers the same distance from zero but on different sides of zero on the number line (p. 6)

4 and 24 are opposites.

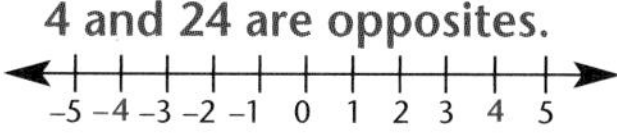

Ordered pair (ôr′ dėrd pâr) a set of two real numbers that locate a point in the plane (p. 250)

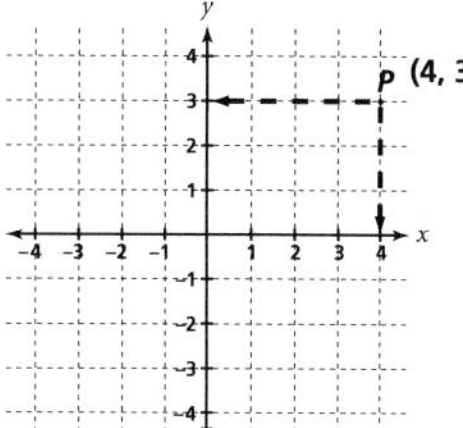

Origin (ôr′ ə jin) the point at which the axes in a coordinate system intersect (0,0)(p. 250)

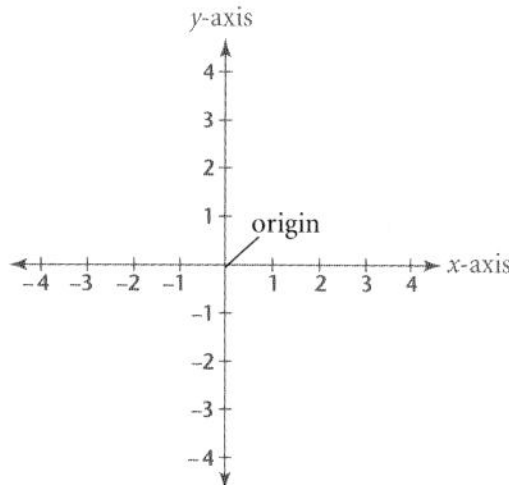

P

Parabola (pə rab′ ə lə) a plane curve generated by a point that moves so that its distance from a fixed point is always the same as its distance from a fixed line (p. 398)

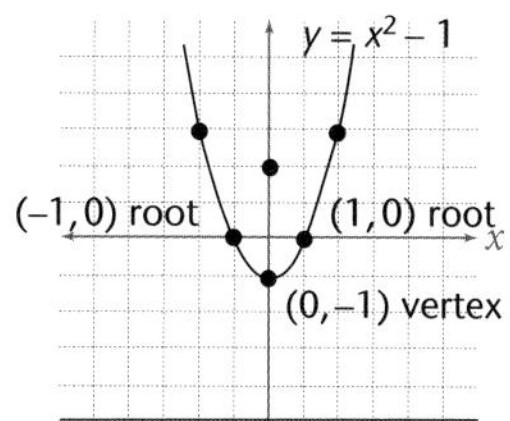

Parallel lines (par′ ə lel līnz) lines that have the same slope (p. 288)

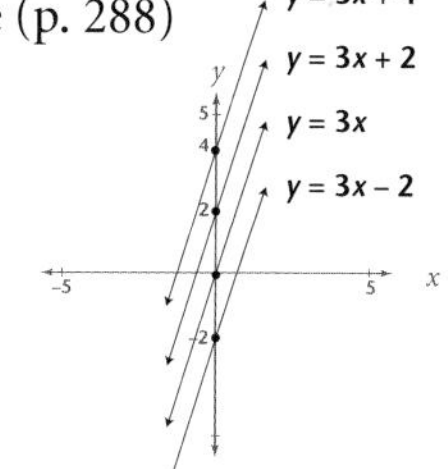

a	hat	e	let	ī	ice	ô	order	u̇	put	sh	she	ə { a	in about
ā	age	ē	equal	o	hot	oi	oil	ü	rule	th	thin	e	in taken
ä	far	ėr	term	ō	open	ou	out	ch	child	ᴛʜ	then	i	in pencil
â	care	i	it	ȯ	saw	u	cup	ng	long	zh	measure	o	in lemon
												u	in circus

Parallelogram (par ə lel′ ə gram) a four-sided polygon with two pairs of equal and parallel sides (p. 370)

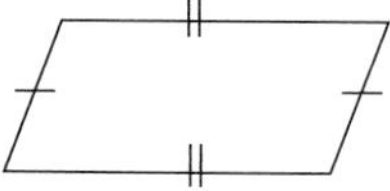

Percent (%) (pər sent′) part per one hundred (p. 98)

Perfect square (pėr′ fikt skwâr) the square of an integer (p. 166)

Perfect square trinomial (pėr′ fikt skwâr trī nō′ mē əl) the result of multiplying a binomial by itself or squaring a binomial (p. 168)

$(a + b)^2 = a^2 + 2ab + b^2$

Perimeter (pə rim′ ə tər) the distance around the outside of a shape (p. 22)

Permutation (pėr myü tā′ shən) an arrangement of some or all of a set of numbers in a specific order (p. 211)

Plane (plān) a two-dimensional flat surface (p. 360)

Polynomial (pol ē nō′ mē əl) an algebraic expression made up of one term or the sum or difference of two or more terms in the same variable (p. 134)

$2x^3 - 3x^2 + x - 3$

Positive integer (poz′ ə tiv in′ tə jər) a whole number greater than zero 1, 2, 3. . . (p. 6)

Power (pou′ ər) the product of multiplying any number by itself once or many times (p. 20)

$2^1 = 2 \quad 2^2 = 4 \quad 2^3 = 8 \quad 2^4 = 16$

Prime number (prīm num′ bər) an integer that can be divided only by itself and 1 (p. 156)

$7 = 7 \cdot 1$

Principal (prin′ sə pəl) the amount of money deposited, borrowed, or loaned (p. 111)

Probability (prob ə bil′ ə tē) the chance or likelihood of an event occurring (p. 196)

Product (prod′ əkt) the answer to a multiplication problem (p. 12)

$3 \cdot 4 = 12$ **12 is the product.**

Proportion (prə pôr′ shən) an equation made up of two equal ratios (p. 116)

$\frac{1}{2} = \frac{2}{4}$

Pythagorean theorem (pə thag′ ə rē ən thir′ əm) a formula that states that in a right triangle, the length of the hypotenuse squared is equal to the length of side *b* squared and the length of side *a* squared (p. 80)

$c^2 = a^2 + b^2$

Q

Quadrant (kwäd′ rənt) regions of a coordinate plane bounded by the *x*- and *y*-axes (p. 250)

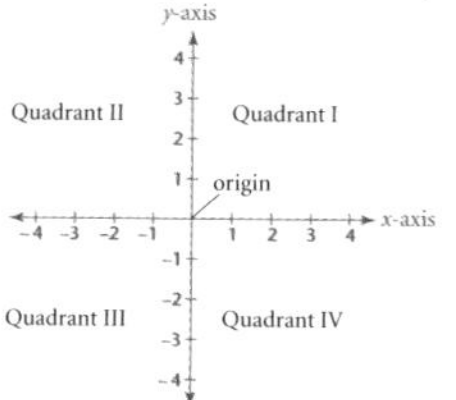

Quadratic equation (kwä drat′ ik i kwā′ zhən)an equation in the form of $ax^2 + bx + c = 0$ (p. 174)

$2x^2 + 3x + 4 = 0$

Quadratic formula (kwä drat′ ik fôr′ myə lə) the formula that can be used to find the roots of any quadratic equation $x = \frac{-b \pm \sqrt{b^2 - 4ac}}{2a}$ (p. 397)

Quotient (kwō′ shənt) the answer to a division problem (p. 14)

$20 \div 5 = 4$ **4 is the quotient.**

R

Radical (rad′ ə kəl) a number that is written with the radical sign (p. 334)

$\sqrt{9} \quad \sqrt[3]{8}$

Radical sign (rad′ ə kəl sīn) the mathematical symbol ($\sqrt{\ }$) placed before a number or algebraic expression to indicate that the root should be found (p. 334)

$\sqrt{16}$ $\sqrt{\ }$ is the radical sign.

Radicand (rad ə kand′) a number under the radical sign ($\sqrt{\ }$) (p. 346)

$\sqrt{3}$ **3 is the radicand.**

Range (rānj) the difference between the greatest and least values in a set of data (p. 188)

$\{2, 3, 5, 6\}$ $6 - 2 = 4$ **4 is the range.**

Range (of a function) (rānj) the dependent variables, or set of *y*-values, of a function (p. 268)

Ratio (rā´ shē ō) a comparison of two like quantities using division (p. 116)

$a : b \quad \frac{a}{b} \quad a \text{ to } b$

Rational expression (rash´ ə nəl ek spresh´ ən) an algebraic expression divided by another algebraic expression (p. 222)

$\frac{(x^2 + 2)}{(x + 2)^3}$

Rationalizing the denominator (rash´ ə nə lī zing ŦHə di nom´ ə nā tər) changing a fraction with an irrational denominator to an equivalent fraction with a rational denominator (p. 340)

Rational number (rash´ ə nəl num´ bər) any number that is expressed as an integer or as a ratio between two integers when 0 does not serve as the denominator (p. 220)

$2 \quad \frac{1}{3} \quad -3 \quad \frac{-2}{5}$

Ray (rā) a set of points that is part of a line. It has one endpoint and extends infinitely in one direction. (p. 356)

ray

Real number (rē´ əl num´ bər) a number on the number line (p. 6)

−5 −4 −3 −2 −1 0 1 2 3 4 5

Reciprocals (ri sip´ rə kəlz) multiplicative inverses (p. 48)

$\frac{1}{2} \cdot 2 = 1 \quad \frac{1}{2}$ **and 2 are reciprocals.**

Rectangle (rek´ tang gəl) a four-sided polygon with four right angles and the opposite sides equal (p. 370)

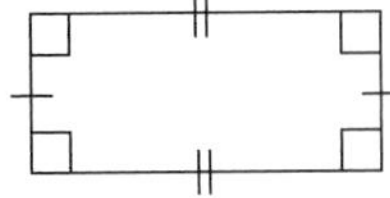

Repeating decimal expansion (ri pē´ ting des´ ə məl ek span´ shən) a decimal sequence in which the numbers repeat in exactly the same order (p. 329)

$\frac{1}{3} = 0.3333\ldots = 0.\overline{3}$

Rhombus (rom´ bəs) a four-sided polygon with four parallel sides the same length (p. 370)

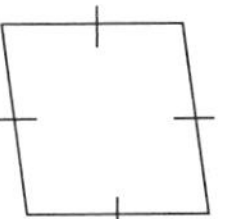

Right triangle (rīt trī´ ang gəl) a three-sided figure, or triangle, with one right, or 90°, angle (p. 80)

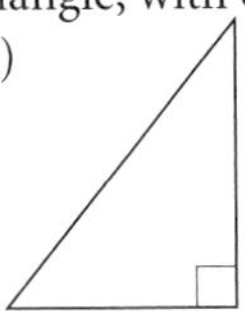

Root (rüt) an equal factor of a number (p. 50)

$\sqrt{25} = 5 \quad \sqrt[3]{64} = 4$

5 is the square root; 4 is the cube root.

S

Sample space (sam´ pəl spās) the set of all possible outcomes of an experiment (p. 204)

Scalene triangle (skā lēn´ trī´ ang gəl) a triangle with no equal sides (p. 368)

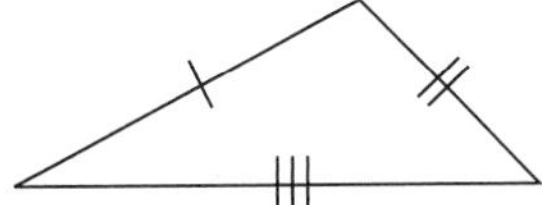

Scientific notation (sī ən tif´ ik nō tā´ shən) a number written as the product of a number between 1 and 10 and a power of ten; any number in scientific notation = $(1 \leq x < 10)(10^n)$ (p. 129)

$5{,}000 = 5 \cdot 10^3$

Set of roots (set ov rüts)the set of numbers that make an equation true (p. 386)

Similar (sim´ ə lər) figures that have the same shape but not the same size (p. 374)

Simplest form (sim´ pəl est fôrm) a fraction in which the only common factor of the numerator and denominator is 1 (p. 220)

$\frac{1}{2} \quad \frac{1}{4} \quad \frac{2}{3}$

a	hat	e	let	ī	ice	ô	order	ů	put	sh	she	ə { a	in about
ā	age	ē	equal	o	hot	oi	oil	ü	rule	th	thin	e	in taken
ä	far	ėr	term	ō	open	ou	out	ch	child	ŦH	then	i	in pencil
â	care	i	it	ȯ	saw	u	cup	ng	long	zh	measure	o	in lemon
												u	in circus

Simplify (sim´ plə fī) combine like terms (p. 16)
$2a + 3a = 5a$

Slope (slōp) the measure of the steepness of a line (p. 258)

Solution (sə lü´ shən) the value of a variable that makes an open statement true (p. 174)

Square (skwâr) a polygon with four equal sides and four right angles (p. 370)

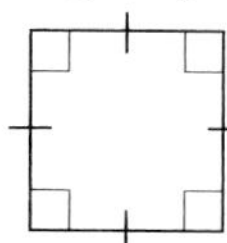

Standard form (stand´ dərd fôrm)arrangement of variables from left to right, from greatest to least degree of power (p. 135)
$x^3 + 2x^2 - x + 5$

Statement (stāt´ mənt) a sentence that is true or false (p. 2)
$5 \cdot 2 = 10 \quad 5 \cdot 2 = 8$

Statistics (stə tis´ tiks) numerical facts about people, places, or things (p. 196)

Stem-and-leaf plot (stem and lēf plot) a way of showing place value by separating the data by powers of ten (p. 184)

Stem	Time Spent Studying (in minutes)	leaves
1	0 0 5 5 5	
2	0 5 5	
3	0 0 0 5	
4	5	

Subtraction (səb trak´ shən) the arithmetic operation of taking one number away from another to find the difference (p. 10)
$10 - 3 = 7$

Sum (sum) the answer to an addition problem (p. 8)
$6 + 4 = 10$ 10 is the sum.

Supplementary angles (sup lə men´ tər ē ang´ gəlz) two angles whose sum of their measures is 180 degrees (p. 358)

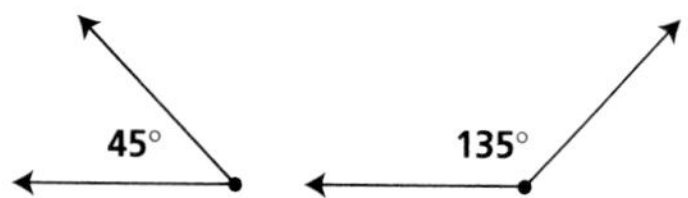

Symmetry (sim´ ə trī) the exact agreement of parts on opposite sides of a line (p. 399)

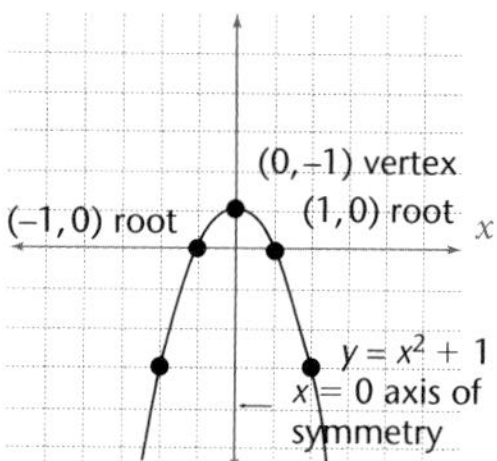

System of equations (sis´ təm ov i kwā´ zhənz) equations describing two or more lines (p. 294)

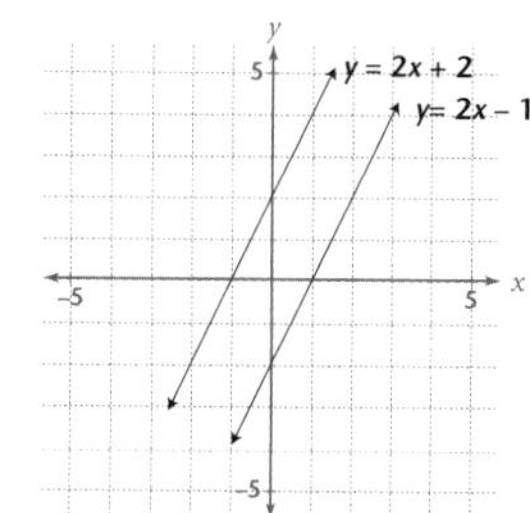

T

Terminating decimal expansion (tėr´ mə nā ting des´ ə məl ek span´ shən) a decimal sequence that ends in all 0s (p. 329)
$\frac{2}{5} = 0.4000\ldots = 0.4\overline{0}$

Term (tėrm) part of an expression separated by an addition or subtraction sign (p. 16)
$3x + 2x + x$ 3x, 2x, and x are terms.

Theorem (thir´ əm) a statement that can be proven (p. 361)

Theoretical probability (thē ə ret´ ə kəl prob ə bil´ ə tē) the predicted likelihood of what should happen in an experiment (p. 197)

Transversal (trans vėr səl) a line that intersects two or more lines (p. 360)

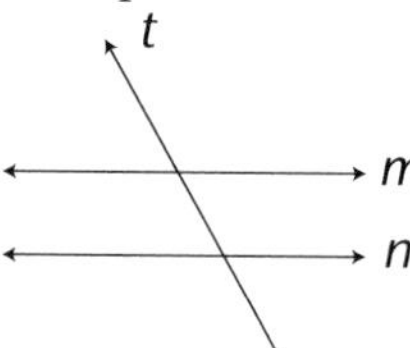

Trapezoid (trap´ ə zoid) a four-sided polygon with one pair of parallel sides and one pair of sides that are not parallel (p. 370)

Trigonometric ratios (trig ə nə met´ rik rā´ shē ōs)angles measured by ratios of the sides of a right triangle (p. 376)

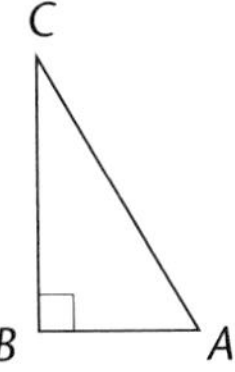

Truth table (trüth tā´ bəl) a table of true and false values (p. 85)

p	***q***	**Disjunction *p* or *q***
T	T	T
T	F	T
F	T	T
F	F	F

Undefined (un di fīnd´) a term used without a specific mathematical definition (p. 242)

$\frac{1}{0}$ $\frac{a}{0}$

Unlike terms (un līk´ tėrmz) terms that have different variables (p. 18)

Upper quartile (up´ ər kwȯr´ tīl) the median of the scores above the median (p. 192)

{2, 3, 5, 6, 8, 9, 11} **9 is the upper quartile.**

Variable (vâr´ ē bəl) a letter or symbol that stands for an unknown number (p. 4)

$5x$ ***x* is the variable.**

Vertex (vėr´ teks) a point common to both sides of an angle (p. 356)

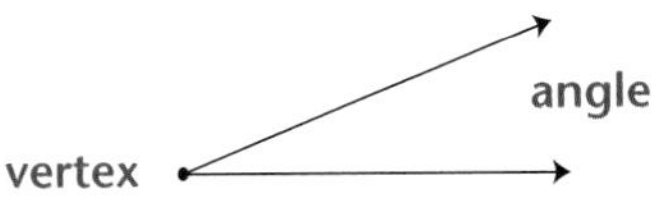

Vertical angles (vėr´ tə kəl ang´ gəlz) pairs of opposite angles formed by intersecting lines. Vertical angles have the same measure. (p. 357)

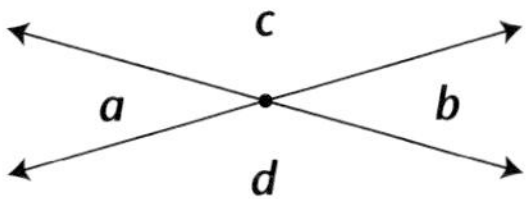

angles *a* and *b* are vertical angles; angles *c* and *d* are vertical angles

Vertical line test (vėr tə kəl līn test) a way of determining whether a graph is a function; if a vertical line intersects a graph in more than 1 point, the graph is not a function (p. 265)

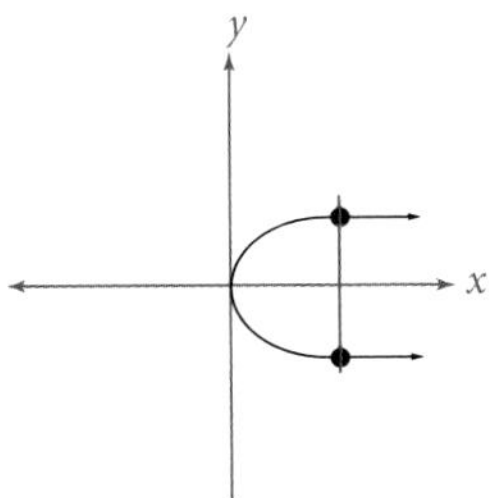

This graph is NOT a function.

X

***x*-axis** (eks´ ak sis) the horizontal axis in a coordinate system (p. 250)

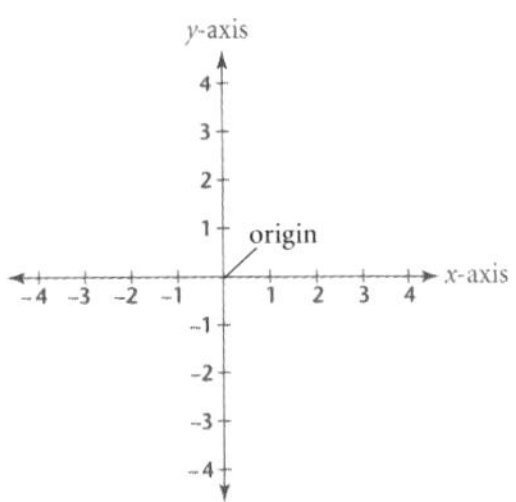

a	hat	e	let	ī	ice	ô	order	u̇	put	sh	she	ə { a	in about
ā	age	ē	equal	o	hot	oi	oil	ü	rule	th	thin	e	in taken
ä	far	ėr	term	ō	open	ou	out	ch	child	ŦH	then	i	in pencil
â	care	i	it	ȯ	saw	u	cup	ng	long	zh	measure	o	in lemon
												u	in circus

***x*-intercept** (eks′ in tər sept′) the point at which a graph intersects the *x*-axis (p. 257)

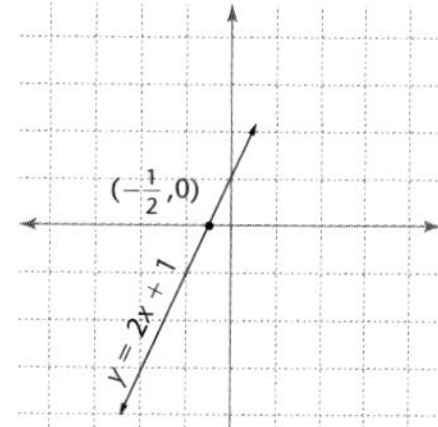

$(-\frac{1}{2}, 0)$ is the *x*-intercept.

Y

***y*-axis** (wī′ ak sis) the vertical axis in a coordinate system (p. 250)

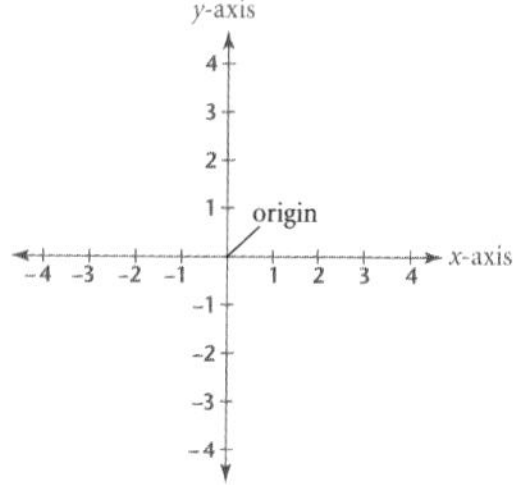

***y*-intercept** (wī′ in tər sept′) the point at which a graph intersects the *y*-axis (p. 256)

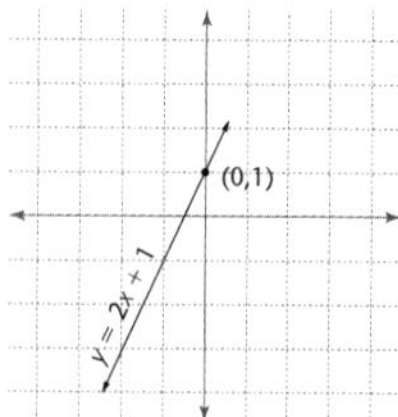

(0, 1) is the *y*-intercept.

Index

D

E

F

G

N

O

P

Q

R

S

T

Photo Credits

cover image: © Cosmo Condina/Getty Images; p. xviii, © MacDonald Photography/ Photri–Microstock; p. 5, © Bill Gallery/ Stock Boston; pp. 24, 244, © Photri–Microstock; p. 26, © Peter Vanderwarker/ Stock Boston; pp. 30, 354, © E.R. Degginger/ Color–Pic Inc.; p. 40, © Aaron Haupt/ Stock Boston; p. 47, © Inga Spence/ Visuals Unlimited; p. 49, © Ray Nelson/ Phototake; p. 57, © Jon Riley/ Stone; p. 58, © Mark Gibson/ Visuals Unlimited; p. 62, © Michael Dunning/ Taxi; p. 80, © Science Photo Library/ Photo Researchers, Inc.; pp. 83, 94, 326, © Tony Freeman/ PhotoEdit; p. 90, © Dwayne Newton/ PhotoEdit; p. 99, © J. Howard/ Stock Boston; p. 105, © Don Johnston/ Stone; pp. 107, 218, 241, 253, © David Young–Wolff/ PhotoEdit; p. 110, © Gary Randall/ Visuals Unlimited; p. 113, © Bob Daemmrich/ Stock Boston; p. 115, © Luis M. De La Maza, Ph.D. M.D./ Phototake; p.122, © Ken Fisher/ Stone; pp. 141, 237 (left), 379, © Gibson Stock Photography; p. 150, © Christopher Bissell/ Stone; p. 154, © S. Callahan/ Visuals Unlimited; p. 178, © Stephen Frisch/ Stock Boston; pp. 182, 350, © Minden Pictures; p. 185, © Doug Martin/ Stock Boston; p. 186, © Will Hart/ PhotoEdit; p. 196, © Neil Lavey/ Phototake; p. 209, © Roger Allyn Lee/ SuperStock; p. 212, © Joe Bator/ Corbis; p. 213, © Robert W. Ginn/ PhotoEdit; p. 214, © Courtesy NASA/ Color–Pic Inc.; p. 237 (right), © Glenn Oliver/ Visuals Unlimited; p. 248, © Jose Azel/ Aurora & Quanta Productions; p. 258, © Spencer Grant/Photo Edit; p. 262, © Royalty-Free/CORBIS; p. 282, © Alfred Pasieka/ Science Photo Library/ Photo Researchers, Inc.; p. 286, © Frederica Georgia/ Photo Researchers, Inc.; p. 297, © Thomas R. Fletcher/ Stock Boston; p. 300, © Michael P. Gadomski/ Dembinsky Photo Associates; p. 313, © Chuck Pefley/ Stock Boston; p. 344, © George Goodwin/ Color–Pic Inc.; p. 380, © Cary Wolinsky/ Stock Boston; p. 384, © Gerald & Buff Corsi/ Visuals Unlimited; p. 389, © Karl E. Deckart/ Phototake; p. 399, © A & E Morris/ Visuals Unlimited